Old World Empires

This book is a sweeping historical survey of the origins, development and nature of state power. It demonstrates that Eurasia is home to a dominant tradition of arbitrary rule mediated through military, civil and ecclesiastical servants and a marginal tradition of representative and responsible government through autonomous institutions. The former tradition finds expression in hierarchically organized and ideologically legitimated continental bureaucratic states while the latter manifests itself in the state of laws. In recent times, the marginal tradition has gained in popularity and has led to continental bureaucratic states attempting to introduce democratic and constitutional reforms. These attempts have rarely altered the actual manner in which power is exercised by the state and its elites given the deeper and historically rooted experience of arbitrary rule. Far from being remote, the arbitrary culture of power that emerged in many parts of the world continues to shape the fortunes of states. To ignore this culture of power and the historical circumstances that have shaped it comes at a high price, as indicated by the ongoing democratic recession and erosion of liberal norms within states that are democracies.

Ilhan Niaz is the author of *The Culture of Power and Governance of Pakistan, 1947–2008* and *An Inquiry into the Culture of Power of the Subcontinent* and teaches history at the Quaid-i-Azam University, Islamabad.

Routledge Studies in Cultural History

Old World Empires

Cultures of Power and Governance in Eurasia

Ilhan Niaz

Routledge
Taylor & Francis Group
NEW YORK   LONDON

First published 2014
by Routledge
711 Third Avenue, New York, NY 10017

and by Routledge
2 Park Square, Milton Park, Abingdon, Oxon OX14 4RN

*Routledge is an imprint of the Taylor & Francis Group,
an informa business*

Library of Congress Cataloging-in-Publication Data
Niaz, Ilhan.
   Old World empires : cultures of power and governance in Eurasia / by
Ilhan Niaz.
      pages cm. — (Routledge studies in cultural history ; 25)
   Includes bibliographical references and index.
  1. Eurasia—Politics and government.   2. State, The—History.
3. Imperialism—History.   4. Power (Social sciences)—Eurasia—
History.   5. Law—Eurasia—History.   6. Political culture—Eurasia—
History.   7. Politics and culture—Eurasia—History.   I. Title.
   DS33.3.N53 2014
   950—dc 3
   2013042201.

ISBN13: 978-0-415-72597-2 (hbk)
ISBN13: 978-1-315-85080-1 (ebk)

Typeset in Sabon
by IBT Global.

To my wife, Uzma

Contents

Maps

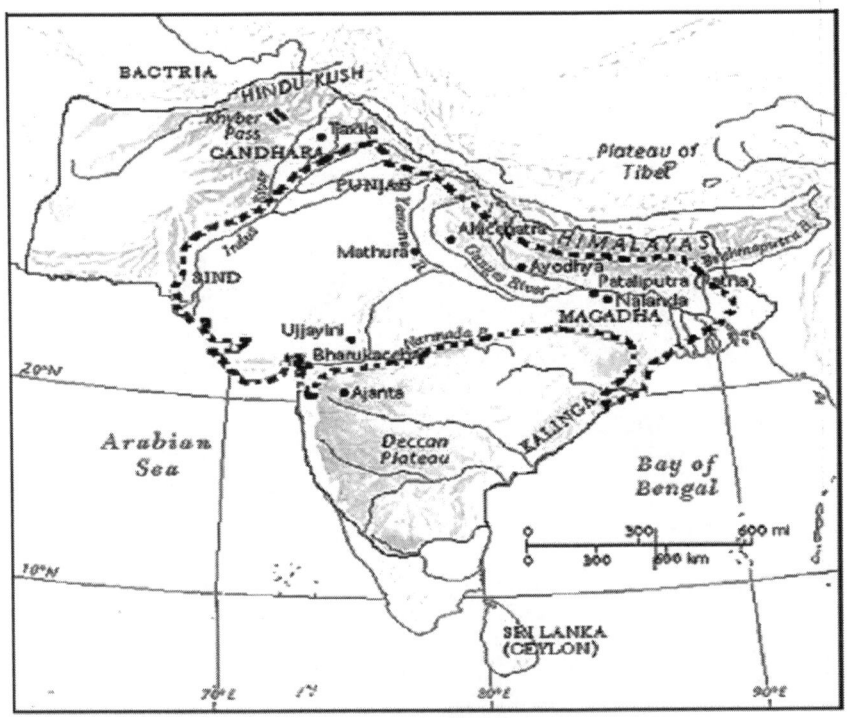

Maurya Empire C 232 BC _____
Gupta Empire C. A.D. 400 ▪▪▪▪▪▪

Map 1   South Asia Under the Mauryas and Guptas

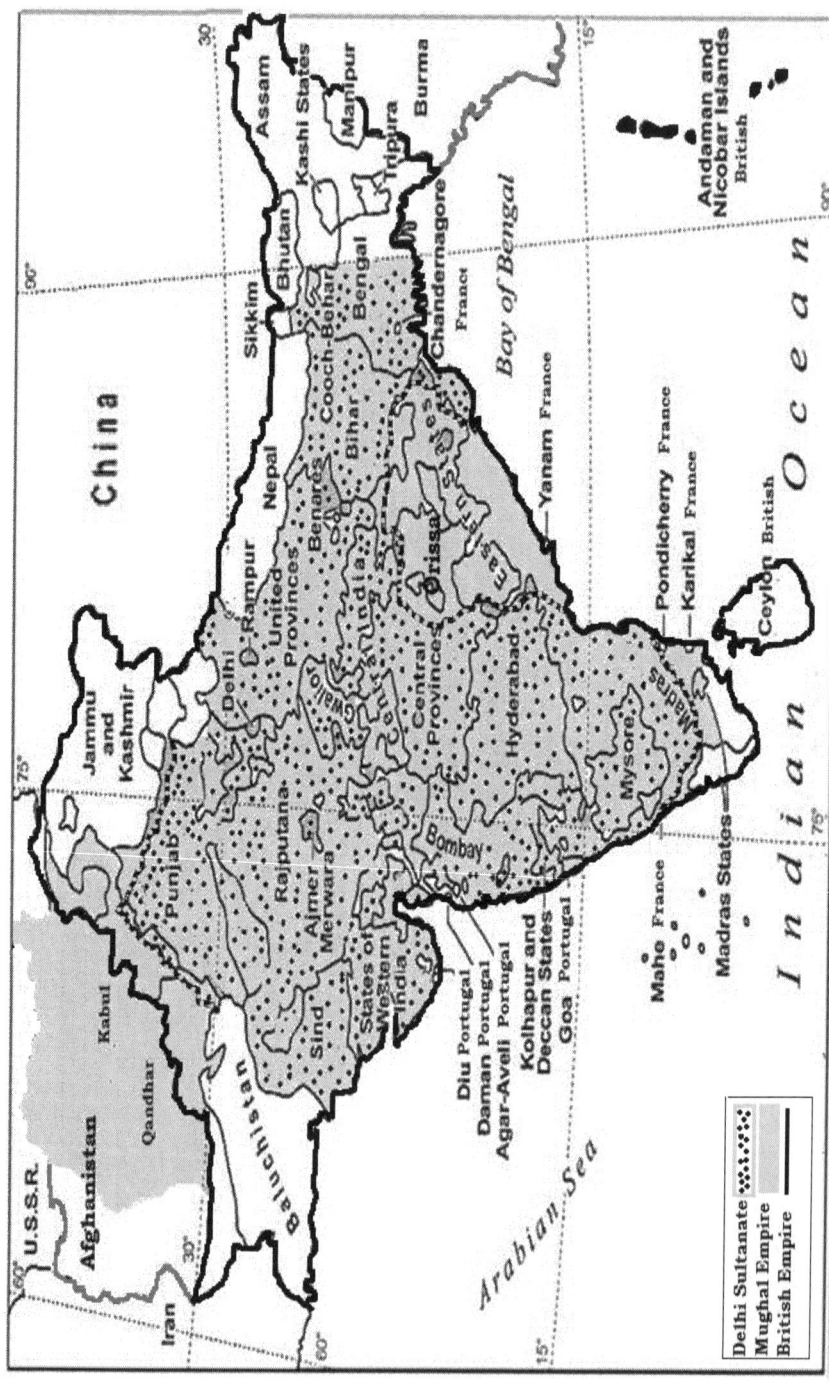

Map 2   South Asia Under the Sultanate of Delhi, the Timurid/Mughal Empire, and the British Empire in India.

Map 3 Contemporary India.

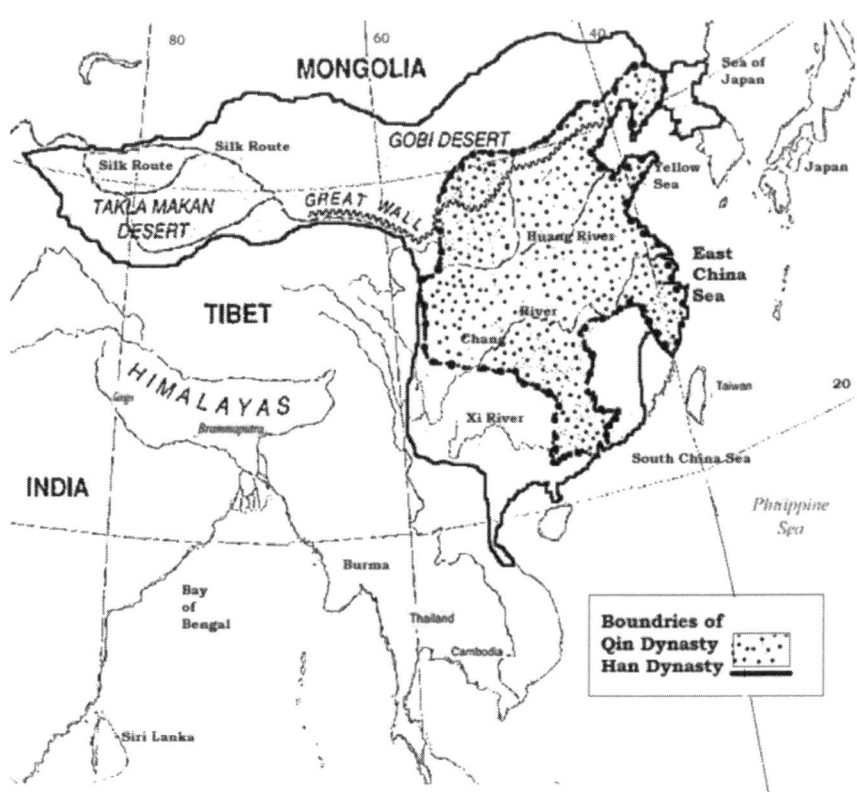

Qin Dynasty (221-206 BCE) and Han Dynasty (202 BCE- 220 CE)

Map 4   Early classical China—Qin and Han.

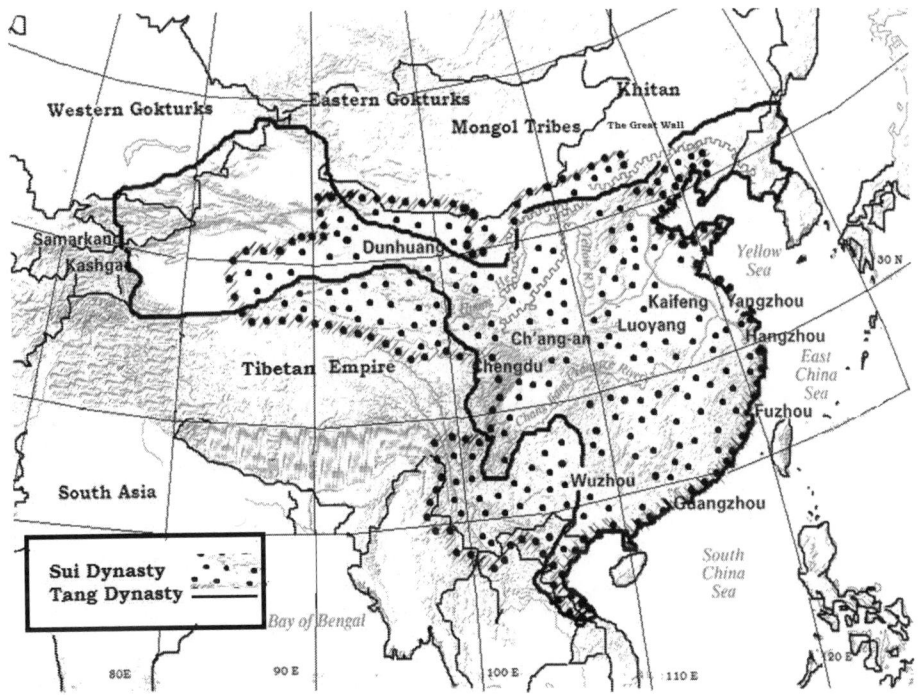

Late- Classical China, Sui Dynasty (AD 581-618) and Tang Dynasty (AD 618-907)

Map 5 Late-classical China—Sui and Tang.

Neo-Classical China and the Mongols: United Song Dynasty (960-1127), Southern Song (1127-1279), Mongol Yuan Dynasty (1271-1368)

Map 6   Neo-classical China and the Mongols—Song and Yuan.

Early Modern China: Ming (1368-1644) and Qing (1644-1911) Dynasties

Map 7   Early modern China—Ming and Qing.

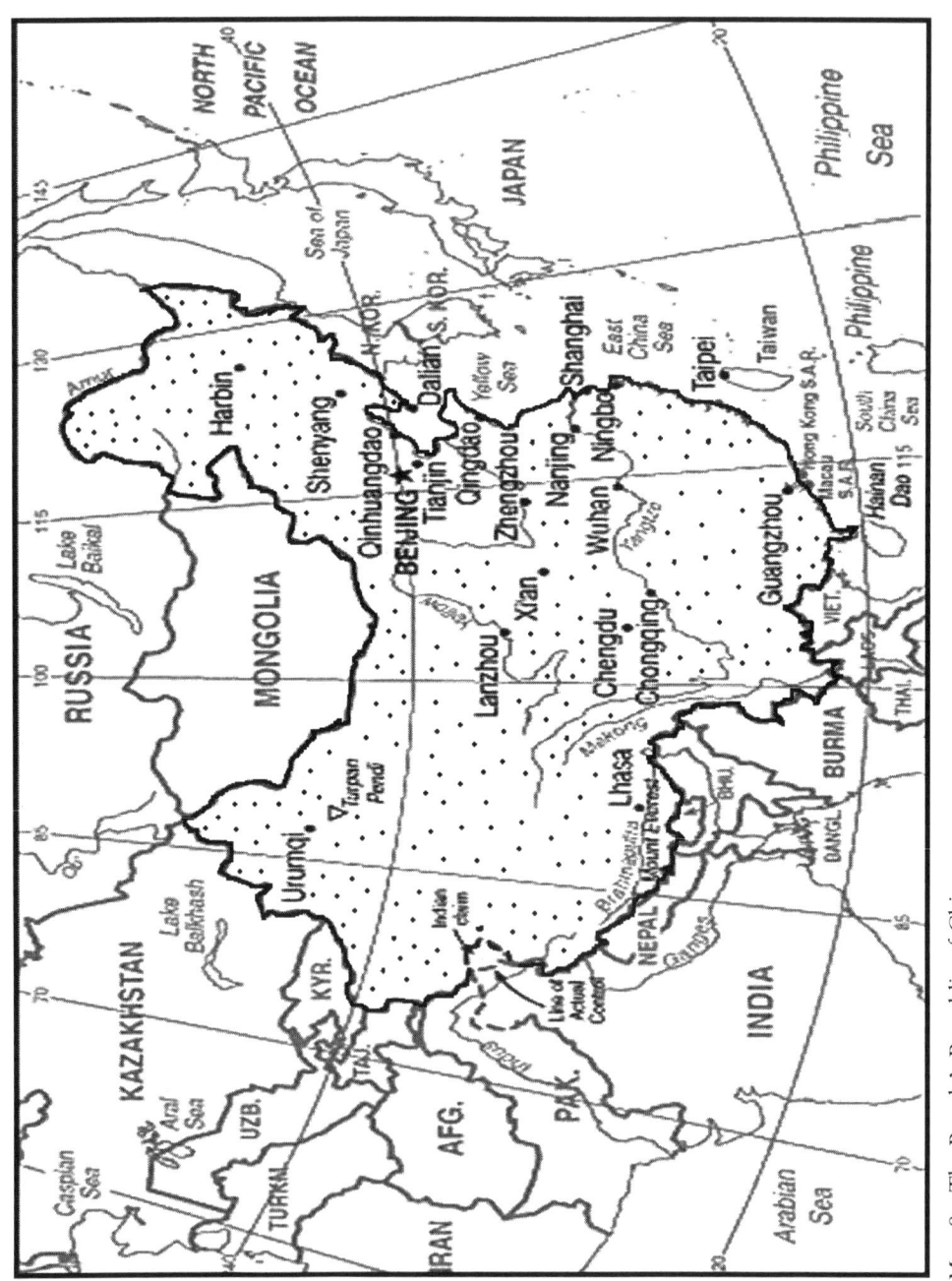

Map 0.2   The People's Republic of China.

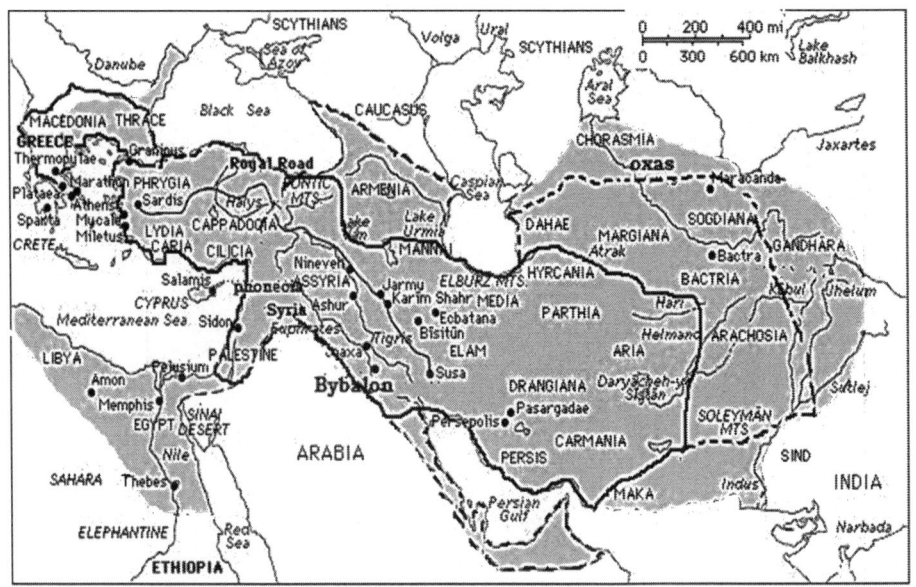

Achaemenid Empire (550-330 BC)
Seleucid Empire (312 BC- 60 BC) ——————
Parthian Empire (247 BC- 224 AD) - - - - - -

Map 9   Ancient Persia—Achaemenids, Seleucids and Parthians.

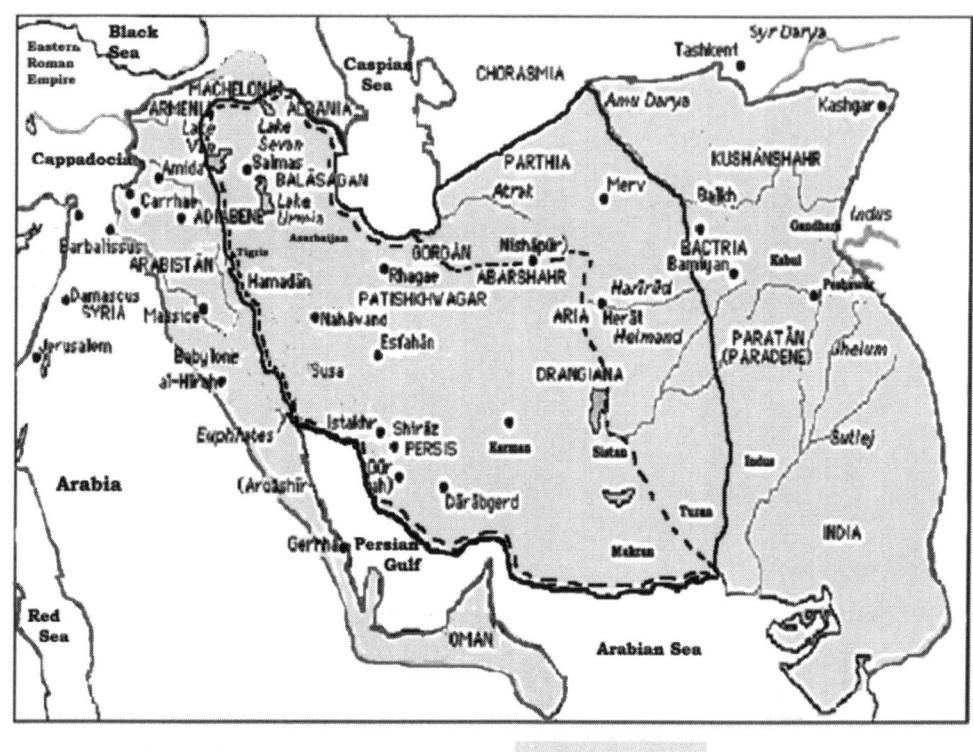

Sasanian Dynasty (224 CE - 651 CE)
Safavid Dynsaty (1501 CE- 1722 CE)
Qajar Dynasty   (1785 CE - 1925 CE)

Map 10   Persia under the Sassanids, Safavids and Qajars.

Political Map of Europe

Map 11   Europe, contemporary boundaries.

Boundries of The Ottoman Empire in 1683

Map 12 The Ottoman Sultanate at maximum extent.

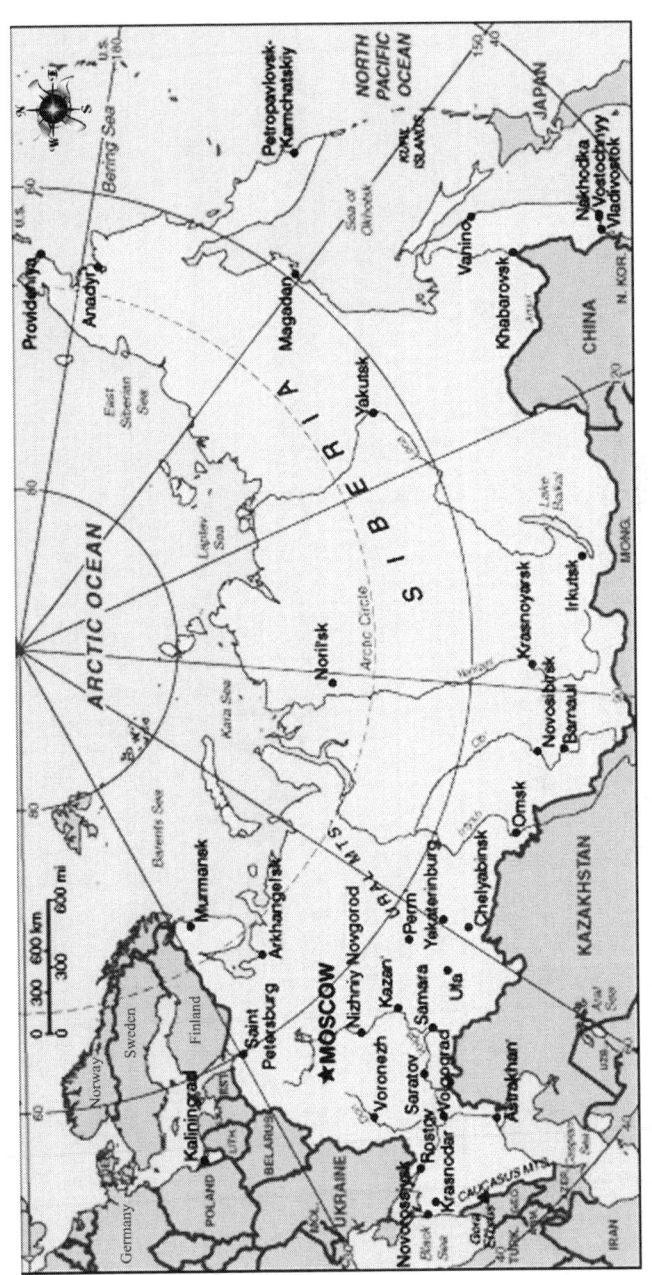

Map 13   Political map of Russia.

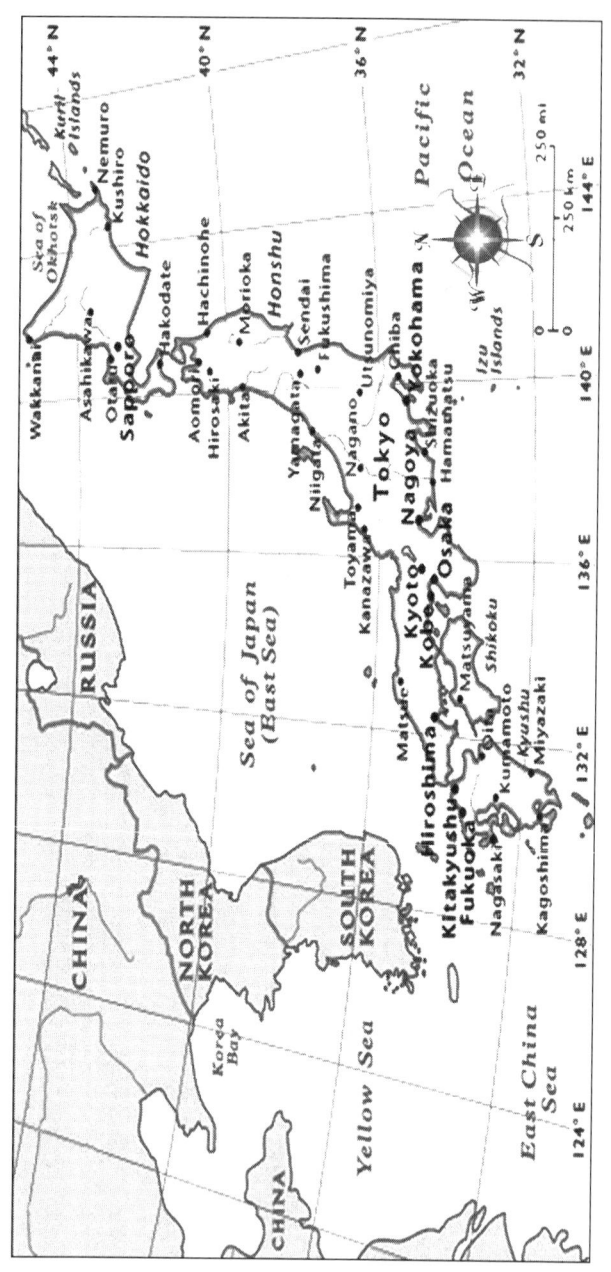

Map 14 Modern Japan.

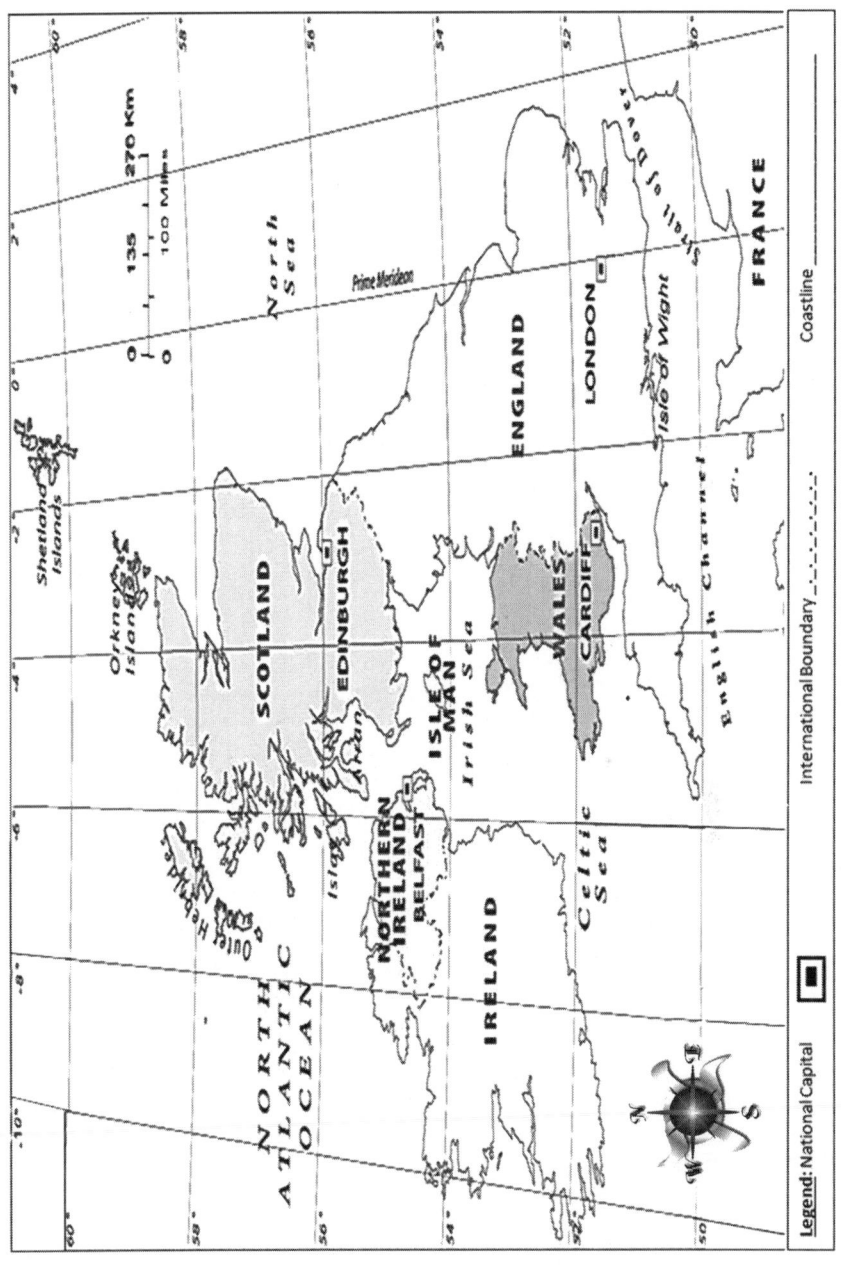

Map 15   Modern Britain.

Preface

"Commending obedience to the dictates of reason and reproving a slavish following of others need the aid of no arguments."

—Emperor Akbar the Great (b. 1542–d. 1605)

To Ibn Khaldun history was the best means of learning about the character of states and peoples. Aided by logic, rhetoric and philosophy, history helped detect and explain broad patterns of human development alongside providing a rational account of what had gone before. The need for integrating wisdom arising from historical perspective was great in light of human narcissism and forgetfulness. To know ourselves better, to avoid falling prey to flattery and self-deception, and to remind ourselves of the selfish and evil behavior we are all capable of, history was essential. Moving beyond the need for memory, correlation, and causation, history served as an antidote to our transience and mortality by helping us occupy a point within a continuum of experience that stretched far beyond a lifetime. Making sense of the past, rather than contending that the past is innately immune to being made sense of, is the basic purpose of historians who regard their subject as a reliable body of knowledge (*scientia* or science). This entails building coherent frameworks that account for similarities and differences in the human condition over time. *Old World Empires: Cultures of Power and Governance in Eurasia* is an attempt to do just that in relation to the historical experiences and behavioral patterns of states and ruling elites in India, China, Persia, Continental Europe, the Ottoman Sultanate/Modern Turkey, Russia, Japan, and the United Kingdom.

The idea of undertaking a survey of cultures of power and governance came to me in 2004 when I had the good fortune to visit my parents in Tokyo. The following year I went to Tokyo again, having completed the manuscript of my first book, *An Inquiry into the Culture of Power of the Subcontinent*. It was in Summer 2005 that I wrote the skeleton outline of *Old World Empires* and alongside my PhD research on Pakistan, which was published in 2010 as *The Culture of Power and Governance of Pakistan, 1947–2008*, continued to work towards applying the framework developed in my first two books to other parts of Eurasia. After March 2010, with the publication of my second book, I was able to concentrate on writing *Old World Empires*.

What follows, then, is the application of a framework originally developed for understanding South Asian history and the patterns of governance that it yields to other regions. The effort is to place before the reader the similarities and differences between South Asia's culture of power and governance and those of others. In some respects *Old World Empires* reverses the gaze though, given the common Eurasian tradition of learning, diffusion, and circulation of ideas, it is perhaps better to move past a "West versus the Rest" binary for Europe is, after all, an integral part of Eurasia. I hope that in the not-too-distant future I will be able to study the culture of power and governance of North and South American states and further the application of the ideas that guide the present volume. For now, let us turn to the Old World and see what lessons it holds for its present denizens, as well as for those who inhabit the New World, about the exercise of power.

Ilhan Niaz
Islamabad
August 2013

Acknowledgments

Old World Empires: Cultures of Power and Governance in Eurasia would never have been written were it not for the guidance, generosity and constant encouragement of Zafar Iqbal Rathore, a retired Police Service of Pakistan officer who is, in my estimation, the wisest public servant to have served Pakistan. My father, Kamran Niaz, was instrumental in helping with the draft and bringing to bear his thirty-five years of diplomatic service on the problems and arguments presented in the work that follows. My mother, Nuzhat Niaz, read the entire manuscript and edited it. For the maps, I am grateful to my brilliant colleague, Fouzia Farooq. Ahmed Fasih, Jibran Riaz, Mohammad Suleiman, and Khurram Afzal, have in the course of the researching and writing of this book provided countless insights from their own reading and experience. My wife, Uzma, has through her warmth, understanding, good humor, patience, and, not to mention, editorial feedback, made the entire writing process as painless as possible. I would like to thank Jennifer Morrow and Max Novick, my editors at Routledge, for believing in this project and for their help at each stage of the book's preparation for publication. Eleanor Chan, the copy editor for *Old World Empires* merits special mention. Although Tanvir Ahmad Khan, a former Foreign Secretary of Pakistan, did not live to see this book published I benefited greatly from his perspective on Iran and Russia. And last, but by no means least, I am forever indebted to the hundreds of authors whose works I have read in order to write what follows.

Introduction

Two centuries ago the vast majority of states were monarchies.[1] In stating this fact about the form of government a monarchist might draw great satisfaction. Such satisfaction, however, would not withstand serious scrutiny of the substance and actual working of monarchies. Some monarchies, like the Persian variant, were non-hereditary, arbitrary, and theocratic.[2] Others, like the Chinese, were bureaucratic, humanistic, and ideological. South Asian monarchies were authoritarian, arbitrary, and chaotic. The Roman monarchy founded by Octavian Augustus was technically a hereditary *principate* in which the Senate reigned and the emperor ruled. This gave way by AD 96 to a non-hereditary adoptive monarchy, which continued to preserve the form of republican government. During the European Middle Ages feudal monarchies with powerful aristocracies emerged alongside the Church, which was a non-hereditary, elective, theocratic, monarchy. Other monarchies, such as the Russian, were absolutist and autocratic. These, and many more examples, help establish that while monarchy was not too long ago almost universal as a form of government, monarchies differed greatly in their actual exercise of power and state organization.

This long view brings us to the contemporary era where democracy is the form of government that is in vogue in the majority of the world's states. The ideological dominance of democracy is such that many states organized as one-party dictatorships claim to be democratic. For our purposes, the bare minimum needed to qualify a state as a democracy is multi-party elections held regularly and in such a manner that a relatively peaceful change from one party's government to another's can materialize. Within the camp of such democracies there is tremendous diversity in how power is exercised. India is a superb illustration of how a remarkably stable constitutional and democratic order can coexist with utterly arbitrary governance, plunder, chaos, and growing religious fundamentalism, at a day-to-day level. Nuclear neighbor and archrival Pakistan combines all the deficiencies of India's arbitrary democracy with constitutional instability and praetorian domination. In both countries, the nature of state power is arbitrary, increasingly corrupt, and even at the highest levels, demonstrably incompetent. Turkey, a multi-party democracy since 1946, has a

Kemalist state apparatus and ideology protected by military guardians and, tellingly, democracy is not one of the six principles of Kemalism. In its quest to achieve parity with the contemporary universal civilization founded on the Enlightenment epistemology of reason, logic, and evidence, the Turkish state has stood above its society and, as the 1950s and the era of Justice and Development Party rule that began in 2003 illustrate, democracy and the Kemalist state are uncomfortable bedfellows.[3] France, constitutionally quiescent since 1958 after a century and a half of sometime violent experimentation, is a republican monarchy mediated by a transcendent national bureaucracy. Japan, superficially a multi-party democracy, does not in its actual state behavior and ethos conform to Western standards of political liberalism. The United Kingdom, substantively the world's oldest surviving parliamentary state, is constitutionally a monarchy. Russia, since 1990, has evolved into an illiberal, democratically elected autocracy dominated by the security establishment that picked up the pieces after the fall of the Soviet Union. In Southern Europe, the behavior of politicians in Greece, Spain, Italy, and Portugal, has more in common with their counterparts in India, Pakistan, and Turkey, than it does with those in Scandinavia, post-war Germany, and the Low Countries.[4]

One of the great lessons of history then is that it is unwise to assume that growing homogeneity in the form of government necessarily results in convergence in terms of the exercise of power. In the world of monarchies that persisted until the 1800s and early 1900s enormous differences existed in the behavior and organization of states. In a world of democracies, which is of recent vintage and dubious authenticity, and may well end soon in the wake of the recession of Western power and impending ecological catastrophe, vast gulfs separate India, Japan, France, and Turkey from each other, and an even greater chasm lies between these imitative democracies and the home-grown, genuinely participatory, variants prevalent in the United Kingdom, Canada, Australia, New Zealand, and the United States of America.[5] To acknowledge this inequality and divergence in the human condition, while necessary, hardly suffices to explain what can be observed. In pursuit of that explanation, which may very well prove elusive or unconvincing, this study examines the world in a certain light whereby the importance of some causal factors is recognized above others.

The first and most important component of these factors is geography, which, taken holistically, extends to biogeography, and the broad environmental conditions in which societies and states are situated.[6] As Jared Diamond has effectively demonstrated, it is no coincidence that agriculture emerged in those parts of the world that had a reliable supply of fresh water, an abundance of wild grasses, and species of herd animals that fed on these grasses and kept close to their water source.[7] Nor is it a coincidence that human communities confronted with climate change and desiccation at the end of the last Ice Age became sedentary once they figured out how to get a steady and productive yield from the soil, grasses, and herd animals. This triggered a rise in population density in these favored locations in and around the Fertile Crescent. More people meant that bands of hunters and gatherers grew into small tribes, and these small tribes grew into chiefdoms. Control and distribution of the food supply needed some kind of organization, record-keeping and central leadership, while society became more complex and capable of supporting specialists. It is this combination of growing numbers and complexity that led, by about 4000 BC, to the birth of civilization in Mesopotamia. Even using primitive methods, early farmers in the Fertile Crescent and along the banks of Chinese rivers, could feed one person per year per acre, compared to four hundred acres needed to support one hunter-gatherer.[8] The spread of farming in Eurasia radiated from epicenters in the Fertile Crescent and China, and spread successfully wherever local conditions were suitable,[9] much as industrialism has spread ever since the early 1800s. The spread of agriculture tells us a lot about the importance of location not only in the mundane context of real estate prices but also for the fate of civilizations and empires. Location is integral to geography and to historical development for Eurasia has a large temperate and sub-tropical band that makes diffusion along an East-West axis feasible even with bronze-age communications.[10] This gave Eurasia a huge advantage in terms of the rate at which its civilizations could develop as compared to the Americas and Sub-Saharan Africa with their North-South axes. Imagine for the sake of illustration if each and every civilization had to discover each and every idea, technology, and method for itself.[11] In such an autarchic world civilizations would develop far slower than in a world where they could learn and borrow from each other or in a world where multiple centers of power and creativity were competing with each other. Many of histories greatest triumphs and most horrific tragedies have flowed from the varying rates of growth imposed on civilizations by the objective facts of geography.[12] History is at an almost subconscious level an account of asymmetries.[13]

Geography and environment, of course, are not everything, though combined they do constitute the initial causes of subsequent historical progressions even if the kaleidoscope of events ends up obscuring these origins.[14] As humanity likes to remember and relive its victories over nature, many of the most celebrated people in history are those who became the first to transcend apparently hard geographic and environmental limits. Fa-Hien, Leif Ericson, Marco Polo, Ibn Battuta, Zheng He, Christopher Columbus, Vasco da Gama, Lewis and Clark, David Livingstone, Charles Lindberg, Yuri Gagarin, and Neil Armstrong, to name a few, deservedly occupy a special place in the human narrative of triumph over natural obstacles and distance. Lest we become excessive in our self-congratulatory fervor it may help to put these achievements in context. Fa-Hien, for instance, traveled from China to South Asia between AD 399 and 414 in pursuit of the Buddhist books of discipline. Buddhism, an Indian religion, had spread to South East Asia and to China in the preceding centuries, and the motivation to endure the rigors of a long and dangerous journey came from the need to satisfy religious knowledge. Zheng He's massive naval expeditions to South East Asia, South Asia, West Asia and East Africa, between 1405 and 1433 were made possible by the resources and technology of Ming China. Likewise, European explorers were bankrolled by governments, motivated by religion, armed with weapons, and, driven by inter-state rivalries to become the first to stake a claim to territories beyond the oceans. In modern times, the dependence of explorers on tech-ingenuity, their desire to bring glory (and sometimes empire) to their motherlands, and pursuit of celebrity status made possible by the mass media, are all factors that spur attempts to push the limits.[15] The space programs of Cold War rivals, the United States and the Soviet Union, were meant to demonstrate the superiority of their respective political and socioeconomic systems as well as satisfy scientific curiosity, and required, quite literally, astronomical sums of money. There are good reasons why Marco Polo and Ibn Battuta stuck to the classical East-West Eurasian axis, which, in the latter case, took the intrepid explorer through the sultanates, emirates, and empires of North Africa, West Asia, South Asia, and China, and didn't, instead, head off into the Arctic or try their luck at crossing Sub-Saharan Africa. Human conceit, which is universal and indefatigable, leads us to celebrate individuals, including ourselves, out of context. Geography and history, in contrast, teach hard but necessary lessons in the ways of humility before the power of context.[16]

States, the next item in our explanatory chain, have long furnished the context of power.[17] Their origins can certainly be said to vary or be shrouded by time. In order to get past this shroud the Western intellectual tradition developed the concept of the social contract, with many different shades and types, which boil down to a community giving birth to a state by some kind of agreement within a group of people.[18] This view is almost certainly incorrect but as it flatters the ego to believe that human beings secured peaceful evolution of communities into states by some archaic and ill-defined mechanism of consent, it is a persistent and influential idea. In actual fact, states are born out of demographic concentration and danger, the twin fears of internal disorder and external aggression.[19] A group within a larger community seizes power, starts to collect taxes from its subjects, and provides protection as well as managerial control for undertaking the increasingly large-scale activities needed to sustain the society.[20] States are exercises in artifice that arise from and then perpetuate domestic asymmetries and try and concentrate power and wealth in the hands of a small elite, which, in turn, becomes self-perpetuating. These elites can be military, bureaucratic, and ecclesiastical, and collectively wield power over others. Power is what states are all about, rather than morality or the greatest happiness of the greatest number, for humanity's triumphs and achievements, many of those that survive as archaeological ruins and end up as tourist attractions, were built through coercion and the inequitable concentration of resources and produced enormous human misery. This misery can be internal, external, or both, but it arises from the ability of states to organize violence and provide it with a sense of greater purpose and inspiration. This is why states are generally religious or ideocratic in their orientation. This religious aspect of states may be civil, ideological, some "ism", or a combination of these, but the end is the same—to legitimize power, provide it with a moral justification, and ensure greater loyalty or passivity amongst the subject population. This has to be done for at an individual level people want to believe in their own morality, and in the morality of the community or state in which they live. This personal morality is rooted in religion, culture, and ethics, and establishes a hierarchy of values, a code of what is desirable and what is repugnant. The problem with power is that it produces its own logic, its own morality.[21] That logic is the logic of self-aggrandizement, status and wealth, and the ability to command others, while that morality is one that justifies otherwise unconscionable behavior in light of the dictates of preserving and extending power.[22] Thus, the same military officer who has a happy family life and loves his wife, calmly, and with hardly a pause, participates in the degradation and slaughter of innocents. Otherwise humane and reasonable academics develop policies that necessitate wars, invasions, and brutal displacement of weaker communities. Zealous and deeply religious priests seeking to purify the souls of their countrymen will see no harm in the employment of torture and fire to do God's work. Civil servants and corporate executives, daily engaged in mismanagement, corruption, and the strip-mining of the Earth's resources, merrily go about dinner parties as if they are not responsible for the wider specter of deprivation. Development consultants grow fat at five-star hotels earning hundreds or thousands of dollars a day for churning out reports full of meaningless jargon that are preconfigured to suit the interests of their funding agencies. The human capacity for cognitive dissonance is so great that it is easy as well as profitable to engage in self-deception about our actual moral worth when placed in a structure of power.[23] The combination of the manufacturing defects inherent in human nature combined with the wear and tear of history, which is essentially a record of how power has been exercised, has produced vast accumulations of rationalizations and moralizations that help perpetuate arbitrary and selfish behavior—from the invisible hand to the Mandate of Heaven.[24]

The accumulation of experience, its ritualization, and elaboration into formal and informal norms of behavior and expectations, produces the continuum commonly referred to as culture. Culture, in itself, is not the object of the study, for it is too amorphous to be a useful category of analysis. The emphasis here is on how the acquisition and exercise of power affects human behavior and shapes the fortunes of states and empires for good and for ill. The culture of power is the aggregated historical experience of a people, state, or empire, in relation to power. Rather than plunging into a fruitless debate about what is or isn't acceptable as a definition of power, history teaches us that power is the ability, actual or perceived, to do, to execute. A society may spread power out, or it may concentrate it. A state might legitimize its power on the basis of religion or civic sense. A ruler may wield power through an army, a bureaucracy, a party, or a clergy. At the end of the day, power is capacity. The culture of power responds and evolves in relation to the exercise of that capacity and generates norms that are transmitted from one generation to the next. In South Asia, for instance, if a police official approaches a citizen the instinctive reaction of the latter is fear and a desire to get away. In the United Kingdom, Sweden, or Japan, law-abiding subjects are not by default fearful of the approach of the police. This difference is due to conditioning and the expectations constructed and perceived in the societies in question.[25]

The combination of geography, environment, the state, legitimacy paradigms, and the culture of power, produce the historical experience of governance. This historical experience, as it is rooted in factors that are primordial, structural, and alterable only at a glacial rate, generally works to reinforce the culture of power.[26] In this manner an autocatalytic cycle is set in motion whereby the nature of a particular culture of power determines the historical experience of governance, which, in turn, reinforces the culture of power. Changes in lifestyle, improvement in technological capability, increase or diminution of wealth, as well as conscious attempts to adopt reforms from more conventionally successful polities, all matter, but they do so very often in ways that aggravate asymmetries and accelerate tendencies already in evidence, making cultures of power more authoritarian, arbitrary, and delusional. No one familiar with the history of the twentieth century ought to have any illusions on this score, reference the chilling mechanized efficiency with which fascist and communist regimes built and operated factories of death or the brutality with which even constitutional states, like the United Kingdom, France, Belgium, and the Netherlands, dealt with their colonial subjects. Herodotus realized some two and a half millennia ago that the effect of power on human mentality was to warp it, in most cases beyond redemption, leading inexorably to hubris and nemesis. Since human nature has not changed and is everywhere the same the adaptive diversity of societies owes much to the hard factors mentioned above and very little to our apparent idiosyncrasies. While it may inflict grievous injury on human pride to think of ourselves as organisms operating in and adapting to an environment and circumstances largely beyond individual control, it is nonetheless a view that needs to gain wider currency if the Earth is to be saved from ecocide and if civilization is to have more than an evanescent innings.

Since this study focuses on the state as the basic structure or unit of analysis it is pertinent to introduce here the two major traditions of the state that evolved in Eurasia. One is the continental bureaucratic state or continental bureaucratic empire and the other is the state of laws. The continental bureaucratic state is a complex of administrative hierarchies that culminate in a master or sovereign. Servants or slaves of the ruler staff these hierarchies at the higher levels though the ruler's advisors may also have a say in appointments. The basic principle of the continental bureaucratic state is that the territory and the people it governs are the property of the ruler. The function of the hierarchies in place is to act as personal servants of the ruler and enforce his proprietorship over the state, which is therefore more of an estate. Religion or ideology are instrumented through an official intelligentsia or priesthood that constitute an ideocratic complex. The function of this complex is that it helps legitimize the ruler, places him above lawful public criticism, and makes it appear that the regime serves some higher purpose that can justify its routine excesses. The combination of the concentration of power, a servile class of state servants, universal proprietorship, and divine or ideological sanction, breeds megalomania, insecurity, militarism, and secrecy. The state of laws is in many ways the opposite of the continental bureaucratic state. In a state of laws the ruler is not the universal proprietor and there is no powerful hierarchy of personal servants that can act as sub-sovereigns who are dependent on the ruler's whim. The ecclesiastical or intellectual establishment is autonomous of the ruler's control though it is amenable to being influenced. The state is constituted as a complex of autonomous institutions that interact with each other and require considerable persuasive skills, popularity and wisdom to lead. The combination of private property, limited bureaucratic control, and autonomous institutions, serves to restrain the power of the supreme executive and disperses that power amongst many different entities.

Continental bureaucratic states typically manifest arbitrary cultures of power. In an arbitrary culture of power the ruler treats the country as a vast personal estate to be used to enhance his personal wealth and to do with as he pleases. In effect, the ruler's effort is to use the wealth of the country in order to build a network of patronage centered on the throne while arbitrarily confiscating the property of others, imposing taxes, and hoarding. The weakness of property rights and the fluctuating character of tax assessments mean that no one is safe from the ruler's caprice. The arbitrary power of the ruler is channeled through his servants who are simultaneously the ruling class and the most vulnerable to their master's direct displeasure. As the servants can be dismissed, transferred, liquidated, or financially ruined, at a moment's notice, they are highly insecure. The combination of being entrusted with arbitrary power by the ruler and perennial personal insecurity leads these servants to treat the subject population with the same arbitrariness that they are treated with. The effort then on the part of these servants is to try and amass as much wealth as possible, to go on working and accumulating till the last possible minute, so that at least some of their wealth survives their fall from favor and accompanying confiscation of property. This way, the family can survive long enough till one of its members manages to worm his way back into the ruler's favor. For ordinary subjects the continental bureaucratic state is normally experienced as an externality imposed by force and fraud that establishes an extractive relationship, quite literally mining the society for the resources and manpower it needs. In terms of social responses to the state, the range typically includes flight, concealment, fatalism, apathy, and, when driven to desperation, rebellion. These complement obedience to the ruler and servility when the state is effective or comes knocking on your door.

When a continental bureaucratic state weakens, things normally go from bad to worse. Rival gangs and potentates carve out their own estates and fight it out with each other. These smaller estates are operated on the same principles as the continental bureaucratic state they are carved out from. The multiplication of power centers leads to civil wars and greater insecurity, which can drag on for centuries until a new state or imperial elite emerges and imposes order from above. During such periods of chaos, the costs to society are enormous, and a resurgent despotism is deemed preferable to continued anarchy and warlordism. The atomized societies of continental bureaucratic states need strong central power to maintain order and fall into disarray in the absence of such a center.

The quality of governance in a continental bureaucratic state depends primarily upon the wisdom and strength of the ruler and the competence of his servants. It is thus not surprising that mirrors for princes and advice for rulers constitute the substance of Eurasian administrative wisdom. A wise sovereign in a continental bureaucratic state is one who understands the difference between the trappings of power and heedless selfishness on the one hand and the requirements of regime stability and the relative well being of his subjects on the other. This insight is, for example, what differentiates a true sovereign from a selfish ruler in the Mughal tradition. The most important function of the ruler is choosing capable servants and assigning them the right duties. The basis for determining capability may vary from one ruler to another or one state to another, and it can be very subjective and dependent on circumstances, but making such judgment calls and deploying the correct personnel in the appropriate positions is central to the governance of such states. Normally, the officer class in a continental bureaucratic state is not very large given the population and the overall size of the state apparatus, which is one of the strengths of this design—the ability to run a large state with a relatively small number of high quality, high powered, officers. The weakness is that there is no reliable way to ensure the succession of competent rulers and a peaceful transfer from one government to the next is often difficult to manage.

The state of laws possesses a moderate culture of power. The core elements of this moderate culture of power are the diffusion of power amongst different centers and the tendency of the rulers to view power as a public trust. This does not by any means imply that corruption and abuse do not take place. They can and do, often on a massive and institutionalized scale, such as policy fixing, or rigging the taxation system to favor one group over others, or funneling vast sums of money from private donors with vested interests into electoral campaigns. Corruption and abuse are only some-what moderated due to the relative inability of one institution or office to deliver without the cooperation of others. The institutional multi-polarity of a state of laws renders it necessary for a political process to be in place through which members of the elite can trade favors, maneuver, and com-pete against each other, with a view to coming to power. This is different from the continental bureaucratic state in which administrative fiat and sycophancy to win over the ruler and his senior servants replace the politi-cal process, and lead to violent conspiracies and rebellions when things go awry. In a state of laws, the political process helps prevent any one group from dominating all major institutions at once and provides for a legitimate and relatively peaceful means of periodic transfers of power from one gov-ernment to the next. At the same time, the state of laws is a fragile plant precisely because it requires so many different elements to work together. It is very vulnerable to military or subversive threats that necessitate emer-gency provisions, arbitrary decisions, and intrusion into the private lives of citizens. To some extent the presence of powerful associations that are independent of the state and legitimately integrated into the political order help guard against this possibility but prolonged threats often lead to their exhaustion. The absence of an ecclesiastical or ideological establishment under the direct control of the executive means that states of laws are not as hard in dealing with differences of opinion as is the case with continental bureaucratic states. There is a higher threshold for criticism and rulers are conditioned to accept contrary views as a part of normal political life. This may have no effect on their behavior and fail to inform their policies, but even then it helps release pressure and provides catharsis to those who are not in power. The multiplicity of legitimate power centers in a state of laws renders the law a fixed point of reference for the participants in the political process. Another implication is that the state of laws represents at least the wealthy section of a community and is born out of their concord over the rules of the game.

Historically, continental bureaucratic states have been the most success-ful. In the Eurasian landmass practically all the major empires adopted the hierarchical configuration that corresponds to the continental bureaucratic model. The Ancient Roman state of laws collapsed under the pressures of expansion. The Ancient Greek states of laws succumbed to Macedonian and then Roman imperial expansion. In feudal Europe a semblance of such states reemerged as free cities, and independent fiefs, but few survived the rise of absolutism after 1600s and the consolidation of national states. The major exception to this rule was Britain, where a state of laws has survived with some interruptions since 1215. From its island home, the state of laws was exported to the dominions of settlement and, in the 1800s and 1900s, attempts were made to spread its norms in the dominions of conquest in the main Eurasian landmass. This represented, at least superficially, a spectac-ular reversal of historical trajectories. In the past, it was states of laws that had collapsed and been replaced by continental bureaucratic empires, but now, the former was intruding in the sphere long dominated by the latter. In British India reforms introduced, among other things, the rule of law, private property, autonomous institutions, an army subordinate to civilians, and a secular state, alongside the classical executive-centric apparatus of a continental bureaucratic empire. There is perhaps no greater example than British India for students of institutional development of the success and limits of human agency in altering the structure of a region in relation to the exercise of power. The successes are obvious, in that India is a stable constitutional democracy. The limits are far stronger, however, the moment one moves beyond the ritual superficiality of Indian parliamentary politics and examines the administrative substance of the country where arbitrary rule has reasserted itself with a vengeance.

In the examples briefly touched upon above as well as in the details to follow, the relevance of cultures of power to the actual behavior of states is the central assertion. Without factoring in the historical experience of governance and the culture of power, along with the structures and habits of the heart that animate them and condition them, attempts to understand the world, let alone change it for the better, shall continue to prove elusive. After all, one can believe that reality is simply a collective of subjective narratives, or deny the importance of geography, history, and culture, to the exercise of power, but doing so does not prevent reality from asserting itself. Therein lies the heart of the notions of objective reality and reliable knowledge that appeal to human reason and direct it towards greater understanding through the articulation of statements of probability to be tested against experience, logic, and forensic evidence.

The major states, empires, countries, or regions, examined in this study are India, China, Persia, Continental Europe, the Ottoman Sultanate and modern Turkey, Russia, Japan, and the United Kingdom. India, China, and Persia, represent the classical tradition of continental bureaucratic empires in Eurasia. Continental Europe reveals a history of fluctuations, alternating between different forms, though remaining bureaucratic during times of prosperity. The Ottoman Sultanate represents a supremely successful variant that incorporated many of the features of the Persian and Chinese traditions and constituted what was arguably the most long-lived and successful dynastic state.[27] The Ottomans are particularly relevant on account of the rise of Turkish nationalism and the establishment in Turkey of a secular republic after the fall of the dynasty. Russia, a latecomer to agriculture on account of its location and harsh climate, nonetheless emerged a great power in the modern world and competed for world hegemony in the 1800s and 1900s. Now a shadow of its former self, Russia faces a difficult process of revival and one that has already occasioned a return to its autocratic roots. In modern times Japan became a bureaucratic state drawing upon Confucian roots and selective borrowing from the West to avert the fate that befell most of the Asian countries in the 1800s. Japan makes for a fascinating study precisely because it does not really fit into any framework. The other island polity taken up by this study is the United Kingdom, which represents the modern template for a state of laws, inherited by the dominions of settlement, imposed on former colonies like India, and imitated by others. Since this framework is derived from South Asia's historical experience of governance let us turn to it first.

1 The Realm of Chaos
The Indian Subcontinent[1]

INTRODUCTION: MORE EBB THAN FLOW

The Indian subcontinent is known in history for a number of vast empires that managed to unite most of its territory and population under a single regime. The earliest of these was the Mauryan Empire (320 BC–180 BC), followed by the Gupta Empire (AD 300–AD 500), the Delhi Sultanate (1206–1526), the Timurid Empire (1526–1707) and the British Empire (1757–1947). These dates can, however, be somewhat misleading given that they often include the period of conquest and consolidation or cover up recurrent rebellions and, in the case of the Delhi Sultanate, recurrent dynastic revolutions. There is also relatively little historical data available for the period before the Delhi Sultanate, which might as well be referred to in the plural (Sultanates) given that it represents a succession of dynasties (Slave, Shamsid, Khalji, Tugluq, Saiyyid, and Lodhi), none of which managed to provide more than a generation of effective government. In the case of the Timurid Empire, the first two rulers (Babur and Humayun) failed to consolidate the empire and it wasn't until the reign of Akbar (1556–1605) that the imperial project really took off. By the 1590s, Akbar had managed to bring most of the Indian subcontinent directly or indirectly under his control. Akbar's successors unwisely sought to expand towards Central Asia and into the South Indian peninsula and got bogged down in long and bloody wars that did great harm to the sustainability of the Timurid Empire. By the 1680s the Timurid Empire was in decline, and in the 1720s it broke up into warring states nominally loyal to the emperor in Delhi. The British Empire that succeeded the Mughals took at least a century to take shape (1757–1857) and eventually provided most of South Asia with a centralized and effective government made up of autonomous institutions. Partly for that reason, British withdrawal in 1947 led to a mitigated breakup of the empire (India and Pakistan), which has been followed by a gradual breakdown of governance structures in the successor states.

What this means is that for much of its history the Indian subcontinent has been in chaos.[2] Invasions, rebellions, fragmentation, and warlordism are the conditions that have prevailed for the most part in this region.

Chaos, in turn, has only occasionally given way to order imposed by unification brought about by a powerful imperial elite. As soon as the quality of the imperial elite has declined, or, the will to hold on diminished, as was the case with the British Empire in India, terminal decline set in paving the way for the resumption of chaos. This is a pattern as old as the history of the Indian subcontinent itself and the precarious present condition of many regional states combined with the rise of religious fundamentalists and militancy indicate that the historical legacy of chaos is threatening to reassert itself. Understanding why the Indian subcontinent's historical experience of governance is characterized by such overwhelming and persistent failure necessitates an examination of those few states that managed to hold chaos at bay for a few generations, which, in turn, is the key to understanding the present and future direction of governance in the region.

EARLY INDIA AND THE ARTHASHASTRA STATE 2000 BC–AD 1000

There is a distinct possibility that the Indus Valley civilization was a continental bureaucratic empire. The environmental conditions that facilitated the emergence of hydraulic civilizations along the Nile and in Mesopotamia are found in the Indus region—aridity, flood plains bounded by natural obstacles such as mountains, deserts, and plateaus and a ready source of fresh water that served as a communications system. The exploitation of this environment required the capacity to organize labour on a large scale, a food distribution system, and an effective central authority. By 2250 BC this central authority appears to have exercised control over the heartland of the Indus River Valley and exerted influence through commerce and diplomacy as far as the Oxus and northern and western India. Greater in territorial extent than its contemporaries in Egypt and Mesopotamia, the Indus Valley civilization manifests several signs of effective governance.

The most important is this civilization's urban development. In a later age Ibn Khaldun observed that urban centres "with their monuments, vast constructions, and large buildings" required "united effort and much co-operation."[3] Given the exertion and sacrifices required, people "must be forced and driven to build cities."[4] Either the "stick of royal authority is what compels them" or "reward and compensation" on such a large scale that only such authority could furnish, are necessary.[5] In the Indus Valley civilization the cities displayed a striking degree of uniformity. Each city drew upon a hinterland for food and resources. The production and distribution of these involved scribal intervention on the Egyptian and Sumerian pattern. The regimentation and orderliness, of the cities also point to the existence of a powerful executive that operated through an effective enforcement mechanism. The instrument of control was probably a bureaucracy responsible for managing the agricultural cycle, maintaining order, collecting taxes, and supervising large construction projects. The rulers of what is sometimes described as the Harappan[6] Empire were also quite possibly legitimated by a homogenizing religion or ideology. Until, however, the writings of this civilization are deciphered the nature of governance that prevailed in it will remain a mystery.

Less mysterious is the Aryan period for evidence indicates that in the sixth century BC continental bureaucratic empires emerged in the Ganges river valley. These states were able to mobilize resources and manpower more effectively than tribal republics or petty chiefdoms, and outfought less centralized and authoritarian forms of government.[7] By the fourth century BC the Nanda dynasty had brought most of the northern plain under its control and is said to have fielded an army two hundred thousand strong. In or around 320 BC the Nandas were overthrown by their former army chief, Chandragupta Maurya, in collusion with his advisor and future prime minister Kautilya and other elements disaffected by Nanda oppression and harshness.

It is to Kautilya that posterity owes a remarkably precise and detailed account of the exercise of state power in Early India.[8] At the heart of the absolutist *Arthashastra*[9] State was the ruler who was advised "A king can protect his kingdom only when he himself is protected from persons near him, particularly his wives and children."[10] Few moral relationships could exist in this culture of power. Princes, compared to crabs, vipers, and fighting rams, were a grave threat to the ruler and so "It is better to kill them quietly if they were found wanting in affection."[11] Queens and other members of the royal household are to be kept perpetually under surveillance by spies.[12] All those with access to the king were considered covetous of the throne. This was perfectly understandable as the reigning monarch was often a usurper and his arbitrary powers excited fear, resentment, and greed amongst his subordinates. As long as the monarch, who was "the embodiment of the state," employed "without hesitation, the methods of secret punishment" against real or perceived enemies, the calculus of fear and greed produced servility.[13] When the royal resolve or capability to inflict punishment was felt to weaken the same logic produced rebellion and instability.

The Mauryan ruler was the universal proprietor and "The metropolitan area was under a highly centralized system of administration."[14] The ordinary cultivator paid rent to the imperial treasury. The servants of the ruler were paid cash salaries and granted lands as transferable revenue assignments. The official priesthood and other recipients of imperial patronage also received revenue assignments in land. Arable land was held by the cultivators so long as they paid taxes and by imperial servants during their employment. The ruler owned or controlled hydraulic infrastructure, settled villages as insular caste-based units, and maintained a fine network of royal highways and state-owned caravanserais. Merchants operated under the threat of confiscation with their trade, organizations and profits, regulated by the state.

The management of the Mauryan imperial estate, which, at its height, stretched from Bihar to the Oxus, necessitated its organization into sub-units. The base unit of the administrative pyramid was the village. Ten villages made a sub-district, twenty sub-districts (two hundred villages), made a district, and two districts (four hundred villages) constituted a division. Two divisions (eight hundred villages) formed a province. Cities were organized into four divisions further divided into multiple wards. At the center, some three-dozen ministries or departments performed functions that included the maintenance of order, tax collection, regulating trade and industry, espionage, prostitution, and enforcing detailed rules and regulations for washer-men.[15] Every task was entrusted to a salaried official hierarchy whose members were recruited, promoted, transferred, or liquidated at the ruler's will with the *adhyakshas*, or department heads, reporting directly to the emperor. Kautilya warns aspirants to official posts "Service under a King has been compared to living in a fire. A fire may burn a part of one's body and, at its worst, all of it; but a King may either confer prosperity or may have the whole family; including wives and children killed."[16] An intelligent officer, therefore, made "self-protection his first and foremost concern."[17] This goal was best achieved through complete obedience in action, word, emotion, and thought, for the imperial presence in the form of spies was pervasive, sensitive to the smallest signs of disloyalty.

The secret service or *gudapurusha* of the *Arthashastra* state had three principal objectives. The first was that it kept the ruler and his trusted servants informed of developments inside and outside the empire. The second was that the secret service conducted covert operations aimed at undermining both domestic and foreign enemies. And third, the secret service was responsible for the internal discipline and loyalty of the bureaucracy and military. A major operational principle that was not to be violated except in emergencies was that intelligence reports from three different sources were needed for the state to authorize action.

The intelligence apparatus was organized into distinct categories. Stationed agents constituted the heart of the machine and comprised all those operatives who stayed primarily in one location and answered to the well-paid and highly trained intelligence officers (*kapatikas*). Mobile agents comprising the secret operative (*sattri*), the assassin (*tikshana*), poison specialist (*rasada*) and wandering nuns (*pariuvajrika*) stood at hand to execute covert action and report on happenings within their circuits. Double agents, counter-espionage, and financial surveillance, had separate hierarchies and operational radii. Kautilya advises the ruler to ensure that the intelligence officers and secret operatives be particularly well paid, honored, and educated so that they may be able to make sense of the information and pass it on in a digested form. It was equally vital that spies of one category and in one post did not know the spies in other categories and posts. The collectors and interpreters of intelligence ought not to know much about field agents engaged in gathering information. Inefficient, disloyal and indiscreet spies were to be killed without hesitation. Disguise, secrecy and silence were vital to the entire enterprise for, "Miraculous results can be achieved by practicing the methods of subversion."[18]

Disloyal elements within the country with the power and wealth to collude effectively with external rivals were particularly worthy objects for the secret service's attention. In essence the *Arthashastra* state waged a continuous and largely unseen war to retain its internal cohesion and disrupt the internal equilibrium of its rivals. The most valuable intelligence operation toward this end was to corrupt or compromise high officials in both hostile and friendly states. This secured valuable insights into the workings of other states and led to a more accurate estimation of their motivations and capabilities. The next best use of spies was the assassination of rival rulers and troublesome dissidents. Given the personalized nature of absolutist states, the removal of the ruler was likely to trigger a civil war, which could be exploited. Properly deployed, "A single assassin can achieve, with weapons, fire or poison, more than a fully mobilized army."[19]

The effectiveness and majesty of the empire depended upon the intellect and work ethic of the ruler and his servants. Of every twenty-four hours, the ruler was to spend separate ninety-minute periods to review reports on defence and finances, grant audiences, receive revenue and make official appointments, draft correspondence and consult with spies, inspect military forces, confer with his defence chiefs, manage secret agents, discuss matters of state with senior officers and appoint spies, respectively. In addition to these twelve hours of regular work, an additional six hours were devoted to secret deliberations and security-related matters. The ruler who stood at the heart of the *Arthashastra* bureaucratic machine was supposed to work eighteen hours a day and in doing so set an example for his servants to follow.

It was in the ruler's own interest that his servants, obedience granted, were recruited, transferred, and promoted on merit. Candidates for imperial service underwent tests of *dharma* (morality and law), *artha* (finance and worldly affairs), *kama* (recreation and aesthetics), and courage. Candidates who excelled at all tests were appointed to the emperor's personal service. Candidates that excelled at morality and law received judicial, police, and district management assignments. Demonstration of excellence in *artha* led to appointments in the financial administration. Success in recreation and aesthetics secured jobs in the establishments responsible for managing brothels, training musicians, and the like. Excelling in the test of courage was the path to the ruler's personal bodyguard and the intelligence service. Candidates that did poorly on every test retained hope of appointments in the departments of mines, forestry, elephants, or workshops and other inglorious assignments.

Salaries ranged from forty-eight thousand *panas* (silver pieces) a year for the royal councillors, guru, priest, defence chief, crown prince, queen, and queen mother, to four thousand to twelve thousand *panas* a year for the bureaucratic officer class that comprised, among others, governors, auditors, and comptrollers, to three thousand to five hundred *panas* for a field bureaucracy that included district officers, brothel managers, local spies, and village headmen. Between the apex and the officer class was a grade of high palace officials paid twenty-four thousand *panas* a year. Beneath the officer grades there existed a mass of clerks, runners, peons, and workers, all paid small but regular cash salaries. Thus, there were effectively four classes of pay (ministers, administrative heads, administrative officers, and administrative support staff). A vast standing military establishment estimated as high as six hundred thousand strong, organized on the same principles, and paid regular salaries, complemented the civilian side of the bureaucracy.

Controlling and sustaining the state machinery was no easy task. Extensive economic controls had to be introduced lest the cost of living diminish the purchasing power of salaries and encourage officers to abuse their powers. A system of regular correspondence between the palace and the districts combined with royal inspections enhanced the ruler's control of his servants. The most effective instruments of royal control were spies. Royal agents installed in covers as varied as senior officers, innkeepers, wandering ascetics, and poison specialists disguised as cooks in the households of royal servants, reported to the emperor and his senior officers. The major objective of the intelligence apparatus was not to prevent corruption. This was recognized as impossible given the size and complexity of the Mauryan Empire. Rather, the aim was to instill fear of imperial omniscience and omnipotence. In so doing, corruption (i.e., stealing from the sovereign) would be reduced and any adverse impact on the ruler's writ minimized.

The ideocratic complex of the Kautilyan continental bureaucratic empire comprised an official religious establishment and a bureaucratic intelligentsia. The ruler assumed the mantle of divine sanction and tongues that committed sacrilege and treason by speaking ill of him were to be ripped from their indiscreet owners' mouths. Religious ceremonies imbued the ruler and his servants with an aura of cosmic significance, as did the employment of *pandits* (learned Brahmins) in the judicial service. In the districts and cities holy men, gurus and tricksters, all on the imperial payroll, projected the ruler's infallibility and godly attributes, while spies found out and secretly punished the dissatisfied and seditious. When the last of the great Mauryan rulers, Ashoka, converted from Hinduism to Buddhism, the state religion also changed. However, while the rhetoric of the state changed, the basic structure of the ideocratic complex did not—a Buddhist bureaucratic intelligentsia and official priesthood took shape.[20] The new ideocratic complex reflected the use of the ruler's arbitrary powers for self-justification and self-aggrandizement and while Ashoka was proclaimed the "Beloved of the Gods"[21] the officers of *dharma* or *dharma-mahamattas* "appear to have been powerful officers with special privileges, possibly fully aware of their role in propagating an imperial ideology."[22] The hollowness of Ashoka's proclaimed pacifism and Buddhism is evidenced by the fact that he "renounced violence only *after* he had done away with all conceivable threats to himself and his realm."[23]

After the disintegration of the Mauryan Empire in the second century BC the Indian subcontinent broke up into numerous kingdoms and principalities each governed along the lines of the Kautilyan continental bureaucratic empire. In the fourth century AD another great continental bureaucratic empire under the Gupta dynasty emerged. A series of wars brought much of the region under Gupta rule by the fifth century. The core of this empire was the old Maurya heartland and its capital, Pataliputra, was the old Maurya capital. The Gupta rulers proclaimed themselves god-kings, exercised universal proprietorship, and brought the country under the direct rule of their appointed servants distributed across the administrative subunits of the empire. The key figure was the *visayapati* (district officer), who controlled rights in land and performed executive and judicial functions. Village headmen were official nominees and the state undertook extensive hydraulic projects to increase yields from agriculture and settle new villages on an insular caste basis. The state monopolized armed force, mobilized labour on a vast scale, minted currency in gold, and maintained an official priesthood and intelligentsia that mythologized the past, preached the virtues of obedience, and projected the ruler as a divine being. After the Gupta Empire fragmented in the sixth century the new states that emerged modelled themselves on the same pattern regardless of size. From the smallest Rajput principality to medium-sized successor kingdoms, the same combination of universal proprietorship, militarism, bureaucracy, and divine sanction, prevailed.

The continental bureaucratic empires of Ancient India manifested an ideocratic and arbitrary culture of power. The country was the personal estate of the ruler. The day-to-day running of this estate was entrusted to a complex bureaucracy subject to the ruler's arbitrary interventions. An official priesthood and bureaucratic intelligentsia, both dependent on the ruler's favour for pay and privileges, furnished the illusion of legitimacy. Wealth, status, and honour flowed from the ruler's will and could be arbitrarily withdrawn. An impressive network of reporters, agents, and spies, kept the ruler informed and punished those believed guilty of thinking, speaking, or acting, against the supreme hegemon. A large military establishment organized on bureaucratic principles stood at the ready to restore order, respond to emergencies and expand frontiers.

Society was atomized by the state into sub-political, insular, caste-based units placed in direct contact with officers representing the overwhelming powers of the central state. The Mauryan state, for instance, "took the precaution of keeping its peasants unarmed."[24] Society responded with servility when the state was strong and with rebellion if the state was perceived to be weak.[25] Successful rebellion, however, led to anarchy and the rise of warlords and petty tyrants who were even more arbitrary, capricious, and unenlightened. Indian society lacked adequate horizontal or vertical associations capable of creating an organic political order when the external force of the imperial state ceased to be effective. After many centuries of breakdown, an apathetic and brutalized society was, once again, brought under the direction of an imperial overlord. The new order, however, was basically a replica of the old and endured only so long as the intellectual and moral qualities of the rulers remained high. This, was often the product of luck or circumstance and if the war of succession that often followed the death of a ruler failed to produce a competent heir, the state would fail and society would be left at the mercy of master-less, fragmenting, arbitrary, and remorselessly selfish, bureaucratic instruments. Kautilya warned that in the absence of a *chakravartin*, there was a real danger of a foreign invader successfully conquering the Indian subcontinent and establishing an empire of his own.[26] Six centuries after the fall of the Guptas, the Turks invaded an Indian subcontinent convulsed by conflict and emerged as the supreme hegemonic element by the mid-thirteenth century.

THE DELHI SULTANATE AND THE TURCO-PERSIAN IMPERIAL AGE, 1206–1526[27]

The Turks were a tribal people on the margins of civilization that came into West Asia and North Africa as military slaves of the Arab Empire. In the mid-800s the Abbasid ruler, Mu'tasim, established an imperial guard "a few thousand strong but tough, disciplined and devoted to their master" comprising only Turks.[28] By the late-800s AD the Turks established themselves as the ruling class of a disintegrating Abbasid Caliphate.[29] Like the Arabs before their imperial rise, the Turks had no experience of ruling a bureaucratic state. Again, like the Arabs, once the Turks acquired power they quickly absorbed the ideocratic and arbitrary cultures of power of the continental bureaucratic empires that fell under their sway. At a more formal level this transition meant the adoption and practice of Ancient Persian conceptions of statecraft. The significance of Turkish adoption of a Persianized culture of power was that before the Turks ventured into the Indian subcontinent they had already come to exercise power in the ideocratic and arbitrary manner common to continental bureaucratic empires.

The core organizational principle of the Delhi Sultanate was the universal proprietorship of the sovereign. The test of a sultan's strength was his ability to enforce his universal proprietorship. Ghiyathudin Balban, through a policy of terror and confiscation, brought his fellow slaves under control. Allaudin Khalji confiscated the properties of his predecessors' servants, converted their *iqtas* (transferable revenue assignments in land) into crown lands, and confiscated all privately held property, inclusive of charitable endowments and lands granted as gifts.[30] Similar acts of mass-confiscation characterized the reigns of later sultans. The pre-existing insularity, apathy, and atomization of Indian society helped the sultans establish their arbitrary rule. Village headmen became the sultan's highway watchmen, were often forbidden from possessing arms or horses, and subjected to beatings and confiscations. Property in the form of capital was similarly under the ruler's control. Leading merchants were coerced into living in or near the capital. A network of market superintendents, reporters, and spies regulated prices and profits, with violators punished with torture and confiscation. The sultan owned his own manufacturing establishments that converted taxpayers' money into luxuries, such as robes of honour (hundreds of thousands of which were doled out each year) and handicrafts, and weapons. Merchants required official permits, licenses, and passports, and existed at the sufferance of the sultan and his servants.

The sheer size of the Delhi Sultanate meant that the ruler had to rely upon appointed servants to do his bidding. These servants, be they judges, tax collectors, military governors, or city magistrates, were granted *iqtas* in exchange for their services. The central government comprised a royal council, ministries for revenue, local administration and communications, war, and markets, and separate departments for justice, agriculture, river navigation, canals, land clearance, subsidies, and the admiralty. The sultanate was divided into provinces, divisions, districts, villages, and urban areas, each administered through a hierarchy of appointed servants or local notables dependent on imperial patronage.

Like Achaemenid Persia and the Abbasid Caliphate, the Delhi Sultanate made extensive use of slaves to fill administrative and military posts. Indeed, the first sultans were slaves themselves. In the early thirteenth century the sultan owned about fifty thousand slaves. By the late fourteenth century the sultan owned nearly two hundred thousand slaves. In addition to these slaves thousands of migrants from Persia, Central Asia, and the Arab world poured into the Indian subcontinent seeking employment in the sultan's service. It was not uncommon for half or more of a sultan's high officials to have been born outside the Indian subcontinent. Slaves, as property of the sultan, were often imported from abroad, and owed everything to their master. Moreover, as the slaves were equal to each other they sought to preserve that equality even if it entailed perpetuating their own servitude. The greatest advantage of this system was that the sultan's arbitrary power, if wielded effectively, could rapidly and without encumbrance operate through a bureaucratic elite that was talented, highly educated, hardworking, and obedient. The greatest disadvantage was that the bureaucratic class was heterogeneous, atomized, lacked moral relationships, and, in the absence of a strong ruler capable of inspiring fear, fell apart.

The sultan's two most vital weapons were the army and spies. As with the Mauryas, the size of the Delhi Sultanate's armies under competent rulers is estimated at between three hundred thousand and six hundred thousand. Even with the lower estimate, the cost of maintaining such a standing armed force on fixed salaries entailed a heavy fiscal burden. Like the Mauryas, the sultans used a combination of economic controls and regulations to keep prices and shortages in check. Unlike the Mauryas, the sultans did not appoint a permanent army chief and, instead, performed that role personally or appointed commanders as needed. Repeated failures of dynastic succession meant the territories of the Delhi Sultanate had to be re-conquered every two generations. When not engaged in re-conquest, the army expanded the frontiers of the sultanate and quelled internal rebellions.

Spies and reporters were used for a diverse range of functions. The most important was providing the sultan with an independent source of information. Regular reports coordinated by the postmaster general, were delivered through an impressive courier-relay system that managed to move official communications ten times faster than otherwise possible.[31] Ibn Battuta recounts how at Multan his party stopped for a routine inspection by the intelligence service.[32] Normally, the journey from Multan to Delhi took "fifty days march but when the intelligence officers write to the sultan . . . the letter reaches him in five days" thanks to the postal service.[33] Besides regular reports, spies were employed in the households of the sultan's relations and senior officers, given undercover assignments in the administration and military, investigated the full extent of officers' assets, pried into household expenses of ordinary subjects, watched markets, and wandered the streets as beggars. There prevailed an "atmosphere of perpetual suspicion and distrust" in which "spies and reporters poked their noses into everyone's private business."[34]

The Delhi Sultanate was an ideocratic state in which the ruler styled himself the Shadow of God and disobedience was equated with opposition to the divine will. The punishment for speaking against the sultan was death. An official priesthood and bureaucratic intelligentsia paid from state funds and grants in land, dispersed across a country with an overwhelming Hindu majority, and thus abjectly dependent upon the sultan, provided him with adulation and the illusion of legitimacy. From the class of Muslim clerics and scholars were drawn the judicial officers (*qazi*s) responsible for settling disputes unrelated to the administration. The sultan appointed the *qazi*s and their decisions could be appealed to him and changed, countermanded, or confirmed as he saw fit. The sultan personally dispensed justice, as did his governors, according to their caprice. Many sultans pursued a policy of destroying Hindu temples and converting them into mosques, albeit with varied zeal. The idea was to humiliate the gods of the Hindus and so demonstrate that divinity was on the side of the sultans. Elaborate and lavish court ceremonial, on the Ancient Persian pattern, complete with prostration and ground kissing, served to dramatize the distance between the ruler and the ruled, "was highly artificial and reveals anything but a virile and healthy environment."[35] By the mid-fourteenth century, Sufi orders were also brought under the patronage and control of the state.[36]

The Delhi Sultanate was a continental bureaucratic empire that periodically rivalled in extent and powers its Gupta and Maurya predecessors. The sultan was the universal proprietor, sanctioned by divinity, and operated through a hierarchy of slaves and servants. So long as the sultan was intelligent enough to wield the instruments at his disposal effectively his arbitrary rule prevailed. As soon as the ruler proved incompetent or indecisive he would be overthrown. If the period of disorder did not quickly produce a competent successor the central administration, which "was practically the only unifying force in the country,"[37] collapsed and anarchy ensued. The sultan ruled only so long as he was successful for "one little disaster, one chance defeat, and the whole fabric of the state broke down. Under such a scheme of government, the masses of people, already living in intellectual isolation, became ever more indifferent to the fortunes of their monarch and the political destiny of their kingdom."[38]

The culture of power of the Delhi Sultanate manifested the same arbitrariness, bureaucratization, militarism, lack of trust within the ruling class, ideocratic delusion, perpetual surveillance, and disregard for private property as the *Arthasastra* State. The differences were in the formal organization of the state, and the preferred idiom in which the discourse of power took place. Like the Hindu rulers the sultans ultimately failed to heed Kautilya's warning of the presence of great outsiders. In 1526, a force of Chingezi Turks and disaffected Afghans under the leadership of Babur, including blood relatives of the incumbent sultan whose pretensions dwarfed his capabilities, defeated the decaying Delhi Sultanate. This inaugurated the Timurid Empire.[39]

THE TIMURID EMPIRE AND THE CLIMAX OF THE TURCO-PERSIAN IMPERIAL AGE, 1526–1707

Though established in 1526, it took the Timurid Empire thirty-four years to emerge as the largest and most powerful of about twenty states in the Indian subcontinent. From 1564 to 1591 the Indo-Gangetic plain was brought under Timurid rule and by the first decade of the seventeenth century the empire pressed with some success into the Deccan and peninsular India. When Akbar the Great (1556–1605) died, the Timurid Empire stretched from Kabul to Bengal and from Kashmir to the Deccan. Akbar's three able successors, Jahangir (r. 1605–1627), Shahjahan (r. 1627–1658), and Aurungzeb (r. 1658–1707), provided a century of strong leadership.[40]

In the classical tradition of continental bureaucratic empires the basic principle of the Timurid dominion was that the entire country was the personal estate of the ruler.[41] The sheer size of the estate meant that to manage it without sharing power an imperial bureaucracy distributed across administrative subunits was needed. These subunits, in the early 1600s comprised twelve provinces, one hundred divisions, and about three thousand districts. The imperial bureaucracy of the Timurids were known as *mansabdars* or office holders, and the system through which they were recruited, promoted, transferred, and remunerated, was known as the *mansabdari nizam*. The *mansabdars* were organized into a hierarchy of grades starting at twenty and going up to seven or ten thousand. Remuneration consisted of salaries and revenue assignments in land or *jagirs*. The military rank of the officer determined the number of heavy cavalry he had to maintain.

The size and complexity of the central financial administration and the wealth and privileges of the warrior-bureaucratic elite were almost without parallel in Eurasia. While in Persia and Turkey there was only one principal treasurer appointed to the royal court "here in India, the amount of revenues is so great, and the business so multifarious" that twelve royal treasurers were needed to help manage imperial finances.[42] Each of the emperor's one hundred workshops had its own treasurer bringing the total to about one hundred and twelve in all.[43] In 1647, when the annual revenues of the empire stood at 220 million rupees, the 445 *mansabdars* of grade five hundred and above accounted for 61 percent of total revenue, while the 68 princes and nobles at the top accounted for some 37 percent of total revenues.[44] When Yamin-ud-Daula, a prominent provincial noble based in Lahore, died in November 1641 and imperial officers took account of his possessions, his estate was assessed at 25 million rupees[45] inclusive of three million rupees in jewels and 12.50 million rupees in cash.[46] At that time, the Safavid Shah of Iran had an annual income of 24 million rupees.[47] Great wealth was also the source of great insecurity for the emperor was "himself the heir of all the *Omrah*s, or lords, and likewise of the *Mansabdar*s, or inferior lords, who are in his pay."[48] When an officer fell from favour, or died, his possessions were seized by the emperor's agents. This practice was the logical outcome of the ruler being the "proprietor of every acre of land in the kingdom, excepting, perhaps, some houses and gardens which he sometimes permits his subjects to buy, sell, and otherwise dispense of, among themselves."[49] As transfers were frequent and confiscation assumed, officers extracted "as much as they could from the peasantry without any concern for the economic future of the areas temporarily under their control."[50] Local notables, such as *zamindars*, *chaudaries*, and even Rajput princes, were confirmed in their possession of land, served either as *mansabdars* or under the direction of imperial officers and could be expropriated if they misbehaved. Merchants operated under numerous restrictions, were subject to arbitrary confiscation, and city magistrates appointed guild leaders. To protect themselves and secure better terms, many merchants sought the patronage of imperial officers. This protection racket was a lucrative source of informal income for the warrior-bureaucratic ruling class who abused its powers to amass great trading fortunes.[51]

Controlling imperial servants and through them the country was no easy task. The Timurids relied on their military machine to maintain order and collect taxes, one of the advantages of the *mansabdari* system being that it allowed for the dispersal and flexible use of armed force. The size of the military establishment according to Abul Fazl's figures, including the heavy cavalry, musketeers, royal guard, and auxiliaries maintained by local notables, comes to 4.40 million.[52] Based upon these figures and the total revenue demands of the Timurid Empire, which amounted to between one-third and half of the GNP, as many as 26 million people may have depended directly and indirectly upon the military for their livelihood and thus sustained a dominant military-agrarian complex.[53] In the royal stables alone there were seventeen distinct categories of employees.[54] Another estimate is that by the mid-seventeenth century the total number of paid soldiers was about one million.[55] Of these soldiers the emperor kept enough of the best with himself and the royal princes, and retained the most important nobles at the imperial court. The general trend was that so long as the emperor was strong, rebellions by local notables, imperial servants, or disgruntled peasants, were crushed.

The ability of the Timurid warrior-bureaucratic elite to unite against their arbitrary overlord and gain a measure of personal and collective security was circumscribed by a number of factors. One was that at the provincial level two officers of equal importance, the provincial revenue ministers and provincial governors headed the financial administration and general administration, respectively. Both officers were often rivals and reported upon each other to the emperor. Another factor was the heterogeneous and alien nature of a ruling class that comprised Turks, Mongols, Uzbeks, Persians, Arabs, Rajputs, Marathas, Afghans, a smattering of Indian Muslims and a few exceptional Hindus. Turks, Persians and Afghans accounted for 60 percent of the imperial higher bureaucracy between 1595 and 1678, Rajputs 13 percent and Indian Muslims 13 percent.[56] Many of the imperial officers were of mean origins, had been raised quite suddenly to high office, and were thus completely dependent on royal favour. Many were foreigners and lacked knowledge of local conditions. Even after experience was acquired the system of regular transfers combined with the imperial bureaucracy's preference for living in the cities and sending agents and soldiers to collect revenue from *jagir*s ensured that the rulers remained strangers to the land they governed and regarded their subjects as intrinsically inferior.[57] Intense rivalries between ethnic and religious groups meant that the rebellion or disobedience of one noble, or group, provided others the opportunity to gain royal favour at the upstart's expense. An intelligent ruler could manipulate the calculus of fear and greed to control his demographically diverse apparatus. However much the imperial servants feared their master, they knew that if one of their own seized power he would assert his universal proprietorship and redistribute assets amongst his favourites. For all practical purposes "the absence of any constitutional body or permanent authority in the state to control and supervise the administration" meant that "the only guarantee to avert, check, or overcome the dangers to the Empire, and to ensure smooth working of the administration, was the vigilance of the ruling monarch."[58]

In 1560, for instance, when word got out that Akbar was upset with his guardian and tutor, Bairam Khan, "all men turned their backs upon him and their faces towards the Emperor" in "the hope of receiving dignities and *jagir*s suitable to their condition."[59] About twenty years later, Akbar, having raised Khawja Mansur, a former clerk in the imperial perfumery department, to the post of *diwan* (revenue minister), threw him in jail upon receiving complaints of his pettiness and obstructionism.[60] After a while, Akbar relented and restored Khwaja Mansur to his ministerial post. Soon, letters fell into Akbar's hands indicating Khwaja Mansur was disloyal. His anger fanned by nobles dissatisfied with Khwaja Mansur, Akbar ordered the revenue minister's arrest and execution, which were immediately carried out. After the execution, Akbar decided to have his "confidential servants" investigate the letters, which proved to be forgeries.[61] Akbar "regretted the execution" but didn't pursue the matter further.[62]

Another vital instrument of control were "confidential servants" or reporters, spies, informants, and secret operatives. Each district had its news-writer whose job it was to report everything of note that occurred in a district. At the centre, fourteen "zealous, experienced, and impartial" imperial secretaries summarized reports, prepared accounts, handled routine correspondence, and performed other vital paperwork.[63] Away from the emperor's watchful eye, in the provinces and districts, the news-writers often opted for collusion and concealment with local officers.[64] One can imagine that diligent reporters were unpopular with the local governors and given the latter's military powers, exposed to considerable physical risk.

Spies and informers were thus necessary for providing the emperor with more reliable information. These agents were deployed to check the household expenditures of royal subjects, infiltrate the harems of nobles and report political and personal information, spy on the royal princes, check accounts, investigate cases, prevent rebellions or provide early warning, and report on military efficiency. The postmaster general acted as the head of the formal and informal system of correspondence carried by a courier-relay system. To be on the safe side, the Timurids employed spies to spy on other spies. Pervasive suspicion meant ordinary subjects and state servants resorted to concealment and theft as and when possible. The former lived in studied indigence and buried their valuables in the ground and in wells. The latter spent lavishly and secretly hoarded ill-gotten wealth knowing that sooner or later it would be investigated and the emperor would confiscate the uncovered amount. So, the logic went that it was advisable to steal so much that even if most assets were confiscated enough was left to maintain the family until another one of them became an imperial servant. Given the Timurid preference for fair-skinned foreigners, however, chances of imperial employment declined with each succeeding generation.[65]

The ideocratic complex of the Timurid Empire consisted of an official priesthood and a bureaucratic intelligentsia. The state paid subsidies to religious establishments, regular stipends to religious scholars, and employed the Muslim priestly class as judges much as the Delhi Sultanate did. The ruler was divinely sanctioned and to oppose him was blasphemous and treasonous. Although great attention has been paid to Akbar's infallibility decree and creation of a royal religious cult based on emperor and sun worship (*Din-i-Ilahi*), taking imperial rhetoric seriously obscures the underlying arbitrary power of the sovereign.[66] There was nothing new in the infallibility decree extracted, as it was from a servile, cynical, and worldly official priesthood. Since ancient times the rulers of the Indian subcontinent assumed the mantle of infallibility. The creation of a new religious cult or legitimating ideology was also not without precedent. Alauddin Khalji and Mohammed bin Tughluq contemplated founding religions. In ancient times, Ashoka changed the official religion, which subsequently alternated between Buddhism and Hinduism, depending on the ruler's personal inclination. That Akbar chose not to spread his religious cult beyond the military and bureaucratic elite does not alter the fact that, ultimately, it was his choice.

Akbar's successors drifted towards an increasingly orthodox ideocratic complex characterized by the wanton desecration of hundreds of Hindu temples and the culmination of this process was reached under Aurungzeb. Aurungzeb, like his predecessors, used religion for political ends and to cloak himself in an aura of divinity. Part of this policy was to employ religious scholars and judges, normally at the base of the Timurid power pyramid, in financial and administrative posts. This led the lay nobles to bemoan the emperor's reliance on abjectly servile "hypocritical mystics and empty-headed scholars."[67] Much like the consultants and development experts of today, "these men are selling their knowledge and manners for the company of kings" and "to rely on them was," and is, "neither in accordance with the divinely prescribed path, nor suited to the ways of the world."[68] Indeed, "these men are robbers in every way" and "(As the saying is), the finances are given over to the Qazi and the Qazi is satisfied only with bribes."[69] Lavish court ceremonial involved the circulation of tens of millions of rupees of gifts every year, and emphasized the ruler's universal proprietorship even as it legitimized bribery.[70]

Society's response to the Timurid imperial machine was even greater insularity and apathy. As the Timurid Empire extracted more resources out of a stagnant economic base in pursuit of military glory and monumental extravagance, flight from the land, concealment, and rebellions became more common. By the 1670s and 1680s order in the vicinity of Delhi and Agra started breaking down. The atomization of society meant that when the external force holding the country together waned the results were anarchy, bloodshed and spiralling arbitrariness and confusion. The end came swiftly for the Timurid Empire. After Aurungzeb's death in 1707 the succession of competent rulers ended. Wars of succession and dislocation at the center caused fragmentation, spread anarchy, and invited foreign invasions. By 1721 the central government ceased to be effective. In the 1730s and 1740s local officers carved out kingdoms for themselves. In 1764, the last vestiges of Timurid power vanished with the British victory at Buxar. The dynasty survived as British dependents until 1857 though its effective power barely encompassed the palace grounds at Delhi.

The Timurid continental bureaucratic empire exceeded its predecessors in territorial extent and centralization. The ruling class of the Timurid state were the servants of the emperor, organized into a bureaucratic hierarchy recruited, transferred, and liquidated at the ruler's will. The ruler was also the universal proprietor and legitimized by his preferred interpretation of divinity. The bureaucratic classes also served as the academic elite while scholars and priests depended on imperial patronage. Within the Timurid omni-estate all wealth, status, and position, emanated from the favour of the ruler and his servants. To keep his flocks and shepherds in line, the emperor employed military coercion and espionage on a vast scale. The Timurid Empire, as its megalithic textual remains indicate, was essentially a government that operated by correspondence, remote decision, and, so long as the ruler was capable, outward respect for refined bureaucratic routine.

The arbitrary powers of the sovereign pre-empted moral relationships from developing even within the ruling family. The emperors' brothers, sons, and relations, revolted repeatedly. Akbar's son and successor, Jahangir, revolted and had Abul Fazl murdered out of personal and political enmity. Jahangir's son, Khusrau, revolted against his father, but failed, was imprisoned, and three hundred of his partisans were impaled outside Lahore. Shahjahan's third son, Aurungzeb, who, in a series of campaigns, defeated and killed his fellow royal princes, imprisoned the aging emperor. Imprisonment and exile were the fates of Aurungzeb's own sons. In 1707, upon Aurungzeb's death, a war of succession failed to produce a competent ruler and the heterogeneous and conspiratorial nature of the imperial warrior-bureaucracy combined with the apathy of the ruled, caused the empire to fragment into hundreds of petty bureaucratic estates, exponentially increasing the levels of arbitrariness, mismanagement, corruption and insecurity. Eventually, out of the maelstrom of wars of Timurid succession a new power willing and able to unify the Indian subcontinent emerged.

This new power was Britain, or, more precisely, the British East India Company. The British, possessed a culture of power anomalous even by European standards that found formal expression in the State of Laws. After the British conquest of Bengal in 1757 it remained to be seen if the British culture of power so admired by Enlightenment thinkers such as Voltaire and Montesquieu, could reform the ideocratic and arbitrary culture of power of the subcontinent. The State of Laws and the continental bureaucratic empire were set to confront each other. Far more was at stake in this struggle than the future of India or the validity of philosophical liberalism. At stake was the idea of the alterability of the human condition in relation to the exercise of state power so central to the Enlightenment and the Revolution. After thousands of years history was about to offer a choice.

THE BRITISH ADVENT, THE STATE OF LAWS, AND REFORMS TO THE CULTURE OF POWER OF THE INDIAN SUBCONTINENT, 1757–1947[71]

The environmental setting in which the state of laws evolved was relatively poor, isolated, and quite literally, at the margins of civilization. Britain lacked agricultural resources, and it was not until the Roman conquest of the first century AD that civilization reached its shores. Till the Roman withdrawal three centuries later, Britain was governed as an imperial province. After the barbarian invasions of the fourth and fifth centuries, which brought the Anglo-Saxons to Britain from Germany, the island was overrun and descended into chaos. It took more than four centuries and the threat of Viking attack for the Anglo-Saxon nobles to realize the necessity of some form of central leadership. Under Alfred the Great (r. 871–899) the country was governed with the advice and consent of the *witena gemot* (council of the wise) and the *folkmoot* (semi-annual gathering of freemen).

The successful Norman invasion of England in 1066 resulted in the establishment of military feudalism and a strong monarchy. The Norman rulers dispersed the Anglo-Saxon aristocracy and replaced it with nobles from Normandy. These nobles were considered tenants by the ruler and owed him military service which, if not properly fulfilled, could result in the confiscation of their lands. An important feature of the Norman system that militated against the ruler's universal proprietorship was that the estates were normally held for life and stood to be inherited by the eldest son. The Norman nobility also maintained order, dispensed justice, and collected taxes, from their estates. Over time, the Norman nobility developed a strong proprietary interest, made long-term investments in developing trading centres and towns on their own initiative, secured a local power base, and, through marriage and enculturation, ceased to think of themselves as foreigners. Royal focus, distracted by continental entanglements ranging from relations with the French monarchy to the Crusades, failed to fathom the growing power of what soon became an Anglo-Norman aristocracy.

The attempts made at circumventing the power of the aristocracy by rulers like Henry II (r. 1154–1189) actually decreased their own arbitrary powers over the long-term. For example, Henry II constituted royal courts that administered the Common Law assisted by juries of twelve freemen. His objective was to draw litigants away from the manorial courts. The Common Law judiciary, however, became one of the champions of a limited monarchy. Later attempts to manipulate judicial power in order to enhance royal control, such as the Nottingham Declaration and the crisis precipitated by Richard II (r. 1377–1399), the High Commission employed by James I (r. 1603–1625) and the Court of the Star Chamber used by Charles I (r. 1625–1649) to enhance royal power by intervening against aristocrats in their disputes with peasants, ended in defeat for the monarch. Indeed, royal efforts to use the judiciary were an admission of executive weakness and indicated the absence of centralized means of administrative control.

If circumvention proved futile, confrontation brought disaster. Practically all attempts by the executive to impose centralized control failed and actually provoked important groups to establish autonomous institutions, most famously the Lords and the Commons, to deter further efforts. In 1215, for instance, King John tried to compel his nobles to join a royal expedition to re-conquer Normandy, which was lost to France in 1204. In order to finance the expedition King John vigorously collected taxes, imposed fines, and abused his powers of escheat and wardship. He also relied on favourites from Normandy and raised a mercenary army which, complemented by feudal levies, was to invade Normandy. The aristocracy, wary of the king's grasping and arbitrary ways, and fearful of what might happen if the army were turned upon them, rebelled. They managed to catch the king off-guard and extracted from him the Great Charter (*Magna Charta*) of 1215.

This charter limited the powers of kings in important areas. The king could not interfere in property-related matters. The appointment of local officials was formally entrusted to the local governments dominated by the aristocracy. Free subjects could not be arbitrarily thrown in jail and had the right to trial by jury. Additional taxes and customs could not be levied on towns and cities and their privileges and exemptions were confirmed. The king could not demand additional funds beyond those derived from the royal lands without the consent of the lords and the higher clergy. Mercenaries were to be disbanded and foreign favourites sent home. The state, in other words, was not the personal estate of the ruler. Lawful opposition was possible, even expected, should the king try to govern the country as his personal estate. The law "was an independent power" supported by important interests to which the ruler was answerable.[72] Between 1215 and 1688, the monarchy, the Church, the Lords, the Commons and the judiciary, engaged in a complex struggle for power and while the alignment of these institutions changed, broadly speaking, the parliamentary and judicial institutions overcame the executive and ecclesiastical combination. At a cognitive level the state of laws rested on the twin realizations that "There is no liberty, if the judiciary power be not separated from the legislative and executive"[73] and "If the legislative power was to settle the subsidies, not from year to year, but forever, it would run the risk of losing its liberty, because the executive power would no longer be dependant."[74]

The culture of power of this state of laws was characterized by the existence of lawful and effective means of defying the sovereign, the prevalence of autonomous institutions, the rule of law, and private property. The soil in which this anomaly grew was England and, eventually, her overseas dominions of settlement. Alexis de Tocqueville, a contemporary of the Marquis de Custine[75] who travelled in the opposite direction to the United States found,

> The English colonies—and that was one of the main reasons for their prosperity—have always enjoyed more internal freedom and political independence than those of other nations; nowhere was this principle of liberty applied more completely than in the states of New England.
>   . . . All the general principles on which modern constitutions rest, principles which most Europeans in the seventeenth century scarcely

understood and whose dominance in Great Britain was then far from complete, are recognized and given authority by the laws of New England; the participation of the people in public affairs, the free voting of taxes, the responsibility of government officials, individual freedom, and trial by jury—all these things were established without question and with practical effect.[76]

The laws and political morality identified by de Tocqueville were transplanted from England. In England, however, aristocratic and class privileges placed limits on the democratic principle. In the dominions of settlement where the feudal legacy was weak the result was faster movement towards greater representation and self-government. Indeed, it was not until the twentieth century that England made the final transition from aristocratic liberalism to representative democracy as practiced in its dominions of settlement.[77]

Most notions of constitutionalism, civil liberties, and the rule of law, are derived from the historical experience of governance of the English and their dominions of settlement. Through the medium of the British Empire aspects of the state of laws were exported to many parts of the world. British prosperity and military superiority were envied by the bureaucratic states of Continental Europe. Some of these states attempted sincerely but with limited success, like France and liberal-conservative Italy in the nineteenth century, to incorporate some of the habits and practices associated with the state of laws. Others, like Bismarck's Germany, were cynical and created a representative façade to obscure despotism. Some states, like Russia, openly held the state of laws in contempt and resisted all attempts to share power with the executive, with ultimately tragic consequences in the early 1900s. One of the greatest challenges to the state of laws as a historical phenomenon came in 1757 with the advent of British rule in India after the East India Company defeated Nawab Sirajud Daula of Bengal at the Battle of Plassey. India was too densely populated to become a dominion of settlement along the lines of Canada and Australia and in spite of domestic pressure the British authorities did not encourage emigration to India. As the ascent of the British Empire in India through craft and coercion has already been dealt with exhaustively by others we limit our survey to those factors most relevant to the continental bureaucratic empires and their cultures of power.

It was not inevitable that the avaricious rule of the East India Company in Bengal would be brought under parliamentary regulation. The constitutional problem with such intervention, the horror stories and wealthy "nabobs" coming from Bengal aside, was that the Company was a chartered body and had a lawful sphere of autonomy ceded to it by the sovereign that could not be arbitrarily interfered with. Even as evidence grew of criminal incompetence and rampant corruption after the conquest of Bengal in 1757, the Company's chartered status protected it. The British state of laws was full of chartered bodies ranging from the hundreds of privately owned turnpike trusts that built and operated the country's road system to the City of London. Parliamentary power and legitimacy flowed from the Great Charter of 1215. An attack on the lawful autonomy of the Company would motivate other chartered bodies to come to its defence to protect a legal principle from which their liberties and that of the country at large were derived. Fortunately for the Company's Indian subjects, the costs of fighting wars combined with manifest administrative ineptitude brought the Company to the verge of bankruptcy. In 1772, the Company's liabilities, at nine million pounds, far outweighed its assets, estimated at five million pounds. Parliamentary intervention took place in the context of the Company's request for public funds to avert collapse. In exchange for a bailout, the government received regulatory powers that created a governor-general, a council of officials appointed by the British cabinet, and a reduction of the annual dividend from 8 to 6 per cent.

Under the new framework Warren Hastings, a company official with decades of experience in India, became the first governor-general (1774–85). Hastings was principally concerned with making the Indian tradition of arbitrary rule effective and expanding the Company's territories. Like Indian rulers, he amassed a considerable personal fortune, patronized scholars, and used whatever means necessary, including extortion, to maximize his powers. His relationship with his council was, at best, ambivalent, and very often hostile. With the Supreme Court at Calcutta, constituted by the Bengal Judicature Act of 1781, and initially headed by his class-fellow and friend, Justice Impey, Hastings had a better relationship. Hastings's tenure was important in two respects as far as the culture of power is concerned. The first was that after Hastings the post of governor-general went almost exclusively to British aristocrats and reflected the realization that continental bureaucratic empires can only be governed from the palace—the counting house mentality being utterly ill suited.[78] Having said that, few in England understood the problems Hastings faced "in constructing the framework of civil administration from want of local knowledge, from the inefficiency of a refractory and corrupt Civil Service, and the venality of native officials."[79] The second was in part a consequence of this lack of understanding and entailed Hastings's impeachment in a trial that dragged on for nine years.

On April 4, 1786, Hastings was charged with "sundry high crimes and misdemeanours."[80] If convicted, Hastings faced the death penalty. On 1 May, Hastings began his defence by asserting that his decisions were "invariably regulated by truth, justice, and good faith" when the better choice was to plead necessity of state and show some contrition.[81] On July 1, 1787, Edmund Burke, the leader of the campaign against Hastings, thundered: "I impeach him in the name of the people of India, whose laws, rights, and liberties he has subverted, whose properties he has destroyed, whose country he has laid waste and desolate."[82] Burke's impassioned plea on behalf of a collective ("The people of India") that did not exist, and of rights and laws and liberties that had no indigenous variant in India, must not obscure the "nuggets of truth" in the accusations or the deeper implications of this rhetorical flourish.[83] The accusations were based on Hastings's arbitrary exercise of power and established the earthly accountability of the supreme executive. That such arbitrariness and excess were the norm in India did not matter. It was in principle wrong and every English officer of the Company was responsible for upholding the state morality of the British state of laws whilst in India.

Actually doing so was the task of Hastings's successor, Lord Cornwallis (1785–93). A product of the Enlightenment, Cornwallis believed that operating an efficient despotism on indigenous principles was morally and politically unacceptable as "The principle of despotic government is subject to a continued corruption, because it is even in its nature corrupt."[84] For Cornwallis "the essence of the problem was to limit government power and so prevent its abuse."[85] The judicial powers of the boards of revenue and collectors were taken away even though his closest advisors, such as John Shore, argued in favour of a strong district executive as the Indians "being accustomed to a despotic authority should only look to one master."[86] Secret inquiries were launched into the illegal activities of the Company's servants and despite the difficulties inherent in trying to prosecute white-collar crime, by February 1787, the Advocate General was moving against the corrupt.[87] Cornwallis refused to exercise his discretion in order to favor candidates for official appointments simply because they were backed by the monarch or leading aristocrats.[88]

The sovereign ended his universal proprietorship and vested it in the local landlords, or *zamindars* in the hope that an aristocracy would emerge. In each district of Bengal the district judge was given control of the police and received greater status and pay than the collector. The armed retainers of the *zamindars* were disbanded and Indians removed from offices of importance. Officers were discouraged from accepting presents and, if they were placed in a situation where they couldn't refuse, the gift was made over to the public treasury. Cornwallis made it clear through word and deed that he did not see the country as his personal estate and that the government machinery and servants of the state were beholden to the law. The greater reliance on Europeans was justified on the grounds that Indian officials were greatly influenced by their superiors' character and competence and thus "under an active collector of scrupulous integrity, all gross abuse of powers" could be prevented.[89] Cornwallis thought that by "giving the landholders a permanent establishment in their possessions" a number of advantages would be reaped.[90] First, the landlords would secure "the benefit of future improvement" and save and invest wisely and contribute to a general increase in prosperity.[91] Second, the landlord would naturally contrast the security and assured importance granted by the British with their immeasurably more "precarious" condition under Indian rulers.[92] Third, this would gain their attachment to British rule and provide it with a broader social base especially in the countryside. Cultivating the landed elite was vital given that it was dangerous to "over-rate the advantages . . . from a favourable disposition on the part of the peasantry" who, in India, "pass with the land from ruler to ruler, with scarcely any consciousness of the change."[93] To make the law more effective and clear, Cornwallis began the process of codification.[94] Cornwallis's successors, John Shore (1793–1798) and Lord Wellesley (1798–1805), continued along this trajectory by expanding the scope of property rights, leaving dispute settlement to the judicial power, and limiting the executive function to the bare minimum required to maintain order and collect taxes.

The Cornwallis system did not work as intended. The judicial power was too slow, alien, and expensive to be the core element of the administration. By 1824, there were nearly 124,000 cases in arrears in Bengal alone.[95] It took time for the British to realize that whereas back home the "grandest and most expensive undertakings" could "be left to individual enterprise or the excitement of public spirit"; the "opposite duty" fell upon their shoulders in continental bureaucratic empires such as India where an arbitrary culture of power had over centuries substantially crushed both.[96] Here it was expected that the rulers and their servants would provide the initiative, resources and organization, necessary for "the construction and maintenance of works of great public utility."[97] Learning from Indian history, it was increasingly appreciated that its sovereigns had "long been in the practice" of providing agricultural loans, manufacturing subsidies, building hydraulic and communications infrastructure, maintaining the intelligentsia, ensuring order, collecting taxes, and defence.[98] Continental bureaucratic empires were ruled from palaces, not counting houses, and the ethos of leadership and management in such states were inspired by princely, not mercantile, values.[99] This was a point that Wellesley asserted with effect when he argued that the East India Company's officials "could no longer be considered as the agents of a commercial concern" and must behave as the "officers of a powerful sovereign."[100]

The *zamindars*, deprived of their coercive powers, relied on loans to finance their lifestyles. When they were unable to repay the loans, their lands were auctioned. The result was the emergence of a new class of absentee-merchant-landlords based in large measure in Calcutta who, much as the parasitic Turco-Persian *zamindars* they dispossessed, did little to improve agriculture. Furthermore, territorial and demographic expansion placed immense strain on a system that was structurally deliberative. By 1815, the British Empire in India had forty million subjects. Forty years later, it had about one hundred and fifty million with even more difficulties to grapple with.[101]

In opposition to the Cornwallis program emerged the Munro school.[102] Munro and his supporters critiqued the Cornwallis system on two major points. The first concerned the transfer of proprietorship from the state to the *zamindars*. This had proved ineffective, if not counterproductive, because the *zamindars* could not shake off their cultural hangover from the Timurid period. Research into the tax records of Indian states annexed by the British indicated that in many places the earliest known revenue settlements were made with peasants and villages.[103] It also made sense that villagers and kinship groups, provided a predictable arrangement, would make a greater effort to improve their lot than *zamindars* accustomed to a life of extortion and ease. Thus, the state should transfer property rights to peasants or villages and settle revenue with them directly.

The second line of criticism addressed the role of the executive function in continental bureaucratic empires. The Cornwallis system relied on judicial power to settle disputes. While Montesquieu would have appreciated this decision as a step towards a state of laws, the Munro school argued in favor of making the executive superior to the judiciary. This was necessary because over centuries Indians had become accustomed to arbitrary rule through appointed servants. The number of disputes and the difficulty of applying standards of proof meant that the Cornwallis system bred delay, confusion, and diluted the effectiveness of the state. It led to widespread abuses as landlords continued to resort "to nothing but arbitrary demands" enforced on the tenants "by stocks, duress of sorts, and battery of their persons."[104] Meanwhile, the local moneylender greatly aggravated "the evil by his own usurious practices" which drove both landlord and peasant to desperation.[105] The peasant had no one to appeal to as the collector lacked the authority to redress his grievances and the judiciary was too remote, complex, and expensive, while the moneylender had the means to move the courts for protection and engage in litigation, often frivolous, to secure his interests. The judicial approach to governance in a continental bureaucratic empire thus raised the cost of securing justice and was incomprehensible to the rural masses. A strong executive presence was therefore needed to negotiate the rural minefield.

Eventually, the views of the Munro school prevailed and were accepted by William Bentinck, Governor General of India from 1828–1835. Bentinck became convinced that the separation of judicial and revenue powers had led to "inefficiency, misrule, and injustice."[106] The courts were overwhelmed at all levels, the detentions of prisoners under trial were being illegally extended, while the one official to whom ordinary people could appeal, and from whom the wealthy and powerful had anything to fear, the district collector, lacked the authority to settle problems as they arose.[107] Bentinck was certain that if things continued, as they were the British Empire in India would be very short-lived. His dire observation, on December 10, 1828, put the situation in perspective:

> . . . if I were obliged to draw an inference from the facts and reports which each council brings more or less before us, as well as from the information received out of doors, I am afraid that I should be obliged to say, that the administration of civil and criminal justice, if not a

complete failure, was so defective and inefficient as to demand our instant and most serious attention.[108]

Given Bentinck's realism, the proposal for drastic reorganization of the district administration was approved at the highest level.

Starting in 1829, India was reconstituted as a hierarchy of administrative subunits (provinces, divisions, districts, sub-districts) ruled through collector-magistrates with supervisory powers over the police (commissioners). Each district was small enough to be personally inspected by its commissioner. The commissioners acted in the classical generalist tradition of other continental bureaucratic empires and directed nearly all the activities of the British Empire in India. They were also the academic elite of the empire and expected to engage in substantial abstract and practical thinking. Their salaries and privileges, though pitiable by Timurid standards, were, in absolute terms, enough to secure an upper middle-class living in Britain. The thousand to one thousand five hundred members of the Indian Civil Service (ICS) were the functional equivalent of the Timurid Empire's five hundred senior-most *mansabdars*.

Unlike the cosmetic differences between the pre-British continental bureaucratic empires, important features of the state of laws and culture of power seeped into the British Empire in India. The organs of the state, be they the civil service, police, customs, or the forestry department, were constituted under laws that could not be arbitrarily changed. Second, the recruitment, transfers, promotions, and discipline, of public servants were merit-oriented and conducted autonomously of the sovereign. The officers were not the personal servants of the governor-general and could lawfully oppose and campaign against approved policy provided they did so professionally. Third, the cohesion and *esprit de corps* of the state service was remarkable when compared to the atomized and self-seeking nature of earlier South Asian bureaucratic elites.

Comparable developments took place in the relationship between the armed forces and the sovereign. Since ancient times, the military was an intensely political institution. The officers were insecure personal servants or slaves of the ruler and should he show any weakness, insurrection and rebellion broke out. There was little theoretical or practical distinction between the civil and military power. The British understood that the actual basis of the power of states in general, but empires in particular, was the ability to apply force effectively.[109] However, it was in the interest of the rulers themselves "that Government should disguise, as much as possible, the principle of its support."[110]

The idea that armed men should obey unarmed servants of the law, which is the critical difference between the rule of force and the rule of law, would have elicited nothing but contempt from pre-British rulers. Many rulers rose from the military to supreme power and thus it was simultaneously the deadliest instrument of arbitrary power and the greatest source of danger to the ruler. Their unique culture of power guided the British response to the same danger faced by rulers of continental bureaucratic empires for millennia.[111] The solution was to insulate the military from politics and create a parallel political dimension within which the recruitment, transfers, promotions, and discipline of officers and enlisted men would take place through an autonomous process. While concerns had been raised before the 1857 revolt, which began as a mutiny in the Bengal Army, it was not until after this trial by fire that more comprehensive policies were implemented. It was imperative that the military be separated from all civil functions, such as policing and taxation, and constituted as a full-time professional force governed by a combination of seniority and merit.

Finding the balance between the seniority and merit systems, then, as now, proved a difficult and controversial task. It was decided that European officers' promotions would be primarily based on seniority to prevent the exercise of patronage by the government and to create certainty within the officer corps.[112] However, "the promotion of Native commissioned and non-commissioned officers" was to be based primarily on efficiency rather than seniority.[113] Even those who disagreed with these decisions and argued for a system based solely on efficiency were constrained to admit that "security against favouritism and jobbery" could only be achieved through the seniority system.[114] That said, the peasant communities and castes of northern India were to be the principal recruitment base for the army within which "castes should be placed upon a perfect equality."[115] The Bengal Army, moreover, was too numerous and its "fixed and most undeserved position of superiority with the Government of India" after the revolt was forfeit.[116] The system worked because the formulation of strategy remained in the hands of a combination of British parliamentarians and civil servants, which thus left the armed forces to focus solely on developing their operational proficiency in relative isolation from Indian society.

The ideocratic complex of the British Empire in India also manifested substantial differences from earlier empires. The most obvious was the freedom to criticize the rulers. The most important was the secularism of the state.[117] There was a bureaucratic intelligentsia but there was no official priesthood. Individual members of the apparatus did patronize Christianity and missionaries, but the consistent effort of the state was to place as much distance between itself and religion as possible.[118] The experience of the 1857 uprising by units of the Bengal army, which was fuelled by belief in a Christian missionary conspiracy, drove this particular point home. In Britain and India missionaries came in for considerable criticism "which amounted in some quarters to the charge that missionary provocation was the primary cause" of the rebellions of 1857–58.[119] By the 1880s, "most British officers had reverted to the habit of their predecessors of the 1820s in regarding missionaries as, at best; absurd; at worst subversive."[120] Even those officers who remained sympathetic to the cause of Christian proselytizing in India began "avoiding any direct association with missionary publications or with public debates."[121] After 1857, as advised by prominent Indians, such as Syed Ahmed Khan, the founder of Muslim modernism in India, some aspects of Indian court culture, such as durbars, and the distribution of prizes and honours, were revived.[122] Generally, British India was lacked the kind of ideocratic complex and behaviour characteristic of other continental bureaucratic empires.[123]

Self-government and the institutions required to sustain it was in many respects the great project of the British Empire in India and the ultimate test of the exportability of the British state of laws. The process began in the early nineteenth century in Calcutta, Madras, and Bombay. From 1850 to 1893 steady progress was made in local government institutions. The first four decades of the twentieth century saw the extension of the representative principle to the center and the provinces in British India and the Indianization of the civil service and military officer corps. In the course of applying the representative principle to the higher tiers of the state, such as an Imperial Advisory and Legislative Council (1909), or debating the relative merits of elections as opposed to nominations for local government, a sustained process of consultation and dialogue with Indians and Englishmen of all shades of opinion unfolded. A retired assistant commissioner, Raja Aurungzeb Khan, told the commissioner of Jhelum district in 1907 with reference to the input asked by the government about the desirability of establishing advisory and legislative institutions at the central level that secret consultations rather than open assemblies were better suited to India.[124]

Narindra Nath, the deputy commissioner of Gujrat (Punjab), advised the government to consider questions of political economy and social change in framing its policy observing that "the enormous value attached to proprietary rights in land" was of "recent origin" and a departure from the pre-British period when "Husbandry was looked down upon as an inferior occupation."[125] Furthermore, "Indian society" was "rapidly changing" and just as the "India of today is very different from India" a generation earlier, another couple of decades "may see changes in economic and other conditions which it is difficult to foresee."[126] At the other end of the Indian subcontinent another civil service officer posted in East Bengal, Babu Hari Charan Das, warned that the representative principle would wreak havoc upon "The Indian—nay the Asiatic—idea of Government" which "is that it derives its sanction from the Creator of the Universe."[127] On balance, while many expressed reluctance about the viability of the representative principle, consciousness of the phenomenon of change and the need for the state to adapt and develop without compromising on the performance of its core functions, prevailed. By the 1920s many people with experience of power would have agreed that it was "absurd to suppose that a handful of foreigners from across the seas can continue to rule indefinitely hundreds of millions of Orientals on the patriarchal lines pursued, with no essential modification."[128]

Although the turbulence wrought by the two world wars and a global economic depression accelerated the demise of the British Empire, its legacy in the Indian subcontinent was different in important respects from previous empires. The country was no longer the personal estate of the sovereign. The officers of the state, military and civil, were not personal servants of the ruler. The state was secular and almost anti-ideological in its ethos and laws. Representative institutions and a culture of constitutionalism and lawful opposition were in place, albeit in an underdeveloped form at the center. A substantial body of politicians had emerged with decades of experience in local, provincial, and national affairs. The higher judiciary inspired confidence while the lower judiciary, though overburdened, kept the wheels of justice spinning at a tolerable pace.

Post-imperial writers have fixated on individual acts of brutality and oppression, such the siege of Delhi in 1857, the Amritsar massacre at Jallianwalabagh in 1919, the Mopilla Uprising of 1921, or the numerous flare-ups along the turbulent Indo-Afghan frontier. These atrocities are worthy of condemnation and should not have taken place. Compared, however, to other imperial powers, such as the Belgians in the Congo or the French in Indo-China and Algeria, the Russians in Central Asia and Eastern Europe, the Spanish in Central and South America, or the Japanese in China, British imperialism was astoundingly restrained. It is perhaps precisely to this restraint that the British owed their imperial success for it made possible collaboration and led many subject peoples to participate in the imperial project.[129] Certainly, the kind of systematic violence employed by the British Empire in India's contemporary imperial formations was not engaged in by the British in India. Some of the greatest innovations instituted by the British were lawful opposition, agitation politics, and civil disobedience. These acted to release pressure, prevented armed insurrection and revolution, and ensured that while the British transferred power in August 1947, the change of regime did not fundamentally and immediately alter the nature or composition of the state. India and Pakistan had a choice between continuing along the path of legal democracy and building upon the institutions and habits bequeathed by the British or reversion to ideocratic arbitrary rule.[130]

INDIA'S SINCE 1947: THE CONTOURS
OF ARBITRARY DEMOCRACY

It was perhaps inevitable that an empire acquired in a fit of absentmindedness would be abandoned without adequate preparation.[131] This opportunistic abandonment was in partly made possible by the formation of a Labor government in Britain under Clement Attlee in 1945. Labor lacked the stamina required to stay engaged in the Indian subcontinent and commit the necessary resources for a reasonably orderly transition to complete self-government given pressing domestic and international constraints.[132] Lord Pethick-Lawrence, the new Secretary of State for India, was a "gentle and manifestly well-meaning intellectual" who "effusively admired" Gandhi.[133] Stafford Cripps was himself quite fond of his socialist "old friends in Congress",[134] had "been busy mending his fences"[135] with them, and "did everything he could to ensure Mountbatten's success."[136] Attlee and his team wanted out of India but did not give themselves, or the Indian parties, time to resolve the complex communal tangle. As the executive will faltered, the political parties armed their members and formed paramilitary organizations. By June 1947, the Muslim League had mobilized nearly a 140,000 national guards, the Congress and its allies could muster about 100,000, while the Hindu fundamentalists had armed more than 190,000.[137] The change of the date for independence from June 1948 to August 15, 1947, made it almost certain that these legions of armed men would be afforded an opportunity to operate in an administrative vacuum.

Under the pressures generated by partition and independence,[138] the steel frame of the Raj bent but did not break. In India, order had been restored within a year of independence in nearly all parts of the country. The Constituent Assembly, in 1950, after about four years of deliberation, completed the task of formulating a constitution for the new state. This constitution incorporated the British values of "democracy, pluralism, secularism, and, in the best sense of the word, liberalism."[139] Here was a continental bureaucratic empire determined to govern a large part of South Asia in the manner of the state of laws amidst bewildering diversity in terms of the languages, castes, and religions of its citizenry. In many respects, the Indian experiment with democracy has been a success. Thanks in great measure to the Election Commission, elections have been held with regularity and produced changes in the composition of provincial and federal legislatures reasonably reflective of public opinion. The British Indian tradition of keeping the military insulated from politics has survived practically unaltered since 1947.[140] The judiciary is substantially independent at the higher levels and the federal constitution has remained in effect at the all-India level for all but two years since its adoption.[141] There exist thousands of autonomous institutions that lawfully challenge government directives and policies, and the press enjoys freedom comparable to several western countries. Furthermore, in urban areas with populations greater than half a million that have attained a suitable level of development, the criminal justice system has been reconstituted on the Calcutta, Bombay and Madras model with the commissioners deprived of magisterial powers. Admirable as these achievements are, Indian legal democracy has not substantively altered the manner in which power is exercised by the ruling classes. It has altered the forms that the culture of power of the Indian subcontinent takes, and delayed open reversion to ideocratic arbitrary rule.

It must be borne in mind that the Constituent Assembly that drafted the Indian constitution was elected by a franchise limited by property and

educational qualifications to about fourteen percent of the adult population. In the course of the debate on the nature of the electorate, Jawaharlal Nehru[142] "brushed aside" objections to universal adult franchise.[143] His
cousin, the civil servant B. K. Nehru, observed that one of the consequences
of the decision to grant universal adult franchise was that the representatives elected to legislatures since 1951 have generally lacked the ability to
comprehend Anglo-Saxon state morality or appreciate "what the position
of the permanent civil service is in a modern state."[144] Another unintended
result was that the financial cost of campaigning in elections increased
while the drastic reduction in the proportion of educated and propertied
voters going to the polls reduced the quality of debate, made it much easier
for politicians to evade accountability, ignore policy issues, and use their
new powers arbitrarily.

The first and greatest casualty of the arbitrary exercise of power by
elected representatives was the institutional autonomy of the civil service. Civil servants who resisted the unlawful and irrational demands of
politicians were, and are, suspended, transferred, and denied promotion.
Many of those that manage to get ahead do so through servility and not on
account of merit thus perpetuating spinelessness at the higher levels, which,
in turn, demoralizes subordinates:

> The *esprit de corps* of the civil service had been undermined . . . When
> young men and women enter the civil service, they are competent, cor-
> rect and enthusiastic . . . Unfortunately, they do not get the support
> they need from their disillusioned seniors . . . If their seniors in the
> headquarters of the State Governments stood by them, they would be
> able to resist political pressures. All too often, the senior members of
> government services do not resist the politicians' demands to transfer
> uncooperative officers.[145]

Then again, the senior members of the bureaucracy themselves did not
fare any better. As Madhav Godbole, the Union Home Secretary who sought
early retirement in 1993 in response to political pressure rather than being
packed-off to some non-post following the razing of the Babri Mosque at
Ayodhya in 1992 by Hindu fanatics writes in his memoirs:

> I had to relinquish the post of Chairman, Maharashtra State Electricity
> Board, for resisting the pressures of the then minister in the award of
> contracts; I had been hounded in the past by the 'all-powerful Amban-
> is'[146]; I had proceeded on long leave from the post of Principal Finance
> Secretary, Maharashtra, when the Sharad Pawar government took the
> decision to scrap the zero-base budgeting; I had been shifted from the
> Petroleum Ministry . . . again under the pressure from the Ambanis
> and also from Chimanbhai Patel, the then Chief Minister of Gujarat
> . . . The three months of vilification[147] since the Ayodhya debacle had

finally taken its toll. I decided to seek premature retirement and to proceed on leave from the very next day.[148]

Godbole's experiences are well known but hardly unique. The Indian Administrative Service (IAS) is the apex administrative cadre of the Indian State and constitutes the bureaucratic leadership. Numbering 5000–6000 officers, the "IAS has been considered to be the only 'multi-functional' government service, as an IAS officer is in charge of running virtually every sector in the country."[149] In spite, or perhaps because, of this the IAS has borne the brunt of political interference as the politicians seek to use it as an instrument to control the rest of the apparatus. It is estimated, for instance, that between 1976 and 1986, about 54 percent of IAS officers were transferred in less than a year from their current charges, with 28 percent managing to last in a post for one to two years, and only 11 percent surviving more than two years in a single post.[150] Politicians have managed to find a way around the Election Commission's ban on transferring officers once elections are announced by back-dating transfer orders and engaging in large-scale reshuffles prior to elections.[151] One consequence of such arbitrariness is flight to the center. Honest and capable officers seek postings in New Delhi, while provincial political bosses are happy to see such officers get out of the way. Once in the capital the effort is not to go back to the provinces thus depriving the field administration of capable civil servants. Work in the capital is more professionally organized and oriented towards policy, which appeals to the better officers. Micro studies of individual districts and boards present a depressing picture in this regard. For instance, in the Kalahandi district in the province of Orissa the post of district collector changed hands 18 times between 1974 and 2000, inclusive of a total period of five years when there was no collector.[152] In the case of the Tamil Nadu Pollution Control Board (TNPCB), which was created in 1982 to monitor environmental pollution in Tamil Nadu, the chairmanship of the board changed hands 18 times between 1982 and 2000.[153] Except for two chairmen, "the rest remained in their posts for less than a year and eight chairmen were given terms of less than three months each."[154]

Demoralization produced by the inability to resist the arbitrariness of politicians is complemented by vast increases in the size of the lower and middle orders of the bureaucracy and the collapse of the purchasing power of public sector salaries. The number of government employees rose from four million in 1953 to some sixteen million in 1983.[155] In 2003, after about fourteen years of economic liberalization, nineteen million persons "out of a total organized wage-earning workforce" of about twenty-seven million were government employees.[156] By 1977, the purchasing power of the salaries of senior officials, who are responsible for supervising and directing the apparatus, had fallen to one-fifth of 1947 values.[157] As the pay scale lost real value and the number of government employees expanded beyond the ability of the officers to exercise control, the bureaucracy was entrusted with

productive assets ranging from rock quarries and handlooms to national-
ized banks and large industrial units. Add to this mix incessant political
pressure on the civil service to abuse its powers and it is inevitable that
corruption will spread from the lower and middle levels to the senior levels.
Once the integrity of the officer corps of the civil service is compromised
the state is bound to start failing in the performance of its core and elabo-
rated functions, for a single corrupt and incompetent officer inflicts more
damage than hundreds of support staff.

The collapse of civil service morale and the decline in the intellectual
and moral qualities of its officers coupled with the absence of a rational
directing impulse from above has had a highly adverse impact on the
financial administration of India. The proportion of direct taxes fell from
nearly 40 percent of the total revenue in 1948–49 to about 16 percent in
1974–75.[158] This trend did not shown signs of reversal for several decades
and the share of direct taxes in total revenue stabilized in the 16 -20 percent range before starting to rise again in the early 2000s to 1948 levels.
The ratio of taxes to GDP is also low, especially for a democracy that is
required by the constitution to establish a welfare state and has been governed by the socialistic Congress Party for all but three of the first fifty
years of independence.[159] At present (2012–2013), the state collects taxes
equal to about 15 percent of GDP, with direct taxes accounting for about
37 percent of the total revenues.[160] It is, therefore, not surprising that the
center and provinces ran up deficits in the eight to ten percent range during the first decade of the 21st century and the fiscal deficit hovers between
4–5 percent of GDP. Strangely, in spite of steady deficits, India's ratio of
public debt to GDP fell from more than 80 percent in 2003 to about 67
percent in 2012.[161] The key to this has been double-digit inflation and low
interest rates giving the rich access to cheap private debt that can be used
to fuel growth in the nominal value of GDP faster than the increase in the
state's debt liability.[162]

Self-government without self-taxation in India has long enabled corruption to thrive though the scale has expanded considerably since 1991.
During the first twenty-five years of independence,[163] according to "conservative official estimates", the amount that escaped the tax net rose
from about half a billion rupees to nearly forty-five billion rupees.[164] A
generation later, corruption is "endemic" and widely perceived to be a
"ubiquitous feature" of India's "governance".[165] Tax officials, threaten
people with over-assessment, secure bribes and then under-assess the
same income. The large industrial groups, in collusion with politicians
and tax-officials, made a mockery of the socialistic controls implemented
by Nehru after 1951, and effectively turned their own country into a cap-
tive market from which excessive profits at the expense of the consumer
were derived. One favorite method of engineering distortions was to purchase "import licenses in the name of firms and individuals" that did not
exist, while another was to "obtain licenses for amounts much larger than

they actually were".[166] Bribery became endemic and the socialist controls and rhetoric proved handy for justifying seizures of private property and assets and terrorizing businessmen:

> . . . the jungle of laws, regulations and controls that sprang up in the name of socialism undoubtedly gave it a bad name and provided a happy hunting-ground for corrupt politicians and bureaucrats. One example is that of an Indian industrialist who says there are no less than thirteen government inspectors who can close his factory down. None are apparently interested in inspecting the safety, quality, pollution levels, or whatever else they are supposed to inspect. All that they are interested is in collecting their pay-offs.[167]

Another example is that of the rock quarries some fifteen miles from Delhi, that were seized by the government under pressure from social workers campaigning for the workers' rights. Once the quarries had been seized, however, the government proved unable to run them and "so they have been handed back to the contractors. It is not the workers who have benefited from the nationalization, but the officials. They now have greater power over the contractors, so they demand greater rewards."[168] This excess pales in contrast to the seizure of fourteen banks by the state in 1969 on Indira Gandhi's orders during the height of her struggle against Morarji Desai in order to present the dispute as one of policy rather than ego.[169] The political leadership spends lavishly on elections and looks upon such expenditures as something to be recouped from the dispensation of patronage in the event of victory. Consequently, "irrespective of which party wins, the nature and quality of political leadership remain largely the same and the people end up being the losers."[170]

Economic liberalization in India has gone hand-in-hand with escalating corruption, embezzlement, and maladministration.[171] While the number of rupee billionaires has soared from 125 in 2001 to more than 300 in 2010[172] corruption and incompetence in the financial administration mean that only 10 percent of welfare spending actually reaches the intended beneficiaries.[173] In 2008/9 the Government of India announced a Rs. 720 billion debt-relief scheme for farmers, which turned into "a bonanza for state officials, non-governmental organizations (NGOs) and *panchayats* rather than those for whom relief was intended."[174] India's Planning Commission estimates that between 70 percent and 90 percent of "rural development funds are siphoned off by a web extending up from the *panchayat* . . . to the local MP with officials too claiming their share."[175] In May 1992, at the outset of India's economic liberalization, then finance minister Manmohan Singh was embarrassed by the revelation of a Rs. 450 billion "financial scam, involving insider trading by banks in collusion with top officials of the State Bank of India and foreign-owned private banks."[176] Speaking of foreign banks, it is estimated (2010) that wealthy Indians have stashed away US $ 1 trillion in secret Swiss bank and offshore accounts.[177] Far from moving forward,

> The state, backtracking from its previous role of provider, has become a vociferous facilitator of private capital, pitching heavily for a "politically neutral" practice of developmental governmentality. While the country targets an annual growth rate of 8 percent, growth in regular employment in recent years has not exceeded 1 percent. India also accounts for the largest number of homeless, illiterate, and malnourished people in the world. For the ruling classes in India, which continue to believe in the power of finance capital and trickle-down economic theory as the panacea for all the evils related to poverty, 'development' does not mean the improvement of the quality of life or wellbeing of ordinary people.[178]

The arbitrariness and injustice of the financial administrative machinery is complemented by the excesses committed on a regular basis by the police, often with the connivance of higher authorities and politicians. One common practice is to levy a protection tax on shopkeepers, small businessmen, service providers[179] and beggars, by threatening them with violence. The police demand bribes for performing routine work, and murders, kidnapping, and arson, can be arranged in exchange for money. In the 1970s, in the United Provinces, for example, "hundreds of beautiful girls were abducted" for the pleasure of Chief Minister Bahuguna and his supporters.[180] In Haryana, during the same period, the sister-in-law of Chief Minister Bansilal was in charge of the female ward of the central jail. She mercilessly exploited the women under her charge or did not bother to show up for work at all.[181] The senior officers dared not stop her because of her relationship with the chief minister. On one occasion, she nearly beat a prisoner to death for possessing a literacy manual.[182] The prisoner was hospitalized for three weeks. After she returned, however, her tormentor elevated her to the position of supervisor, which completely turned the girl's head who:

> Dreaming of the power she would now have over everybody . . . began to show an aspect of herself about which all the women, and the matrons too, had long since warned us . . . the spite and vindictiveness which she now displayed were a revelation. Sita laughed at our disbelief and dismay. 'What did I tell you?' she said. 'They're all the same. Each one of them will bite the hand that feeds them without hesitation if they think it is to their advantage. I've lived with them for twenty years and I know what I am talking about'.[183]

Where the police "are themselves the most dangerous and disorderly forces in the country" and rendered "pliable and responsive" to political interference,[184] law and order will break down. N. A. Palkhivala[185] wrote in the *Illustrated Weekly of India* on April 17, 1977, that "Fear, born of terror, was more acute—particularly among the innocent—during the twenty months of the Emergency than it was during the two centuries of British rule".[186] Five years later, Palkhivala observed, in the *Illustrated Weekly* on November 21, 1982, that:

> Not since the abolition of thuggery by Lord William Bentinck in the 1830s has violence characterized our national life on a scale so widespread and so unchecked as today . . . life is too easy for the criminals and too difficult for law-abiding citizens.[187]

The law and order situation continued to deteriorate and towards the end of the 1990s "more than 200 out of 535 districts" were "experiencing insurgency, ethnic conflict, extremism, caste-clashes, and other crises" while "In many areas the police themselves have become co-opted by criminals, who wield considerable political influence"[188] and "there is increasing lawlessness and anarchy in most parts of the country."[189] During British rule, laws enacted to restrict liberties in the interests of public order generated intense opposition and "It was taken for granted that the governments in free India . . . would not emulate" the British.[190] This belief has been proven false for, not only were repressive laws maintained but those pertaining to the accountability of the state and its officials before the law ". . . were rendered more illiberal."[191] It remains a matter of "shame" that "after independence a Law Commission and a Parliament felt that 'in the circumstance prevailing in India'" state officials needed "a far larger measure of protection . . . than was required even by foreign rulers."[192] This behavior is hardly surprising given that in 2010, 75 percent of Indian parliamentarians had criminal records or were being investigated by the Central Bureau of Investigation (CBI).[193] Combined with repressive laws, the Indian state has sought to bring down the spiraling levels of mismanagement, corruption, and disorder, through greater material investment in the police.[194]

The irony is that the numerical strength of the police and its firepower has increased dramatically since independence. The former rose from about four hundred and sixty-eight thousand to more than nine hundred thousand in 1981[195] and presently stands at about two million.[196] The armed component of the police force, which is given basic infantry training, increased from fifteen percent of the total strength in 1950 to about fifty-six percent in 1970.[197] The central reserve police, created in 1949 with one battalion, increased to sixty battalions by 1973.[198] In spite of these measures, the army was called out to assist civil power four hundred and seventy-six times between 1951 and 1970, and three hundred and sixty-nine times between 1980 and 1990.[199] Large parts of India, include some 60 districts in the east and center of the country, as well as Jammu and Kashmir[200] continue to be affected by revolutionary or secessionist insurgencies.[201]

One of these interventions, conducted in 1984, was codenamed Operation Bluestar, and entailed storming the Golden Temple at Amritsar in order to dislodge Sikh insurgents.[202] The significance of this episode is not derived from the exceeding incompetence and brutality with which the insurgents were put down.[203] Nor was it extraordinary that thousands of Sikh soldiers, outraged by the Indian army's operations, mutinied and more than a hundred of them were killed in the process.[204] What does shed light on the oppression inherent in the Indian subcontinent's culture of power is that following Indira Gandhi's assassination on October 31, 1984, by her Sikh bodyguards a countrywide pogrom against Sikhs was organized by the ruling Congress party:

> The pattern was similar all over; the people living on the periphery of society as well as habitation, led or instigated by local Congress (I) men, looting property and then setting fire to it and even killing or burning the owners and occupants. In Delhi, the worst affected city, there was virtually no law and order for three days. . . .[205]

One institution that has done better than most in containing the arbitrariness of executive power and taken a public stand against excesses committed by the state apparatus is the higher judiciary. Almost immediately after independence, the judiciary ruled "in favor of the traditional landlords who had fallen out of favor with the ruling Congress" and stood to have their properties confiscated in the name of scientific socialism.[206] Nehru, ever the revolutionary without a revolution, "chastised the courts for standing in the way of socialism"[207] and drew distinctions between those judges committed to upholding the directive principles, which could be interpreted to allow arbitrariness in order to attain socialistic goals, against those who gave priority to maintaining the fundamental rights of individuals.[208] On April, 24, 1973, seven supreme court justices ruled in the *Kevananda Bharati* case that Parliament could not "alter or destroy the basic structure or framework of the Constitution" regardless of the size of the government's majority.[209] The right of the Indian Supreme Court to exercise judicial review is more important than in presidential systems because in a parliamentary democracy the prime minister and his allies are almost certain to command a majority in the central legislature. However, the rapid increase in the volume of litigation handled by the courts has put them under immense pressure. Between 1977 and 1983, for example, the number of cases pending in High Courts rose from nearly six hundred thousand to "more than one million", while the Supreme Court's backlog stood at nearly one hundred and forty thousand at the end of 1983.[210] By the first decade of the 21st century there were more than thirty million cases pending before Indian courts "and most people have lost faith in the capacity of the justice system to resolve disputes in time or to punish culprits."[211]

The rise in litigation reflects the mass of legislation and regulations that have been enacted since independence. It is estimated between 1947 and 1967, one thousand six hundred "statues", one hundred "regulations", one hundred "presidential acts", and one hundred and fifty "ordinances" were passed, most on executive direction.[212] In addition, "government departments" during the same period issued five thousand or so rules and directives annually.[213] The snail's pace and technicalities of the court system also help explain why a police force, whose institutional autonomy is daily undermined by elected politicians, and whose service conditions have deteriorated since independence, finds it easier to administer vigilante justice than properly investigate cases and send them for prosecution.[214] Another complication is that at present the Indian state is itself "the biggest litigant" while "the entire scheme by the framers of the constitution to ensure proper appointments to the judiciary has been reduced to a farce."[215] The resulting "Demoralization breeds corruption and other judicial vices such as favoritism."[216] At the highest levels the judiciary has failed to rule decisively on issues vital to the integrity of the Indian state of laws, such as secularism,[217] and police accountability for torture and custodial deaths.[218]

The Emergency of 1975–77 damaged the reputation of the Supreme Court as the upholder of individual liberties and fundamental rights against executive overstretch. Out of a bench of five judges only one, Justice H. R. Khanna, dissented against the decision to suspend habeas corpus.[219] Incidentally, the declaration of an emergency in 1975 was precipitated by the Allahabad High Court's conviction of Indira Gandhi for electoral malpractices, including the use of government assets in her 1970 election campaign. Once emergency was declared, the court reversed its decision. After the emergency was lifted, and Indira Gandhi voted out of power in 1977, the new Janata Party government under Morarji Desai tried to bring the former incumbent to justice. Special courts were constituted to try Indira for corruption and a reference was filed challenging her dismissal of nine provincial governments. Neither the corruption charges nor the reference could be made to stick, the proceedings turned into a farce, the Janata government itself disintegrated into its component parties, and Indira emerged from this episode a martyr and was reelected in 1980.

Far more dangerous than any backlog of cases is the apparent inability of the courts, police, and investigating agencies to get a handle on corruption. Indians generally believe their politicians,[220] civil servants, landlords, and successful businessmen, to be corrupt. Yet, between 1950 and 1975, not one minister was brought to justice. Bribery is often done openly and without any understanding or fear of the law, which is treated with impunity and contempt by the ruling classes. In August 1970, for example, Sanjay Gandhi, Indira Gandhi's younger son, was granted a license to manufacture fifty thousand small cars a year (the Maruti) that were to be marketed by the government for six thousand rupees each. The site selected for the project was in Gurgaon, in the province of Haryana, where the "notoriously corrupt, arrogant, and vindictive" Chief Minister Bansilal, who later rose to the position of minister for defense, "had placed himself and the whole of Haryana, which he ruled like a despot, at the service of the personal needs of the Prime Minister and her son."[221] The Punjab National Bank, the Central Bank of India, and the Industrial Finance Corporation, without any security, approved a 170 million rupees investment within a week. About 1500 farmers were strong-armed into selling their land at one-fifth of its market value to make way for India's rising son and his wonder of scientific socialism. Sanjay never got around to producing a single unit and, in 1975, with the projected per unit cost having spiraled upwards to about 25,000 rupees, he turned his attention to population control and slum clearance. The resultant program of "forced vasectomies" and urban renewal "targeted the poor and lowly, leading the wits to comment that having failed to get rid of poverty[222] the Congress had taken to getting rid of the poor".[223]

While the "pervasiveness of corruption in India is a well-established and often reiterated fact"[224] it is one of the most important "symptoms of the collapse of the institutions of governance that are supposed to manage the relationship between citizens and the state".[225] Not surprisingly, "corruption in the private sector is as deep as that in the public sector"[226] and feeds off the arbitrariness of the political leadership, financial administration, and criminal justice system. Amongst the more telling effects of corruption is its ability to render the writ of the state ineffective and brings about consequences diametrically opposed to policy objectives. Fifteen years after economic liberalization began it was asserted that "Deregulation has made almost no impact at the district and village level" while "In many ways, *the poor actually subsidize the rich*."[227] Equally alarming is the growing "social acceptability of corruption", stringent provisions in the Indian Penal Code and the 1998 Prevention of Corruption Act notwithstanding.[228] According to the Government of India's own estimates (2009–10), 350 million Indians live below the official poverty line of Rs. 12 per day, and 600 million live on less than Rs. 20 a day.[229] India is labeled a development state but 650 million Indians, as opposed to 50 million Chinese, have no access to toilets—a telling indicator of Indian democracy's responsiveness to basic human needs.[230]

Politicians treat government assets and funds, and the possessions of ordinary Indians, as if they were personal property. In 2003, Mayawati, the Chief Minister of Uttar Pradesh, on her forty-eighth birthday, declared it an annual official function and spent thirteen and a half million rupees from the province's contingency funds, on its celebration. Official transport, security, and personnel were commandeered for the function. Later that year, Laloo Prasad Yadav and Rabri Devi,[231] the elected rulers of Bihar, celebrated the wedding of their daughter. In order to provide transport for the wedding procession, Laloo Prasad's henchmen confiscated forty-five luxury cars from showrooms in the provincial capital.[232] To provide bedding and furniture for the wedding, one hundred sofa sets and other items were seized from shops. To provide gift clothes, seven hundred thousand rupees worth of fabric were confiscated from Raymond's outlets alone. To provide sweets and dry fruits, bakers and vendors were compelled to hand over tens of thousands of rupees worth of their stocks. Before the Tatas, one of India's leading business and industrial families, lodged a First Incident Report with the police, they first locked down their showrooms and evacuated their employees to Calcutta for fear of reprisal.[233] It appears that B. K. Nehru's understanding of India has proven better than Jawaharlal Nehru's, for, both Laloo Prasad Yadav, and Mayawati, style themselves deliverers of the downtrodden from upper-caste oppression. Their actions demonstrate that being of the people, and being for the people, are not naturally compatible. Ordinary Indians can easily justify their excesses by pointing out that their leaders—political, bureaucratic, and entrepreneurial—have, with few exceptions, gotten ahead by looting and defrauding the state and its citizens.[234]

The Congress had undergone changes for the worse under Indira Gandhi, and its leaders sorely lacked the intellectual and moral qualities necessary for ensuring even a tolerable level of quality in governance. Indira, unlike Nehru, did not tolerate dissent. Lacking her father's stature or ability, she destroyed the autonomous political process within Congress, packed it with "hand picked protégés",[235] and,

> During the Emergency even the pretence of democratic functioning was given up and her favorite son and heir apparent, Sanjay, ran the party apparatus like a mafia boss, hiring and firing people and distributing patronage without any reference to the formal organizational structure.[236]

The presidency of Congress "became not only a non-elective but also a hereditary institution"[237] and the organization came to be characterized by "arbitrary decision-making, corruption, opportunism, and encouragement of incompetent sycophants."[238] While Sanjay lived, he was "the most important extra-constitutional center of power" and even chief ministers could only secure appointments with Indira through him.[239] Indira Gandhi had also created the Research and Analysis Wing (RAW) in the Union Cabinet Secretariat in 1967, placed it under her direct supervision, and took for herself the power to make appointments and recruit new personnel—tasks that should have come under the purview of the Union Public Service Commission (UPSC). RAW was designed as an instrument in Indira Gandhi's arsenal "available for whatever purpose she thought fit", and it was "more active gathering intelligence at home than abroad."[240]

Rajiv Gandhi, Indira's eldest son, who stayed away from politics until his mother's assassination in 1984,[241] entered the arena with a clean image. Rajiv began an anti-corruption drive and pledged to shake up Congress. Within months, however, Rajiv found himself defending socialism, allegations of corruption emerged against his own government, and V.P. Singh, the minister in charge of the much vaunted anti-corruption drive, resigned complaining that the prime minister was not serious about the accountability process. This was hardly surprising as the electoral process is characterized by "massive rigging by impersonation, booth-capturing and various other malpractices", the "electoral rolls are notoriously flawed all over the country".[242] Political parties nominate "Notorious criminals and rapaciously corrupt persons . . . for public office with impunity",[243] and "function as closed oligarchies and personal fiefdoms."[244]

After Rajiv Gandhi's assassination in 1991, a right-wing party inspired by Hindu revivalism and intimately linked to the fundamentalist Rashtriya Swayamsevak Sangh (RSS)[245] began to stake an increasingly convincing claim to being the national alternative to Congress. This was the Bharitya Janata Party (BJP), founded in 1980. In the 1984 national elections, the BJP won two seats. In 1989, the BJP won eighty-five, in 1991 one hundred and twenty, in 1996 one hundred and sixty-one, and in 1998 one hundred and eighty seats. The BJP's share of the popular vote more than tripled from about 7.5 percent in 1984 to nearly 26 percent in 1998.[246] The growth of the RSS has also been phenomenal. In 1977, it had six thousand branches, in 1983 about nineteen thousand branches and seven hundred thousand volunteers, and in 2000 forty-five thousand branches, thirteen thousand educational institutions, one million seven hundred thousand students and seventy-five thousand teachers.[247]

As early as March 1944, the Home Department of the Government of India described the RSS as an organization that "concentrated on the formation of a militant body on fascist lines."[248] This evaluation is shared by many:

> "The RSS line is very clear. It is a supra-party, paramilitary organization which wants to take over the state and the nation and establish an authoritarian regime in the manner of the Nazi Leaders", wrote the ideologue and leader of the Janata Party, Madhu Limaye, in an article in *Sunday* on 10 June 1979 . . . Limaye was only echoing something which Gandhi had said long ago. According to his secretary Pyarelal, Gandhi had described the RSS as a "communal body with a totalitarian outlook" and compared them to the Nazis and fascists.[249]

The Hindutva ideology espoused by the BJP and RSS is based upon an uncompromising cultural nationalism,[250] calls for the creation of a Hindu State (*rashtra*), the nullification of the existing constitutional order, autarky, the establishment of an empire stretching from the Khyber Pass to Rangoon, and no tolerance for minorities and other communities or points of view. Though leading members of BJP think tanks, like Balbir K. Punj, who is also a member of the Rajy Sabha, assert that "India is a secular and vibrant democracy because it is essentially Hindu",[251] The ultimate objective of the Hindu revivalists is to establish an omnipotent, centralized state, where the rulers and their appointed servants are legitimized by divine sanction—in other words, ideocratic arbitrary rule.

The desire to revert to a Hindu *rashtra* is sustained by "A paranoid, pathological kind of Islamophobia" combined with an intense "sense of inferiority"[252] vis-à-vis both Islam and the West. Indeed, Hindutva's "self-perception" is one of "aggression, machismo, virility and militancy" and "while Ayodhya and Gujarat are the laboratories where these ideas are being tried and tested with considerable success" the inspiration comes from adaptations of nineteenth and twentieth century Western concepts such as fascism.[253] The Hindu revivalists overcompensate for historical humiliation by seeking to indoctrinate others, through their impressive network of schools and cultural organizations, in the "Hindutva notion of India's incomparably glorious" ancient past.[254] The ideological father of the RSS, Golwalkar, "was notoriously fascinated by Nazism and Italian fascism and directly praised Hitler's view of racial purity".[255] Hindutva's unimaginative and recycled version of social Darwinism, has found an audience amongst "India's globalizing middle-classes" that "are seceding from, and turning against, the mass of the people" who they treat with "horrendous callousness".[256] Globalization, consumerism, and the information technology boom, have combined to produce an elite that "is strongly drawn to the culture of authoritarianism" and obsessed with force and coercion:[257]

> The Bajrang Dal functions like the modern-day equivalent of stormtroopers and uses physical violence to intimidate opponents. Bajrang Dal goons and ruffians periodically smash public property and burn churches and mosques, as happened in Orissa, where an Australian missionary and his two young sons were burnt alive in 2001. This is just when Prime Minister Vajpayee was calling for a "national debate" on religious conversion.[258]

Another interesting case study of what Hindutva means in practice can be found in the province of Gujarat on India's west coast, which has been ruled by the BJP since 1998. At the time of the 2002 Gujarat Massacre the province with fifty million people, was home to five percent of India's population but generated about twelve percent of the country's industrial output.[259] Gujarat has a very prominent and cosmopolitan mercantile elite with centuries of trading experience and is the ancestral home of both India's M. K. Gandhi and Pakistan's founder, Muhammad Ali Jinnah.[260] Gujarat is one of India's relatively industrialized provinces[261] and has averaged an economic growth rate of nearly 9 percent a year since the early

1990s.[262] More than six-tenths of the population is literate, life expectancy in the mid-sixties, and the infant mortality rate, at sixty-three per thousand, is good by regional standards.[263] Material progress, however, has not led to intellectual or moral enlightenment:

> ... the land of Gujarat is known for housing some of the most dedicated communal arsonists, and there are signs in the form of painted graffiti and billboards which announce that this is a Hindu *rashtra* ... A clear and incontrovertible marker of this culture of political authoritarianism is the staging of state spectacles, whereby theatrical and dramatic public demonstrations of authoritarian power [are] displayed.[264]

The former Chief Minister of Gujarat, Kehubhai Patel, for instance, attended an RSS camp, dressed in RSS uniform, standing besides L. K. Advani.[265] The massacre of thousands of Gujarati Muslims in February 2002 by the RSS in association with the provincial government, drew a poignant response from Khushwant Singh, one of India's leading novelists, critics, and political commentators:

> These are dark times for India. The carnage in Gujarat, Bapu Gandhi's home state, in early 2002 and the subsequent landslide victory of Narendra Modi in the elections will spell disaster for our country. The fascist agenda of Hindu fanatics is unlike anything we have experienced in our modern history ... Far from becoming *mahaan* (great), India is going to the dogs, and unless a miracle saves us, the country will break up. It will not be Pakistan or any other foreign power that will destroy us; we will commit hara-kiri.[266]

An equally sobering thought is the possibility of "despotism by invitation" motivated by the increasingly "desperate quest for order":

> As the propertied and educated middle and upper classes, which have a great stake in peace and order, become disenchanted with the governance process, they are coming to the dangerous conclusion that freedom and democracy are synonymous with chaos and anarchy. Most of the urban middle classes have already become votaries of some form of authoritarianism that can bring order and peace, at whatever cost ... the threat of dictatorship does not lie in a possible coup d'état but may creep into the system with the acquiescence of the middle and upper classes ... [267]

Apparently, India's public mind is shrinking:

> The malign upper-caste orientation of Hindutva, and its utility as an instrument of domination not just of religious minorities but all

underprivileged groups, finds its highest expression in what might be called the Golwalkar Programme, outlined by the RSS's most important ideologue. The Golwalkar Programme consists in systematically assaulting modern-liberal ideas, weakening and undermining all democratic institutions, and using coercion to disenfranchise the minorities politically so as to turn them into second-class citizens without any rights.

The Gujarat pogrom of 2002, in which 2,000 Muslims were massacred with state complicity under BJP Chief Minister Narendra Modi, shows the extent to which the Hindutva forces can go in implementing the Golwalkar Programme. The Vajpayee government has shamelessly colluded with Modi and shielded him in a variety of unseemly ways. This not only proved the secularists' contention that Vajpayee's image as a "soft" leader or half-liberal is totally deceptive: he is as steeped in Hindutva's toxic ideology and communal politics as anyone else. It also showed that Hindutva remains the most serious and deadly menace to democracy in India.[268]

The Hindu revivalist challenge involves more than cosmetic changes to the ideocratic complex of the Indian state, which, until recently, was characterized by a mixture of socialism, secularism, Gandhian philosophy, and a loud commitment to democracy and reform. This, "the common but debased rhetoric of power"[269] of the Congress party is giving way to a new set of ideological certainties equally "grounded in illusion"[270] but rendered far more dangerous for the state of laws due to the fact that in their use of Hindu idiom they tap into the emotional basis of Indian civilization. As Al-Beruni's *Kitab-ul-Hind* made clear nearly a thousand years ago, the objective of the Indian subcontinent's oldest intellectual tradition is to help the educated elite avoid contact with reality. That the *New Cambridge History of India* devotes an entire volume to "argue that caste has been for many centuries a real and active part of Indian life, and not just a self-serving orientalist fiction"[271] is one indication that the state of mind described by Al-Beruni is not only alive and well, but has become sufficiently aggressive and self-confident to intimidate foreign scholars. In the absence of a reality check from outside, a splendid edifice of rhetoric has been erected, which, if it were one's principal source of information, would make it seem that the Congress was the center of British India's political universe, that the caste system was produced by the machinations of the Raj, the Timurid Emperor Akbar was a great liberal-secular-nationalist, or that the Mauryan Empire was the original socialist utopia.[272] Perhaps the greatest indicator of the extent to which the Indian elite is wrapped up in a world of make-believe is,

> Mohandas Gandhi . . . he looked at India as no Indian was able to; his vision was direct, and this directness was, and is, revolutionary. He sees exactly what the visitor sees; he does not ignore the obvious . . .

He sees the Indian callousness, the Indian refusal to see . . . he looks down to the roots of the static decayed society. And the picture of India which comes out of his writings and exhortations over more than thirty years still holds: this is the measure of his failure . . .

It is as if, in England, Florence Nightingale had become a saint, honored by statues everywhere, her name on every lip; and the hospitals had remained as she had described them.[273]

The ideocratic complex of the Indian state, which is extraordinarily elaborate and multi-faceted, is, in effect, a grand attempt to justify "Inaction" through loudly "proclaimed function."[274] A recent example of this phenomenon was the organization of the Commonwealth Games 2010 in New Delhi. Unfortunately, re-branding was a poor substitute for effective organization and invited comparison, to India's detriment, with the organization of the 2008 Beijing Olympics.[275] The mantra about the rise of India is in part a nervous reaction to the far more real rise of China.[276]

CONCLUSION

In the preceding survey of the nature of state power in the Indian subcontinent several important features merit recapitulation. First, the dominant form of the state in the Indian subcontinent was the continental bureaucratic empire. Second, the culture of power of continental bureaucratic empires whether ruled by Hindus, Turks, or Europeans, exhibited high levels of arbitrariness. Third, under British rule serious and sustained efforts were made to reform the nature of the state. The motivation for these reforms came from the contradiction between the British experience of the state at home and the profoundly different reality that prevailed in India. This, in turn, evolved into a gradual movement towards the establishment of a state of laws in India that incorporated many features of the continental bureaucratic empire. The objective of this synthesis was to establish a state that could achieve and sustain effective constitutional government along representative lines on a continental scale[277] and potentially establish a truly "imperishable empire" of reason, laws, and state-morality.[278]

In order to understand where we are going it is imperative that we be cognizant of the broader historical patterns that have unfolded on the South Asian canvas and see how the present situation stands in comparison. In broad outline, the recorded history of South Asia begins with the advent of the Mauryan dynastic empire around 320 BC and continues in patches until the rise of the Delhi Sultanate in AD 1206. From 1206 onwards, the record is much better and improves the closer one gets to the contemporary era.

What this record reveals, even in its outline, is sobering. From 320 BC to the present day, a time span of 2300 years, South Asia has known, at best, 500 years of effective government and relative peace. These 500 years correspond to the peak periods of major empires (Mauryas, Guptas, Delhi Sultanate, Mughals, and the British Raj). The rest is taken up by different degrees and kinds of chaos. The Indus region, that forms the core of Pakistan, was subjected to 70 major invasions between AD 1000 and AD 1800 and countless rebellions and raids. Even the most dynamic and aggressive regimes struggled to keep one step ahead of chaos. Akbar, for instance, crushed 140 plus rebellions during the first 40 years of his reign. Aurungzeb spent the better part of his reign trying to crush revolts in Peninsular India. British India, which eventually succeeded the Timurids, faced constant problems along its frontiers and repeated rebellions in the heartland, in spite of its regard for institutionalism, the rule of law, meritocracy, civilian supremacy, and its seeding of South Asia with the basic prerequisites of constitutional democracy.

With the termination of the British Raj in August 1947, South Asia broke up into warring states determined to exacerbate each other's internal problems even as they failed to cope effectively with their own. Since 1947, the general trajectory of South Asia is towards greater political and administrative chaos set against the backdrop of unsustainable and uncontrollable demographic pressure. To a limited extent, the institutional legacy of the British Empire in India has mitigated the severity of the return to arbitrariness and chaos in India though other regional countries, such as Pakistan, have not been even that fortunate.

One scenario for the Indian subcontinent that is already upon us in many respects is that the state ceases to exist as a means of improving the lives of its citizens and delivering public services. In this scenario a quasi-representative but criminalized political system exhibiting high levels of corruption and mismanagement may continue to preside over a society in which public services are steadily breaking down. The rich will be able to move into gated communities, hire private security, produce their own utilities, and send their children and surplus capital abroad. The rest will stew in their own juice without food, electricity, gas, water, law and order, quality education/health care, but with mobile phones and televisions to communicate and heighten their perception of deprivation. The state will not, however, have the administrative capability to respond to this deprivation, no matter how many times civil society stages demos or people burst into protest.

The second, which is not yet upon us but may materialize in the next 5–15 years, is that the state machinery in the Indus region and the Indo-Gangetic plain breaks down and South Asia descends into criminal anarchy with local mafias and sectarian fanatics carving out their own spheres of influence. Regional states will continue to exist as cartographic and diplomatic entities but their administrative writ will cease to operate except for selected areas (cantonments, upscale suburbs and city centres) and a few other key regions. In this scenario the fortunes of the state might be revived by intervention from two sources, together or separately. One is that a military saviour emerges and pursues salvation by the sword. The other is that the most motivated elements in Indian and Pakistani society, the religious fundamentalists, overcome obstacles and fill the vacuum.

The third scenario is one with which many are already familiar owing to the West's well-known fears of Pakistan becoming a failed state—a gigantic Yugoslavia-like entity with hundreds of nukes and legions of militant obscurantists determined to build a jihadist utopia guided by an operational calculus incompatible with the logic of deterrence and interest-based statecraft. This projection can be called the supernova scenario and would have truly global implications if it were to emerge. Once again, hardy and religiously motivated warriors would descend on the Indo-Gangetic plain bringing in their wake chaos and terror a foretaste of which was provided by the attack on Mumbai in 2008.

One of the basic deficiencies that the Westernized elite of the Indian subcontinent is afflicted by is sheer ignorance of regional history. More interested in the national security and democracy and development discourse, hardly anyone in positions of authority cares to know about this part of the world. The reaction then of India and Pakistan's educated to the crisis that threatens to overwhelm the state varies between delusional optimism and a longing for miracles that "should" happen and a despairing cynicism.

The point to understand is that the future is neither absolutely predetermined nor completely random and alterable. India and Pakistan[279] are both troubled states confronted by enormous challenges that can be overcome with determination and rational leadership. The way to deal with these challenges is to improve the quality of the state apparatus, which, in the Indian subcontinent's own history, means improvement of the executive arm of the state. That can only be done if Indian and Pakistani leaders and intellectuals stop mindlessly parroting fashionable clichés and learn rational lessons from their tragic history.

The ability of the Indian state to perform even its core functions has been steadily compromised by the reassertion of the culture of power of the Indian subcontinent since independence. Indian politicians are arbitrary, corrupt, incompetent, driven to self-aggrandizement and devoid of that minimum of enlightened self-interest necessary for the discharge of their duties as elected representatives. The survival of India's legal democracy appears to have more to do with the institutional and intellectual inheritance from the British Raj and inertia imposed by India's intractable social structure than the competence of the indigenous ruling classes of politicians, big businessmen, and bureaucrats.

The behavioral pattern of these classes manifests a level of arbitrariness incompatible with the survival of the institutions upon which the governance of India depends. These institutions, instead of being consciously nurtured and strengthened, were, and are, derisively categorized as relics of the British colonial legacy, a steel frame possessed of a vision limited to the maintenance of law and order and the collection of taxes rendered obsolete by the new sophistries of the age of development paradigms. Thus, there was a failure at the highest level to understand that the British, far from teaching India bureaucracy and authoritarianism, had learnt how to contain the two and reduce the level of arbitrariness inherent in the exercise of state-power in continental bureaucratic empires. This was done by recasting the state as a complex of autonomous institutions governed by rational laws, in contradistinction to the subcontinent's tradition of governance through servile instruments dependent on the ruler's will. Of course, the responses accumulated by Indians over thousands of years could not be miraculously changed or wished away. They could only be reformed with patience and persistence derived from rational thought.

The post-independence leadership's perception of the state, however, was based upon an unsound grasp of the Indian subcontinent's historical experience of governance, and rapidly gave in to the indigenous culture of power. Instead of protecting private property, the state undermined that institution under the cover of socialist rhetoric. The civil service was reduced to servility through arbitrary transfers, promotions, and suspensions. The police suffered a similar fate, and became criminalized and politicized. The financial administration, instead of being empowered by self-government to make tax collection more progressive, became reliant on indirect taxation, thus reversing the positive trends evident under British rule. India's democracy, now in its seventh decade, does not rest on the foundation of self-taxation and shows little inclination of ever doing so. The judiciary, though it has performed reasonably well in rearguard actions, cannot be expected to escape the general institutional decay and, thus, single-handedly bring about a reversal in fortunes. Even the military, if state failure persists, may be drawn into the political vortex. The legislatures, provincial and central, far from being India's salvation, are the major cause of system-wide deterioration. Their failure to have a meaningful impact on the manner in which power is exercised is underscored by the fact that Hindu revivalism is seeping into the state structure through the electoral process. This revival is a symptom and a cause of the inability of the Indian leadership to exercise power through the state rationally, lawfully, and with due respect for institutions.

India is trapped in a crisis from which there is no real escape. The culture of power and historical experience of governance both militate in favor of Hindu revivalism and the rebirth of an *Arthashastra* state or breakdown and warlord-ism. The first outcome terrifies minorities, leftists, liberals, and many political parties including the Congress, which headed the opposition to the BJP-led government and has formed the government at the center since 2004. The latter outcome may galvanize support for a party of order and help the Hindutva phenomenon make a serious comeback. The groups ranged in opposition, however, are only marginally less irrational than the Hindu revivalists. The Congress, having governed India for the longest since 1947, has done more than any other group to render the state ineffective, corrupt, and incapable of rational comprehension, and thus paved the way for the open reassertion of the indigenous Indian culture of power.

It needs to be understood is that when some Indian politicians abduct girls to satisfy their carnal appetites, arbitrarily transfer civil servants, use state funds to finance lavish expenditure on their birthdays, seize the assets of their people, otherwise abuse their power to enrich their personal connections, or use religion for political purposes, they do not really believe that they are doing wrong. As far as they are concerned the part of the country over which they wield power is a personal estate. The civil servants are their personal servants. The people are their personal subjects. State and private property is their personal property. If they win the election, then it is taken as a sign of divine favor solicited by paying homage to gurus and filing nomination papers on the auspicious date determined by astrologers.

The idea that the country is not a vast personal estate, over which power is gained by divine sanction and sustained by personal servants operating servile instruments, is imported from the British. Barring a dramatic realization amongst the Indian political class that their real struggle is against their own culture of power, it appears that ideocratic arbitrary rule either in the form of a Hindu *rashtra* or some other shape, or a descent into chaos are the probable futures.[280] India's free media and the openness with which the government is criticized, are important assets that might help avert these dire outcomes but the sensitivity of the state and its capacity to respond are both compromised by weak coalitions and the habituation, since independence, to arbitrary rule punctuated by elections.

2 The Dragon and the Phoenix
The Chinese Civil Service State

INTRODUCTION: DYNASTIES AND EMPIRE

In terms of territorial and demographic extent, material prosperity, social stability and inventiveness, the historical experience of China stands out in world history. China is credited with having the world's oldest living state/civilization.[1] It is also credited with pioneering concepts such as meritocracy, performance legitimacy, an administration based on laws and regulations, and a humanistic system of ethics.[2] China's infrastructural and architectural achievements, ranging from the iconic Great Wall and Forbidden City, to the canals and roads of the imperial era, are also testaments to endurance and capability. From a South Asian perspective the patterns of Chinese history and the achievements of Chinese culture and civilization almost inevitably invite comparison. To some, China and India are Asia's two distinct ancient civilizations and their ongoing economic transformation heralds the return of these cultures to their historical preeminence. Without taking anything away from the cultural or intellectual achievements of the South Asian region, there is one point on which the two civilizations differ fundamentally. That point is the experience of the state.[3]

Counting from c. 300 BC to the present day, a period of about 2300 years, a centralized Chinese state governing most of the population centers and many of the territories that are presently part of the Peoples' Republic of China has existed for around 1500 years. For South Asia, during the same period, an effective central government that exercised power over Northern India plus Pakistan and Bangladesh, has existed for perhaps 500 years. For China, centrally imposed and maintained order has been the historical norm while for South Asia it has been the exception. China and India are both inheritors of a great and ancient tradition of civilization but it is only the former that has managed to remain a great and effective state.[4]

In China, as in South Asia, the dominant configuration for the exercise of power has been rule by an absolute monarch whose writ was enforced through a hierarchically organized state bureaucracy. Like South Asian rulers, the Chinese rulers exercised arbitrary power over their bureaucratic servants who, in turn, comprised the principal element of the ruling class.

In the Chinese case, however, the most outstanding and well-known of these state functionaries were civil servants recruited through a competitive process from a talent pool that consisted of the educated elite. There were also a large number of eunuchs who were ineligible for the exams but could be allowed to serve in the royal palace, while in the early stages of dynastic rule military officials also exercised great influence.[5] In addition to the civil service officers, palace eunuchs, and military officials, a large field bureaucracy made up of clerks, runners, spies, record keepers, postmen, and guards, staffed the lower rungs of the administration and were most often in contact with the population. The elite that officered the Chinese state was recruited from a social base formed by scholars from the rural gentry and urban merchant class. These scholars acted as the ideological and intellectual props of the Chinese state and blended legalism, Confucianism, Taoism and Buddhism into a worldview that served to legitimize the state and extol service to it as the highest social virtue.[6] The basic configuration of the Chinese state has survived fluctuating geopolitical fortunes, invasions, rebellions and regime change and continues to thrive under present circumstances. Some clues that can help us better understand the extraordinary perseverance and resilience of the Chinese state are to be found in its formative experiences some 2300 years ago.

THE BIRTH OF THE QIN DYNASTIC EMPIRE AND THE UNIFICATION OF CHINA

China's unification as a single state-empire was brought about by conquest. The state of Qin annihilated and absorbed its rivals in a series of wars, intrigues and annexations that occurred in various phases between 500 BC and 221 BC.[7] In the process, millions died or were displaced, entire populations were enslaved and exiled, and blood and iron used to crush dissent. The rise of Qin began during the Spring and Autumn Period (770–476 BC) when China was divided into hundreds of aristocratic fiefdoms notionally subject to the authority of the Zhou emperors. By 476 BC, these hundreds of petty states had given way to seven warring states leading to the Warring States Period (475–221 BC) that ended in Qin victory over its competitors.[8] Of these competitors, Wei and Qi had advantages of location and resources as they occupied the most fertile areas and were protected from barbarian incursions by the other states. There was nothing inevitable about the Qin victory or the unification of China. If China's pre-unification history offered any lesson on the unity of China it was that like India, China was destined to become a civilization with many competing power centers.

The Qin state, however, benefited from the services of a radical reformer named Shang Yang.[9] Patronized by the Qin ruler from 380 BC onwards, Shang Yang reorganized the Qin state in accordance with the precepts of the legalist philosophy, which represented a world view that embraced practicality, order, regimentation, bureaucracy, military discipline, and took a basically dim view of human nature.[10] Legalism maintained that a state should be organized on the basis of laws that were to apply equally to all segments of society and that in order to deter misbehavior punishments should be as harsh as possible. The ruler ought to consider the laws as representing his own writ and ensure their implementation with minimal interference. The Qin state turned itself into a Chinese Sparta and by focusing on agricultural and infrastructural works was able to shift the balance of power in its favor. Culturally backward as compared to the other Chinese states, Qin proved pragmatic in its employment of outsiders and pursued the strategic vision of a united Chinese state with ruthlessness and vigor. The outcome of the Qin struggle to unify China had enormous ramifications for world history for without it "China" may never have existed as a state encompassing the core areas of a civilization.

The Qin state possessed a strong standing army that was led by the military-service nobility, as opposed to the feudalistic armies of the other warring states. Internally, the Qin state was divided into administrative subunits administered by centrally appointed civil servants that could be transferred or eliminated if the ruler wished, as opposed to the relatively aristocratic structure of the other warring states. Qin society was divided into units of ten households that were responsible for reporting criminal activity, including anti-state activity, directly to police and judicial officers. If they made reports that resulted in convictions the household groups could be rewarded. Conversely, if they failed to report crime to the authorities the households would be subjected to collective punishment. Idleness was punished by enslavement and thousands of slaves, prisoners of war and enemies of the state, along with ordinary criminals, were converted into forced labor and expendable frontier colonists. The conscious objective of the Qin state was to organize society in order to maximize the power and wealth of the state. It was this "harsh fascistic society of snooping neighbors and hungry soldiers" that unified China by defeating its more easygoing and aristocratic competitors.[11]

The Qin ruler who finally succeeded in completing the unification process was Yang Sheng, better known as Qin Shihuangdi (First Sovereign Emperor of the Qin). The First Qin Emperor, unlike the founders of many other states and dynasties, was reviled as an upstart and oppressor. Oppressor though he was, the harsh legalism that Qin espoused meant that Confucianism and traditionalism were suppressed, the hereditary aristocracy marginalized, and the literati exposed to the wrath of the state. The Han dynasty (206 BC–AD 220) that succeeded the Qin had a vested interest in emphasizing the brutality and excesses of the preceding dynasty even while continuing many of its practices.

What is known of the First Qin Emperor is that he became the ruler of his state at the age of thirty-three and asserted his authority through bloody reprisals against those he suspected of disloyalty, which led to the executions of twenty senior officials and the exile of 4000 others.[12] His authority consolidated at home, the First Qin Emperor embarked on a final series of campaigns to bring the remaining states under his direct administrative control. In one of these campaigns, directed against the State of Zhao, 100,000 adult males were beheaded in order to demonstrate the price of resistance.[13] Owing to his mother's less than glorious involvement in court intrigues at the time of his accession, the emperor forbade mention of her name and put to death twenty-seven courtiers who, unwisely, did not take their master seriously on this point.[14] The unification of China under the Qin dynasty in 221 BC meant that the emperor could deploy his energies, and those of his servants, towards internal consolidation.

The First Qin Emperor introduced a number of important reforms to ensure control of the newly unified country. Well-advised by his ministers, the Qin did not parcel the empire out amongst family members for this could easily lead to the resumption of aristocratic rule by families claiming imperial descent. Instead, the empire was divided into thirty-six provinces each headed by a centrally appointed governor and administered by political and military secretaries. The population was disarmed and an agricultural census was launched in order to determine the tax and population resources of the empire. The basic principle of the taxation system of the Qin was that taxes were levied in accordance with the needs of the state to make them easier to collect. One aspect of this fiscal administrative exercise was the standardization of weights and measures as well as axles (to make road construction easier). Language reform created a single standardized official script that did not vary when written down but still allowed for differences of dialect when spoken. The law of the ruler was made effective through a justice system designed to compel the accused to concede the wisdom of the state while torture, or the threat thereof, was freely employed to extract the needed confession. In this way, the imperial justice machinery ensured in a manner worthy of a modern police state that only guilty people were brought to trial.

The harshness of this system served a number of purposes. One was the levying of fines in place of carrying out punishments. Since the objective of the justice system was to strengthen the state and preserve order, depriving people of their money rather than killing, maiming or exiling them, was a source of revenue and introduced an element of clemency. When linked with the household groups responsible for prying and spying on each other and their own members, the ability of the state to terrorize its subjects into obedience was quite considerable. That said, the maimed and the dead might have been useful as deterrence but they were of no use to the state once the punishment had been carried out. The interest of the state dictated that the spirit be suppressed but the body kept in one piece and thus the most practical punishments were exile to the frontier and enslavement for use as forced labor. Indeed, for a convict "to be sent to the farthest edges of the Qin Empire, perhaps never to return, often accompanied by his equally doomed family", was arguably the worst punishment—a sort of living death.[15] Qin police and judicial officers were under intense pressure to either produce convicts and impose punishments such as exile and enslavement, or risk being hauled up themselves on charges of leniency if they failed to throw enough meat into the imperial grinder. Exile to the frontier, or forced labor on one of the large construction projects, was the fate that awaited tax evaders and purged government officials.

Many of those exiled and/or enslaved ended their lives as workers on the First Qin Emperor's tomb—the spectacular Terracotta Army. It is estimated that 700,000 convict laborers worked on the project for forty years and the secrecy of the project was so well maintained that it wasn't until the 1970s that the tomb of China's unifier was discovered.[16] The emperor also ordered the construction of the Qin Long Wall and entrusted the project to one of his favorite generals. Billed as a defensive structure, the Long Wall was also "the Qin gulag, a huge, arbitrary building project designed to swallow up soldiers demobilized after the big push to unify China" and put thousands of convicts to good use.[17] The Long Wall became, in the popular imagination, a symbol of the state's arbitrary power and the "bleak, lonely graveyard of ordinary Chinese."[18] In addition to these vast undertakings, the Qin embarked upon a road construction program, which added 4000 miles of roads, and built 1200 miles of canals. The First Qin Emperor's increasingly bizarre obsession with immortality, his attempt to destroy non-legalist literature, the purge of the intelligentsia, and expensive mega-projects, established his reputation as a radical and mercurial despot. Unfortunately for his dynasty, his successors proved incapable, while feuding within the Qin state hierarchy gave rebellions a chance of success and paved the way for the fall of the Qin and rise of the Han. At this stage we can pause and reflect on the nature of the Qin state and its impact on China's culture of power and governance for some of its features have continued into the modern period.

The Chinese state founded by the Qin was remarkably centralized. This centralization was made possible by reliance on civil servants and military officers who earned rather than inherited their rank. The state was organized in order to maximize the power of the ruler over society, while the society was organized in order to maximize the power of the state. This was achieved through the ruthless enforcement of harsh laws, the atomization of society into small household units, and by keeping social energy employed in large-scale projects. The Qin state also attempted, almost like a revolutionary government in modern times, to root out all pre-unification thought and crush internal dissent through police state methods. The emperor commanded the people and resources of the country as if he were the sole proprietor and was, on top of that, worshipped as the representative of the will of Heaven. For all practical purposes, there was no morality above the state, and Confucian pieties, never a real challenge to a strong ruler and not much of a restraint during the Warring States Period, were entirely rubbished. Later regimes would modify these features to suit their own interests and inclinations, but the underlying nature of the Chinese state—hierarchical, authoritarian, arbitrary, bureaucratic, formally ideological, and actually personalized—would remain intact.[19]

THE APPARATUS IN FORM

The continental bureaucratic empire founded by the Qin survived in different incarnations for most of the 2200 years of Chinese imperial history. Although this empire was highly centralized, it delegated decision-making powers to the provincial, regional and district administrations. Civil servants recruited through a combination of patronage and competitive exams were responsible for running the day-to-day affairs of the state. These civil servants answered to their superiors while the governors and their staff answered directly to the central government. The role of the emperor in this system had three major dimensions. First, the emperor was the head of the administration and ultimately responsible for its operation. This responsibility was borne by the emperor in his capacity as a policy maker who was also supposed to maintain a broad superintendence of the administration. Second, the emperor acted as a referee between court factions, the civil service and other cliques. And third, the emperor had a large number of ceremonial and protocol functions to attend to. The professional civil servants in conjunction with the governors and ministers best handled administrative routine. Of course, the emperor could intervene whenever he chose and discipline or reward his servants. Strong emperors were either energetic to an almost superhuman degree and took a keen interest in running the state or displayed good judgment in choosing competent ministers and governors to take care of routine matters for them.

The organization of the Chinese imperial state reflected the practical delegation of power to appointed sub-sovereigns in the provinces and districts. During the Han dynasty, the number of divisional administrative units varied from 103 to 105 while the number of counties, or what South Asians would understand as districts, varied from 1100–1600. The Han dynasty also recognized a number of kingdoms ruled by members of the extended royal family. In Tang China (618–907) the number of administrative divisions grew to 300–330 (circa 750) while the districts numbered about 1600. For the united Song dynasty (960–1127), the number of divisions was similar to the Tang period but the number of districts fell to between 1200–1300 (circa 1000). Towards the end of the Ming dynasty (1368–1644) the number of divisions stood at 159 and the number of districts ranged between 1100 and 1200. During the Qing dynasty (1644–1911), there were 400 divisions and 1700 districts.

One of the administration's major tasks was to keep count of the population and resources of the empire. The Chinese empire excelled at keeping records and it is possible to determine the population of China to an extent that is unusually precise for a pre-industrial society.[20] Even the smaller dynastic empires that emerged during periods of imperial collapse managed to compile statistical information about the populations they ruled. One figure that seems to be widely accepted is that China's population ranged from 60–100 million between the Han and Ming dynasties, before growing considerably during the Qing period so that by 1741 the census counted 140 million people, which nearly doubled to 260 million by 1775. There are questions about the counting procedure and periodicity of the counting and there is little doubt that people would have wanted to avoid being counted if possible as that would lead to tax and labor demands on the part of the state.[21] Population growth also seems tied to the fortunes of the state, increasing steadily or, as in the case of the Qing very rapidly, during periods of political stability and effective administration, and falling during periods of imperial disintegration. A growing population did not translate directly into changes in the structure of the administration and could have also stressed the bureaucratic capacity of the imperial Chinese state. Assuming a population of 60 million in 1600 spread over 1100 districts gives us an average district population of 54,545. With a population of 260 million in 1775 spread over 1700 districts, the per-district population comes out to 152,941.

At the central level the structure of the Chinese empire demonstrated unparalleled resilience. During the Han dynasty the emperor had three senior advisers for the chancellery, secretarial affairs and the military, and a cabinet of nine ministers responsible for protocol, the royal household, imperial security, imperial stables and communications, diplomacy, agriculture, finance, justice, and ancestral shrines and state records. Later dynasties, such as the Tang and the Ming, favored a trifurcation with an imperial chancellery, an imperial secretariat and a department of state, with other functions placed under boards or commissions responsible for establishment, fiscal administration, law and order and judicial administration, and military affairs. The Ming merged the three departments into a single Grand Secretariat but retained three to six Grand Secretaries to operate six boards (personnel, rites, war, justice, revenue, public works). From the time of the Qin dynasty a special institution known as the Censorate was responsible for maintaining discipline within the state apparatus. During the Ming period there were two chief censors and 100 investigating officers plus numerous administrative staff needed to handle finance and correspondence. In theory, since the united Song dynasty, the censors had the power to criticize the emperor's decisions and suggest alternatives. In practice, the censors' ire was directed against errant officials and not the sovereign.

Whatever the formal structure of the imperial state, much depended on the quality of leadership provided by the rulers and the competence of the imperial servants responsible for running the state machinery and advising the emperor. It is here that the Chinese truly stand apart from *all* other pre-industrial societies, and most post-industrial ones as well; in terms of its ability to create and perpetuate a civil service elite drawn from the literate classes through a system of examinations. Early in the Chinese imperial history, China's rulers constituted a partial meritocracy to recruit their servants and in so doing made a contribution to administrative thought and practice that is imperfectly understood and under continuous assault in South Asia where the indigenous tradition made for a far more whimsical process of recruitment until the advent of the British Empire in India.

SERVANTS OF THE STATE

One of the greatest contributions of legalism to the Chinese administrative tradition was the idea that ability rather than birth should be the principal basis of recruitment to state service. The radical nature of this concept is perhaps difficult for Western societies to appreciate in the contemporary world although it was not until the 1800s that many of them internalized the need for merit-based recruitment to state service as feudal culture with its aristocratic pretensions slowly receded. There are still some Western societies, like the United States of America, that allow the elected chief executive to nominate thousands of individuals to bureaucratic and advisory positions and reject the need for a permanent higher bureaucracy on the pattern that prevails in France or the United Kingdom. The fact remains, however, that for most of human history, birth, race, caste, kinship, religion, and political clout, mattered far more than ability in securing official positions. This was as true of feudalistic Europe as it was of absolutist South Asian and West Asian empires. Some of these states also adopted the practice of selling offices and noble titles as a means of generating revenue and binding newly emerging groups to the old regime. In South Asia, the ruler's discerning eye was considered sufficient for the purpose of determining merit (sometimes it was, most of the time it wasn't). Often caste or belonging to a racially distinct group of outsiders, determined initial access to positions in government service. In some West Asian empires the rulers' officials were his slaves though many of them would have been manumitted at some stage in their careers. The idea of recruiting civil servants through a series of examinations held at regular intervals was a Chinese innovation that began with the Han dynasty and matured under the Sui and Tang.

The Han dynasty founded an Imperial Academy in 124 BC, which produced some 30,000 graduates over the next 150 years, and developed a system to recruit civil servants that took advantage of the Qin-era reforms.[22] The practice under the Han was to allow provincial administrations to select from amongst the educated classes apprentices that would serve in the local administration. The bureaucracy was divided into 12 levels or grades with clerical staff at the bottom and ministers at the top. Starting in a clerical position, the apprentices would be trained in law, drafting, finance, protocol, and rites. Periodically, the central government would instruct the provincial governments to nominate candidates to serve in the capital. If the emperor so desired, the candidates could be put through a written examination. These examinations were conducted as needed but the incentive structure was clear. Anyone with the right educational qualifications could become an apprentice and rise to senior positions in the state machinery. The education required included subjects like law, ethics, philosophy, poetry, prose writing, and aesthetics, with Confucian classics forming the core of each subject. As one can imagine, such an education was expensive and time consuming and only families with some land and wealth could afford to educate their sons. Sometimes, wealthy but dim-witted families would adopt the children of poorer but brighter relations and pay for their education in the hope that someone from the family could make it into state service.

During the Sui and Tang dynasties a more comprehensive and centralized mechanism for recruitment through competitive examinations was adopted and the principle that local officials should be appointed directly by the center was adopted. The Tang dynasty gave particular attention to the establishment of schools at the local level for the purpose of training candidates who could then participate in the exams for the local, provincial and central bureaucracies. By the united Song period, most senior officials were recruited through the examinations that were held once every three years and the emperor himself acted as the final examiner. The Ming dynasty saw the format of the examinations changed to three stages. The first was a local level examination that made successful candidates eligible for posts in the local bureaucracy. The second was a prefecture-level exam that made successful candidates eligible for appointment to the provincial government. The final stage was the central exam held in the capital that enabled successful candidates to secure posts in the central bureaucracy. One important aspect of this system was that the local, provincial, and central bureaucracies were staffed by an administrative elite recruited through the same process and from the same social class.[23] Candidates could re-take exams and improve their position and one had to pass the lower level exams in order to be eligible to take the higher level of examinations.

In order to ensure the integrity of the recruitment process a number of practices were followed. One was the use of roll numbers to prevent examiners from knowing whose paper they were grading. Another was the use of cubicles to prevent candidates from cheating off each other. Examination papers would be checked by two different examiners and in the event of a major difference in grading be referred to a third. Candidates would be evaluated on the basis of how well they wrote, the information they used, and the overall quality of their arguments and answers. The grading was so rigorous that only a small percentage (actually less than 1% during Ming rule) managed to clear the provincial exams and become eligible for sitting in the central examinations.

After the central examinations the passing candidates were divided into first class, second class, and third class, and assigned to vacancies in different departments or given field postings. Once in service, confidential evaluations of officers were conducted every three years while the censors kept a close eye on the performance of government officers. Postings were also classified into difficult, busy and easy categories, against which the performance of the officers could be judged. In addition to such safeguards, from the Ming dynasty onwards, officers could not serve in districts or departments where their relatives lived or were employed. The Chinese evidently understood the concept of conflict of interest and sought to avoid putting officers in positions where their kinsmen would have easy access to them. The education of the civil servants was basically considered complete upon qualification at the local level and new recruits were expected to learn on the job often from more experienced local staff over which they had administrative powers. The total numerical strength of the central officer cadre varied from 10,000 to 30,000 from AD 1000—1800, against a population of 60 million to 300 million.[24] Even if China had a literacy rate of 5–10% during this entire period, that would create a pool of 3 million to 30 million people from which to recruit the central, provincial and local bureaucracies.

For literate Chinese families representation in the imperial service was the key to property, status and protection. Frank Ching's *Ancestors*,[25] which is an account of one family's history through a thousand years of Chinese history, reads like a repetitive saga. Each generation of young men grows up preparing for the examinations. A few succeed and help make the family fortune. Some manage to pass the basic or intermediate stage of the exams and serve respectably in the local or provincial administrations, while those who cannot make the grade become local poets and scholars who tend to their lands and prepare their sons to attempt the competitive exams and get onto the bureaucratic fast-track. In Imperial China there was no greater honor than service to the state and the best and brightest sought to join the ranks of the civil service elite and defined their self-worth by their performance in the competitive examinations.

Prestige was not, of course, the sole motivation for joining the ranks of the imperial servants. In China, administrative power was the key to accumulating wealth and the presence of even one member of a clan in the civil service at a senior position could alter the entire clan's fortunes. Without a landed aristocracy to speak of, China never developed primogeniture to keep landed estates intact on the feudal pattern. The practice of polygamy amongst the landed classes meant that even a large estate established by an enterprising patriarch would be, in one or two generations, divided into dozens of small ones. The only way to climb back up the economic ladder was state service. The Chinese accepted that corruption was inevitable and that the ruler could never hope to eradicate it. Confucian pieties and legalistic harshness could only do so much to prevent bribery, maladministration, and the abuse of power. The Chinese solution was to allow certain practices that would today be condemned as corruption. One of these was the giving and taking of presents. So long as the officers did not extort gifts or neglect their duties they could receive gifts from grateful or expectant subjects. Another was allowing government officers to accumulate landholdings whether as gifts or through purchase. Since these landholdings were going to pay for the education of the next generation of civil servants, it made little sense to prevent their accumulation. Although the Confucian-minded civil servants frowned upon the merchants as base and unworthy creatures, the state needed them and they needed the state. It behooved merchants to cultivate the favor of civil servants and vice versa. The real earnings of a Chinese civil servant ranged from four to nineteen times as much as the regular paid salary.[26] As long as the government got its share of the revenues, the emperor's instructions were followed, order and infrastructure maintained, and important targets met, corruption was tolerated. The nexus between landholding, education and state service, meant that the landed elite, the intellectual elite and the administrative elite were all drawn from the same group and a basic harmony of interests prevailed. Landlords needed the civil servants to enforce their property rights and collect rent while those who joined the imperial service soon became, if they weren't already, landlords. Both landlords and civil servants invested in classical education designed to get the next generation of young men ready to serve the empire and, of course, helping secure the future of the clan for another generation or two. The intelligentsia itself subscribed to the same statist ethos as the civil servants (whose ranks they aspired to join) and the landlords (the social group to which most educated young men would have belonged to).

It is perhaps to this highly integrated administrative, landed and intellectual elite, which shared a worldview and sense of loyalty, that Imperial China owed its resilience as a state and a cultural unit. Here there is a marked difference between China and South Asia for in the latter such integrated elites never emerged and the ruling class comprised invaders keen to disassociate themselves from the land and people they ruled. China's relative stability is often taken as a case of conservatism and the country's failure to industrialize in time to stave off the Western onslaught is often attributed to Confucianism and the statist nature of the Chinese upper stratum.[27] There is some truth in this but such Euro-centric fixation on the developments of the last 250 years misses several important points. First, the Chinese elite possessed a humanistic worldview that was largely untroubled by the metaphysical and eschatological obsessions of the Western Christian churches. Second, in terms of sheer inventiveness, China stands out as the most brilliant of the pre-industrial civilizations and there is compelling evidence that on the eve of the Mongol invasions of the 1200s China had developed the basic dynamic of coal-dependence, iron manufacturing, and mechanical innovation to boost textile production, that mark the initial stages of an industrial revolution.[28] Third, in terms of literacy, education and communications, China easily surpasses all other cultures prior to 1600 and was second to none until the late 1700s owing to printing and paper-making (both Chinese inventions). Fourth, China's continental size economy and large population facilitated monetization and led to the adoption of paper currency centuries before other countries. Finally, the same effectiveness of the state that made the above possible also meant that the central government could impose policies on the whole country that proved unsound in the long run. One such policy was the decision taken by the Ming regime in the 1430s to concentrate on the in-land threat from Central Asia and abandon the promising policy of naval expeditions. Another policy, adopted by the Qing dynasty, was to limit trade relations with foreign powers. In the competitive environment of Europe, governments did not have the power to impose policies on a continental scale but in China the apparatus of empire was ready and able to execute the wishes of the imperial court. Once a policy was decided upon the inertial momentum of the state elite kept it going until it met some irresistible internal or external force.

The statist attitude of the Chinese elite meant that merchants and mercantile wealth were viewed with suspicion and distaste. This did not mean that the Chinese were inherently opposed to mercantile wealth or lacked an appropriately rational ethic. What it meant was that in Imperial China land and status derived from public office were coveted markers of identity and the strength of the state meant the intelligent merchants curried favor with the state elite. Commerce was taxed and subjected to the operation of government monopolies and thus merchants cultivated state officials and tried to educate their own sons for a career in the imperial service. While some merchants may indeed have had themselves castrated to join the palace as eunuchs,[29] most did not and managed to work profitably within the framework of the imperial system. The fault of the system was that it failed to anticipate *unprecedented* threats from across the seas and happened to be in a condition of internal decline when they materialized.

While the civil service elite may have publicly scoffed at the merchants, they had to be far more careful in their dealings with the eunuchs in the imperial service. The emperor's own household and establishment were staffed by eunuchs even though career bureaucrats normally staffed senior official positions. Only the eunuchs had direct personal access to the emperor and the royal family. Emperors regarded their eunuchs as loyalists and used them to balance the power of the competitively recruited civil servants. A strong emperor—and China was blessed with an unusually large proportion of competent and assertive absolute monarchs—kept the balance tilted in his own favor. A weak emperor, however, could quickly find himself hostage to his personal retainers and be isolated from the state machinery. During the Ming decline, for instance,

"There was no area of government devoid of eunuchs competing with and spying on their civil servant counterparts."[30] There was even, during this period, a eunuch "secret police, an organization reaching out far and wide across the empire" that tortured and imprisoned those suspected of disloyalty to the emperor.[31] Balancing the need for loyalty to the national leader with the requirements of administrative efficiency was then, as now, a delicate matter.

The relationship between the civil and military arms of the government was one of the most interesting aspects of governance by the civil service elite. Initially, the dynastic regimes that ruled China were militarized in nature and leadership. It was, for example, the obsessively militaristic Qin that unified China. The founder of the Sui dynasty was also a military man, while the last dynasty, the Qing, maintained a distinct role for the ethnic-Manchu banner-men that formed the hard core of their military strength. In spite of these developments, once order was restored and the frontiers stabilized, the Chinese civil service elite gained ascendancy over the military elite. The emperor was the supreme military commander and all senior military commands depended on imperial favor. However, unlike the *mansabdar*s of the Timurid Empire in India, which fused military and civil functions into a single hierarchy, the Chinese had separate hierarchies for the men of learning and culture (*wen*) and the men of violence and action (*wu*). A career in the civil service was far more prestigious than a career in the military and civil servants could actually be appointed (temporarily) to military positions, especially for the purpose of crushing internal rebellions—something that requires administrative skill as much as military might. Even the most militaristic of China's dynasties, the Yuan, "learned that empires could be conquered on horseback but not ruled on horseback, much as the nineteenth-century European imperialists would learn that bayonets were no use for sitting on."[32]

This did not mean that resources were not lavished on the military and military-related projects. The Qin constructed 5000 kilometers of walls along the frontier, the Han built 10,000 kilometers of walls, the Sui deployed over 100,000 men to rebuild the Han-era walls, while new fortifications in 1576 cost 3.30 million ounces of silver or 75 percent of Ming central revenues.[33] Successive dynasties also experimented with military land grants systems that allocated land and the rent from it to the military officers and soldiers in exchange for their service with surplus rent sent to the treasury. Under the Ming dynasty, 41.30 million hectares of land were thus alienated with the revenues from the land split evenly between the army and the imperial court.[34] In spite of these megaprojects, financial outlays and alienation of land revenues, that military policies dictated, the internal administration of China was in the hands of the civilian bureaucratic elite, which enjoyed a considerable measure of control over the military. This superiority of *wen* over *wu* was an integral part of the Chinese conception of empire and the legitimate exercise of power.

ALL UNDER HEAVEN AND IMPERIAL CONFUCIANISM

Legalism, the harsh and morally pessimistic philosophy of laws, deterrence and order, and Confucianism, the relatively benign and morally optimistic philosophy of hierarchy, ethics and education,[35] served as the basis for the Chinese imperial ideology and intellectual discourse since the Han dynasty. Under successive dynasties the structure of the Chinese state apparatus was modeled on the legalist Qin dynasty. The intellectual discourse, ethos and rhetoric of power, during the same imperial period, viewed the harshness and violence of the Qin system with transparent distaste. Nothing perhaps captured the Yin/Yang dichotomy better than the competitive exams for recruitment to state service. The meritocracy thus promoted went against the aristocratic grain of Confucianism but, the curriculum, was dominated by Confucianism and Neo-Confucianism. The apparent contradiction was reconcilable if understood in terms of the different needs of the state. In order to be effective, Confucian-minded rulers incorporated the legalist model into the state structure. However, Confucianism provided the moral basis of the state and served to justify it in ethical terms. To rely completely on legalism would condemn the empire to severe and unstable despotism. To rely principally on Confucianism would risk rendering the state ineffective.

During the pre-unification period, which covers at least 1000 years, China was an "ideal" empire with a theoretically suzerain center that conferred legitimacy on practically independent aristocratic fiefdoms.[36] The Chinese empire in its pre-Qin incarnation resembled the Abbasid Caliphate post-868 or the Roman Empire during its long decline in Europe or even the Japanese Empire during pre-Tokugawa period—titular sovereignty devoid of substantive power. The Chinese "empire experienced revolutionary reform in 221 BC when the [Q]in Emperor the Great conquered China and created a country with central governance over many provinces instead of sub-states."[37] The practical triumph of a centralized bureaucratic state (*jun xian*) over decentralized feudal-aristocratic governments (*feng jian*) was followed by a brief period during which the Qin dynasty sought to impose its world-view on the rest of the country. An essential component of that world-view was that there ought to be no power-sharing between the center and the provinces (formerly independent states) and that the soft unity of China as a broad cultural unit and civilization was insufficient and had to be replaced by a hard unity of laws, armies, bureaucracies and infrastructure, so that the emperor could rule and not merely reign over the empire. The Qin carried out brutal purges of the intelligentsia and destroyed as many Confucian texts as they could find in an effort to alter the philosophical base of China's elite. While the Qin dynasty itself capsized in 206 BC and was succeeded by the Han, the imperial state that it had founded and the idea of a unified empire to govern all under heaven persisted and, arguably, persists to the present day.

While succeeding dynasties would mix legalist practice with Confucian and neo-Confucian ideals, leading to the emergence of Imperial Confucianism as the ideology of the ruling elite, the purpose of this exercise was to cover the iron hand of the legalist state apparatus in a velvet glove so as to reduce the outward manifestations of coercion.

As the Chinese philosophical tradition did not develop organized religion or a universal teleology and eschatology rooted in mystical and spiritual experiences, the state, in and of itself, came to represent the will of Heaven that was, in turn, manifested within the natural world. From the Chinese perspective, the regime enjoyed legitimacy or the Mandate of Heaven (*Tian ming*) as long as it met at least one of two conditions. The first was that the regime had come to power in a time of great calamity and saved the people from being consumed by it and in so doing won their acceptance.[38] The other was that the regime was running the state effectively and preserving order to the satisfaction of its subjects.[39] If a dynasty was too harsh then it might indeed come to power and save the land from chaos, as was the case with the Qin and Sui, but such a dynasty might not last for very long. Legitimacy depended on performance and performance depended on being effective without being excessively tyrannical and striking a balance between the needs of the state and the pain threshold of the society.

At an ideological level the emperor was the Son of Heaven and had to maintain harmony "between heaven and earth."[40] This meant ruling in accordance with the Mandate of Heaven and balancing strength with moderation. Natural calamities, barbarian invasions, court intrigues and popular rebellions were all portents or signs that the ruler was being too harsh or lax in the performance of his duties. By reacting effectively to these challenges the emperor could prove that the Mandate of Heaven remained in his grasp. The odd failure could be accommodated so long as it was not repeated anytime soon. However, repeated failure to respond successfully to challenges meant the regime had lost the Mandate of Heaven and it ought to be replaced by another regime that would hopefully prove more capable.

While the popular saying was that "He who succeeds is an emperor; he who fails is a bandit"[41] and some rulers, such as the founders of the Han and Ming dynasties were actually from poor rural backgrounds, the Chinese concept of legitimacy countenanced a difference between the empire and state on the one hand and the ruling dynasty or regime on the other. The empire was a cosmological or an ultimate reality. There was no morality above the state. The ruling dynasties were the temporary manifestations of the Mandate of Heaven and had a right to rule the empire only so long as they husbanded its strength, compensated for its flaws, preserved stability, and guarded the frontiers. The persistence of the Celestial Empire and the trans-millennial coherence of its ethos, indicate that the Chinese may well have been one of the earliest societies to understand the difference between the state/empire, which was ideally permanent, and the dynasties/regimes which waxed and waned in accordance with their ability to cope with circumstances and preserve the state.

This development required the active and sustained involvement of human agency. It is here that, as we have seen earlier, the statist ethos of the scholar class and the high regard that China's rulers had for scholarship, reinforced the idea of the empire. Liu Bang, the founder of the Han dynasty, though from a humble background, appreciated the need for advice and counsel and restored Confucian scholars to favor. The preceding Qin dynasty had patronized the legalist school of thought and Liu Bang wanted to distinguish his government from the brutality of the Qin without, however, dismantling the structure of the legalist state apparatus. In Imperial China scholars were recognized as the "apex" of society and were followed by landlords, military men, merchants and peasants.[42] It was the duty of scholars to place their knowledge at the disposal of the state as civil servants, advisers and ministers. It was the duty of the state to provide its subjects with educational opportunities to become scholars, and reward scholars with titles, exemptions from tax and labor burdens and encourage them to impart their wisdom to others. It was this harmonization of interests between the scholar class, which provided the administrative talent needed to run the state, on the one hand, and the leadership of the ruling house that exercised political power, on the other, that helped make the empire such a near-permanent fixture of the Chinese political landscape. Post-unification, therefore, the main challenge was to recruit the best to serve the state and help it act so that it preserved the Mandate of Heaven. Service to the state was thus the greatest virtue and those who served the state, or had the potential to serve it, were recognized as the highest social group. This meant that while society was hierarchical and class conscious, both hierarchy and class were defined by their relationship to the state. It is easy to see how Enlightenment thinkers in Europe developed a favorable impression of China.[43] Here was a state that transcended dynasties and was administered by civil servants drawn from the intelligentsia through competitive exams, posted and evaluated on merit and deriving their powers from a complex system of laws made by men for men. The contrast with the European old regimes, with their archaic aristocratic privileges, half-baked bureaucracies, venal offices and titles for sale, and grasping bourgeoisie could not have been greater.[44] Imperial China was far more "modern" and rational-bureaucratic in its administration than any of its contemporary states and would still compare favorably to many.

One aspect of the Chinese imperial legitimacy lay in the antiquity of the state and the preservation of records relating to it. Indeed, "With thousands of years of written history, China is one of the longest-lasting civilizations in the world" while the "account of Chinese archival development is as long as the written records of Chinese history."[45] China's rulers had long shown an interest in "controlling" as well as preserving the records and it was standard practice to write the history of the previous dynasty and then destroy superfluous materials that may enable a fundamental revision of the official text.[46] There was also the problem of physical destruction during changes of dynasties with local and central archives often suffering terrible attrition. Even with these limitations in mind, the archival records of the Chinese empire are impressive and coherent. The Qin dynasty, for instance, standardized the characters that comprise the Chinese language under a reform program executed by Li Si, the prime minister. A complex classification system for official records was developed and different types of documents were classified under different headings and stored separately.[47] Stone inscriptions for public displays of laws and regulations along with wooden strips were the principal materials used by the Qin. The Han developed a system of archives that stretched from the center to the local government level and continued the apprenticeship system of recruitment.[48] It was from the material in these archives that the Han historian, Si Ma Qian, wrote *Shi Ji* or *Record of the Historian* that covered some 3000 years of the Chinese past, including the history of the Qin. Later dynasties, including those in the period of disunity (AD 220–581) presided over an impressive increase in the volume of publication owing to the use of paper and "As many more people became involved into archival administration of various regimes, there were more than fifty official titles and ranks for archival personnel of that time."[49] Each smaller dynasty "basically followed the central government model set by the Han" which was, in turn, an adaptation of the Qin model.[50]

The Tang dynasty went several steps further by developing "color-coded papers" and requiring that each document deal with only one topic.[51] 1600 or so courier posts dotted the empire and ensured the timely and secure transmission of orders while every three years files deemed unimportant were systematically destroyed.[52] The Song dynasty benefited from the development of block printing which made duplication much easier. The Mongol Yuan dynasty basically kept the Song system in place and assimilated into the Chinese culture to such a degree that the competitive exams for recruitment to state service were restored in 1313–15. The Ming and the Qing went even further in their archival techniques and developed comprehensive rules governing the production and distribution of state documents.

This did not mean that China was a historian's paradise. The political risks of writing history were considerable and each dynasty tried to portray its predecessors as wicked and unworthy of the Mandate of Heaven. Si Ma Qian himself suffered dire consequences when he differed with the emperor about a general who had fallen from favor. Si Ma Qian was offered a choice between castration and death and chose the former and finished writing his historical account. During the Qing dynasty the historian Zhuang Tinglong wrote a history of the Ming dynasty. Even though the history came to light after Zhuang Tinglong's death, the Qing regime was incensed by its relatively positive portrayal of the Ming and "reacted to it with a vengeance":

Zhuang Tinglong's corpse and that of his father were dug up and burned and the Zhuang family and the families of other scholars implicated were almost wiped out. The printers and purchasers of the book were executed. In all, seventy persons were killed and many others exiled.[53]

The Qing dynasty also exerted its authority over the intelligentsia by cancelling tax exemptions granted by the Ming on the grounds that these exemptions had become sources of tax evasion and fraud and undertaking a reorganization of Chinese knowledge designed to minimize criticism of foreigners.[54] In China, then as now, criticism of the state, explicit or implicit, carried grave material and physical risks for a dependent intelligentsia and contributed to conformism in political matters. Han Fei, a Qin-era scholar, laid bare the precarious nature of the scholarly elite's relationship with the sovereign and observed that the advisers of an absolute monarch were perpetually torn "between flattery and insult."[55] The absolute power of the monarch meant that his advisers were inclined to tell him what he wanted to hear. Han Fei felt that such self-serving validations of the emperor's opinions did not constitute advice and argued that in secret free discussion should be encouraged by the ruler in his own enlightened self-interest.[56] China's bureaucratic intelligentsia promoted an ideal of unity, order, hierarchy and obedience to the state and was thus not in a position to act autonomously of the state when the need arose. China's greatest strengths could at times be terrible weaknesses and "may contribute to explain why China at the time of Renaissance Europe developed the world's best and largest ships, sent fleets to India and Africa, and then dismantled those fleets and left overseas colonization to much smaller European states."[57]

The absence of autonomous or semi-autonomous religious establishments has also characterized much of Chinese history. Given the religious wars and persecutions that have racked other parts of the world, especially Europe, this could well be seen as a blessing. The arrival of Buddhism in China from India did for several centuries promise to create a Church-like institution that might have competed for power with the Chinese state. However, in AD 845, the Tang regime pulled the proverbial prayer rug out from under the feet of the Buddhist clergy and laicized 260,000 nuns and monks while confiscating ecclesiastical property.[58] After this episode, it would take another 1000 years before the arrival of Christian missionaries backed by European imperial powers would allow an organized religion independent of the state to emerge. Communist rule from 1949 onwards, however, suppressed religions and restored an ideology (in this case Marxism/Maoism) to the status of dominant philosophy. Like the Tang ruler in 845 or the Japanese shoguns in the 1600s, the Chinese communists regard autonomous ecclesiastical establishments with great suspicion—as potential if not actual enemies of the state. At the heart of the Chinese state there was ultimately one sovereign who allegedly maintained a cosmic balance. Of course, like elsewhere, the masters of the Chinese empire were mere mortals.

AUTOCRATS

At the end of the day the Chinese government during the imperial era was an autocracy. The autocrat was advised by councilors, his orders were executed by complex state machinery, and his person aggrandized by the official intelligentsia, but the buck stopped and started with him. The final say in important affairs, indeed, in any affair that the emperor chose to pay attention to, lay with the emperor. He could legislate, allocate, reward, punish, declare war, make peace, interfere in the internal matters of the civil and military bureaucracy, and envision and order the implementation of great projects. An effective emperor was capable of controlling the state apparatus through a combination of fear, charisma and inducement, and using that apparatus to secure his reign and, hopefully, his dynasty. The emperor lived in legendary luxury isolated from those he governed by mental, physical and administrative barriers.

Ideally, the emperor would have been a man of discretion who allowed his advisers and servants to implement the laws of the state in his name. The emperor's task was one of superintendence rather than running the day-to-day affairs of the state. Thus, the most important task before any emperor was choosing competent servants for advisory and ministerial positions. These ministers and advisers would be in charge of different departments and report directly to the emperor. Through these ministers and advisers the emperor could control the higher levels of the state bureaucracy and military. Given the sheer size of the empire and its population, the emperor was necessarily a distant figure even for many civil servants. The Chinese emperor had to delegate powers to officers in the secretariat as well as in the field. The challenge of control, however, could be met in several ways.

One instrument of control was fear of the emperor's wrath. The First Qin Emperor was notorious for his harshness towards his officials and his willingness to make examples out of them. Thus, judicial and police officers suspected of being lenient towards criminals were subjected to the same punishment as the offender they let off the hook.[59] The most terrible of punishments was exile to the frontier to work on the fortifications being built and officers and commoners alike had reason to fear. Indeed, "on the statute books, this most terrible of sentences could be identified by a single distinct word: Wall."[60]

While exile to the wall(s) would be the fate of hundreds of thousands of undesirables, direct personal interventions by the emperor and purges were also instruments of control. In 1380, early during the Ming period, the emperor ordered the elimination of his prime minister and all his clansmen. Some 40,000 people were executed while later purges claimed an additional 60,000 lives.[61] In 1519, 146 officials were flogged for incurring the emperor's displeasure and in 1524, 134 were beaten for objecting to the award of imperial honors to the emperor's parents.[62] In the first case, eleven officials died from their wounds and in the second case sixteen died.[63] The

Ming emperor's Embroidered Uniform Guard, numbering 16,000 at the beginning of the dynasty and 75,000 towards the end, served as a political police that operated parallel to the regular civil service machinery and reported directly to the imperial court.[64]

Another practice was to employ loyalists in key positions as spies and overseers and task them with reporting on the regular civil service. The Mongol Yuan dynasty and Manchurian Qing dynasty employed a practice different from the Chinese dynasties. In the case of the Yuan, Mongol or Central Asian supervisors were appointed under which Chinese officials worked. The Qing relied on Manchu kinsmen in much the same way, operating a joint administration with the Chinese civil servants. In both cases the ethnic identity of the dynasty was different from the subject population and the rulers tried to control the state machinery through the strategic deployment of kinsmen. In time the power of China's culture was so great that the Mongols and Manchu became culturally Chinese even though the anti-Mongol rebellions of the 1350s and the anti-Manchu risings in 1911–1912 indicate strong reservoirs of ethnic hatred.

While fear of the emperor's wrath and fear of being reported to the emperor in unfavorable terms by his eunuchs/spies/kinsmen were important elements of control, prestige, reward, and censure, were just as important in securing the emperor's writ. One of the most important institution was the censorate and "Since the time of the First Emperor, there had been censors whose job was to keep other officials under surveillance and to report any wrong-doing to the emperor."[65] During the Song dynasty, the Chief Censor was appointed for a 12-year term, could criticize the emperor's actions, and did not have to reveal the sources of information upon which his recommendations were made.[66] The censors traveled across the country and recommended rewards for the virtuous and efficient and punishments for those who failed in the performance of their duties. The triennial evaluation of junior officers by their superiors and the allocation of posts on the basis of such evaluations provided further incentives to the ambitious to work hard. While the Imperial Chinese approach towards asserting the emperor's authority was prone to abuse and arbitrariness, there was a serious and sustained effort to reward the imperial servants on the basis of academic and professional merit as determined by a number of routine procedures and checked by the censorate. It was partly the realization that competent servants are good for both the empire and the emperor that guided the recruitment and personnel management structure of the Imperial Chinese state. Mistakes in the evaluation of papers by the examiners and subversion of merit were criminal offences that carried punishments as terrifying as death or exile.

The emperor's personal control was also asserted by keeping the size of the civil service elite within reasonable limits. With a total strength of between 10,000 and 40,000 for most of the imperial period, China's higher bureaucracy did not experience excessive inflation relative to the size of the population.[67] This had the singular advantage that an energetic emperor could get to know a substantial percentage of the officers and, assuming he had the ability to demonstrate his intellectual and moral superiority, impress them. Civil servants with proximity to those in power tend to talk about them and given that most of their colleagues will not have the chance to judge for themselves it is these impressions that get passed on and accepted as truth. In 1380, the founder of the Ming dynasty, is recorded as having personally gone through 1600 dispatches over an eight-day period, or 200 dispatches a day, dealing with 339 issues.[68] Taking a personal interest in the final stages of the exams and personally reviewing the top papers was another means of asserting imperial skill in scholarship. Kublai Khan, the founder of the Yuan dynasty, took a keen interest in the development of a new script to help cut down on translation work and kept a close watch on the affairs of his civilian (Chinese-dominated) bureaus.[69] The Kangxi Emperor (r. 1662–1722) of the Qing dynasty was a "Military leader, patron of the arts and poets, student of Latin under Jesuit tutors, familiar with the latest thinking in mathematics, science and western technology" and an exemplar "of careful executive rule."[70]

The public display of the ruler's wealth and power was also a critical element in the exercise of control. The Tang dynasty bequeathed to its successors "an immense three-volume corpus of imperial rituals" detailing 150 different rituals that combined aspects of Confucianism with Buddhism and Taoism.[71] The emperor's mastery of ritualism and protocol required the employment of hundreds of officers in the Board of Rites even as all (10,000–40,000) "scholar-officials of all the other departments were expected to have intimate knowledge" of the relevant "rituals in their own areas of expertise."[72] This vast apparatus, which would today be dismissed as mumbo-jumbo, "picked up where the criminal code left off, for it did not coerce people or punish them. It affirmed the benevolence of the cosmic order, and the emperor's role in mediating between heaven and earth."[73] Combined with the strict protocol that surrounded the emperor and the formalism and hierarchy of the central government, this ritualistic aspect of governance sought to inspire awe amongst the servants of the state and the subjects of the empire. The First Qin Emperor had gone so far in this respect that:

> None dared look at him or speak his true name . . . As for original sources, we have decrees issued in the name of the First Emperor, but little of his personality, although the *Record of the Historian* includes biographies of his ministers, his generals and even the man who tried to kill him. The First Emperor himself is that silence in between, the subject they dare not mention or the distant sovereign in whose name they claim to act.[74]

However terrifying, awe-inspiring, ruthless, efficient and charismatic many of China's emperors may have been, they and their dynasties were all transient manifestations of the Mandate of Heaven. All would necessarily perish through a natural process of decay so the Celestial Empire could be reborn.

DYNASTIES FALLING

The short lived Qin and Sui dynasties fell due to poor leadership and over-extension wrought by simultaneously undertaking multiple great projects. The Han and Tang fell due to gradual deterioration in the effectiveness of state. The otherwise brilliant Song dynasty fell victim to insufficient military preparedness, losing control over the northern part of the country in the early 1100s before falling to the Mongol onslaught (1215–1271). The Mongol Yuan dynasty proved relatively short lived and was overthrown by a popular rebellion against misrule. The Ming dynasty fell on account of internal decay and the advent of the Manchu (Qing) invaders. The Qing dynasty died a slow and painful death at the hands of foreign invasions, internal rebellions, and administrative cum political failure. Each time, however, the empire would be reincarnated in a slightly different form.

The Qin and the Sui are particularly instructive with regard to the phenomenon of dynastic decline because they completed in two generations a process that normally took 150–200 years. The First Qin Emperor united the country and gave it the basic form of imperial bureaucratic government that would be continued by later dynasties. The Qin built 5000 km of walls, the magnificent Terracotta Army, 4000 miles of roads and 1200 miles of waterways. Any of these projects could have singlehandedly undermined a pre-modern state and it is no wonder that by taking up so much at the same time the Qin went into imperial overstretch almost immediately after consolidating their rule. Upon the First Qin Emperor's death the succession was to pass to his eldest son, Fusu, but the secretary who withheld news of the emperor's death decided to make a power play for himself and sent the royal letter and seal to the younger son, Huhai. Huhai was persuaded to stake his own claim and a forged letter was sent to Fusu instructing him to commit suicide, which he promptly did. General Mien Tian, in charge of building the Long Wall, suspected a plot but could not react in time to prevent the coronation of Huhai. Soon thereafter, 12 royal princes were executed along with other loyal servants of the First Emperor. Huhai decided to press ahead with his father's projects and made the Qin laws that enabled collective punishment of families even stronger.

Rebellions began in 209 BC when a military official (originally a conscript) named Chen She tried to seize power. Chen She's rebellion flopped after six months and his followers killed him for behaving like the emperor he sought to replace. While rebellions raged, Huhai concentrated on completing a giant hall with place for 10,000 people and his two principal advisers (and co-conspirators), Zhao Gao and Li Si, fell out with each other. Zhao Gao emerged successful from this power struggle and Li Si and his whole family were executed. In 206 BC, however, "Liu Bang, who had been a gang master on the construction of the First Emperor's tomb . . . led a force of 3000 into the Qin capital" and seized power.[75] Liu Bang and his followers burned the Qin capital to the ground and founded a new capital nearby. Thus began the long-lived Han dynasty.

The Sui dynasty, which reunited China in AD 581 and lasted a mere 37 years, manifested many similarities with the Qin. Like the Qin, the Sui unified the country after centuries of warfare between rival states. Upon establishing control, the Sui embarked upon a program to rebuild the frontier defenses dispatching hundreds of thousands of laborers to the walls. Most famously, the Sui commenced construction of the Grand Canal system, which would ultimately stretch for more than 1000 miles.[76] True to the legalist spirit of the Qin, the Sui inaugurated the competitive exams for recruitment on the pattern that would survive with modifications until the Ming period, and set about codifying China's laws. The construction of a new capital city for the Sui alone required the mobilization of over a million workers. Like the First Qin Emperor, the Sui seemed determined to do many things at once without regard to the costs. The Second Sui Emperor, convinced by a prophecy that a man named "Li" would destroy the dynasty, started executing people with that name. The dead included 32 members of the royal family and the emperor's servants soon retaliated by killing him and the crown prince in 618. In the struggle for power that ensued, Li Yuan founded the Tang dynasty that would rule China for nearly 300 years.

The experience of the Qin and Sui rise and fall are particularly instructive. In both cases a ruthless ruler (or succession of rulers) unified the country and put an end to the warring states. Having attained victory through war, the new dynasty set about rapidly mobilizing people and resources for big projects. Many of these projects proved of lasting value to the empire.[77] Others, such as military expeditions on the frontier or building/expanding the capital, proved of little lasting use. These projects combined, however, strained the economy and brought misery to the millions press-ganged into serving the state. While a backlash was inevitable, in both cases it coincided with a leadership crisis born of imperial paranoia and bureaucratic meddling. The main lesson to be learnt from the Qin and Sui is that regimes that act in great haste and do not consider the human and material costs of their reforms will fall sooner rather than later. Gradualism and pragmatism are the keys to prolonging the duration of the Mandate of Heaven.

In the case of the Han and Tang dynasties the decline and fall occurred after centuries of rule. The Han and Tang benefited from the infrastructure and reforms of their predecessors but proved far more easy-going in their political attitudes. The Han dynasty tolerated the existence of semi-autonomous kingdoms within the empire and thus balanced bureaucratic absolutism with elements of aristocratic rule. This meant that the Han dynasty experienced a long decline in which power steadily shifted from the imperial court to local grandees originally appointed by emperor. Tang absolutism, though bureaucratic and centralized, tolerated powerful landed elites carried over from the warring states periods and left it to the gradual working of the competitive exams and imperial bureaucracy to consolidate its power. Until 845, the Tang also tolerated a semi-autonomous Buddhist clergy. The Han and the Tang had the ability to assert total power but tempered its exercise in the interests of continuity. Thus, the Han and Tang are considered prime examples of successful dynasties and their longevity can be cited as proof of their moral merit.[78]

With the Song and Qing repeated foreign invasions and failure to deal with them effectively ultimately spelled doom. The Song fought and lost to the Jurchens and the Mongols while the Qing were defeated by the Europeans and, more gallingly, after 1895, by the Japanese. The Song managed to hold out for 50 years against the Jurchens and the Mongols while the Qing, counting from 1841, lasted till 1911. The bloodshed and chaos that characterized these dynastic declines eventually led to the revocation of the Mandate of Heaven. During the Taiping rebellion of 1851–64 some 600 walled cities changed hands between government and rebel forces and some 20 million Chinese may have died in the process. Interestingly, the Taiping rebels soon recreated what they imagined to be the grandeur of the imperial court they sought to overthrow, elaborating ranks, nobility and status, even as they split into rival factions (1856 onwards) leading to a civil war among the rebels. The culture of power of the rebels was even more arbitrary than the dynasty they sought to replace while the influence of a linear eschatology that promised utopia, injected into Chinese culture by Christian missionaries, made the Taiping rebels considerably more delusional than the imperial court. The Song and the Qing reacted too late to the foreign threat and were overwhelmed by the consequences.

The Ming decline and fall follows a pattern similar to the Han and Tang in that the gradual accumulation of stress on the fiscal, administrative and military system of the state combined with a leadership crisis set in motion the dynasty's decline and fall. Some structural flaws within the Ming system, such as the centralization of secretariat work under the emperor, a financial system that pre-allocated revenues from certain taxes to certain heads of expenditure and reliance on military farms, are alleged to have compounded the problems of the Ming regime. These structural deficiencies don't seem to have adversely affected the duration of the Ming dynasty (276 years) as compared to the Qing (267 years) or the Tang (289 years). This longevity of Ming rule indicates that its fiscal, military and administrative policies were not altogether ill-advised and did serve the interests of the state until the late 1500s and early 1600s.[79]

Three major long-term trends that worked against the Ming dynasty were the growing numerical strength of the secret police, the drain on the tax base caused by a royal family that came to number in the tens of thousands, and the exemptions granted to the scholar class.[80] The critical breakdown in the Ming fortunes evidently occurred during the reign of the Wanli Emperor (r. 1590–1620). At this time many problems were making themselves felt and reform was needed if the dynasty was to survive. Unfortunately for the Ming, and millions of ordinary Chinese, the Wanli emperor's only "interest in affairs of state" was the levying of "taxes . . . to satisfy his whims" and these were collected by his eunuchs.[81] Between 1603 and 1614, the emperor "held only one meeting with his grand secretaries" and between 1615 and 1620, he held two more meetings.[82] Without imperial approval, vacancies could not be filled and the administration could not function—soon half the posts in the provincial administration were lying vacant and "Yet no one could assume responsibility for the government because such an act would amount to usurpation."[83] The resultant "paralysis" produced "deep-seated factionalism and a weakened bureaucratic as well as military structure that was to lead to the eventual downfall of the dynasty."[84] The Wanli emperor's legacy was an empty treasury, a demoralized bureaucracy, a faltering administration and a million-man army that existed primarily on paper and operated at less than 20% of its nominal strength. As a parting gift, the Wanli emperor spent 10.4 million ounces of silver on his tomb.

It still took until 1636 for a large-scale rebellion to break out against Ming misrule. Li Zicheng, a postman by profession, proclaimed himself the Dashing Prince and promised justice and an end to oppression. Although the Dashing Prince didn't have a clue as to how to govern the country, his message appealed to a people reeling from the "crushing burden of taxation and corvée".[85] The rebel army, however, lived off plunder and took its time getting to the Forbidden City. Early in 1644 the rebel army reached the capital but found its hopes dashed by an empty treasury. Angry and frustrated, the rebels began torturing Ming officials to extort money and "1000 died by being slowly crushed to death in special vices."[86] Still not satisfied, the rebels started looting the capital. It was in this context of tragedy compounded by tragedy in which the state faced the prospect of dissolution that the Manchu invaded and drove the rebels from the capital. It would take until the 1660s to consolidate the Qing dynasty.

The Yuan dynasty was one of the shorter-lived dynasties and its collapse was well under way by the 1320s when Emperor Yingzhong (r. 1321–23) was overthrown in a coup launched by royal princes. While Kublai Khan captured the western imagination owing to Marco Polo's visit, the fact was that the Yuan dynasty never attained the administrative stability of other dynasties and was handicapped by its Mongol-steppe connections. The Yuan divided their subjects into a racial hierarchy with Mongols at the top, followed by Central Asians, Northern Chinese and South Chinese. The Mongols and Central Asians were less than 2% of the population and less educated than the Northern or Southern Chinese but they held key positions by birth. Although the competitive exams were restored in 1313–1315, the devastation and humiliation of the Mongol conquests combined with Yuan attempts to invade neighboring countries, led to rebellions. By the 1350, the Red Turban Rebellion started to galvanize the countryside against the Mongol rulers and led to the fall of the Yuan dynasty in 1368. The human cost to China of the Mongol rule can be gauged by the population estimates—during the United Song Dynasty, c. AD 1000, China had a population of 100 million whereas in 1400 it had a population of 60 million. The Ming would, like earlier dynasties, demonstrate their grandeur through architecture and expeditions, gradually rebuilding the frontier fortifications into the Great Wall recognizable today, mobilizing 200,000 laborers to build the Forbidden City, and, between 1403–1419, building a fleet of 2000 ships, including 100 treasure ships that displaced 3000 tons apiece, and reorganizing the Grand Canal system.

It is perhaps understandable, in view of the foregoing, that the rulers of the Celestial Empire failed to appreciate the danger posed by the Europeans. The oft-quoted response of the Qianlong emperor (r. 1735–1796) to the British ambassador reveals a parochial sense of superiority that did not seek to civilize others.[87] This cultural arrogance was brutally punctured by the wars and rebellions of the 1800s. Between 1841 and 1949 China was in a state of chaos and warlordism aggravated by foreign invasions. The communist regime that came to power under Mao's leadership in many ways corresponded to earlier rural rebellions that had driven off invaders and restored unity. The communist regime was, however, animated by a Chinese version of Marxism, much as the Taiping rebellion had been animated by a Chinese interpretation of Christianity. Mao himself, like the first Han and Ming emperors, came from a humble background. Self-educated in military and political affairs and a voracious reader of history, Mao admired the First Qin Emperor and shared his disdain for Confucian pietism and ethics.

THE RED EMPEROR: COMMUNIST CHINA, 1949–1976

There are several worthy biographies of Mao written from a number of different perspectives[88] and Mao's own selected works were widely disseminated by his regime.[89] The one point on which most of his biographers agree is that Mao was a radical despot who used all means at his disposal to create a new modern China capable of prevailing in a far more competitive global environment than hitherto encountered. Mao detested traditionalism with a violence worthy of comparison with the First Qin Emperor and wanted to shake Chinese society out of its Confucian stupor. Deeply versed in Chinese history and thought, Mao ruthlessly embarked upon a systematic attempt to eradicate the legacy he studied so closely and almost succeeded at the height of the Cultural Revolution of 1966–69.[90] Having led and organized a rural rebellion of staggering proportions, waged a peoples' war upon the Nationalist Chinese and the

Japanese, and developed his own school of Marxism (Maoism), Mao was unquestionably a great leader.

Mao's policies and attitudes, however, were pitiless towards real and imagined enemies and tried through the Great Leap Forward of the late-1950s to leapfrog into industrialization causing a famine that claimed the lives of tens of millions of his fellow citizens. A man of great intellect and fluency, Mao displayed a pathological hatred towards dissenters and other intellectuals, luring them out into the open by pretending to believe in free expression (the Hundred Flowers campaign of 1957) only to liquidate or re-educate them once they had shown their capitalistic or traditionalist inclinations. Coming from a modest rural background of the kind that would have enabled him to try his hand at the competitive exams, Mao rejected meritocracy in favor of absolute personal loyalty. A cold blooded realist in the conduct of diplomacy, Mao sought to restore the Celestial Empire to a position of independence and employed the strategy of playing more distant barbarians (such as the United States of America) against closer ones (such as the Soviet Union). As had happened in Russia in the 1920s, a pre-industrial autocracy with an ideological and arbitrary culture of power, fell into the hands of left-wing revolutionaries determined to engage in utopian social engineering. Armed with a charismatic "modern" ideology and, more importantly, modern weapons and means of communications, Mao and his henchmen, like Lenin and company, converted their traditional autocracies into totalitarian police states.

One of the policies instituted by the new regime was land reform. In Xingjian, the Communists divided the predominantly Muslim landed elite into two categories, namely, "goats" and "sheep":

> Heading the goats were landowners with political power such as hereditary Muslim nobles. They were automatically shot. Next in line were landlords and smaller landowners, who were certain to lose their property but who might, if small enough, keep their lives. After these came middle-class enemies who were considered capable of redemption.[91]

The sheep included workers, tenant farmers and leftist members of the middle-class.[92]

This is not to say that landlords and the bourgeoisie had it any easier in other parts of China. One of Mao's specialties was tapping into social hatreds and frustrations and using the Communist Party to channel this negative energy into violence directed at enemies of the regime. Maoist terror was truly democratic and involved the local population in acts of violence against those deemed enemies. The state used the people to butcher other people and thus established a regime of participatory terror. This was somewhat similar to Qin efforts to divide society into mutually suspicious households and Mao consciously modeled himself on the First Qin Emperor:

Mao knew by heart the lessons of the dynastic histories. It was not chance that led him to choose, among all his imperial predecessors, the First Emperor of Qin—who throughout Chinese history had been feared and reviled as the epitome of harsh rule—as the man against whom he wished to measure himself. 'You accuse us of acting like Qin Shihuangdi', he once told a group of liberal intellectuals. 'You are wrong. We surpass him a hundred times. When you berate us for imitating his despotism, we are happy to agree! Your mistake was that you did not say so enough.'

To Mao, the killing of opponents—or simply of those who disagreed with his political aims—was an unavoidable, indeed a necessary, ingredient of broader political campaigns. He rarely gave direct instruction for their physical elimination. But his rule brought about the deaths of more of his own people than any other leader in history.[93]

Within a few years, millions of landed and capitalist enemies of the revolution lay dead and their wealth stood confiscated by the state. Mao, however, lived in imperial splendor surrounded by sycophants and luxuries and was deeply interested in finding ways to keep his sexual appetite strong, much to consternation of his personal physician.

Under Mao's leadership the Communist Party embarked upon the Great Leap Forward. The objective was to turn China into a modern industrial economy within a few years. Communist party cadres were ordered to motivate the population to build their own crude industrial facilities and raise output. In an atmosphere of mass hysteria and police-state terror reports started flowing in of glorious successes. Chairman Mao was pleased and ordered his followers to press on. Press on they did and soon China found itself in the midst of a massive man-made famine as requisitions completely lost touch with actual output. Prior to launching the Great Leap Forward, the 1957–58 Anti-Rightist Campaign had purged at least 300,000 skilled professionals from the state machinery. The political hacks that replaced them had neither the competence nor the integrity needed to deliver on Mao's outlandish promises.

Then, from 1966 onwards, Mao would unleash the Cultural Revolution and take the promotion of his cult of personality to an extreme that might have even given Hitler pause. Mao's objective was to purge the party of all those who opposed him and had gotten in the way of his Great Leap Forward. For achieving this end Mao enlisted China's youth and the Chinese military. The youth were encouraged to rise up and their violence was unleashed on senior party men and ancient monuments. 60 percent of the officials were purged and at least 400,000 died with tens of millions traumatized by the public humiliations, trials, beatings, and struggle sessions, inflicted upon them, their loved ones, colleagues and elders by fanatical youngsters organized into Red Guards units.[94] Most civilian institutions were adversely affected by this exercise in permanent revolution and many ceased to function as people were terrorized by Mao's youth-in-governance initiative. China, and the Communist regime, seemed doomed to collapse at the hands of a senile emperor and his juvenile vigilantes. The only institution that remained functional was the People's Liberation Army (PLA).

Under Mao, there were party branches at all levels of the PLA and the "closed-party-army" structure relied on political commissars to educate soldiers and officers.[95] In the context of Imperial Maoism, education meant Maoist thought and correct thinking. Mao was personally in charge of the Military Affairs Committee and determined strategic and defense priorities. As Mao was convinced that foreign invasions could take place at any moment, and believed firmly in the principle of local autarky, about 25 percent of "the entire national defense industrial complex was rebuilt in the mountainous regions of ten provinces" at a cost of RMB 200 billion over a 20 year period starting in 1964—an amount that represented two-thirds of fixed military expenditure.[96] Mao's obsession with self-sufficiency even at a regional level meant the defense forces had a vast manufacturing base that could be used to manufacture everything they needed, even for non-military needs. The military, one of the main props of the Maoist regime, benefited enormously from the economic liberalization of 1978–1989 with its industrial profits soaring by 700 percent during the same period and sales of goods manufactured by the PLA fetching RMB 20 billion domestically and RMB 140 billion in exports, in 1989 alone.[97]

For Mao, the PLA was explicitly a political army. An officer corps lacking in professional or academic qualifications led the PLA's overstaffed ranks, and in the early 1980s only 10% of its officers had received college-level education.[98] While being politicized due to party interference, the PLA was also factionalized and characterized by a high level of "Nepotism and favoritism" during the Maoist era.[99] Mao steadily expanded the role of the PLA, lavished resources on it, and during the Cultural Revolution ". . . the PLA was the only functioning institution in the PRC, as Mao deliberately destroyed China's administration and party mechanism."[100] That said, with 6 million men under arms, the PLA was the largest but also one of the less professional militaries in the world and lagged behind qualitatively in nearly every field.

Mao, like the first emperors of the Qin and Sui, and also to some extent the Ming, was a brutal and unforgiving man whose mania for control over thought, society, economy, politics, administration and the military, matched or exceeded the worst excesses of Stalinism without, however, producing comparable economic development. China, at Mao's death, was an overpopulated agricultural country with a per capita income of US$ 280, endemic poverty, and malformed social services. The mercilessness of Mao's regime, its complete disregard for human life and dignity, and the administrative and political chaos it unleashed draws comparison with either the Mongol conquest of China in the 1200s or the Taiping rebellions of the 1850s. After Mao's death, his wife (Jiang Qing) and her supporters tried to seize power but were outmaneuvered by Deng Xiaoping. Deng inherited a legacy of despair, a brutalized and impoverished population, a barely disciplined military, and a political and administrative structure on the verge of collapse. If effective and wise decisions were not made and implemented, the Communist regime would go the way of the Qin and Sui dynasties, lose the Mandate of Heaven and potentially plunge China into decades of chaos. Fortunately for China, Mao's successor was no utopian romantic revolutionary, had his feet firmly on the ground and was eager to restore China's indigenous practices of pragmatism and order to favor.

THE LAST EMPEROR

Mao is worshipped as a distant deity or ancestral spirit. Officially, Mao's ideology and guiding principles retain most of their sanctity. A vast bureaucratic intelligentsia is employed in churning out exegeses of Maoist and Marxist-Leninist thought.[101] The rhetoric that Mao built the base while his successors raised the structure is sold for the consumption of the gullible some of which may well have a romantic fascination with the founder of Communist China. Mao of course was a great dreamer and wanted to see China strong and prosperous.[102] He did not understand the relationship between intentions and effect and became so obsessed with his personal power and aggrandizement that he drove the country to the verge of dissolution.[103] Mao's successor, the diminutive Deng Xiaoping, who had been lucky to survive Mao's purges, actually set in motion China's emergence as a world-beating economic power and steered China, through reform and firm guidance to a point where, arguably, the growth and development process became self-sustaining.[104] Statisticians cannot and do not do justice to the enormity of Deng's achievements for he saved the world's most populous state from economic collapse, social destabilization and political disintegration.[105]

Contrary to the notion that Confucianism or Chinese values had stifled economic growth, or that the Chinese lacked the socio-cultural apparatus to be intellectually curious and materially acquisitive like the "modern" West, Deng reached back into the best of China's own traditions of pragmatism, meritocracy, administrative rationality, and social stability. Deng overturned the Confucian and Maoist disdain for merchants and rejected the post-Ming insularity of the Chinese state. Deng, in other words, changed government policies in critical areas, rebuilt the administration and let people get on with their daily lives. In order to achieve his objectives, Deng prioritized civil service reform, the professionalization of the army and bureaucracy, and the gradual lessening of the state's grip on the productive assets of the country. Like his predecessor, however, Deng did not tolerate open defiance of the state and used ruthless means to preserve order.[106]

Rebuilding the bureaucracy meant opening the door to recruitment on merit and educational qualifications and only then absorbing such candidates into the party machine. De-politicizing the army meant easing out Maoist generals, reducing the role of the commissars, laying the foundations for civilian control over the military, and professionalizing the military officer corps. In 1978, Deng restored competitive exams for entrance to universities and started recruitment to the civil service on the basis of exams. At present, some 800,000 university graduates compete for 13,000 vacancies in the Chinese state bureaucracy on an annual basis. On the military side, greater emphasis was laid on promotions based on educational credentials and the percentage of PLA officers with college level education went from 10% when Deng came to power to over 70% at his death in 1997.[107] Between 1982 and 1997 "the proportion of the central committee who were college educated rose from 55.4 per cent to 92.4 per cent" while for the top leadership all had a graduate level education.[108] Deng was aware that he was a transitional ruler who "would be the last leader to exercise personal control of the PLA"[109] and that the only way to get the military under civil control was to rebuild the civil service and restore meritocracy in both civil and military affairs. Deng played a key role in convincing the military to accept policies that favored civilian economic development over immediate investments in military modernization.[110]

Deng was successful in terms of restoring overall civilian authority even though problems such as factionalism and favoritism persisted in both the civil and military bureaucracies. Deng, who receded into the background as the Paramount Leader and left the day-to-day running of the state to the heir apparent, guided the rise of Jiang Zemin, in 1989, to the Central Military Committee (CMC). Jiang Zemin became "The PLA's first real civilian leader with limited personal authority" and represented the emergence of "an unprecedented institutional base, which enabled him to preside over a vast central bureaucracy encompassing the party, the state and the military."[111]

The civil service assumed more policy-making and advisory functions as it became more confident while the Party itself became more technocratic and entrepreneur-dominated, with some one-fifth of its members drawn from the business community by 2000.[112] Party loyalists remained in key positions but their role was now similar to that of kinsmen in the imperial period. In 1988, the Ministry of Personnel was constituted and in 1993, the Provisional Regulation on Civil Servants formalized the law insofar as the initial recruitment and subsequent promotions, discipline, and commendations, were to be conducted and awarded.[113] In 1998, shortly after Deng's death, village level self-government was introduced in thirty-one provinces and 626,655 villages with seventeen provinces opting for open nomination of village heads.[114] This re-introduction of village authority had nothing to do with democracy and basically represented the realization within the center that it was better to delegate certain functions to local authorities. Indeed, in China "grassroots democracy and local self-government is motivated by government, civil society is led by government, and the market economy is initiated by the government."[115] Even as "cronyism and *guanxi* connections" pose a problem at the local (and higher) tier of government, the state has presided over substantial economic growth that increased China's per capita income from US$ 280 in 1980 to US$ 3744 in 2009.[116]

1998 and 2002 represented critical milestones for the Chinese state. In 1998, the Chinese civilian leadership began the process of dismantling the PLA's economic empire having already substantially reduced the number of employees in State Owned Enterprises (SOEs) while aggressively pushing ahead with raising the tax-to-GDP ratio to 20 percent. In 2002, China became the first communist country to manage a peaceful and legitimate transfer of power from one set of leaders to another. Hu Jintao succeeded Jiang Zemin as China's president. In 2006, a Chinese Academy of Social Sciences survey found that the central government enjoyed a confidence rating of 3.56/4.00 and the local governments managed a rating of 2.80/4.00.[117] While continuing to press ahead with growth friendly policies, Hu Jintao extended tax relief to the rural areas and by 2006, all 31 provinces had adopted agricultural tax exemptions.[118] Prior to this reform a complex web of rural taxes forced farmers to pay a disproportionate share of taxes to the state and exposed them to arbitrary assessment at the hands of corrupt civil servants.[119] The central government was, and is alive to the problems of the countryside even though China's fifteen metropolitan areas account for 40 percent of its GNP. After all, the Chinese communists came to power through a rural rebellion and are aware of the possibility of another Maoist or Taiping style uprising.

With 40 million state employees of whom 6.5 million are classified as civil servants, China's state apparatus is certainly the largest and arguably the most complex and dynamic in the world.[120] This is nothing new for China has long enjoyed the distinction of having the world's most intensive and extensive state apparatus. The restoration of competitive recruitment in 1978 has steadily improved the quality of China's civil servants while political stability and pragmatic policies have unleashed the socioeconomic potential of the Chinese people. China's present rulers preside over a merit-based civil service state that stakes its legitimacy on its competence and ability to improve the quality of life while maintaining China's territorial integrity and domestic stability.[121] Marxism, Leninism and Maoism remain part of the official propaganda but the state's focus is on substantive rights and efficiency, not adhering to the utopian delusions of nineteenth century European intellectuals and their Russian and Chinese acolytes. The Chinese communist regime, like the imperial dynasties of the past, holds the Mandate of Heaven not by virtue of its ideological pretensions but on the basis of its secular achievements.[122]

THE FUTURE OF THE PAST

Centuries prior to the advent of modernity in the West, China was a civil service state run by men chosen on academic merit from an educated elite whose world view was far more secular and humanistic than that of Europeans from comparable positions in their social hierarchies until the late-1800s. In engineering, navigation, printing, military technology, medicine, astronomy, law, administration, and demographic/economic expansion, the Chinese empire set the standards of achievements until the 1800s. After falling behind in certain critical sectors in the 1800s, China experienced one of its periodic decline phases at precisely the time when the European states were reaching the height of their ability to project power. The political and revolutionary chaos that lasted from 1841 to 1976 left China lagging behind. Since 1978, however, China has made a dramatic comeback on all fronts.[123] The 2008 Beijing Olympics represent one aspect of its success. Another is that in 2010, students from Shanghai secured the number one position in a global ranking of academic achievement, edging out Finland. The world's oldest surviving state is reasserting its historical primacy guided by a rational leadership willing to make and implement difficult decisions, such as the one-child policy.[124] The Chinese leadership also reacts harshly to demands for power sharing and greater autonomy from minorities as evidenced by the Han colonization of Tibet and Xinjiang. Chinese history offers compelling evidence that political and administrative authoritarianism and centralization can coexist quite happily with socioeconomic dynamism and technological development.

That said, all is not well behind the Great Firewall. China's environmental problems are becoming more intense and in spite of tremendous growth, China remains in per capita terms a poor country in comparison to the Western powers it seeks to emulate. China's population is simply too large to be sustained at a much higher standard of living and the situation seems ripe for a Malthusian correction or the perpetuation of deep inequalities that could prove destabilizing for the present regime. The political succession process is opaque and if an incompetent leader comes to power the situation could well unravel. The centralized absolutism that has been China's greatest political strength in the hands of able rulers has also proven time and again to be its greatest weakness under less able ones. In the Chinese civil service state, where these days there are plenty of new developments to take note of, the past is forever threatening and inspiring the future.

A continental bureaucratic state needs to possess three qualities if it is to be successful in the long-term. The first is leadership that commands respect on the basis of its competence and achievements. The second is a body of capable servants of the state to advise the rulers and effectively implement policies made after mature consideration. The third is a mechanism that allows for a periodic peaceful transfer of power from one set of leaders to another worthy of the mantle. China has been fortunate in that the crisis of succession after Mao's death eventually brought to the helm Deng Xiaoping. While Mao deserves credit for restoring Chinese sovereignty after nearly a century of chaos, Deng's contribution to China's modernization was pivotal. Deng restored meritocracy in China's education system and encouraged it in the professions and in the state apparatus. He also saw beyond his own tenure and realized the need to step down gracefully after a decade and groom capable successors. In doing this Deng invented a new tradition of succession, one almost without parallel in the history of authoritarian regimes, and one that helped secure the transition from Hu Jintao to Xi Jinping at the Eighteenth Party Congress in 2013. The resulting stability and pragmatism of China's governance at the top level since 1978, has translated into phenomenal economic growth, rising standards of living, a burgeoning knowledge sector, and sufficient wealth to rapidly build up military power if the need arises. The challenges China faces after 35 years of solid economic achievement are, however, enormous.

On the demographic front, the one-child policy halted runaway population growth, which has peaked at 1.35 billion and will start declining in the 2030s, while skewing the gender balance (120 males for every 100 females). It has also had the effect of altering China's age demographic as the proportion of elderly increases faster than the workforce needed to sustain them. In the late-1970s, when Deng began his reforms, for each Chinese pensioner there were seven workers. Twenty years from now there will be between two and three workers per pensioner. China is facing the unenviable prospect of a population that is still too large, a per capita income that at about US $ 5000 is still far less than the advanced economies of the West, and a prospective labor shortage.

Economically, China's growth is set to decelerate and as personal incomes grow the inexpensive labor that made the country such an attractive destination for investment in manufacturing is likely to face competition from poorer countries. Managing deceleration will be difficult since so much of the Chinese government's moral authority and performance legitimacy has been derived from its ability to deliver high growth rates year after year. The temptation to borrow and spend to sustain growth, or encourage consumerism, or both, will be hard to resist. Current economic policy settings have nurtured powerful vested interest groups as well as national pride—taking them on will require intellectual rigor and moral courage.

The environment is another challenge, and one that is increasingly impossible to ignore. China presently accounts for about half of the world's coal consumption and thus employs this highly polluting energy source to power its industrialization. Going by Western standards, China's air is fast becoming un-breathable. In January 2013, for instance, for nearly three weeks Beijing's air pollution index was above 300—meaning the air was unsafe to breathe without the aid of air purifiers. Rapid and unsustainable use of water and biological resources means that at present some 25 percent of China's territory is experiencing desertification. China's faltering attempts to halt the spread of deserts, painfully slow official acknowledgement of local environmental disasters owing to the lack of press freedom, and the feeling that as China is still a poor country it should not be held to high environmental standards, all stand in the way of effective response to what is a slow-motion catastrophe. More mundane issues, such as day-to-day frictions, abuse of power by officials, corruption and mismanagement, and growing social inequalities, pale in comparison with the broader structural changes in economy, demography, and environment, but are nonetheless serious. Addressing them will take great skill and strength on part of China's new leaders.

And yet, it is here that the silver lining lies. China has a state that is strong enough to carry out wide-ranging reforms and pursue them consistently over a long period of time.[125] The great challenge before China's current leaders is to understand that the economy-first approach needs to give way to an environmentalist framework. In the past, China's governance faltered when rulers fell into the practice of blindly imitating their illustrious predecessors and ignored the phenomenon of change. The reasoning in favor of this imitation was that the source of past greatness could be reemployed in present circumstances without modification, which had the effect of making Chinese dynasties victims of their own success. The basic lesson that Chinese leaders ought to draw from their own history is that just as Deng broke with Mao's legacy to make China rich and industrialized, they need to break with Deng's legacy to ensure ecological resuscitation and demographic balance.[126]

3 Empires of Will
The Rise, Fall, and Rebirth of Persia

INTRODUCTION: MIRRORS FOR PRINCES

Persia's empires have had considerable influence on the culture and world-view of its neighbors.[1] In South Asia the ruling class was Persian-speaking for some six and half centuries (1200–1857) and a courtier at the time of the Delhi Sultans would have had little problem securing employment in the Sikh Kingdom of Ranjit Singh for the language of power of both was Persian. For much of this time period in South Asian history the dominant regimes preferred recruiting their service nobilities from the ranks of Persian-speaking settlers from what are today the states of Iran and Afghanistan. The Arab Empire of the Pious Caliphs (632–661), the Umayyads (661–750) and the Abbasids (750–1258) drew upon the Persian administrative and political traditions and the Turkish-dominated sultanates that succeeded the fragmenting Arab super-state from the late 800s also operated in accordance with Persian norms. In terms of political theory, administrative organization, espionage, and diplomacy, Persia provided the template for some 2000 years.

Achaemenid Persia (c. 559 BC–330 BC) was the first world empire and brought under its control territories from the Indus in the east to the Sahara and Mediterranean in the West. The Achaemenians almost brought western classical civilization to a premature end, conquering Ionia (now Turkey) but failing to annex mainland Greece. The dramatic rise of Achaemenid Persia and its expansion into Greek territories provided the inspiration for the birth of history as a critical inquiry into causes, courtesy Herodotus, and still provides fodder for Hollywood war epics and contemporary academic discourses on the conflict and confluence between the East and the West.[2] One long-term outcome of the conflict between the Achaemenids and the Greek city-states was that under Alexander the Great, who was an admirer of Cyrus the Great, a Hellenic world empire almost came into being. In a series of military campaigns Alexander overthrew the Persian monarchy, though his premature demise led to the fragmentation of his empire with the territories corresponding to Persia falling under the control of Seleucus, one of Alexander's generals, who founded the Seleucid monarchy

(312 BC–160 BC). The Seleucids were in time replaced by the Parthians (160 BC–AD 224) whose mounted archers frustrated Roman ambitions to neutralize all possible threats to their Mediterranean-based empire.

The Seleucids and the Parthians were never regarded as authentic Persian dynasties. It was under the Sassanians (AD 224–641) that a self-consciously Persian Empire was restored along with the religion of Zoroaster. The Sassanid dynasty clashed with the Roman Empire but was never able to match the Achaemenids in terms of imperial success. The Persian-Roman wars, however, exhausted both sides with the conflict escalating dramatically in the first three decades of the seventh century AD. The combination of economic exhaustion and, after 627, political instability, left the Sassanids vulnerable to the desert Arabs who, united and energized by the new Islamic creed, were increasingly formidable opponents. Geography also conspired against the Sassanids for their capital Madain/Ctesiphon was within easy reach of the Arabs. The Arabs thus absorbed Persia into the Arab Empire.

The Arab Empire, however, far exceeded the Achaemenid in that it stretched from what is today Pakistan and the Oxus in the east to the Pyrenees and the Atlantic in the West. Within the Arab Empire, opposition to the Umayyad dynasty was concentrated in the eastern territories of Khorasan and it was from there that in the 740s a movement aiming at returning the government of the empire to the hands of the Prophet Muhammad's direct descendants began and grew into a full-fledged revolution. The Abbasids, therefore, more Persianized in their outlook, shifted the capital of the empire from Damascus to Baghdad, and openly adopted Persian institutions and practices. The period of effective Abbasid government (750–900) was brought to an end by the Turkish military slaves employed to protect the regime. From the late-800s a number of smaller dynasties nominally loyal to the Caliph in Baghdad started to emerge, most notable amongst them being the Samanids (903–999), the Ghaznavids (962–1040), and the Seljuks (1037–1157). These dynasties presided over the rebirth of Persian culture, letters and political thought and saw in the Sassanids, in particular, an ideal model of absolute monarchy worth emulating, Islamic sensitivities in favor of a caliphate or imamate as opposed to *milkiat*/sultanate, notwithstanding.

This Persian Renaissance was interrupted by the Mongol advent, first under Genghis Khan in the early 1200s and then under Amir Timur in the late 1300s. The period of Mongol domination lasted over two hundred years but never really got around to establishing a stable state. That task was eventually taken up by the militant Safvi order of Sufis and the Turcoman Qizilbash tribes that recognized the Safvi Shaikhs as their absolute temporal and spiritual masters. The birth of the Safavid regime marked the third restoration of a distinctly Persian Empire, albeit under a Turkic dynasty, which in adopting and enforcing Shia Islam as the official creed created a new and enduring political distinction within the Muslim world. In spite of recurrent internal turmoil and military pressure from the Ottomans, Uzbeks and, on occasion, the Timurids (Mughals) of India, Safavid Persia thrived for about two centuries (1501–1722). The chaos that followed the decline and fall of the Safavids witnessed Afghan invasions, the rise of Nadir Shah Afshar, the Zand amirs, and, eventually, the Qajar dynasty (1796–1926).

During the Qajar era, Persia was drawn into the Anglo-Russian rivalry. Qajar diplomacy compensated as best as it could by manipulating the competing agendas of these antagonists and a semblance of independence was retained even though domestic development faltered. The Qajars were eventually overthrown by Riza Shah, commander of the Cossack division, and replaced by the Pahlavi dynasty (1926–1979). The overthrow of the Pahlavi regime resulted in the establishment of an Islamic Republic that is in many respects a combination of effective control by the religious establishment led by a jurist-king with a small measure of popular participation.

From the rise of the Achaemenids onwards Persia's culture of power has manifested certain core characteristics. First, in Persia the ruler was neither a king in the European sense of hereditary rule, nor a despot or dictator as would correspond to modern notions of authoritarianism. Rather, in Persia the ruler had no inherent right of hereditary succession to the throne and normally seized power through conspiracy and violence with the help of powerful tribal, bureaucratic, military and religious interests. Once on the throne, the ruler either succeeded in marginalizing those who had brought him to power or, failing that, was reduced to a cipher. If the ruler proved able to control the factions that supported him in his bid for power, arbitrary personal rule would emerge and if he failed then arbitrary rule by his "servants" carried out in his name would prevail alongside fragmentation as rival factions fought it out for monopoly control over access to the nominal ruler.

Second, the most successful regimes managed to fuse the political interests of the state with a particular ideology or religion that in turn came to be identified with the rulers. Of course, other empires also patronized religion and had ideologies but the Persian Empire was more overtly theocratic than other more pragmatic or cynical dispensations. In the case of the Safavids this tendency was particularly pronounced as the Safavids were simultaneously regarded as manifestations of the divine will by their Sufi adherents and prosecuted the task of converting their empire to mainstream Shia Islam with ruthlessness and vigor.

Third, the combination of arbitrary rule and theocracy was complemented by the absence of security for private property. This did not mean that people did not own property in land and capital, but what it entailed was pervasive insecurity with members of the regime and the ruler himself having the power to confiscate whatever he pleased. Within tribes property was insecure in the face of factionalism, polygamy and the absence of primogeniture. Constant upheavals within the tribes as well as elite families prevented the emergence of a stable aristocracy and exacerbated the arbitrary nature of governance.

Fourth, the Persian bureaucratic model that was believed to have reached its zenith under the Sassanids was designed to ensure concentration of power in the central apparatus while delegating power to the field officers subject to inspection and surveillance by the center. The apparatus itself was made up of diverse elements with Turks and slaves dominating the army during the Safavid period and Tajiks dominating the secretarial functions. Under an energetic ruler, the state apparatus could work very effectively towards a number of goals simultaneously, though it was prone to disruption under a weak ruler.

Taken together the Persian model of governance was, and substantially still is, that of a theocratic or ideological empire ruled arbitrarily through a set of hierarchical instruments subject to the personal control of the supreme leader or dominant group. The charisma and effectiveness of the rulers is thus a major determinant of overall state success. This model might seem archaic from a contemporary Western perspective but it is actually quite flexible and has enabled the Persians to meet tremendous internal and external challenges. Indeed, Persia has for much of its history been a great power with enormous cultural influence and prestige. The most successful incarnation of this Persian Empire was arguably that of the Achaemenids and it is to them that we now turn.

EARLY PERSIA AND THE RISE OF THE ACHAEMENIDS

The Persian civilization owes it origins to the convergence of two major factors. The first was the eastward expansion of urbanism and imperialism of the major Mesopotamian powers and the consequent rise of the kingdom of Elam by 1200 BC. The second was the westwards and southwards migrations of various Aryan tribes and their eventual contact with the early civilizations of Mesopotamia.

The kingdom of Elam was a player in the struggle between the Babylonian and Assyrian empires for mastery over the Fertile Crescent. Elam benefited from the rivalry that prevailed between Babylon and Assyria and was able to take advantage of their mutual antagonism and internal difficulties and made its own bid for supremacy in the 1100s BC. Susa became the capital of Elam and under Shutruk-Nakhunte (1160 BC) a centralization of records and monuments at the seat of government combined with the construction through royal patronage of temples in major cities point to the presence of an effective government.[3] The kingdom of Elam extended along the Persian Gulf, occupied and controlled the caravan routes that linked Mesopotamia to the Iranian Plateau and, in 1160 BC, occupied Babylon itself. The semi-nomadic tribes of the Iranian Plateau and outlying areas were forced to pay tribute while in Mesopotamia and adjacent territories the writ of Elam was established over hundreds of settlements.

Under Kutir-Nakhunte (c. 1140 BC) and Shilak-in-Shushinak (c. 1130 BC) Elam emerged as a major imperial power. Shilak-in-Shushinak launched a dozen military campaigns, conquered at least one hundred cities and villages, and aspired "to control the country between the Tigris and the Zargos which touched his northern borders."[4] While public works and temple construction took place throughout Elam's empire the state seems to have prospered. One important indicator of this growing prosperity was a switch from unbaked bricks and mud in favor of baked bricks for construction, which represented a labor and fuel-intensive investment. After Shilak-in-Shushinak, Elam went into decline. The two major causes of this reversal of fortunes were the revival of Assyrian power and the inability of Elam's rulers to sustain the tour de force of their ancestors. By 1100 BC, the western bank of the Tigris was lost for good to the Babylonians and Susa itself was in jeopardy. Elam fades into obscurity soon after this while the Assyrians start penetrating the Iranian Plateau and exploiting oases and fertile river valleys. In 843 BC, the Assyrian Empire launched a campaign against a recalcitrant Aryan tribe that had migrated into the imperial periphery. The Assyrians called these tribesmen the Parsua and it is thus the Persians enter history.

In 689 BC the Assyrians conquered Babylon and razed it due to its rebelliousness. Although the city was rebuilt it rebelled again in 648 BC and was once again destroyed by the Assyrians. While Mesopotamia tore itself apart under Assyrian oppression and militarism the semi-nomadic tribes of the Iranian Plateau, strengthened by migrations and tempered by encounters with Assyria's military, gained in strength. One of these tribes was that of the Medes and in the 7th century BC, according to Herodotus, a wise man by the name of Deiokes, son of Phraortes, was chosen by his tribesmen to be their king. Deiokes set about imitating the Assyrians and established a permanent capital (Ecbtana), raised a royal guard, and successfully projected himself as a beneficent but firm judge. The Medes were able to bring the other tribes under their control through a combination of force and diplomacy and around 650 BC the Persians submitted to their authority. What followed was a major war against Assyria and in 606 BC the Assyrian capital of Nineveh fell to the Medes and their tributaries. It seemed that a new Medean empire was destined to replace Assyria as the regional hegemonic power. This destiny, however, was disrupted by the Persian rebellion led by Cyrus, the head of the Achaemenid family of the Pasargadae. The Medean ruler, Astyages, had, in 559 BC, married his daughter to Cyrus in order to win him over but it seems that the marital alliance backfired. By 546 BC the Medes had been overthrown and Cyrus established in their place the Persian Empire. Cyrus the Great, as he was soon known, thus became the founder of the Persian monarchy, the Persian state, and, arguably, Persia's imperial civilization.

In contrast to the ruthlessness of the Assyrians, Cyrus was prepared to offer defeated adversaries generous terms. The Medes, for example, were made part of the administration and even placed in charge of the army. Although willing to use violence to further his ambitions, Cyrus appreciated that once military superiority was established, offering a fallen rival the option of honorable collaboration could win allies, even if some were only biding their time. The other advantage that Cyrus reaped was that the emerging Persian Empire was able to project itself as benign compared to the bloodthirsty Assyrians. Cyrus, wise autocrat that he was, also realized that the empire would need fresh leadership if it was to outlast its first emperor. In preparation for the transfer of power Cyrus nominated his elder son, Cambyses, as the crown prince while appointing his younger son, Bardiya, governor of Bactria, Khorsmania, and Carmania. When Cyrus died in 529 BC, the crown passed with little difficulty to Cambyses.

Cambyses was harsher than his father and allowed his outrage and fears to govern him. In one instance, Cambyses ordered one of the seven high judges to be flayed on charges of corruption and then forced the slain judge's son to sit in his father's judicial chair now covered in his father's skin.[5] Cambyses was also jealous of his younger brother's popularity amongst the nobles and the common people. Given Cambyses's reputation for harshness and the competing ambitions of Persian and Medean nobles, political tensions rose steadily.

Cambyses, whatever his reputation may have been, achieved great victories on the field of battle. The most important of these was the conquest of Egypt in 525 BC. With that victory the Persian Empire had become the master of the Nile, having already subdued the Tigris-Euphrates and reached the Indus. The Persian Empire could now draw upon the resources of three major river valleys to fuel the imperial engine of conquest. Between 525 BC and 522 BC Cambyses put Egyptian affairs in order while growing increasingly suspicious of his brother. What happened next makes for riveting drama but leaves many key historical questions unanswered. One version of what happened is that Persian and Medean nobles encouraged Bardiya to claim the throne for himself. This conspiracy, however, "could hardly be kept quiet for long. Spies were everywhere" and Cambyses, in early 522 BC, set off for Persia determined to put an end to his brother's ambitions once and for all.[6] In March 522, Bardiya claimed the throne and it seemed Cyrus's great work was about to be undone. At this stage fate intervened for Cambyses injured himself, fell ill, and died, effectively leaving Bardiya as the new emperor.

The story, however, gets more interesting from here. Bardiya evidently proved to be far worse than Cambyses and used populist measures, such as remission of taxes, to buttress his rule. In 518 BC, Bardiya was murdered by a group of Achaemenid noblemen led by Darius. After the deed was done, Darius and his co-conspirators claimed that the man they had killed was not Bardiya but an imposter and heretic named Gaumata. Cambyses had murdered the real Bardiya years ago. Darius and company stuck to the agreed narrative and, for good measure, claimed to be acting in accordance with the divine will of Ahura Mazda, the Zoroastrian deity.

If Herodotus is taken at his word, the manner of Darius's elevation to the Persian throne was the outcome of a debate between Darius and his companions. Otanes argued that a monarchy in concentrating power in the hands of one person would inevitably corrupt that person and lead to tyranny.[7] Megabyzus argued in favor of oligarchy asserting that "there is nothing so void of understanding, nothing so full of wantonness, as the unwieldy rabble" so that it was best to "Let the enemies of the Persians be ruled by democracies"—a sentiment probably shared by the Ayatollahs.[8] Darius then intervened in favor of monarchy arguing that in democracies outrages were committed by feuding parties while oligarchies were prone to breaking down into civil war. An enlightened and just monarch was thus the best possible type of ruler and monarchy, because it permitted for optimal leadership to achieve optimal results, was the best form of government. Darius successfully connived to get himself picked as the monarch and carried the day while his former companions became his servants. Darius, thus empowered, set about remaking the Persian Empire.

The situation Darius faced was complicated by Bardiya/Gaumata's rebellion and the stubbornness of his followers. Although Gaumata was killed and the rebellion crushed, Darius learned important lessons from the experience. One was that greater centralization was needed if the empire was to survive. Cyrus's approach of conquest and collaboration was not as sustainable as it may have appeared and, at any rate, the political skills needed for such a strategy eluded Darius and the other Achaemenids. Another lesson was that the Persian Empire needed a more coherent and enforceable religious orthodoxy that legitimized the dynasty and the wielding of autocratic power. Cyrus's policy of universal tolerance and attempts to portray his dynasty as being favored by all the gods and goddesses his subjects worshipped required great wisdom and self-assurance but left the regime open to charges of heterodoxy by conservatives and deprived it of a religious-administrative base. When rebellion occurred the absence of a state sponsored class of theocrats meant that the propaganda advantage went to the rebels.[9] There was also a need for greater regular taxation to pay for the maintenance of an empire that had, following the conquest of Egypt in 525 BC and the navigation of the Indus in 518 BC attained certain natural limits. Further expansion, as Darius's frustrating campaigns against the Scythians and the Greeks demonstrated, ended up costing more that they could yield, making the financial administration and security of existing territories a key priority.

Administratively, Darius decided to centralize power in his magnificent new capital of Persepolis and place the day-to-day running of the provinces (satrapies) in the hands of three powerful officials all directly answerable to the emperor. The first was the governor or satrap, the second was the secretary of state, and the third was the commander of the military forces. Land in the conquered provinces was allotted by the state to Persian nobles responsible for maintaining troops that could be called up for service. The

Persian imperial highway linked the remotest parts of the empire to the capital and the courier-relay system ensured that official communications traveled much faster than anything or anyone else. The imperial highway was dotted with check-posts, stations, wells, and caravanserais. Herodotus was impressed and noted that "Nothing mortal travels so fast as these Persian messengers . . . these men will not be hindered from accomplishing at their best speed the distance they have to go, either by snow, or rain, or heat, or by the darkness of night."[10] A more precise estimate is that news and orders traveled at the speed of 100 miles per day along the imperial highway,[11] which is more or less consistent with what is known about the Abbasid Caliphate or the Delhi Sultanate. On the ideological front, Darius promoted worship of Ahura Mazda and made Zoroastrianism the official ideology and religion of the Persian Empire. Darius claimed that all his successes were due to the favor of Ahura Mazda and it was the duty of his government to suppress the Lie propagated by upstarts like Gaumata. The Persian monarch emerged as "almost a mediator between God and man."[12] By the reign of Artaxerxes (465 BC—421 BC) a hierarchy of Magi, comparable to the Brahmins of India, had effectively hijacked Zoroastrianism and operated under state patronage.[13] That said, during Darius's lifetime, the officially patronized religion coexisted more or less peacefully with the traditional religions of the subject peoples.[14] The policy of centralization, expenditure on improved communications such as the Nile-Red Sea Canal, monumental construction of a new capital, the patronization of a religious establishment and the maintenance of a large standing and reserve military force, all required a new revenue settlement.

During the reigns of Cyrus and Cambyses there was no pre-determined revenue demand on the satrapies and each year the ruler would assess and try to collect the amount he deemed necessary.[15] While Cyrus gravitated towards generosity and assessed lightly and Cambyses tended towards pushing the demand up, Darius hit upon the idea of a more stable settlement. The first step was that Darius ordered a survey to determine the tax to be levied upon each of the provinces although Persia itself was declared exempt from taxes. These taxes were to be valued in terms of Babylonian talents[16] of silver, livestock, and food supplies. The only exception was India, which was assessed in terms of talents of gold dust, while tributaries were assessed in terms of commodities (horses, ivory, incense, etc.). The first satrapy, which included Ionia proper, paid 400 talents of silver in annual taxes, while the second satrapy, centered on northwest Anatolia and the outermost Greek islands paid 500 talents of silver.[17] From across the Hellespont the third satrapy paid 360 talents of silver per year while Cilicia, the fourth satrapy, furnished 360 white horses and 500 talents of silver per year.[18] The fifth satrapy, which comprised Phoenicia, Palestine-Syria and Cyprus paid 350 talents of silver per year.[19] Egypt, the sixth satrapy, was one of the most important as in addition to yielding annual taxes worth 700 talents of silver it supplied the profits from its fisheries to

the imperial treasury and provided grain to feed the 120,000 Persians stationed at Memphis.[20] The seventh satrapy, centered on the Gandarians near
the Kabul river, paid 170 talents of silver per year, while Susa, the eighth
satrapy, paid 300 talents of silver per year.[21] Babylonia/Assyria, the ninth
satrapy, was another major source of wealth providing 1000 talents of silver per year, provisions for one-third of the imperial army, and 500 boy
eunuchs for the imperial court.[22] Media, the tenth satrapy, paid 450 talents
of silver per year, while the eleventh satrapy, comprising, among others, the
Caspians and Pausicae, paid 200 talents of silver per year.[23] From Bactria,
the twelfth satrapy, came 360 talents of silver per year, while Armenia,
the thirteenth satrapy, paid 400 talents of silver per year.[24] The fourteenth
satrapy, which included the Persian tribe of Sagartians, paid 600 talents of
silver, while fifteenth satrapy of the Caspians and Sacans paid 250 talents
of silver.[25] From the sixteenth satrapy of the Parthians and Chorasmanians
came 300 talents of silver per year while the Paricanians and Ethiopians of
Asia who were counted as the seventeenth satrapy paid 400 talents of silver
per year.[26] The eighteenth satrapy extended into the northeast Caucasus
and paid 200 talents of silver per year while the nineteenth satrapy, possibly
located in what is today Georgia, paid 300 talents of silver per year.[27] The
twentieth satrapy was that of the Indians "who are more numerous than
any other nation" and "paid a tribute exceeding that of every other people,
to wit, three hundred and sixty talents of gold dust."[28] Thus, the regular
annual income of the Persian Empire under Darius was about 7740 talents
of silver and 360 talents of gold. The whole regular amount was housed in
the imperial treasury after being carefully counted by scribes and melted
down and stored to be minted into currency as the need arose. The concentration of tax demands in Egypt and Babylon may have contributed to
rebellions in these provinces after the reign of Darius, but, on the whole,
the cost of holding on to the ancient agrarian heartlands was well worth
the occasional rebellion.

The major expenditure was the military and the maintenance of the
temples and nobles affiliated with the state. Initially, the Achaemenians
employed light cavalry and revenue assignments in land were given to
noblemen to raise the required number of horsemen.[29] Under the early
Achaemenid rulers the nobles were required to fight at the head of their
contingents and thus earn their place in the imperial social hierarchy.[30]
Inspectors and spies kept the ruler informed of the performance of his
nobles though by the later Achaemenid period, noblemen resorted to using
mercenaries to meet their military obligations while the highly motivated
light cavalry gave way to expensive heavy cavalry and multitudes of poorly
trained infantry.[31] An imperial guard of 10,000 Immortals, plus Persian
and Medes cavalry provided the core of the Persian military. Royal troops
were garrisoned in major cities while the satrapies were responsible for
maintaining local troops and raised additional forces as the need arose. The
exact size of the Persian military is difficult to assess. Herodotus provides

figures to the effect that the Persian force invading Greece under Xerxes (r. 486 BC—465 BC) included 1.7 million infantry and 100,000 cavalry.[32] While the infantry figure is incredible, the cavalry figure, given the size of the empire, is not. It seems unlikely that the Persian Empire could have mobilized more than 100,000 cavalry for any particular campaign though even that figure would have represented a massive mobile army.

The culture of power of Achaemenid Persia can be described as a pragmatic though arbitrary autocracy in which the emperor's temperament and competence determined the effectiveness of the apparatus. There was no recognized framework for hereditary succession and thus princes and pretenders repeatedly came to blows over the throne and control of the state apparatus. That apparatus comprised a powerful military, efficient communications and espionage, central and provincial bureaucracies responsible for financial administration and record-keeping, and a state-patronized religious establishment that helped project imperial ideology. Taxes, from Darius onwards, were assessed in kind as well as in silver or gold value and were convertible into coinage. The wealth of the state was effectively the wealth of the ruler who dispensed it as he pleased, waging wars, building monuments, endowing temples and engaging in conspicuous consumption at court. The division of the satrapy administration under three heads made for divide and rule and encouraged rivalries and appeals to the emperor. Darius had the governors of Lydia and Egypt killed on suspicion of disloyalty and royal inspectors backed by troops and empowered by the ruler to punish errant provincial officials were sent out as the need arose. A scribal bureaucracy in which positions could be purchased kept the state machinery running while state functionaries were paid through revenue assignments for specific purposes associated with raising cavalry or running temples or were allowed to intercept a share of the wealth that passed through their offices. While relatively tolerant of other faiths, Achaemenid Persia developed an ideocratic complex that patronized Zoroastrianism as the state religion, provided the Magi with state lands, and recognized the Persian ruler as a cosmic mediator and the executor of the divine will. Subsequent to the dramatic collapse of the Achaemenids at the hands of Alexander the Great and his Macedonian and Greek army in the 330s BC no Persian empire would come close to the first of the Persian dynasties in terms of temporal success. Later empires would, however, be shaped by the administrative structures and culture of power of the Achaemenids which proved to be one of the most enduring legacies of Cyrus and his successors.

EMPIRE INTERRUPTED: SELEUCID AND PARTHIAN

From 330 BC to AD 224 Persia was under foreign rule. The Seleucid dynasty founded by Alexander's general, Seleucus, managed to gain control over the Mesopotamian heartland of the Achaemenid Empire. Expansion into India was evidently checked by the rise of the Mauryas while Egypt fell under Ptolemy, another of Alexander's generals. The Seleucid dynasty peaked between 300 BC and 240 BC in terms of its control over territory but thereafter went into decline so that by 175 BC two-thirds of the empire had been lost and by 80 BC only a rump state centered on Syria was left. The Seleucids appear to have kept the satrap system intact but replaced Zoroastrianism with worship of Olympian gods as the official religion. The Seleucids also failed to deal effectively with rebellions and fragmentation of their authority. An important reason for this could be economic. The Achaemenids were able to draw on the resources of the Nile, the Tigris-Euphrates and the Indus, and dominated ancient overland and land-sea trade routes. The Seleucids, however, only controlled Mesopotamia. Much of the territory controlled by the Seleucids was rough and the imperial core was too small to cope with the demands of effective governance. Thus, in 245 BC, the satrap of Bactria declared his independence and success-fully founded a dynastic state of his own. Around the same time as Bactria broke off, the Seleucid satrap of Parthia also rebelled and tried to found his own dynasty. While the satrap was able to secede he was soon overthrown by Parthian tribesmen led by Arsaces, who proceeded to found his own dynasty, in 238 BC. The successors of Arsaces were known as the Arsacids and eventually supplanted the Seleucids to form a Parthian Empire.

The Parthians, as well as rebellious satraps, were advantaged by the Seleucids declining military fortunes further west. Ptolemy Egypt defeated the Seleucids in 217 BC and further defeats in Anatolia and Greece meant that by 188 BC the Seleucids were forced to abandon Anatolia and pay reparations. Seleucus IV (187 BC—175 BC) was overthrown and killed by one of his ministers and from then onwards major rebellions in the east and west of the empire combined with civil war at the center left much of the country in the hands of local warlords. While the eastern territories were swallowed up by the Parthians the western territories came under Roman military pressure. In 63 BC, Rome annexed Syria and turned it into a province putting an end to the Seleucid dynasty.

As Seleucid power receded westward the Parthians under the Arsacids (238 BC—AD 224) apparently filled the vacuum. On the surface, the Parthian empire was a monarchy and claimed to be the successor of the Achaemenids. The Parthians also made Ctesiphon (near Baghdad) their capital. Further westward expansion was checked by the Roman Empire even as the Parthians managed to hold their own against Roman efforts to defeat them. Mesopotamia, however, remained under Roman military pressure.

In contrast to the Roman Empire, the Parthian Empire was a low-maintenance state that allowed sub-kingdoms with their own coinage to exist. There were also satrapies and subdivisions but the central government had no standing military force at its disposal. The tribal nature of the government meant that Parthian nobles had considerable freedom to do as they pleased within their domains and could act with impunity. These nobles eventually came to dominate the throne as kingmakers and administrators in key positions at court and in the religious establishment. The fragmented and warlord-dominated polity of the Parthian Empire was an example of *para-kandeh shahi* and as such was far removed from the administrative and political genius of the Achaemenids. The decline of Parthian power and the failure of the Parthian nobility to establish a strong state, however, paved the way for an imperial restoration under the Sassanids.

THE PERSIAN EMPIRE REBORN: THE SASSANIDS

Around AD 200 an ambitious Persian noblemen with close family ties to the priests associated with the goddess Anahita became the satrap of Persis. His name was Ardashir and in 208, after killing his brothers, he proclaimed himself the sovereign ruler of Persis. The Parthian nobility were fighting for control of the throne and thus did not move to deal with the upstart Persian effectively. This enabled Ardashir to consolidate control over Persis and the south of Persia. Belated attempts by Parthian nobles to check Ardashir proved futile and added to his reputation. In 224, the last Parthian king, Artabanus, tried to rally his noblemen and took the field against Ardashir but was defeated and killed in battle. Ardashir moved westwards and took control of the capital and thus inaugurated the Sassanid Persian Empire. The emergence "of a new autocratic ruler from more or less obscure origins, taking power by force after a period of disorder, and claiming the decision of God for his victory" would, with the Sassanid advent, become a "recurring theme" in Persian history.[33]

Ardashir, like Darius, proclaimed his victory as being due to the favor of Ahura Mazda and set about the consolidation of the new regime. Zoroastrianism became the state religion and the Magi were patronized through the creation of a centralized priesthood under royal control. Hellenistic influences, Parthian customs and Christianity were all corruptions and manifestations of the Lie that Darius had so successfully banished. Ardashir's successor, Shahpur I (r. 240–271) proceeded to purge the empire of the Manicheans putting to death their leader, Mani. Bahram II (r. 275–282) began his rule "so tyrannically" that a conspiracy was formed to murder him, but, before it could be put into motion he is said to have repented and relented.[34] The idea was that a just ruler was always religious while tyranny was always irreligious. Of course, there was nothing wrong in being tyrannical in implementing the true faith—indeed, it was impossible for a religious-minded ruler acting on good faith to be considered a tyrant. Thus, Shahpur II (r. 309–379) embarked upon a general persecution of Christians and required them to pay double the taxes owed by other subjects. The bishops were instructed to collect the additional amount due but when they protested that their community was too poor the Catholicus, five bishops and a hundred priests were executed on Good Friday, AD 339 and a general anti-Christian campaign was launched. For the next forty years Christians were massacred, Churches desecrated and destroyed with "monks and nuns, especially being subject to pitiless persecution."[35] Although the Christianized Roman Empire was hardly any better towards its minorities, the systematic persecution of religious dissent distinguished the relatively effective and ruthless theocratic state of the Sassanids from the relatively pragmatic and easy-going Achaemenids.

The decision to allow Christians to worship publicly in 409 did not mean that Sassanids would not respond with great violence to religious dissent. The campaign launched against the Mazdakites—followers of Mazdak who believed that property and wives ought to be held communally—was prosecuted with vigor by Khusraw I Noshirvan (r. 531–579). Also known as Noshirvan *Adil* for his love of justice, he presided over the liquidation of 100,000 Mazdakites and restored the Magi to full favor. Indeed, by Noshirvan's reign the Sassanids employed some 25,000 salaried priests to run the religious establishment.[36] That said, when it suited them politically, the Sassanids could be enlightened as well. Noshirvan had provided refuge to Greek and Roman classical scholars fleeing persecution in the Byzantine Empire. Ardashir I, Shahpur I, and Khusraw I were wary of beliefs that might challenge the legitimacy of their state and wedded their empire to Zoroastrianism. Far more so than the Achaemenids, the Sassanids transformed Zoroastrianism into an imperial ideology and "So close was the link between the Zoroastrian religion and the Sassanian Empire that the collapse of one meant the downfall of the other."[37]

The ideocratic nature of Sassanid Persia was complemented by administrative and fiscal development along bureaucratic lines. Initially, the anarchic autonomy that characterized the Parthian era was tempered only in parts of the Sassanid Empire with Mesopotamia and Persis administered as metropolitan regions. By the reign of Shahpur II, however, the Sassanids had adopted "a tight centralized bureaucratized administration" that had much in common with post-Darius Achaemenid governance.[38] The key players in the Sassanid administration were scribes, judges, priests, treasurers, tax collectors, inspectors, spies, and a service gentry that raised troops in exchange for grants of land as revenue assignments. Prominent Persian and Parthian nobles were initially accommodated by the Sassanids but successive wars and internal disturbances guided the evolution of the state towards greater reliance on bureaucracy and centralization. Towards the end of the Sassanid Empire the old nobility had been deprived of power, "the sub-kings had all but vanished" and "[e]ven the Arab buffer state of the Lakhmids in Iraq had been absorbed into the centralized, bureaucratic, Sassanian empire."[39] With each passing reign, the "nobility of service supplied a salaried officer cadre" that supplanted tribal leaders and local potentates.[40] The Sassanids were also capable of putting fairly large armies in the field, suffering heavy losses, only to raise fresh armies in a manner that the Parthians could never have entertained. What makes this feat of centralization all the more impressive is that the Sassanid Empire was about the same size as the loosely structured Parthian domain and controlled a similar revenue base.

The difference was in the financial administration of the realm. Land revenue was settled as a fixed percentage graded with reference to the productivity of the soil and then left to stabilize. Farmers could therefore keep the surplus for themselves since the tax demand of the state would not arbitrarily increase.[41] Reclamation of wastelands was made a priority with incentives and facilities offered to settlers willing to make the move. Separate taxes were levied on orchards and property alongside a poll tax. Lands were granted to the Magi for the maintenance of temples and the priests also acted as inspectors for the financial administration and helped settle legal disputes. A class of service nobility known as *dehqans* received lands from the state and had to maintain troops subject to regular inspection and recorded in registers or muster rolls. These troops were responsible for keeping the roads and highways secure for trade and official communications, protected towns and villages from brigands and tribal aggressors, and were called up for military campaigns as and when required by the central government. The creation of the institution of vizierate or prime minister (great commander) at the center and the appointment of special executive officers sent out to the provinces to enforce the ruler's wishes also helped consolidate power. The prime minister was responsible for overseeing the day-to-day running of the state, especially the financial administration, and keeping the ruler informed and well advised. That taxes were collected at four-month intervals, or thrice a year, meant that the administrative machinery was constantly on the move, assessing, taxing, inspecting, and remitting, as the need arose.

To further facilitate imperial control Noshirvan divided the empire into four super-satrapies with high-ranking governors that reported directly to him. The Eastern Command comprised Khorasan and Kerman, while Mesopotamia, which also included the imperial capital, constituted the Western Command. The Northern Command consisted of Amernia and Azerbaijan while the Persian heartland of Persis (Fars) and Khuzistan made up the Southern Command. Each command had its own revenue minister, with an ombudsman to protect poorer subjects against the tyranny of the rich and state officials. The *dehqans* also collected taxes from villages in their revenue assignments but were answerable to the provincial and central financial administrations. Noshirvan neatly summed up the causal chain that went into making the Sassanid Empire such a formidable entity:

> Royal authority exists through the army, the army through money, money through taxes, taxes through cultivation, cultivation through justice, justice through the improvement of officials, the improvement of officials through the forthrightness of wazirs, and the whole thing in

the first place through the ruler's personal supervision of his subjects' condition and his ability to educate them, so that he may rule them, and not they him.[42]

Actually ruling the subjects, however, required great personal ability on the part of the ruler. Sassanid emperors that were inadequately ruthless and cunning had relatively short life-expectancies and stood to be killed by their kinsmen and senior officials. Thus, Ardashir II, Shahpur II, and Bahram II were murdered by their own officials. Noshirvan, whose words are quoted above, killed all his brothers and nephews to ensure his own throne. Khusraw II, who led Sassanid Persian in a quarter-century-long war against Byzantium that substantially exhausted both powers, was deposed in 628. This triggered a crisis of succession after his immediate successor, Kavad II, who had massacred his brothers upon assuming the throne, died of the plague. This caused another crisis of succession to erupt and anarchy ensued between 628 and 634 with six emperors and two empresses ascending the throne only to be killed by their kinsmen or officials. By the time Yazdgerid III became emperor (634) the bloodletting at the highest levels combined with the ruinous legacy of the war against Byzantium, had compromised the integrity of the Sassanid state. It would have taken a truly great ruler along the lines of Ardashir or Khosraw I, to rally pro-regime elements and restore order, but perhaps even such a leader could not have remedied the situation in time to stem the rise of the Arab Caliphate.

The culture of power of Sassanid Persia is more vividly apparent than earlier empires. Of the Achaemenids the design of the empire and major tendencies, rebellions and wars are known, while of the Seleucids less is clear and the Parthians do not appear to have set up an organized state machinery. The Sassanids, like the Achaemenids, sought administrative consolidation, promoted an official religion and relied on a regular military paid for through a systematic financial administration. As the empire prospered it displaced local notables, tribal leaders and other allegedly "feudal" elements and relied increasingly on a service nobility, regularized clergy and official administration. The day-to-day running of the empire was entrusted to the prime minister, governors, provincial finance ministers (*diwans*), and *dehqan*s. The ruler retained the absolute right to arbitrarily punish or reward his servants and wealth and status depended on state service. The ruler also had the ability to dispose of the property of his subjects as he wished though it was recognized that such arbitrary exactions were not productive in the long run. The effectiveness of the state depended a great deal on the personal charisma and competence of the ruler and in the context of arbitrary rule *sans* a recognized right of succession moral relationships were stunted even within the royal household.

Sassanid Persia exhibits many structural similarities with continental bureaucratic empires in South Asia and China though it seems to have been more aggressively theocratic than the former and less oriented towards meritocracy than the latter. The Sassanid ruler held arbitrary power that was exercised through his servants who were in effect the ruling class and comprised civil, military and ecclesiastical officials organized in hierarchies and distributed over the sub-units of the empire. The ruler was legitimized by divine sanction and had unlimited powers over the country which may be considered the estate of the ruler. While there were geographic and phys-iological limits to the ruler's power, the governing elite was exposed to con-siderable arbitrariness and through them the population at large was also vulnerable. The Sassanid Empire appears to have developed a more vigor-ous and complete ideocratic complex than its predecessors and also seems to have maintained a more regular military force. The Sassanid model of ideocratic and arbitrary personal rule through a state apparatus compris-ing hierarchical official instruments would greatly impress the Arabs who defeated and conquered Persia in the 630s and 640s and Turks who eventu-ally overthrew the Arabs in the 800s-900s.

THE SECOND INTERREGNUM, ARABS AND TURKS

The Arabs of the peninsular desert were divided into tribes, practiced agri-culture on a small scale,[43] and took part in the caravan trade of West Asia. For the mighty empires that bounded Arabia, there was little to be gained from the penetration of such a vast, hostile, and desolate expanse. Yemen, where archaeological remains confirm the existence of an urban civiliza-tion that practiced irrigation agriculture, had been reduced to the status of a zone of conflict between the Persian and Abyssinian empires by the 500s. The Arab tribes of the north were in contact with imperial state formations since the ninth century BC and enlisted alongside rival powers as auxiliaries and confederates. An Assyrian inscription of 854 BC reveals that "Gindibu the Arab" led a force of one thousand camels against Shalamaneser III.[44] Punitive expeditions aside, direct control was not exercised over the barren lands inhabited by these turbulent and hardy nomads.

At the advent of Islam, the desert Arabs had no experience of a cen-tralized, omnipotent, continental bureaucratic empire. Mecca was gov-erned by an assembly within which each of the ten kinship groups were assigned special functions, and the Prophet of Islam entered into a for-mal compact with the citizens of Medina after his flight from Mecca in 622. The republican and egalitarian ethos of Islam, however, rapidly gave way to the exigencies of managing a vast continental empire follow-ing the Arab conquests.[45] After the Arabs expanded into Sassanid and Byzantine territory, they adopted the administrative systems and public ethos of their vanquished rivals.[46] By 661, the republican experiment was over and the rise of the Umayyad dynasty completed the process by which power was concentrated in the hands of the central execu-tive.[47] Government by consultation was replaced by pledges of loyalty to the caliph *after* his ascension and to refrain from doing homage invited all "the consequences of rebellion".[48] During the reign of Walid (d. 715), the Umayyad dominion expanded to include both Spain and Sindh, the subjugation of the latter being entrusted to the Governor of Khurasan, Hajjaj bin Yousuf, and the field command of the invasion force being entrusted to Mohammed bin Qasim. The Arab imperial advent sheds light on the culture of power of the Arab Empire as well as that of its adversaries.

The ruler of Sindh, Raja Dahir, had married his own sister based on an astrologer's prediction that her son would be a great ruler, and defeated his brother Dharasaya, who sought to capitalize on the indignation caused by this incestuous union.[49] Dahir's unstable and violent temperament prevented his officers from giving him "any sane advice", and this hesitation was reinforced by the murder at their master's hands of the messenger who bore "news of the Arab crossing of the Indus".[50] Kaka, one of Dahir's senior officers, deserted his camp and found justification in "astrological calculations" that predicted Arab victory.[51] Hajjaj, in the meanwhile, was in constant touch with Mohammed bin Qasim as letters were sent and received every three days.[52] The policy adopted by the Umayyad satrap was to uphold the prerogatives of the upper classes, offer security of life and property to those who surrendered, and ensure that the taxes paid to local rulers were redirected to imperial coffers.[53] Hindus in general, but Brahmins in particular, were recruited for public service, local notables were to collect taxes, and tax incentives were given to encourage conversion.[54]

Mohammed bin Qasim's proven competence did not save him from death and disgrace after his patron died in the summer of 714. In 715, the Caliph Walid followed the proconsul to his eternal rest, before he could alter the succession in favor of his son. Soon after the change of ruler, an official messenger "arrived with orders for bin Qasim's arrest".[55] Hajjaj had executed the brother of Salih al-Wasit, who now found favor with the imperial court and took revenge by torturing Mohammed bin Qasim to death.[56] A similar fate was the reward of the royal servant who brought Iberia, at the opposite end of the known world, under his sway. It is only natural for an order that lacks legitimacy and is operated on the arbitrary wishes of a single individual and his personal favorites and servants, to view successes achieved without direct supervision with suspicion. The victorious general or brilliant administrator of today could well be the emperor or kingmaker of tomorrow. The annals of the Abbasid dynasty, which succeeded the Ummayads in 750,[57] also contain many references to viziers and subordinates arrested or killed by the Caliph and his favorites, which reveal an atmosphere of mutual suspicion and intrigue. One of the most valuable examples of this behavior is that of the rise and fall of the Barmarkids, a succession of powerful ministers of Persian origin who dominated the Abbasid court from 770–803. These ministers ". . . developed and streamlined the administration of the state: after their fall the mail piled up unopened in sacks. . . . They provided leadership and inspiration for generations of secretaries."[58] In 803, the Barmarkids suddenly met their nemesis when the Abbasid ruler, Haroun al-Rashid (immortalized in the *Arabian Nights*), stunned "almost everyone at that time" and "ordered the destruction of the Barmarkids. Yahya and his son Fadl were placed under arrest and his favourite Ja'far was summarily executed in the middle of the night, his body being cut in pieces and displayed on the bridges of Baghdad for every passer-by to see. Their possessions were confiscated and their officials arrested."[59] Given the unreasonably high rate of attrition, it is hardly surprising that viziers had no compunctions against eliminating or manipulating a ruler who showed weakness.

One group of people who impressed the Arabs on account of their toughness and warlike nature were the Turks. The Turks originated in the Southern Siberian plains, and were organized into small family groups headed by a paternal figure.[60] By the 500s, the Turks had founded two large confederations stretching from the northern reaches of China to the Black Sea.[61] Tang China evidently saw the presence of these entities as a threat and managed to subvert them by 660.[62] Seven years later, the Arabs crossed the Oxus and raided Bokhara, Samarkand, and other tributaries of the Turks.[63] Until their contact with the Arabs, the Turks essentially had a tribal-confederate political organization and practiced shamanism. Transition from a tribal society on the margins of civilization, to the most successful dynasts in Muslim history took three forms.

First, some Turkish clans on the periphery of the Arab Caliphate that accepted Islam and pledged loyalty to the caliph were granted governorships. In this manner, four grandsons of Saman-Khudat were made governors of Samarkand, Ferghana, Shash, and Herat in 819 by Ma'mun al-Rashid and laid the foundations of the Samanid dynasty.[64] The second way in which the Turks established their dynastic rule was through the institution of military slavery. By the ninth century, the Abbasids had come to rely heavily on Turkish slaves for military purposes. Caliph Wathik (842–846) began granting Turkish chiefs governorships and, consequently, in 868 Ahmad bin Tulun became sovereign of Egypt[65]—the first Turk to carve an independent principality for himself out of the Caliphate. [66] At about the same time as Egypt's secession from the Abbasid dominion, the Turkish military leadership at the capital, Samarra, murdered the sovereign after having forced him to "voluntarily" abdicate through a written instrument solemnly and spinelessly "witnessed by the judicial establishment."[67] The junta also had the imperial secretaries flogged, an act that "made a deep impression" for the secretaries ". . . were respected figures, well-educated in the great traditions of Abbasid bureaucracy, and this barbarous assault showed both the power and the savagery of the Turkish leadership."[68] The third mode of transition consisted of migration from the steppes to Anatolia and gradual settlement with war against the Byzantines a near permanent feature of Turkish statecraft after the Battle of Manzikert in 1071.[69] Thus, by the time Mahmud of Ghazni assumed control of his principality in 997 and styled himself "Sultan", the decline of Arab power was terminal. The Ghaznavid state consciously modeled on the ancient Persian dynasties even as it employed Islamic rhetoric to justify its plunder of India.

Subuktagin, Mahmud's father, was succeeded on the throne by his elder son Ismail, who proved to be "an incompetent spendthrift".[70] Seven months after Subuktagin's demise, Ismail was forced to abdicate and Mahmud ascended the throne.[71] Sultan Mahmud led seventeen expeditions into India, and arranged for the administration of subject territories in the Punjab during the latter half of his thirty-three year reign. The wealth looted from India allowed Mahmud to establish a glittering court adorned by some four hundred poets[72] churning out tributes to the sultan's magnificence. Firdausi, who composed "by the special order of the king", fled the court, having satirized the sultan because of the insufficient "reward" given to him for the *Shahnama*.[73] The punishment for those who dared oppose the sultan was death by the particularly awful method of "being trampled by elephants".[74] Shaik Bu Ali Sina (Avicenna), the famous physician and biologist, was forced to seek asylum in Ray upon his refusal to come to Mahmud's court.[75] Al-Beruni, the author of the unmatched *Kitab-ul-Hind* also suffered imprisonment and royal disfavor at the hands of Sultan Mahmud.[76] Some satisfaction can be derived from the superior endurance of the "monuments of the pen"[77] left behind by these luminaries of the "Persian Renaissance"[78] of which the Ghaznavids were comparatively transient manifestations.

The language of power and refinement of the age was Persian, and Sultan Mahmud exercised power in the manner of Achaemenid or Sassanid rulers.[79] The daily routine of administration was left to salaried ministers and officials who were at the absolute mercy of the sultan in whose name they wielded power, and from whose will came their status and wealth. The most accurate gauge of the power of the sultan over his officials is the status of the office of the vizier, who, for all practical purposes, was the first minister due to his charge of the revenue department. Sultan Mahmud's first vizier was Abul Abbas Fazl bin Ahmed.[80] His eventual fall from royal favor was due to "alleged" financial corruption, the jealousy of some nobles, and his refusal to transfer one of his "favorite slaves" to the sultan.[81] Fazl bin Ahmed was "cruelly treated" and "died under merciless torture".[82]

Next was Abul Qasim Ahmed bin Hasan al-Maimandi, a "class fellow", and "foster brother" of the sultan.[83] After eighteen years of loyal service, the sultan's sister and partisans secured his dismissal from office and imprisonment in an Indian fort.[84] The vizier who served Sultan Mahmud until the end of his reign in 1030 was his close friend and confidante, Hasanak.[85] In the war of succession that followed Mahmud's death, notwithstanding the will he left in favor of his son Mohammed, his other son, Masud, emerged victorious. When Hasanak realized that Mohammed was doomed, he tried to switch sides to Masud's party but was arrested, executed, and his property was confiscated.[86] The throne having been successfully usurped from the hands of Mohammed, Masud developed the habit of inviting advice only to reject it. Masud was eventually imprisoned by his own slaves and his blind brother Mohammed was placed on the throne while the affairs of state were entrusted to his mad son.[87]

One is reminded by these examples of Nizam-ul-Mulk Tusi, author of the *Siyasatnamah*, and vizier to the Seljuk Turks. Tusi was dismissed from office in his early nineties due to the queen's intrigues against him over the issue of succession, suffered accusations from his enemies, and was conveniently murdered by a religious fanatic. Tusi had come to power in 1064 by killing Amid ul-Mulk Kunduri, loyal vizier to Sultan Tughril for twenty years, soon after Alp Arsalan's enthronement. Amid ul-Mulk is reputed to have cursed Nizam ul-Mulk shortly before being killed telling his executioners to inform their master that by "killing viziers" he had brought a "hideous practice" into existence and that it wouldn't be long "before this practice will befall you and your descendants."[88] The Seljuk Sultanate in Persia was organized along three mutually reinforcing principles and Nizam ul-Mulk took these to a new level of efficiency. The first principle was that the empire was the estate of the sovereign but that a portion of that estate could be alienated in the form of an *iqta* or transferrable revenue assignment in exchange for the maintenance of military forces or service to the state. The second principle was that the state was an ideological-religious enterprise legitimized by divine sanction, and that this legitimacy was to be reaffirmed by campaigns against heretics, such as the Ismailis, as well as service, whether he wanted to be served or not, to the Abbasid caliph at Baghdad.[89] The third principle was that the official postal system or *barid*, with the surveillance agents or *sahib khabar*, and the espionage agents or *jasusan*, would work to neutralize all opposition and ensure that orders were carried out. The vizier was supposed to handle the routine running of the state and advise the ruler on what course of action to follow. The fact that Amid ul-Mulk managed to survive for two decades as vizier to Tughril, and that Nizam ul-Mulk served both Alp Arsalan and Malik Muhammad Shah as vizier for nearly three decades, indicates that the Seljuk rulers, for all their faults, recognized talent and had the sense to let their ablest servants take care of things. Of course, a change of ruler could spell disaster for the vizier as his enemies would try and use the opportunity to discredit the incumbent. Ultimately, no one could "elude the endless cycles of intrigue and accusations of heresy" in the Seljuk regime—"not even the masterful" Nizam ul-Mulk.[90] Nizam ul-Mulk was eventually murdered at the instigation of his successor in office, Taj ul-Mulk, who was also a favorite of the queen. At the time of his murder, Nizam ul-Mulk personally held about one tenth of the agricultural produce of the realm as *iqta*, and had used his wealth to further the interests of his family and found the famous Nizamiyya Madrassah at Baghdad.

One of the principal advantages of appointing a vizier, from the sultan's perspective, was that it spared him direct association with the administration of a state that was even at the best of times heavy-handed and structurally prone to concentrating power in unscrupulous and often unaccountable officials. Appeals directed against the behavior of the apparatus were heard by the sultan and provided him with the option of making examples of some officials. Their ill-gotten property, of course, would go into the royal treasury. A timely change of vizier accompanied by the incumbent's death or disgrace would further project the sultan as a good man misled by evil advisors who had, mercifully, been found out and punished.

The Ghaznavids twice attempted to reform the administration. Sultan Mahmud had his senior officials nominate a panel from which he would select a vizier.[91] This practice was abandoned after Mahmud's death. The other attempted reform was the separation of military from civilian government in the Punjab. Ali Ariyaruk was entrusted with regional command of the former and Qazi Sherazi took charge of the latter from the seat of government in Lahore,[92] and to keep the two in control Bul Hakan was made superintendent of news carriers.[93]

This reform misfired and soon Qazi Sherazi was running around in military robes and Ariyaruk "bore down all opposition".[94] The immediate crisis ended when Ariyaruk was arrested in 1031 and replaced by Niyaltgin who, in turn, rapidly developed differences with the Qazi.[95] As soon as Niyaltgin went on a campaign deeper into India, the Qazi sent reports to his superiors informing them of the corruption from which his military counterpart had benefited at the sultan's expense.[96] Niyaltgin was not amused by these shenanigans and laid siege to Lahore, but suffered defeat at the hands of imperial forces under the command of a Hindu named Tilak.[97] This second failure led to the restoration of the old system of viceroys that combined in their person supreme military and civil authority, subject to review, transfer, dismissal, or liquidation, by the sultan. Prince Majdud, Masud's son, was thus made viceroy and sent to Lahore.

Perhaps the greatest good that came of Masud's reign was his restoration to favor of Al Beruni, now granted a pension that freed him from mundane worries.[98] The *Kitab-ul-Hind* sheds light on the culture, philosophy, and religion of Hindu India around 1030, prior to Turco-Persian colonization and Islamic proselytism. Al Beruni observed that the Hindus had a classical language spoken and understood "only" by the "upper and educated classes", and a "neglected vernacular" for the masses.[99] Indian scribes are described as "careless" individuals who neglected "to produce correct and well-collated copies".[100] Only "that which is known by heart" was considered "canonical", which further devalued the written word.[101] The embarrassing lack of written historical knowledge for India before the Turco-Persian conquests appears to confirm Al Beruni's harsh evaluation, though instability and chaos were also doubtless contributing factors.

The people Al Beruni interacted with were arrogantly insular to the extent that "if you tell them of any science or scholar in Khurasan or Persis, they will think you to be both an ignoramus and a liar".[102] Hindus were also divided into castes called *varnas* (colors), and a mass of humanity existed beneath the caste-system, who performed degrading menial work, and *antyaja* (guilds) that rendered services.[103] Each caste had special functions and the lower orders were criminally culpable if they violated the restrictions placed on them by divine sanction as represented by *dharma*. Al Beruni recounts Ram's murder of a *candala* who performed rituals forbidden to his kind and the subsequent justification that "I kill thee on account of a good action which thou art not allowed to do".[104] Al Beruni also confirms the existence of state managed prostitution to raise revenues.[105] The practice must have continued at least since the time of Kautilya (c 300 BC) and is comparable to a policy devised by: "the Buyide prince 'Adud-aldaula . . . who besides also had a second aim in view, viz. that of protecting his subjects against the passions of his unmarried soldiers".[106]

The Ghaznavid state that alternately terrorized and patronized Al Beruni was well on its way to collapse by the time the *Kitab-ul-Hind* was completed. This was largely due to the deficient leadership of Sultan Mahmud's sons. Ghaznavid rule, however, would endure in parts of the Punjab until 1186 when a fresh wave of Turkish invaders descended from the northwest and laid the foundations for the political order of the Delhi Sultanate. The Persianized Arab and Ghaznavid empires had, by then, congealed the culture of power later Muslim invaders would carry deeper into the Indian subcontinent. In both cases, the central executive was omnipotent, praetorian, legitimated by divine sanction, and recognized no lawful opposition. The personal favorites and appointed servants of the central executive constituted the ruling class. Private property, landed or otherwise, maintained a precarious existence as evidenced by the frequent Abbasid practice of levying "monetary fines" on the rich in the range of "fifty thousand to a hundred thousand dinars".[107] The Caliph Muqtadir, in 914, "confiscated the fortunes of a jeweler, valued at four million dinars".[108] The country, in other words, was the personal estate of the ruler.[109]

The dominant religion of Islam was bent and broken to provide the system with divine sanction on account of factors grounded in a historical experience of governance long determined by geography, climate, and the compulsions of hydraulic civilizations in Mesopotamia, Egypt, and Persia, that predated Islam by millennia. Thus, the Abbasids, who took power in the name of religion and promised a return to an earlier age of purity, rapidly founded their dominion "on a solid foundation with a paid professional army of mostly Khurasani soldiers and an efficient tax system to collect the money to pay for them." [110] Within a generation, revolts by the Alids were brutally crushed and the Abbasid imperium ". . . looked very much like the Umayyad one it replaced, but with different people in charge."[111] The Umayyad, during their innings, maintained the structure of the bureaucratic state they inherited from the Byzantine and Persian empires. Whether Arab or Turk, Persia's rulers' during the post-Sassanid period depended greatly on the Persian inheritance and organized their states proprietarily and bureaucratically, maintained a bureaucratic intelligentsia dependent on royal largesse, and could do as they pleased with their officials and subjects. In short, all the characteristics consistent with the behavior of continental bureaucratic empires in Persia before the Arab conquests also manifested themselves in the governance of the states during and after the Arab imperial age.

EMPIRE RESURGENT: SAFAVID PERSIA

While the Arabs and Turks had sought conquest and administrative consolidation and in pursuit of the latter gravitated steadily into Persian practices, the Mongol and Timurid advent heralded a new kind of challenge in terms of the intensity of violence. Mongol armies devastated major urban centers in the Muslim world and spread chaos and terror as no previous, or subsequent, invader. Persia and its extended zone of influence bore the brunt of the Mongol onslaught that culminated in the fall of Baghdad of 1258 and the massacre of some 800,000 refugees and residents while earlier, during the Mongol conquest of Merv, perhaps as many as 1.3 million people were slaughtered. [112] In spite of this catastrophe, the Mongol rulers of Persia, styling themselves the Il-Khans, were soon dependent on Persian administrative personnel and practices to govern what was left of the land and people they had conquered. By the early 1300s the Mongols had embraced Islam and a slow revival of trade and agriculture enabled a return to normalcy. This normalcy, however, did not last long.

In 1370, a Chingezi Turkish warlord name Timur seized power in Central Asia and brought the feuding Mongol horde under one banner. Amir Timur, like Genghis Khan, wanted to establish a world empire and embarked on a series of military campaigns. Once again, Persia bore the brunt of the onslaught. At Isfahan, the population was put to the sword and 120 pillars of skulls taken from 70,000 victims were erected outside the ruined city. At Baghdad, the same fate was meted out and skull towers made from the heads of 90,000 victims were erected. In 1398, South Asia bore the brunt of Timur's limitless ambition with the Delhi Sultanate facing the same ruinous outcome as Persia and Mesopotamia. In 1402, the Ottomans were given a severe chastisement that involved the defeat of Sultan Beyazid *Yildirum*, though, amidst the horror of this campaign, Timur would find time to host Ibn Khaldun, the great Arab philosopher of history.[113] Having reduced the major centers of Muslim power, from Delhi to Anatolia, to smoldering ruins, Timur turned his attention towards Ming China but died en route in 1405. No sooner was the warlord dead that his commanders and relations fell out amongst themselves and started fighting for control over the Timur's dominion, which fragmented into hundreds of petty states.

It was against this backdrop of ceaseless violence and Mongol depredations that a response started to take hold. The rally started in the town of Ardabil in Azerbaijan with the founding of the Safavid order of Sufis under Sheikh Safi-ud-Din (d.1334). The Safavid order wasn't a group of sensitive ascetics seeking escape from an oppressive reality. They were, rather, a militant order that drew strength from the Qizilbash Turcoman tribes of eastern Anatolia. These warriors believed that the Safavid Sheikh was a miracle-working *murhsid-i-kamil* (peerless guide) vested with divine attributes. Advocating a messianic interpretation of religion that broadly fell within the fold of Shia Islam, the Safavid Sufi order was also a political movement guided by charismatic and infallible leaders determined to acquire power and crush the Mongols, Timurids and other religious denominations. While such movements had arisen in the past, the Achaemenid and Sassanid empires had proven strong enough to resist and overcome them. This time, however, there was no large, highly organized state—only fractious warlords. The Safavid Sufi order would thus emerge as a state building instrument and in this respect it has some resemblance to the movements that established totalitarian-ideological regimes in the aftermath of the First World War.[114]

By the 1460s the Safavids had become important political players and in spite of setbacks, commanded the loyalty of twelve Turcoman tribes. One important aspect of this loyalty was Shia Islam and a desire to convert the population of Persia. By 1501, the Sheikh of the Safavids proclaimed himself the ruler and the new Shah Ismail (r. 1501–1524) set about enforcing Shia Islam as the state religion. On the face of it this decision seemed unwise given the number of Sunni Muslims in the country but Ismail had "harnessed the driving power of a dynamic religious ideology" and placed it at the service of the new dynasty.[115] A test case of the new policy was the forcible conversion of the people of Tabriz to Shia Islam even though two-thirds of them were Sunnis. Even Ismail's Qizilbash felt that such measures could backfire, but they were told by their master that "God and the Immaculate Imams are with me, and I fear no one. By God's help, if the people utter one word of protest, I will draw the sword and leave not one of them alive."[116] The plan worked, at least in the larger towns and cities where the congregational prayers presented the new regime with an excellent opportunity to herd the male population and employ the argument of power to convince them to convert. To ensure that was no relapse the ritual cursing of the first three caliphs was instituted and armed officials patrolled the streets with orders to execute anyone who did not approvingly join in the heaping of abuse. Other than the Sunnis, Sufi orders also endured persecution at the hands of the Safavids. Shah Ismail was in theory as well as in practice a "theocratic and absolute ruler."[117]

Another way to explain Shah Ismail's power is that he was an absolute ruler *because* of the theocratic nature of the Safavid dispensation. The Qizilbash loyalists were fanatical in their determination to execute their spiritual master's orders for if they fell trying to obey him they were assured a place in paradise.[118] The willingness of the Qizilbash to go into battle lightly armored and throw themselves at the enemy gave them a morale advantage over the petty warlords of Mongol-Timurid Persia. The terror that these loyalists were able to generate was quite considerable and for the petty rulers and warlords (*Muluk u't-Tawaif*) irresistible for "[n]one of them long stood in Shah Ismail's path."[119] Rebellious warlords faced dire consequences as Rais Muhammad Kora found out to his peril after having briefly seized control of Yazd. Ismail's forces retook the city and crushed his rebellion. Kora was put in a cage after being smeared with honey and eventually executed at Isfahan. The idea was to terrorize petty rulers into maintaining their submission and making it clear that while the odd rebellion might surprise the new regime, retribution was certain. The Qizilbash commanders and soldiers worshipped the Safavid Shah and were "willing to die for their master."[120] The Kurds, Lurs, assorted Mongol and Timurid warlords, and the Sunni ulema, were flattened by the Safavid's fanaticism fuelled steamroller.

While the fanaticism of the Qizilbash was one of the key sources of strength for the Safavids, the organization of a bureaucracy and a praetorian guard helped the regime stabilize. The ancient Persian tradition of administration flowered once again and it was in the bureaucracy that Iranians predominated while the army was dominated by the Qizilbash. However, both the men of the sword and the men of the pen were the Shah's personal servants for "[a]nyone who held office in the state was considered to be the slave of the Shah: his property, his life and the lives of his children, were at the disposal of the Shah, who held the absolute power of 'loosing and binding', to use the terminology of that time."[121]

The Shah's ability to exercise absolute power depended on his personal qualities as a ruler and his ability to manipulate rivalries within the state apparatus.[122] The Qizilbash tribes that provided the military strength of the state were fractious and semi-nomadic. Shah Ismail rewarded their loyalty with grants of land as revenue assignments in exchange for which they continued to furnish troops. The Shah could take these assignments away and give them to any other tribe or tribesmen. By circulating the land revenue assignments within a particular tribe or clan internal rivalries could be encouraged and the Shah's power assured. An added precaution was the retention of a 3000 strong royal guard for the ruler's personal security and enforcing orders, but without effective leadership even these troops were potentially a threat to the ruler. An illustration of this can be found in the example of the Tekelu tribe of Qizilbash.

Under Muhammad Khan Tekelu they rose to prominence during the reign of Shah Tahmasp (r. 1524–1576). Muhammad Khan Tekelu was noted for his fanatical loyalty to the Shah and rose to be governor of Herat and Khorasan in 1536–37. Muhammad Khan Tekelu even executed his own rebellious tribesmen when they sought protection with him in 1531. The next generation of Tekelu, led by Qazeq Khan Tekelu, was patronized by Shah Tahmasp, given Muhammad Khan Tekelu's loyalty. However there was trouble within the tribe as in 1564, two of Qazeq Khan Tekelu's younger brothers betrayed him by warning Shah Tahmasp against a likely rebellion. Qazeq Khan Tekelu had apparently become drunk with power as the governor of Herat and Khorasan and started to raise his own corps of slave soldiers. In 1565, Shah Tahmasp sent a military force to eliminate Qazeq Khan Tekelu. The force succeeded, aided by intrigues within the Tekelu tribe, and the younger brothers, Ahmad Beg and Musayyb Beg, were granted official positions, though not in Herat and Khorasan, which were now placed under Ustajlu governors. In the chaos that followed Shah Tahmasp's death, the Tekelu did not fare well and aligned against the dominant court faction, with the result that in 1586, many Tekelu amirs were killed in a battle against royal forces. Later, in 1596–97, Shah Abbas I, ordered ". . . the final destruction of the Tekelu tribe as such, which was achieved by royal order by means of a well-planned and well-conducted massacre" concentrated in Hamadan where the Chingezi Turk governor was more than happy to win the Shah's favor.[123]

Shah Ismail died in 1524 leaving his ten-year old son, Shah Tahmasp, in charge. Due to Shah Tahmasp's youth the Qizilbash fought each other to dominate the court. It wasn't until 1533 that Tahmasp was able to assert his authority though he did so with a ruthlessness and vigor that Shah Ismail would have commended. Taking advantage of rivalries within the Qizilbash, Tahmasp managed to purge by execution the most powerful commanders and chieftains and replace them with men noted for their personal loyalty. In order to enhance his own power, Tahmasp developed marital relations between the Safavid dynasty and leading tribesmen but also hedged against the military power of the Qizilbash as he took a page out of the Ottoman book and employed slaves, typically from Georgia, as soldiers and spies. Thus, slaves, Qizilbash, and Iranian bureaucrats, came to constitute the three pillars of the Safavid regime under Tahmasp.[124] In the 1550s and 1560s the theocratic fervor of Safavid absolutism was directed against the Nuqtavi heresy by massacring or exiling as much of the sect as possible. Tahmasp probably saw in the Nuqtavis a mirror image of the Safavid order during its rise to temporal power, and, like the Achaemenids and Sassanids, decided to take to no chances.

Tahmasp's greatest fear was that one of his sons would overthrow him. To keep factions at court guessing Tahmasp refused to nominate a successor. Prince Haider was the apparent favorite and enjoyed the support of the royal slaves and the powerful Ustajlu tribe. Another son, prince Ismail had been locked away in jail by his father but many of the Qizilbash hoped to install him as the ruler and curtail the power of the slaves and Ustajlu. When Tahmasp died in 1576 all hell broke loose as the Qizilbash freed Ismail and placed him on the throne, liquidating Haider and his backers. Shah Ismail II (r. 1576–1577), however, had become warped on account of his long confinement and was vengeful and extremely paranoid. Hundreds of Safavid sufis were massacred, while two of his younger brothers were murdered and a third was blinded. Shortly before he died in November 1577, quite possibly from poison, Shah Ismail II had ordered the execution of his remaining male relatives. His death stayed the order but triggered another succession crisis.

This time, the harem party gained the upper hand with Shah Sultan Muhammad a puppet in the hands of Khair-al Nisa Begum. Khair-al Nisa had her rivals, Peri Khan Khanum and Ismail II's infant son, killed and made her eldest son, Prince Hamza regent. The Qizilbash amirs revolted, killed Khair-al Nisa begum, but kept Hamza on as the regent. The weakness at the center prompted major religious and tribal rebellions in the 1580s, some led by Sufis claiming messianic powers, and others involving the Lur tribesmen from the Zargos mountains and the Kurds. These rebellions were suppressed with characteristic brutality but the inability of the Qizilbash to govern the state as a corporate body encouraged further disturbances. Internal divisions combined with the arbitrary nature of power led to violence when one faction tried to dominate the court. If this chaos, however, went unchecked for much long, Safavid Persia could well disintegrate. The Qizilbash amirs then threw their support behind Prince Abbas, son of the blind Prince Muhammad Khodabanda and a grandson of Shah Tahmasp. Abbas had been sent away from court when only eighteen months old and appointed titular governor of Herat. There he remained for sixteen years before making a triumphant return in October 1588, after Prince Hamza was killed. Shah Abbas "showed no mercy towards the amirs who had backed his younger brother Abu Taleb, and whom he held responsible for the murder of Prince Hamza. He had them disarmed and brought one by one in the audience hall of the palace, where they were killed."[125]

Shah Abbas then took steps to rid himself of his *vakil* Murshid Quli Khan and cut the Qizilbash down to size. Murshid Quli Khan never suspected that the young ruler would betray him and felt confident enough to take Isfahan as his revenue assignment and double the tax rates. This oppressive act led the Shah to call on other Qizilbash amirs "to rally to him on the basis of *Shahsevan* or 'love of the Shah'."[126] Those officials accused of disloyalty to the Shah soon found themselves hunted by loyalists appointed to their positions with the instructions that they should send the severed heads of the regime's enemies to the court by way of a joining report. On July 23, 1589, Murshid Quli Khan was murdered in the Shah's presence and a general purge of the *vakil*'s supporters ensued. Shah Abbas increased the strength of his personal guard from 3,000 to 12,000, expanded the slave-soldier corps to include cavalry, and raised a force of 12,000 musketeers recruited from the Iranian peasantry. These measures diluted the Qizilbash's military importance to the state though they remained a vital element in the regime's social base and campaigning strength.

In 1591, Shah Abbas appointed the brilliant Hatem Beg Ordubadi as the Grand Vizier. Hatem Beg was entrusted with the task of reorganizing the financial administration of the realm in order to provide the resources needed to maintain an expanded military, a slave corps and a centralized bureaucracy. Even more extraordinary than Hatem Beg's brilliance was his ability to survive in the toxic atmosphere of the Safavid court for he retained Shah Abbas's favor for twenty years. Among the most important changes introduced was the creation of additional crown provinces that were directly administered by the Shah's appointees and paid taxes directly into the central treasury.[127] Hatem Beg also relied on slaves to fill senior administrative positions such as governorships so that by the end of Shah Abbas's reign eight out of fourteen of the major provinces were headed by royal *ghulam*s. A revenue census was carried out in order to assess taxes more fairly and productively while patrol men or *rahdar*s were appointed to secure trade on major roads. Hatem Beg proved industrially efficient in dealing with the day-to-day running of the state and it was estimated by one trader that the vizier dealt with 200 petitions each morning and even hours of taxing work failed to disrupt his impenetrable serenity.[128]

One major problem that had the potential to cause even Hatem Beg alarm was the resurgent Nuqtavis. The Nuqtavis, mentioned above, believed in cyclical time and denied the resurrection. With the approach of the first Islamic millennium in 1591–92, their propaganda intensified and it was declared that the next millennium was going to be dominated by the Nuqtavis. What made this sect especially dangerous was that since Shah Tahmasp's repression it had gone underground with Nuqtavis pretending to be orthodox Shia Muslims in public. Darvish Khusrau of Qazvin, the Nuqtavi leader, thus claimed in public to be orthodox and many Qizilbash, bitter at Shah Abbas for his curtailment of their clout at court, became Khusrau's disciples. Shah Abbas appears to have consorted with suspected Nuqtavis in order to get them to reveal their real identity and agenda. Darvish Khusrau was delighted at the prospect of making such a powerful convert while Shah Abbas seems to have played the role of an earnest disciple to perfection. Khusrau's disciples revealed their true beliefs and told Shah Abbas that come the new year, 1002 (September 27, 1593), "he would lose his throne to a Nuqtavi disciple."[129] What triggered the crackdown on the Nuqtavis was their leader's arrogant offer to send Shah Abbas troops to help deal with a Lur rebellion. The crackdown, however, was methodical and was probably prepared well in advance. It began with a surgical strike on Qazvin[130] that resulted in the arrest of Khusrau and the killing or capture of many of his closest disciples. Khusrau was then tried by the orthodox Shia ulema for his heretical beliefs and found guilty. Shah Abbas then devised a particularly painful death for Khusrau and "He was tied by his throat to the saddle of a camel and dragged around the city, after which the body was exposed to public view for a week."[131] This accomplished, the government launched a general massacre of suspected Nuqtavis on the ground that they were all heretics like their leader. Shah Abbas personally led this campaign, his "ruthless purge of the Nuqtavi ... prompted by his realization that they were an extremist religious movement which was aiming at political power, just as the Safavid movement itself had done so successfully."[132] In order to shore up the ideological base of the Safavid regime, Shah Abbas identified the Shia ulema as the rightful custodians of morality and legality and set about patronizing them through donations and endowments of land.

Success against internal enemies was accompanied by victories against Uzbeks and Ottomans, duly followed by largesse for both priests and the people. After victory over the Uzbeks in 1598, the tax on sheep in Khorasan was abolished, taxes lowered by 25 percent throughout the realm and all taxes in Isfahan remitted for one year. Following victory over the Ottomans in 1607, made possible by the fielding of a 60,000 strong fighting force, Shah Abbas donated his estates and private library to the Shrine of Imam Reza at Mashad. It appeared that aligning with the orthodox Shia ulema had after all helped secure divine favor.

The suppression of internal rebellions also furnished opportunities to demonstrate the power of the regime. Thus, in the 1590s, the major silk-producing region of Gilan, was subjected to extensive state terrorism. A special squad of five hundred enforcers used to police Qazvin were sent ahead of the regular army to massacre the locals into submissions. Khan Ahmad, the leader of the Gilanis, fled while his Safavid wife and daughter were taken by Shah Abbas for the royal harem. In 1595, the region was annexed and made a province of the empire. In 1614, expecting a renewal of hostilities with the Ottomans, 15,000 families were deported from the Caucasus to help populate the less vulnerable interior. In 1616, following the defeat of a 15,000 strong Persian force in Georgia, a general massacre of the Georgians was launched in which 60,000 were killed and 100,000 deported to the interior. In 1625, another Georgian rebellion would be crushed and Ottoman attempts to retake Baghdad would be frustrated. In examining these figures it is fruitful to bear in mind that the population of Safavid Persia was about 6 million under Shah Abbas.

In making the orthodox Shia ulema part of the ideocratic complex of the Safavid Persian Empire, suppressing rebellions, curtailing the power of the Qizilbash, beating the Ottomans and Uzbeks, setting up a sound administration and putting the state finances in remarkably good order, Shah Abbas was eminently successful. One problem, however, that vexed Shah Abbas was controlling his sons and providing for the succession of one of them to the throne. In the Persian tradition of arbitrary rule all the ruler's sons had a claim on the throne. The Qizilbash amirs, of course, regarded only Safavid royal princes as legitimate successors but regularly shifted loyalties from one prince to another. Shah Abbas had alienated many of the Qizilbash and, in shifting emphasis towards the orthodox Shia ulema, had also distanced himself from the Safavid Sufi base. The practice until Shah Abbas was that royal princes were placed under guardians and sent to administer provinces. The idea was to train the princes in administration, politics, and warfare, so that if at a later stage they assumed power, they would be able to provide effective leadership. While the efficiency argument militated in favor of keeping this practice in force, from the perspective of stability, there were problems. Royal princes sent out to the provinces gathered around them their own coteries of supporters. Each clique had a vested interest in propelling *its* prince to the throne as soon as possible and using the arbitrary power of the sovereign to reconfigure patronage relations within the empire to its own advantage. Shah Abbas thought it best to stop appointing princes as governors, but during the war with the Ottomans in 1614, Prince Safi fell victim to his father's fears, fanned by court intrigue, that the prince was in a hurry to sit on the throne. Shah Abbas had Prince Safi assassinated while his other two sons were later blinded and it was decided that all royal princes would be confined to the royal harem and kept under house arrest. This Safavid version of the Ottoman cage[133] was designed to prevent rebellion and ensure that royal princes did not acquire power bases independent of the incumbent at the cost of the competence and training of a future sovereign.

Shah Abbas's death in 1629 did not lead to a sudden decline in the empire's fortunes or catastrophe. The imperial bureaucracy and army combined with the officially patronized ulema provided the regime with enough of a base to keep the state going while the Qizilbash were no longer in a position to dominate politics in the absence of a strong ruler. Shah Abbas's financial reforms, encouragement of trade, and internal pacification, produced a modest prosperity. There were, however, reversals, which took their toll as Baghdad fell to the Ottomans in 1638 and the Timurids of India repeatedly managed to threaten Kandahar. Shah Abbas II (1642–66) tried to meet these challenges by converting Qazvin, Gilan, Mazandaran, Yazd, Kirman, Khorasan, and Azerbaijan, into crown provinces, but such centralization could do only so much. With a population of perhaps 8 million by the mid-1600s, Safavid Persia was dwarfed by Timurid India (100–150 million) and much smaller than the Ottoman Empire's 20–30 million subjects. The Safavids struggled to generate the wealth they needed to compete with much larger and better-placed rivals. The growing reliance on slaves and peasants to fill the ranks of the army, as opposed to the Qizilbash, also meant that the quality of the Safavid army deteriorated. Under Shah Sulaiman (1666–1694) and Shah Sultan Hussain (1694–1722), Safavid decline accelerated as the rulers failed to provide the leadership needed by the empire. By the early 1700s the authority of the Shah was collapsing, tribal Afghan and Persian rebellions were brewing, and the breakdown of order, gathered steam. Shah Abbas I's reforms, particularly the isolation of princes, ensured that the later Safavids could not provide dynamic leadership. In 1722, the Afghans deposed the last Safavid ruler, set about despoiling Isfahan, and triggered a war of succession that would rage until the advent of the Qajar dynasty in 1796.

In terms of its culture of power Safavid Persia's governance was highly arbitrary and driven by ideological-religious fervor. This was accompanied by substantial centralization or concentration of power at the imperial court that was in turn mediated through a bureaucracy and army. The Safavid Shah ruled by virtue of his personal qualities of leadership and did not have any inherent right to succession by seniority or consensus. Rulers seized power by eliminating their rivals, moral relationships within the power elite were almost impossible, and the arbitrary nature of state power remained even if the ruler proved personally weak for in that event his clique would do the governing for him, albeit in his name. During the early Safavid period the Qizilbash were the most important players though after Shah Abbas I, slaves, Iranian Tajik civil servants, and orthodox Shia ulema, gained in power and prestige. The Safavids found the Qizilbash very difficult to control and while strong rulers could manipulate rivalries within the tribes to their own advantage, a weak ruler would quickly be overwhelmed and chaos would start to engulf the state. Thus, while the morale of the Qizilbash tribes and their special spiritual connection to the Safavid ruler as their disciples was instrumental in restoring order and converting the population to Shia Islam, their volatility meant that once internal peace was restored they had outlived their usefulness.

The Safavid state seems to have been highly effective by the standards of the day. In spite of its small population and lack of adequate domestic sources of gold and silver,[134] Safavid Persia successfully warded off Ottoman, Uzbek and Mughal military pressure for almost 200 years, while conducting an impressive international diplomacy and maintaining internal peace and security. Major roads and trade arteries were remarkably safe owing to police patrols and "merchants, even in small caravans, could travel without need for armed guards, at least until the late Safavid period, when security conditions deteriorated."[135] Trade was quite substantial given that in the 1600s, some 20,000–25,000 camels carrying textiles from Timurid India arrived in Isfahan annually.[136] The ability of the state to concentrate land revenues through extension of crown lands also points towards effective administration, as does the marginalization of the Qizilbash during the reign of Shah Abbas I. Another vital indication is the ability of the state to convert the population to Shia Islam, the vicious crackdowns on Sufi orders and religious deviants, and the relocation/resettlement of hundreds of thousands of people. The contemporary Timurid rulers of India, their enormous wealth and demographic base notwithstanding, come across as indolent liberals when compared to their counterparts in Safavid Persia.

The resilience and effectiveness of the Safavid state cannot be explained through economic structure or demography. Safavid Persia was much poorer than Timurid India or the Ottoman Sultanate and had a relatively small population. It was also exposed on three fronts to inland warfare and much of its territory was wasteland. The explanation then seems to lie in human agency, particularly religious fanaticism and organizational genius. Safavid Persia was a regional powerhouse due to the kinetics of its religious base, the ruthlessness and charisma of its rulers, and its superior administrative organization, which was greatly admired by the Timurids in India who eagerly sought to appoint Persian migrants to high offices. Forced by the poverty of their circumstances to do more with less, the Safavids rose to the challenge and became exemplars of ideocratic arbitrary rule and recreated with great drive the behavioral norms and administrative design of earlier Persian continental bureaucratic empires.

QAJARS AND PAHLAVIS

As the later Safavids "gave less and less attention to government", and left power in the hands of their servants and favorites "a miasma of inefficiency and neglect descended on the system."[137] Shah Sultan Hossein, the last Safavid ruler, had, in 1706, sent a retinue of 60,000 pilgrims to Qom and Mashad causing huge expense at a time when Isfahan, a vast metropolis of more than half a million people, was suffering from food shortages. The trouble was that due to the ruler's weakness "Any individual among the court officials that appeared to be about to take decisive action against the various threats to the State immediately brought upon him the hostility of the other court factions."[138] Safavid military decline and failure to cope with the Afghans was also due to a lack of leadership, which is absolutely lethal for an arbitrary autocracy. In 1722, an Afghan rebellion placed "Shah" Mahmud of the Ghilzai tribe on the throne. Over a hundred members of the Safavid royal family were killed, the royal guards were massacred, and the city of Isfahan subjected to the avarice and violence of its Afghan overlords. So terrible was the plunder that by 1726, Isfahan's population had been reduced to 100,000. The Persians did manage to rally but they did so under the leadership of Nader Khan Afshar who formally declared himself Nader Shah and became the founder of the short-lived Afsharid dynasty in 1732.

Nader Shah was single-minded in his focus on acquiring and provisioning a large standing army. By 1736, at the height of his power, this army was 200,000 strong, and, compared to the population (maximum 6 or 7 million) represented a very large force. Paying for this army was very difficult and Nader Shah tried to make it finance itself by waging wars and plundering others. His signature success in this effort came in the 1739 Indian campaign. Delhi was taken, and wealth amounting to 700 million Rupees, or nearly 90 million pounds sterling in the currency of the day, was looted and brought back to Persia.[139] The wealth looted was so great that Nader Shah proclaimed a three-year tax holiday as he had enough to maintain his military. The loot from India did not, however, stimulate any qualitative changes in trade or industry for Persian society lacked the institutions and practices to benefit from a wealth transfer that was, at any rate, consumed by the military. The respite from confiscatory taxation, did, however, allow a modest revival of domestic trade and agriculture. This was sorely needed as in the years before the invasion of India, Nader Shah's government had centralized all land revenue leaving the provinces with the bare minimum needed to keep their administrations going, and brutalized the commercial classes. The merchants of Kerman, Bandar Abbas, and Isfahan, were particularly vulnerable to Nader Shah's propensity to arbitrarily levy taxes and then use torture and imprisonment to get the wealthy to pay up. This extortion helped pay the army in the short-term but depleted Persia's capacity to generate wealth needed by the state in the long-term.

Nader Shah also seems to have become increasingly paranoid and greedy with each passing month. His success in India made him even more fearful of rivals and led him to accuse his son Reza Qoli Khan, of conspiring to have him assassinated. Reza was stripped of his offices and eventually blinded on his father's orders. Additionally, campaigns in Daghestan exhausted the treasury and led to the re-imposition of large tax demands. The ulema, already strong-armed by Nader Shah into toeing the line, something which included easing the more vociferous practices of Shia Islam to placate the Sunni soldiery, could offer neither counsel nor relief. By 1746, Nader Shah's "cruelty and avarice had become obsessive, and as soon as he arrived in Isfahan, he set about beating the citizens to get their money."[140] Leaving Isfahan in February 1746, Nader Shah toured the country en route to Mashad and at each stop along the way local officials were brutalized and forced to pay whatever sums they were accused of stealing from their ruler. By this time, Nader Shah's network of spies was feeding its master's paranoia and while he amassed a spectacular personal fortune of 4.5 million *toman*s of gold and silver "a great storm of poverty and misery" engulfed his empire.[141] The following year, Nader Shah was assassinated by his officers and chaos erupted anew across the realm.

If Nader Shah's rule represented arbitrary rule at its worst, the rise of the Qajars, who claimed Mongol descent, offered some hope that order might be restored. In December 1781, under Aqa Mohammad Khan, the Qajar tribesmen began a program of conquest. By 1788, Gilan, Khorasan, Qazvin and Yazd were in Qajar hands while control of Isfahan was being hotly contested. While Aqa Mohammad Khan provided political leadership, his brother, Jafar Qoli Khan, was the commander of the Qajar army. As military successes piled up, however, Aqa Mohammad Khan became fearful of his brother and suspected him of coveting the leadership. Jafar Qoli Khan was consequently assassinated in 1791 on his brother's orders by "special officers of the court. . . ."[142] In his youth, Aqa Mohammad Khan had been captured and castrated by an Afsharid rival and was thus no stranger to the kill-or-be-killed ethos of Persian politics or to the violence and suffering that arbitrary power was the cause and the consequence of. Aqa Mohammad Khan also appreciated the value of terror in restoring the writ of the state. In the winter of 1794–95, after Kerman fell to the Qajar forces, Aqa Mohammad Khan "ordered the slaughter of the inhabitants. . . .About 8000 women and children were distributed as slaves among the army; all the men were either killed or deprived of their sight."[143] Later in 1795, Tiflis was sacked and 15,000 "boys, girls and young women" were enslaved.[144] Aqa Mohammad Khan was also very acquisitive when it came to jewels, especially those reputed to have been owned by royalty in the past. He took great offense at anyone else possessing such jewels and made it a point to insist that they be made over to him as gifts.[145] Nader Shah's grandson, Shahrokh Shah, was tortured until he revealed where the remnants of the Afsharid stash were located. Jewels aside, Aqa Mohammad Khan, also took the precaution of taking "women and sons as hostages from all the emirs of Khorasan" and collected them in Tehran.[146]

Initially, the strength of the Qajars came from their tribal army, some 60,000 strong in 1795, and the ruthlessness and ability of their leaders in pacifying the country. Once in power, the dynasty lavished funds on securing support from the orthodox Shia ulema and distributed subsidies to some 100,000 people to win them over to the Qajar side. The Qajars also reconstituted the state apparatus with four main ministries for establishment, finance, correspondence, and military. The vizier in charge of the establishment also acted as the prime minister and enjoyed seniority over the other ministers. Governors ruled provinces, tribal leaders ruled their people with the support of the central government and district governors (*boulkat*) handled the day-to-day running of the state at the local level in tandem with the village headmen. The effectiveness of the Qajar dynasty's power is debated in academic circles as is the nature of that power. One view is that the Qajar dynasty lacked a highly-developed modern bureaucracy and thus ruled primarily by cooption and influence.[147] Another view is that the Qajar, like previous dynasties, were highly arbitrary and under strong rulers, like Aqa Mohammad Khan, wielded concentrated power effectively.[148] What is interesting is that to an outside observer familiar with the patterns of governance in South Asia the debate appears more complementary than contradictory since both views cite numerous instances of the arbitrary exercise of power either by the Shah or by other elements in the society on basis of their accord with the ruling dynasty.

It also helps to divide, for the purpose of understanding this problem, Qajar Persia into three broad zones. The first zone was that of the major cities and in it the power of the state was most visible and perhaps effective. The second zone comprises the settled rural hinterland and here landlords with rights of possession and taxation derived from the state, ruled over peasants who paid them rent. The third zone is that of the tribal regions where tribal leaders were dominant and, in times when the state was weak, in a position to directly challenge the state. The population of Qajar Persia was between 6 and 10 million and of these about one-third were tribal, perhaps one-tenth lived in the cities, and the rest were peasants and rural tenants. The Shah's power was strongest in the cities and in the settled agricultural areas but it appears that by the late 1800s "tribal Khans became incorporated into the state system of control."[149] Mayors appointed by the

Shah from the local population ruled the towns and cities while a police force under the control of *darugha*s maintained order. This police force "was often brutal and venal and although shopkeepers paid a monthly rate to prevent robberies, the police themselves could be connected to the robbers."[150]

The tribal leaders were no aristocrats in the European sense of the term. In the case of the prominent Bakhtiyari tribe, for example, each male scion competed against others as there was no recognized mode of succession within the tribe meaning that "Aspiration to greater power required outside assistance."[151] Holding lands outside the tribal regions, which were pastoral or semi-pastoral, was critical to the power of the tribal leaders in terms of having the wealth to secure clients and supporters within the tribe. These lands, however, could only be acquired with the support of the state and made the tribal leaders vulnerable to manipulation and coercion by the central government. The most prominent tribal khans were "landlords and government officials", the two being sides of the same coin, and thus linked the tribes to the state.[152] The chaotic nature of politics within the tribal peoples meant that the Shah could play a decisive role through grants of land and official positions. The central government was often in a position to use the tribal leaders thus ensnared "to collect taxes, maintain order, and conscript" soldiers.[153] Further compromising the tribal social base and reducing its capacity to preserve tribal autonomy were the twin practices of polygamy and division of inheritances, in contrast to the European practices of monogamy and primogeniture.[154] The combination of large numbers of offspring and marriages served to intensify rivalries within the tribes. Taqi Khan, for example, killed his uncle to seize control of the leadership of the Bakhtiyari, only to be abandoned by his family members and supporters when the state demanded he pay back taxes and, upon his non-compliance, accused him of treason for being in communication with the exiled uncle of Mohammad Shah Qajar. Ali Raza Khan, the son of Taqi Khan's murdered uncle, was named the new tribal leader and Taqi Khan's supporters were killed or captured. Taqi Khan was arrested and sentenced to life imprisonment, eventually dying in 1851 after ten years in jail. Later Bakhtiyari chiefs set up a loose bureaucratic administration of their own modeled on the Qajar state apparatus. This, however, in no way impeded the Qajars from executing the Bakhtiyari chief in 1882. Indeed, "the Bakhtiyari cannot be considered apart from the state"[155] and this episode, as well as others like it, "underscored the weakness" of the tribes "when confronted by a determined central government."[156]

Whatever doubt exists about the effectiveness of Qajar power across Persian territories and demographic groups, at the center itself, there was no doubt that the Shah and the court elite exercised power arbitrarily. The Qajar Shah, like the rulers of earlier dynasties, held power by divine favor and was "not bound by any earthly contract."[157] There was no established norm for succession and each son could stake a claim in his father's lifetime, which made it almost impossible to maintain moral relationships even within the royal family. The reigning monarch used this ambiguity to play his sons off against each other however much uncertainty such politics might create:

> Nevertheless, it is extremely instructive that Naser-al-Din Shah—who was by no means the worst example of an arbitrary ruler of Iran—almost withdrew the right of succession from his son and heir-designate, Mozaffar-al-Din Mirza (the governor general of Azerbaijan) and sold it to his other son, Zel al-Soltan, the governor general of Isfahan. He wrote to the former that the latter had offered him [one million *tomans*] for the position. Zel was well known both for his shrewdness and lack of scruple. Mozaffar was lucky, therefore, that in reply to his father the Shah, his able secretary, Amir Nagan Garrusi, warned that Zel might well spend another [five million *tomans*] for the Shah's position itself.[158]

The absence of moral relationships and the arbitrary nature of the Shah's power meant that members of the elite had "no choice, but at the slightest thought, imagination or supposition of rebellion, irrespective of who it might be, to try to put it down forthwith and not to hesitate even for a moment."[159]

One rebellion that helped the Qajar dynasty and the orthodox Shia ulema come closer together was the Babi rebellion of the 1840s and 1850s. The story of the rebellion is one that ought to be familiar in its pattern to students of Persian history. In 1844, Sayyid Ali Muhammad, a merchant from Shiraz, claimed to have become the gateway (*bab*) to the Twelfth Imam and the receptor of divine knowledge and soon he had disciples spreading his message, which caught on in a number of places. As the movement grew in strength its leaders became more confident and broke with the pretence of falling within the ambit of the officially patronized Shia Islam. This set off a cycle of repression and rebellion in Mazandaran, Nayroz, Zanjan, Shiraz, Qazvin, Isfahan and Tehran. In some cases, as in Zanjan, it took the state forces nine months to crush the rebellion leaving some 3000 dead.[160] The government mobilized the orthodox ulema, the city administrations, levies and the regular army to crush the rebellion, which looked dangerously like an extremist religious movement aiming for power. Had such a movement been launched in the chaotic aftermath of Safavid collapse or Afsharid excesses it may well have succeeded but in the mid-1800s the Qajars had sufficient strength and organization to dispatch the rebels to the other side of the gateway. This episode, like others before it and after it, including the politics of the Constitutional Revolution (1906), helped underscore that the flipside of arbitrary power was delusional and fanatical resistance:

> During the millennia of arbitrary rule, the practice and theory of righteousness, self-sacrifice and martyrdom, which belonged to the realms of religion and mysticism, had also been extended to resistance against

unjust arbitrary rulers. People would fight for a cause often without regard to the worldly interests of themselves and others, and defeat, death and even total annihilation would not matter at all because they too were seen as means, if not the only means, of redemption. There was no politics and no notion of conflict management: there was either win or lose. If the rebels won, they would probably become oppressors themselves and lose their previous legitimacy. If they lost, they would be regarded as martyrs irrespective of the mistakes they had made.[161]

Qajar decline and the emergence of the Pahlavi dynasty was due to a number of failures on part of the former. The first was that the Qajar military organization remained a ramshackle affair with irregular payment of salaries, massive corruption within the army, and excessive brutality towards the enlisted men. The Qajars also did not undertake policies aimed at modernizing their country, even to the limited extent of military reforms and support industries and services. The second was that the Qajar dynasty lacked the ideological dynamism and religious fervor of the Safavids. Relying on their tribesmen, patronage, and support from the Shia ulema, the Qajars were more of a traditional absolute monarchy and their leaders, though at times effective, never possessed the inspirational qualities of the great Safavid rulers. The third was that the Qajars sought to maintain their country's independence through playing the Russians and British off against each other. Unlike the Safavids, who also conducted a vigorous diplomacy with the Ottomans, Timurids and European powers, however, the Qajars negotiated from a steadily deteriorating position on account of domestic underdevelopment. This policy was partially successful but it ended up turning Iran into a zone of competition between Britain and Russia and both powers started interfering to protect and advance their interests. Fourth, soon after the Constitutional Revolution of 1906, the British and Russians decided to temporarily put aside their differences and work together to contain the rising power of Hohenzollern Germany. This change pulled the Persian rug out from under the feet of Qajar dynasty's diplomatic balancing act. Finally, the outbreak of the First World War resulted in Iran being dragged into the conflict between the Ottoman Sultanate, allied to Germany, and the Russians and British. Unable to cope with the situation, the Qajar leadership seems to have abdicated all responsibility, leaving the country vulnerable to the depredations of outside powers, internal fragmentation and economic collapse. It was in this context that new leadership emerged from the only professional military force in the country—the Cossack division.

The Cossack division comprised 8,000 Persian infantrymen, about 3,000 cavalry, and was officered by 64 Russian officers and 202 Persian officers and NCOs. It was deployed in Tehran, Isfahan, Mashad, Hamadan, Gilan, Mazanderan, Ardabil, and Urmiyah. Compared to the rest of the military, the Cossack division was much better trained and equipped and enjoyed higher morale. By 1920, the situation in Iran was dire. 100,000 people had died of starvation during the war, 10,000 farming villages lay abandoned, millions of heads of cattle had been requisitioned by the Russian and British forces, the state was financially bankrupt and warlords were asserting themselves as the center weakened. The constitutional government had no power while the last Qajar ruler was not interested in affairs of state. Riza Khan, as the chief of the Cossack division, saw his opportunity to seize power and took it in 1921, becoming the prime minister. Between 1921 and 1926, Riza Khan took steps to build himself up as an alternative to the Qajar ruler and was convinced that he alone knew what Iran's problems were and how to go about resolving them. Having strong-armed the cabinet to give the army direct control over the Ministry of Indirect Taxation, Riza Khan also benefited from Ahmad Shah Qajar's decision, in 1923, to proceed to Europe leaving the prime minister in charge of affairs at home. Riza Khan then financed a media campaign that spread propaganda in favor of abolishing the monarchy altogether and making Iran a republic. Conservatives rallied to the defense of monarchy but were persuaded by Qajar non-seriousness to consider a change of dynasty. In the meanwhile, Riza Khan launched punitive expeditions to reassert control over areas that had become practically independent. At the military level Riza Khan divided the army into five divisions and placed loyal officers of the Cossack division in charge. The result was that more and more people came to see Riza Khan as a strongman who had emerged from obscurity to restore order and place Iran on the path of modernization. Success, in other words, brought legitimacy and Qajar leaders, Shia ulema, journalists and professionals, started to bandwagon. In 1926, the Majlis, or national assembly, voted unanimously via a secret ballot to replace the Qajar dynasty with Riza Khan's Pahlavi dynasty. Riza Shah Pahlavi, as he was now known, moved quickly to establish his arbitrary rule, centralize power, crush opposition, and reduce all nascent non-executive institutions to mere ciphers. By 1928, the new Shah was acting as a classical arbitrary ruler especially keen to introduce changes that would make the state machinery more powerful.

Riza Shah's rule was "absolute and arbitrary" and was made even more dangerous by the introduction of modern technology into a medieval culture of power.[162] For dissenters "There was literally no where to hide" and the police, army, gendarmerie, and intelligence organization, were tasked with eliminating opposition ranging from nomads who didn't want to be resettled to tea and coffee house aficionados who engaged in "harmless gossip about the Shah or his policies."[163] The Shah was proclaimed through "crude and ugly public propaganda" as "the symbol of perfection" and a "god incarnate".[164] The Shah regarded the state as his personal estate and expropriated the property of landlords and businessmen at will, while "state institutions" became "instruments for the promotion of the Shah's public wishes and private property."[165] The state factories and the banking system became notionally modern means of perpetuating the ancient

Persian practice of arbitrary rule through patronage and oppression. The peasantry, about 60 percent of the population, was in particular victimized by state procurement monopolies, regressive taxes, and major expenditure in a few main cities. While 13,000 kilometers of new roads were no doubt a boon, the trans-Iran railway project was "an unmitigated economic folly paid for by taxes on tea and sugar."[166] This vast railway project "connected Tehran to Riza Shah's own province of Mazandaran—where he had acquired extensive estates, and was about to confiscate many more" while "beyond it, on the edge of Iranian Turcomenistan" lay "the lucrative cotton-producing estates he was to purchase, usurp or requisition."[167]

Even the most favorable account of Riza Shah's rule is compelled by the volume of examples to concede the arbitrary and despotic nature of the Pahlavi regime. Indeed, Riza Shah was proud of his arbitrariness as he regarded it as the expression of justice flowing naturally from his regal disposition. In November 1929, when a murder was committed in Tehran and brought to the Shah's notice the city police chief, General Muhammad Daroghi, was informed that he would "be shot on the scene of the crime if the murderer was not apprehended within forty-eight hours."[168] Any one who promoted "the cause of 'freedom'" found that it "was a very unrewarding enterprise during his regime, for nearly all its exponents ended up in prison."[169] The press, to create a feel-good atmosphere, "suppressed all stories of crimes, suicides and motor accidents"[170] while the purging and disgracing of officials was a matter of routine and helped deflect criticism away from the benevolent autocrat to his evil and self-serving servants who were disposable and could be accused of leading the country astray.[171] When the special train sent to transport the Egyptian queen and her daughter, Princess Fauziah, to Tehran suffered battery failure and ran out of food and water "Riza Shah was furious and had the director general of the railroads and numerous other officials arrested."[172] Riza Shah's "secret police was active throughout the country" and reflected its master's maliciousness.[173] There was no recourse to the traditional Persian practices of sanctuary and mediation admitted by all but the most absolute of arbitrary rulers in the past. Under Riza Shah "Hardly anyone dared to plead for clemency" out of "fear of turning his anger and suspicion towards himself."[174] One exception was the crown prince and "No individual other than the young Muhammad Riza Shah could influence" Riza Shah's "decisions and actions."[175] Riza Shah's downfall was occasioned by his tilt in favor of the Axis powers in the early stages of the Second World War, which led to a Soviet invasion of Iran in 1941 and his abdication. By that time about a tenth of the country's agricultural land including "the most productive cash crop producing estates" were Riza Shah's personal property and one of his greatest worries following the Soviet military moves into northern Iran in August 1941 was the future of his lands in the occupied areas.[176]

Between 1941 and 1953, Iran experienced political instability and Great Power interference. The parliament became more assertive and in 1952–53 it seemed that Iran might achieve a modicum of stability as a left-leaning democracy under Mossadeq. Mohammad Riza Shah's henchmen, ably assisted by Montague Woodhouse, Kermit Roosevelt and the MI6-CIA combine, together with royalist elements within Iran, staged a successful counter-revolution. The restoration of monarchical absolutism in 1953 would eventually come to haunt Iran for "the revolution of 1979" was led by people who realized that "If the Shah was ever to be dethroned, there could be no flirtation with constitutional rights, no half-measures, no counter-revolutionaries left to restore Western power in Iran."[177] Rather, "A future revolution would embrace more than five thousand dead" and would be "final, absolute—and unforgiving."[178]

The ferocity, repressiveness, and arbitrariness of the restored Pahlavi monarchy are both well documented and disconcerting even when set against Persian political standards. The twin pillars of the regime were the army, 200,000 strong by 1960, and the civilian bureaucracy, 260,000 strong by 1960. "The Shah" was by then "in complete control of the army and the Savak" and there was "no love lost for the landlords, nor for any of the religious leaders."[179] Although estimates vary, the Savak (State Security and Information Organization) had, at the height of the Shah's power, some 60,000 agents while one third of the adult male population were informers.[180] Other than the Savak, the Special Intelligence Bureau, which was housed within the Niavaran palace, and the J-2 branch of the armed forces, were also employed fulltime in gathering intelligence and eliminating opposition. These organizations went far beyond anything earlier arbitrary rulers, including the founder of the Pahlavi dynasty, had attempted in terms of their scope and effectiveness. Iranians settled abroad and students in foreign universities were especially targeted for surveillance.

Iran's oil wealth as well as its land and capital were at the disposal of the Shah as if they were his personal property. A pliant parliament had restored the Pahlavi's ill-gotten estates with some 2167 villages, employing 235,800 persons, falling directly in the Shah's possession.[181] In sectors other than agriculture, "Few industrial or commercial undertakings" were "launched in Iran without the blessings of the Shah. To secure these blessings, the Shah" was "often made the gift of a share in the ownership of the venture, just as Reza Shah was the recipient of estates from favor-seeking elites."[182]

On the administrative side the Shah was a great believer in expanding the bureaucracy to meet the needs of the expanding bureaucracy—to adapt a famous witticism for the purposes of this discussion. Multiplying the number of bureaucracies, increasing their size, and creating redundancies within the executive arm of the state, all paid for, of course, with oil revenues, led to a phenomenal expansion in the size of the state apparatus, which had swollen to 700,000 employees by 1979. The sheer size of the machinery and the absence of any objective criteria for appointment, promotion or discipline, meant that the Shah's favorites could carve out their own petty estates and were encouraged in their rivalries with other's vying for the ruler's favor.

Even within the Iranian elite, by the late 1960s, some 70% thought that their state had very much or much injustice in it which meant that "the overall level of perceived injustice" was "higher among the Iranian elite than among the French and Italian industrial proletariat."[183] One of the major sources of this sense of injustice was "the realization by the members of the elite, that they exercise[d] virtually no control over their tenure in a given position or over their appointment to any other position" for no "well-established or generally understood criteria for the maintenance of office appear to exist. In fact, the same [was] true for achieving office."[184]

The Shah's fatal mistake in prosecuting his arbitrary rule was his confrontation with the traditionally quiescent Shia ulema and his attempt to impose superficial Westernization on his people who perceived him, quite accurately, as a neo-colonial puppet of the West. Historically, religion had not posed a serious challenge to arbitrary rule unless that rule had become degenerate and ineffective and some religious or dynastic force started to emerge as an alternative. The most successful Persian rulers, with the notable exception of the enlightened Cyrus, were those who brought the religious establishment under state patronage and thus aligned the interests of the throne and pulpit. In exchange, the state-patronized theocrats helped the state by declaring opposition unlawful, encouraging people to accept the existing regime, mobilizing public support in response to rebellions and heresies, but otherwise keeping out of the ruler's way. The ruler's personal lifestyle was nobody's concern—Persian rulers drank, womanized, enjoyed all the luxuries and refinements their age had to offer, hunted, confiscated, pronounced arbitrary judicial verdicts, and engaged in any other behavior they wanted to. As long as the ruler was effective, preserved the independence of the country, and paid formal respect to the official religion, there was no basis for conflict.

Muhammad Riza Shah, however, was seen as a puppet imposed on his people by foreign powers. His management of the state and its resources was woefully whimsical and wasteful and made sustainable only by its vast oil wealth while his ceaseless propaganda about the Light of the Aryans and the Great Civilization made him appear pompous and callous. In spite of this, the break between the Shia ulema and the Shah was not foreordained. The ulema had kept quiet during the Shah's counter-revolution of 1953 and did not protest until the early 1960s. The Shah's growing autocracy, rigging of elections, land reforms, and introduction of legislation giving women the right to vote in local elections, however, led some ulema to criticize the regime. The Shah reacted aggressively, using the secret police to break up gatherings and ordering, in April 1963, "the conscription of seminarians, who until then had been exempt from military service, into the army."[185] With all other means of opposition silenced, Ayatollah Khomeni emerged as the heroic counter-figure to the Shah. Khomeni urged the ulema to abandon quietism and challenge the Shah's regime openly for its subservience to the West and insulting and arrogant attitude towards the religious sentiments of the masses.[186] The regime, by targeting Khomeni, made him the de facto head of the resistance to the Shah's unjust arbitrary rule. The politics of martyrdom and resistance in face of such rule had great emotional and historical resonance amongst the people who, at any rate, had lost confidence in what the state media told them and were tired of the Shah's megalomania and incompetence. Behind an apparently stable façade, publicly lauded by Western governments, the Shah's Iran started to come apart in the 1960s and 1970s. Rioting against the regime and bombings, some 400 of which took place between 1971 and 1975, indicated that a storm was gathering. The Shah tried to strike at the economic support of the Islamists by targeting the conservative bazaar merchants. The 1975/6 anti-profiteering campaign required the mobilization of thousands of the Shah's agents and "approximately 10,000 merchants were imprisoned by the end of 1977."[187] The Shah's failing health and growing restiveness amongst the youth gave Khomeni and his followers the opportunity to go mainstream with their concept of state and sovereignty.

THEOCRACY

All great Persian empires have been theocratic in the sense that the ruler was legitimated by divine sanction and ruled with the support of a religious establishment. The Safavid dynasty was different in that it drew support from a militant Sufi order and took advantage of the political vacuum prevailing at the time. During the reign of Shah Abbas I, however, the Qizilbash/Sufi element within the state was marginalized and a more traditional combination of monarchical absolutism supported by an official clerical establishment emerged. Direct rule by the ulema or holy men was something aberrant and rebellions, from Gaumata to the Babi movement, aiming at this outcome had met with failure. The protracted failure of the Qajar and Pahlavi dynasties to restore Iranian independence combined with the latter's systematic destruction of any moderate opposition and alienation of the ulema, paved the way for a fusion of popular religiosity with anti-imperialism and Iranian nationalism.

Khomeni's moral stature as the leader of the opposition to the Shah's unjust arbitrary rule gave him the confidence to openly propagate a different vision of the monarchy—one that would be completely theocratic and utopian, ruled by a succession of jurist-kings selected on the basis of their Islamic learning. The solution then to Iran's problems lay in the establishment of an Islamic government, which may "be defined as the rule of divine law over men."[188] Such a government would be neither a popular democracy nor a hereditary monarchy. Rather, the proposed government would be one of experts in the divine law and traditions as they alone, by virtue of their superior spiritual insight and esoteric knowledge, had the potential to rule justly.[189] However, since one could not dispense justice without power, the ulema had to set about becoming rulers for the sake of the collective good.[190] The key to victory was propaganda for "Tyrannical rulers, for their part, stood in terror of the Imams" precisely because the latter represented divine law and justice.[191] In developing the theory of the rule of the jurist or *vilayat-i Faqih*, Khomeni was challenging the quietism of the Shia ulema and advancing his own candidacy for this all-powerful position should the Shah be overthrown. Many jurists actually saw through Khomeni's propaganda, none more important than Grand Ayatollah Kho'I, who considered these ideas to be stretching the idea of ward or guardianship exercised by ulema over orphans and widows rather far. The opposition within the ulema, however, added to Khomeni's stature and helped contribute to the overt and aggressive politicization of the ulema against the Shah's regime.[192]

The Iranian Revolution of 1979 was a popular reaction to unjust arbitrary rule and humiliation at Western hands. The people saw in "Imam" Khomeini a savior and a redeemer who would set things right and restore Iranian sovereignty and rescue the people from the Shah's brutality and oppression. Khomeini for his part manifested all the psychological insight, ruthlessness and cunning, worthy of an aspiring "just" arbitrary ruler. Upon returning to Iran, he set about seizing control of the state apparatus while calming fears he intended to establish a dictatorship by appointing a moderate prime minister. This encouraged the United States of America and the Iranian army to believe that a moderate outcome was a distinct possibility. Prevarication produced a split within the armed forces between pro-Shah and pro-Khomeini elements. Fighting erupted between these factions with popular and religious militias joining the fray against the royalists. Khomeini responded by ordering his followers to join the fight, defy curfew, and for good measure, proclaimed holy war against any military units that did not immediately surrender. The royalists, already leaderless, collapsed and the morale of pro-Shah elements within the armed forces was broken. Khomeini seized the opportunity to turn popular hatred of the Shah and his supporters into a vehicle for steamrolling all opposition. A purge was launched of the Shah's real and alleged sympathizers as Khomeini allowed "the voice of moderation" to be "drowned by a clamour for blood."[193] Executions and incarcerations followed and soon the notorious Qasr prison, which had housed 2,000 inmates under the Shah, was overflowing with 8,000 prisoners detained as guests of "Imam" Khomeini.[194]

On the streets, Hezbollah, or the Party of God, emerged as a force of radicals loyal to Khomeini determined to crush all those who dared disagree with the supreme leader. By the end of 1979, a revolutionary guards corps of 25,000 men (eventually 120,000 strong), carefully selected to ensure their loyalty to Khomeini, had been raised, and the moderates, liberals and leftists were marginalized by the turn of events. Following a referendum in 1981 that declared in favor of an Islamic Republic, without actually defining what that meant, Khomeini proceeded with putting his jurist-monarchical political system into practice. The jurist-monarch was chosen for life by other jurists and was the head of state, having control over the army, the militias, and the intelligence apparatus. A toothless parliament and a popularly elected but powerless president were conceded as sops to democratic sentiment. The leftists were arrested or killed, Savak reappeared as the Ministry of Intelligence (1983), and the *basij* militia, Khomeini's "army of twenty million", acted as a social and religious police. In August 1982, all un-Islamic laws passed since 1917 were nullified by the Supreme Judicial Council, effectively making the ulema the judicial administrators of the country with power to dispense justice as they saw fit. Khomeini would personally authorize the massacre of thousands of political prisoners in 1988 after a rebel group (the Peoples' Mujahideen) invaded Iran from Iraq. This was done in spite of protests by Ayatollah Montazeri, who pleaded for clemency and pointed out the blatant illegality of arbitrarily pronouncing death sentences on thousands of people who were already serving jail sentences. The Iraqi invasion of Iran had played into the hands of the regime, justifying national economic controls and suppression of dissent due to wartime emergency. This conflict also, however, demonstrated the superior morale of Khomeini's followers, who, like the Qizilbash in the ascendant phase of the Safavid, threw themselves into battle hoping to be martyred. Oil revenues helped keep the country fiscally afloat even as revolution, war and Western sanctions bit deep into Iran's economic prosperity.

The regime survived the death of its founder and managed a peaceful transition to Ayatollah Khamenei's leadership. After the war ended, oil revenues enabled reconstruction and a gradual return to normalcy. The new jurist-king, though not nearly as popular or charismatic as the founder, remained in power through manipulation, patronage and coercion, even as presidents Khatami (1997–2005) and Ahmadinejad (2005–2013) tried to share power more equitably with the clerical establishment that dominated the decision-making bodies. Attempts to peacefully reform the system have generally come to naught while more aggressive protests, such as those that erupted after Ahmadinejad's disputed 2009 election, resulted in effective repression by the regime. In effect, a popular mandate "was no match for the institutional might of the conservatives" who held all the cards in terms of control of the state apparatus.[195]

Vigorous indoctrination over the past three decades have produced a believing population that is young and has no personal memory of the pre-revolutionary days. The religious police, the military, revolutionary guards, seminaries, legal system, intelligence apparatus, and media, are all loyal to the regime and ruthless in crushing opposition to it. The achievement of the current system of jurist-monarchy is that Iran has recovered its sovereignty and with the fading of Western military interventions in Iraq and Afghanistan seems poised to reemerge as a major regional power in its own right. Should contemporary Iran acquire nuclear weapons its leaders would have the perfect screen for deterring conventional retaliation even as they project their power through proxies and asymmetric means. Whether this means that a new Persian Empire is in the making is open to speculation but such an outcome is one the region is quite familiar with. This outcome might also make strategic sense given the ongoing implosion in the Arab world as the crisis wrought by failed modernization and corrupt westernized elites deepens and widens. That this new empire-in-the-making is a theocratic arbitrary state ruled by a non-hereditary jurist-monarch wielding nearly absolute power places it firmly within the great tradition of Persian imperial governance that stretches in history from the Achaemenids to the Ayatollahs.

4 European Orders from the Roman Empire to the Eurozone

INTRODUCTION: A MATTER OF TIMING

In the late 1600s Louis XIV, the Sun King of France, ruled the wealthiest, most powerful, and best-organized state in Europe.[1] With its standing army of 200,000, a population of nearly twenty million, a temperate climate, a brilliant academy, and an opulent court culture, France was *the* state in Europe. Feared, admired, and imitated, the luminescence of Versailles reflected the absolutist spirit of the French monarchy that was given practical form through the operation of an organized civil administration spearheaded by royally appointed intendants. While French courtiers basked in their master's radiance and imagined themselves the rightful hegemons of Europe, the Timurid monarch of India drew revenues ten times greater than the Sun King, ruled five times as many subjects and could mobilize field armies of half a million men.[2] In contrast to the semi-feudal apparatus of France with its offices of purchase and encumbering aristocratic and clerical immunities, the Mughal ruler appointed his servants directly and paid them through a combination of cash salaries and revenue assignments. While Louis XIV proclaimed without being able to pursue the claim that all land in France was the property of the king, his Mughal counterpart practiced universal proprietorship without feeling the need to openly assert it. Further east was China, an empire twice as large and wealthy as Mughal India and one that consequently dwarfed France to an even greater degree. Had China's emperors known "that French philosophers such as Voltaire were writing paeans praising them, they would probably have thought that that was exactly what French philosophers ought to be doing."[3] In pre-industrial times, when land was the major source of wealth, Europe was the relatively impoverished extremity of Eurasia and, as such, lacked the wealth necessary for the maintenance of a hierarchically organized state in which the ruler and his servants were the dominant element. In China and India the density of population per unit of arable land was thirty to forty times greater than Europe, and by 1200, Chinese agriculture could support 1000 people per square kilometer of arable land.[4]

It is only logical that bureaucratic states comparable in power to Imperial China or the Timurid Empire emerged in Europe in the 1700s and

1800s enabled by newfound wealth generated by trade and manufacturing centered on the Atlantic economy that emerged after 1492. Except for brief and highly traumatic periods under Napoleon I and Adolf Hitler, Europe, even the western or central parts of it, were never united as large empires. If anything, attempts to overcome Europe's underlying diversity, through conquest, ideology, or, in more recent times, economic integration, repeatedly ran aground. The underlying fractures of geography, demography, national cultures, aristocratic privilege, clerical autonomy, civil society, and work ethics proved too great to overcome. Indeed, these attempts, often brutal and fanatically motivated, reinforce Ibn Khaldun's realization that civilization is about power, not morality, and in this respect the European record is as traumatic as that of other regions in the pre-modern period. In the modern period, especially when one factors in the cost of fascism, communism and colonialism, the European record of arbitrary power assumes unprecedented proportions.

Europe's historical experience of governance can be broken down into a number of stages. The first corresponds to the period of Roman supremacy and covers the period from the rise of the Republic (c. 509 BC) to its evolution into an absolute monarchy (c. 27 BC) and its decline and fall in the west (c. AD 200—500). The second is the feudal age and broadly covers the period from the aftermath of the fall of the Roman Empire (500—800) to the emergence of consolidated feudal polities (800—1200), to the eclipse of the lords and the rise of monarchies (1200–1500). The third stage, or early modern Europe, canvases the period from the Reformation to the French Revolution and Napoleonic Empire (1500–1800), while the fourth stage takes up the modern period (1800–1945). In the third and fourth stages the historical experience of governance of France and the Germanic alternatives of Prussia and the Habsburg dominions are examined here. The fifth, and for our purposes final, stage examines Europe from the end of World War II to the post-Cold War bid for European unity and the reassertion of a statist paradigm (1945–2012).

THE ROMAN MARCH TOWARDS EMPIRE, DESPOTISM, AND COLLAPSE

One of the basic tenets of western perspectives on political order is that it emerges from the consensus of a community as a kind of contract. Ideally, this consensus should be based on *Concordia ordinum* (cooperation of all classes). The practical difficulty of bringing everybody on board for every decision, however, means that the *consensia omnium honoram* (consensus of the honorable) can be used to frame policies, laws and take important decisions.[5] In either case, once political order emerged out of consensus and contract, the state could legitimately claim to be acting on behalf of the group of people whose collective will gave rise to it. These individuals together constituted a "public" or "a numerous gathering brought together by legal consent and community of interest."[6] The state, as a consequence, was "the property of the public."[7] The idea that the state emerges out of a contract negotiated by members of a community remains firmly fixed in the western tradition. Twelve hundred years after the fall of the Roman Empire, Jean-Jacques Rousseau confidently asserted that as "no man has any natural authority over his fellows, and since force alone bestows no right, all legitimate authority among men must be based on covenants."[8] Rousseau adds that if the notion that might makes right is accepted in domestic politics then "cause and effect are reversed, and every force which overcomes another force inherits the right which belonged to the vanquished."[9] Between the social contract theorists of the Enlightenment and the triumphal discourse of the contemporary era, emboldened by victory in the Cold War, the thesis that legitimacy flows from capacity, rather than capacity from legitimacy, has been for all practical purposes discarded. The concept of the state as the expression of the community thus stands validated from a contemporary European perspective.

The origin of this idea lies partly in the history of the Roman Empire, particularly during the Republic (509–27 BC), and partly in the political philosophy of the Ancient Greek city-states, some of which developed constitutional orders with a degree of public representation in the seventh and sixth centuries BC. The sense of community formally expressed created "public virtue" amongst the citizens of Rome.[10] Public virtue generated a spirit of self-sacrifice and desire for glory that "rendered the legions of the republic almost invincible."[11] As inspiring as the virtue of the ancients "derived from the strong sense of our own interest in the promotion and prosperity of a free government of which we are members"[12] might have been, the actual trajectory of Roman governance was from republicanism to absolute monarchy mediated by appointed servants and legitimized by divine sanction. Rome started out special in terms of its political institutions. Over time, these institutions became more numerous and complex while finding it harder and harder to assert control over the dominions of conquest. This led to increasing reliance on the army, governors, and administrators whose ascendancy made Rome more like continental bureaucratic empires in other parts of Eurasia. The *Pax Romana* resulted from the abandonment in substantive terms of republicanism and stabilization initially as a hereditary monarchy (27 BC–AD 68) and then as a non-hereditary monarchy (AD 96–180).

The Roman march towards empire and monarchical absolutism was powered by the difficulties inherent in accommodating additional representation within the structure of Rome's institutions. The Roman Senate, a patrician body of three hundred elders, was in theory the most powerful and certainly the most prestigious in Rome. The senators regarded themselves as the best suited to govern but nonetheless had to contend with assemblies that represented voting districts, tribes, and the plebian elite.

Citizens thus simultaneously owed political allegiance to their tribe, senator, local forum, assorted assemblies and councils, and electoral areas. A
social contract with so many sub-clauses is more likely to produce and
sustain massive conflicts of interest rather than preserve order and dispense
justice. To participate in politics required immense wealth for popularity
was often a question of purchasing enough votes as well as street muscle—a
phenomenon that is familiar to South Asians and other developing states
that have experimented with democracy. Each leader had a network of
patronage and clients that he could maneuver or manipulate to move closer
or further away from public office. Such leaders moved "in and out of titled
government continually" and employed their own slaves and favorites to
help them get things done while in public office.[13] These rotations were so
frequent that "one can in fact almost ignore the distinction between public and private."[14] While Roman rhetoric inveighed that "there is no more
degenerate kind of state than that in which the richest are supposed to be
best",[15] Roman politics required such vast sums that riches were the major
route to political power, and power thus acquired served to help amass
greater riches. Between 509 and 390 BC, the senatorial elite enjoyed a near
monopoly of power for from its ranks emerged consuls, heads of temples
and, at a pinch, a legally-sanctioned dictator. As Rome grew and a class of
wealthy commoners emerged, the senatorial monopoly was challenged. The
genius of the senatorial class was that when the risk of disorder became too
great it responded through concessions that effectively co-opted wealthy
commoners. Some patricians exploited the grievances of the commoners to
carve out larger power bases, while highly successful plebs could look forward to rank and official position and thus had much in common with the
senatorial elite. The patrician/plebian dichotomy is in some ways misleading for other than the senators the upper classes or *honestiores* included
equites or freeborn property owners and *decurions* or wealthy townsmen.
The lower classes or *humiliores* comprised the "freeborn poor, freedmen,
and slaves."[16] Julius Caesar, a patrician *par excellence*, "made his way to
the top by championing the popular interest at Rome", much to the chagrin
of conservative senators.[17] That these conservatives aligned themselves with
Caesar's colleague in the First Triumvirate, Pompey Magnus, is revealing.
Pompey's father was a wealthy provincial who rose to noble status, a new
man as it were, while Pompey had risen to prominence as the dictator Marcus Sulla's sword arm.[18]

   The crisis of the Roman republic can be understood as a triangular
disequilibrium in which the privilege of the senatorial aristocracy at the
center, the growing power of governors and military commanders in the
provinces, and the popular sentiment within Italy in general and Rome in
particular, combined to render the Roman Empire ungovernable. Roman
expansion within the Italian peninsula had followed a "low end" strategy
of imperial maintenance.[19] This strategy was based on a combination of
treaties, internal autonomy for cities that recognized Roman supremacy,

partial representation in the Senate, and pledges of mutual military support. This approach worked well enough within Italy where city-states and polities similar to Rome existed. Its success meant that the Roman army remained a seasonal force drawn from citizens as the need arose and permanent deployment was unnecessary.[20] Expansion outside the Italian peninsula was a different game altogether and one in which a "low end" strategy could not work for three major reasons.

First, some of the territories (such as Gaul) were still at an early stage of agricultural development and required continuous military exertion and colonization to be kept under Roman control. Granting the indigenous inhabitants titles like "Brothers of Roman People" and bribing or intimidating their leaders was all well and good but only the demonstration of military superiority could keep them from rebelling.[21] Julius Caesar was keenly aware "that almost all the Gauls" were "eager for political change" and on account "of their fickleness" could easily be "roused to war" against the "state of servitude" recently imposed upon them by Roman arms.[22] Maintaining the "state of servitude" required permanent garrisons, a colonial administration, and powerful governors with practically despotic powers. Second, some of the territories (such as Egypt, Carthage, or Syria) rivaled or surpassed the wealth and sophistication of Rome itself. Effective rule over densely populated agrarian heartlands and maritime powerhouses required the means to remote control the local administration and sufficient Roman penetration of an already developed apparatus to extract the food, gold, and services needed by the empire. The wealth of these territories was such that Rome needed to be ready, willing, and able to protect them through military means, which meant governors and garrisons. The third problem was distance and the need to maintain communications for administration, trade, and warfare. Here Rome could not escape responsibility for organizing communications around itself ("All roads lead to Rome") or investing in public infrastructure and managing the production and distribution of food so that surplus regions could feed deficit regions. The "low end" strategy worked well enough when it came to sending out armies and expanding the empire. Control, however, over far-flung areas that existed at varied levels of development and had diverse populations, required a "high end" strategy of centralization, militarization, and bureaucratization.[23]

The evolution of the Roman military reflected these trends and pressures. In 107 BC the Roman army was converted from a citizen army mobilized as and when needed to a standing force of volunteers. These volunteers received regular pay, a share of any loot, land, and Roman citizenship. In this way Roman citizenship now became a benefit of military service rather than a prerequisite. This reform undoubtedly improved discipline, professionalism, and made it possible to deploy the army on long campaigns. By 60 BC the organization of the army had taken the familiar form of legion (6000 men), cohort (600 men), maniples (200 men) and centuries (100 men), with distinct detachments of cavalry, auxiliaries and siege weapons, added as required. Armies were raised by the legion and these units were maintained even if they fell below fighting strength so that fresh recruits could be brought in to replenish the ranks. Command of legions was entrusted to generals appointed by the Senate or, in emergencies, by the dictator. The Roman army lacked overall unity of command and legions were loyal first and foremost to their generals rather than to Rome or its Senate. This loyalty was due in part to the personal identification of soldiers with their commanders and the very real arbitrary powers of discipline and reward possessed by military superiors. The experience of shared hardship, common danger and sacrifice was cemented by the voluntary long-term service structure of the legions (twenty years). In the absence of overall unity of command, every general was an army chief with political interests and rivals back in Rome. Soldiers had contempt for the luxury-loving patricians and wealthy commoners in Rome and regarded their commander as sons would their father. To disobey one's commander through mutiny or desertion was almost incomprehensible.[24] In other empires, the ruler himself was often the army chief or appointed a chief of staff to run the day-to-day affairs of the military. The Roman army had no overall chief, much as the Roman Empire lacked an emperor. This contradiction was temporarily resolved by Julius Caesar in 49 BC when he refused to disband his legions and instead marched into Italy. Pompey fled and was eventually killed at the hands of the Egyptians when he sought refuge in their lands. Julius Caesar moved quickly to conciliate his enemies and avoided proscription, cancelling debts or confiscating property. His government struck 170,000 fake paupers off the welfare rolls and increased the size of the Senate from 300 to 900, making new senatorial appointments dependent on the dictator's favor. Provincial governors were now directly appointed by, and answerable to, Caesar, and so "no Roman magistrate could look forward at the end of his year of office to the prospect of enriching himself by the plunder of a fat province. He went forth as the agent of a jealous sovereign."[25] The sovereign's assassination at the hands of jealous and indignant aristocrats, who reasoned that Caesar was out to establish an absolute monarchy, in 44 BC, led to another round of civil war. In the first phase, populist-monarchist forces loyal to Octavian, Caesar's nephew and adopted heir, defeated aristocratic republicans. In the second, dissension within the Caesarian camp broke out into fighting between Octavian and Mark Antony supported by the Ptolemaic Cleopatra (r. 51–30 BC). By 27 BC, the war was over, Octavian Augustus (r. 27 BC–AD 14) was the First Citizen or *Princeps* and the Roman Empire became an absolute monarchy called the *principate*.[26]

Augustus benefited from the bloodletting of the civil wars and the severity of the confiscations and executions[27] carried out between Caesar's assassination and his own victory. The Senate was sufficiently cowed to accept monarchical power, the populace was relieved at the restoration of peace, and the *Princeps* was wise enough to leave the form of constitutional order in place thereby preserving the appearance of republican government. Behind this façade, power was concentrated in the hands of the emperor who "alone was the general of the republic, and his jurisdiction, civil as well as military, extended over all the conquests of Rome."[28] The Senate was effectively a council of imperial advisers and a pool from which the emperor appointed senior civilian and military officials. Augustus felt secure in this delegation on account of senatorial vulnerability to imperial displeasure for they could lose all if they proved disloyal. The agents of the emperor's displeasure were the Praetorian Cohorts now permanently deployed at Rome as the imperial bodyguard and political police. Augustus successfully set about "seducing the military with donations, the masses with grain allowances, and everybody with the pleasures of peace."[29] The emperor "gradually increased his powers, drawing to himself the function of Senate, magistrate, and laws."[30] Augustus amassed a vast fortune and left a bequest of 43.50 million sesterces[31] for the Roman poor, 1000 sesterces for each praetorian guardsman, and 300 sesterces for every legionary.[32] Augustus was a compulsive organizer and personally prepared a detailed list of all the resources of the Roman state including population, allies, fleets, clients, provinces, revenues, expenses, and gifts.[33]

The eye for detail and largesse that characterized Augustus combined with outward reverence for republican forms and reflected the inherent fragility of a political order that depended on the personal abilities of the ruler and the support of the army. This support had to be carefully cultivated and could not be taken for granted. Augustus thus eschewed further territorial expansion hoping to prevent through moderation the rise of powerful and popular new generals, like his uncle, Julius Caesar.[34] The state also provided land to soldiers as part of its policy of internal colonization and expansion of agriculture though the rank-and-file grumbled that they did not receive enough of the most fertile land and had to make do with hills and marshes.[35] Some 300,000 soldiers were settled in this manner throughout the empire at the cost of nearly a billion sesterces during Augustus's reign, though by AD 5 it was decided to provide a retirement payment equal to twelve years' pay to soldiers and let them decide how to spend it. To reduce the chance of soldiers falling prey to idleness they were kept busy with employment on construction projects when not training or recuperating.[36] Augustus's restraint and generosity notwithstanding, the vast military machine "was a blind and irresistible instrument of oppression" while the centralization and personalization of power had reduced the Senate and other republican institutions to imperial ciphers, incapable of correcting the quality of decision-making by the ruler.[37] The precariousness of personal rule was brought home at the time of Augustus's death in AD 14. Mutiny broke out in the Pannonian legions motivated by the hope amongst the soldiers that "the change of emperors offered the prospect of unrestrained rioting" and "profit from civil war."[38] The mutiny, however, remained isolated and Tiberius (r. AD 14–37) became the new emperor.

The reigns of Augustus's four successors from the Julio-Claudian family, Tiberius, Caligula (AD 37–41), Claudius (AD 41–54) and Nero (AD 54–68) serve as examples of absolute power corrupting absolutely. Tiberius, arguably the best of the four, had certain fixed notions about how a state ought to be run. Troubled by allegations that the courts were not delivering justice fairly, Tiberius took to sitting in them personally to ensure the right decision was made and limiting lawyers' fees. Larger decisions that affected the well-being of the empire were put off on account of indecisiveness. Often unable to decide upon important appointments, Tiberius opted "to extend commands and keep numerous people in the same armies or jurisdictions to the end of their lives."[39] Hurt by rumors and poetic lampoons, Tiberius instinctively distrusted merit and relied on spies and informers who quickly gained his confidence by playing on his suspicions. Rome was soon drowning in accusations of disloyalty accompanied by torture, exile, the suspension of honors and confiscation of property. Laws were passed to target individuals while "many people found their fortunes severed from them" and all were "threatened with terror."[40] Sometimes, when things went too far, Tiberius would personally intervene in particular cases, these interventions confirming the personal and arbitrary nature of imperial rule. Complaints often had lethal consequences for the accused without bringing about improvement in the delivery of services. Thus, the official appointed by Tiberius to inspect roads in Italy complained that government contractors were not doing their job properly and set about levying charges and confiscating the property of the accused.[41] The public continued to suffer on account of poorly maintained roads while the inspector and his touts grew wealthy on expropriations. These acts violated due process and the contractual agreements between the state and contractors, which were, in fact, remarkably modern in terms of their attention to matters of conflict of interest and their subjection to public scrutiny.[42]

Aelius Sejanus, the prefect of the Praetorian Cohorts, made it his business to slander others for to do so was eminently profitable as accusers got a share of the property of their victims. Tiberius prevented the Senate from eliminating rewards for the accuser if the accused committed suicide before the case was decided and so ensured that "informers, a class of men devised for the destruction of society, and never sufficiently checked even by legal penalties, were now being given the inducement of rewards."[43] As terror intensified Rome was enveloped by "tension and panic" and people avoided each other and sought refuge in isolation.[44] The atomization that results from arbitrary rule is well known in South Asia as is the fact that such a development has the effect of enabling the rulers to pick their victims at leisure for it ensures that a collective reaction will not materialize. The perpetrators and instruments of tyranny also suffer the effects of atomization when their master turns against them. Thus, when Sejanus fell from royal favor, his property was confiscated and added to the emperor's wealth. Tiberius became increasingly unhinged, putting to death an elderly lady for "weeping over the execution of her son", trying to stabilize interest rates at 8 percent per annum only to cause a crisis that forced the state to inject 100 million sesterces of liquidity into the banks, and having his daughter-in-law, nephew, and grandchildren killed.[45] Sextus Marius, a wealthy miner from Spain, was accused of incest with his daughter and executed and the emperor confiscated his gold and silver mines.[46] Eventually, everyone accused of involvement with Tiberius's former favorite, Sejanus, was put to death.[47] Such cruelty was accompanied by acts of generosity as well. Thus, when the Aventine Forum burned down, Tiberius sanctioned 100 million sesterces for its reconstruction, and after an earthquake in Asia, a tax-holiday of five years was proclaimed in the affected territories in additions to tens of millions of sesterces in reconstruction money. Generosity, of course, is also a form of power and in the case of Augustus's successor was hardly adequate to balance the capriciousness with which power was generally exercised.

Tiberius's successors, Caligula, Claudius, and Nero, continued along the path of unenlightened despotism and plunged the center into chaos. Caligula earned the distinction of becoming the first emperor to be killed by the imperial bodyguard, which, fortunately for the royal family, remained loyal to the dynasty and elevated Claudius to the throne. The essential problem that Rome now faced was one familiar to other arbitrary monarchies—the problem of the bad emperor or selfish ruler. Only a monarch with absolute power could manage a state as large and complex as the Roman Empire that ruled diverse subject multitudes. So long as the monarch was wise and able the state ran smoothly but ensuring the succession of a competent ruler appeared almost impossible. Strict hereditary rule from father to son made for the greatest stability but did not guarantee competence and was not always practically possible. Loose hereditary succession within the Julio-Claudian family had worked for a while, but generated terrible intrigues and since the death of Augustus had produced rulers significant for their mental derangement and heartlessness. Overthrowing the dynasty risked reverting to the civil war conditions that led to the creation of a dynastic state in the first place, and even if a new dynasty emerged there was no guarantee it would avert the disasters that befell the Julio-Claudians.

The Flavian dynasty (AD 69—96) that succeeded the Julio-Claudians after Nero committed suicide in AD 68,[48] emerged victorious in the civil war and tried to adhere to a strict interpretation of hereditary rule. Vespasian (r. AD 69–79), founder of the dynasty, ruled for a decade and was followed by his son Titus (AD 79–81) who died after just two years. Domitian lasted longer (r. AD 81–96) but was assassinated by his courtiers and succeeded by Nerva (AD 96–98). For nearly a century after Nerva, the practice was for the reigning emperor to nominate his successor by legally adopting an heir that possessed qualities of leadership. In this manner, a competent successor could be selected and groomed and the transfer from one ruler to the next could be managed peacefully and legitimately. The good fortune that adoptive succession secured a line of capable rulers helped cement the impression that for a century the "vast extent of the Roman empire was governed by absolute power, under the guidance of virtue and wisdom."[49]

Monarchical virtue and wisdom were channeled through a complex class of imperial servants. These servants can be broadly divided into five categories. Some were direct appointees of the emperor and were paid salaries and given critical coordination and administrative assignments. Others were members of local councils and municipal committees who were elected or nominated and drawn from the *equites* or *decurion* orders. Then there were a host of contractors, tax farmers, transporters, etc., who worked for the government under contracts awarded by magistrates but who were not technically civil servants. At the top of the food chain were Senators who were deputed by the emperor for important civilian commands such as governorships. And finally, there was the emperor's own household establishment, complete with its secretaries, treasurers, slaves, guards, spies, entertainers, favorites etc.

The most important field officials as far as ordinary people were concerned were the *publicani* and the civilian *decurions*. The former were tax farmers under the republic but in Augustus's time were converted into tax collectors. They collected imperial taxes and acted with the support of provincial governors. The most important taxes were those on land, income, and sales, and the tax burden was calculated on the basis of a periodic census that originated in republican times.[50] The latter were councilmen and were drawn from urban property owners. They sat as members of town and city councils and were responsible for collecting taxes from their constituents, running the day-to-day affairs of municipalities, ensuring transparency in the award of contracts at the local level, and assisting the imperial administration in any major undertaking. Above the collectors and councilmen were elite salaried officials bearing the title of procurator. Paid between 60,000 and 300,000 sesterces per year, procurators could rise to become governors of minor provinces, i.e. provinces where no legions were stationed. Most often, they were appointed to oversee the collection of taxes in all provinces, to run the emperor's lands and properties, organize indirect taxes in groups of provinces, and act as administrative heads of different departments. The highest appointments went to members of the Senate, a club whose strength was fixed at 600 by Augustus with a minimum property qualification of one million sesterces. Membership of the Senate depended on imperial favor and while the son of a Senator had a right to stand for his father's office, election was by no means guaranteed. Being part of the Roman Empire's millionaires' club meant that Senators had their own administrative establishments of servants and slaves that they took with them on official appointments. Through the Senate the greatest wealth and talent within the empire could be harnessed to the imperial chariot. The civil administration of the empire thus depended on the quality of imperial servants ranging from appointees drawn from the

Senate, to procurators, local officials and contractors. Of course, a lot of the agricultural, construction, and domestic work that melded into official business on account of the porous frontier between private life and public office was performed by slaves who constituted as much as a third of the total population in Italy. State power, however, "was everywhere exercised by the ministers of the senate and of the emperors" and this "authority was absolute, and without control."[51]

The greatest Roman bureaucracy, and the one that emperors had the greatest interest in controlling, was the military. A standing army and navy defended the borders, guaranteed internal peace, and stood ready to crush rebellion—as the Jews, Gauls, Britons, and Spartacus's slaves, among many others, learned the hard way. Lightly armed local militia forces also helped maintain order under normal circumstances. The republic had created an army that had conquered an empire and that army was the ultimate argument in favor of the absolute imperial monarchy. During the civil war that preceded the *Pax Romana*, the size of the military had swelled to seventy legions and nine hundred warships. This was obviously beyond the ability of the Roman state to sustain and so Augustus demobilized scores of legions and limited the number of war-fleets to two. The steel core of Roman military strength was represented by the twenty-five legions (each legion having 6000 men), which made for a standing force of 150,000 heavy infantrymen. The soldiers were recruited on the basis of a long-term voluntary service contract of sixteen to twenty years and served as disciplined armored infantry. In addition to the Roman legions, a regular force of auxiliaries drawn from non-Roman subjects were maintained through a combination of voluntary long-term service contracts of twenty-five years and conscription. At the end of their service auxiliary troops received Roman citizenship. Unlike the legions, which were large units of 6000 men, the auxiliaries were organized into cohorts (600 men). At total of 200 to 400 auxiliary cohorts were maintained during the *Pax Romana* making for a minimum strength of 120,000. Combined, the legions and auxiliaries numbered 150,000 plus 120,000 under Augustus, or 270,000 in all.

The legionaries were paid regular salaries three times a year (January, May and September). Each salary was equal to about three *aurei* or three hundred sesterces.[52] Thus, the salary of an ordinary Roman legionary was about nine hundred sesterces a year during the *Pax Romana*. The annual salary bill of the Roman legions under Augustus would therefore have worked out to nine hundred sesterces multiplied by 150,000 legionaries or 135,000,000 sesterces/1.35 million *aurei* per year. The salary bill for the auxiliaries was probably not as large as that for the legions. However, even if we assume that 120,000 auxiliaries were paid half of what the legionaries received, the amount would still add 50–60 million sesterces to the salary bill. When one accounts for variations in pay, such as the double salary paid to the Praetorian Cohorts, the retirement bonus equal to 12 years pay given to legionaries, the enormous sums spent on veterans' colonies as part of the demobilization after the civil war, etc., the flat rate calculations made above probably furnish a conservative estimate of actual military expenditure—somewhere in the range of 180–220 million sesterces per year. The logistical exercise and infrastructure needed to feed, equip, and deploy such a large force were enormous, as evidenced even today by the ruins of Roman roads and aqueducts, and by information that has survived pertaining to the shipping of millions of tons of grain around the empire. The Tunisian Sahara alone exported some 500,000 tons of grain to Rome every year until overrun by the Vandals in 429.[53]

The ideocratic complex of the Roman Empire merits special attention given the powerful hold it exercised, and continues to exercise, over the Western imagination. Until the early 300s AD the religion of the state was primarily a matter of ritual rather than formal doctrine. A hierarchy of ecclesiastical officials drawn from the upper classes presided over the ceremonial culture of the state and produced auguries to placate the superstitious masses. Many of the members of that same elite subscribed to skepticism, Epicureanism, stoicism, Platonism, or some version of natural theology compatible with the philosophical tradition of the Greeks. For the five million or so citizens of the empire (AD 48) their elevated status was also a matter of pride and helped them adhere to the state and its laws, which privileged them. Gibbon perhaps overdoes it when he declared that the "policy of the emperors and the senate, as far as it concerned religion, was happily seconded by the reflection of the enlightened, and by the habits of the superstitious, part of their subjects."[54] He did, however, have a point that the kind of systematic religious persecution and propaganda that characterized the late-Roman, medieval, and early-modern West, was alien to the spirit of Rome. Roman emperors were deified and had an official cult, but tolerated other belief systems so long as they did not lead to rebellion or disruption of the state. The sophistication of the Roman senatorial and service elite also made the pursuit of doctrinal conformity undesirable while the diversity of the subject peoples made the pursuit of such an objective highly problematic. Roman "magistrates could not be activated by a blind, though honest bigotry, since the magistrates were themselves philosophers; and the schools of Athens had given laws to the Senate."[55]

The exception to the practice of tolerance, as indicated above, was the deification of emperors and the patronage of an official cult, and the suppression of groups, such as the Jews, and later the Christian and Manicheans, who refused to acknowledge Caesar as a divine being. Here, polytheistic cultures had an easier time adjusting to Roman pretensions as compared to monotheistic or dualistic religions that found adding a deity doctrinally untenable. The policy of elite assimilation through education and employment in the provinces or extension of citizenship in exchange for military service meant that collaboration paid. This also helped diffuse Greco-Roman culture throughout the empire and lessened the need for naked coercion with the passage of time. Masking the iron hand of the Roman army upon which the continuity of the empire ultimately depended was the velvet glove of continued deference to republican institutions and practices conveying the impression that constitutional government still prevailed. When Augustus "framed the artful system of the Imperial authority" his objective was "to deceive the people by an image of civil liberty, and the armies by an image of civil government."[56] That such subterfuge was considered necessary reflects the supremacy and majesty of the law in the Roman worldview even if the reality of monarchical absolutism prevented that theoretical superiority from being actualized. Beyond such self-projection and constitutional pieties, the Roman state pacified strategically-located groups, such as the Roman masses, through subsidized food and mass entertainment. Under Augustus, some 200,000 residents of Rome received grain from the state, which meant that 80,000 tons of grain imports were dedicated to the dole every year.[57] Accompanying the bread, were circuses, quite literary in the case of the Circus Maximus, where the great chariot races took place, and other entertainments including the display of exotic animals and gladiatorial combat. All told, some sixty to one hundred and thirty-five days of the year were devoted to games, many sponsored by wealthy citizens, and major events organized by the state. The Roman emperors and provincial governors took personal interest in building the infrastructure needed and in organizing the "supply of gladiators and animals for entertainment" in the arenas, amphitheaters, and circuses of the empire.[58]

The Roman Empire was a continental bureaucratic state that relied on a social elite (senators, *equites*, *decurions*), a permanent bureaucracy, and a standing army. The ideocratic complex of the empire was relatively soft on account of a long tradition of quasi-representative government, the ritualistic as opposed to doctrinal emphasis of Roman religion, and the humanistic education program that the elite subscribed to. The Roman emperors wielded arbitrary power and could, if they wanted, treat the state as a vast personal estate. Enlightened rulers, like Julius Caesar or Augustus, diverted this impulse to territories outside Italy, such as Egypt, which became a personal fiefdom of the emperor after 27 BC, off-limits to prominent Romans except with the emperor's permission. Unenlightened rulers, like Tiberius, Caligula, Claudius and Nero, were unable to restrain themselves and targeted members of the Roman elite. In either case, it was the wisdom and character of the ruler rather than formal institutional checks that moderated the Roman version of arbitrary rule. Like other continental bureaucratic empires, Rome wrestled with the problem of the bad emperor and for about a century (AD 96–180) solved it through the practice of non-hereditary succession through the reigning emperor legally adopting an able individual as his "son" so that power would be transferred peacefully and predictably. This policy benefited from the Roman legal practice in which adopted heirs had the same rights as biological heirs and the good fortune that the army and the senatorial elite backed this arrangement. The decline and fall of the Roman Empire is often attributed to the abandonment of adoptive succession after the death of Marcus Aurelius (AD 180). Aurelius's son, Commodus, was nominated by his father but proved unworthy of the imperial office. He was killed in AD 192 and imperial Rome entered a period of chaos and civil war that lasted for nearly a century and altered the character and competence of the state.

Rome's downfall appears dramatic only in hindsight due in part to the continued emotional resonance of that process as told and retold by generations of historians. Compared to other empires in our survey, Rome's remarkable ability to survive even after the onset of political degeneracy and for brief periods reassert itself during its long and ultimately terminal crisis indicates that the bonds of administrative and military cohesion and a sense of loyalty to the idea of a united empire were resilient. This resilience is further evidenced by the ability of the Eastern Roman, or Byzantine Empire, to survive substantially intact in the Near East until the Arab blitzkrieg of 633–661, and endure in a reduced form until the Turkish onslaught under the Seljuks and finally the Ottomans (1071–1453). In the context of the European and North African territories (the Western Roman Empire), decline and fall can be divided into three distinct phases. The first begins with the murder of Commodus and ends with the reorganization of the empire under Diocletian (r.284–305). The second takes us from the conversion of Emperor Constantine to Christianity (r. 306–337, converted in 312) and the eastward shift of the imperial center to Byzantium/Constantinople (330) to the sacking of Rome in 409 by the Goths. And the third covers the period from 409 to the final overthrow of the Roman Empire in the West in 476. During the first of these phases terrible chaos at the center and demographic decline notwithstanding, the Roman Empire revived with a larger and more powerful army and bureaucracy and a more intolerant, ideologically inclined and arbitrary leadership. In the second phase, the transition from a soft ideocratic complex to a theocratic state with a hard religious-ideological orientation gathered pace while administrative and military exhaustion set in. The third phase was characterized by widespread administrative and military breakdown and the collapse of Roman authority in the western regions.

Commodus (r. 180–192) inherited a functioning state, a disciplined army, and a capable civil service. Unlike his father and predecessor, Marcus Aurelius, Commodus soon fell prey to the intrigues of his attendants and lost his psychological balance. An assassination plot instigated by his sister in 183, convinced Commodus of the need to punish malcontents. His suspicions inflamed by clever courtiers, Commodus unleashed vengeance on the senatorial elite, accusing some of treason and putting to death entire families for the alleged crimes of individuals. When rebellion and discontent surfaced, Commodus was glad to allow his favorites to visit retribution while shutting himself in the palace and proceeding to enjoy the trappings of power rather than personally attending to the onerous burden of its actual exercise. Having "shed with impunity" the "noblest blood of Rome",

Commodus "perished as soon as he was dreaded by his own domestics."[59] Pertinax, who had participated in the conspiracy against Commodus and was a respected senator was proclaimed emperor by the Praetorian Cohorts. Pertinax reigned for less than three months as he refused to provide the Praetorian Cohorts with a large donation and tried to restore discipline. The Praetorians then auctioned the imperial office to the highest bidder, which was Senator Didius Julianius. This unleashed further chaos and civil strife as Julianius was soon overthrown by Septimus Severus (r. 193–211), who then defeated rival generals in a brief civil war.

The new regime restored stability in the sense that a monarch was now wielding power effectively. Effectiveness, however, was not tempered by wisdom and Severus treated "the Roman empire as his property."[60] Forty-one senators and their families were executed and their wealth was confiscated. New senators were created from the Eastern provinces to fill the void. A kinsman of the emperor was appointed as the prefect of the Praetorian Cohorts who, in "every department of administration" soon "represented the person and exercised the authority of the emperor."[61] The emperor's sons, Caracalla and Geta, were given free rein by their father and acted as viceroys with arbitrary power. The senatorial elite and wealthy commoners were obliged to attend to the caprices of these princes and furnished large sums to pay for gifts, palaces, and entertainments. The wealthy were "ruined by partial fines and confiscations" while the poor were burdened with heavier taxes and the casual brutality of an increasingly undisciplined imperial guard out to join in the loot and plunder of the empire it was supposed to protect.[62] More taxes were needed to pay for a larger army as the old Praetorian Cohorts were disbanded (they had numbered between 5000 and 19,000) and replaced by a larger Praetorian guard of 50,000 soldiers. To keep the legions happy, wages for the legionaries were raised by 60 percent and the number of legions grew from twenty-five to thirty-three. To pay for this "the imperial bureaucracy took charge of supplying oil and wine from Spain" thus establishing state monopolies.[63] Steady expansion in "state control of resources", the debasement of coinage, and higher taxes, meant a larger and more predatory bureaucracy, one that was no longer restrained by wisdom and discretion from above.[64] The great problem with corrupt and incompetent rulers, as Cicero realized centuries before Severus and sons, was that "They are a menace, not just because they are corrupt themselves but because they corrupt others. They do more damage by example than by their misdemeanors."[65] Control over public construction, which had gradually become more centralized and bureaucratic from Augustus onwards on account of the need for large-scale public works had ensured greater efficiency when guided by a strong and relatively impartial hand.[66] Now, that concentration became yet another source of wealth for corrupt and irresponsible imperial servants. These same servants were now entrusted with moral policing as Christians were now liable to be reported to the authorities and as a test of loyalty to the emperor compelled to condemn Jesus Christ and offer a ritual offering to the Roman gods.

In spite of these and many other excesses, Severus's death was followed by the accession of his sons Caracalla (r. 211–217) and Geta (r. 211) as co-emperors. Geta was soon killed by Caracalla who preferred to rule alone and accused his brother of plotting against him. The Praetorian Cohorts were bribed and everyone suspected of being pro-Geta was murdered—perhaps as many as 20,000 people in all. In 212, Caracalla approved an edict granting all freemen within the empire Roman citizenship. This democratic equality was a meaningless gesture given the arbitrary culture of power that now pervaded the Roman state. The complex of institutions that had once protected citizens no longer functioned effectively and thus extending citizenship entailed increases in tax and service obligations without furnishing liberty or security. The powerlessness of these institutions was demonstrated repeatedly during Caracalla's reign though two examples help illustrate the unchecked power and structural fault-line upon which the Roman monarchy rested. In 215, Caracalla ordered the massacre of tens of thousands of Alexandria's citizens for ridiculing his claim that he had killed his brother only in self-defense.[67] These citizens had assembled in order to receive the emperor as he visited their city. Earlier during his reign, while still in Rome, Caracalla was attending a chariot race at the Circus. When the crowd abused the charioteer that Caracalla favored, he ordered his soldiers to kill the offending spectators. Since it was impossible to identify which spectators had actually abused the charioteer, the soldiers started killing everybody, making exceptions for those who agreed to pay a worthwhile ransom.[68] The fact that Roman soldiers would, at imperial whim, massacre Roman citizens peacefully assembled in major cities revealed the servile character of the officers. That such opportunities were used to plunder indicated that for all the tax increases and additional allowances, and new legions, the discipline and morale of the army was breaking down. Caracalla eventually got the just reward of his deeds when the Praetorian prefect, Marcinius, murdered him in April, 217. Marcinius's brief reign was inglorious as it involved payment of an indemnity of 200 million sesterces to the Parthian kingdom after inconclusive but costly warfare along the frontier. Rebellion in the army soon put an end to Marcinius reign and his life and restored the Severus family to the throne—a perch they sat precariously on until 235 when Maximinius, the first of the barracks-emperors, took over and triggered a series of succession crises that lasted nearly fifty years.

Maximinius (r. 235–238) in many ways established the pattern for the next fifty years. Politics degenerated into an extended cycle of conspiracy and violence that makes the later-Mughals or decadent Ottomans seem tame by comparison. The insecurity of the ruler drove him to find ways to keep his troops satisfied and led to confiscatory taxation being imposed. Maximinius, for instance, seized the revenues dedicated in cities to the purchase of grain for the poor and confiscated the cash, gold, silver, and other valuables held by temples. Such unpopular and "impious orders could not be executed without tumults and massacres."[69] Maximinius's hatred of the senatorial elite meant that the emperor did not set foot in Rome while intrigues divided the army into factions to a degree not seen since the civil war during the dying days of the republic. Rival commanders increased the size of their military forces leading to unsanctioned increases in the size of the army, which grew to nearly four hundred thousand men by 284. The rule of gangs was now upon the Roman Empire with, on occasion, half a dozen rival claimants running around trying to grab the imperial mantle. By 260 the Roman Empire had de facto fragmented into central, eastern, and northwestern, zones. Rome's military savior, Diocletian, emerged too late to prevent lasting damage to the state and society and his reforms purchased temporary respite at the cost of ever greater administrative and military overstretch that became evident within decades of his abdication.

Diocletian's solution to the problem of Roman *Sikha Shahi*[70] was to expand the civilian and military bureaucracy, double the number of provincial units, and eventually divide the empire into four zones each with its own co-emperor. Coordination required additional layers of officialdom as the machinery became more complicated. In 285, Diocletian elevated one of his generals, Maximian as co-emperor and Caesar responsible for the Western Roman Empire. In 293, two more co-emperors were appointed, Galerius for Syria, Palestine and Egypt, and Constantius for Gaul and Britain. The rule of four emperors meant that each region had to support a separate court and royal administration. Diocletian's calculation was that by sharing power in this manner within the army he could placate factions and divert conspiracies away from himself. The combination of administrative reform, military reorganization and power-sharing helped stabilize the Roman Empire but made it more bureaucratic and militarized and set the stage for formal division.

In order to implement the Tetrarchy, the central structure of the state was now replicated four times over, as there were four courts. The division of provinces meant more governors and the replication of provincial administration. It meant that the semi-autonomous local bodies and councils that had existed during *Pax Romana* were now exposed directly to a larger bureaucracy. Given that the population of the Roman Empire had fallen since AD 160 from about 100 million to about 60 million in 285, a situation emerged in which more imperial servants were administering far fewer people. Each co-emperor naturally made appointments and inflated the size of the imperial service elite. As late as AD 200, the number of "career civil servants" appointed directly by the emperor was a few hundred,[71] and with the senators and their private staff thrown in, plus governors and their appointees, the total figure was less than 5000. But by AD 300, the number of career civil servants had risen to between 30,000 and 35,000.[72] The increase in the size of the imperial bureaucracy was matched by the growing numbers of the standing army, which was swelled through the reintroduction of conscription. Its strength grew from about 400,000 in 285 to nearly 600,000 by the end of Diocletian's reign. During the *Pax Romana* a population of 100 million supported a standing army of about 300,000 (legions plus auxiliaries). By AD 300, a population of 60 million supported an army of twice the size that Augustus had commanded. The expansion in the size of the army required additional investments in infrastructure, which, in turn, required heavier taxes. Conscription had the effect of raising numbers but depleted the economic base and lowered morale. It also led to logistical difficulties, as the construction of infrastructure could not keep up with recruitment. Soldiers were thus left to live off the land and some 250,000 of them were "in a position to enjoy a stimulating proximity to the civilian population."[73]

A hardening of the ideocratic complex of the Roman state closely followed rampant militarism and bureaucratization. The Senate, long deprived of real power, lost all connection with the government owing to the multiplication of co-imperial centers, each with its own royal council, and Diocletian's own absence from Rome. Diocletian styled himself *dominus*, the title by which slaves addressed their masters, and his government was the *Dominate*. Persian court practices, such as prostration before the emperor (*zaminbos*) and the employment of eunuchs, were introduced and Roman religion was now made the doctrinal basis for loyalty to the government.[74] The latter tendency boded ill for Manicheans, Jews and Christians, whose uneasy relationship with the Roman state now degenerated into large-scale persecution. In 302, Diocletian ordered the massacre of all poor Manicheans and deportation to the mines for wealthy members of this community, attended by confiscation of their property. In February 303, general persecution was extended to the Christians. Diocletian ordered that Christian religious texts be seized and burned, their property forfeited, and communal worship was outlawed. These measures could not be sustained for very long but they did enormous damage to prospects for co-existence and radicalized the communities that were victimized. Diocletian voluntarily retired in 305, leaving a superficially reinvigorated empire, but civil war soon broke out and between 306 and 312 Constantine defeated his rivals and reunited the empire under a single ruler. By 311, the religious restrictions were eased by Constantine, and following his conversion to Christianity in 312, the Edict of Milan (313) extended religious toleration and restored confiscated property to the Christians. Constantine's conversion to Christianity, his personal antipathy towards fanaticism aside, set the stage for further a shift toward theocracy and persecution of non-Christians as well as Christians with interpretations that differed from the official version of religion.

Constantine divided the Roman state elite into three classes. At the top were the illustrious, below them were the respectable, and below them the honorable. Imperial prefects of the illustrious class were answerable to the emperor and appointed to head departments dealing with finances, currency, highways, posts, and the administration of justice. The Praetorian prefect was given the responsibility of supervising provincial governments, exercising magistracy on the emperor's behalf, and watching over the rest of the apparatus. The emperor personally handled appeals or complaints against illustrious class officials, which gave him the opportunity to make examples and ensured that these officials did not last very long. The use of arbitrary power by the ruler to punish the servants who exercised that power on his behalf was a practice common to many continental bureaucratic empires and one that was conducive to the perpetuation of the benevolence myth associated with despotic rule, i.e. the emperor wishes his people well but is misled by evil servants who he is happy to punish when the truth is brought to his attention. Appeals and complaints against provincial officials were handled by prefects while titles such as vicar and count were added and the empire was divided into eleven domains (the East, Egypt, Asia, Ponticia, Thrace, Macedonia, Dacia, Italy, Gaul, Spain, and Britain). The domains were further divided into one hundred and sixteen provinces, three of which were headed by pro-consuls, thirty-seven by consuls, five by correctors, and seventy-one by presidents. The regional and provincial heads were responsible for the collection of taxes, the maintenance of order, and the dispensation of justice, served at the emperor's pleasure and reported to prefects. The army was organized into a parallel hierarchy of salaried master-generals, provincial generals (dukes), and commanders, while soldiers were given land to farm by the state in exchange for service and with the obligation that their sons would join the army. The shift towards remunerating in land as opposed to the earlier practice of payments in cash provided one of the major foundations of feudalism in the Western regions of the empire. The construction of a new imperial capital at Constantinople created a transfer of population from other urban centers as its population grew to 800,000 by 400 before collapsing to 250,000 by 450 under the weight of disease, warfare and erratic food supplies.[75] Constantinople was the new Rome, and the emperors who resided there were more concerned about protecting it rather than other imperial centers, including the old Rome. The hold of the empire on its western territories weakened considerably as barbarian tribes started moving in, with and without permission, sometimes in collusion with a declining imperial elite that desperately tried to placate the barbarians closer to them in order to turn them against other barbarians. The movement of Goths, Vandals, and Huns, into Roman territories, the Anglo-Saxon migration into Roman Britain, and the spread of Christianity combined to sap the residual strength of Rome.

By the late-300s the empire in the West was falling apart administratively and territorially. Government even in Italy degenerated into plunder a generation before Alaric sacked Rome. As chaos spread the state resorted to selling offices to raise money, and those who acquired office through purchase were only interested in making a profit for themselves. The armies under the command of the Roman Empire withered away. We know that Diocletian was able to raise fifteen legions to stabilize the Danube region alone as part of his over all program of increasing the size of the army to 600,000. Fifty years after Diocletian, "the size of Rome's armies was contemptible", with difficulty numbering 20,000 regulars, though normally these were no more than "four or five or six thousand at various other crucial moments."[76] The imperial authority in the Western Mediterranean, Gaul, Spain, Britain, and North Africa, evaporated between 350 and 400 as the state succumbed to institutional exhaustion and poor leadership. The exhaustion at least can be attributed to the steroidal policies of Diocletian, the poor leadership in an autocracy being a matter of fortune more than anything else. Heavier taxes and larger armies had set in motion an inflationary spiral that undermined the interdependence of regions and led to a turn towards subsistence farming. In Egypt, the granary of the empire, the price of wheat rose from eight drachmas[77] per *artaba*[78] to twenty-four per *artaba* by the mid-200s, and 220–300 drachmas per *artaba* by AD 300.[79] The state responded to this by tying peasants to the land, abolishing freedom of movement for agricultural labor, turning artisans into hereditary craftsmen, and imposing, in 301, price controls on over one thousand items.[80] The tax on land, which accounted for nine-tenths of the total revenue and had become more important as the mercantile and manufacturing sectors contracted, was tripled between 300 and 350, crushing productivity and leading to flight from the land and the shrinking of the cultivated area.[81] The state, "From the time of Constantine onwards" responded to these diminishing returns through "the exaction of taxes by violence and torture" and confiscations.[82]

The sack of Rome by Alaric in 409 stimulated St. Augustine to write *The City of God*, one of the most important works ever produced in terms of its impact on the Western worldview.[83] St. Augustine interpreted history as a struggle between the true believers, who would be saved, and all others, including false believers, who would be damned, and argued that the calamities that were then falling upon the Romans were not due, as some were arguing, to the abandonment of the worship of the Roman pantheon. Battered by waves of barbarians, exhausted due to its own ineptitude and a lack of wise leadership, and demoralized by the spread of Christianity with its combination of isolationist spirituality and willingness to employ violence against real and imagined enemies, the Roman Empire fell in the West, in 476, though it continued in much diminished glory in the East as the Byzantine or Eastern Roman Empire. While the dream of reviving the Roman Empire never died, the collapse in the West left behind a powerful legacy of fragmentation and disunity from which the historical experience of feudalism and the early modern orders of

Continental Europe in terms of society, religion, and the state, would gradually emerge.

FALLEN EMPIRE, FEUDAL ORDERS

Ibn Khaldun drew a sharp distinction between tribal leadership, or a chiefdom, and royal authority as manifested in state (*dawlah*) power. In the former, the leader must convince others of the need to follow him and there is no basis for systematic coercion if agreement is not forthcoming. In the latter, the ruler has the ability to compel obedience to his wishes regardless of whether these are wise or utterly deranged. In chiefdoms, leadership operates by persuasion, appeals to honor, and the careful manipulation of antagonisms and ambitions. In a state, persuasion is of course desirable but it is not a necessary requirement for the exercise of power. During and after the collapse of the Roman Empire royal authority in the sense that Ibn Khaldun, Kautilya, Shang Yang, Nizam-ul Mulk Tusi, or Abu'l Fazl would have understood it ceased to function in Europe. This western peninsula of Eurasia descended into chaos from which, over centuries, an aristocratic feudal order emerged. In this order local magnates and kings exercised limited powers that became ritualized in custom through long usage and repetition. Cut off from the wealth of Asia and Egypt, European elites lacked the resources and trained manpower to counteract the centrifugal effects of a fragmented geography, relatively short growing seasons and limited agricultural yields, a low intellectual and cultural level, and a lack of great river valleys. So substantial was the resulting disparity that prior to the early modern period, as discussed above, China and India supported population densities per unit of arable land forty times greater than Europe.[84] So comprehensive were the ravages that attended the twilight and destruction of the Roman Empire that in 1500, Western social development was still lower than it had been 1300 years earlier during the *Pax Romana*.[85] Imperial China's annual iron output in 1078, at 125,000 tons, was greater than that of all of Europe combined in 1700.[86] Given the harsh objective limitations that hindered state building in Europe it is not surprising that it took more than a thousand years for continental bureaucratic states to reemerge at all, and even then, in an uneven and confused fashion owing to the historical experience of feudal governance.

Feudal governance evolved out of the maelstrom of Roman collapse, barbarian migrations and warfare, and Christian missionary zeal. The system of relationships associated with feudalism reached its apogee in the 1200s and 1300s before slowly coming under pressure from mercantile city-states, religious reformers, and more assertive monarchs and magnates. Alexis de Tocqueville provides a succinct summary of feudal development within Europe reference the situation in the 1300s:

. . . government was conducted according to the same principles, political assemblies were formed from the same elements and given the same powers. Society was divided in the same way, and the same hierarchy was displayed between the different classes: the nobility occupied an identical position in each society; they had the same privileges, the same appearance, the same character . . .

The constitution of the towns resembled each other and the country was governed the same way. The peasantry's condition varied little; the land was owned, inhabited, and farmed in the same way, the farmer subjected to the same burdens. From the borders of Poland to the Irish Sea, the manor, the lord's court, the fief, the services to be performed, the feudal dues, the corporations, everything was similar. Sometimes the names were the same, and what is even more remarkable, a single spirit animated all these analogous institutions.[87]

The core element around which feudalism was organized was a landowning aristocracy that held a substantial portion of its estates as private property.[88] Private ownership had come about owing to the disintegration of the Roman state and the vacuum it left as it dwindled in terms of public authority. In the late-Roman period "private property was what could be held and defended" and this established the principle that individuals could own and alienate lands as they wished, and organize themselves to defend their property.[89] Initially a form of possession, prolonged occupancy and the absence of a central power or even a local power capable of asserting itself as universal proprietor meant that over time "conditional tenure evolved by an irresistible momentum into outright property."[90] Thus a hierarchy of landowners gradually came into existence tied to each other, and the Church, through a web of service and family obligations that bound the more powerful and less powerful as lord and vassal. The Church was an integral part of this system owing to its extensive property and status as a lord in its own right. It also absorbed the younger sons of the aristocracy as high church officials, clerical aristocrats if you will, and maintained extensive records of land ownership as well as demographic information that gave it a say in disputes. The Church also received lands from the penitent as donations and endowments for churches and monasteries. At the apex of the lord-vassal pyramid were kings and the Holy Roman Emperor. Kings and emperors were themselves feudal magnates and had to contend with their vassals, who were great lords and had their own vassals, who in turn, might have their own dependents. Mutual recognition of social inequality and different degrees of prestige combined with mutual obligations held to be honorable were what governed the lord-vassal relationship that was central to feudal governance. This interface was arguably the most important political relationship in Europe for over a thousand years and one that had a profound impact on the subsequent development of European institutions and ideas as they relate to the individual.

Exploring the lord and vassal relationship reveals a pattern of proprietary rights and service obligations tied to a concept of social order that has few if any effective parallels in other parts of Eurasia and indicates that feudalism was a specifically European type of landlordism. The feudal nobility in Europe possessed by AD 1000 two distinct types of land in the form of the *allod* and the fief. The *allod* was the personal property of a noble and could comprise farmland, castles, coastal strips, pastures, mines, and some forests. The noble was free to sell it or add to it by buying from others as he or she pleased. Addition to the *allodial* holdings could also be made through inheritance though this might require litigation and more physically intense forms of feuding. The fief was land granted by a higher lord, the king, or the emperor, in exchange for service. The lord and vassal swore oaths of mutual loyalty and protection that tied their fortunes together. A fief would normally pass from father to eldest son, though if the eldest were not fit for military service he could be disinherited in favor of a younger son. Land held as fief was not strictly speaking private property as it could not be alienated by the fief-holder, and the higher lord who had granted the fief could take it away. In practice the absence of a central military force or monarchical bureaucracy meant that once a fief was granted, or recognized, it could only be resumed with difficulty. The feudal custom was that the lord had to demonstrate before an aristocratic jury that his vassal had failed to live up to his end of the bargain. An excellent example of this process was when the Holy Roman Emperor Frederick Hohenstaufen I "Barbarossa" (r. 1152–1190) sought to dispossess the Welf Duke, Henry the Lion, of lands granted to his family as fiefs. Henry the Lion was put on trial and in 1180 a jury of his aristocratic peers ruled in favor of the emperor and stripped him of his Saxon and Bavarian duchies. Of course, Henry the Lion did not lose his *allodial* dens, which remained in his possession, as they were private property held free of service obligations.

Feudal monarchs could also manipulate property disputes between and within the Church and nobility. The Holy Roman Emperor Otto III (r. 996–1002), famous for his attempt to revive the Roman Empire, supported bishops in their disputes with nobles that had fallen from royal favor.[91] In the cases involving the Margrave Arduin and Count Lantbert, the imperial tribunal's support helped the Church confiscate land from these errant noblemen.[92] On other occasions, Otto III, favored one group of clergymen against another, helping, for instance, Abbot Hugh of the monastery of Farfa defend himself against the "priests of St. Eustachio" (998) and press his claims "against the monastery of Sts. Comsa and Damiano in Mica Aurea" the following year.[93] Ottonian and Hohenstaufen pretensions as regards reviving the Roman Empire were not backed by the substance of royal authority. Monarchs and lords had to be very "careful when dealing with" their vassals.[94] Even in the event of rebellion or serious disobedience, aristocrats "could typically count on intermediaries to negotiate a surrender of some sort" predicated on stopping punishment "well short of any physical injury."[95] Reconciliation would be effected through the submission of an apology and expression of contrition at past acts of disobedience followed by the swearing of fresh oaths, and the monarch, or higher lord, was well advised to accept such olive branches for to do otherwise left him with few good options short of raising an army and visiting chastisement on his vassal who would in many cases be the owner of castles capable of withstanding a royal siege for months.[96]

Kings and emperors probably derived *schadenfreude* from the fact that they were far from alone in terms of being defied by their vassals. High lords had as hard a time controlling their vassals and managing relations with the Church, and later the townsmen, in their patrimonies and fiefdoms. A key figure at the local level was the castellan, or castle commander. Castles were strong points that helped defend territory by housing knights and soldiers and acted as administrative and economic centers. High lords, such as the dukes of Aquitaine, Normandy or Burgundy, dealt with dozens of important vassals many of whom were in command of one or more castles. This lesser nobility did much of the heavy lifting when it came to fighting, tax collection, maintaining order, gathering intelligence, and generally keeping the serfs in their place. Like those higher up the ladder, lesser nobles received fiefs and held *allodial* lands. The duke or count, could, in theory, dispossess his vassal of lands granted as fief if the oath or covenant was grossly violated or demand that his vassal seek service with another lord. In practice, doing so was risky for it could lead the vassal to rebel, seek aid from another lord, appeal to the king or emperor for justice, and even antagonize the Church.

A particularly potent illustration of the complexity of the lord and vassal relationship is provided by the dispute between Count William of Poitiers and one of his castellans, Hugh of Lusignan.[97] From the record of the dispute three vital features of the lord and vassal binary emerge. The first is that Hugh the castellan acknowledges Count William as his superior and always addresses him with the utmost deference. There is no pretence of equality as Count William is a high lord and Hugh is a relatively humble local baron. Second, deference in language granted and the high lords social superiority accepted, Hugh is not happy with some of the demands being made of him, such as Count William's desire to transfer Hugh's services to another lord, and Hugh is displeased with some of his complaints made in his lord's court being decided against him. Third, the count appears rather disdainful in the sense that he does not address Hugh by name and tells him that he should obey whatever orders are given, but as the record of the dispute progresses it turns out that "the count loses his preemptory bluster and his orders and threats change to suggestions and exclamations of frustration at his own helplessness."[98]

The dispute between Hugh the castellan and Count William helps establish that the lord did not own his vassal. Instead, lords and vassals entered into covenants. The lord had an obligation to consult his vassals, just as the king or the emperor had to consult their high lords, before making important decisions. The lord was required to resolve disputes involving his vassals, which was often a delicate affair. Vassals had a duty to protect the fief, defend their lord, and perform civil and military duties associated with maintaining castles, which included seeing to it that the lord got his share of the land-rent on time and in full. If the lord failed to consult his vassals or passed orders that hurt them materially in the absence of a military emergency or constituted a grievous insult to aristocratic honor, the vassals had the right to resist. The lord could deal with this resistance by withdrawing fiefs or taking to the field to beat some sense into a stubborn vassal but such options had a chance of succeeding only if the vassal lacked *allodial* holdings and castles. In the dispute between Count William and Hugh, the latter's position was strengthened as he owned "his home castle at Lusignan", plus "two others nearby" and had "received his uncle's castle" as well.[99] Furthermore, Hugh was pressing his family's claims to castles at three other locations.[100]

Up in Normandy, the local dukes had their own problems when it came to establishing their writ and controlling their vassals. The dukedom of Normandy, was formally recognized by the King of France, Charles the Simple, (r. 898—922), in 911. Rollo, a Viking war-chief, thus became the first Duke of Normandy, and gradually expanded his private holdings. Given that Rollo had besieged Paris, the French king was glad to have a negotiated settlement that recognized lands under the Viking's military control in exchange for a respite. Rollo was encouraged to direct his expansion towards Brittany, which, though not part of the French kingdom was ceded by the king, who turned out not to be so simple after all, as *allodial* holding to the Normans. Duke William Longsword extended the family's possessions to Breton lands and secured the coastline areas, though a resurgence of Breton power under Duke Alan II (r. 938–952) of Brittany, who deftly acknowledged the supremacy of the French King, Louis IV in 942, after expelling the Normans from much of Brittany in 939, threw a spanner into the works. Alan II was, however, forced to give up his claim to the Cotentin Peninsula and recognize its occupation by the Normans. For the Norman dukes, the Cotentin Peninsula was their frontier region and they sought to establish a presence by building churches, contracting marriages, and settling their Scandinavian kinsmen.[101] By expanding their *allodial* holdings the dukes were able to enter into agreements with vassals as well as making donations to the Church, which was also assisting in converting the Viking settlers to Christianity.[102] William the Conqueror, Duke of Normandy (r. 1035–1087) and King of England (r. 1066–1087), waged a long struggle to consolidate power in his domains and was able to assert his authority only through constant touring, attendance at church councils, and personal supervision of the collection of taxes. After 1066, the conquest of England provided him with a chance to settle many Normans in place of the Saxon lords who had fallen in battle. Later rulers, however, were not able to maintain the balance between their commitments in England and in Normandy and William's bid to rule the latter by "isolating, dividing and conquering the aristocracy" was not sustained.[103]

The Kingdom of Leon in the northwest of the Iberian Peninsula confronted problems similar to other feudal polities especially when it came to managing the relationship between the king and his magnates. Government in the 900s and 1000s was essentially an exercise of "royal concessions to agents" so as to draw them into "the regulation of justice" in areas beyond those under direct royal ownership.[104] The kings had practically no direct tools to speak of, though the Church was much better in this respect at least when it came to keeping records, so the only instruments were the "magnates."[105] The king negotiated with his magnates and issued charters that transferred responsibility to royal agents and local nobles for working together for the common good.[106] The monarch was the *de jure* head of the political system while feudal lords and the Church did more or less as they pleased. On balance, the aristocracy was sufficiently satisfied with their privileges and secession from the kingdom was not seriously contemplated.[107] To the extent that kings owned their lands they could hear complaints, decide cases and make donations. Like other monarchs, the kings of Leon could withdraw titles, honors and fiefs, "but they were mostly happy to allow families to retain this honor; to re-appropriate land and title was potentially troublesome, and sustained loyalty within families depended in some measure on the development of precedent."[108] It is no surprise, therefore, that land and title became hereditary and integral attributes of nobility in the northern corner of Iberia.[109]

The powerful role of the landed aristocracy is further evidenced by the tussle between the Hungarian monarchy and its vassals from its inception in 1000 to its liquidation at the hands of the slave soldiers of the Ottoman Sultan in 1526. As in Germany, France and Northern Iberia, the crown sought to consolidate power by granting lands as fiefs in exchange for military service. The nobility, however, soon became hereditary and assumed a corporate identity when it came to defending aristocratic privilege from monarchical aggrandizement. Extraordinarily charismatic and able kings were able to periodically increase royal power but time and again the nobility reasserted itself. By 1386, only nobles were represented in the Hungarian Diet and even the military threat from the Mongols (1200s) and Ottomans (1400s and 1500s) failed to trigger the formation of a royal authority. The resurgence of aristocratic power in the 1490s, which saw funds for the royal army cut, made sense constitutionally in terms of limiting the power of the king but was disastrous for the state given that it faced a persistent threat to its existence. In choosing aristocratic liberty over state security, the Hungarian nobility ended up losing both.

In Northern Italy, royal authority proved abortive as well. This is established by the 1183 Peace of Constance agreed between the Lombard League "and its overlord" Emperor Frederick Barbarossa.[110] This agreement was important as it recognized "the autonomy of Italian cities (including most of those of the Po Valley) collectively" and was employed "by medieval lawyers to argue about the limits of imperial power."[111] These arguments, combined with the incapacity of the empire in terms of asserting royal authority, meant that when Frederick II Hohenstaufen (r. 1220–1250) repudiated the 1183 Peace of Constance in 1226, the Lombard League was revived and open defiance of the emperor followed.[112] This open confrontation between the emperor and his Italian vassals, who felt entitled to rebel on account of violation of the covenant granted in 1183 by the Hohenstaufen dynasty, allowed the Papacy "to provide arbitration in the continually renewed disputes between the League and Frederick II."[113] The emperor tried to assert his authority by waging a long and ultimately unsuccessful war against the Italian city-states that ended in a rout of imperial forces at Parma in 1248. During this struggle, Frederick II won many victories in terms of forcing individual city-states to capitulate but resistance always flared up elsewhere and without an imperial bureaucracy or sufficiently large army to actually garrison his conquests, the strategic balance was not in his favor. One policy adopted by Frederick II in order to weaken resistance was to try and undercut the University of Bologna, which was a strong center of support for the Lombard League and adept at coming up with legal arguments against direct imperial rule. Frederick II responded by helping the University of Naples, which he founded in 1224, to train lawyers and secretaries for employment by his royal court, as well as to lure faculty and students away from the University of Bologna.[114] Amidst the feudal diffusion of power, the force of persuasion had some chance of balancing persuasion by force.

During the feudal period the most effective institution in terms of its ability to mobilize, organize and terrorize, was the Roman Catholic Church. Here the European experience between 500 and 1500 diverges considerably from other parts of Eurasia. In Europe, the ideocratic complex of the society was far wealthier, stronger and more coherent than its fragmented political order.[115] The strength of the Church is partly evidenced by the preponderance of ecclesiastical over lay records until the 1200s. It is also attested to by the ability of the Church to own vast amounts of property and earn revenues from the population at large, and the co-option of the aristocracy in the form of appointments to high offices in the Church, a development that helped weave it securely into the tapestry of a feudal society. Finally, the Church had the capacity to unleash considerable violence on account of its organizational integrity, near monopoly on learning, and ruthlessness in harnessing spirituality and sentimentalism for securing its economic and political interests. The success of the Church ensured in Europe a remarkable degree of religious unity amidst political fragmentation. The fact that up to the 1400s Europe was divided into hundreds of aristocratic chiefdoms and lacked royal authority in the Chinese or Persian sense of the term facilitated this process.

The Church was the single largest landowner in Europe. By the 600s about one third of the "productive land" in France was under Church ownership.[116] Between 700 and 900 Church landholdings in Germany, France, and Italy, benefited from close association with the Carolingian monarchy and effectively doubled.[117] By the 1200s between one-fourth and one-third of the cultivated land in Europe was owned by the Church.[118] Land meant revenues with which the Church could support members of the aristocracy in a style comparable to the wealthiest feudal lords and thus kings and nobles vied to fill high ecclesiastical offices with their nominees and kinsmen. For such appointments the Church could often extract, without much resistance, special concessions. Bishops in key places, such as Metz, were often appointed from families drawn from the "highest Frankish nobility."[119] In 775, Charlemagne (r. 768–814) granted Metz "a diploma of immunity" which prohibited the Frankish aristocracy from taxing or dispensing justice within Church lands.[120] The near monopoly of learning that the Church exercised also made clergymen vital to the functioning of the lay government. Thus, Charlemagne's most important advisers on political affairs, diplomacy, religion and education were Alcuin, St. Paulinus, and Abbot Fulrad—all clergymen, Fulrad having served the earlier Frankish monarchs in administrative and diplomatic capacities as well. The standardization of rituals and administrative practices under Pope Gregory the Great (r. 590–604) meant that for nearly a thousand years the Church was Europe's only functioning bureaucracy.[121] These qualities made it an indispensible ingredient of the feudal order and led to a nexus between secular authority and ecclesiastical power.

The unity of politics and religious rites found early expression in the relationship between the Carolingians (effective period was 718—888) and the Church. Charlemagne relied upon an aristocracy led by some three hundred counts to provide soldiers and maintain Frankish military superiority. The paucity of educated administrative personnel meant that there was no formal mechanism through which the monarch could communicate with or direct his lords except in terms of calling them up for military service. The Carolingian monarchy functioned, to the extent it could be said to function at all, "through a finely calibrated articulation of local and central interest" with the king ruling through the manipulation of a network of negotiated relationships with his aristocrats.[122] A ramshackle confederation of high lords led by an able and charismatic chief like Charlemagne, needed a sense of mission, a unifying purpose, to survive. That unifying agent was Christianity and entailed employing the chivalric vigor of the Frankish aristocracy to assist the Church in establishing a religious community. This was a pressing task for the Carolingian dynasty which, at is height, claimed sovereignty over one million square kilometers that included "180 dioceses, 700 monasteries, 750 royal estates . . . 150 palaces" and nearly seven hundred "administrative districts."[123] The religious program undertaken by the Carolingians with the assistance of the Roman

Catholic Church proceeded along four main lines. The first was providing space for missionaries to preach and backing them up with force wherever necessary. The second was cracking down on heresy and upholding orthodox Christian doctrine as expressed by Rome and the Frankish-dominated ecclesiastical establishment of the empire. The third was enforcing a basic minimum amount of religious observance, and the fourth was promoting the worship of relics and saints.

The sword cleared the way for the cross and Charlemagne hoped, erroneously as it turned out, that religious uniformity would hold his conquests together. The war against the Saxons, which consumed much of Charlemagne's energies from the 780s, dragged on for about thirty years and ended in a victory for the Franks. The solution to the problem of Saxon rebellion was to spread Christianity by rewarding those leaders who accepted and stayed loyal with gifts, titles, and incorporation into the aristocracy. Fortified churches were set up to act as the local centers for Christianization. When the Saxons rebelled in 782, Charlemagne responded by massacring rebels and ordering all those who refused baptism, attacked churches, conspired against Christians, or broke their oaths of loyalty, be put to death.[124] The struggle against the Saxons, and later the Avars, was converted into a Holy War that ended in military victory, political adjustment, and religious conversion.

While expanding the frontiers of Christendom was a virtuous and rewarding exercise, attacking fellow Christians posed a moral dilemma resolved by the need to act in order to preserve the purity of Church doctrine. By siding with the orthodox views of the Roman Papacy Charlemagne not only won for himself an imperial title in 800, but secured Church support for his dynasty. The Adoptionist controversy that came to a head when Pope Hadrian I appealed to Spanish bishops to reject adoptionism and return to the true path furnished an opportunity to demonstrate Charlemagne's seriousness on religious matters. The Adoptionists claimed that Christ "in his human nature was the adoptive Son of God by Grace" though otherwise he remained "the true Son of God."[125] Charlemagne's adviser, Alcuin, was displeased that the Adoptionists used "the word *adoptivus* rather than the orthodox *assumptus* to describe" Christ in his human form and thus regarded Adoptionism as a rejection "of the unity of Christ's two natures in one person."[126] As the Frankish kingdom expanded into the Spanish March it took upon itself the responsibility for eliminating this heresy.[127] Successfully doing so would prove that unity in religion could overcome the diversity of laws and peoples that lived under Carolingian rule. In 796, Alcuin reported that some 20,000 heretics had been brought back into the fold and that the people at large were coming around to seeing the error of their ways.[128]

Enforcing a minimum amount of religious observance was a logical extension to Holy War and eliminating heresy. The religious justification for compulsion was based on the belief in "the inherent truth of Christianity and the entrance into that truth through baptism."[129] While negotiation and correspondence with infidels was possible, there could be no negotiation with an individual or a community that became Christian but didn't adhere to religious practices or relapsed into paganism. Carolingian laws deemed it compulsory for all subjects to have basic religious knowledge and be able to recite the Creed and the Lord's Prayer.[130] Avoiding baptism was declared a capital offense and, of course, relapse into paganism invited similar consequences.[131] All children had to be baptized before they turned one and parents who proved lax in this respect suffered fines and were forced to do penance.[132] With the passage of time the system of ecclesiastic courts, censorship, and special offices designed to seek out and destroy false believers became more elaborate—the Index and the Inquisition serving as the divine razor's edge.

The worship of Saints and Holy Relics, closely connected with belief in miracle-working, added an element of mysticism and the supernatural to the daily routine of Christian worship. The veneration of relics was "relentlessly promoted by the Carolingian establishment" in order to provide "unity to the empire" and compensate for the relatively small number of holy men on the ground.[133] This establishment helped consolidate the system of parishes, brought individual churches under Episcopal control and tried to collect the tithe on a regular basis.[134] Relics were important as the miracles attributed to them helped prove the truth of Christianity and thus encouraged the faithful to make donations and follow religious practices. In 794, six years before Charlemagne accepted an imperial title from the pope, the ecclesiastical council of Frankfurt brought together bishops from Italy, Germany, Gaul, and England, as well as papal legates, to condemn the Adoptionists and reject some of the findings of the Second Council of Nicaea held under the auspices of the Byzantine Empire.[135]

The relationship between the monarch and the high lords on the one hand and the Church on the other was rarely smooth, but the cultural dominance and wealth of the sacred institution placed it in a position where it could manipulate religious belief and popular superstition to keep the aristocracy in its place. The sheer number of aristocratic chiefdoms and their complex networks of potentially unruly vassals gave the Church enormous advantages in organization, discipline and propaganda—a bit like a modern Multinational Corporation operating in poor countries. At opportune moments, these strengths could be converted into the crusades, inquisitions, purifications, expulsions, and intensified censorship that figure prominently in Europe's medieval and early modern history. Seeking out and destroying witches, for instance, was effected "through spies" that reported to the Church which followed up by securing "confessions using various torture techniques" and executing those "who failed the test."[136] The Spanish experience during and after the re-conquest saw this potential fully realized owing to the special confluence of aristocratic, royal and clerical zeal. The Moriscos, formerly Muslims who had been forced to accept

Christianity, were expelled in 1609. Some 400,000 were forced to leave and of these it is estimated that two-thirds died.[137] It is a "terrible paradox" that the Inquisition was motivated by the "ardent and often sincere desire to combat evil" but ended up perpetuating "evil on a grander scale than the world had ever seen before."[138] Europe's gradual economic recovery, the revival of trade, and the great opportunities opened up by the discovery of the New World, meant that the commoners, especially townsmen, also emerged as actors on the political scene.

In the early 1400s, the annual revenue of the city-state of Venice was 750,000 ducats, while its population was 150,000.[139] If one adds to these totals the amounts for revenues and population of Venice's colonies they would stand at 1.615 million ducats and about 500,000 people.[140] In 1423, the revenue of France as a whole amounted to one million ducats while its population was in the range of 10–15 million.[141] In Florence, at about the same time, out of a total population of 100,000, some 10,000 were children enrolled in primary schools, 1,000–1,200 were enrolled in high schools, and three hundred to four hundred were attending universities.[142] The ability of Italian city-states to defy the Holy Roman Emperor was formally recognized by the 1183 Peace of Constance and confirmed by Frederick II's eventual defeat in 1248. While defying the emperor, the Italian city-states were able to bring in the Church as a collaborator and arbitrator without falling under its direct control. The rise of the Italian city-states and their humanistic ethos reflected the growing tri-polarity of European social and political orders as the townsmen began to assert themselves against ecclesiastical and feudal-aristocratic excesses. In some parts of Europe, this led to the emergence of city-states,[143] in others the alignment of townsmen with monarchs helped accelerate the rise of a central government strong enough to resist the parochial privileges of the aristocracy and the supra-territorial intervention of the Church. By the 1600s monarchies had generally triumphed over city-states on account of superior war-making capabilities and their increasingly bureaucratic though still semi-feudal administrative practices. This was the case in France where the early modern European variant of the continental bureaucratic state first emerged, it is to its historical experience of governance that we now turn.

LA GRANDE NATION AND THE FRENCH MONARCHICAL TRADITION

Continental bureaucratic empires eventually emerged throughout Europe, the only major exceptions being England (discussed later) and the Netherlands. The process took many centuries (1500–1900) and proceeded from the logic of modernization, classicism, and the pressures of economic and military competition in a geographic and demographic environment conducive to multi-polarity. The reemergence of the "Roman law tradition, which did not . . . give the habit of local self-government a primordial value" coincided with the reemergence of continental bureaucratic empires.[144] This was understandable from the ruler's perspective given "the greater difficulty of state-making on the continent, where recalcitrant regions and cities were often subdued only by force or ruse."[145] The oldest, and for many centuries the greatest, continental bureaucratic state in Europe was France.[146]

The Hundred Years' War (1337–1453) had necessitated the creation of a standing royal army as the old feudal levies proved incapable of resisting the English invasion. With the war over in 1453 and with France victorious, the French aristocracy reasserted its independence. Louis XI (r. 1461–1483), known as The Spider, was determined to cut the aristocracy, led by Charles the Bold, the Duke of Burgundy, down to size. In 1477 the royal army defeated the nobility, the Duke of Burgundy fell in battle, and Louis confiscated the greater part of the fractious duke's estate. Four years later the feudal states of Anjou, Maine, and Provence, were brought under royal control. Louis made and broke laws and raised taxes as he pleased, presented royal authority as the savior of the peasantry and middle-classes from aristocratic hegemony, and embarked upon a program of royal works inclusive of canal and road construction unprecedented by medieval European standards. France's internal divisions and restlessness meant that the monarch had to be firmer and emerged "as the natural arbiter and policeman."[147]

Francis I (r. 1515–1547) used the royal army to defeat the Swiss and capture Milan at the outset of his reign and inherited a class of officials some seven thousand strong. In 1516 he negotiated the Concordat of Bologna with Pope Leo X from a position of military superiority. Under the Concordat the king gained control of all appointments of material significance in the Catholic Church in France, which also became the king's source of divine sanction. Consequently, ". . . the best posts in the Church were used by the king to reward service to the crown."[148] Once the Reformation began, Francis I persecuted Protestants in France and sparked nearly a century of religious warfare within the country. Judicial institutions, such as the Parlement of Paris, or the seven provincial parlements that had emerged between 1443 and 1532 at Toulouse, Grenoble, Bordeaux, Dijon, Aix-les-Bains, Rouen, and Rennes, and feudal representative institutions in the provinces were not able to compensate for the executive function.[149] The Estates-General, in 1439, had surrendered its right to raise taxes other than feudal dues, enabling the monarch to maintain an army and rule through an appointed council, and so could not play the role of the English Parliament as a centralizing *and* representative body invested in maintaining the authority of the state while simultaneously checking the power of the king and his appointees.[150] In France the state would evolve as the consequence of the ascendancy of royal authority maintained by the army, administered by a bureaucracy, and legitimized by the Church and a royalist ideology. The alternative was chaos.

Widespread civil strife set the context for the next step towards absolutism. In order to coordinate and improve the responses of local governments, which were still in the hands of aristocrats and rich commoners, the royal council began deputing extraordinary agents who represented the sovereign's will and possessed royal sanction for taking measures and securing the resources necessary to restore order. The propertied classes, aristocrats and commoners alike, who had the most to lose from a breakdown of order, submitted to the will of royal representatives. The rise of the Bourbon dynasty under Henry III of Navarre, later known as Henry IV of France (r. 1589–1610) helped established the principle of absolutism as a superior form of government to feudal power-sharing. In 1598, the Edict of Nantes, which granted religious toleration to Protestants and allowed them to maintain military forces in cities they governed, brought the civil war to an end. This edict recognized "the power of the Protestants" and the need to bring an end to internal feuding till the state was strong enough to assert itself rather than representing an authentic royal commitment to upholding freedom of conscience.[151] The respite, however, was used fairly well by Henry IV and his financial chief, the Duke of Sully, to consolidate royal superiority. This was done by centralizing all tax-related matters by forbidding provincial governors from raising or collecting taxes without royal approval so that a central budget document could be drawn up.[152] This also helped fix the size of the royal army at about 100,000 in peacetime and paid for military pensions and a hospital to cater to the army's medical needs.[153] A postal service was organized to facilitate communications within France and central inspection of roads and public infrastructure was introduced.[154] To oversee all this activity centrally appointed royal commissioners were sent to the provinces on a regular basis. These royal commissioners represented an extension of the king's person and thus, while being of common origin, enjoyed a direct line to the monarch that aristocratic governors and parlements, and nobility-dominated provincial estates, could not match. By the 1620s these commissioners were referred to as intendants and were regularly appointed and rotated royal officials. These royal servants focused on matters of finance and reported to the king through his finance minister. With their aid, a crackdown was launched by the central government on fraudulent practices in the tax administration, which relied heavily on tax farmers and venal office holders for collection. Tax farm terms were stabilized so that collectors had more predictable ten-year tenures and strict book-keeping ensured that more money made it to the royal coffers. Attempts to establish tax tribunals and eliminate life-time pensions and annuities failed on account of vested interests, but increases in the salt tax, special taxes on officers being transferred, and the regularization of an annual donation by the clergy did produce positive effects.[155] In 1598, France's debt stood at 300 million *livres* and expenses were 50 percent greater than revenues.[156] By 1609, bankruptcy had been averted and there was a surplus of twelve million *livres* in the royal treasury.[157]

The contrast with Spain, where the king received gold and silver from the American colonies and spent lavishly on imperial wars and royal magnificence could not have been greater. Spanish monarchs declared bankruptcy in 1557, 1560, 1575, 1598, 1607, 1627, 1647, 1652, 1660, and 1662.

By 1610, the French state had become stronger and better organized than any individual group in French society.[158] Henry IV's assassination in 1610 triggered nearly half a century of uncertainty that ended with a comprehensive triumph for royal authority. Under Louis XIII (r. 1610–1643), the ascent of Cardinal Richelieu to the Royal Council, where he served as First Minister from 1624 to 1642, provided the absolutist cause with an able leader. Richelieu, a delegate to the Estates-General of 1614, sought to further strengthen royal authority within France. In 1627, Richelieu waged a successful war against Protestant-controlled cities in France, which concluded with the Peace of Alais. This arrangement confirmed the religious toleration extended by the Edict of Nantes but deprived Protestants of the right to maintain troops in cities that they governed. For Richelieu, only the state, which is to say the monarchy, could possess the means of perpetuating organized violence and the freedom granted to Protestant cities as the price for peace a generation earlier had to be rescinded now that the center was strong enough to assert itself.[159] Notwithstanding the opposition of the "Parlements" and nobility to Richelieu's centralization,[160] the cardinal steamed ahead.[161] All fortifications controlled by the nobility within France were destroyed or brought under royal control courtesy of the royal army. Exile or execution awaited the real or perceived enemies of absolutism.[162] Richelieu "terrified the nobility", punishing those who violated royal edicts and placing restrictions on noble prerogatives such as dueling with confiscations, exile, and executions, though "he did nothing to make them useful members of society."[163] Within the clergy, Richelieu appointed persons of administrative talent and loyalty to the crown to key positions, spiritual merit being of inferior importance in the eyes of the Machiavellian cardinal.[164] The Parlement of Paris was thus allowed to deliver judgment on Church matters though state prisoners were excluded from its ambit.[165]

France was organized into provinces and Richelieu began the conversion of the extraordinary agents used during the civil wars and employed frequently by Henry IV into regular salaried, appointed, royal commissioners recruited from the middle-classes and gave them the imposing title of "*intendants de justice, de police et de finances*,"[166] and subdelegates. The intendant could "preside over any court within the province," personally "try cases," assess and collect the poll tax, and "intervened more and more" in the affairs of the local governments.[167] These officials were similar to collectors and collector-magistrates in the South Asian tradition. Within France, provinces fell into two major categories. In the *pays d'etats*, which included Languedoc, Brittany, Burgundy, Provence, Dauphine and Normandy, provincial estates dominated by the local aristocracy and wealthy commoners continued to function with limited fiscal powers.[168] Here the intendants had to contend with the residual power of the aristocracy on a daily basis. In the rest of the country, however, the provinces were *pays d'elections* in which "enterprising and able intendants might carry out reforms impossible in provinces subject to moribund and reactionary assemblies."[169] Press, police, and pubic opinion were controlled by these royal servants, and Richelieu saw to it that official news bulletins, such as the *Gazette* and *Mercure*, were complemented by apparently independent pamphleteers secretly subsidized by the state to spread pro-regime propaganda.[170] In 1631, the formation of a special tribunal, the *Chambre de l'Arsenal*,[171] provided Richelieu with the means to go after political opponents with the help of royalist judges. By the end of Richelieu's tenure, the French king had a royal bureaucracy that numbered, from the highest to the lowest grade, about forty thousand strong, out of a population of about nineteen million.[172] The continental bureaucratic state had arrived.

Its survival, however, was put into question soon after Richelieu's death in 1642, followed in 1643 by Louis XIII's passing away. The aristocracy, taking advantage of the minority of Louis XIV, combined forces with venal office holders and staged an uprising known as the *Fronde*. The aristocrats wanted to restore their past power and bring the monarchy under their influence. The venal office holders were troubled by the financial direction that France had taken after it intervened (in 1635) in the Thirty Years' War (1618–1648). The cost of this war meant that in 1643, out of total revenues of 58 million *livres*, some 48 million *livres* had already been committed to military expenses.[173] By 1645, the entire revenues for the next three years had been spent against loans taken to pay for the war.[174] The fiscal pressure led to tax farmers committing excesses and triggered protests and rebellions that merged with aristocratic opposition to the royal regime.[175] Fortunately for the young king, his council contained an absolutist able to rise to the aristocratic challenge—Cardinal Mazarin. Mazarin responded by using the army to crush the commoners who refused to pay taxes, billeting troops in homes until the residents submitted to the state's demand.[176] Tariffs were raised, additional financiers were appointed to squeeze Paris, and the tax levied on house building outside city walls was increased. The ultimate Kautilyan maneuver was executed in 1648. Mazarin announced royal bankruptcy, which predictably caused the value of state bonds and financial papers to collapse.[177] Panic selling meant that royal agents were able to buy up about nine-tenths of the bonds at throwaway prices—sometimes one-fiftieth of the nominal price.[178] Once this was accomplished Mazarin announced that the government had accidentally underestimated its ability to pay interest on its debt.[179] The price of these papers now rose rapidly and they were sold off to venal office holders and tax farmers at a profit.[180] The end of the Thirty Years War in 1648, combined with dissensions within the rebels, whose aristocratic leaders were acting out of personal motives and despised the commoners even more than they hated Mazarin, created more space for the royalist camp. By May 1651, the aristocrats had broken away from the commoners and their war of the "gutters and the chamber pots", while Mazarin appeased Paris by sacrificing unpopular subordinates.[181] In October 1652 Louis XIV (r. 1643—1715) returned to Paris while the royal army led by Turenne defeated the rebels.[182] By February 1653, the rebels were on the run and Mazarin was summoned to Paris by the king so as to resume charge of the government.[183] Despite initial successes, the organized force of the state apparatus created by Richelieu, when wielded with skill, proved too great for the rebels who were crushed. In 1661, Mazarin passed away and Louis XIV decided to rule without a first minister and manage the affairs of state personally. During the first twenty years of his reign "all those institutions which might curb in some degree the power of the Crown—the *Parlements*, the governors of provinces, the provincial Estates and town councils—were gradually stripped of any effective power."[184] It was under Louis XIV, that an ideocratic and arbitrary culture of power similar in many of its characteristics to other continental bureaucratic empires discussed, took hold of France.

Louis XIV began his reign by imprisoning his aristocratic superintendent of finances, Nicolas Fouqet, ostensibly for embezzlement and for maintaining a small private army, but in actuality for building a "court far more glamorous than the king's," on which eighteen thousand men toiled at the cost of 18 million *livres* on his feudal estate.[185] Fouqet, who had probably embezzled funds to build his palace, died in prison. Fouqet was replaced by Jean-Baptiste Colbert, a commoner and son of a merchant, as superintendent of finances. Colbert focused on improving the collection of taxes and more than doubled the net revenues of the government between 1661 and 1667. By 1689, three-fourths of the French population lived in provinces whose assemblies had fallen into disuse and in all of France the system of intendants, subdelegates, and mounted police, was rendered effective. A former controller of finances, Mr. Law, confessed to a contemporary ". . . the kingdom of France is ruled by thirty intendants. You have neither a parlement, nor estates, nor governors; it is thirty subordinate officials detached for duty in the provinces, on whom the happiness or misfortune of these provinces, their prosperity or their poverty, depend."[186] A more accurate statement would be that the intendants, being the instruments of the king, reflected his intellectual and moral strengths and weaknesses. As long as the former outweighed the latter, the machine worked with reasonable efficiency and arbitrariness was restrained by the ruler's enlightened self-interest.

So long as the center was strong, rebellions could be dealt with. Louis XIV's "ruthless taxation policy" and conscription of the peasantry, sparked "sporadic" rural revolts that were "mercilessly suppressed."[187] In 1662, at Boulougne, rebels suffered six hundred casualties and three thousand were arrested.[188] In 1670, at Vivarais, one hundred were executed. In 1675, in Brittany, "innumerable executions took place, and the soldiers robbed, tortured and killed as they made their way through the province."[189] The strength of the standing army doubled under Louis XIV to about 200,000. Ably administered and led by la Tellier, Louvois, Vauban, and Turenne, the French military stood a cut above others in terms of its organization, discipline and morale.[190] With a fully developed commissariat that took care of logistics and an ambulance service, the army's need to live off the land was greatly reduced.[191] The state was the sole and direct employer of troops[192] while the navy was maintained through selective conscription from coastal communities managed through detailed registers compiled by the royal bureaucracy.[193] Commissions could still be purchased but candidates also had to pass qualifying examinations and some branches of the army, such as the artillery and siege-craft, became substantially merit-oriented.[194]

When Louis XV (r. 1715–1774), decided to eliminate begging from France "The mounted police were ordered to arrest at one blow all the beggars to be found in the kingdom" and "more than fifty thousand were seized."[195] The mounted police, under the control of intendants, became the principal instrument of order as the eighteenth century unfolded and men of property asked for police units to be deployed close to their residences and places of work. By today's standards, the Old Regime was tolerant of crime and disturbances and left dealing with such behavior to the local bureaucracy and aristocrats. Such behavior was regarded as inevitable and accepted provided that it did not spread upwards. The state, however, took a dim view of violence directed towards the royal servants. Thus, murdering state officials, obstructing the collection of taxes, and threatening state security, all merited the military being sent in.[196] The judicial system in France was "inquisitorial", "operated in private," and relied extensively on "the use of torture," the purpose being not "to discover and establish the facts" but "confirm guilt."[197] Given the option, however, the French monarchy preferred circumvention to direct confrontation. For example, instead of abolishing the post of *Chancelier*, the head of the French judicial system and an aristocratic life officer of the crown with security of tenure, his powers were transferred to the *Garde des sceaux*[198] who was "appointed and dismissed at will by the king."[199]

An essential component of French absolutism was the financial autonomy of the king derived from the sale of offices, titles, and privileges.[200] Licenses were sold to guilds, titles of nobility to commoners, election rights to municipalities, and thousands of offices were created for the express purpose of being sold to the highest bidder. Periodically, and this emphasized the arbitrary power of the king, the offices, titles, privileges, and licenses, were revoked en masse only to be re-created for sale at even higher prices. Richelieu, for instance, abolished about one hundred thousand venal offices and saw to it that they ". . . were immediately reborn under other names."[201] A generation later, Colbert estimated that half a billion *livres* were "sunk in this miserable kind of property."[202] Between 1693 and 1709 Louis XIV created forty thousand posts for sale.[203] He also "annulled all the titles of nobility acquired in the last ninety-two years, the majority of which had been given by him" and stipulated that keeping one's title was possible "by furnishing an additional sum."[204] Between 1689 and 1715, Louis XIV created an additional two thousand offices to manage the ports and markets of Paris alone.[205] These measures were needed to pay for the enormous costs of France's wars and the growing opulence of Versailles. It is estimated that from the War of Devolution (1667–68) to the War of Spanish Succession (1701–1714), France spent 1.5 billion *livres* and 1.2 million Frenchmen paid the ultimate price for their monarch's pursuit of glory.[206] Louis XV did much the same as his predecessor though defeat in the Seven Year War saw the loss of much of the overseas French empire (1763). The ease with which tens of thousands of posts and titles were arbitrarily created, abolished, and recycled, reveals the extent to which the aristocracy had declined as an autonomous institution and the degree to which French society was imbued with a mania for public office and bureaucracy.

Such measures were accompanied by more enlightened reforms. Thus, the tax tribunal set up in 1661, provided an incentive to cooperate with the government in the form of offering complainants a share of the ill-gotten wealth of financial offenders.[207] The budget was improved and made a proper balance sheet while taxes, like the *taille* or tax on land, were recalibrated and a formal appeals mechanism created to deal with complaints.[208] The state provided subsidies for shipbuilding and invested in improving the quality and competitiveness of French manufactures such as linen, leather-goods, silk, cloth, and tapestries.[209] The policy of the government was to discourage the export of raw materials and encourage the export of manufactured and luxury goods that could bring in more gold and silver than went out of the country. The wealthy commoners benefited from Louis XIV's absolutism. They could buy titles of nobility and get official status, which was a matter of great pride for them. Even military service, the traditional preserve of the aristocracy, was open to them though here aristocrats continued to dominate the officer corps until the Revolution. Nevertheless, in 1789, out of an officer corps of 10,000, about 1,000 were bourgeoisie, while in technical arms like the artillery, the percentage was closer to one-fourth.[210]

The decline of noble power, albeit without a corresponding decline in privileges, becomes evident when one considers that in Louis XIV's entire reign only two aristocrats became ministers. The aristocratic governors of the provinces were kept at the royal court, as were many other leading nobles, where ". . . they outdid one another in flattery," piled up debts "in lavish entertainments," and were transformed from "turbulent semi-feudal lords" to "docile courtiers" dependent on royal patronage.[211] The policy of the government was to exclude the nobility and clergy from offices of any consequence and rely on official families drawn from the bourgeoisie, such as the Colbert family, to fill key positions. Louis XIV became so certain of his power over the aristocracy that he "in his edicts had publicly proclaimed the theory that the lands of the kingdom had been originally leased on terms by the state, which thus remained the sole real owner."[212] Louis

XIV thought nothing of ordering his engineers to build roads in straight lines with forced labor[213] even though "they cut across a thousand inheritances" and the "proprietors thus devastated or destroyed were always paid arbitrarily and late, and often not at all."[214] The palace of Versailles was completed at a cost of 116 million *livres* and 30,000 workers were deployed during its construction only to divert the local river to provide the palace complex with fresh water.[215] Further evidence of Louis XIV's subjugation of the aristocracy is that other than the *Fronde*, only the rebellion of Rohan involved noblemen. Rohan, however, was motivated by pressure to pay his debts and his dislike for Louvois, and tried to sell Quilleboeuf to the Netherlands in 1674.[216] Rohan and "his few accomplices paid for the revolt with their lives."[217]

French society's absorption of a statist culture of power found expression in the behavior of the bourgeoisie. Like the merchants of China, the greatest "ambition of a well-to-do *bourgeois*" was "to rise out of his own despised class into the nobility" through purchase of title, or service to the king.[218] Tax farming, royal favor, abuse of venal offices, and government contracts, not trade and manufacturing for the market, were the sources of the greatest wealth in France. The French bourgeoisie ". . . was heavily dependent on royal favor, subject to royal regulation, and oriented toward the production of arms and luxuries for a restricted clientele" and thus "the situation" resembled "late Tokugawa Japan or even India of Akbar's day somewhat more than" England at that time.[219] The intensely political nature of the French economy combined with an arbitrary taxation system provided the taxpayer:

> . . . a direct and permanent interest in spying on his neighbors and reporting to the collector on the increase of their wealth; everything was listed there, from envy, informing and hatred. Would one not think that these things were happening in the domains of some rajah of Hindustan?[220]

The ideocratic complex of the French State elevated the king to godlike status. Louis XIV adopted the symbolism of sun worship common to Japan, Egypt, Persia, and India, and styled himself the "Sun King." At a more practical level, the king legitimated his absolute power through the combination of an official priesthood and bureaucratic intelligentsia common to other continental bureaucratic empires. That said, the advent of the Enlightenment compromised the ability of the French monarchy to avoid fundamental questions being posed, especially when many of the leading members of the court, bureaucracy, and intelligentsia, subscribed to the Enlightenment ideals of reason, humanism, and liberalism. Within France opinion was polarized between supporters of the Enlightenment and Catholic fundamentalists, with both factions seeking control of the state in order to impose "one, and only one" conception of the state and the nation upon society.[221] The revocation of the Edict of Nantes in October 1685 through the Edict of Fontainebleau withdrew religious toleration for Protestants and led to the emigration of perhaps 400,000 out of the one and half million strong community.[222] This was a serious blow to the French economy for many of the migrants were skilled artisans, traders, and manufacturers, who had earlier been encouraged by Colbert's policies.

Ultimately, the French monarchy fell for reasons similar to other continental bureaucratic empires. The king, "a Grand Bureaucrat," presided over a complex, cumbersome apparatus, and was "the central figure of the whole machine, who provided the source of power" and direction, suffered from human failings.[223] The concentration of administrative, fiscal, judicial, military, and diplomatic powers in the hands of the king placed immense strain on his intellectual and moral capabilities and required a great deal of hard work. Louis XIV spent his days "in a routine of official business so regular" that one could "tell the time of day from his acts."[224] When ill, Louis XIV convened the royal council in his bedchamber and carried on directing the work of government, thus setting a personal example of diligence and rigor.[225] During the early decades of Louis XV's reign his first minister, the Cardinal de Fleury (1726–1743) and controller-general, Philibert Omy (1730–1745) kept the ship of state on course.[226] After de Fleury's death, Louis XV decided to personally handle the affairs of state as his illustrious predecessor had done. Unfortunately for France, Louis XV was, quite simply, "bored with the duties" of his office and invested much of his time in "hunting and women."[227] His greatest weakness "was the fatal incapacity for decision" which paralyzed the center while his protégés "and mistresses competed for influence."[228] The discipline of the state broke down and king lost control of his subordinates. In this context, the level of arbitrariness increased, the ability of the state to perform its basic duties declined even as its functions multiplied ridiculously, confusion reigned, and the country descended into fiscal and ideological crisis.

One particularly damaging effect of the slowdown after Louis XIV was the indiscipline with which tax farms were allotted. Another was the recurrence of famine on account of the inability of the government to move grain quickly enough from where it was in surplus to deficit areas. Without royal vigilance and effective intervention to check abuses the tax farmers became a mafia that intercepted revenues and rotated assignments within a narrow circle. Finance officials, rather than representing the interests of the king in their dealings with tax farmers did the opposite. Thus, indirect taxes were left to the tender mercies of sixty millionaires who provided an initial outlay of 1.56 million francs each.[229] The trouble was that tax farms were being granted for decades at a time with little or no regard for delivery after the initial payment.[230] The famines inflicted or aggravated by state incompetence and corruption were perhaps the most terrible punishment visited on France through the malevolent apathy of her sovereign and the mendacity of his servants. During the reign of Louis XV a dozen famines struck the country and the single most important cause of these tragedies was the royal grain monopoly and attendant restrictions on internal trade in essential food items.[231] The need for a thorough revamp of the royal grain administration was acute for by 1774, the price of a loaf of bread was nearly nine *sous* against a daily wage for agricultural and urban workers of between ten and twenty *sous*, having doubled in twenty years.[232] Assuming a laborer was able to find work two hundred days in a year, he could barely afford to feed himself let alone a large family.[233]

The Old Regime's last king, Louis XVI, though pious and personally untainted by scandal, was like Louis XV, prone "to let events take their course,"[234] and unable to take the hard decisions necessary to preserve, initially, his absolute power, and ultimately his own life. One of the decisions that needed to be taken involved reform of the royal household, another entailed doing something about the hopelessly inefficient royal monopoly on grain while another involved increasing revenues. On all three Louis XVI struck out. The royal household remained a drain on the treasury for it now comprised some fifteen thousand persons employed or associated with the king, queen, or their immediate relatives.[235] On the grain monopoly, Louis XVI brought in Turgot and allowed him to have a go at reforming the system. Turgot had great confidence in the free market and was convinced that liberalizing the grain trade would automatically correct the imbalances that resulted from the royal monopoly. Of course, when free market reforms are introduced into a badly managed state dominated by mafias the situation deteriorates further. The price of grain shot up after the liberalization and the reform was abandoned after Turgot's dismissal in May 1776. Opposition within the royal household stymied tax reforms as the only way to balance the books was to extend regular taxation to the nobility and clergy who still enjoyed various immunities. The king could have overruled opposition and supported his ministers but lacked understanding of the problem and was inclined to avoid making hard decisions. One method that could have been used was to reintroduce the 1715 inquiry into corruption and malpractices in the tax farms in order to force tax farmers to readjust their payments to the state and pay arrears. This would have required political will and was technically well within the capacity of the state. After years of doing nothing, it was the fiscal crisis that triggered the general crisis of 1787–88, the declaration of bankruptcy,[236] and the convening of the Estates-General that set the stage for the overthrow of the Bourbon monarchy.[237]

The Revolution resulted in the creation of an even more centralized and bureaucratic state whose basic features remain intact to this day.[238] The provinces were swept away and replaced with administrative departments, mass conscription raised the size of the army to 800,000 and was accompanied by drastic economic controls to stabilize prices. The property of the Church and nobility was confiscated on a large scale and during the Reign of Terror unleashed by the democratic Jacobins in 1793–94, tens of thousands were guillotined or killed as the revolutionary army moved to crush internal rebellions. A new cult involving the worship of reason was introduced along with a new calendar to mark the beginning of a great new age of liberty, equality and fraternity, that were to be secured through a leveling terror. Given that the new regime was acting for the common good it was perfectly acceptable to use coercion to secure compliance with the new social contract, to force people to be free.[239] The overthrow of the democratic dictatorship of the Jacobins and its replacement by a republican oligarchy called the Directory (1795–1799) weakened the executive power and paved the way for military dictatorship under Napoleon Bonaparte (r. 1799–1815). Napoleon I restored the French state, modernized the bureaucracy, and made talent and merit rather than birth the key indexes against which state servants could be judged. Napoleon I thus represented the restoration of high quality authoritarian rule.

Napoleon I relied upon multiple bureaucratic hierarchies to maintain order, collect taxes, administer justice, and carry out development work. Napoleon understood that the servants of the state were the key to effective government. In this spirit, "One of Napoleon's first acts as Consul was to create a special body of 840 officials, eight to a department, whose sole job was the levying and collecting of tax".[240] This worked remarkably well for within a few years of the coup the state collected 660 million francs from income tax and property tax, which was 185 million more than "the old regime had obtained from dozens of different levies in 1788."[241] The purchase of offices was replaced with direct appointments and regular salaries. To ensure financial discipline separate institutions, such as the Bank of France and the Audit Office, were founded although Napoleon personally "checked the budget of all his ministries and nothing escaped his thrifty eye."[242]

Law and order was designated a special function and placed under prefects and the jury system copied from the British during the Revolution was abandoned by the Napoleonic regime on the advice of the Council of State, even though Napoleon himself thought it was not a bad innovation.[243] Napoleon made it a point to post prefects and judges only in departments where they had no relatives and set about standardizing French laws into proper Codes.[244] The initial appointment of the prefects was managed on the advice of the Ministry of the Interior. Lists of notables were drawn up and Napoleon, together with Lucien (the Minister for the Interior) made about one hundred initial appointments, of which fifty-seven had served as members of assemblies during the Revolution.[245] Once appointed, the prefects could operate autonomously, which is to say, that within the law, they were free to take whatever decisions they thought fit. Napoleon interfered so rarely in the field administration that the few occasions on which he intervened (once to chastise a prefect for banning an opera, and on another to rebuke a prefect for forcing people to get vaccinated) confirm the rule.[246]

Napoleon, like Louis XIV, or, for that matter, most great executives in continental bureaucratic empires, realized that the quality of the state and the prosperity of the country depended upon the intellect and character of the bureaucracy.[247] Napoleon worked a sixteen-hour day and drove his ministers, advisors, and civil servants to match his energy and devotion to duty. The result was that the Napoleonic regime worked twenty days more per year than the Old Regime had at its height.[248] Those that served in the Napoleonic administration lauded "this apparently super-human effort" while royalists of the old school, perhaps forgetting how hard Louis XIV had worked, poked fun at the workaholic emperor and his civil servants.[249] That 40,000 exiled nobles chose to return to France after an amnesty was enforced in 1801 and 1802, and that the Concordat of 1804 helped normalize relations between the state and Church, indicated that even while hating the Napoleonic regime few could resist its magnanimity when it came to healing wounds inflicted during the Revolution.[250] Napoleon's sound judgment on internal affairs and willingness to take advice was not, however, replicated in the military field and in foreign policy. Here, French military successes generated hubris so dense that wise counsel, such as that proffered by Talleyrand against weakening Austria and Prussia too much or intervening in Spain's internal affairs, was rejected.[251] On January 28, 1809, Talleyrand was summoned to the Imperial Council to answer for his disagreement with Napoleon's foreign policy. Napoleon thundered at Talleyrand that "to doubt the emperor . . . was to betray the emperor, and to differ with the emperor was treason."[252] The emperor hurled abuse at his former foreign minister for an hour, after which, Talleyrand left quietly dragging himself on account of his limp, remarking quietly to a courtier who followed him, "What a pity that so great a man should be so ill bred."[253] Talleyrand had the last laugh, for after the disastrous invasion of Russia (1811–12),[254] Napoleon asked him to rejoin the cabinet as foreign minister.[255] When Talleyrand refused, Napoleon accused him of treason, to which he replied: "No sire, I cannot assume office because in my opinion your policies are contrary to my own conception of the glory and happiness of my country."[256] After Napoleon, there wasn't much by way of military glory or constitutional happiness to go around though as France vacillated between monarchical restoration, citizen kingship, the return of Napoleonic "plebiscatory dictatorship," unstable republics, military defeats, and imperial presidencies, the state apparatus compensated for the lack of constitutional consensus and political stability.[257]

After the restoration of the Bourbon monarchy and the Congress of Vienna, Talleyrand submitted a memorandum to the king, Louis XVIII (r. 1814–1824). He advised the king not to get carried away by the principle of monarchical legitimacy that was a major plank of the Vienna settlement and a source of comfort to the ultra-royalists led by the Count of Artois. The legitimists, feared Talleyrand, were guilty of confusing "two completely different things—i.e. the source of power and the exercise of power."[258] On account of this confusion, the legitimists seemed to think that hereditary right justified absolutism, and through absolutism they could regain all they had lost during the Revolution.[259] Although Louis XVIII did not like Talleyrand and soon dismissed him from ministerial service, he did accept the need for moderation and thus allowed constitutional guarantees manifested in the Charter of 1814[260] to remain in place. Without fanfare, Louis XVIII set about manipulating the electoral system of the Restoration era to securing pliant majorities. This meant that the most important official for the king was the departmental prefect, successor to the intendant of the Old Regime, originally appointed by Napoleon I. The prefects of the Restoration were, in a sense, vassals of the king employed to keep local mayors in line, control the rural police, discipline anti-royalists in the education department, and deliver their departments come election time.[261] In 1820, the double-vote law gave the wealthiest one-fourth of electors two votes instead of one, which made it much easier for prefects to pressure voters to opt for pro-regime candidates.[262] At the same time, within their departments, prefects were supposed to be sub-sovereigns and respond to local challenges as they saw fit so long as they enjoyed the confidence of the monarch.[263] Like the intendants of the Old Regime, the prefects "mediated between legitimate authority", which is to say the monarch (Napoleonic, Bourbon, or Orleanist), and the people.[264]

The succession of Charles X (r. 1824–1830) represented a turn for the worse when it came to relationships between the royal executive and the people. Charles X attempted to narrow the electorate by increasing the qualifications needed to vote, arbitrarily retired 150 generals due to their Napoleonic origins, and imposed redemption payments to compensate nobles who had lost property during the Revolution. The National Guard was disbanded and the Sacrilege Law imposed the death penalty for insulting the Church. These excesses sparked the July Revolution of 1830 that brought the king's cousin, Louis-Phillipe, to the throne. The new king "was required by law" to demand that civil servants swear a fresh oath of loyalty, an experience that left many bitter and demoralized.[265] The aftermath of the July Revolution was that relations between the aristocracy and bourgeoisie deteriorated to the point where it became difficult even for friends to visit each other informally across class lines.[266] The new government used the threat of a leftist takeover to get the small property owners on its side and conflated republicanism with socialism, which was not altogether implausible given the excesses of the Jacobins during the Revolution. Though less assertive than his predecessor, Louis-Phillipe was soon resorting to the usual tricks. Associations were harassed by the 1834 law that made threats to the state allegedly arising from them subject to summary judgment while a failed assassination attempt on the king the following year led to the ban on citizens declaring themselves republicans, allowed trials *in absentia* for those deemed rebels, and imposed censorship on the press.[267] The French attempt to reconcile the administrative order of a bureaucratic state with the representative order of a parliamentary government and constitutional monarchy was stumbling along when disaster struck the House of Orleans.

On July 13, 1842, the Duke of Orleans, the heir apparent and by far the most respected and well liked of the royal family, was killed in a carriage accident. The duke's death "was a dynastic catastrophe" that left an insecure seventy-year old monarch in Paris while the duke's son, next in line, was only five years old.[268] This created the prospect of regency and raised expectations that the House of Orleans would not survive.

Discontent with the regime, partly due to economic conditions and its growing repressiveness, led to its overthrow in 1848. A new assembly of 750 was convened in which conservatives, including legitimist supporters of monarchy, had 450 seats. Prince Louis-Napoleon, nephew of Napoleon I, was elected president of this Second Republic. Under the new constitution the president was limited to one four-year term. Surrounded by his cronies, Louis-Napoleon carried out a coup as his term reached its end, on December 2, 1851, and was proclaimed emperor.[269] Louis-Napoleon mastered the art of appearing to be above politics as the president during the Second Republic while building "an extensive propaganda machine, a growing entourage identified specifically with his leadership, and support within the military and civil administration."[270] To turn Clausewitz on his head, in France, politics became the continuation of war by other means and centered on the expression of hatreds and deep divisions that long prevented the normalization of politics. The apparent primacy of politics did not mean that the French state became less bureaucratic. Indeed, on the eve of the First World War, the total strength of the French civilian state apparatus was about 800,000, and would rise to 1.25 million by the mid-1920s out of a population of about forty million.[271]

In France, political processes remained contested well into the 1960s. Thus, the recent internal harmony of even the wealthy and developed Continental European states is of recent vintage. Between 1944 and 1946, Charles De Gaulle, in his capacity as premier, set about "resurrecting the unitary and centralized state" and prioritized restoring order, communications, finances and managing shortages caused by wartime dislocation.[272] The short-lived Fourth Republic was brought to an end by a combination of rebellion brewing in the Algerian army that was set in motion on April 27, 1958 and popular discontent against the regime in France. The rebels had the support of the police and the French state security organization (CRS). The French Parliament started working under pressure and President Rene Coty agreed to receive de Gaulle on May 29, 1958. De Gaulle was sworn in as prime minister with emergency powers for six months starting June 1, 1958. On that day the French Parliament legitimized the coup by voting approval of his appointment as premier with emergency powers by 329 votes to 224. A referendum in September 1958 turned out a massive 79 percent approval in favor of de Gaulle's plan for what amounted to a republican monarchy.[273] De Gaulle's worldview was that "all human activity is ordered around the nation, which in turn is shaped by history and geography, armed by the State, held together by common interests, animated by culture and led by a hero."[274] In France, de Gaulle himself was the hero, at least for now, and he set about, with the aid of his ministerial and bureaucratic sidekicks, extricating France from Algeria and setting the economic house in order. The ardent nationalist saw that it was in France's interest to free currency transactions within the European Economic Community (EEC) and moved towards economic integration with erstwhile enemies. This would help maintain demand for French goods and services far better than trying to hold onto a colonial empire that required, in Algeria alone, 50,000 elite French troops plus half a million men in the colonial army. De Gaulle's desire to rationalize French external commitments provoked a coup attempt in April 1960 in which five generals were involved in addition to seven regiments in different parts of Algeria. The coup-makers, however, lost their nerve when de Gaulle took to the airwaves and addressed the nation. The army might have made the emperor, but de Gaulle's popularity and competence were too great for the army to unmake him so soon after his installation.[275] That task was taken up by the people in the crisis of May 1968 that dragged on till de Gaulle stepped down on April 28, 1969. By May 1968 "the regime was ossifying into a huge, prosperous enterprise"[276] and, as de Gaulle observed, his country was "in the midst of transformation. There is fear neither of war nor of misery. When the French are no longer afraid, they challenge the authority of the State."[277] General Fourquet, the army Chief of Staff, had the armored gendarmerie of one thousand crack troops and a dozen AMX tanks stationed at Versailles, but he was unwilling to use force out of the fear that the soldiers would join the protestors.[278]

The eventual triumph of the "spiritual principle" of the Enlightenment[279] and conscious attempts to reform the culture of power have led to the stabilization of a French legal democracy that manifests regard for the rule of law, individual rights, social and political autonomy, and a considerable measure of private enterprise, though not nearly so much as the British state of laws. An essential component of the French attempt to graft the rule of law onto its absolutist tradition was the expansion of executive accountability through the Council of State. Originally established by Napoleon in 1799, the Council of State stayed aloof from politics and thus earned public confidence. Its essential function became to regulate "administrative practices by enjoining on the administration to respect the law and to avoid arbitrary methods."[280] During the Third Republic (1871–1940), the Council of State had tried to avoid political questions and acquired the ability "to annul the illegal acts of the administration and to ensure their legality."[281] The Council of State thus came to exercise "a control over the nominations and promotions of government servants" while the latter, individually and organized as associations, relied on it to counter favoritism and deviation from merit.[282] The formal structure of the Council of State was made sacrosanct by administrative precedent, and so, without formal security of tenure, the bureaucratic support and popular prestige enjoyed by this body ensured it in practice.[283] The modus operandi of the Council of State "is inquisitorial" with junior officers carrying out investigations and reporting their findings in writing.[284] Hearings are possible and carried out as necessary and in public but "deliberations are secret" and the Council demands that the state be able to defend its action on rational and legal grounds.[285] France is thus an unusually enlightened and humane continental bureaucratic empire at the heart of which lies to this day the "grand corps of the state,"[286] unrivalled in competence and intellect, and drawn from the National School of Administration. Indeed, "The rescue of the Republic was carried out in the name of defending the state: with General de Gaulle's formally proper return to power in December 1958, the state regained its majesty in a Fifth Republic ruled by a strong executive" complemented by a new class of politicians drawn from the higher ranks of the civil service.[287] Under the Fifth Republic even the French left "abandoned the utopia of civil society, rediscovered the state," adapted to "the trappings of power," and relinquished "the idea of challenging" the establishment.[288]

HABSBURGS AND HOHENZOLLERNS: GERMANIC ALTERNATIVES

The story of the Habsburg monarchy that governed dynastic territories across central Europe until 1919, Northern Italy until 1866, and Spain and Latin America until 1713, is one of gradual transition from a feudal confederation led by a monarch to a continental bureaucratic empire. This empire had, since 1356, seven electors,[289] an imperial assembly in which nominees of the electors met, and separate assemblies for the townsmen. The empire was divided into ten to twelve groupings or circles within which the local aristocracy and clerical elite enjoyed a mosaic of privileges and immunities.[290] Between 1500 and 1648, the Habsburgs, strengthened by the inclusion of Spain in their dominions (1506–1700), sought to capitalize on the resulting gold injections and potential for mercenary recruitment to impose political and religious unity on Europe.[291] An alliance of states including Sweden, France, the Netherlands, and north German principalities eventually frustrated this ambition and established the ascendancy of France (in Continental Europe) and England (at sea). Ultimate strategic failure and the enormous bloodletting of the Reformation Era[292] did not mean that administrative consolidation did not take place in the 1500s and 1600s. Tax collection by the Habsburg emperor rose from 4.3 million florins in 1521 to 23.3 million by 1607, while in Bavaria the number of officials increased from 162 in 1508 to 866 by 1571.[293]

An important figure in this process was the *kreishauptmann* or circle officer, initially an aristocrat with local roots, answerable, in theory, for the supervision of the local administration, to the emperor. In 1526, the Estates gained control of the district officers' appointments but lost these powers in 1620 to the emperor. In 1668, the post was regularized with a salary and benefits. In the mid-eighteenth century Empress Maria Theresa (r. 1740–1765) extended the system of district officers to Styria, Carinthia, Carnolia, Lower Austria, and Tyrol, and thus increased their total numbers to forty-seven.[294] In 1765, the district officers were placed at the head of the district police, educational institutions, local bodies, churches, and commercial institutions and fifteen years later a pension system was added to the benefits they received.[295] The recruitment of district officers entailed a test of the applicants' knowledge and character. Once appointed, the security enjoyed by district officers was enviable.

Maria Theresa left her successor Joseph II (r. 1765–1790) a "Civil Service State" that, though confined to the German core of the Habsburg Empire, employed the middle-classes, was staffed by "honest and devoted officials" and, by the standards of the day, "intensely efficient."[296] Joseph II continued the advance towards "bureaucratic absolutism"[297] and "much of what he created still exists."[298] His legacy includes a highly educated, motivated, and technically competent bureaucracy, a press "unctuously submissive to authority," and the ". . . overwhelming presence of the state in the media, the education, and the economy clearly reflects the Theresan and Josephenian traditions" even in today's Austrian Republic.[299] Another indicator of the rise of the center is the number of courtiers in attendance upon the emperor. When Emperor Maximilian died in 1619, there were only "six" courtiers "officially in attendance."[300] In 1780, when Joseph II purged his court, there were about one thousand five hundred courtiers in attendance.[301]

Aside from the civil service, which, in 1914, numbered three million out of a total population of fifty-two million, and did everything from policing and taxation to administering pensions and hospitals,[302] the power of "His Imperial and Apostolic Majesty the Emperor"[303] rested on the army, spies, the Church, and a bureaucratic intelligentsia. The army, which communicated in eleven languages and included contingents from the empire's many nationalities, was primarily a tool of domestic control used to crush revolts and insurrections, for attempts to share power with the center were perceived as assaults upon a divinely sanctioned order. In the nineteenth century, to counter the challenge posed by the French Revolution, a "system of police spies, censors, and prosecutors" was instituted to seek out and eliminate non-conformists.[304] The Church, after Joseph II, served the state and encouraged unquestioning obedience to the emperor and his servants. The practice was also developed of transferring "outspoken academics to posts in the government service, where they could be effectively muzzled."[305] Through control of the universities, the state discouraged philosophy, political science, and history, and encouraged practical scientific subjects.[306] The Habsburg Empire's postal service became notorious for its expertise in opening, copying, and re-sealing correspondence between both foreign governments and its own subjects. The greatest opposition to the advance of absolutism came from the bi-cameral Hungarian Diet, a feudal institution that provided the aristocracy and rich commoners with representation, and, for that reason, was convened as irregularly as possible.[307]

Though not as centralized or arbitrary as France, the Habsburg's dynastic dominion did eventually become a continental bureaucratic empire. The ruler was divinely sanctioned and exerted control through a central bureaucracy distributed across administrative subunits. The diversity of the empire fuelled the ruler's propensity to take a particularly neurotic view of local attempts to share power and resort to military and political repression. The Habsburg Empire, however, was eclipsed in the realm of state formation by Hohenzollern Prussia. The Hohenzollern state was an assortment of territories in Germany and Poland often separated by other small states. Located on an open plain, with a miniscule population and few natural resources, and surrounded by greater powers (France, Austria, Russia) the survival, let alone rise, of Prussia was remarkable. The emergence of Prussia was principally the work of a succession of effective sovereigns between 1640 and 1786, Fredrick William the Great Elector (r. 1640–1688), Fredrick William I (r. 1713–40), and Fredrick the Great (r. 1740–86).

In the seventeenth century the Great Elector improved the management of his personal lands, introduced indirect taxes, secured French financial assistance, and thus made "the central power virtually independent financially" of aristocratic assemblies.[308] By carefully husbanding these resources the foundations were laid "of a new centralized bureaucracy" and a professional standing army.[309] In the military "men received a rudimentary education . . . and were conditioned to habits of order and obedience" that permeated the society as the "lower ranks of the civil service" were retired soldiers.[310] To maintain a standing army on fixed pay, price controls "enforced partly by . . . garrison commanders"[311] were introduced. Manipulation of the level of indirect taxes enabled the state to cultivate those trades and industries that maximized "tax yield."[312] By the early eighteenth century Prussia had become the exemplar of "the Power-State,"[313] that is a state that organized and regimented society for the maximization of its strategic and operational capabilities. Prussia was undoubtedly a "military state and much of what was produced went to the maintenance of the army."[314] This increasingly "compact military state" was administered by centrally appointed governors and civil servants, communications were maintained by the postal system and the treasury was kept full by renting out the army whose standing strength at this stage was about 27,000.[315]

In the eighteenth century town councils were supplanted by boards of civil servants with life appointments answerable directly to the center. These boards dealt with order, taxation, justice, and development work. The countryside received rural commissioners drawn from the gentry and middle-classes. Fredrick the Great continued the process of centralization and systematically inspected his state and army, relied extensively on written reports, deprived his officers of the right to take initiatives, encouraged them to spy on each other, and appointed agents called fiscals to spy on his servants. New ministries headed by officials personally responsible to the king were created to manage mining, forestry, the mint, and government trading monopolies. The state vigorously took on the tasks of settling villages, improving agriculture, and building a network of canals to link major rivers to each other.[316] The codification of laws was begun and court procedures were simplified even as the king "often" interfered "in criminal cases, and freely removed or punished judges who seemed to him unsatisfactory."[317] Although "actual corruption was rare" within the Hohenzollern continental bureaucratic state, the apparatus sought to please the king "with a little window-dressing rather than report unpopular truths. The same still happened under Hitler."[318] The ideocratic complex of Prussia comprised acceptance of the king's divine right to rule, an official priesthood, and a self-consciously militaristic public ethos. A bureaucratic intelligentsia that idealized the Prussian state as intrinsically superior, above politics, and the culmination of human history was also an integral component of the ideocratic complex. The significance of Prussian emergence as the engine of German unification was that more liberal currents of opinions were discredited and the Prussian culture of power, defined by militarism, bureaucratization, and a conformist ideology that glorified the central state and leadership, became dominant in Germany as a whole. Prussianization lay at the core of Chancellor Otto von Bismarck's policies as the creator and effective ruler of Germany from 1871 to 1890.

Although Bismarck was an aristocrat who regarded "the bureaucratic Prussian state" with ambivalence and "Contempt," as chancellor he "knew well how to use it."[319] Prussia's ascendance, Bismarck believed, was based upon the achievements "of strong, decisive and wise rulers," not "liberalism and free thought."[320] Bismarck's primary objective was the preservation of the "essential" element of Prussian statecraft, that is "the monarchy's direct control of the army."[321] The constitution that he crafted for a united Germany was extremely complex and left the arbitrary powers of the executive, including the power to interpret the constitution, make war, conclude peace, dismiss governments, and declare martial law, untouched. There were no guaranteed rights on the English, American, or French pattern. The chancellor answered to the king and depended on his favor. The deputies to the Reichstag were not paid salaries, which turned it into a social club for wealthy dilettantes and retired civil servants. Bismarck did have to cope with a vocal opposition and it was expected that he would be replaced after the death of Emperor William I who was in poor health by 1880. But William I's surprising ability to survive combined with Bismarck's apparent indispensability for running foreign policy ensured he stayed put.[322] That didn't mean that Bismarck didn't have a back-up plan. In fact, Bismarck "contemplated a coup against the constitution" that would have eliminated the Reichstag and replaced it with new assemblies "that would produce the majorities" required for his "legislative program."[323]

Of course, Bismarck's style of leadership thrived on the *appearance* of crisis while the nervous and easily excited nationalism of the masses and conservative fears of leftism and liberalism provided the perfect context for the brinksmanship and maneuvering that the Iron Chancellor excelled at. In order to neutralize the threat he saw emanating from the crown prince's apparent sympathy for a liberal reworking of German domestic institutions patriotism was successfully invoked to divide liberals.[324] The spat with the United Kingdom over Bismarck's 1884 decision to make noises about acquiring colonies, while eschewing a naval buildup that might actually pose a threat to the maritime superpower, had the desired effect when "the Anglophile Freisinnige party" ended up splitting on this issue.[325] The threat from the socialists, particularly the Social Democratic Party (SDP) was harder to deal with on account of their popularity with the workers. Bismarck thus set about creating a welfare state that, in 1883, introduced compulsory health care insurance for blue and white-collar workers followed in 1884 and 1887 by the extension of accident insurance to sectors of the economy and in 1889 with old age insurance.[326]

Away from the imperial court, at the local level, the rural commissioners were fully integrated into the bureaucracy, and the press and academia were barred from "criticizing the fundamental aspects of the existing order."[327] Indirect taxation was preferred over direct taxation as the latter invited demands for representation, and the police were given arbitrary powers to handle socialists, communists, and dissidents.[328] In 1882 a civil service regulation was passed that "required public servants to support the government at election times", be unquestioningly loyal to the emperor, and thus undermined "the position of officials and judges" critical of the government and enforced "a conservative recruitment policy to the public service."[329] Vigorous persecution of the Catholic Church succeeded in rendering it, at least outwardly, subservient to the state.

The legacy of two centuries of centralization, bureaucratization, militarism, and indoctrination, was an ideocratic and arbitrary culture of power. Bismarck represented in his person the continental bureaucratic empire that sought to reduce its subjects to a sub-political role in exchange for protection and welfare and the embrace of a great leader. It was this culture of power that motivated

> ... those German conservatives whose parliamentary representatives rose in demonstrative applause to the ringing challenge of Herr von Oldenburg auf Januschau: "The King of Prussia and the German Emperor must always be in a position to say to any lieutenant: 'Take ten men and shoot the Reichstag!'"[330]

This attitude was not isolated for Bismarck's reign, which was made better by comparison with the tragedies that followed, was widely regarded as "the good old days" by later generations.[331] This perception was particularly strong in Prussia, which was the dominant component of Germany for it contained some six-tenths of the population, was the major recruiting ground for the military and civil service elite, and viewed itself as the state that had finally brought about the long desired German unification.[332] The glory and success of Bismarck's time went to the head of his successors who lost all sense of proportion and allowed hubris to prepare the way for nemesis.[333] Indeed, for Kaiser Wilhelm II (r. 1888–1918), "the whole of Germany was nothing but a giant toy created by the Almighty to please His Imperial Majesty."[334]

That the fate of the country depended upon "the succession of supermen"[335] was confirmed in the eyes of many Germans by the foreign and domestic disasters that befell their country after the exit of Bismarck.[336] It was in this context that Hitler and the Nazis became the largest political party in the Reichstag in the early 1930s and, once at the head of the government, erected a *fuhrer-stat* that combined in a single artifice a pharonic culture of power with the techniques and resources of one of the world's scientifically and industrially advanced societies.[337] No one had seriously contemplated what would happen if the superman at the head of the apparatus were simultaneously insane, charismatic, and effective. To these qualities one must add popular, for the Nazis had increased their share of the popular vote from 800,000 in 1929 to 17 million by January 1933 and enjoyed widespread support in the middleclass and the working class. Indeed, Nazism's "mass psychological effect" proceeded "from the presupposition that a *fuhrer*, or the champion of an idea" could only succeed "if his personal point of view, his ideology, or his program" was consistent with the world-view "of a broad category of individuals."[338] Among the regimes less well-known victims were 200,000 handicapped persons euthanized along with 400,000 forcibly sterilized to maintain the purity of the gene pool between 1933 and 1945.[339] The "societal essence" of Nazi totalitarianism was "cowardly minor bureaucratic bullies involving bigger bullies to grind the critical and non-compliant into submission."[340] Movements like Nazism and Communism were rooted in Europe's long tutelage in utopian morality and eschatology courtesy of the Catholic, and later Protestant, churches.[341] And like the Church, such movements, while ostensibly political or socioeconomic, produced wild enthusiasm among the believers in the apocalyptic-utopian future.[342] The result of such utopian delusions taking over in the German case[343] was the application of that country's proverbial efficiency to the pursuit of objectives that ranged from the elimination of handicapped children, to the killing of "enemies" in staged police encounters, to the mass murder of millions of undesirables and "two legged animals" and the conquest and depopulation of Soviet Russia which was itself a state designed as an exercise in egalitarian utopian social engineering.[344] Ultimately, at the cost of more than fifty million lives, about half of them Russian, man overcame the Nazi superman.[345]

STATIST EUROPE SINCE 1945

After the Second World War Europe was divided by the United States of America and the Soviet Union into spheres of influence turning the colonizers into the colonized. In the American sphere, constitutional democracy and economic reform led to the creation of modern welfare states. In the Soviet sphere, police states ruled by communist party elites were installed and perpetuated by repression.[346] On both sides of the divide, however, Europe experienced the growth of the state bureaucracy accompanied by systematic attempts by governments to raise standards of living. Europe remained highly militarized during the Cold War as rival alliances (NATO and the Warsaw Pact) squared off against each other, but this militarization was sustained primarily by the exertions of the American and Soviet states. On the American side of the Iron Curtain, arbitrary rule was substantially restrained by the post-war dispensations though the spread of liberalism did not in any way impede the strengthening of the state. In the Soviet sphere of influence, the Eastern European states were not nearly as fortunate. In Hungary, for instance, some 200,000 people, about one in fifty people, fled after the Soviet military intervention in 1956, 22,000 were sentenced to prison, 13,000 to internment camps, 2,700 were killed by Soviet forces and 341 were eventually tried and executed.[347]

While in the communist economies of Eastern Europe a career in the state service was perhaps the default option,[348] the success of the statist model in the capitalist economies of Western Europe merits mention. Between 1950 and 1973 state spending as a percentage of GNP rose in France from 27.60 percent to 38.80 percent, in West Germany from 30.40 percent to 42 percent and in the Netherlands from 26.80 percent to 45.50 percent.[349] In Belgium, in the late 1970s, some six out of ten university graduates opted for careers in public service, while the bureaucracy in France easily drew the most enterprising and diligent into its ranks.[350] In Scandinavia, there was extensive state control of practically every sector with high social spending and high levels of taxation.[351] Though normally benign, Scandinavian states were sensitive to matters of racial hygiene well into the 1970s. Between 1934 and 1976, forced sterilization programs in Sweden processed 60,000 people, while in Norway some 40,000 were processed.[352] Nine-tenths of those sterilized were women.[353] In West Germany, where one in three members of state banks between 1948 and 1990 were former Nazis,[354] 98,700 men were convicted for homosexual offenses (1953–65), against some 38,000 convicted between 1933 and 1945.[355]

For all the rhetoric of deregulation and the need to reform statist economic systems in Continental Europe, the percentage of the total workforce employed by the state actually rose between 1973 and 1990. In West Germany the increase was from 13.10 percent to 15.10 percent, in Italy it was from 13.40percent to 15.50 percent and in Denmark from 22.20 percent to 30.50 percent.[356] Statist Europe promised its citizens that the state would take care of them from the cradle to the grave. This led to a sense of entitlement to being well taken care of by those who grew up under the nanny-state regimes that came into existence in Europe. Paid for by the wealth generated by industrialization, the postwar economic boom, and high tax rates that in 2011 averaged out to 44 percent for wage earners in the European Union,[357] the European state became both functionally pervasive and intellectually *passé*. Europeans growing up in the semi-capitalist version of statist Europe came to accept the omnipotent, omnipresent, welfare-oriented bureaucratic state as part of the background even as it extracted heavy taxes to pay for the EU-topia.[358] In Austria, the real tax deduction on an average income is about 55 percent, in France more than 56 percent, in Germany 52 percent, in Hungary over 57 percent, in Sweden over 52 percent.[359] In France, a responsible economy in the context of the present crisis, state spending presently accounts for nearly six-tenths of GDP and since 1973 no government has been able to balance the budget. Even with such high levels of taxation, the absurdly high entitlement demands have pushed contemporary Europe deep into a debt and employment crisis.

The economic orientation of policy-making in Europe paid rich dividends in the first generation after the Second World War, sustained in part by reconstruction and American aid and investments. Thus, in the 1950s West Germany's economy grew at more than six percent a year, while Italy managed annual growth rates of over five percent and France, burdened as it was by imperial commitments, grew at a respectable three to four percent a year.[360] In the initial stages, the need for economic growth and the pursuit of mutually beneficial integration was itself the product of an "international order imposed by the superpowers" which made "intensifying economic and legal cooperation" among some European states "seem rational."[361] However, once set in motion a number of vested interests in trade, industry, politics and administration, that gained from the process needed to perpetuate it and could do so relatively free from a Europe-wide challenge so long as the internal prosperity of the cooperating members was reasonably assured.[362]

For civil servants in parts of the new Europe regulation, economic planning, and political acquiescence in the face of technical expertise ensured a privileged place and plenty of power. In France, as discussed earlier, civil servants could move into politics. They could also move into the private sector and the system of the great schools (administrative and polytechnic) ensured synchrony amongst state and private sector elites.[363] In Italy, the Industrial Reconstruction Agency (IRI) and the lucrative Ministry of Public Works became key instruments of political consolidation (the latter used successfully to tame the socialists) and patronage.[364] In Italy, between 1973 and 1990, some 350,000 people were appointed to public service without going through a competitive recruitment exam.[365] Against this, about 250,000 were recruited through entry and qualification examinations.[366] This establishes patronage, rather than merit determined by autonomous bodies, as the principal means through which Italy recruited public servants in the late-twentieth century.[367] In 1998, "a legislative decree tied the occupants of the upper echelons of the civil service to incoming government" and "allowed for the appointment not only of civil servants but also of politically loyal (but 'external') experts to the *cabinet ministeriels*."[368]

Italy is, of course, not alone in moving towards arbitrary and personalized appointments to the civil service, a journey that inevitably reduces the competence and integrity of public servants.[369] In Portugal, the legacy of authoritarian arbitrary rule until the mid-1970s combined with democratic politicization since then has meant that there is no autonomous higher bureaucracy in the German, French, Scandinavian, or British, sense. In October 1995, the Socialist Party government proceeded to make 6,000 "political appointments", though this was not "an exceptional situation."[370] In 1974–76, and again in the mid-1980s, governments had resorted to large-scale politicization of the state services through such inductions.[371] In Spain, erosion of the civil service structure since 1982 led to the emergence of a spoils system though without large-scale lateral recruitment to the state services.[372] The Spanish practice evolved along lines more familiar to India and Pakistan, with politically-oriented reshuffles within the existing civil service cadres.[373] The Greek state services were politicized to a much greater degree at the higher levels with civil servants and managers of state corporations shuffled with the Cabinet on a regular basis.[374] The pattern of recruitment reflected the patronage orientation of political elites in Southern Europe. Typically, "state-owned enterprises, such as the Italian postal services or the Greek state airlines" were and are overstaffed, while important technical and support services had to make do with insufficient personnel.[375]

Since 1990, the rhetoric of European integration, which, in substantive terms moved far more quickly on economic issues than on political and constitutional ones, articulated a concept of common values shared by all Europeans. In a very superficial sense this idea of common European values is plausible. After all, European states by the 1990s were democracies of the ostensibly liberal variety, their economies were mixed though with a substantial state sector, and their people enjoyed individual liberties that Enlightenment *philosophes* would have approved. And yet, in spite of these apparently common values, Europeans are very different from each other in terms of the emphasis of their historical experience of governance, administrative traditions, and attitudes towards politics. France is a republican monarchy mediated by an almost imperial bureaucracy recruited on merit, which is regulated by the Council of State, and capable of moving into and out of politics and the private sector. Germany is a federal state and the regional economic powerhouse with a deeply divisive and embarrassing past. Italy, politically unstable for much of the Cold War in terms of the rotation of governments, has evolved into a centralized but politically patronage-based bureaucratic state. Other Southern European states are relatively recent converts to any kind of democracy and were prematurely integrated into the Euro-zone.[376] The Scandinavian states are welfare states with small and highly educated populations and effective merit-based apolitical bureaucracies.[377] Eastern Europe, ruled by communist parties and their secret police forces until the early 1990s is seeking to converge with Western and Northern Europe but has a lot of catching up to do. The European Union itself is a remote bureaucracy that does not really command the political allegiance of the European peoples—a civil service without a state that performs uninspiring technocratic functions easily lampooned by popular comedies. As the Euro-zone's economic crisis continues, with average debt-to-GNP ratios hitting 90 percent and persistently stubborn unemployment and unpopular austerity measures in the spendthrift economies that dragged the others down with them,[378] there is a growing realization that a serious constitutional debate is needed and that the European Union, in order to remain viable, will have to evolve into a centralized or at least concentrated state with effective control over finances. In January 2013 in France, the labor minister's comment that his country is basically bankrupt was criticized by politicians but validated by public opinion—two-thirds agreed with his dire diagnosis.[379] Political and constitutional federalism combined with fiscal centralization can power Europe out of the present impasse, but will require an idea to motivate Europeans; something more powerful than extra paychecks, paid vacations, and secure pensions. The place to perhaps begin this search is, as Siedentop realized in 2000, Europe's historical experience of governance.[380]

5 From Sultanate to Secular State
The Rise and Fall of the Ottomans and the Successes and Limitations of Kemalism in Modern Turkey

INTRODUCTION: WHEN IBN KHALDUN MET AMIR TIMUR, DAMASCUS, 1401

Ibn Khaldun saw history as a cyclical process in which hardy pastoralists and nomads invaded and occupied decadent sedentary cultures. In the process, they infused their tribal and religious solidarity, or *asabiyah,* into the decaying polity and established a new dynasty strong enough to restore order. With the passage of time, the tribal conquerors would be softened by luxury and the spectacle of obedience secured through hierarchical instruments. The tendency towards concentration would inevitably lead to rifts within the conquering elite and the monopolization of power by one family, and, eventually, by one person. Slaves and clients would replace kinsmen, ritualism and clericalism would replace genuine religious fervor, and the pursuit of war and magnificence would consume the resources of the state. As the rulers became more remote and their government more extravagant the state would start to decline. Sooner or later this decline would lead to fragmentation into petty estates ruled by gangs and ostensible servants and chaos would be relieved only when a new set of tribal conquerors appeared from the margins of the empire. These conquerors were nemesis incarnate sent by the very nature of geography, culture and history, to bring down those unfit to rule. The old dynasty would soon be wiped out, or, if they were lucky, allowed to subsist as pensioners and stooges of the new rulers. In time, however, the new rulers would succumb to the same tendencies manifested by their predecessors and the cycle would reset. This process normally took four or five generations to complete, which corresponds to roughly a century of effective rule for a dynastic state.

In 1382, Ibn Khaldun bade farewell to Tunis and headed to Egypt where the emir, Altunbugha al-Jubani (d. 1395), an intimate of Sultan Barquq (r. 1382–1399) and chief of his council of commanders, took him under his protection. Ibn Khaldun's fame had preceded him and he soon found himself in the enviable position of a protected client of the slave-soldier or *mamluk* sultanate. The *mamluks*, which literally means the ones who are owned, were a military elite constituted as the one-generation service nobility of the state, replenished through the purchase of fresh Turkish and Circassian slaves, though, to Ibn Khaldun, the *mamluks* were primarily Turks. The greatest threat to the *mamluks* was the growing all-conquering empire of Amir Timur, whose house later ruled India from 1526 to 1857, as the Timurids. Timur was a ruthless, charismatic, military genius whose generosity towards his own men and cold cruelty towards all who dared oppose him, forged the Turkic and Mongol tribes of Central Asia into a seemingly invincible war machine. Timur's appeal to his people rested on a mixture of good old-fashioned tribalism, religion (jihad), greed, and his astonishing successes on the battlefield. These successes naturally secured the adherence of more followers whose added weight enabled further victories. Religious pretensions aside, most of these victories were at the expense of fellow Muslim rulers and after devastating the Sultanate of Delhi in 1398–99, Timur turned his armies towards Syria, Anatolia, and Egypt. The Ottomans under Beyazid I "Lightening"[1] (r. 1389–1402) controlled most of what is now the Turkish republic, minus Constantinople, plus parts of the Balkans. Syria and Egypt were ruled by the *mamluks*. In effect, three Turkic empires were about to square off for control of West Asia and the Eastern Mediterranean.

The Timurid storm struck the *mamluk* sultanate first. Aleppo was sacked, Damascus[2] was besieged, and the surrounding countryside was devastated to provision Timur's army of 100,000 horsemen. Ibn Khaldun was in Damascus when the city's communications with Egypt were compromised in November 1400. Timur personally encamped outside the gates of that ancient city as the siege dragged on into winter. This was a dark omen for the inhabitants for the imperial presence considerably upped the ante for Timur's commanders. Timur had, through his spies, heard that Ibn Khaldun, the great scholar from Tunis, was in Damascus. When not acting in his capacity as the chief mass-murdering sociopath of the realm, Timur was a man of culture and refinement and wanted to meet Ibn Khaldun.[3] The feeling was mutual for Ibn Khaldun hoped to secure his personal survival by impressing Timur with his learning and wisdom and perhaps convince the conqueror of the veracity and wisdom of his theory. Messages were exchanged and on January 10, 1401, Ibn Khaldun was lowered from the walls of Damascus. To show how much he valued the scholar's arrival, Timur had sent officials, including the governor-designate of Damascus, to receive him.[4] Ibn Khaldun was announced and ushered into the imperial presence as soon as he arrived at the camp. Timur invited Ibn Khaldun to sit at his side and had soup brought in. Ibn Khaldun presented his host with gifts, which included a poem, a prayer rug, and sweet meats. Timur asked that Ibn Khaldun remain in attendance at his camp/court and granted him free access as a mark of trust and respect.[5]

Timur wanted to learn from Ibn Khaldun and in the thirty-five days that the philosopher spent at the camp a range of subjects were discussed. Timur was keenly interested in geographic and historical information about the north coast of Africa and quizzed Ibn Khaldun at length and asked him to prepare a report on the subject.[6] Ibn Khaldun also got opportunities to explain his perspective on history, the role of leadership, and *asabiyah*. Timur "listened attentively" to Ibn Khaldun's fascinating extempore lectures and was greatly "impressed."[7] When an Abbasid claimant to the caliphate showed up asking for Timur's support, Ibn Khaldun was invited to advise on the matter and presented a critical and balanced view of the subject that acknowledged the absence of consensus on the matter.[8] Ibn Khaldun also managed to secure amnesty for himself and his colleagues in Damascus while Timur, who was fond of collecting rare animals, asked the philosopher if he was willing to sell his gray mule.[9] Ibn Khaldun gifted his mule to Timur though the latter sent him generous compensation in Egypt.[10] Ibn Khaldun's encounter with the living manifestation of *asabiyah* left him greatly impressed, and he later opined about Timur that he

> . . . is one of the greatest and mightiest of kings. Some attribute to him knowledge. Others attribute to him heresy . . . still others attribute to him the employment of magic and sorcery, but in all this there is nothing; it is simply that he is highly intelligent and very perspicacious, addicted to debate and argumentation about what he knows and about what he does not know.[11]

One thing that Timur did not know was defeat. After beating the *mamluks* in Syria he turned his attention to the Ottomans. The Timurid and Ottoman armies met at the Battle of Ankara on July 28, 1402. The 85,000 strong Ottoman army was defeated by Timur's 100,000 horsemen, and the victor restored the petty Anatolian emirates that the Ottomans had gradually rolled back. For the next eleven years the Ottoman Sultanate teetered on the verge of dissolution as chaos reigned in the absence of a strong sultan. And yet, fifty years after Beyazid I, and his army, met their doom at the hands of Timur, the Ottoman Sultanate had staged an astonishing recovery and was poised to successfully conquer Constantinople, which fell in 1453. The *mamluks* of Egypt and Syria would become servants of the Ottomans after their defeats in 1516 and 1517. The Ottoman Sultanate would endure until 1923–24 and remained a formidable military power to the very end before the rebirth of the Turkish heartland as a nation-state under Mustafa Kemal. The longevity of the Ottoman Sultanate challenges Ibn Khaldun's timeframe for the waxing and waning of group solidarity that he believed underlay the rise and fall of dynastic states. The rise of the Ottoman Sultanate unfolded over two centuries (1299–1517), its period of glory lasted another two hundred years (1517–1730) and its decline and fall, much derided in the West, took yet another two hundred years (1730–1924). Even then, collapse was not total for the core Turkish territories of the Ottoman Sultanate galvanized themselves to resist Allied occupation after the First World War. Nationalist Turks rebuilt the army and established a nation-state amidst the ruins of a fallen sultanate.

At one level, the Ottoman Sultanate was a classically arbitrary state in which the sultan owned much of the arable land and the instruments of his rule.[12] At another level, the Ottomans prided themselves on their *kanun* or law derived from royal edicts, as well as the application of the Islamic *sharia*. This, however, did not mean standardization for many communities and religious groups were managed by imperial nominees drawn from their own ranks and enjoyed freedom in their private civil affairs provided that taxes were paid, service to the state was rendered as required, and loyalty to the sultanate was maintained. This tolerance by exclusion was accompanied by the flexible and inclusive nature of the Ottoman household. Slaves, servants, eunuchs, military commanders, local notables, and even pirates, could join the royal household and become Ottomans for it was an official rather than ethnic identity. The sultans themselves were not pure Turks on account of the diversity of their harems and the concubines therein. Even for the royal household, being an Ottoman was a social and cultural, rather than genetic, identity, leaving obsessing about aristocratic bloodlines to European monarchs and their vassals. The Ottomans were proud of their Turkish heritage but considered themselves cosmopolitan members of the House of Osman, Muslims by faith, imperialists by tradition, and administrators by duty. The cultural pull of Ottoman identity was so intense that during the long decline of the sultanate local power players sought greater recognition for themselves without breaking the empire up. This stands in stark contrast to the House of Timur where break-up and breakdown of the empire proceeded almost immediately after the death of the last great ruler. In India, the Muslims turned towards the Ottoman Sultanate as a source of solace and pride as other parts of the Islamic world fell to the European colonizing onslaught.[13] In the Ottoman case, some parts of the sultanate, such as Egypt, even climbed the first few rungs on the ladder to an industrial revolution and modernized their local military forces providing a blueprint for reforms at the center. Since the collapse of the Ottoman Sultanate, West Asia and North Africa, have experienced a crisis of imperial succession which as the lengthening and darkening Arab Spring indicates, is far from over. The Ottoman Sultanate was, interestingly, itself the product of the prolonged crisis of Abbasid imperial succession and the rise of the Turkish slave soldiers and emirs.

ABBASID TWILIGHT, SELJUK DAWN, MONGOL NEMESIS

The political eclipse of the Abbasids was brought about by the policy they adopted in the early 800s to ensure the effective concentration and centralization of arbitrary power. Propelled to the caliphate in the 750s by loyalists from the eastern provinces of the Umayyad domain, and having waged a struggle to restore the prophet's family to government, the Abbasids sought to distance themselves from their kinsmen and partisans once the throne was theirs. One strategy was to employ Persian civil servants in key positions while another was to liquidate troublesome kinsmen. Emphasizing the Islamic credentials of the new regime, discrediting the Umayyad dynasty on grounds of insufficient piety, and reducing the ulema to quietism,[14] were also meant to serve the purpose of elevating the Abbasids above their rivals and their subjects. By keeping the army busy on the Byzantine frontier the jihad aspect of the caliphate was tapped as well though unlike their Umayyad predecessors, the Abbasids did not expand the frontiers of Islam very much.[15] At the end of the day, the Abbasids still felt the need for greater remoteness and sought a radical solution that would preserve, at least in theory, the autocracy of the imperial center from all who dared make a claim of familiarity. This solution was to procure Turkish slaves, hardy nomads from the Central Asian steppes, and organize them into an elite imperial guard. Mamun ar-Rashid (r. 813–833), who was based in Merv during his princely career, realized the military and political potential of slave soldiers and became the first Arab ruler to raise a corps of Turkish *ghulams* or slaves.[16] The Samanid family was important suppliers of Turkic slaves to Baghdad and during the reign of al-Mutasim (r. 833–842) some 3,000 to 4,000 slave soldiers were in royal service.[17] These slaves were employed for important administrative positions as well. Thus, Ashinas, was appointed governor of Egypt in 834, Itakh was made governor of Yemen in 839 and later became chief of security in Samarra, the city to which the capital was shifted in 836.[18] The slave soldiers soon took the caliph and his senior civil servants hostage. After a generation, new Turkic commanders, such as Bugha al-Kabir, Bugha al-Saghir, Wasif, and Otemish, realized that the caliph's isolation in Samarra could be turned to their advantage. Mutawakil thus became the first caliph to be overthrown and killed by his slave soldiers while his successor, al-Muntasir (r. 861–862) and al-Musta'im (r. 862–866) suffered similar fates.[19] Abbasid clients, like the Samanids and the Tahirids, imitated the Abbasid example with identical results—a turbulent and willful slave soldiery[20] that wielded power disproportionate to its numerical strength due to its concentration at the center.

The first slave dynasty was that of the Tulunids in Egypt. Ahmed bin Tulun, originally a slave of al-Mamun, seized power in Egypt in 868. The caliph legitimized this usurpation in exchange for a tribute payment of 300,000 dinars.[21] Ahmed bin Tulun was succeeded by his son, Humarawayh, who ruled till his assassination in 896, which predictably triggered a chaotic succession struggle. Tulunid rule benefited Egypt in that after two centuries under the caliphate its surplus wealth was no longer being diverted to the imperial center. Though short-lived, Tulunid rule was popular and blazed the trail that other Turkish adventurers and slave soldiers would follow—usurp power, extort legitimacy from the caliph, try and establish a new dynasty, and succumb to factionalism within the military elite. Within the Abbasid Caliphate, the royal share of revenues declined as *iqtas* were granted on terms favorable to the slave-soldiers. By the early 1000s, *iqtas* had spread all over Iraq and Persia and Turkish successor states effectively replaced the Abbasids as the rulers and eagerly adopted the sophisticated protocol and bureaucratic organization of their Persianized Arab masters.[22] The fragmentation of the secular power of the Abbasid Caliphate was not, however, something that was easily digestible for orthodox Muslims. The unity of the caliphate and its perseverance over the core territories of the contemporary Islamic world for some two hundred years were not achievements that were easily forgotten and reunification remained (and remains) on the agenda.[23] This task was not one that the Arabs were in a position to take up on account of their displacement from the military organization of the caliphate. Instead, the effort to revive the unity of the caliphate in some form was taken up by the Seljuk Turks and their clients.

The Seljuk were Oguz Turks of the Kinik tribe and entered Transoxiana in the late-900s, securing control of the territories around Samarkand and Bokhara. The name Seljuk by which the tribe became known is that of their leader who converted to Islam along with his tribesmen. The Seljuk Turks led by Tugrul and his son, Alp Arsalan, spread throughout the domains of the decadent Abbasid dynasty and decisively defeated the Byzantines, led by Emperor Romanus, in 1071, at the Battle of Manzikert. The Seljuk Sultanate was highly unstable on account of its approach towards the critical matter of succession. All the sons of the sultan had an equal claim to the throne. This presented the Seljuk polities with three possibilities when a ruler died. First, there could be an immediate outbreak of a war of succession. Second, different parts of the sultanate could be given to the sons of a sultan, which probably meant fragmentation or an eventual civil war. The third was that powerful emirs would carve out their own emirates (*beyliks*) and throw their support behind the claimant to the throne they thought most likely to let them exercise power undisturbed at a local level.

Seljuk political history thus follows a pattern similar to that of other arbitrary monarchies with tribal origins confronted with the problem of maintaining political order amongst a diverse settled population. Seljuk history is punctuated very regularly by wars between brothers, uncles and nephews, plus their factions of emirs, for control of the throne.[24] Alp Arsalan, thus had to fight a war of succession with Katalamis in which the latter was killed while fleeing from battle. The death of Kilic Arsalan in 1107 left the Seljuk Sultanate of Rum (Anatolia) in deep trouble as none of his sons was in a position to immediately take over (three were hostages, and one was with his mother in Malatya). Kilic Arsalan II, hoping to avoid bloodshed, divided the realm amongst his *eleven* sons, granting the title of sultan in his final testament to his youngest, Giyassedin Keyhusrev I. This left ten angry older brothers and an indeterminate number of unhappy emirs to cause trouble though Keyhusrev I managed to hold on to power. When he died, his three sons contested the throne, with many of the emirs supporting the eldest, Keyferidun Ibrahim, though it was the middle son, Keykubad, who emerged victorious. When Keykubad died in 1237, a crisis of succession emerged between his three sons. This time, the emirs backed the winning horse, Keyhusrev II, who seized the throne and had his half-brothers and their mother executed. This was the first instance of cold-blooded royal fratricide. By this time, however, the Seljuk Turks of Anatolia were under intense pressure from the Mongols. The Seljuk army, number-ing some 80,000, engaged the Mongols on June 26, 1243, and was badly defeated, though not yet destroyed. When Keyhusrev II died in 1246, recov-ery from the Mongol defeat was far from complete and all his sons were minors, which allowed his senior officers to seize power. Amir Shams-al Din married the mother of Prince Ruknuddin and sent an embassy to the court of Batu, who invested the prince with the title of sultan. The Seljuk Sultanate of Rum thus became a vassal state of the Mongol empire, more specifically, the Emirate of the Il-Khans that dominated Persia and Meso-potamia. The Il-Khans, faced the same problem with regard to succession as the Seljuk Turks, and fell victim to a civil war in 1282 when Tegudar seized the throne from his nephew, Arghun.

The Seljuk Sultanate established by Tugrul and Alp Arsalan spawned a number of sub-dynasties like the Zengids in Syria and the Ayyubids in Egypt and Palestine under Salahuddin Ayyubi (r. 1173–1194), who was a Kurd and a former servitor of the Zengids. In these times, local emirs, grasping sultans, nominal caliphs, and zealous crusaders, plunged the region into instability though the emergence of strong leaders, such as Nuruddin and Salahuddin, could establish islands of relative prosperity. Salahuddin's governance of Egypt is instructive in this regard. The Nubian soldiers of the defunct Fatimids were driven off or killed, trusted Turks and Kurds from Syria were brought in to take over the military, a royal guard of slave-soldiers was raised, dismissed officials were conciliated through the grant of pensions, grain prices were stabilized at 100 kg of wheat for one dinar, additional taxes were abolished, while the government imposed a 25% duty on mercantile traffic and used some of the resulting revenues to pay for armed protection for caravans and the construction of trading posts.[25] While the lower ranks of the state apparatus continued to be filled by Coptic Christians, at the higher levels Salahuddin opened the doors to talent drawing into his service men of outstanding ability and learning. Salahuddin thus ran a state whose elite guard were *mamluks*, soldiers were Turks and Kurds, senior administrative personnel were Persians, clerks were Copts, and the economy was run by merchants of diverse nationalities. One important reason for Salhuddin's success at gaining and retaining adherents was the generosity with which he treated his soldiers, paying them out of his own share of the loot and normally keeping little for himself. He earned such a reputation for justice and good sense that the day-to-day abuses of the administration were blamed on corrupt and deceitful officials who suc-ceeded in keeping their wrongdoings secret from the sultan.[26] This was the benevolence-myth at its finest, and Salahuddin is perhaps its most worthy exemplar for more than most rulers of his time he did make an effort to be gracious and kind. After Salahuddin, the Ayyubid dynasty soon fell prey to their slave-soldiers. By the 1250s, the *mamluks* had taken over the government and established a slave dynasty (almost contemporaneously with the slave dynasty of the Sultanate of Delhi, half a world away). The situation in Anatolia, more exposed to Mongol depredations, was complicated by the emergence of *beyliks* nominally under the patronage of the horde. These emirates included the Aydinid, Dulgadir, Eretnid, Hamidid, Karamanid, Karasi, Mentese, Ramazanoglu, and Osmanli (Ottomans). The Ottomans would mount a successful response to the challenge of Abbasid imperial succession—a question that had become more pressing after the devastation of Iran and the destruction of Baghdad, and much of Mesopotamia's hydraulic infrastructure, in the wake of the Mongol invasions.[27]

SLAVES OF THE PADISHAH: THE RISE OF THE OTTOMANS, 1299–1517

According to Ottoman tradition, an Oguz chief by the name of Ertugul became a servant of the Seljuk Sultan in or around 1275. In 1281, upon Ertugul's death, his son, Osman, succeeded him. Osman is considered the founder of the dynasty that bore his name and that would, over the next two centuries, establish an empire that eventually rivaled Rome, the Arab caliphates, and Achaemenid Persia, in its wealth, power, and cultural florescence. Little is known about Osman, though in 1302 he attracted Byzantine attention by defeating two imperial contingents. These victories drew other Turks to his banner and made him a *ghazi*, or holy warrior, tested in this case in battle against the Byzantines. Orhan succeeded his father, Osman *ghazi*, in 1324, captured Bursa in 1326, and minted his own coin in 1327, which was a strong indicator of sovereign pretensions. The Ottomans, wedged between the Byzantines and other emirates expanded slowly and deployed their forces in sieges and blockades that could last years. The challenge was holding on to conquests and ensuring a steady supply of loyal and competent civil and military officials. The Ottomans were already familiar with the practice of military slavery from their acquaintance with the Seljuk Turks. It would not, therefore, have been surprising for Orhan to have raised a royal guard of slave soldiers that would have served alongside tribal and levied forces. Nevertheless, it is, his successor, Murad I (r. 1362–1389), the first Ottoman ruler to proclaim himself sultan, who is formally credited with raising the slave corps of new troops, or janissaries. Murad I conquered Adrianople (Edirne) and expanded Ottoman power to Serbia, Macedonia, and Greece, while absorbing the emirates of Germiyan, Hamidid, and Teke, and effectively encircling Constantinople on land. The ability of the Ottomans to wage long wars and campaign every year was impressive while their janissaries earned a reputation for discipline and professionalism that invites comparison with the legions of Rome under Octavian.

Within the Ottoman Sultanate "the decree of the Sultan" was the only basis for "any income or privilege."[28] This did not mean that the Ottomans displaced the local elites that they defeated in battle. Given a choice, the Ottomans rather preferred to incorporate local notables into the power structure while clearly subordinating them to the sultan's household, which is to say his slaves, and Turkish nobles. In the Balkans, the combination of inducing collaboration while imposing a higher bureaucracy backed by superior military force allowed "a centralized administration" to replace "feudal decentralization."[29] For the ordinary cultivator this meant that local feudal dues and obligations were counter-balanced by a higher authority to which they could, at least in theory, appeal. In Anatolia, the same process meant the absorption of the emirates and their conversion into provinces of the Ottoman Sultanate. The Ottomans readily adopted "the bureaucratic tradition" of the region as necessary, remained flexible in accommodating local diversity even as they firmly imposed their writ and dealt effectively with rebellion.[30] The sultanate's basic organizing principle was that the subjects and all the land belonged to the sultan.[31] The primary objective of the sultanate's machinery was thus to ensure the effective exercise of the sultan's universal proprietorship. In this regard, the system of military and administrative slavery meant that the elite corps of the army and the civil service was also "owned by the ruler."[32] The Ottoman Sultanate, like other continental bureaucratic empires, confronted the problem of securing able and motivated servants that would also remain loyal to the dynasty. Simply importing Turkish slaves, as practiced by other Muslim polities, was never a truly satisfactory solution as evidenced by the numerous rebellions and uprisings staged by these servants.[33] Relying on Turkish nobles from the defeated emirates worked well enough in terms of securing order at the local level, but elevating them to the highest offices was deemed too risky for they could mobilize their kinsmen and exert pressure on the sultanate. The turbulent history of the Seljuk Sultanate had already demonstrated the unreliability of Turkish nobles while that of the Abbasids and Ayyubids testified to the difficulty of controlling slave-soldiers. The solution Orhan and Murad I apparently felt, lay in perpetuating a particular kind of slavery that would greatly expand the ruler's household while preserving its *asabiyah*—creating, as it were, an artificial tribe.

The first step towards manufacturing *asabiyah* was to enslave non-Muslim boys in the Balkans and Anatolia through the child-tax (*devshirme*). Once collected, the boys were sent to live with loyal Turkish families to learn the language and the tenets of Islam, were converted, and entrusted to the sultan's care. The second step was to train and educate the youths in a disciplined environment and identify those with the potential to join the officer class. Isolated, indoctrinated, and tightly controlled, these slave-cadets gradually came to identify with the sultanate at an emotional and moral level, regarding the sultan as the head of *their* very special Ottoman household.[34] The third step was to sort the cadets by ability and thus decide the future course of their careers as imperial servants. Those cadets who performed well at all academic disciplines, which included subjects as diverse as history, literature, art, engineering, and law, and at physical training and military subjects, could look forward to becoming palace officials. Cadets who excelled at military subjects and were notably courageous and hardy were marked for becoming officers in the janissary corps. Cadets with exceptional academic performance in particular subjects could become elite technocrats and serve the state as engineers, architects, and doctors. All cadets were subject to the same Spartan discipline and the training and education imparted was designed to produce a class of guardians worthy of the Platonic ideal expressed in *The Republic*. This was far from a speedy process for a boy enslaved at the age of ten or twelve would not receive his first official assignment until his mid-twenties. The emphasis was also on quality rather than quantity for the size of the slave corps was small, in contrasts to the tens of thousands or hundreds of thousands, of slaves in the possession of the contemporary Sultans of Delhi. The total strength of the Ottoman Sultanate's household slaves was, in the mid-1400s, about 700 palace officials, 1000 or so military officers, 12,000 janissary infantry and 7,500 imperial cavalry.[35] These slaves of the *padishah* were paid regular salaries on a quarterly basis, drew pensions, and could marry and have children though their status died with them and their children were disqualified, as free men, from higher imperial service. Although normally manumitted, the members of the Ottoman officer class continued to think of themselves as slaves. Their high level of education and culture meant that Ottoman officers, in general, but palace officials, in particular, were an academic as well as imperial elite rivaling the scholar-bureaucrats of China:

> In the Ottoman Empire . . . bureaucrats were required to possess an encyclopedic knowledge, and for this reason they displayed an interest in all fields of practical and useful knowledge—literature, language, calligraphy, law, history or geography, the principles of the calendar, surveying and agriculture. The ulema had no direct interest in these subjects, and the most important Ottoman writings in these fields are the work of professional secretaries.[36]

These officials were, like other members of the ruling class, "professional Ottomans"[37] and saw themselves as part of the royal household and stood at the top of the sultanate's social pyramid. Since fresh recruits were slaves, status was not transferable from father to son and so the officer class of the sultanate was a single-generation service nobility. By the mid-1400s, the sultanate's "crack troops were Slavs, its leading general Greek, its admiral Bulgarian, its sultan probably half Serbian or Macedonian."[38] The ability

of the sultanate to Ottomanize its royal slaves meant that the elite's loyalty to the household was far greater than that found in the *mansabdars*
of Mughal India, or the *ghulams* of Egypt and the Qizilbash adherents of
the Safavid order. Loyalty to the sultanate, in the Ottoman case, did not
translate automatically or necessarily into loyalty to every individual sultan. Even able rulers had to be wary of discontent within their slave corps.
Thus, in April 1512, Beyazid II "The Just" (r. 1481–1512),[39] was forced to
abdicate by a janissary rebellion in favor of his son, Selim I "The Stern"
(r. 1512–1520), which was the first instance of a change of sultan being
brought about the slave-soldiers.

The Ottoman Sultanate clearly grasped the connection between the
employment of a high quality officer class and the overall stability and
prosperity of the state. After all, the sultan could not be everywhere and
was often fully absorbed with strategic matters such as the conduct of
diplomacy and the leadership of military campaigns. Adopting a different approach from relatively homogenous imperial China, the Ottomans
enslaved, trained, and deployed a cadre of royal servants that would stand
comparison with the mandarins. While the Ottoman Sultanate excelled
at maintaining an outstanding imperial service class, like other continental bureaucratic empires, its Achilles heel was the problem of succession
and ensuring that competent rulers occupied the throne. Servants can be
trained and indoctrinated but the quality of the sovereign is almost everywhere accidental. The Ottomans, however, succeeded in producing a practically unprecedented succession of strong, effective, autocratic rulers for
nearly three centuries (1326–1603) and even during the late-Ottoman
period several sultans displayed qualities of leadership worthy of their great
ancestors, to say nothing of the continuation of that legacy in the modern
Turkish Republic's Mustafa Kemal, Ismet Inonu, and Kenan Evren. The
contrast with the Arab Caliphate, Persia, India, and other Turkish dynasties is almost embarrassing and only the Chinese have a historical tradition
of high quality autocracy that arguably exceeds the Ottoman example.[40]

One major contributing factor to Ottoman success was that they thought
very little of bloodlines, or the notion, quite prevalent in aristocratic
Europe, that qualities of leadership are somehow hereditary. Like their
slave-soldiers and administrators, the Ottoman princes were genetically
diverse products of the imperial harem. Sultans generally did not marry
and thus it was concubines who bore children, with the mothers of male
offspring elevated to higher status. Within the royal family any son capable
of commanding an army and managing the administration could succeed
his father. Failure to emerge as the de facto successor meant death or exile,
with the former being the preferred practice. By killing his brothers and
nephews, the new sultan monopolized the position as the only surviving
candidate. To overthrow or kill him would mean an end to the dynasty and
this was not something that the imperial slaves could contemplate. The first
recorded instance of royal fratricide among the Ottomans occurred at the

accession of Beyazid I in 1389. In February 1451, when Mehmed II "The Conqueror" succeeded Murad II, the former sent an assassin to kill his half-brother, Ahmed. After the murder was carried out, Mehmed II had the assassin put to death. Mehmed II formalized the practice of fratricide by enjoining his successors to do away with their male siblings and nephews in order to preserve the state. Royal princes were thus sent to govern provinces under the tutelage of high officials who would also help them master the art of war and military command. When their father died, a race for the capital would begin in which the winner took all and the losers lost their lives. It was expected that the years of practical experience followed by the trial by fire of a fratricidal Ottoman succession struggle would bring to power the most ruthless, hardened, and strategic-minded prince. Here the Ottoman Sultanate's peculiar brand of official slavery helped it avoid the fate of other empires where wars of succession were the normal method of deciding the next monarch. Many of these empires risked disintegration into their regional and sub-regional units during succession crises while the heterogeneous nobility, if it gained the upper hand, could plunge the country into a prolonged civil war. In the Ottoman Sultanate, however, the loyalty of the slaves to the state and dynasty meant that while they might support one brother against the other, there was no question of a slave becoming the ruler or taking advantage of a succession crisis to carve out an independent state. The result of the Ottoman variant of a game of thrones was thus decisive—the Rose Pavilion for the victor and the silken cord for the vanquished. This doubtless seems harsh, but the arbitrary Ottoman culture of power did not permit moral relationships even within the royal family and the practice of royal bloodletting increased the "chances for an extended line of competent rulers."[41] Field experience gained by young princes as governors of provinces, the existence of a centripetal officer class, and periodic fratricide, combined with formal education to help improve the chances for able leadership. In South Asia it is often pointed out that as Emperor Akbar and Maharaja Ranjit Singh were unlettered, formal education is not essential to leadership. The Ottoman attitude was that while leadership qualities cannot be magically conjured up through formal education, a lack of book learning is a serious handicap for the ruler of a state. To this one can add that one should not confuse literacy with a meaningful and reflective education. Akbar and Ranjit Singh were great leaders because they constantly sought to educate themselves though they were hampered by a lack of literacy.

Mehmed II's princely education is a classic example of the Ottoman respect for learning. Mehmed was a troublesome child and did not take well to his studies. To his father this was utterly unacceptable and so he authorized Mullah Ahmed Gurani, Mehmed's tutor, to beat the prince if he did not study. After the first time he was disciplined, Mehmed fell in line and became an exceptionally able and inquisitive student. Later, as sultan, Mehmed remained a voracious consumer of knowledge being particularly fascinated by history, languages, gardening and military science. The combination of learning and experience cultivated in the prince an attitude of heroic pessimism, cold patience, and an inscrutable demeanor. Thus, after emerging victorious in the 1453 siege of Constantinople, Mehmed entered the city in triumph one day after it had fallen.[42] Flanked by his janissaries and ministers who were in a celebratory mood after the military triumph of the millennium, Mehmed was characteristically quiet. After he laid eyes on the ruined Hippodrome he expressed his sadness regarding "the impermanence and instability of this world" and recalled the destruction of the mighty Sassanid Persian state in the mid-600s.[43]

The Ottomans were strangers neither to bringing about the destruction of those states that stood in their path nor to surviving terrible defeats such as the one inflicted by the Timurids in 1402. Like other states, the Ottoman Sultanate was a war machine that sought to conquer territory, dominate sea-lanes, and gather the resources needed to sustain further expansion. Sultans were war leaders and though the Ottomans did not risk their rulers' lives in battle it was not unusual for them to assume direct personal command of important campaigns. The Ottoman military was, like other militaries covered by our survey, divided into distinct categories of troops. The janissaries, imperial cavalry, artillery, and engineers, were elite units under the direct control of the sultan and his trusted officers. The total strength of these elite units was not particularly large by modern standards. In the mid-1400s, the janissary infantry and imperial cavalry did not exceed 20,000 in number, though the artillery, with about seventy heavy cannons, needed thousands of non-combatants for transport and deployment. Then there were provincial cavalry forces maintained through royal grants of the right to collect revenue from the land (*timars*). The *timar*-holders were called up for active service as needed with the sultan paying the mobilization cost. The provincial cavalry numbered between 30,000 and 50,000 in the 1400s. The poor cousins of the *timar*-holders were the *akinci*, or irregular light cavalry. These were forces raised from Muslim and non-Muslim communities and paid with war booty. In the mid-1400s, some 50,000 *akinci* were in the sultan's service. Rounding out the army were volunteers recruited as infantry on a seasonal basis as well as highly motivated holy warriors who joined campaigns in the hope of attaining martyrdom—an expectation sultans were happy to exploit for it helped preserve the janissaries, imperial cavalry, and *timar*-holders, for the purpose of delivering the decisive blow. The actual numerical strength of the army, including support staff, depended on the requirements of the individual campaign. In 1453, at the siege of Constantinople, some 80,000 troops and 120,000 non-combatants were deployed. At the failed invasion of Rhodes in 1480, perhaps 60,000 troops were dispatched, while in 1526, during the Hungarian campaign, the Ottomans fielded 50,000–100,000 troops.

While no European state would have the capacity to consistently mobilize campaign armies in the range of 100,000–200,000 men until the mid-1600s, some two hundred years after the fall of Constantinople, it was not numerical superiority alone that helped the Ottomans prevail so frequently. In terms of organization, the war department operated bureaucratically and took logistics very seriously. Ottoman war planning was scientific and made effective use of intelligence and maps. Within the military, the sultan's special messengers and reporters ensured that his orders were obeyed and that meritorious deeds were rewarded, while indiscipline and cowardice was punished. The Ottoman camp was quiet, calm, and adhered to effective principles of sanitation designed to preserve the health of the troops for as long as possible. The attitude towards new technology was pragmatic. The janissaries had originally been formed as a slave corps skilled in archery but by the mid-1400s firearms had become their weapon of choice.[44] The sultans embraced artillery enthusiastically and its value in sieges was rapidly understood. One of the major reasons for Ottoman victory in 1453 was the fact that Constantinople's fortifications had not yet entered the gunpowder age. Ottoman victories over the Persians (1514), *mamluks* of Syria and Egypt (1516, 1517), and the successful siege of Rhodes (1521), were triumphs of organization, firepower, and leadership, as well as strategic superiority. The discipline, devotion, and capacity for self-sacrifice of the janissaries were unmatched and acquired proverbial status in South Asia. South Asian history is replete with examples of smaller but better trained, equipped, and motivated, mobile invading armies making short work of larger but more traditionally organized defending forces. The success of Ottoman arms against forces as diverse as fanatical Qizilbash, heavily armored Christian knights, and Egyptian *mamluk* cavalry, is comparable to the success of modern European militaries during the wars of overseas colonial expansion in the 1700s and 1800s.

Armies can conquer territories and help hold on to them but a durable political order needs much more than just military strength to support it. This was the problem faced by conquerors ranging from Alexander the Great to Amir Timur, and in modern times, by Napoleon, Hitler, and imperial Japan. The Ottomans ruled through a combination of conservatism and generosity backed by the capacity to unleash terror if needed. Conservatism in the Ottoman context meant that the sultanate tended to accept the geographical and cultural realities of the territories that came under its sway. Thus, the Ottomans had little interest in converting their non-Muslim subjects to Islam, for doing so would necessitate terrible oppression, lead to disturbances, and diminish the revenues generated through the poll-tax on misbelievers. Beyazid II, for instance, actually sent his navy to rescue Jews being persecuted in Spain after 1492, granted them special permission to settle in the Ottoman Sultanate and decreed the death penalty for anyone found guilty of obstructing the refugees. The Jews, and other non-Muslim communities, excelled at trade, manufacture, learning, and were law-abiding, tax-paying subjects—it made no sense to harm them for a difference of religious opinion in pursuit of some impractical St. Augustinian notion of theological purity. Such pragmatism was lost on many European rulers, ranging from Ferdinand and Isabella of Spain, to Louis XIV of France, various German polities during the Reformation, and on twentieth century leaders, such as Hitler, Lenin, Stalin, and Mussolini. Recognizing different groups as communities (*millets*) and letting them enjoy civil and religious freedom in exchange for taxes, service and loyalty to the state, was the deal offered by the Ottoman Sultanate.[45] Co-opting elites displaced or marginalized by the Ottoman conquests was another method of bringing potentially troublesome subjects into the fold of loyalty. Thus, in North Africa, Ottoman power rested on the recognition of local notables, many of them no better than pirates, as part of a respectable imperial elite that merited the sultan's military protection and administrative support. In the Syrian provinces of Aleppo, Damascus and Tripoli, direct Ottoman rule was confined to major cities and their arable hinterlands.[46] Outside these directly administered zones, the Ottomans entered into arrangements with local families and tribal leaders who received official recognition from Istanbul. It was far cheaper to employ a "policy of manipulation, of setting one family or one member of a family against another" and in so doing "preserve the balance between imperial and local interests."[47] In Egypt, where seven janissary regiments were deployed after the conquest in 1517, the *mamluks* continued to exist, though now as a lesser nobility employed primarily to retain control over the countryside.[48]

The state apparatus was hierarchically organized and designed to run a vast empire with a relatively small number of highly competent elite imperial servants. At the center was the *sadr-i-azam* (Grand Vizier), with additional viziers appointed for the establishment, the military, and provincial affairs. The sultan presided over his viziers in the supreme council or *divan*, which was assisted by high officials below the rank of vizier. The council articulated policy, listened to appeals from the provinces, heard complaints directed against the administration, debated matters of war and peace, and oversaw the daily functioning of the central government. Assisting the high officials were members of the ordinary bureaucracy (*kalemiye*) and an assortment of inspectors, supervisors, messengers, spies, and collectors. These civil servants were responsible for maintaining the records of taxes, population, laws, council decisions, and drafting communications in the stylized and ornate pattern of the Ottoman Sultanate in which the physical size and composition mattered as much as the mundane contents. The Ottoman bureaucracy was "without parallel in the world of Islam" when it came to the preparation, preservation, and organization, of "Documents and accounts."[49] In the Ottoman administrative structure the officer class was drawn from the sultan's household, which is to say that they were his slaves, while routine business was left in the hands of a salaried secretarial bureaucracy drawn from subject local populations of the empire. In this way the central control and relative impartiality possible through the rule of strangers was combined with the detailed local knowledge of the provincial bureaucracy—much like the Indian Civil Service drawn from Britain and the local staff employed in the district administration—an imperial officer class and their indigenous *munshis*.

The central apparatus was replicated in the provinces (*eyalets*) and local governments (*sancak*s). Imperial governors were appointed from Istanbul and served at the sultan's pleasure with regular transfers from one province to another. Imperial troops, provincial cavalry, and local levies, were garrisoned at key points in the provinces and were ultimately answerable to the provincial governor. The typical governor "had his elaborate household, his secretaries and accountants, and his council of high officials meeting regularly."[50] The local administration varied considerably and depended on the practices inherited from the pre-Ottoman period. In territories where the preceding regime already had bureaucratic system of governance the Ottomans installed their own high officials and troops and continued as before.[51] In the Balkans, the Ottomans reduced the powers of the local aristocracy and limited feudal obligations on the peasantry, while subjecting European notables to the same principles of manipulation and disposal as those in other parts of the empire.

Taxes were assessed on households, while land revenue, which in theory was a tax of ten percent on produce, combined with levies on markets and trade to furnish most of the state revenues. The sale of slaves captured in war as well as booty were important though irregular sources of income for the sultan and his servants and helped replenish the navies' galleys.[52] Protected non-Muslim subjects paid the poll tax (*jizya*) and were exempted from military service. As discussed above, the poll tax provided the sultans with a strong incentive to preserve religious tolerance. Until the 1600s direct assessment of taxes and collection by the sultan's agents or those of his governors, was the preferred method of revenue collection. Land revenue assignments in the form of *timar*s helped support the provincial cavalry while the janissaries, *mamluks*, and royal family members, ran networks of foundations, ostensibly charitable, that helped provide for them over and above pensions and salaries. Foreign traders were encouraged to invest in the Ottoman Sultanate through concessions called capitulations and this helped secure a supply of gold and silver bullion.

The army, bureaucracy, royal household, fiscal administration, and provincial and local authorities, were governed by the sultan's regulations, or *kanun*:

> The 15th-century Ottoman historians Aşıkpaşazade and Tursun Bey provided important information about the Ottoman rulers' making of *kanun*. One extract from Aşıkpaşazade's history in which Osman Gazi, the founder of the Ottoman principality, proclaims *kanun*, reads as follows:[53]

Kadı and *sübaşı* were appointed. And a market was opened. And *hutbe* was delivered after the Friday prayer. And these people began to ask for *kanun* to be established. A person came from *Germiyan* and said "sell the *bac* of this market place to me". The people answered "you should go to the Khan". That person went to the Khan and repeated his words. Osman Gazi said "What is *bac?*" and the person answered "Whoever comes to sell something in this market will give me some money". Osman Gazi said "Do the people of this market owe you something? The person said "My Khan! This is *töre* and it is in use in all cities and the rulers take it". Osman Gazi said "was it ordered by God or did the rulers order it? That person again said "It is a *tore,* my Khan, and it has been in use for a long time". Osman Gazi got angry with the person and said "when someone earns money why should other people have a share in it? The one who earns it owns the money. I did not put money in his trade and so I cannot ask him to give me money. O man! Go away and do not say these words any more to me or I will punish you". This time the people said "My Khan it is an *adet* that when a person watches a market place he is expected to get some money from the traders". Osman Gazi said "since you put it like this, anyone who brings goods to the market and sells them will give two *akças,* if he does not sell he will not give any money". And he added "whoever breaks my *kanun* God may disturb [in] his religion and [in] his world . . . may God be pleased with whoever follows my *kanun* . . . "[54]

These, and many other royal laws, overruled all other laws and filled the gaps with regard to practical administration and finance left by the religious law or *sharia* as well as custom. Technically, the Ottoman Sultanate subscribed to the Hanafite school of jurisprudence though, in practice, Sufi influences on the janissary corps were strong and non-Muslims administered their own civil and religious laws. Other than *kanun* and *sharia*, which were formally declared consistent with each other thanks to the compliant ulema, tribal and local custom, were also taken into account, especially outside the settled areas. The Ottoman legal system, somewhat like British India's, operated on the principle of uniformity where possible and diversity where necessary. One important concession made by the Ottoman Sultanate was its tolerance of *waqfs*, or charitable endowments. Ottoman household slaves often sought to invest their wealth in such endowments to protect at least some of it from confiscation, either by the sultan or by their colleagues.[55] As for crafts guilds, "they were constituted by Ottoman recognition" and "were not self-sufficient."[56]

The Ottoman Sultanate during its rise was, like Achaemenid Persia, a pragmatic autocracy mediated through a class of royal slaves and a subordinate quasi-hereditary secretarial bureaucracy. The army was led by the sultan's slave-soldiers, the provincial governments were headed by governors drawn from the high palace officials and senior military officers, and the ruler's advisers were, for the most part, slaves as well. Beneath this extended household was a mosaic of local variations that the sultanate tolerated and manipulated. The sultan quite literally owned the sultanate and the officer class though, like other arbitrary rulers, he alienated a share of his estate in the form of revenue assignments to pay for provincial cavalry and patronized local notables with tangible and intangible rewards. The law was complex with the sultan's edict constituting the de facto supreme law, the *sharia* the de jure supreme law, and numerous communities and sects enjoying their own civil and religious laws. Of course, the sultan could always set aside any legal tenet that proved inconvenient and edicts, such as the fratricide law of Mehmed II, that enjoined the murder of siblings in order to ensure effective monarchy, were declared consistent with Islamic principles. The sultan was the *padishah*, the subject communities were recognized as *millets* and *jamaats* while the subjects were generally considered a flock of sheep or *reaya*. The Ottomans took a dim view of open rebellion and purged officials and hunted down rebels mercilessly. The sultan held the power of life and death over his servants and subjects and had hundreds of executioners who, when not strangling, amputating, or hanging, doubled as the royal gardeners. Policy debates took place with these executioners standing by, for to end up on the losing side of an argument meant death or exile. Halil Pasha, Mehmed II's vizier who counseled caution in the siege of Constantinople, lost his life soon afterwards, much to the glee of the hawks, led by Zaganos Pasha. The violence and arbitrariness that the sultans meted out to their minions were inexorably directed at the royal family itself, which underwent a bloody internecine purge with every change of ruler since Murad I. There was no kinship in Ottoman kingship. What prevented the sultanate from exploding or disintegrating was the loyalty to the dynasty that pervaded the slave elite that was the product of the extraordinary lengths that the Ottomans went to in order to groom and educate its officer class.

THE ROSE PAVILION AND THE SILKEN CORD:
THE OTTOMAN SULTANATE AT ITS HEIGHT, 1500–1730

In 1500, the Ottomans had already been around for two hundred years. At this point South Asia was divided into warring states and the Mughal invasion of 1526 was still a quarter of a century away. Persia was in chaos though the Safavids were on the move and about to restore her to imperial status. The Russians had barely shaken off the yoke of the Mongol horde and still confronted that, and many other, formidable enemies. England, France, and Spain were still in their infancy as states worth the name. England and France were locked in an enduring rivalry that had resulted in the Hundred Years War while Spain, the blood from its re-conquest from the Muslims having not yet dried, had unleashed the Inquisition and aimed at nothing less than a genocide of its non-Christian population. Italy and Germany were geographical and cultural expressions divided into a patchwork of city-states, feudal domains, and imperial territories. Hungary was in its death throes, trapped in strategic and political quicksand on account of an aristocracy that refused to recognize the need for a strong royal authority and a regular army to resist the Ottomans. Europe as a whole was on the verge of the Reformation and would soon be torn asunder by sectarian violence and *raison d'état*. The only state that exceeded the Ottoman Sultanate in size, splendor, wealth, and population, was Ming China, though geographic location, the continuing inland threat from the north, and cultural disposition, prevented the Chinese from playing the role of a world power. Many great Ottoman victories still lay ahead of them in 1500 including Chaldiran (1514), Syria (1516), Egypt (1517), Algeria (1521), Rhodes (1522), Hungary (1526), Preveza (1538), Libya (1551), Cyprus (1570), Tunisia (1574), Georgia (1578), Azerbaijan and Armenia (1590). True, there would defeats as well—Vienna, Malta, and Lepanto to be precise, and had the Ottomans won these engagements the history of Europe would have played out very differently—but a sixteenth century Ottoman could be forgiven for seeing these losses as temporary pauses on the road to an even greater and more glorious empire. As late as 1683, the Ottomans were still hurling armies 200,000 strong at Vienna, while after Lepanto (1571) it took them only two years to rebuild their entire navy. In terms of internal organization the 1500s saw the acceleration of three major trends. The first was the growing remoteness of the sultan and the delegation of more and more decision-making powers to viziers and governors. The second was a gradual softening of the janissary ethos, as the slave-army became more of a garrison force than a field force. The third was increasing violence within the empire perpetrated by the ruler or his servants in an effort to reinvigorate the sultanate.

Ibn Khaldun appreciated that once a dynasty was established the need to protect the ruler from threats necessitated tighter security, more elaborate protocol, and increased physical isolation. At the same time, it also became desirable to rely more on viziers to carry out the routine administration with minimal royal supervision so that the ruler could focus on the pursuit of war and magnificence or, at a more degenerate stage, immerse himself in the pursuit of pleasure. Mehmed II had made it a point to spend more time in seclusion and hoped that by doing so he could foster "an aura of mystery and power."[57] His successors follow him in this and sultans appeared with diminishing frequency in public.[58] Suleiman I "The Lawgiver" (r. 1520–1566) stopped accepting petitions from the public and preferred to sit silently behind the screen in council meetings.[59] Selim II (r. 1566–1574) became inaccessible even to his viziers and by the 1590s personal access for the grand vizier "became less usual, replaced by written correspondence in which the sultan indicated his desire on a range of affairs of state."[60] Growing royal isolation from the running of the state produced a slackening of discipline in the administration for no vizier, however wise, could be more than a first slave. The moral authority of the sultan as the father of his household and janissaries was gradually undermined by his absence. After Suleiman I, it became rare for the sultan to accompany his troops on important campaigns. In 1566, rank and file janissaries were granted permission to marry and after 1568 the regular enslavement of Christians via the child tax was abandoned in favor of occasional harvests. The janissaries quickly settled down and grew accustomed to the pleasures of civilian life and domesticity and used their military and administrative clout to intervene in business, amass fortunes, and enroll their children in the janissary corps. The number of janissary infantrymen on the imperial payroll rose rapidly, from 13,500 in 1574 to 40,000 by 1609.[61] Many of these later janissaries were not in the military to fight wars and thus the state faced a shortage of troops in the early 1600s. The Ottoman Sultanate responded to this through the short-term enlistment of peasants as musketeers, it being relatively easy to impart basic training in firearms.[62] The *askeri* had become self-interested businessmen while the *reaya* were being pressed into military service—a stunning reversal for a state that prided itself on the professionalism of its military and had set the standard to beat in this regard for some 250 years. Increasingly confident in their power and hubristic in their attitude towards external enemies, the janissaries assumed the role of a mafia engaged in extorting resources from the state. If those resources were not forthcoming, or if the state was forced to economize, the janissaries revolted. In 1589, they revolted in Istanbul, while in Egypt mutinies occurred in 1589, 1598, 1601 and 1604.

Like practically all states, the Ottoman Sultanate reacted violently to rebellion. Within the Ottoman slave elite the sultan's powers of life and death were often asserted, even against intimates. Sultan Selim I, ran through six viziers in his eight years in power and ordered the execution of three of them. His predecessor, Beyazid II, in contrast, employed seven grand viziers in 29 years. Selim I was also determined to crush the pro-Safavid Qizilbash in Eastern Anatolia, and presided over the massacre of some 40,000 of this community. Suleiman I had his grand vizier, Ibrahim Pasha, "suddenly executed" in March 1536 soon after his return from the "the campaign of the two Iraqs."[63] The room where Ibrahim Pasha was executed was evidently left bloodstained as a warning to other palace officials. Ibrahim Pasha, for his part, had amassed a considerable personal fortune and encouraged the sultan to spend extravagantly, even putting to death a treasurer who criticized the vizier for spending on a helmet crown for Suleiman I during the 1529 Vienna campaign.[64] Suleiman I personally oversaw the execution of his most capable son, Mustafa, in 1553, and secured the execution of another son, Beyazid and all his sons, in 1561, by bribing the Safavids under whose protection they were living. The apogee of royal bloodletting was reached a generation later with the accession of Mehmed III (r. 1595–1603). As was custom, Mehmed III ordered the execution of nineteen of his brothers and half-brothers, the largest batch of royal executions in Ottoman history. Ahmed I (r. 1603–1617), was so appalled by the practice of royal fratricide that he decided to break with tradition and the *kanun* and introduced the practice of imprisoning Ottoman princes within the palace complex in what was called "the cage".

The cage was meant to serve humane and political purposes. With regard to the former, the cage seemingly eliminated the need for a fratricidal struggle for succession that ended up producing substantial collateral damage and sometimes led to preemptive rebellion by anxious princes. Insofar as the latter were concerned, the cage was supposed to ensure dynastic stability by preserving Ottoman princes so that if the elder brother died the younger one could take over. As it turned out the cage failed in both its humane and political objectives and produced the unwholesome side effect of depriving future sultans of administrative and military experience. Locked up in protective custody, princes became pawns in the hands of court factions and lived in dread of execution. As a result of this "most of [the Ottoman princes]" soon "suffered psychological disorders."[65] Rather than being active participants in a struggle for succession, princes became passive and paranoid spectators while janissaries, palace eunuchs, and elite civil servants, engaged each other in intrigues of Byzantine complexity and ruthlessness. The rule of gangs at the center provoked tumults and chaos throughout the empire. By 1635, the Anatolian countryside lay devastated by rebellion and state oppression. Sultan Murad IV (r. 1623–1640) responded by ordering refugees to return to their destroyed homes or be executed but relented at the insistence of his mother and ordered a report on the situation to be prepared.[66] Murad IV, in a fit of administrative piety ordered the closure of coffee houses and the enforcement of sumptuary laws, which indicated a slight hardening of the official religiosity of the Ottoman Sultanate. His successor, Ibrahim "the Mad" (r. 1640–1648) proved to be an unusually imbalanced specimen of derangement even among the alumni of the cage. Sultana Mustafa (r. 1617–1618), had appointed infants as provincial governors. Deposed in 1618, he was succeeded by Osman III, whose favorite pastimes included archery practice with live human targets. Osman III was not only overthrown by the janissaries but earned the distinction of becoming the first sultan to be murdered by them. Murad IV enjoyed ordering executions and put some 25,000 of his subjects to death. Sultan Ibrahim had 280 of his concubines tied up in sacks and drowned in the Bosporus. He was also a hypochondriac and convinced everyone was plotting against him, a belief which represented a plausible hypothesis for in the end, driven to desperation by his depravity, even the queen mother turned against him. Fed up with misrule and imperial insanity, the janissaries deposed Ibrahim in 1648 and executed him.

In 1648, the Ottoman Sultanate was more than three hundred years old. The experience of South Asian empires, or Persia's empires, indicates that the end of the succession of able rulers is followed by the fragmentation of the state and the overthrow of the dynasty within a few years, or, at most, a few decades. In Timurid India, the death of Aurungzeb in 1707 triggered a succession crisis that was followed by rapid dissolution for by the 1720s successor states had emerged in different parts of the former empire. So rapid was this collapse that by 1739, a briefly reinvigorated Persia under Nader Shah, who had replaced the fallen Safavids, invaded South Asia and plundered Delhi. The Ottomans, for all the concern about their decline, defied the laws of regime mortality in evidence elsewhere in Eurasia. Fuad Pasha is said to have quipped to a Western interlocutor that the Ottoman Sultanate was the strongest state in the world on account of the fact that in spite of the best efforts of the West *and* the Ottoman elite to destroy it, it doggedly refused to succumb to the deadly combination of external machinations and domestic ineptitude.[67] Far from collapsing after 1648, the Ottoman Sultanate underwent a remarkable resurgence, as it would again in the 1820s.

The janissaries, the palace officials, enlightened members of the harem faction, and provincial notables, all realized by 1648 that things were going terribly wrong. With thirty million subjects spread across three continents the Ottoman Sultanate needed wise leadership and determined management, both of which had been in short supply since the 1580s. Mehmed IV "The Hunter" (r. 1648–1687) who succeeded Ibrahim seemed oblivious to this reality during the first eight years of his reign and disposed of ten viziers in that time. The sultan had little interest in governing but indulged his whimsicality by making and breaking senior palace officials. Thus, when Koprulu Mehmed took over as Mehmed IV's eleventh grand vizier in September 1656 few could have expected him to survive long in power, let alone establish a dynastic vizierate that provided the empire with solid leadership for another fifty years.[68] Koprulu faced an apparently impossible task, which was, that he had to save the Ottoman Sultanate from the Ottoman Sultan. In spite of this, Koprulu had three aces up his sleeve. The first was he did not seem to covet the grand vizierate and insisted on the sultan giving him a free hand to fix the administration and not to listen to any negative feedback against Koprulu were he to take the assignment. The second was that Koprulu had resolved to move quickly and violently against those who threatened the state. If he got the job, then swift retribution would fall upon any and all who dared stand in his way. The third was that Koprulu understood that Sultan Mehmed IV was an overgrown child and needed to be treated with a combination of firmness in public matters and indulgence in private matters. Ruthless, brilliant, and relentless in the pursuit of restoring royal authority, Koprulu was able to draw upon the residual esprit de corps of the slave elite, which, also feared the breakup of the empire and was threatened by the rising tide of disorder. The janissaries, the ulema, the old elites that had been accommodated by the Ottomans, all thought of themselves as loyal subjects of the sultanate and many longed for the reassertion of its strength.

Mehmed Koprulu took on corrupt officials, their networks of patronage, and rebels who were exploiting the growing chaos within the sultanate. Brutal purges of the apparatus followed and between 50,000 and 60,000 people were executed—these included corrupt officials as well as the Orthodox Patriarch. Such harsh measures produced appeals to the sultan, but Koprulu had seen to it that the sovereign was out of the capital enjoying hunting expeditions while the silken cord and scimitar did their work. Severity restored the writ of the state and made defiance a costly, if not catastrophic, proposition. In pursuit of accountability Ottoman-style, Koprulu spared no one—thirty pashas were executed in 1658–1659 for rebellions while ordinary cavalrymen who mutinied were massacred until discipline was restored. Here Koprulu used the janissaries against other forces to crush rebellion while, with the sultan no longer in Istanbul, the ability of senior military commanders to gain direct access to the monarch was undermined. Koprulu apparently realized that once the authority of the state has broken down to the point where the rule of gangs became the norm, only massive violence directed at a cross-section of gangsters, could bring about the needed restoration. When, in the summer of 1660, fire leveled parts of Istanbul, the grand vizier took personal charge of the rebuilding with the state taking over the damaged areas in order to pay for the reconstruction effort. Improvements on the domestic front brought victories against external rivals as well. Venice was defeated in 1657 while Transylvania was annexed in August 1660. The mercilessness with which failed commanders were treated may have had something to do with it, for the Ottoman admiral who failed to break the Venetian blockade in January 1657 was executed for this lapse. Koprulu's time, however, was running out for, born in or around 1575, and inducted into the sultan's service as a slave via the child tax, he was eighty years old when he became grand vizier. This unusual longevity meant that unlike his sons and nephews, Koprulu knew the old ways firsthand and understood, in a manner that later generations could not, what had made the Ottoman Sultanate great in another time. In some ways Koprulu's position was similar to the Indian Civil Service officers from the British Raj that continued in the service of India and Pakistan after 1947. They sought to resurrect the state they knew best amidst the chaos, populism, and militarism unleashed by the termination of the British Raj and succeeded in restoring its basic structure and some of its ethos, which is what still keeps India and Pakistan going. But later generations simply didn't have the needed exposure and as the Raj became more remote the indigenous variant of arbitrary rule reasserted itself.

Mehmed Koprulu's son, Fazil Ahmed succeeded him as grand vizier in 1661 and governed the empire until 1676. Fazil Ahmed benefited from the hardheartedness of his father's regime as the elite had been so thoroughly cowed that continuous employment of terror and confiscation could be set aside. Kara Mustafa, who took over from Fazil Ahmed in 1676, was eager to deploy Ottoman armies for further conquests and set his sights on Vienna. In 1683, mobilizing an army of 200,000 men for the Vienna campaign he set off for the Habsburg capital but failed in taking the city as had Suleiman I in 1529. Even in defeat, Kara Mustafa set an example as "a model of the old Ottoman virtues. He received his executioners with courtesy, and when shown the [silken cord], praised the sultan's honor and generosity, prayed briefly and submitted silently to his doom."[69] This was only to be expected for in the old days failure in battle meant that the commanders' lives were forfeit, though the sultan could be merciful and reduce the punishment to dismissal from service and confiscation of property, as Mehmed I had done with his admiral during the siege of Constantinople when some enemy ships disrupted the Ottoman naval blockade. Even after Kara Mustafa's fall, the dynastic vizierate established by Koprulu the slave-official continued for another twenty years, though it was no longer as effective or successful as before.

One area of particular concern had always been tax collection. In the cities the commissioners or *emins* were centrally appointed, as were market officials, and drew regular salaries. These functionaries were allowed to receive gifts from supplicants and operated within networks of patronage that extended to the governors above and the wealthy *reaya* below. Like the secretarial bureaucracy in the capital, these officials were not of servile origin and thus, under the classical Ottoman system, their prospects of advancement were limited. In the countryside the practice had been for the sultan to collect revenues directly from royal estates or grant lands as revenue assignments in exchange for civil and military service. The growth of the empire and the relaxation of its founding ethos led to the emergence of rural tax farmers by the early 1600s. The right to collect taxes on land was auctioned off to the highest bidder who was expected to operate a private bureaucracy to realize the assessed revenues. Such tax farms were insecure, as demonstrated by the purges carried out by Koprulu, and could be withdrawn in an instant for all land was ultimately the domain of the sultan. This meant that tax farmers had little interest in the long-term improvement of the lands that fell under their jurisdiction and had every incentive, in the absence of effective coercion from above, to cheat the central government of its share of the revenues while extracting more than the legitimately assessed amount from the cultivator. In 1691, to aid transparency and increase revenues, poll taxes were reassessed on individuals and payments were to be monetized. In 1695, tax farms in South-eastern Anatolia and the Arab provinces were granted for life, the idea being that greater security would lead to less rapacity and, in the long-term, increases in productivity that would also bring about the growth of state revenues. In 1697, tax farming was extended to the royal domains, the *timars*, and the vizier's estates. Here, in the case of the royal domains, tax farms were granted for three-year terms.

When Ahmed III (r. 1703–1730) was brought to power by the janissaries, these reforms misfired badly. The sultan, his family, and his favorites, started buying up tax farms. In 1715, the titles of life-term tax farms were arbitrarily revoked, and two years later, in another exercise in extortion, the sultan offered to sell the rights back to the original tax farmers for a fee equal to half the current price. Ahmed III and his successor, Mahmud I (r. 1730–1754) presided over an empire that had become complacent. Victories against the Russians, then pressed by the Swedes, and Austria (Banjaluka was recaptured in 1737, Belgrade in 1739) and the collapse of Safavid Persia in the 1720s, appeared to validate the notion that the Ottoman Sultanate was a realm protected by Heaven. Culture flourished during the Tulip Era (1718–1730), the frontiers expanded or were stable, the sultan reigned, his officials ruled, and troubles in the provinces, such as the near civil war in Egypt on account of rivalries between groups of slave-soldiers and janissaries were barely audible to the sultan's ears. The Ottoman Sultanate had lasted four hundred years by 1730 and as such had exceeded practically all other dynasties in terms of its period of effective rule. Since 1517, the Ottoman Sultans had also been caliphs, their descent from the Quraysh conveniently secured by the pliant ulema whose head, the *Sheikh-ul-Islam* was a servant of the ruler.[70] In 1634 and 1656, troublesome *sheikhs* had been executed. Furthermore, the major Sufi order in the empire, the Bektashi, which had some seven million adherents, was enmeshed with the janissaries who were its patrons and most fervent adherents. The sultans and viziers of the 1700s, however, would have done well to heed Mehmed "the Conqueror's" reflection after he entered Constantinople in triumph in 1453 about the basic instability of human fortune.

THE DESCENT: OTTOMAN DECLINE AND ATTEMPTS AT RESURGENCE, 1730–1839

The "Sick Man of Europe" almost outlived them all for Romanov Russia, the Habsburg Empire, and the Hohenzollerns of Imperial Germany, fell during or immediately after the First World War. By the time the Ottomans made their exit from the stage of world history the Mughals and Safavids were long gone while the Qajars of Persia were in their death throes. After the First World War, the technically triumphant but badly mauled empires of Britain and France would limp along for another generation before they too succumbed to the march of time and changing circumstances. That the Ottoman Sultanate declined over two centuries is itself unusual for in so much time most dynasties and regimes rise and fall. During its decline, even towards the very end, the Ottoman Sultanate remained militarily formidable, as the British learned the hard way at Gallipoli[71] and Kut, and a politically independent polity—a vestige of the secular might of the Muslim world. As late as 1867, the Ottoman Sultanate ruled some five million square kilometers of continental expanse and it wasn't until the First World War that the empire's hold on the Arab world was broken.

The late-Ottoman state, like the late-Roman Empire, was beset on all sides by powerful predators and internally fractured by strengthening currents of identity formation that ran counter to the imperial idea and steadily delegitimized the state. Late-Ottoman sultans were engaged in a desperate holding operation that involved manipulation of the antagonisms of their rivals while trying to buy time and political space for internal reforms.

The Ottoman Sultanate, as noted above, was conservative and pragmatic in its approach to the problem of control. In the provinces this meant investing in a variety of local elites and making them feel a part of the extended Ottoman household. An essential component of this was recognition. Thus, in the Arab provinces, for instance, the ulema, landlords, and local government officials, were recognized as *ayan* (notable, or elite).[72] The *ayan* exercised an inferior level of patronage (*intisap*) and associated with the Ottoman administration as intermediaries between ordinary subjects and the royal authority. Rather than trying to reinvent the wheel, the Ottoman reforms of the mid-1800s built upon the historical experience of governance even as it sought to channel it towards more modern objectives, such as local representation.[73] They did so by creating sub-district councils chaired by the sub-district officers (*qa 'immaqam*). These councils had seven members, three elected and four ex-officio.[74] Eligibility criteria for standing for elected office included being an Ottoman subject, having attained the age of thirty, and paying at least 150 *qurush* a year in taxes.[75] With regard to the Bedouins, the traditional approach had been to let the governors use the patronage at their disposal to play one group against another to keep the caravans, and pilgrims performing *Hajj* (some 70,000 per year by 1814) safe. This required the holding of strong points and punitive expeditions. The reform of the Ottoman military after 1826 strengthened the central government as did the establishment of a regional police in the late-1800s, though these changes complemented rather than replaced the traditional approach.[76]

As the center weakened in the 1700s local power players led by Ottoman officials stepped in. These civil servants, judges, and decadent janissaries/ *mamluks* were not as aloof towards local concerns as the classical slave elite had been but they too sought to make their careers and fortunes within the great framework of the Ottoman Sultanate. In this respect, "even the bey of Tunis andthe *dey* of Algiers wished to be formally invested by the sultan as governor."[77] In Tunis in the late-1500s, junior officers of the janissary corps formed a council and chose a leader (the *dey*) "who shared power with the governor."[78] These janissaries were loyal to the sultanate and wanted it to continue, though, after the relaxation of the child-tax and the easing of restrictions on marriage and settling down, the official Ottomans grew local roots. Key positions remained in the hands of the sultan's elite officials, the secretarial bureaucracy was dominated by locals, and the janissaries continued to play the leading military role.[79] The growth of urban centers also helped consolidate Ottoman influence. Cairo grew from 200,000 to 300,000 between the late-1500s and late-1600s. Aleppo, Damascus, Algiers, and Tunis, had about 100,000 people each by the late-Ottoman period. One result of the Ottoman peace was that the "walls of most of the great cities were no longer useful", on account of population growth, "the order the Ottomans maintained in the surrounding country-side" and the spread of artillery.[80]

Egypt, arguably the most important province of the sultanate on account of its rich agriculture and high population density, provides a useful test case of the phenomenon of decline in the late-Ottoman period. Here, it is necessary to clarify that Egypt itself was not in decline until it was incorporated into a British protectorate and subjected to dual misgovernment. In fact, in the 1800s, Egypt benefited from the strong rule of an Albanian soldier, Muhammad Ali (r. 1806–1849), and his successors. Egypt started its industrialization under a strict mercantilist regime, trained and equipped a modern army that helped preserve the Ottoman Sultanate in the Arab provinces, and introduced scientific education in its schools to help the country stay competitive with the West. In Egypt, central authority was maintained by the imperial regiments of janissaries though the *mamluk*s continued to enjoy a local presence. Between 1670 and 1700 the janissary regiments became practically autonomous of the center and more local in their thinking. The *mamluk*s benefitted from the relaxation of janissary discipline and gained control of much of Egypt's rural areas, which is where most of the wealth was. This change in the balance between janissary and *mamluk* destabilized the military. Factionalism was no stranger to the Ottoman bureaucracy but after 1713, the status quo nurtured by the stick of central intervention broke down.[81] The center, realizing the difficulty of using the janissaries for military purposes, started to raise fresh forces of mercenaries and irregular levies. The mercenaries quickly became another cause of disorder, as they were afraid of being dismissed by the sultan.[82] The levies, primarily infantrymen pressed into service from the peasantry, soon numbered between 100,000 and 150,000, but were no match for the increasingly professional and disciplined armies of the western powers.[83]

Egypt's importance was augmented by its role as the major route through which Abyssinian slaves, especially eunuchs, destined for royal or provincial service, passed. Beshir Agha, the Chief of the Black Eunuchs in Istanbul, was the most powerful person in the sultanate during the early and mid-1700s, and could make or break viziers. Beshir Agha's career spanned two reigns (Ahmed III and Mahmud I) and he spent the last sixteen years of his life determining who would run the Ottoman Sultanate.[84] The functions of a chief black eunuch included running the royal harem and managing the religious endowments constituted by the royal family. This gave the office tremendous power that combined daily access to the ruler with managerial control of enormous wealth secured in royal foundations. In contrast, the viziers dealt with the sultan through correspondence for the rulers had long abandoned the practice of direct involvement with the supreme council. In

Egypt, Beshir Agha's agent was Osman Agha, and when the former died there was a scramble for his estate, which was subject to both imperial confiscation and the claims of his subordinates and collaborators. When the Qatamish and Dumyati associates of the late Beshir Agha held up shipments of grain due to pious foundations, Osman Agha prevailed upon the governor to assassinate the overstepping grandees.[85] The assassinations were carried out and consequently the "Qatamis and Dumyati households" were "eliminated" from Egyptian politics.[86] While he lived, Beshir Agha was involved in factional politics in Syria and Egypt and sought to tilt royal favor towards his own allies.[87] These allies, in turn, looked for powerful patrons who could help them secure Istanbul's sanction for satiating their lust for status, office, and wealth, at the local level.

In Egypt, a struggle for effective power at the local level broke out with the recession of central control.[88] Local janissaries and *mamluks* fought it out amongst themselves and carved out small estates. As was the case elsewhere in the Ottoman Sultanate, the peasant and the tax farmer "had no property rights" over the land, which was all royal domain, save charitable endowments (*Waqf*).[89] As royal authority weakened, tax farmers, local officials, janissaries, and *mamluks* took to plundering the sultan's wealth and, in the process, exactions on the peasantry grew. Heightened insecurity meant that those benefiting from plunder sought to secure their fortunes by transferring their wealth into religious endowments.[90] The result was that by the late-1700s one-fifth of Egypt's arable land had been converted into *waqf*.[91] Peasants responded to the situation through concealment, flight, and rebellion, and prayed for deliverance.[92] Ali Bey, a Georgian *mamluk* who had risen through the ranks, seized power in 1760 and proceeded to "massacre his opponents", inclusive of janissaries.[93] He employed the confiscated wealth of his fallen enemies to equip his forces with firearms and cannons, appointed trusted officials, especially Syrians, as customs officials, deposed the Ottoman governor in 1768, and stopped paying tribute to Istanbul.[94] The sultan, however, was able to win over Ali Bey's commander in Syria, and the upstart died in 1793 with his allies deserting him and Egypt sliding back into chaos. To make matters worse, plague struck Egypt in 1785 and killed one-sixth of the population, the price of wheat more than doubled between 1784 and 1792, and the local strongmen engaged in confiscatory taxation to satisfy their whims.[95] Salvation and the sultan's justice took until 1801 to materialize in the form of a fresh army comprising Albanian volunteers and Syrian troops. Muhammad Ali became the senior commander of the Albanian contingent on account of the deaths of his superiors. Though a merchant by heritage and a tax collector by profession, Muhammad Ali proved a competent military commander with a grasp of strategy. Rather than risk his army in engaging the rival janissary and *mamluk* factions, the Albanian contingent let their enemies maul each other. As the fighting dragged on from 1801 to 1805, Muhammad Ali's forces gained the support of the townsmen, merchants, and ulema. Egyptian notables begged him to seize power and put an end to the fighting, a coup that was carried out in May 1805 and the sultan recognized Muhammad Ali as the new governor. Muhammad Ali was well aware of the practice of rotating governors frequently and Egypt, in particular, was a revolving door for high officials. Muhammad Ali secured his position by approaching the sultan's mother, Asma Sultan, in 1807. Asma Sultan agreed to ensure that Muhammad Ali stayed put as governor of Egypt in exchange for "monetary advantages."[96] While in Istanbul the janissaries soon put an end to the sultan's reforming ambitions, which included badly needed military modernization, Muhammad Ali was able to carry out his own *nizam-i-cedid* in Egypt. Any residual *mamluk* power was taken care of in March 1811, when Muhammad Ali lured rival military commanders with invitations to an investiture ceremony, and massacred twenty-four *beys* and forty *kushaf*. The Ottoman Sultan, Mahmud II (r. 1808–1839), commended Muhammad Ali for this brutal but effective exercise in restructuring.

Muhammad Ali ended the immunity from taxation enjoyed by religious endowments (1809), confiscated all tax farms in Upper Egypt (1811) and reinvested the capital in setting up modern war industries. In 1814, Egypt was divided into fourteen governorates, subdivided into departments, with groups of departments reporting to superintendants. The governor and his ministers formed a cabinet while the governor's suite became a central secretariat in which officials were appointed on the basis of their educational qualifications. Muhammad Ali appointed his son, Muhammad Ibrahim, as his deputy and entrusted the finance department to his care. Later in his reign, Muhammad Ali constituted a consultative assembly (*majlis-i-shura*) that comprised thirty-three high officials, a hundred lesser officials, and twenty-four notables. In the countryside, with tax farmers and military commanders sidelined, village headmen granted lands by the state were made responsible for handing over the land revenue to state collectors as well as providing the army with conscripts. A state grain monopoly was made effective and it purchased wheat at fixed rates, selling them for a surplus at home and abroad. State patronage of industries, the restoration of peace, effective collection of taxes, and the enforcement of the *corvée* (albeit with monetary compensation) on the peasantry produced considerable progress. By 1835, there were 230,000 industrial workers in Egypt (4% of the total population) and the foundations of an industrial revolution had been laid.[97] Egypt enjoyed a positive trade balance by the 1820s, with exports, in 1823, amounting to 1.455 million pounds sterling and imports 656,490 pounds sterling.[98] The most stunning turn around was in revenue collection, which rose from 158,724 pounds sterling in 1798 to 1.88 million in 1822 and stood at nearly three million by 1842.[99] The upward spike in revenue collection between 1798 and 1822 was due to the centralization of taxes, the ending of immunities, and the confiscation of the wealth and property of intermediaries. Muhammad Ali also enriched himself in the process and by 1845 his family owned about 19 percent of the arable land in Egypt—a position they retained until the revolution of 1952.[100] Even so, Muhammad Ali tried to bring Egypt into the modern world, while the "rest of Egypt's rulers were content to treat the country as a milch cow and the Egyptians as serfs on a fief."[101]

Egypt's successes had not gone unnoticed by Sultan Mahmud II, who was brought to power by a janissary revolt that ended the reforms (and life) of Sultan Selim III (r.1789–1807) and resulted in the death of Mustafa IV (r. 1807–1808). Mahmud II, however, was no ordinary sultan, and possessed many of the attributes of Mehmed II, "The Conqueror". These included inscrutability, patience, vision, and ruthlessness. In great secrecy, Mahmud II raised a new army, 14,000 strong, modeled on the Egyptian. Mahmud II also secured the support of the ulema for military reforms, and persuaded them that he was only imitating the example of one of his Muslim governors. By the time the janissaries realized what the sultan was up to, it was too late to stop him, and they were isolated and massacred on June 16, 1826 when they gathered to protest, an occurrence officially referred to as "the Auspicious Event."[102] The janissaries who opted for loyalty were allowed to keep their lives and their property but lost their status as the sultan's officers. The Ottoman army was now recruited primarily from Turkish peasants in Rumeli and Anatolia and residual slave forces, such as the *mamluks* in Iraq, were greatly reduced in significance. These changes were being implemented even as external blows fell upon the Ottoman Sultanate. The European conquest of North Africa, in which the French invasion and colonization of Algeria played a leading role, began in the 1830s. In 1832, Greece's independence was recognized by Istanbul after a prolonged rebellion that enjoyed the support of the western public. The stimulus of these shocks was felt not only in terms of military modernization but also in terms of administrative changes. Provincial governors were stripped of their power to condemn people to death, the court of confiscation was abolished, the collection of poll taxes was entrusted to committees, western-style clothing was introduced at court, and palace officials were prohibited from living off the land while on tour.

Mahmud II and Muhammad Ali had breathed new life into a five hundred year old empire.[103] The dysfunctional equilibrium imposed on the Ottoman Sultanate by the janissaries and *mamluks* had at last been broken and military modernization, legal and administrative reform, and even economic success (in Egypt) were on the cards. The take-off, would not, however, succeed for the Ottoman Sultanate was about fifty years too late. Had reforms been pursued in the mid-1700s they would have probably revitalized the empire but the problem was that since the Ottomans were hubristic they did not sense the need for reform at the time. Escalating military pressure, growing central government debt, assaults on the periphery, rebellions within, and the unrest produced by improved communications and more coherent subject national communities, all worked to push the Ottoman Sultanate towards breaking point. Mahmud

II's reforms, however, did succeed in buying more time for the Ottomans and their empire and planted the seeds of new ideas that would in time mature into Turkish nationalism.

THE EMERGENCE AND TRIUMPH OF
TURKISH NATIONALISM, 1839–2002

The Ottomans are of particular importance to any study of nationalism in the Muslim world. Not only did the Ottomans rule a considerable portion of the Muslim world, but they were also in continuous contact with the West for nearly six centuries, and may well have retained the throne of Turkey had Kemalism not emerged as the dominant political trend in the 1920s. The political and cultural regeneration of the Muslim world after three centuries of Christian Crusades and Mongol massacres (1095–1405) can be credited to Turks, be they Seljuk, Ottomans, Safavids, or Timurids.

The Ottoman Sultanate had to solve the fundamental economic problem of getting food from rural producers to urban consumers while extracting a sufficient share of the surplus to pay for the court, military, and administration. The sultan ran the empire as his personal estate and answered to no one—the only limits to his power were those imposed by geography, rebellion, his personal character, and the abilities of his advisors. Arbitrary rule meant that the quality of the state and the prosperity of the land depended upon the intellectual and moral capabilities of the sultan and his servants. Wise rulers, such as Suleiman I, took a keen personal interest in the management of their sprawling dominions, tempered arbitrariness with enlightened self-interest, and sought to ensure that their corps of military and civilian officers, many of whom were slaves, operated on principles of merit. Ottoman administration of a diverse multitude of communities spread across three continents coupled with the Sublime Porte's unrelenting pursuit of war and magnificence presented a dilemma common to other continental bureaucratic empires. It was simply not possible to pay the servants of the state, who wielded enormous arbitrary power in the name of the sultan and were often hundreds of miles away from his supervision, a regular salary that would keep them subservient and reasonably honest. The Ottomans, in order to solve this problem, resorted to the sale of offices and tax farming by the sixteenth century.[104] "The political repercussions of the 'privatization' of the state resources were the incremental loss of control. . . ."[105] Another manifestation of the deterioration of the ability of the sultan to restrain his officers was that from ". . . the end of the sixteenth century bribery became widespread even in the highest grades of the administration," partly due to the decline in the purchasing power of government salaries.[106] Furthermore, the Ottoman Sultanate, for all its administrative genius and power, never developed a mercantilist economic policy[107] designed to keep wealth in the hands of indigenous merchants and artisans.

The causes of Ottoman decline have been studied exhaustively. Explanations range from cultural rigidity, which made the use of Western technology and knowledge controversial to the point of inducing paralysis[108], to the predatory nature of the janissaries, the *millet* system, and the Capitulations.[109] There was also a widely acknowledged decline in the competence of the sultans from the 1600s onwards although this decline was partly offset by the strength of the central bureaucracy and the abilities of individual ministers. The course of Ottoman decline can be divided into two major parts.

The first period, characterized by the absence of an internal reform impulse, lasted from the late sixteenth to the mid-eighteenth century. During this period the Ottomans went from a position of clear superiority over their Western rivals to one of relative equality. The second period begins in the late-eighteenth century and ends in 1924. It is characterized by growing awareness within the Ottoman elite, including several sultans, that unless their system modernized, at least in military affairs, the empire would be condemned to defeat. Conflicts began to develop between and within pro-reform and anti-reform forces. These conflicts, which often turned violent, prepared the ground for the growth and triumph of Turkish nationalism. As was the case in many countries with a repressive political system and an underdeveloped bourgeoisie, the impetus for fundamental reform ultimately came from the relatively modernized armed forces.

Today, Turkey is the only Muslim-majority country that can legitimately claim to be a nation-state and a secular republic in the modern sense of these terms. With not even one-twentieth of the Muslim world's population,[110] Turkey is the only Muslim country in the G-20, has the eighteenth largest economy in the world, and accounts for fifteen percent of the Organization of Islamic Countries' (OIC) GDP.[111] The Turkish military well trained, properly equipped, and highly motivated. In terms of income, output, employment, physical infrastructure, law, and human development, Turkey is decades ahead of most Muslim countries, which is a phenomenal achievement given its relatively poor resource base. Furthermore, Turkish society is significantly more open and permissive than other Muslim societies—a fact reflected in its multi-billion dollar tourism industry and outward looking nature. Kemalist ideology has enabled Turkey to endure for nearly a century as a secular republic and accumulate wealth, military power, and democratic experience.

Turkey's attempts to catch up with the West are not new. An early example was that the first printing press in the Ottoman Sultanate was established in 1727 by a Hungarian and operated for fifteen years during which seventeen books were printed.[112] In 1729 and 1773 army reforms and a school of mathematics for the navy, respectively, were instituted with French assistance.[113] These cosmetic measures did not have any impact on the fortunes of the Ottoman Sultanate, which suffered defeat after defeat from 1683 onwards at the hands of Europeans who, in the eyes of the janissaries, fought like machines devoid of valor or honor.[114] The need for military reform had become desperate. Fortunately, for the Ottoman Sultanate, two rulers of relatively superior vision and determination ruled in close succession in the late-eighteenth and early-nineteenth centuries.

Selim III established the *Nizam-i-Cedid* (New Order) with the support and counsel of twenty-two reform-minded imperial dignitaries.[115] The principal objective was the creation of a military contingent ten thousand strong, trained and equipped along European lines, and personally loyal to the sultan.[116] In 1792, permanent embassies were sent to major European capitals with instructions to learn everything they could about their host countries.[117] New regulations for taxation, regulating the grain-trade, and administration, were drawn up, which in time formed the nucleus of a modern administration.[118] With the new armaments, training manuals, technicians, and advisors, Western ideas, especially from France, began to reach the educated elite of the Ottoman Sultanate. Napoleon's fourteen-months occupation of Egypt provided a practical demonstration of the advantages of the new rationality and the weakness of the Ottoman Sultanate. Napoleon established a consultative assembly of notables comprising one hundred and eighty-nine Egyptians and divans of up to nine members in each of Egypt's fourteen provinces.[119] He established a regular postal service, a stagecoach service, a mint to coin French currency, a street-lighting system for Cairo, a three-hundred bed hospital for the poor, four quarantine stations to check the bubonic plague, windmills, and Egypt's first Arabic language printing press.[120] Napoleon read the Muslim scriptures and reached a compromise with the *muftis,* by which he agreed to protect Islam in exchange for a statement describing him as ". . . God's messenger and the friend of the Prophet."[121] Napoleon's expedition gave birth to the discipline of Egyptology, which has returned to the Egyptian people nearly four millennia of their history. The Egyptians, who called Napoleon *Sultan-el-Kabir,* saw in him ". . . a man who cared about justice as the Turks never had."[122] Napoleon's Egyptian campaign is little more than a footnote to the historians of Europe.[123] For the Ottoman Sultanate, however, its ramifications were profound. Egypt emerged from the Napoleonic occupation as a virtually independent principality. The chaos produced by the slave-soldiers, whose ranks had been decimated by French arms, was overcome by Mehmed Ali, and Egypt continued on the path of reform. The Ottomans were not nearly as fortunate. In 1807, the janissaries revolted against the sultan, who tried to appease them by abolishing the New Order. The reformers were murdered by the janissaries and the sultan deposed.[124]

Mahmud II was the choice of the conservatives who had destroyed the New Order. Until 1826, Mahmud II worked imperceptibly towards the creation of a new army modeled on the Ordered Army of his Egyptian governor.[125] By 1813, the Egyptians had annihilated the Wahabis and regained control of Mecca and Medina for the sultan[126] and, in 1818, Abdullah Ibn Saud was captured by the Egyptians, sent to Istanbul, placed before an inquisition, and executed.[127] In 1822, the archconservative grand vizier was dismissed and executed while the pays and privileges of the religious clerics were increased[128] After the Egyptian army repeatedly defeated Greek rebels in 1825 and 1826,[129] Sultan Mahmud secured a judgment from the clerics to the effect that ". . . it is the religious duty of Muslims to learn military drill."[130] The entire military reform effort was imbued with religious significance, from the blessing of carbines to the propaganda efforts of religious clerics on behalf of the sultan's reforms.[131] When the janissaries revolted, after having agreed to submit to the military reforms, the clerics sided with the sultan and, in a brief struggle, the Janissaries were wiped out. The spirit of reform was symbolized by the sultan's appearance ". . . at Friday prayers on the day of victory, 16 June 1826 . . . surrounded by artillery men and bombardiers . . . this was the measure of the Auspicious Event, as the destruction of the Janissaries was now officially termed."[132]

The *Tanzimat* reforms that began in 1839 and culminated in the 1876 constitution represent the final serious effort on part of the Ottomans to reform the system. The *millet* system was abolished in 1856 and the Reform Edict granted common citizenship to all Ottoman subjects.[133] The 1876 Constitution was the Ottoman dynasty's opportunity to become an integral part of a constitutional order that, in time, could evolve into a national monarchy. This experiment in constitutionalism failed to take off as Sultan Abdul Hamid II (1876–1909) used the pretext of war with Russia to dissolve parliament in 1878.[134] Abdul Hamid II was the product of an arbitrary culture of power in which the sultan was an autocrat legitimated by God. For Muslim subjects the sultan's legitimacy came from his enforcement of the *sharia* and defense of the *Dar-ul-Islam*. For non-Muslims, the Ottomans provided a considerable degree of local autonomy, provided they did not challenge the sultan's arbitrary rule. Abdul Hamid II retarded the task of political modernization by dismissing parliament and cracking down on dissent. He did modernize the administration, which grew to include a formidable espionage system, an improved rail and telegraph network and a more modern military.[135] With peaceful internal change ruled out increased contact between educated Ottomans and the West could only raise expectations and engender dissent.

Ziya Gokalp (1875–1924), the father of Turkish nationalism, was born in the southeastern town of Diyarbakir, and was profoundly influenced by Emile Durkheim's *The Rules of the Sociological Method*, Leon Cahun's *History of the Central Asian Turks*, and Vefik Pasha's *The Ottoman Dialect*.[136] In 1913, he accepted the Chair of Sociology at Istanbul University and served in that capacity until the end of the First World War.[137] A critic of the Ottoman state, Gokalp regarded its universalism as a major cause of the ideological backwardness of the Turks, and realized that Turkish participation in business and industry were proportionately low while the complex official language hurt administration. Gokalp's thought underwent major shifts in emphasis although he continued to regard national regeneration as the first step to establishing a durable and progressive Muslim polity on a global scale.[138] Pan-Turanism remained a major theme in Gokalp's thinking until the end of the First World War. From 1908 to 1918 Gokalp also tried to reconcile the competing ideals of Pan-Islamism, Pan-Turanism, and Modernism.[139] With the defeat of the Young Turks and Ottomans in the First World War, and the risings in Arab lands, the Nationalists emerged as the only group with the will, popularity, and leadership with which to repel the tides of darkness that threatened to submerge the Turkish heartland. In response to changing conditions, Gokalp threw his weight behind the Nationalists. He died on October 15, 1924, shortly after the manuscript of *The Foundations of Turkish Nationalism* was completed, while serving as a Member of the Committee on Public Instruction.[140] The essence of Gokalp's nationalist thought was that Turkey needed to be reborn as a territorial nation-state while social science was indispensible in aiding nation-building. A broad consensus on the importance of nationalism granted, there existed considerable ideological diversity within the Nationalist's camp when it came to the specifics. Many leaders, including some of Mustafa Kemal's closest associates, such as Rauf Hussein and Refet Bele were liberal constitutionalists who wanted parliament to be supreme[141]. Neither wanted the institutions of Caliphate and Sultanate to be abolished and both favored a constitutional monarchy on the British pattern.[142] Like Gokalp, this section of the Nationalist movement did not adopt an actively anti-religious platform though the supremacy of parliament would necessitate a degree of secularization.

Mustafa Kemal's concept of Turkish nationalism was incorporated into Article 2 of the Constitution in 1937 and consisted of the six principles of republicanism, nationalism, populism, statism, secularism, and revolution.[143] Mustafa Kemal understood that a nation of superstitious and largely illiterate, peasants, landlords, clerics, dervishes, and monarchists, after six centuries of arbitrary rule, did not possess the prerequisites for liberal democracy. The first step towards the realization of this goal was the establishment of a secular state that made no apologies for its rejection of the epistemological validity of religious and traditional arguments. In order to create a new state the traditional structures, upon which the old regime rested, would have to be destroyed or marginalized. A great many of these structures, be they religious orders or *sharia* courts, were based upon Islam and tradition. Kemalism is accurately described as the anti-religious center-left trend within Turkish nationalism that represented a revolutionary agenda that sought to create a new basis for Turkish historical experience, which, in time, could make possible the growth of liberal democracy on Turkish soil. The triumph of Kemalism over its less radical competitors effectively determined the reality of Turkish nationalism. Indeed, so great has been Kemalism's impact that chronologically, Turkish nationalism can be divided into three main periods: before, during, and after Mustafa Kemal. The first phase begins with the granting of a constitution in 1876 and ends in 1919 with the Erzerum and Sivas Congresses. The second phase comprises the years 1919–1938 and represents the radical, militant period of Turkish nationalism. The third phase, which takes us to the present day, is characterized by movement towards democracy punctuated by breakdowns in the constitutional order occasioned by public dissatisfaction with the government and instrumented by the military.

In May 1876, students of theology rioted and compelled Sultan Abdul Aziz, who had driven the empire to bankruptcy, to abdicate and allow Midhat Pasha to establish a Council of State and formulate a constitution.[144] Abdul Hamid II was enthroned on the promise that he would abide by the constitution and allow Parliament, which comprised a bicameral legislature of twenty-five nominated senators and one hundred and twenty elected deputies,[145] to function. In February 1877, Midhat Pasha was dismissed by the sultan, imprisoned in the fortress of Taif, and strangled to death.[146] War with Russia in the Balkans in 1877/78 provided Abdul Hamid with a pretext to dissolve the Ottoman Parliament—it would not convene again until 1908. By formally reverting to arbitrary rule the sultan broke his solemn pledge, made obvious his contempt for the aspirations of liberal-minded Ottomans, rejected the democratic legitimacy conferred upon him by the Parliament, and ultimately destroyed whatever chances his dynasty had of adjusting to the modern age. To make matters worse, disaster after disaster followed the dissolution of parliament. Control of the economy was formally handed over to the Council of Administration of Ottoman Public Debt,[147] and the empire lost 232,000 square kilometers of territory and six million subjects between 1878 and 1882.[148] Within the empire the spy system coupled with the systematic butchery of opponents, including entire communities such as the Armenians, led many educated Turks, including the sultan's brother-in-law to flee abroad and join the exiles.[149]

Led by Ahmed Riza (d. 1930), a former member of the Ottoman Parliament, headquartered in Paris, and organized like the *Carbonari,* the Young Turk movement was started in 1889 by students from the Imperial Military Medical School.[150] On July 4, 1908, the Third Army Corps at Salonika mutinied under the leadership of Enver Bey and Major Ahmed Niyazi, and killed the general sent by Abdul Hamid to restore order.[151] A year earlier, the various secret societies and organizations had merged into a single Committee of Union and Progress headquartered in Salonika.[152] When the Second Army Corps also mutinied, the sultan was compelled to restore the 1876 Constitution on July 23, 1908. Elections were held, the Committee of Union and Progress organized itself into a political party, and the liberals under Saad and Kamil Pasha dominated the parliament and embarked upon a policy of "Ottomanization".

Times had changed. The Committee was dominated by Talaat Bey (Minister of Interior), Jemal Bey (Military Governor of Istanbul) and

Enver Bey (War Minister).[153] This triumvirate, which formally seized power in 1913 during ceasefire negotiations in the Balkan's War of that year, ruled through the modernized machinery of oppression created by Abdul Hamid. Together they managed ". . . to transform a dawn of high promise into a fatal nightmare before dying by violence in distant lands."[154] When the Young Turks were forced out of power in 1918, the Ottoman Sultanate had lost an additional one-third of its territory and one-fifth of its population.[155] With the Arab provinces in revolt, the only realistic basis for rebuilding a Turkish state was nationalism. What the Turks lacked was a leadership courageous enough to discard the imperial legacy, and sufficiently competent to renegotiate peace terms with the victorious Allies and drive out the invading Greeks. Into the vacuum stepped Mustafa Kemal, the hero of Gallipoli.

The war against the invading Greeks and the Sultan's government was not sure of success till the Nationalists checked the Greek advance towards Angora at the Battle of Sakarya fought from August 23—September 13, 1921.[156] Successive nationalist congresses at Erzerum and Sivas in 1919, the confirmation of the National Pact as the manifesto after the Nationalists won parliamentary elections, the meeting of the First Grand National Assembly on April 23, 1920, and the Constitution Act of January 20, 1921 spelled out the Nationalist war aims.[157] Anatolian clerics were mobilized in defense of the nationalists and issued counter-*fatwas* against the *Sheikh-ul-Islam* in Istanbul.[158] To improve army organization and effectiveness Mustafa Kemal was granted extraordinary powers as Commander-in-Chief of the armed forces on August 5, 1921.[159] In September 1922, as Smyrna burned and the Greeks retreated Mustafa Kemal remarked "It is only now that our real work is beginning."[160] On October 2, 1923, Istanbul was occupied[161] and on October 29, the Turkish Republic was proclaimed with Mustafa Kemal as its first President.[162] Until he was firmly in power, Mustafa Kemal remained ambiguous on the subjects of political Islam and traditional culture. Given the frequency with which he invoked God's grace, the effective use of Anatolian clerics, and religious appeals to his soldiers, had Mustafa Kemal died shortly after defeating the Greeks, Turks could well have endlessly debated his political vision for Turkey. Power attained, Mustafa Kemal's mask (and gloves) came off.

A letter from the Aga Khan and Syed Ameer Ali that urged the Nationalists to maintain the Caliphate was portrayed as a subversive effort by proponents of imperialism and provided the necessary pretext for the abolition of the Caliphate in March 1924.[163] In the same breath, the Ottoman dynasty was banished from Turkey[164] and the Ministry of Religious Affairs and religious schools were disbanded.[165] To his credit, the sick man of Europe had the satisfaction of outlasting the ruling houses of Germany, Austria-Hungary, and Russia.[166] A month later, the *sharia* courts were declared defunct.[167] In 1925 and 1926, the shock tactics continued, in spite of an uprising by the Kurds led by Naqshbandi dervishes, which enabled the government to assume extraordinary powers.[168] Using these powers, the religious orders were abolished, sacred tombs were closed, and wearing a fez was made a prosecutable offence. In three years the Nationalist regime had dismantled many of the structures upon which the traditional order had rested for six centuries.

While pulling down the old structures the Nationalist regime took care to build upon the Ottoman administrative legacy and focused on making the state effective within the country's new frontiers. The personnel to implement the program of modernization from above came from the Ottoman bureaucratic and military elite. 85 percent of Ottoman civil servants and 93 percent of military staff officers remained in Turkey after the fall of the sultanate and collectively "constituted an intelligentsia."[169] Although Mustafa Kemal did not trust the old Ottoman officials who had opted to serve the new regime only after its victory had become inevitable, he was pragmatic enough to use their talents and experience to subordinate or eliminate all structures that had a traditional orientation and concentrate power in the state. The bureaucratic elite also furnished a steady supply of parliamentarians for legislatures until 1950 were "staffed in large part by deputies of bureaucratic origin."[170] The 1924 Village Law made villages legal persons answerable to the authorities in Ankara and made the headmen and their councils functionaries "of the central government."[171] This centralization of power was followed in 1926 by the adoption of the principle of career advancement on the basis of merit, though here, an important part of competence was adherence to the goals of the republican regime.[172] Mustafa Kemal basically wanted a more powerful bureaucracy grounded in merit but loyal to his party and ideology.[173] Mustafa Kemal dealt directly with subordinates where necessary and bypassed the chain of command and expected his orders to be implemented quickly, efficiently, and without question.[174] That said, the routine affairs of the state as well as important policy debates were entrusted by Mustafa Kemal to his deputy and comrade from the struggle for national salvation, Ismet Inonü. Inonü succeeded, for the most part, in keeping Mustafa Kemal's drinking companions and old cronies from interfering in the government.[175] Inonü had enormous respect for expertise, educated himself rigorously, and stood up for his own views—he only accepted the premiership in 1925 offered to him to crush Sheik Said's rebellion on the condition that the army was to be mobilized and Independence Tribunals established nationwide to root out enemies of the state.[176] Mustafal Kemal and Inonü were on the same page when it came to their conviction that "the state had to function as the guardian of the long-term interests of the community."[177] The country was brought under "the effective control" of the central state and the "gendarme and the tax collector became more hated and feared than ever before" as the razor's edge of a 220,000 strong civilian bureaucracy.[178] Tax collection nearly doubled from 111.30 million Turkish Liras in 1924 to 206.10 million Turkish Liras in 1929, nearly balancing the budget—a remarkable achievement for an agrarian country whose economy had been shattered by the First World War.[179] With the exception of agriculture, where indigenous expertise existed, Turkey had to start almost from scratch when it came to industries. The new regime was, however, reluctant to borrow large sums from abroad or run heavy deficit budgets to stimulate industrial development. The strategy adopted was thus of a fiscally conservative statist economic development program that would gradually establish an industrial base without requiring foreign borrowing or budgetary indiscipline.[180] It was also necessitated by the exchange of population between Greece and Turkey as up to 1926 some 1.26 million Greeks left Turkey and 400,000 Turks migrated to their ancestral homeland. The statist economic policy direction, sustained until 1950, "must be seen not only in the light of the regime's economic aspiration, but also in its very structure, based mainly on the Military and Civil Service, which were rather apprehensive lest the power of the [religiously conservative] middle class increase."[181]

The process of erecting new structures began on February 17, 1926, with the adoption of the Swiss Civil Code.[182] In November 1928, the Latin alphabet was introduced to rapidly raise the literacy rate and to give the new Turkish language a sound academic base the Turkish Linguistic Society was created in 1931.[183] Mustafa Kemal convened a Historical Congress in 1932 under the aegis of the Historical Society with the aim of inculcating ". . . that sense of unity between land and race which creates a spirit of patriotism in the Western sense."[184] In November 1934, a new law required all citizens of Turkey to adopt surnames. That December full political rights were extended to women.[185] Early in 1935, Sunday was made the weekly holiday and the twenty-four hour international clock was adopted.[186] Aside from these legal measures a whole range of social changes, including mixed social gatherings, the opera, theatre, radio, and ballroom dancing were introduced.

When Kemal Atatürk died on November 10, 1938,[187] he left to his successors an effective state apparatus committed to the task of reform. Ismet Inonü steered clear of the Second World War and, with the formation of the Democrat Party on January 7, 1946, under the leadership of Celal Bayar, took Turkey towards multi-party democracy.[188] In 1950, the Democrats swept Turkey's first free elections securing 408 out of 487 seats while the Republicans were reduced to 69 seats.[189] Inonü accepted defeat and, for the first time in the history of the Turks, if not the Muslims, the government changed hands peacefully and constitutionally from one party to another. This was creditable for "some elements within the military seem to have offered to stage a coup" to prevent the Democrats from coming to power.[190] Here it needs to be noted that by 1950 practically all civil servants, judges, and military officers, were committed Kemalists and deeply suspicious of the Democrats whom they considered to be crypto-medievalists.[191] Kemalist misgivings notwithstanding, Celal Bayar, a banker and economist, became president while Adnan Menderes, a rich landowner, became prime minister.

The Democrats allowed *muezzins* to recite the *azan* in the language of their choosing, lifted the ban on religious programs and recitation of the Holy Quran on radio, made religious education compulsory and even bene-fited from the use of pulpits to preach against the Republicans.[192] When the Korean War ended in 1953, the rate of economic growth slowed and dif-ferences between the state and Republicans, which represented the urban, pro-Kemal, segments of society, and the Democrats, who represented the countryside, came out into the open. The Democrats, in 1953, seized the assets of the Republican party in an attempt to quell dissent.[193] To make matters worse, the landlords and rural notables who dominated the Demo-cratic Party adamantly refused to tax themselves to fund their expansion-ary economic program with the result that the agriculture sector, which accounted for one-fifth of GNP, contributed only one-fiftieth of taxes.[194] The Democrats, as the economy sank, continued to pay the Turkish farmer twice the world price for his produce.[195] The 1957 elections took place in the context of deteriorating economic conditions. The Democrats were reduced to 424/610 seats while the Republicans secured 178/610 seats.[196] Key institutions, including the judiciary, civil service, and universities were alienated by the Democrats.

The Democrats passed laws that made public criticism of the govern-ment a crime, the bureaucracy was pressured to be loyal to the party line, the assets of the Republican Party having already been confiscated, even Inonü was targeted. This was, in many ways, the beginning of the end for the Democrats for while they could find courts and collaborators willing to act against the Republicans, nothing "could be done against Ismet Pasha himself."[197] Menderes recognized that he faced "a great hero, a legend-ary rival" in the form of "Ismet Pasha!" for he did "not owe anything to the country; on the contrary, this country" owed a great deal to him.[198] This did not, however, prevent Menderes from escalating the conflict with the Republicans. Eventually, the army was ordered to stop Inonü from campaigning, martial law was declared by the government on April 28, 1960, and a committee empowered to investigate and ban political parties was constituted.[199] General Kemal Gursel proposed a reform package and resigned on May 3, 1960 after it was rejected.[200] Three weeks later middle-ranking officers executed a bloodless coup, to be subsequently purged by the Turkish high command, which established a National Unity Commit-tee to draft a new constitution, abolished the Democratic Party, executed Menderes on charges of treason, held a referendum in July 1961, elections in October, and handed over power to civilians with General Gursel as President.[201] The entire parliamentary Democratic Party (some four hun-dred members) were imprisoned, and after an eleven month long trial, fif-teen Democrats were sentenced to death, with three sentences carried out (including Menderes) on September 16, 1961.

Turkey did not re-stabilize for nearly twenty years. Turkish nation-alism was plunged into two decades of crisis with hung parliaments, behind-the-scenes manipulation by the military, and weak coalition governments from 1961–65 and 1973–80.[202] The latter period also included an energy crisis and war with Cyprus. The democratic process proved unable to find a solution to political terrorism and a renewed Kurdish insurgency. In 1979/1980 an average of twenty deaths in political violence were being reported every day and the state of order was collapsing.[203] On September 12, 1980 General Kenan Evren, the Chief of General Staff, seized power in a coup, abrogated the constitution, dissolved parliament, banned all political parties, and created the National Security Council (NSC).[204] Evren moved rapidly and "Law and order were restored by draconian methods."[205] 180,000 people were arrested, 42,000 were sentenced, and twenty-five were executed, for political violence.[206] The authorities seized 7000 machine guns, 48,000 rifles, 640,000 handguns, and twenty-six rocket launchers.[207] With the state's writ effective again, trade unions were taken on and de-politicized and students' organization affiliated with political parties were disbanded or forced to go underground.[208] In November 1982, a new constitution was approved by 91 percent of voters and Evren became president for a six-year term.[209] Economic liberalization, accompanied by external borrowing and increasing foreign trade, led to unprecedented prosperity but also entrenched a rivalry between middleclass Islamists who dominated local governments and the classical state bureaucracy. Organizationally, Turkey remained a centralized bureaucratic state in which about eighty *valis* (governors) acted as sub-sovereigns representing the central state ministries in the provinces and districts.[210] Deputy governors (*kaymakams*), who were "young graduates" and "bring to mind district officers in the British Empire", assisted the governors at the local level.[211] Directives that issue forth from the governors' mansions, or from the deputy governors' offices are what channel state resources and authority in the field. Islamist mayors, however, gradually became more representative of the people, especially as the urban population swelled on account of migration from the rural areas. Thus, even in Ankara, as early as 1984, the Islamists came to dominate the local government and the municipality, and in 1994 held 340 out of 2710 contested mayoral seats.[212]

After a brief period of political restructuring, elections were held in 1983 contested by the Nationalist-Democratic Party (left), the Populist Party (center-left), and the Motherland Party led by Turgat Ozal (center-right). Although the National Democrats were the establishment's favorites, the Motherland Party secured a simple majority in parliament.[213] The eight years that followed represented a period of relative stability, improved law and order, and market driven economic growth, which spread affluence but greatly increased external debt, which grew from US$ 19 billion in 1982 to US$ 67 billion by 1993.[214] Turkey emerged as an exporter of electricity, the volume of trade increased two hundred percent and tourism grew into a US$ 3 billion a year industry.[215] Exports, which stood at US$ 5 billion in 1981 grew to US$ 50 billion by 2003, while imports rose from US$ 14 billion to US$ 70 billion in the same period.[216] There was a dark side to this economic growth as the state could not keep track of it and it failed to ease ethnic tensions within Turkey. By 2003, according to the Chairman of the Ankara Chamber of Commerce, the grey/black economy was about two-thirds the size of the formal economy, with the black market in the range of US$ 50–100 billion.[217] The political implication of this trend was that crypto-medievalist movements were able to secure funding and resources outside of state regulation or official knowledge, a trend that led to the reemergence of *hizmet* (charity) as the basis of semi-autonomous religious civil society organizations and movements.[218] Though such elements were (and are) still frightened of the Kemalist apparatus, prosperity had a numbing effect on the rigor and determination of the state. It could, however, still be motivated to act harshly against those deemed to be working against the six principles of the Republic. In 2003, for instance, the gendarmerie "detained 1000 suspected reactionaries, and investigated nearly 6,000 state officials, some 3,500 of whom were disciplined for reactionary activities."[219] The Turkish Council of State also acted as an inoculation against religious recidivism, striking down legal and administrative challenges to the secular character of the state even as it disciplined the bureaucracy for excesses.[220] These ideological and socioeconomic challenges to the Kemalist order grew at the same time as Turkey's troubled east, where the Kurdish minority is concentrated, exploded into violence.

The incorporation of Kurdish areas was somewhat of an anomaly given the firmly Turkish orientations of the post-1924 dispensation and its expulsion of the Greek population. Rebellions and insurgencies in the Kurdish areas were put down with an iron hand under successive governments. The most intense and sustained period of insurgency began in 1984 and continues to the present day though a ceasefire is now in effect. The destabilization of Iraq following the fall of Saddam's regime in 2003 considerably eased pressure in the Kurdish areas governed by Baghdad and led to Iraqi military equipment falling into the hands of Kurdish tribal militias. That there are many different factions of Kurdish insurgents has helped Ankara keep control of its restive eastern frontier, as has the ruthlessness of the Turkish military and intelligence agencies and revenge brigades in crushing resistance. In the mid-1990s, for instance, Tansu Ciller, Turkey's first and thus far only female prime minister (1993–1996), gave the security agencies and the army a free hand to crush the Kurdish insurgency, which resulted in a campaign of arrests and assassinations targeting the Kurd leadership as well as the destruction of entire villages associated with the rebels.[221] Confronted with an ethnic tribal rebellion on its periphery, the Turkish state behaves much the same as it often has in the past, with a combination of terror and adamantine resolve not to tolerate subversive identity formation. Since 1984, 40,000 people have died in violence related to the Kurdish insurgency and 2012 was a particularly brutal year with the Turkish military slaughtering hundreds of rebel fighters, launching more than one thousand operations against the Kurdish resistance, and raiding into the notional post-Saddam Iraqi state's Kurdish-dominated north.

Serious challenges, ranging from Kurdish rebellion to growing external debt liabilities notwithstanding, the momentum generated by Ozal's policies enabled Turkey to continue rapid development through the 1990s even as fragmentation reemerged as the dominant trend in politics. When economic growth paused in 2001–2002 people naturally looked to try new leadership that seemed promising and enjoyed popularity in major cities such as Ankara and Istanbul in the local government. In November 2002, the Justice and Development Party (AKP in Turkish) successfully capitalized on Turkey's worst economic recession in sixty years and a deeply divided center-left and secured 363/550 seats in parliament with just 34 percent of the popular vote. The AKP is led by Tayyip Erdogan, who was imprisoned for four months in 1998 and barred from holding public office for reciting a poem imbued with religious fervor at a public rally. Erdogan, who was born in "metropolitan poverty" in Istanbul, was, in 2001, during the election campaign, "asked to explain a large increase in his personal wealth. He replied that the money had been lent to him by his young son who had received gifts of gold when he was circumcised."[222] Since 2003, Justice and Development Party has maintained the fiction that it is a conservative, as opposed to Islamist, party while delivering on the promise of high growth rates—between 2003 and 2013, Turkey's real GDP has more than doubled and nominal per capita income has tripled from some US$ 3500 to US$ 10,000.[223] During the same time Turkey has emerged as the world's leading jailer of journalists, slaughterer of Kurds, and a country in which criticism of the rulers brings with it harsh consequences.[224] The protests in the summer of 2013 and demonstrations against the Justice Party's growing authoritarianism received little coverage in the Turkish media and revealed the extent to which it has been brought under the government's control.[225] In this respect, it is the military, which still enjoys public confidence and is integral to Turkish nationalism on account of conscription and Kemalist indoctrination, which needs to be watched carefully. The smothering of secularist protests, a political center-left that is in disarray and without strong leadership, and an increasingly religious public ethos collectively bode ill for the state.

CONCLUSION: A CREEPING RETURN TO SULTANATE?

The Ottoman Sultanate was arguably the greatest dynastic state in history. It defied the normal pattern of rise and fall and crafted an artificial tribalism sustained by fresh inductions of slaves that provided the state and the dynasty with able and loyal corps of military and civil officials. The Ottoman Sultanate was authoritarian, arbitrary, and governed as a vast imperial estate legitimized by divine sanction. However, it was also pragmatic, accommodating, and flexible in its dealings with subject peoples. The slave elite that ran the empire for nearly three hundred years was renowned for its ability and Ottoman sultans contained an unusually large number of outstanding autocratic rulers. What made this even more remarkable was the geographic and demographic scale and diversity of the empire as it was spread across three continents, faced with the need to maintain naval as well as an inland military power, exposed on all sides to raids, rebellions, and invasions. Amidst such difficult circumstances, the longevity and success of the Ottoman Sultanate was substantially derived from its qualitative superiority in terms of esprit de corps, organization, and leadership. Unlike other autocratic empires, even a succession of incompetent rulers did not produce rapid disintegration. Instead, local Ottomans sought affiliation with autonomy and embarked on reforms that helped inspire and reinvigorate the center.

This capacity for reinvigoration was reflected in the resurgence of Turkey, as a distinct nation state, in the aftermath of the First World War. That this process was led by nationalists committed to the achievement of liberalism, and, if possible, democracy as well, meant that the Turks inherited a quasi-theocratic empire and replaced it with a secular state. This is quite the opposite of what happened in Pakistan, where the westernized elite inherited a secular state from the British Raj and gradually turned it into a quasi-theocratic empire. The decision to move towards liberalism was made by Mustafa Kemal at a time when fascism and communism were competing successfully with traditional and democratic political systems. Today, Mustafa Kemal's historic decision has been vindicated though the growing anti-liberalism of the Justice and Development Party government since 2003, as well as the experience with the Democratic Party in the 1950s, indicates that democracy is still not yet mature in Turkey. It is evident from Mustafa Kemal's policies that he considered a secular state to be the necessary condition for the establishment of liberal democracy, a social order reflective of the highest standards of "contemporary civilization", and the attainment of material progress. To create this necessary condition Islam had to be removed from law, state-management, the military, and representative bodies, and all sources of social allegiance other than the individual family unit and the state had to be eliminated or otherwise contained. The state would have to carefully guard against any deviation from secularism until such a time as religion ceases to be relevant to the political process. In assessing the impact of the Kemalist variant of Turkish nationalism on foreign relations, economy, and society one must bear in mind the basic historical truth that no polity has yet succeeded in living up to its ideals in full.

Some of the most visible changes wrought by Turkish nationalism have been in the external policy field and have amounted to a rejection of the Ottoman imperial legacy. Atatürk dispensed with Ottoman pretensions of universality, referred to the fallen dynasts as "usurpers",[226] and negotiated treaties that have given Turkey clearly defined national borders. Turkey's alignment with the anticommunist camp was, and is, firmly based on ideology, economics, and resistance to Russian influence. As an oil-importer engaged in industrialization, and member of NATO since 1952,[227] Turkey's interests in the Middle East are best served by association with the West. Turkish nationalism has helped overcome the shock of imperial collapse by redefining Turkey's role in the world from an aggressive antagonist that espouses universal objectives, to a fortress of geopolitical equilibrium.

Erdogan's pledge to proceed quickly with greater integration with Europe is indicative of how important accession to the European Union is for Turks, regardless of their political affiliation. Absorption into the EU can be regarded as the logical culmination of eight decades of secularization, industrialization, and democratization, though, here, again, reluctance on the European side and persistent economic and social crises within the EU mean that such integration will have to be carefully considered. Indeed, it may not necessarily be in Turkey's own interest nor should the EU be eager to extend its frontiers to West Asia with the region descending into civil war and chaos since the Arab Spring was sprung. Some successes on this front, made in more stable times, include the 1964 Treaty of Ankara, which created a Turkey-European Community (EC) association, the customs union agreed upon in 1972 and achieved in 1995, and application to the EC in 1987. Turkey's human rights record especially in Kurdish areas, the institutionalized role of the military in politics, and persecution of Islamists and Communists have so far complicated Turkish accession.

Republican Turkey has done reasonably well at resolving the central economic problem of modernization, i.e. transferring economic surplus from agriculture and the export of primary products to the industrial sector, without resort to mass coercion or large scale state-subsidization of living standards based on oil exports. From 1923–1929, Turkey followed free-market policies in agriculture, which, due to war-related destruction and low levels of organization and capital, failed to develop economic capacity quickly. When global economic depression struck in 1929 Mustafa Kemal switched over to flexible statism and Turkey became a mixed economy with centralized economic planning. In the Cold War, Turkey benefited from the Korean War and American assistance. From the 1960s, Turkey has coordinated economic policies with those of the EU, which is also an important source of remittances. The economic expansion of the 1980s and 1990s signified a successful shift from statism and populism, with Turkey now described in World Bank jargon as a "newly industrializing country."[228]

For women Turkish nationalism and the introduction of the Civil Code, has meant an end to legal inequality, civil marriages by consent, equal rights to divorce, the right to legal guardianship, equal inheritance, and equal remuneration for equal work. In 1930 and 1935, the electorical franchise was extended to women at the municipal and national levels, respectively.

That said, the benefits of these reforms are distributed unequally between the cities and rural areas with a great deal dependent on the economic position of individual women.

Democracy has encountered great difficulty adjusting to the social and political environment of Turkey. Kemalism is, at least partially, responsible for the difficult adjustment by strengthening the logic of military intervention in cases where the secular character of the state is perceived to be under assault.[229] The conflict between the state and democratically elected government has led to a compromise in the form of the NSC even though the existence of this institution reduces Turkey's chances of integration into the EU.[230] That said, were Atatürk alive today, he may well be pleased that Turkey has advanced to such a degree that doctrinaire interpretations of his vision and advice no longer correspond to the needs and aspirations of a Turkish society committed by democratic consensus to further integration into the West.

Compare Turkey to the advanced industrial democracies it aspires to emulate and its deficiencies, which range from human rights abuses to the rate of inflation, draw greater attention than its successes. Alter the basis for comparison to the former communist bloc and, provided the observer places a premium on human life, Turkish nationalism and the Kemalist regime compare favorably. Indeed, the revolutionary terror of the Independence Tribunals created and abolished by Mustafa Kemal[231] were neither meant to, nor capable of, undertaking the mass liquidations characteristic of communist and fascist dictatorships. A comparison with other Muslim-majority countries works to Turkey's advantage on nearly every major issue or indicator.[232] Between 1924 and 1950, Turkey developed into a secular republic, with a cohesive national identity that expressed itself within a rationally derived constitutional framework. These were no mean achievements. As a continental bureaucratic state the difficulties experienced by Turkey in operating representative institutions are neither unique nor, given time and effort, insurmountable. The Justice and Development Party, like the Democratic Party of the 1950s, had a historic opportunity to do away with restrictions on individual lifestyle preferences and public expression abhorrent to liberalism without attacking the secular character of the state, though it seems that it is running into growing difficulties as protests and dissatisfaction with its intolerance of dissent grows. Erdogan's ambition seems to be to turn Turkey into a democratically sanctioned presidential autocracy with Islamic leanings, a change, which if effected, would mean a return to sultanate.

6 The Origins and Legacy of Russian Autocracy

INTRODUCTION: PERFECT STRANGERS

A long and distinguished chain of Western observers and scholars from Habsburg and English ambassadors to footloose French aristocrats and brilliant North Americans have asserted and reasserted that Russia is quite unlike the West.[1] From a North American and Western European perspective Russia inhabits a sphere of alienation that removes it from the mainstream of Western Civilization. From an Atlantic viewpoint Russia's historical development was almost antithetical to the matrixes of institutional autonomy, private enterprise and civil society that emerged in North America and Western Europe. This "otherness" of Russia was apparently validated by the ideological struggles of the 1900s that culminated in the Cold War confrontation between the "free" world led by the United States and the communist world led by the post-1917 Soviet incarnation of the Russian Empire.[2] With the collapse of the Soviet experiment in 1991, Russia's disastrous attempts to transition to a market economy and a multiparty democracy have led to the reassertion of authoritarianism and statist tendencies under Vladimir Putin, implicitly calling into question the triumphalism of the early 1990s.[3] Augmenting the confusion is that educated Russians, since the reign of Peter the Great (d. 1725), have been divided about where they belong.[4] The debate continues about whether early Russia would have evolved into a feudal monarchy with an autonomous Church, permanent aristocracy and corporate privileges for towns and cities, were it not for the Mongol conquest and domination of Russia from 1240–1480. Another view is that Russia is different from the West and the rest and has its own traditions that do not need fundamental reform inspired by foreign models though technology transfers are welcome.

While North Americans and Western Europeans will undoubtedly continue to struggle to overcome the difficulties imposed on them by their exceptional historical development, from a South Asian perspective Russia and its empires are almost instantly recognizable as belonging to the great tradition of continental bureaucratic states found in the Eurasian landmass. That the first state-like entities started forming in what became the Russian

Empire only in the 700s and 800s under the Khazars and their Kievan Rus successors means that Russia achieved statehood much later than Persia, China, India, Mesopotamia, and Egypt. This delay owes much to the geography and climate and holds the key to understanding the autocratic and centralizing tendencies of Russia's culture of power.

The growing season in Russia is, at five months, brief even when compared to Western Europe. It compares very poorly to the two or three harvests possible in China and India. The long Russian winter is notorious for its severity and makes movement and communications difficult for long parts of the year for most of Russia's people. The soil in the northern parts of Russia is poor but rain is relatively more abundant than the southern parts where the land is more fertile. Fresh water, in the shape of rivers, is available in key regions, and land is plentiful relative to the size of the population. Subarctic forests provide access to timber though in winter conditions they became hard to exploit. Beyond the rivers and forests there are vast expanses of steppe, historically peopled by martial tribes. Primordial Russia was, therefore, a vast plain, bounded by forests, crushed by ice, devoid of defensible natural frontiers and exposed to banditry, enslavement and slaughter from the pastoral tribes of the steppe. Having very little themselves, early Russians lived in fear that the predators circling their notional frontiers could strike as soon as the long winter ended.

Under such harsh conditions social and political evolution was necessarily slow as the processes of accumulation needed to establish statehood and an organized society took much longer to reach a critical mass. The distances involved, the extremes of the climate, and vulnerability to attack, meant that Russia's marginal position towards the north of the Eurasian landmass and distance from the ancient core zone of civilization constrained its early development.[5] The major ideological and cultural stimulus came from the residual Eastern Roman or Byzantine Empire. Under the Khazar Khakanate of the 700s the land around the Dnieper River was a major trading artery as well as a relatively fertile zone with access to the Black Sea. The Slavic inhabitants of the Dnieper region evidently rebelled against the Khazars in the mid-800s and led by Oleg, an enterprising war leader with semi-mythical status, occupied Kiev in 882. The state of Kievan Rus, therefore, originated in a rebellion against the Khazars, and it drew inspiration from geographically proximate Byzantium[6] rather than distant Rome.

KIEVAN RUS AND THE MONGOLS: 882–1380

Kievan Rus remains mired in controversy. To Russians as well as foreigners keen to establish a direct connection with the rest of Europe, the Rus, or at least the ruling class, were Vikings who came to plunder but then settled down and married into the local Slavic population. The raid on Constantinople carried out in 860 by 8000 men and 200 boats, is cited as an example of a Viking-led attack, even though it was not until the 880s that the Khazars lost control over the core region of Kiev and it would take until the early-900s for their power to be broken to the point where Kievan Rus could claim its place in the Sun. Slavophiles emphasize the indigenous nature of Kievan Rus and reject the Scandinavian connection. The debate about the genetic history of Kievan Rus as it arose from the primordial soup of tribalism, migration and settlement, need not detain us here. What is relevant is that the rulers of Kievan Rus looked to Byzantium for guidance and organized their state and society along lines somewhat different from what prevailed in Western Europe.

The history of Kievan Rus can be divided into three phases. The first covers the birth and consolidation of Kievan Rus between the mid-800s and the late-900s. The second phase is that of ascendancy and follows the establishment of control over the Eastern Slavs through exploitation of Kiev's commanding position along the Dnieper, which enabled it to control key trade routes. This phase corresponds to the reigns of Saint Vladimir (r. 980–1015) and Iaroslav the Wise (r. 1119–1054). The third and final phase is that of decline following Iaroslav's death in1054 and ends with the conquest of Kievan Rus by the Mongol horde in 1240.

The first phase saw the establishment of the *apanage* system that served as the basis of the Kievan Rus state structure. Under it the vast but sparsely populated state was parceled out into principalities or domains ruled by direct relations of the Prince/Grand Prince at Kiev.[7] The idea was that the family of the ruler was less likely to betray him and had a corporate interest in keeping themselves in power. Family members were thought to be more loyal and obedient than strangers. These subordinate princes were required to maintain armies, collect taxes, administer justice, consult the peasants and merchants, and maintain communications. When needed, they contributed troops to the central army. For this purpose the system could muster considerable forces for campaigns. In 970–971, for example, Kievan Rus deployed some 60,000 soldiers in the Balkans against the Byzantines, though, after hostilities ended the strength of the army was reduced to 22,000.[8]

The *apanage* system has been compared to aristocratic feudalism in Western Europe. One plausible argument is that if it had been allowed to operate without disruption it would have produced in Russia a variant of feudal society along Western European lines. There are, however, key differences between the system of landholding and titles in Kievan Rus and what prevailed further West that make this outcome, with or without the Mongols, unlikely. First, landholding in Kievan Rus was not subject to primogeniture. This meant that the estates of princes were divided and subdivided from one generation to the next preventing stability in landholdings. Second, succession to the throne of Kiev often required a civil war among the sons of the incumbent, as there was no legitimate principle of hereditary succession from father to eldest son. Third, by the

1100s succession was further complicated by the practice of first going through the brothers in order of seniority and then, once no more brothers remained, switching to the sons.[9] This produced chaos as lines of succession and inheritance were hopelessly confused as every prince had plenty of brothers, uncles and nephews, to keep political conflict raging. Finally, with the passage of time the royal family grew in size as more and more people claimed descent from it with the result that possible heirs to the thrones and to princely estates became "so numerous that serious genealogical skills would have been needed to establish where sovereignty and precedence should lie."[10]

An illustration of the essentially arbitrary nature of power grabs in Kievan Rus is provided by the reign of Saint Vladimir. In 969, Prince Sviatoslav, assigned the administration of the Kievan heartland to his eldest son, Iaropolk. The second son, Oleg, was assigned the lands of the Drevliane, while Vladimir got Novgorod. In 971, Sviatoslav was killed by the Pechenegs while returning from his Balkan campaign and civil war erupted in Kiev. Oleg was killed, Vladimir fled, and Iaropolk succeeded his father. However, in 980, Vladimir returned and killed his elder brother with the help of mercenaries and occupied the throne. Vladimir ruled for the next thirty-five years and upon his death another civil war erupted. At first, his eldest son had the upper hand but another son, named Iaroslav, operating from his base in Novgorod, pushed back and defeated his older brother in 1019. This victory, however, represented a new stage in the civil war that dragged on till 1026 and was fought between Iaroslav and his brother Prince Mstislav. An agreement was reached in 1026 that effectively partitioned Kievan Rus between the two brothers. Iaroslav got the lands to the west of the Dnieper while Mstislav got those to the east of the Dnieper. It was only in 1036, with Mstislav's death, that the state was formally reunited under a single ruler. This unity, however, was short-lived as Iaroslav, trying to reform the system and stabilize succession before his death, carefully divided Kievan Rus amongst his five sons and made them agree that they would sit on the throne of Kiev in order of their seniority. Succession would therefore pass from brother to brother before it would go back to going from father to son. This reform added a new layer of confusion and caused conflict between uncles and nephews in addition to the already present conflict between sons. Kievan Rus was locked in a perpetual state of civil unrest with no legitimate principle of hereditary succession either in property or in power.

While there was plenty of feuding, Kievan Rus did not develop aristocratic feudalism on the Western European pattern for that would require much greater stability in the inheritance of authority and wealth. In Western Europe, feudalism was based on the practice of primogeniture, the gradual recognition of royalty and hereditary right, and the emergence of customs and institutions that defined the relationship between the monarch, the lords, their vassals, and subjects. Many of these conditions were absent in Kievan Rus. In fact, the cycles of civil war, contested succession, fratricide, and atomization of genealogies and estates seem to have more in common with Persia or India than with France or England.

The conversion of Kievan Rus to Christianity during the reign of Saint Vladimir also had far-reaching consequences. It was Constantinople, not Rome that succeeded in converting Kievan Rus. Though, at the time, there was no formal schism between the Roman and Byzantine churches, the success of the latter meant that Kievan Rus avoided the Latinization of its literate culture. Although the Church became wealthy and powerful in Kievan Rus, it was never quite as powerful as the Roman Church. The Kievan Church acted as a prop of the political order while the princes had a say in appointments other than the Metropolitan of Kiev who was nominated directly by Constantinople.

The sheer size of Kievan Rus and its exposed frontiers made it vulnerable to invasions and necessitated the maintenance of military discipline. Such discipline depended on the ability of the princes to lead their *boyars* and wage war on multiple fronts. The loyalty of the boyars and their peasants depended on their personal relationship with the princes. If a boyar was not happy he could always switch loyalty from one prince to another, a practice that would have made it even harder for the system to stabilize as the number of princes proliferated. This also complicated the management of vassals, an essential component of feudalism, and meant that personal loyalty to a particular individual rather than loyalty to a particular house or domain was what mattered the most. The internal pressure on Kievan Rus, owing to its nihilistic configuration, and the external pressure in the form of military threat from outsiders coalesced alarmingly in the early 1200s. Civil wars erupted in 1212 and 1226 as the Mongols moved towards Kievan Rus. The first military engagement between Kievan Rus and the Mongols occurred in 1223. The Mongols won the battle, but then withdrew only to return in strength in 1237.

The rise and fall of the Mongols represents a uniquely terrifying example of Ibn Khaldun's philosophy of history in action.[11] A charismatic leader (Genghis Khan) united his tribal kinsmen on the basis of their blood ties and infused them with a sense of divine mission. The solidarity (*asabiya*) thus produced created a formidable force capable of overwhelming nearly any static defenses or rival field army through superior mobility and motivation. Those unfortunates that found themselves in the way of the initial onslaught were swept away. Over a generation, however, the successors of Genghis Khan fought amongst themselves and ended up dividing the Mongol dominion into a number of successor states.[12] The fragmentation of the universal empire was followed by the Mongols adapting to local conditions and the manipulation of the survivors of their conquests. As the hardiness and leadership qualities of the Mongol elite declined, the reliance on local clients and practices became greater. Eventually, the conquered were able to turn the tables on their masters bloodily ousting them from their lands.

Astronomers assure us that the planet Jupiter shields the inner planets from harmful cosmic debris that could well prove fatal to life on Earth. In a like manner, Kievan Rus absorbed the full weight of the Mongol onslaught that ran out of steam on its blood soaked plains. Much of the south was converted into pasturelands for the Mongol armies leading to a shift of population, economic activity and spiritual life towards the north expanses of Russia. In these expanses the Mongols appointed local grandees to act as tax collectors, census takers, and dispensers of justice. These grandees were confirmed in their lands by the Mongol Khan at Sarai and obliged to leave hostages at the Mongol court. The Mongols encouraged rivalries amongst their Russian stooges and manipulated local antagonisms to their own advantage.

The Mongols retained overall control through maintaining a capability to intervene with decisive military force. The Russians employed by the Mongols were overseen by Mongol supervisors while the local population was forced to keep at ready the horses, boats and other implements needed to maintain an imperial postal system. Through these assets the Mongols could overwhelm local rebellions while exploiting internecine rivalries amongst the Russians. The aura of invincibility around Mongol arms and slaughter and depredations of the initial conquests also went a long way towards ensuring that the will of the Khan was obeyed. An illustration of Mongol imperialism responding to the challenge of control is provided by the rebellion of Tver in 1327. Ivan, the prince of Vladimir-Moscow, sided with the Mongols as Tver was a local rival. The Mongols mustered a force of 50,000 horsemen, placed them under Ivan's command and sent them to deal with Tver. The rebellion was crushed and additional lands were granted to the loyal ruler of Moscow.

The making and breaking of Russian grandees and the granting of lands appears to have been done in an arbitrary manner. The Mongols were primarily, if not exclusively, interested in plunder and for that purpose were happy to sell the title of grand prince to the highest bidder and execute those who resisted the Court's wishes. It was the Mongol Khan who decided matters of inheritance and succession and mediated between rival Russian underlings. These underlings were constantly pulling each other down and thus could not establish a united front against the Mongols. Resistance was apparently quite futile given the unbeaten record of Mongol arms. Servile towards the Mongols, oppressive towards those below them, and deeply suspicious of each other, the Russian landed elite was atomized, self-seeking, and propped up an arbitrary system of which it was part perpetrator and part victim. The Mongols as a ruling class serve as an effective example of how an armed minority can keep a much larger host population in a state of terror through the selective but rigorous application of violence. What the Mongols did not expect was that the principality of Moscow, one of their most loyal servants, would gradually gain in strength and lead a rebellion that would establish the Russian Empire.

THE RISE OF MOSCOW: 1147–1400

In 1897, czarist Imperial Russia ruled 21 million square kilometers of the Earth's land surface and had nearly 130 million subjects. It was, within the hierarchy of world powers, one of the three global empires alongside the British and French empires. Unlike the British and French, however, the Russians had acquired territories through continental expansion that projected outwards from the core territory of Moscow. Thus, the Russians ruled dozens of different nationalities that were simultaneously dispersed and concentrated along the vast extended periphery of the ethnic Russian population, which was about half the total. Within this empire there were no autonomous institutions that could lawfully challenge the czar. The economy was dominated to an astonishing extent by state monopolies and controls. The country was run, in the czar's name, by civil servants and military officers, and although local government and judicial reforms introduced in the 1860s had created a small space for politics and the rule of law in cases that affected imperial subjects, there was no doubt that Russia was an autocracy. The czar was an arbitrary ruler who, it was believed by loyalists, was alone capable of preserving order and unity in the vastness and diversity of the Russian Empire. The nucleus of this juggernaut lay in a place called Moscow.

The rulers of Kievan Rus evidently founded Moscow in the mid-1100s. Its location places it well north of Kiev, but sufficiently towards the center to have some buffer between itself and the Poles and Lithuanians to the west. In 1237, the Mongols destroyed Moscow during their conquest of Kievan Rus, though the territory reemerged as a small principality under Prince Daniel in the late 1200s. Daniel concentrated on establishing his control over the land around the Moscow River and defeated the Riazan prince to the south to secure control of its mouth. In the early 1300s Daniel's son, Yuri, attacked his western neighbor and secured a monopoly over the entire course of the Moscow river, thus realizing his father's cherished dream. Yuri aligned himself with the Mongol court at Sarai and scored a significant victory in 1318 when one of the Khan's sisters was married to him. The Mongols also bestowed the title of Grand Prince on Yuri as a mark of imperial favor. Yuri leveraged this support and took on the Grand Prince of Tver. For the next 20 years Moscow and Tver went head-to-head. Moscow suffered an early defeat and Tver forces captured Yuri's wife. Unfortunately for Tver, the Mongol princess died in their custody and Yuri appealed to the Khan to intervene. Grand Prince Michael of Tver was summoned to the Mongol court and executed after which the Khan made Michael's eldest son, Dmitri, the new ruler of Tver. In 1325, Yuri and Dmitri both ended up at the Mongol court as they struggled to retain Mongol favor. There, Dmitri killed Yuri and was executed by the Mongols. The Khan appointed Alexander, Dmitri's younger brother, as the Grand Prince of Tver, though, owing to continuous intrigues the Mongols, aided and abetted by Moscow, attacked Tver in 1327. Alexander escaped and spent a decade in exile before being lured back by prospects of reconciliation only to be executed in 1337. In the meanwhile, Ivan I, Yuri's younger brother, had been appointed Grand Prince of Moscow by the Khan.

Ivan I ruled until his death in 1341 and earned the title "money bags" for his administrative and fiscal skills. Ivan I seems to have realized that the best way to stay on the good side of his Mongol overlords was to excel at providing them with the revenue they craved. For his loyalty and talent for extraction, the Mongols elevated Ivan I above other grandees by giving him the task of collecting the tribute due to the Khan from Russian princes. Ivan I was able to employ the money bags thus generated to buy out insolvent princes and landlords, pay ransoms to free prisoners and settle them on his lands, keep the Mongol court happy, acquire additional territory with the Khan's approval, and ward off rivals. By 1341, Moscow had become a substantial principality of 600 square miles and within it the Grand Prince ruled as he pleased with the support of the Mongols.

While the assertion of Moscow's fiscal and administrative leadership was the result of conscious and consistent efforts, Ivan I also benefited from an extraordinary bit of good luck on the religious and ideological side of the power equation. Since the devastation of Kievan Rus by the Mongols and the destruction of Kiev, the Orthodox Church in Russia lacked a permanent headquarters. With the Roman Catholic Poles and Lithuanians to the west and Russian princes locked in internecine struggles punctuated by Mongol interventions, there was no stable center where the Church could find refuge. In 1326, Metropolitan Peter, head of what remained of the Orthodox Church in Russia, died while staying in Moscow. Proclaimed a saint, Peter's grave became a site of pilgrimage. A few years later, Ivan I succeeded in persuading the new Metropolitan, Theognost, to set up a permanent headquarters in Moscow. Theognost agreed and Moscow thus became the new spiritual center of Orthodox Russia while the Church tied itself and its fortunes to the perpetuation, legitimization and enlargement of Moscow's power. If the Roman Catholics and the Muslim Mongols were ever to be driven out, the Orthodox Church would need a powerful secular ally.

Ivan I's successors, Simeon (r. 1341–53) and Ivan II (1353–59) continued to consolidate their power within Moscow while expanding its territory as opportunities to do so arose. They remained loyal to the Mongol Khans, patronized the Orthodox Church and bought off or beat rivals. Nevertheless, Moscow's slow rise was threatened in the late 1360s by two major developments. The first was that between 1357 and 1378, the Mongols experienced a crisis of succession. Twenty Khans came and went in about as many years. For Moscow, hitherto the most loyal of the Russian principalities and one that could call on the Mongols for reinforcements if need be, instability at the Mongol court represented a major crisis. The second was that upon the death of Ivan II in 1359, Prince Dmitri of Suzdal claimed the throne of Moscow as his nephew (Ivan II's son), who was also named Dmitri, was only nine years old. The case of Dmitri vs. Dmitri was referred to Sarai but chaos at the imperial court meant that *both* Dmitris managed to secure Mongol approval. With the aid of the Metropolitan Alexi, the younger Dmitri secured the loyalty of Moscow and the succession passed from father to son.

Pandemonium at the Mongol court meant that Moscow was left to its own devices. Grand Prince Dmitri (r. 1359–89) led Moscow's armies in a series of campaigns that checked the Lithuanians, defeated Tver, and trounced the Volga Bulgars and Riazan. In 1378, Dmitri even beat a Mongol army at the Vozha River—a development that sent alarm bells ringing in Sarai. In 1380, the Mongols gathered a host 200,000 strong to reassert their power over Moscow. Dmitri, fielding an army 150,000 strong, managed to lure the overconfident Mongols into joining battle on hilly terrain broken by streams. After the Mongols were soundly defeated, the Church proclaimed a holy war and twenty leading princes rallied to Moscow's support. Although the Mongols returned to plunder Moscow in 1382 and devastated its territory they did not manage to defeat its armies in the field. Hostilities ended as both parties were exhausted and willing to compromise with Dmitri remaining Grand Prince in exchange for formally acknowledging Mongol suzerainty. A balance of power now prevailed between Moscow and Sarai and in addition to the prestige gained by defeating the Mongols in the field, Dmitri more than doubled the area under his control. Fortune favored Moscow as, upon Dmitri's death he was succeeded, without the usual hitches, by his son, Basil I (r. 1389–1425).

ASCENDANCY AND AUTOCRACY IN EARLY IMPERIAL RUSSIA, 1400–1533

Between 1340 and 1450 Moscow grew in size from a principality of 600 square miles to a sizeable proto-empire of 15,000 square miles. Its central location, military prestige, religious importance, and good fortune in enjoying a succession of relatively able rulers while escaping devastation at the hands of Amir Timur (in 1395), laid the foundations for later greatness. At an institutional level it was between 1400 and 1600 that certain practices emerged that worked to the advantage of the Grand Prince and his personal servants in terms of raising them above other groups within their expanding domains.

One such practice was the service estate modeled on the Byzantine *pronia*. Called *pomestie* in Russia, it was first introduced in Kievan Rus though it competed with landlords who owned their lands. The principle of the service estate was that the Grand Prince granted his servants leases on the revenue generated by specified lands. Maintaining the lease was contingent upon the landlord keeping at ready a certain number of troops. These troops were to be mustered when commanded by the Grand Prince. New conquests and settlements were leased out on such terms making the service gentry more important with time. The lease could be transferred from one generation to the next provided that the heirs agreed to furnish the same number of troops. By the reign of Ivan III, Moscow could raise three or four times as many troops as it did a generation earlier. Larger armies meant faster expansion and consolidation and increased the amount of land that could be handed out as service estates. In this way a self-sustaining cycle of conquest, expropriation, and service leases was set in motion. Old rivals like Tver and Novgorod were finally crushed by the growing militarism and autocracy of the Grand Prince of Moscow. What happened to Novgorod and its representative institutions is particularly instructive and reminiscent of the destruction of tribal republics by the bureaucratic empire of the Mauryas in India c. 300 BC.

Located to the North-West of Moscow, Novgorod emerged as a practically independent principality during the decline of Kievan Rus in the mid-1100s. In 1136, Novgorod expelled the prince appointed by Kiev. The boyars, merchants and common householders convened a *veche* or town council and hired their own prince who was required to consult them on important matters. With a population of about 30,000, Novgorod was divided into streets, neighborhoods, and city districts. Each street chose an elder to represent it while city districts had their own councils, appointed their own officials and received a share of lands to pay for maintenance. The prince, who was the executive head, could not dismiss the officials without a court order and was obliged to appoint only locals to his own staff. The head of the city guard and the chief advisor to the prince were appointed by the *veche*. A permanent secretariat served the *veche* while the impracticality of keeping the whole assembly in permanent session meant that day-to-day affairs were entrusted to a council of notables. Even on the judicial side, trial by jury, rather than torture, was the preferred mode of decision-making.

This admirably democratic system had several flaws that disadvantaged it compared to the authoritarian Moscow model. Conflict between rival factions within Novgorod sapped its military discipline and strength. Moscow, on the other hand, was socially and culturally backward but far more disciplined and relatively free of internal dissent owing to the power of its Grand Prince. By the 1450s, Moscow was able to impose terms on Novgorod that made it a subordinate state with internal autonomy. The aristocratic faction in Novgorod was not happy with the state of affairs and sought help from Lithuania. That said, many of the common people as well as the Orthodox Church, were not on the same page as the aristocrats. Thus, when, in 1471, Ivan III (r. 1462–1505) moved to crush the rebellion Moscow's forces were able to prevail. Ivan III was not unduly harsh and allowed Novgorod to continue governing itself as before in exchange for reparations and reaffirmation of its loyalty to Moscow. When, in 1477–78,

Novgorod's aristocratic faction sought Lithuanian intervention yet again, Ivan III resolved to defeat the rebels and remove the cause of the rebellion. Divisions within Novgorod meant that this time it wasn't even able to put up a fight and Moscow occupied it with ease. Ivan III then eradicated Novgorod's representative institutions, confiscated the property of its landlords, and dispersed rebels to other parts of the country. The offices and assemblies were thus abolished and Novgorod was absorbed into Moscow's growing empire.

Princes and other notables flocked to Moscow's rising star while Ivan III's marriage, in 1472, to a Byzantine princess, added greatly to its prestige. Byzantine court ritual and culture, long an influence on Russia, became more firmly rooted after the fall of Constantinople to the Ottomans in 1453. Ivan III, in 1493, proclaimed himself the czar, autocrat and sovereign of all Russia, and adopted the two-headed eagle of Byzantium as the Russian imperial crest. Ivan III's successor was his son, Basil III (r. 1505–1533) who continued the policies of expansion and autocratization that had matured under his father. In 1511, Pskov submitted to Moscow, in 1514, Smolensk fell, and in 1517, Riazan, the upper Oka, Starodub, and Chernigov-Sversk were subjugated. Kazan, then a khanate, found itself under relentless pressure and Moscow had the satisfaction of playing one faction off against the other, turning the tables on the Mongols. As Moscow's empire grew in size the Grand Prince or czar, as he was now known, became more powerful relative to his boyars who were increasingly reduced to the status of servitors. In the new settlements there was no earlier undergrowth and villages could be settled directly by the state or by landlords under the direction of the czar. The empire was becoming a vast estate owned by its ruler and legitimized by divinity on the classical pattern of continental bureaucratic empires elsewhere in Eurasia.

AUTOCRACY AND ITS DISCONTENTS, 1533–1649

Ivan IV (r. 1533–1584), better known as Ivan the Terrible (or "The Dread") became czar at the age of three and consequently Russia was ruled by an unstable succession of regents from boyar factions until he got around to seizing power for himself. What the factions had in common was their desire to monopolize access to the young czar and rule arbitrarily on his behalf. This practice is a fairly familiar occurrence as far as other continental bureaucratic empires were concerned where, should the ruler weaken or a regency come about, rivals at court would fight each other to control the de jure ruler. This struggle was not aimed at curbing the arbitrary power of the ruler or the autocratic nature of the culture of power. Rather, the effort on the part of ambitious courtiers was to displace arbitrary power from the ruler to their own selves and wield it on the ruler's behalf. In 1547, Ivan

IV, hardened by years of intrigues, the death, possibly by poisoning, of his mother, and the fractiousness of the royal court, killed the regent and had himself formally crowned czar.

Ivan IV moved quickly to consolidate his power and expand his realm. In 1550, an elite guard of musketeers known as the *streltsy* were raised and maintained at the capital. The *pomestie* system was infused with new life and direction with a firm hand to guide it from above. Ivan IV wanted to finish off the Khanate of Kazan and crush the Tartars once and for all. For this purpose, starting in 1551–2, Ivan IV raised a campaign army 150,000 strong equipped with 150 cannon. After Kazan fell in 1552, Ivan IV set his sights on pacifying the surrounding countryside and occupying Astrakhan, which was annexed in 1556. These military successes were accompanied by the import of specialists from the West aimed at improving Russia's technological base, especially in critical areas like gunnery and mining and by administrative reforms, such as setting up a high council of advisers and providing greater freedom to local government. The latter reforms are cited as examples of Ivan IV's benevolence and desire to modernize Russia's political institutions.

While the military success proved lasting, Ivan IV's experiments with government by consultation ended with harsh consequences for those close to him. Ivan IV was deeply suspicious by nature and, having grown up in a maelstrom of court intrigues and savagery, was prone to seeing enemies everywhere. The death of Czarina Anastasia in 1560 appears to have unhinged Ivan IV. Initially, the czar's rage was confined to members of the court and his council of advisers whom he believed responsible for Anastasia's death. Arbitrary arrests and executions followed that engulfed entire families close to those Ivan IV suspected of involvement. When some boyars publicly criticized the extremes to which the czar was going two of the critics were executed and many others fled to Lithuania, a measure that only confirmed their guilt in the czar's eyes and justified victimization of their families and confiscation of their properties. In 1565, Ivan IV, after a bizarre episode in which he left the capital, expressed the desire to abdicate, and condemned his boyars and the clergy, established the *oprichnina*. The *oprichnina* was a special department that ran parallel to other departments and reported directly to the czar. Its function was to seek out and destroy enemies of the regime. This state security organization had its own lands and peasants and an elite corps of cavalry that eventually numbered 6000.

Ivan IV unleashed a reign of terror that would last, with varying degrees of intensity, until the end of his life, though repression peaked between 1565 and 1575 when the *oprichnina* was active. The families of those who had fled into exile were arrested, tortured, forced to denounce others, and either killed or left to rot in jail. The czar's cousin, Prince Vladimir, along with his relations and retainers, were wiped out. Anyone who ever associated with an enemy of the czar became a suspect and stood to lose his freedom, property, honor and, often enough, life. Those who were sufficiently craven and clever directed the czar's ire towards others and became instruments through which lives were arbitrarily destroyed. Absolutely no one was safe. Even the Orthodox Church, which had done so much to plead Moscow's cause and justify its crimes and its autocracy, found itself unable to remonstrate effectively before the czar. In 1566, The Metropolitan Filip, who dared urge Ivan IV to relent in his persecutions, was deposed, condemned by a synod of the senior clergy, handed over to the *oprichnina* and executed. In 1570, Novgorod was paid a visit by the czar's enforcers who massacred 30,000 of its inhabitants and enforced the confiscation of properties.

The terror unleashed against some real though largely imaginary internal enemies, was accompanied by relentless warfare on all fronts, against the Swedes, Lithuanians, Poles, Mongols, Turks and Tartars. These wars account for practically the entirety of Ivan IV's reign, and ended only in 1583, a year before his death. The cost of these conflicts was enormous and provides strong evidences of the resilience and effectiveness of early czarism in Russia. In 1571 alone, the Crimean Tartars looted and pillaged their way to Moscow, taking at least 100,000 prisoners and leaving famine and pestilence in their wake that no doubt killed many more people than the fighting itself. Polish and Swedish offensives in 1578 led to military setbacks and the loss of an entire army, straining Russian organization and finances that nevertheless provided men and material for another five years of warfare. The regime's response was to further centralize power, subordinate society to the needs of the state, and expand on other fronts such as the Urals and Siberia where resistance was less organized.

Ivan IV established the state's monopoly on the sale and distribution of alcohol that was provided through state sanctioned liquor houses. The state monopoly on alcohol was a very important source of revenue until almost the end of czarist times, accounting for one-third to one-half of revenues.[13] The village commune, in which lands were held collectively and assigned to families based on their size in unconsolidated holdings, was also the product of Ivan IV's drive to control movement, ensure recruits for his wars, and increase tax collection. And, above all, there was the institution of serfdom in which peasants were tied to crown lands or service estates and could be transferred or sold like slaves, forbidden to move without authorization.[14] The landlords or the czar's agents were responsible for keeping order and had a free hand to do as they pleased so long as revenue and recruits were furnished on demand. These landlords and agents were vulnerable to dispossession and dismissal, if not worse, and thus had little interest in long-term improvement in productivity. The village communes were sub-political, insular, and fractured by petty rivalries and jealousies. They kept society in a condition of institutionalized poverty in which initiative and enterprise went unrewarded. Further expansion was the only way for the state to increase its wealth and though many peasants did manage to escape into the wilderness (a common practice in South Asia) the state would eventually catch up with them.

Ivan IV's madness eventually caught up with him and undermined the future of his dynasty. In 1581, he attacked his eldest son and heir apparent with a staff and injured him so badly that he died of his wound. When Ivan IV died three years later the crown passed to Fedor I (1584–1598). Fedor was a simpleton who depended on his advisers and allowed them to conduct state affairs unsupervised. One of these advisers was an ambitious boyar of Mongol origins named Boris Gudonov. Gudonov was believed to have orchestrated the murder of the czar's nine-year old brother, Prince Dmitri, in 1591. Though his guilt was never established, Gudonov took full advantage of the czar's trust in him and used him to amass great wealth and power. Like the viziers of Persia, Gudonov had no desire to limit the czar's autocracy for it suited him perfectly to become the primary channel for the exercise of his nominal master's arbitrary power. The czar's failure to produce an heir and his dependence on Gudonov made the upstart so confident that, animated by the audacity of hope; he set up his own court and secured permission to conduct diplomacy with foreign powers. Such pretensions would have led to dismissal, expropriation and death under almost any czar who was in his senses, but Gudonov thrived with Fedor as the ruler. In 1598, when the czar died heirless, Gudonov set about making a play for the throne itself. What followed, however, was not his founding a new dynasty but a period of civil war that brought to power the Romanov dynasty.

THE TRIUMPH OF AUTOCRACY, 1600–1700

In the absence of an effective autocratic ruler Russia descended into chaos. Godunov convened a council of notables and secured approval to ascend the throne but was soon overwhelmed by challenges to his right to rule and changes in circumstances. Poor harvests in 1601, 1602 and 1603, led to famine and epidemics that devastated the population with perhaps as many as 100,000 perishing in the Moscow region alone. It was as if God was punishing Russia for allowing Godunov to rule as czar. On the one hand, word spread that Godunov was a murderer of princes and on the other that Prince Dmitri had escaped assassination and was planning to return and reclaim the throne. The rumor about Prince Dmitri, Godunov was convinced, was a conspiracy against his government hatched by rival boyars. He responded through violent purges of the service nobility aimed at crushing opposition and quashing the rumor mill. Under normal circumstances such tactics could well have worked but with famine raging and a pretender claiming to be Prince Dmitri openly defying him, Godunov was under immense pressure. As boyars, clergy, mercenaries, Cossacks and peasants rallied to support the pretender, Godunov gathered his forces to strike back. In April 1605, before, however, Godunov had the chance, he died, and his enemies moved to liquidate his immediate family and secure control over the capital. The pretender was, in turn, eliminated by the boyars who brought another pretender to the throne in his place. Instability ensued as the state started to breakdown into petty estates. By 1610, rebellions in the south combined with Polish and Swedish military interventions convinced some of the boyars to set up a council of seven members. This council, in spite of heroic resistance by Russian forces, such as at Smolensk where 72,000 out of a population of 80,000 died before the city surrendered to the Poles in June 1611, was unable to bring direction to the war effort. Russia, it was increasingly realized, could not be governed by multiple wills—boyar oligarchy was too unstable while society, atomized into small communes, tended towards anarchy without firm leadership. Without an autocrat Russia would fall apart. Having finally regained control of Moscow in September 1612, a council of notables was convened in which the Church, nobility, and merchants were represented. This council should not be confused with Parliament nor can it be said to represent a constitutional advance. Its objective was to choose a new dynasty that would rule Russia autocratically and arbitrarily for in the absence of such a ruler anarchy within and subjugation without appeared to be Russia's fate. Nearly three hundred members of this council appended their signatures to the proclamation that heralded the onset of the Romanov era (1613–1917) and the accession of Michael Romanov (r. 1613–1645) as czar. Michael Romanov inherited a crisis situation and set himself to three major tasks. The first was to restore order after nearly twenty years of chaos. The second was to raise sufficient revenues to meet the demands of the state. The third was to negotiate and then maintain peace with Russia's neighbors, even if it entailed accepting loss of territory, in order to provide breathing room.

Regarding the first task, Michael Romanov hit upon a simple method. His government, realizing the impossibility of eliminating all the brigands and marauding Cossacks that plagued the countryside, offered them a conditional amnesty. The condition was that they should enroll as infantry and cavalry and muster for duty at Russia's borders. Those that refused to accept the amnesty or were considered too dangerous were isolated and dealt with severely as an example to the others. It took three years but by 1617, relative peace had been restored. The cost of peace was that the czar needed enough revenues to keep his troops paid. Thus, in 1614, the czar imposed a special tax of one-fifth on wealth and/or property on both the urban and rural areas. This was accompanied by emergency loans secured from leading boyars. As money started to flow into imperial coffers and order was slowly restored to Russia, the czar was in a better position to secure the frontiers. Here, the new regime proved supremely realistic and conceded territory to the Swedes and Poles as the price of peace treaties signed in 1617–18. Against the Ottomans, Michael proved cautious and refused to go along with the pro-war service nobility even after Cossacks, on their own initiative, occupied Azov in 1637.[15]

Michael was succeeded by his son, Alexis (r. 1645–1676), who initially relied on a small band of cronies whose depredations led to a rebellion in Moscow just three years into the new reign. Alexis responded by putting some officials to death though the most prominent miscreants managed to escape. Desperate to stabilize state finances, Alexis debased the currency. This led, predictably, to inflation, speculation, and, in 1662, to rioting against the government. Rebellions in the Ukraine and an uprising of Don Cossacks in 1670–71 that had to be put down by the army, indicated that all was not well under Romanov leadership. Alexis did try to bring about reforms, such as a new legal code in 1649 that remained in use for nearly two hundred years, and encouraged specialists from Western Europe to settle in Russia. These attempts, however, ran into a basic problem in that Alexis was reluctant to deal firmly with the service nobility. Thus the antiquated *mestnichestvo* or system of priority continued to serve as the basis for assigning protocols and offices with endless arguments about which noble was entitled to what position. Of course, when the czar chose to assert his power, the ranking system was flexible enough, but left to their own devices, the nobles were too chaotic and mutually suspicious to make it work—they lacked a corporate spirit even when it came to defending a system of priority that might have shielded them from the czar's arbitrary power. Alexis appears to have been fairly well-liked and acquired a reputation for being quiet and quiescent. He also enjoyed luxurious living and had, among other things, 3000 falcons handled by 200 falconers and 100,000 pigeons.[16]

Alexis and his successor, Fedor II (r. 1676–1682), presided over expansion of the central bureaucracy and the consolidation of the service nobility and serfdom. The central administration had long relied on secretariats called *prikazy* that came into existence to enforce the czar's orders. By the late 1600s about forty such bureaus were maintained permanently with about the same number being constituted and suspended as the czar deemed fit. The most important secretariats dealt with the czar's household and office, the service nobility, state lands, manors, the Church, and finance. As secretariats these organizations drafted instructions, maintained official records, and advised or informed the ruler on any subject he wished to be briefed about. The service nobility was responsible for enforcing imperial orders, collecting taxes, conscripting labor for their estates or public works, providing recruits for the army, and serving the czar in any other capacity. Obedience to the czar was secured by the instability of service estates, the fractured composition of the service nobility, the retention, at the center, of the Praetorian guard, some 22,000 strong, originally established by Ivan IV, and the atmosphere of reverence for the czar's person propagated by the Church. It was genuinely believed that the autocrat mediated between the Divine and the mundane, and without his guidance order and society would collapse and Russia's many enemies would feast on her remains.

By the late 1600s Russia had evolved into a "service state" where each group was regulated by the czar's power as mediated through his servants.[17] These servants were divided into distinct though by no means watertight hierarchies of bureaucrats, clergymen, soldiers and service nobles. The service nobility provided additional troops and managed state functions on the czar's behalf on the estates provided to them. The czar patronized them by granting them almost arbitrary power over the serfs in their jurisdictions. The Orthodox Church propagated the cult of the czar and with its spending rituals and esoteric mastery served as the primary ideological prop of the regime, its pretensions to autonomy finally broken after the fall of the zealous Patriarch Nikon in 1658 who had, among other things, triggered a schism by introducing minor changes to Church rituals. The czar also had directly under his control a corps of shock troops, a small (by modern standards) central bureaucracy, and considerable state lands and monopolies administered by his agents. As befits an autocracy, much depended on the temperament and ability of the czar and his senior advisers. The limits on the czar's power were physical rather than legal or moral—a point demonstrated by Fedor II's abolition of the medieval system of noble ranking and priority. Equality prevailed "in the very special sense that no one, whatever their rank or station, possessed any kind of right or privilege which the czar could not revoke at will."[18] The state was thus the personal estate of the czar, "his own private domain which it was his privilege to exploit and manage as he wished."[19] While inequality in liberty prevailed in Western Europe, the Russians had achieved equality in servitude. Russia had long become, in terms of territory, by far the largest state in Europe, and with a population that had grown from 8 million in the early 1600s to about 11 million by the 1680s; a considerable demographic base was also in place.

PETRUS IMPERATOR MAGNUS AND HIS LEGACY, 1700–1796

Peter the Great (r. 1682–1725) is known in the West for his attempts to modernize Russia by importing Western European practices and innovations. While the extent to which Peter's modernization succeeded is still debated, it is undeniable that by the end of his reign Russia had become a major part of the European balance of power. In terms of Russia itself, Peter's methods and reforms were not without precedent. From Ivan IV onwards, Russian rulers had encouraged skilled foreigners to settle in their territories and bring with them advanced techniques. Russian rulers had time and again wielded their autocratic power to kill resistance and push through important legal, social and economic reforms that they felt secured the interests of the state. What set Peter apart, perhaps, was his energy and curiosity, as well as his vision of Russia as a European great power albeit with indigenous norms and practices as far as internal affairs were concerned. Peter's reforms of the military, society, bureaucracy, economy and the Church, were pushed through owing to the sustained exertion of autocratic power. To many of his traditionalist critics, the czar appeared to be possessed of demonic energy as was even believed to be the Anti-Christ. Even his Western admirers questioned his methods as well as his ultimate sincerity in making Russia more of a European country than an Asian one. There was, nonetheless, a method to Peter's madness.

The most pressing reforms, critical to the stability of the czarist regime, were military in nature. Only ten years old when he became czar, Peter's power was handed over to a regency council dominated by his mother, Alexis's second wife, Natalya, and her family and favorites. However, Ivan, Fedor's younger brother and Alexis's son by his first wife, was still alive and though ill and mentally slow, he became a rallying point for those unhappy with the new government. The malcontents had, in Sophie, Alexis's daughter by his first wife, a strong leader. Only a month after being proclaimed czar, Peter suffered a terrible setback. The *streltsy* mutinied, killed leading members of the regency council, and forced the boyars to accept Ivan V as the senior czar with Sophie as the regent. The *streltsy* knew that they were the real power behind the new regency and made financial demands that forced the government to melt the Kremlin's gold and silver plate, levy additional taxes on the population and confiscate property. Sophie gave the *streltsy* little cause for complaint, doting on them as best she could. She did succeed in turning the *streltsy* against the Old Believers,[20] who were purged and forced to flee. The Church establishment warmed to Sophie and assisted her in ridding Russia of the Old Believer heresy. Between 1684 and 1690, some 20,000 Old Believers were executed by burning at the stake. Many more fled to the wilderness beyond the reach (for now) of the regime. Confiscations of property enriched those involved in prosecuting the persecution.

While the regent indulged the *streltsy* at home, she authorized military action against the Crimean Tartars and their Ottoman allies. In 1687, Russia sent an army of 100,000 and lost 45,000 men without engaging the Tartars who wisely withdrew and allowed logistical difficulties to undermine the Russians. Rather than relent, or learn anything, Sophie celebrated this misadventure as a victory. In 1688, another campaign was launched against the Tartars with the mobilization of 112,000 soldiers, 450 artillery pieces and a levy of 16,000 Cossacks. This time, as before, the Tartars withdrew, employing hit-and-run tactics while allowing the Russians to exhaust their armies and 20,000 Russian soldiers were killed, 15,000 captured, and 70 cannons along with nearly all the war supplies fell into enemy hands. These military disasters, while testifying to Russian endurance and capacity for mobilization, knocked the bottom out of military support for Sophie and her clique. Seeing enemies everywhere, Sophie attempted to instigate a *streltsy* revolt aimed at her detractors but found no takers. Peter, in the meanwhile, escaped to the nearly impregnable, and terribly symbolic, fortress-monastery of Troitsky and demanded that his authority as czar be finally acknowledged. Units of the regular army, the Church, leading boyars, and even some of the *streltsy*, came to proclaim their loyalty to Peter. With her allies deserting her, Sophie also pledged loyalty to Peter, stepped down from the regency, and was allowed to live comfortably in internal exile. Her chief advisor, Golitsyn, was stripped of rank and property, others were exiled, and two key aides were executed. Ivan V continued on as co-czar but now everyone knew that Peter was in charge.

Peter clearly understood that the *streltsy*, like the degenerate Ottoman janissaries, were a threat to the state and to his person. The *streltsy* were spoiled beyond redemption and were aware of their power over the czar as a strategically placed minority. While the czar was apparently powerless against the *streltsy* it seemed as if the state was powerless to stop Tartar raids that took a dreadful toll in terms of subjects killed or enslaved. Peter set his sights on succeeding where Sophie had failed and taking control of Azov, breaking the power of the Crimean Tartars. The 1695 campaign against Azov, which mobilized an army of 150,000, failed to achieve its objective but made Peter realize the need for a navy to cut off the enemy naval reinforcements. To this end, the 1696 campaign mobilized 46,000 Russian troops, 20,000 Cossacks, 3000 Kalmucks, 1000 barges and 30 seafaring ships. To build the naval component of the 1696 invasion force, Peter conscripted 30,000 laborers and imposed ship quotas on different regions. This time, Azov fell, and in the aftermath of victory, Peter dispatched 20,000 workers to build a new harbor and 6000 families to settle the land. Thus, between 1687 and 1696, four campaigns, each mobilizing 100,000 soldiers, with the final campaign also entailing conscription of labor to build a new navy, had succeeded in breaking the Crimean Tartars. Given that Russia's population was about 11 million in the 1680s, the mobilization of 400,000 soldiers over nine years was no mean feat. That the armies that eventually won the campaign against Azov was officered by foreigners and trained along foreign lines rankled with the *streltsy*, who mutinied in July 1696. Forces loyal to the czar crushed the rebellion with 130 mutineers executed and 1860 imprisoned. The rebels had wanted to bring Sophie back to power and Peter, believing her to be involved, had her confined to a nunnery. More than a thousand of the Streltsy were eventually put to death after being subjected to prolonged torture, sometimes carried out by the czar in person (who was occasionally moved to pardon some of his victims).

With the *streltsy* crushed and Russian arms covered in glory, Peter set out on the Great Embassy to the European courts. This enterprise cost the Russian treasury 2.5 million rubles, required the czar to be out of the country for some 18 months, and led to the recruitment of 800 specialists who returned to Russia with the czar. Upon his return, Peter was more determined than ever to change Russia, or at least its elite, so that it would appear more European. The assault on Russian traditionalism would take many forms, some of them quite substantive, but it began with an offensive against beards and traditional dress. Peter decreed, in 1698, that Russian gentry and townsmen, except for clergy, would have to shave their beards. This was sacrilege for most Russians, as the male beard was considered holy, something that God himself had bestowed on men while creating them in His image. To enforce this decree, a czarist fashion police comprising censors and barbers was constituted. Initially, "horrified and desperate Russians bribed these officials to let them go, but as soon as they did, they would fall into the hands of another official."[21] Peter decided to convert the ban into a graduated beard tax. Men could keep their beards for a tax payment assessed on their wealth so that peasants paid two kopeks while wealthy merchants paid one hundred rubles on an annual basis. In 1700, Western-style formal wear became compulsory for the noblemen and the following year a similar requirement was placed on noblewomen. As can be expected, in the capital total compliance was secured within a few years while in the provinces implementation took significantly longer. Peter also introduced Russia to the practice of rewarding people by given them membership of an order. This was much cheaper than rewarding with land and money and brought a touch of aristocratic honor to an elite society that had not experienced the concept.

Peter was determined to introduce great reforms in the administration of the country and not just in the sartorial and cosmetic appearance of the elite. Peter's efforts on this front were made even more urgent due to the outbreak of war between Sweden and Russia in 1701. In the early stages of the conflict, Sweden performed superbly. A small country of 1.5 million subjects, Sweden maintained an army 110,000 strong and had the most efficient civil service in Europe (arguably, it still does). Ably led by their king and officers, the Swedish army punched well above its weight and early victories against the Russians led the former to treat the latter with disdain and fall prey to the illusion that it would be possible to inflict a complete defeat on Russia. This was not the first time a more advanced adversary with operational superiority suffered from delusions of total victory over a strategically superior Russia and it certainly wouldn't be the last.

To fight the war, Peter needed a functioning currency system, increased arms production, a stronger navy, the sustained mobilization of hundreds of thousands of soldiers and laborers, and tax revenues to help pay for it all. The standardization of the currency into copper kopeks and silver rubles that exchanged at the rate of 100 kopeks for 1 ruble, accompanied by horrific punishments for counterfeiting currency, achieved the first requirement. Emergency measures that made full use of the czar's arbitrary power helped supply the armies during the first years of the conflict. In June 1701, one out of four church bells in Russia was melted down to be used for military purposes and converted into 300 new artillery pieces. In the meanwhile, between 1701 and 1704, a crash program saw the construction of seven major ironworks beyond the Urals. This iron came in handy for equipping the army with matchlock bayonets and by 1706 production was 30,000 units a year, up from 1000 a year in 1701, and peaked at 40,000 a year by 1711. In the midst of war, Peter decided to found St. Petersburg as a new capital that would project Russia as a major European power. This project required labor conscription with anywhere from 30,000 to 100,000 workers losing their lives during the initial construction. While sustaining all these exertions Russia had also mobilized some 400,000 soldiers for the war by the time it ended in victory over Sweden in 1721.

Peter remodeled his administration on the pattern that prevailed in Sweden establishing new departments for the navy, artillery and mines. In 1708, a new class of about 500 officers called fiscals was created to oversee revenue collection. These officers were kept busy, as Peter was adept at finding new ways to raise revenues as well as push the limits on collection from existing sources. One new way of raising revenue was mandating the use of stamp paper for official business that could only be purchased from the state. State monopolies were strengthened or established for alcohol, resin, tar, playing cards, chess sets, Siberian furs, coffins, salt and flax. Russia was divided into eight large provinces each headed by a governor whose power depended on the czar's favor much like the satraps of ancient Persia. In 1711, a Senate and colleges (ministries) headed by ministers replaced the old council of advisors and departments.

To watch over his officials and subjects Peter established the Secret Office. This bureau "had agents everywhere" and was responsible for seeking out and neutralizing treason, i.e. disloyalty to the czar, whether it was committed by word or deed.[22] It was already a crime to fail to denounce others should they speak or act against the czar. Romodanovsky was in charge of the Secret Office and by employing "a network of pervasive eavesdropping and denunciation, followed by torture and execution"; opposition to the regime was suppressed.[23] The system worked so well that through two decades of war and magnificence financed through rigorous taxation and forced labor, the throne itself was never threatened. That is not to say that there weren't any disturbances. Countless peasants fled to the forests to escape taxation, military service and forced labor. Rebellion in Astrakhan, and uprisings of Bashkirs and Cossacks had to be put down with an iron hand. On the other hand, Peter allowed Old Believers freedom of worship provided they paid double the usual taxes for this privilege. With the *streltsy* neutralized, there was no effective resistance to Peter and his policies.

After the war against Sweden ended, Peter reorganized the structure of the service nobility with the aim of ensuring a steady supply of competent recruits for state service. Members of the nobility and their male children were now required to serve the state on pain of arrest and confiscation of property. On balance, about one-third of young nobles were to go to the civil service and two-thirds were destined for the army or navy. In 1722, a Table of Ranks, which remained in place till 1917, was issued. The table divided service to the czar into civil, military and court hierarchies. All nobles started at the bottom (rank 14) of the military or civil service and worked their way up. The czar directly assigned the top five grades, or higher nobility, while only those civil and military officials who made it to rank 6 were eligible for transition to the court service. Promotions below rank 5 or 6 could be secured by departmental favor or the patronage of a governor though; it is hard to imagine anyone who offended the czar being promoted too far up the hierarchy.[24] Nobles were allowed to own serfs, collect taxes from service estates, and were addressed with respectful titles. Peter also insisted that nobles educate their children for he wanted a literate bureaucratic and military elite to staff the Swedish-inspired ministerial departments he had introduced in 1711.

The effectiveness of the new setup was demonstrated by the census conducted in 1722. That census established that Russia had about six million male serfs and that serfs accounted for more than nine-tenths of the total population. Previously, serfs paid a household tax that was deemed insufficient and prone to enabling concealment. Now, it was decreed that a poll tax would be collected on each individual serf, assessed at between 74 kopeks to 114 kopeks per capita/per annum and peasants now needed a passport to travel within the empire. The poll tax soon accounted for half of total revenues and was being collected by service nobles on the czar's behalf. Where needed, troops were billeted to ensure compliance with the new taxation and passports regime.

While Peter drove himself hard, working fourteen hours a day, lived simply with only two valets and six orderlies on his personal staff, ate and dressed frugally, abhorred sycophants and showed great personal bravery in battle,[25] he was hated by his subjects for his taxes, wars, and attitude towards the Orthodox Church. Peter established a Monastery Office in 1700 and changed the calendar count from the beginning of the world to the BC/AD system used in other European countries. The Monastery Office was placed under the control of a trusted noble, rather than a clergyman, and was given a mandate to shutdown monasteries that were operating fraudulently or not at all. When, in October 1700, Patriarch Adrian died, Peter declined to appoint a successor asserting that he was too busy. In effect, a civil servant, the Procurator of the Holy Synod, ran the Orthodox Church with the assistance of other lay officials, for the rest of the czarist era. The administration of church lands and serfs was brought under the Monastery Office. The effective nationalization of the Church and its blatant subservience to the czar reduced its appeal to rituals and ceremonies. Peter's ideology was that of progress and he propagated it as best he could, establishing, for example, the Russian Academy of Sciences, as well as schools for the nobility.

The nobility, as far as Peter was concerned, was ignoble when it came to corruption, wastage and disloyalty. Peter railed against the pretensions of the highborn and their oppressive sense of entitlement and was willing to appoint anyone who showed talent and seriousness. His closest advisers were often from humble backgrounds and included the sons of clerks and serfs and secretaries who had come to Peter's notice. Peter's preference for the company of foreigners, whom he regarded as more industrious and honest than his own countrymen, was also a matter of dismay for conservatives. The service obligations he imposed on the nobility, which necessitated the education of young noblemen (and noblewomen), were designed to instill the values of hard work and loyalty to the crown Peter so admired in more advanced European nations. Peter's rage when it came to punishing disloyalty, especially from those whom he had earlier favored or were personally close to him, was consuming. Prince Alexis, the heir apparent, fell prey to it after he fled abroad to get away from his demanding father. Betrayed by his mistress, Alexis watched in horror as his friends were struck down and the investigation into the prince's disloyalty ground on, leading to his arrest, torture and execution. The chief of the fiscals, Alexis Nesterov, suffered a similar fate in 1718 when he, who was supposed to crack down on corruption, was himself found guilty of it and was broken on the wheel. Governors, while enjoying immense powers when they enjoyed the czar's favor, were also liable to be executed if evidence of their corruption came to their master's attention. While Czarina Catherine did protect her inner circle and helped mollify Peter at times, everyone knew that a czar who could strike down his own son for disloyalty was capable of destroying anyone else. As in Persia, there was no kinship in Russian kingship.

One of Peter's advisers warned him, in good humor, that if the czar was as harsh as he wanted to be with thieves then he would soon have no subjects left to govern for in Russia everybody was a thief, what differed was the magnitude of their theft.[26] In saying this, the adviser displayed great insight. Peter's Russia was a great state with an army of 200,000 men, 16,000 cannons amassed in its arsenals, a decent regional navy, a powerful service nobility and a subservient Orthodox Church. Between 1710 and 1725 state revenues rose by 250 percent to 8.50 million rubles, and increased even further under Peter the Great's successors to 19.4 million rubles in 1764 and 40 million rubles in 1794. This greatness was purchased at a terrible price that entailed subordinating everything and everyone to the arbitrary power of the czar. Punitively high taxes, insatiable demands for military and labor conscripts, the culture of denunciations, confiscations of property, the flight of hundreds of thousands into the wilderness, and brutal purges that could consume anybody at any time, meant that the subjects of the Russian Empire lived in fear. Some 653,000 Russian soldiers would die in the 1700s on various fronts while half of all Russians conscripted did not live to the see the end of their period of service. The Bashkir rebellion during Peter's reign was crushed with 17,000 killed and 700 villages destroyed. Russian civil servants were paid so little they had to live off the land and could be expropriated by the czar at a moment's notice. Peter had modernized Russia, but that process had increased the power of the state over society and strengthened autocracy with resistance, real or imagined, smothered by police state tactics.

THE SOFTER SIDE OF CZARISM, 1725–1796

Between 1725 and 1796 the Russian Empire was ruled by a succession of seven sovereigns, four of whom were women. These rulers inherited Peter's system and continued many of his policies though the severity and energy with which power was exercised diminished. Peter's successor had to contend with the influence of the imperial guards regiments who took over the role of czar-makers previously held by the *streltsy*. The demonstration of these regiments in favor of Czarina Catherine I (r. 1725–27) meant that other factions at court, including some who wanted more power for the nobility, were driven underground. When Catherine I was succeeded by the twelve-year-old Peter II (r. 1727–30), the czar was quickly reduced to the status of a pawn in the hands of Peter the Great's favorite crony, Menshikov, before coming under the control of the Dolgurky clan. In 1730, Peter II was struck down by smallpox and died having nominated no successor. The Supreme State Council decided to offer the throne to the childless daughter of Ivan V, who accepted and ruled as Czarina Anne (r. 1730–40). The council members, who wanted to keep real power in their own hands, secured from Anne an agreement by which many of the monarch's arbitrary powers were transferred to the council. This agreement proved short-lived as discontent against this appropriation of monarchical power grew in the army and service nobility. With the support of the anti-oligarchs Anne reneged on her commitments, disbanded the council, and restored autocracy. That done, she proceeded to execute thousands and exile tens of thousands for opposition to the regime and placed the task of carrying out purges in the hands of her lover Ernst-John Biron. Estates and titles were bestowed on German families while thousands of others lost everything to the ruler's caprices. While Peter the Great's arbitrary actions had, at the end of the day, been motivated by the desire to make Russia a first-rate military and economic power, Anne's exactions were driven by personal aggrandizement and exemplified unenlightened arbitrary rule.

Anne's nominee to succeed her, the infant Ivan VI, was overthrown in 1741 by the imperial guards who brought Elizabeth (r. 1741–1762) to the throne. The daughter of Peter the Great, Elizabeth was charismatic and reminded people of her father, though she lacked his zeal and capacity for work. Predictably, Anne's favorites were shown the door and a new set of acolytes soon came to orbit around the ruler. Elizabeth styled herself the mother of her people and made a wonderful spectacle of her religious devotion, emphasizing her Russian roots and desire to rule justly. In contrast to her predecessors, Elizabeth didn't liquidate her enemies en masse. In fact, she categorically refused to sign execution orders, preferring to let her enemies keep their lives even if she took their freedom, property, and, on occasion, body parts. Even the deposed Ivan VI was not executed, though the conditions in which he was kept were harsh.

On the question of succession, Elizabeth nominated her nephew, Grand Duke Peter, as the heir apparent. Elizabeth also contracted a marriage with a German princess (the future Catherine II) for her nephew who was infatuated with all things German and idolized Fredrick the Great of Prussia. Being no fool and aware of the mortal danger that designated successors posed to incumbents in Russia, Elizabeth took great care to isolate the Grand Ducal couple and kept them on a short leash. Their every movement was monitored and Elizabeth decided who could and couldn't socialize with them. The iron discipline with which she treated Peter and Catherine was not, of course, applied to her own person. Elizabeth was extravagantly self-indulgent and believed that power was useless unless you knew how to have a good time. Between amassing a personal collection of 15,000 dresses and compelling all the court ladies to dye their hair a particular way, and going off on pilgrimages to repent for her sins and invoke divine favor, Elizabeth took little interest in the boring business of government. She was, however, very popular with the military on account of being the daughter of Peter the Great and intervened when necessary to preserve her position, dealing primarily through a cabinet of close advisers. Intriguingly, Elizabeth's reign did not see a large increase in the number of serfs. When she came to power there were an estimated 3.4 million male serfs and when she died there were about 3.8 million.[27] The number of state peasants, in the meanwhile, had grown from 3 million to 3.3 million.[28] On the military front, a combination of Prussian strategic over-extension and Russian endurance also brought Elizabeth glory. By 1762, the sixth year of the Seven Years War, Russian armies were closing in on Fredrick the Great and were poised to occupy his capital. Not only was Russia capable of fielding larger armies for longer periods but in 1763, with 16,500 civil servants, the imperial government of Russia was over ten times the size of the Prussian bureaucracy, which employed about 1400.[29] On the eve of a decisive victory, however, Elizabeth died and was succeeded by her nephew Peter III (r. 1762).

Having lived under his aunt's shadow, with the imprisonment of Ivan VI a living reminder of the fate that awaited him if Elizabeth chose to dispense with him, Peter III grew up warped by fear. He seems to have remained a child in many ways, preferring to play with his toy soldiers and beating his pet dogs while carousing with favorites who pandered to his delusions of grandeur. Peter III, perhaps as an act of rebellion against his aunt, openly hated all things Russian, modeled himself on Fredrick the Great, and didn't seem interested in learning about the vast empire he would one day have to rule. Thrust into power at the time of what should have been the greatest Russian victory since the Great Northern War (1701–21), Peter III suddenly called the war off. Fredrick the Great couldn't believe his luck and about two hundred years later Adolf Hitler would hope for a repeat of the "Brandenburg Miracle" as this episode became known. Prussia offered Russia concessions as the price of peace but this offer was rejected out of hand by the new czar whose admiration for the Prussian sovereign was too great to permit him from accepting. The czars had long been arbitrary in their disposal of internal affairs and, for the most part, the military didn't particularly care if their master lavished money on dresses or confiscated estates but such an about face when the Russian army was winning produced terrible frustration amongst the service nobility and the imperial army. While Peter III lived in a world of make belief, his wife, Catherine, who had spent the previous seventeen years becoming more Russian than the Russians and was quick to appreciate the imbecility of her husband and his favorites and the need to cultivate the military, was soon the center of a conspiracy to overthrow the czar.

In mid-1762, Catherine and the imperial guards, led by the Orlov brothers, overthrew Peter III. Catherine was proclaimed empress by the imperial guards and her son by Peter III, Grand Duke Paul, was declared heir apparent. Soon, Peter III, as well as the hapless Ivan VI, were conveniently dead. With the military in her favor and potential alternatives permanently out of the picture, Catherine II (r. 1762–96), the French ambassador predicted, could expect "fear and servile obedience" to triumph "as calmly as when the Empress [Elizabeth] usurped the throne."[30] Catherine II lavished funds on patronizing her supporters—gifts worth 800,000 rubles were distributed while 40,000 rubles, it was said, was spent on procuring vodka for the regiments.[31] 18,000 state peasants were made serfs and handed over to the empress's loyal supporters.[32] For her coronation in September 1762, Catherine II distributed 600,000 rubles of silver coins, spent 50,000 rubles, one pound of gold, and twenty pounds of silver, on the ceremony itself.[33] Catherine II's expenditure on herself was dwarfed by the lavish indulgence she showed her consorts and close aids. British and French diplomats came up with remarkably similar estimates of the amount of wealth the empress had granted her intimate favorites by the mid-1780s—around 90 million rubles, equal in the currency of the day to about 460 million francs, or US $ 2 billion in today's money.[34] The five Orlov brothers raked in about 17 million rubles while Gregory Potemkin was far ahead of the others in securing about 50 million rubles worth of state wealth.[35] Other favorites secured more modest fortunes ranging from 300,000 rubles to 10 million rubles.[36] Even 300,000 rubles was a huge sum for in mid-1700s Russia 1000 rubles a year was considered a gentleman's income.

Potemkin's career is particularly instructive when it comes to understanding Russian autocracy. In 1740, Russia had 50,000 noblemen out of a total population of about nineteen million. Of these 50,000 nobles, 82 percent owned less than 100 serfs, about 15 percent owned between 101 and 500 serfs, and only 3 percent owned more than 500 serfs.[37] Gregory Potemkin's father was a middle-ranking country noble who owned about 430 male serfs, which meant that the family were reasonably well off compared to most nobles but were nowhere near the higher nobility whose members owned tens of thousands of serfs. Gregory entered military service as an officer and was in the right place at the time of Catherine II's coup, which he supported. This led to substantial rewards for he was granted 18,000 rubles and 600 male serfs.[38] With this wealth, the Potemkin clan was elevated into the higher nobility, but Gregory wanted to rise to the top and that required further imperial favor. Here, Gregory's personal bravery, ability to work hard while appearing to disdain work, wit, charm, and sexual magnetism eventually got him into Catherine's intimate circle. From there he never looked back—rising to become the Viceroy of New Russia, War Minister, commander of all irregular forces including the Cossacks, created a Prince, and was presented with a gift of 100,000 rubles by the empress on his name days. It so happened that Prince Potemkin was, unlike many imperial favorites, actually competent, and successfully settled the Crimea, built Sevastopol, and refurbished the Black Sea fleet with twenty-four new Ships of the Line. While projecting himself as the epitome of masterly inactivity, Potemkin "ruined his health with the mammoth amount of work" he and his chancery of fifty civil servants carried out.[39] Such success had its enemies and led to accusations and rumors that his achievements were nothing more than smoke and mirrors designed to deceive a doting empress into continuing to pour rubles and serfs into Prince Potemkin's pockets. In actuality, while the prince did enrich himself, he "did not need to falsify towns and fleets" as verified by curious foreigners including the Habsburg Emperor Joseph II.[40] While Prince Potemkin was unusually successful in terms of the amount of material benefit that he drew from association with the empress, his case was fairly typical in terms of the need for imperial favor to secure social mobility within the service nobility.

Catherine II, of course, achieved a lot more than a well-deserved reputation for spending vast sums on her favorites. She also presided over a substantial increase in the number of landlords' serfs and state serfs. At the start of the her reign there were about four million landlords' serfs and 3.3 million state serfs while by its end there were some 6 million of the former and 5 million of the latter.[41] By the late 1700s, the top three serf owners counted 120,000 souls as human chattel.[42] Catherine II also transferred about 800,000 state serfs to landlords as rewards for service.[43]

While condemning hundreds of thousands of her subjects to enserfment on landlords' estates, spending some 90 million rubles on her consorts, and millions on procuring works of art from abroad, Catherine II was also fond of making enlightened noises about the need for reform. In 1767, an assembly convened to recommend an overhaul of the legal system, failed to do so, leaving it to Catherine II's edict or *nakaaz* to pronounce on the subject.[44] By 1782, Catherine was proud of having issued nearly 200 edicts/laws while the poor serfs who constituted nine-tenths of her subjects knew nothing of the reforms, which, at any rate, did nothing to improve their lot given that the service nobility had no interest in implementing Enlightenment-inspired mumbo jumbo.[45] One of these reforms involved increasing the number of provinces from 11 to 50, greatly stimulating the demand for governors and senior officials without, however, doing anything to secure a supply of competent functionaries. Catherine II was highly proficient at paper work and she seems to have realized that the lack of qualified and motivated civil servants meant nothing substantive be accomplished except through the sustained application of terroristic force a la Peter the Great. Catherine, while capable of destroying individuals who posed a direct threat to her position, does not seem to have had the stomach for prolonged efforts at coercion and "rarely dismissed ministers or servants."[46]

Assuming that Catherine II was serious about reforms, Pugachev's rebellion (October 1773-August 1774) sapped the political will needed to push them through. Pugachev, a Don Cossack, claimed to be the (dead) Czar Peter III, and soon rallied a force of 15,000–25,000 men. This army stormed and plundered estates, killed nobles, and pledged to overthrow the empress. Pugachev soon set up his own court and started behaving like an "Imperator". Once the imperial army was deployed, many of Pugachev's supporters found that they had urgent business to attend to at home and deserted and his closest comrades turned him in exchange for pardons. Thus, in 1796, by the time the enlightened reign of Catherine II ended, out of a total population of 36 million, 20 million were landlords' serfs and 14 million were state serfs, with both groups subjected to routine "coercion, arbitrary punishment, and sheer brutality."[47] The problem was that the Russian state had organized society "in such a way that it seemed impossible to deprive the nobility of their sustenance without bringing the state to the ground."[48] This nobility secured privileges that weakened its service obligations without, however, lessening its power over the serfs and remained the basic administrative power at the local level where the formal civil service structure did not penetrate. The czarist autocracy came to believe that it needed the nobles to preserve order and it wasn't until the 1860s that a czar would seriously put this assumption to the test.

RUSSIAN AUTOCRACY'S LONG NINETEENTH CENTURY, 1796–1917

Czar Paul (r. 1796–1801) hated his mother, Catherine II, for hanging on to the throne long after he had come of age. He was also harsh with the service nobility making them liable for corporal punishment and passing laws that limited working days for serfs. In his brief reign, he, among other things, tried to micromanage the realm and transferred or liquidated officials with astonishing frequency. Initially lenient towards those who were out of favor during his mother's reign, Paul quickly vented his anger on anyone he suspected of disloyalty. Soon the prisons were overflowing and peasants, who he favored at a rhetorical level, were dealt with harshly if they expressed discontent. In just five years, Paul transferred 600,000 state serfs to his favorite nobles and made every effort to extend serfdom as far south as possible. It seemed as if the czar wanted to simultaneously extend and intensify serfdom to exploit the resulting antagonisms so as to further his arbitrary power over the nobility.

The czar's arbitrariness, unprecedented transfer of state serfs to nobles, harshness and use of terror tactics were not the cause of his violent overthrow and assassination in March 1801. In fact, in the Russian context, Paul's willingness to use violent means to achieve his goals was actually a state virtue—fear of the czar, after all, was what ensured compliance in the past. Channeled properly, terror could have propelled Russia forward. Paul even tried to reform the Russian monarchy by making it one based on hereditary succession from father to eldest son rather than the arbitrary succession model that normally prevailed in continental bureaucratic empires. Military glory beckoned as a combined Austrian-Russian army led by General Suvarov drove the French out of Northern Italy, winning three major battles in 1798–99. It was, however, the Russian army that was alarmed by one of Paul's policies. Distrustful of the imperial guards, who had, after all, brought his mother to the throne and killed his father, Paul started creating a new military force recruited exclusively from czarist estates. The imperial guards realized that if Paul was successful, their position as a strategically placed minority would be compromised and their fate would be the same as the *streltsy*. A military coup in March 1801 was the result, Paul was killed, and his eldest son, Alexander I (r. 1801–1825) became the new czar.

Alexander I came to the throne by consenting to a conspiracy against his father that resulted in the latter's death. This is hardly remarkable for in an arbitrary and autocratic culture of power moral relationships are almost impossible to forge and maintain. Alexander I had a mania for secrecy and a tendency to be obstinate somewhat mitigated by a mercurial temperament. Like Catherine II, Alexander I projected himself as a reform-minded and benevolent sovereign who wanted to wield arbitrary power in a manner that would do justice to his subjects. Unlike Catherine II, the Napoleonic domination of Europe that culminated in the disastrous French invasion of Russia (1812), meant that Alexander I had to confront a very real menace to his empire's continued existence. The way to deal with the challenge posed by the French Revolution and its Napoleonic incarnation was to strengthen autocracy. Russia's diversity and size meant that only an autocratic ruler with arbitrary power could maintain order and introduce reforms. However, due to the absence of autonomous institutions such reforms needed autocracy to succeed. Any reform that weakened autocracy was a danger to the state.

Alexander I thus set about modernizing Russia by transforming its government "more than ever" into "a bureaucratic apparatus, headed by ministers, directly responsible to the emperor."[49] These ministers formed a committee, somewhat like a cabinet, but were burdened by petty details involving doing favors for powerful people while awaiting the czar's directives on matters of policy. In August 1809, the czar's most brilliant adviser, Count Speransky, persuaded him to make university education and qualification via tests mandatory for recruitment to senior grades.[50] The Council of State was formed on January 1, 1810, comprising "a number of appointed elder statesmen" who represented the "accumulated wisdom of the most experienced bureaucrats."[51] The ministerial-bureaucratic system steadily gained ascendancy over the provincial governors while the Ministry of Police and Special Chancery collected intelligence and rooted out disloyalty to the czar, with the former also dealing with public health issues such as inoculating 2 million people against small pox between 1806 and 1815.[52]

While Speransky retained the czar's confidence on administrative reform, General Aracheyev, war minister and, for the last years of his reign, practically Grand Vizier, dominated the military sphere. The czar was inspired by the discipline and efficiency that prevailed on Aracheyev's estates and wanted the model replicated throughout the empire. Aracheyev was always willing to implement the czar's wishes without a second thought and embarked upon building a network of military-farming settlements that, by 1825, were populated by 750,000 men and their families accounting for perhaps one-third of the peacetime strength of the Russian army.[53] The idea was that soldiers, nearly all of them conscripted serfs, would make better farmers on account of their military discipline and devotion to the czar, which had, only recently, crushed the Napoleonic hordes, catapulted Russia to the status of the most powerful country in Europe and the only global empire other than that of the British. Landowners in areas marked for military-agricultural settlements were compensated with lands elsewhere in the empire or through "monetary compensation, usually below the value of the property they were obliged to leave."[54] The military farms became "a state within the state" that reported to Aracheyev and through him to the czar who was, at any rate, losing the inclination to engage with domestic issues.[55] While those in charge of the new settlements seem to have benefited the soldiers forced to farm seem to have resented this reform and the brutality and corruption of those in charge. Military service was no picnic and, as mentioned above, half of Russia's soldiers never made it to retirement. Harsh conditions were, however, mitigated, by the communal nature of regimental life, honors, occasional plunder, and a solid vodka ration and exemption from farm labor. Mutinies in 1819 and 1831 eventually led to this policy being rolled back.

Ideologically, Alexander I became increasingly mystical and conservative in outlook and this change was reflected in the policies pursued by his cultural viziers, Golitsyn, Magnitsky and Runich. The Enlightenment was decidedly *passé* and as far as these men were concerned the Holy Bible contained everything that was worth knowing. Reaction was not unique to Russia for the Metternich system prevailed in central Europe and archconservatives in France would try and turn the clock back to 1789, contributing to the outbreak of the 1830 revolutions. The difference, however, was that whereas in the rest of Europe there existed autonomous or semi-autonomous institutions and social, economic and academic conglomerations capable of resisting absolutist states, Russia had none. Within reform-minded elite Russian civil service and military circles resentment grew at the czar's turn to a combination of not-so-sublime mysticism and tyranny. These elites had far greater exposure to the Enlightenment and wanted Russia to modernize constitutionally. Calling them liberals might be a misnomer as they lacked a proper constitutional program, central leadership, cohering ideology or even a list of demands. However, they derived some comfort and inspiration from the considerable autonomy granted to Poland, post-1815, and Finland, post-1809, and wanted similar reforms enacted in Russia itself. Frustrated and disappointed by Alexander I, Russia's liberals prepared for a violent revolution that would depose the czar and bring them to power.

The two major centers of the conspiracy were the capital, St. Petersburg, where the imperial guards were stationed, and Tulchin, in Southern Russia, where the Second Army was garrisoned. The two groups had different agendas in that the Second Army officers were animated by pan-Slavism and saw Russia becoming the leader of a democratic and federal Slavic federation. The imperial guards were elitist liberals in favor of constitutional monarchy. When Alexander I died unexpectedly, neither group was prepared to act. Since the czar died without an heir a succession crisis loomed. The czar's oldest brother, Grand Duke Constantine, had given up his right to the throne in order to be allowed to marry a Polish aristocrat of non-royal blood. The czar's younger brother, Nicholas, was a military man obsessed with fortifications, order and discipline. Secretive to the end, Alexander I had approved a protocol that nominated Nicholas as the rightful successor. The hitch was that this decision, taken in 1822, had not been communicated to Nicholas. The confusion as to who was to succeed gave the rebels a chance to improvise a coup by swearing allegiance to Constantine and getting their troops to rally behind them. The rebels' lack of leadership, Constantine's refusal to make a bid for the throne and Nicholas learning of the protocol collectively took the wind out of the revolution's sails. Loyal troops crushed the rebels, killing sixty or seventy of them and arresting the rest. Nicholas I (r.1825–1855) had thus begun his reign with the traditional Russian combination of conspiracy and violence. After the uprising was suppressed, Nicholas I proceeded to dispose of the rebels in a manner that set the tone for the rest of his reign:

> . . . the new Tsar chose to preside in detail over the humiliation of the defeated, question them individually and at length, censuring them, pleading with them, threatening them, as he saw fit, prescribing for each his cell in the fortress of St. Peter and St. Paul across the river from the Winter Palace, the way he was to be treated, how he was to be fed . . . he had established himself, at twenty-nine, as the chief policeman of his realm.[56]

Nicholas I was not just the chief policeman, but also the chief spy, the chief military engineer and the chief administrator. Like Alexander I and Aracheyev, Nicholas I idealized military life with its uniformity and discipline. Unlike Alexander, Nicholas I was hands on in his management of military affairs and went further than his predecessors in seeking to militarize civilian life. The committee of ministers, long taxed by minor matters of patronage, was prevented from acting as a cabinet by the czar's preference for dealing with each minister separately. The Imperial Chancellery, in addition to acting as the czar's secretariat, became the seat of a parallel government that dealt with everything from charities to state serfs. To examine pressing issues, ad hoc committees were constituted in secret and reported directly to the czar. Within the czar's personal bureaucracy was the Third Department, formally created on July 3, 1826, to address matters of state security.

The Third Department had wide-ranging responsibilities. The most vital, given the nature of the 1825 rebellion, was to collect information on civil servants and military officials and watch for signs of disloyalty. The loyalty of the apparatus thus secured, the Third Department kept watch on elements within Russian society who might be hostile to the czar. Foreigners visiting Russia were special targets for surveillance for the Third Department was always suspicious of liberal-minded outsiders infecting loyal Russians. In addition to targeting officials, renegades and foreigners, the Third Department prepared reports on developments within the empire, censored literature, and compiled statistical data as demanded by the czar. In operational terms the Third Department depended on a network of confidential informers to collect intelligence and had at its disposal an elite police force to carry out arrests, deportations and interrogations. This gendarmerie was not bound by ordinary laws and acted under special administrative orders sanctioned by the czar. The Third Department thus added another layer of oppression and surveillance while keeping the czar informed and added to the people's fear of the regime.

Fear, while it did secure obedience, did not gain for the regime active loyalty. Nicolas I was the first czar to have to engage with the question of national identity and integration in the Russian Empire. In earlier times a combination of Orthodox Christianity, ethno-cultural feeling and loyalty to the czar, had sufficed as an ideocratic complex. The rise of the French revolution and the ideology of nationalism, however, had complicated calculations. Educated elites were no longer enthused by tradition. The dozens of subject nationalities that chafed under Russian domination and wanted reform or freedom also needed pacifying. To meet these challenges Nicholas I eventually hit upon the doctrine of Official Nationality.

Official Nationality had three pillars—Orthodoxy, Autocracy and Nationality. Orthodoxy meant that being Greek Orthodox Christian was an essential indicator of loyalty to the regime. Autocracy emphasized the necessity for autocratic rule in a vast and diverse empire like Russia. Nationality referred to Russian culture and language and the need to Russianize subject populations through education and propaganda. The Orthodoxy component was handled by Prestasov, the Procurator of the Holy Synod (1836–55) who ensured that the Church rigidly upheld the czar's legitimacy and right to arbitrary power and in doing so guaranteed that it became "more and more like a regular government department" that reported directly to the czar.[57] Uvarov, the Education Minister from 1832 to 1849, handled the nationality and Russianization component, and it was reckoned that Nicholas I had more officials employed in censoring books than the "number of books published in a year."[58] The combination worked well enough for the autocratic czarist regime managed to stay on the right side of the national and religious sentiments of the 50% of its subjects who were ethnic Russian. For a substantial segment of society loyalty to the country became "more akin to a religious faith" and was exploited by the ostensibly anti-nationalist communist regime that succeeded the czars in 1917.[59] For non-Russians, especially the more rebellious communities, repression and forced indoctrination were prescribed. Thus, between 1800 and 1850, the Russian state deported about 5000 Polish nationalists every year.[60] It also crushed 148 peasant rebellions between 1826 and 1835.[61] These policies were evidently vindicated for when revolution swept the rest of Europe in 1848, the Russian Empire was not affected and famously, or infamously, assumed the role of the gendarme of Europe.

Beneath the formalism, activity and outward discipline of Nicholas I's centralized, ideological police state, lay considerable chaos and oppression born of the arbitrary nature of the apparatus and those it governed. The compliance thus secured was at best "negative, or passive, obedience" compounded by an "abdication of responsibility."[62] Russia's administration was for all practical purposes "the colonial service of an occupying power."[63] The czar's arbitrary power, the secret police and its network of informers and the stifling atmosphere of ideological conformity meant that in "the Russian system nobody at all knew where he was: nobody therefore dared move"[64] unless forced to do so. Since most subjects were not in a position to stand up to the local officials who oppressed them, inducements in the form of bribes and gifts had to be given at nearly all levels of government. Each and every ministry and department was trapped in a web of deceit and double-dealing from which there was no escape. Those in charge of managing state serfs plundered and abused their charges as a matter of right. The Third Department's network of informers told officials what they wanted to hear and settled personal scores. At local levels salaries were so small and powers so poorly defined that officials considered it their right to live off the land. At the senior-most levels governors and advisers stole on a grand scale and neglected official business in favor of petty patronage and self-aggrandizement. Even the military, which the czar adored and lavished resources and attention on, personally designing new uniforms and fortifications, was falling further and further behind other European armies in training, organization and firepower. The czar, blinded by the vastness of his empire, the opulence of his court, the increasing numbers of his subjects, would blunder into the Crimean War of 1853–56, only to realize too late that his attempts to drill the entire country and run the state through ad hoc committees and personal ADCs, had left it vulnerable to defeat.

For all his conservatism and mania for control, Nicholas I was quite possibly the first czar to groom his successor and pay close attention to the crown prince's education and experience. Indeed, throughout the 1600s and 1700s, Russia's rulers had sought to isolate their successors out of fear of being overthrown. This fear was rooted in experience for Peter the Great killed his own son, Catherine II liquidated Peter III and Ivan VI, Alexander I was party to the conspiracy that overthrew and killed his father Paul I, and Nicholas I saw his reign begin with another crisis of succession that could have led to civil war. In spite of this, Nicholas I succeeded in maintaining a moral relationship with his successor, Alexander II (r. 1855–81). Alexander II received a broad liberal education, was sent to study the Russian countryside for himself so that he may acquaint himself with the conditions in which his subjects lived. While Nicholas I was away from the capital, the crown prince acted as regent. A sound education, practical experience, and first-hand knowledge of his subjects, convinced Alexander II that Russia was in dire need of reforms. The central reform that needed to be implemented if Russia was to modernize and avoid humiliations like the Crimean War was the abolition of serfdom.

In expressing the desire to emancipate the serfs Alexander II was hardly being radical or even reformist. For almost a century Russia's autocrats had lamented the evils of serfdom, especially the injustice and oppression it perpetuated, and the huge price Russia had to pay in terms of the institutionalized leveling poverty imposed on the agriculture of the country. Moral repulsion, comparable to what American leaders felt about slavery, and Enlightenment rhetoric did lead to minor tinkering and passing laws was a favorite pastime for some rulers even while they increased the number of landlords' serfs. Russia's rulers did not attack the system itself for it was feared that emancipation would lead to anarchy, economic collapse and the overthrow of czarism.

Alexander II, however, was genuinely appalled and determined to use his autocratic power to push the nobility towards accepting the emancipation of serfs in exchange for monetary compensation for their losses in terms of ownership of serfs and land. If this was not done then the hundreds of minor rebellions that plagued Russia in the first half of the 1800s might well become general rural unrest. In March 1856, the czar made his wishes known to the nobility and asked them to develop proposals to emancipate the serfs before the serfs started emancipating themselves. The initial disbelief was understandable given how earlier rulers had piously exhorted against the evils of serfdom but once the czar's resolve was to act was accepted the nobility fell in line. By 1858, all provinces had formed committees to discuss proposals on the best way in which to implement the autocrat's will. These provincial committees reported to a central committee of civil servants convened by the czar in the imperial capital.

Hardly anyone dared defend serfdom now that the czar's seriousness in enacting reforms was no longer in doubt. As the wheels of the committees moved, Russia fifty million serfs awaited emancipation while the nobility demanded compensation while reformers thought up a new system of local administration that would go into effect after emancipation.

In February 1861 emancipation went into effect. The way it worked was that the peasant communes gained ownership over lands while serfs received basic civil rights such as freedom to marry and buy and sell without the landlords' interference. The serfs were now exempt from forced labor on private estates. In exchange, peasant communes would make redemption payments to their former owners on a collective basis. Landlords complained that the czar had forced them to accept too little compensation for giving up too much land and, in fact, by 1911, nobles owned half the amount of land they had in 1861. Ex-serfs complained that the redemption payments were too high and they had received too little land. On balance, state serfs benefited more than landlords' serfs and a class of independent farmers slowly began to emerge. In 1864, an independent lower judiciary that conducted trial by jury was introduced and in 1866 a system of representative local government in which landlords had about two-thirds of the seats (the *zemstvos*) was introduced. Alongside reforms on the civil side, Alexander reduced reliance on corporal punishment in the military and cut the minimum service obligation from twenty-five years to sixteen years. In 1874, universal conscription was introduced to create a military reserve though the amount of compulsory military service went down as educational level went up. Thus, an illiterate peasant could serve up to six years while and educated townsmen had to serve only six months.

Alexander II's reforms were pushed through with remarkably little organized resistance or dissent—in stark contrast to the difficulties that the United States of America faced in terms of resolving the question of slavery. While democratic America had to fight a civil war that consumed 600,000 lives to liberate three million slaves, autocratic Russia managed to emancipate fifty million serfs with little or no violence. Emancipation in Russia was followed by a new judicial system and local government system, also implemented on the czar's orders. Where Alexander II drew the line was at reforms that might dilute the czar's arbitrary power. The czar believed that the preservation of autocracy was vital to the success of the reforms he had introduced. Thus, there would be no national equivalent to the *zemstvos*, no fiscal autonomy in terms of collection of local taxes by local governments. There was no question even of a cabinet government for Alexander II allowed only the finance and defense ministers to have access to other ministries—everybody else reported personally to the czar who thus retained a synoptic view of the administration of the country. Power-sharing or autonomy within the empire, as the Poles learned the hard way in 1863, or as thousands of students found out in 1873–74 when they headed to the rural areas to sensitize the peasants to the need for further liberation, were also non-starters. In the former case, Russianization was intensified while in the latter the students were attacked, betrayed to the police and deceived by the "sly, suspicious, envious, venal and drunken" peasants they had come to save.[65] Frustration in radical circles grew and some decided to kill the czar. There were failed assassination attempts on the czar in 1866, 1867 and 1879, and a successful one in 1881.

Alexander III (r. 1881–1894) felt that his father's reforms had gone too far and that there was a need to rein in the local governments and peasants. The local governments came under the increasingly strict control of the Ministry of Interior and centrally appointed land commandants gained in strength. Censorship was vigorously imposed on newspapers, universities lost control over academic appointments and were placed under imperial inspectors, and Russianization was imposed upon all nationalities, not just those that rebelled against the regime. The czar's new secret police, the *Okrhana*, received imperial sanction to harass, intimidate, and liquidate enemies of the regime and among those executed was the older brother of the future leader of the Bolshevik revolution. The limited gains made in terms of private property in land were contained. Thus, by 1894, peasants could no longer mortgage their land even after having paid their redemption money in full, and were prevented from purchasing consolidated plots.

Nicholas II (r. 1894–1917), combined conservatism with weakness and indecision at a time when the Russian Empire needed strength in leadership.[66] By 1897, the Russian Empire's nobility was 1.2 million strong, the central government had about 42,000 administrative and judicial officials, 44,000 military officers, and 10,000 gendarmes.[67] The *zemstvos* had about 105,000 employees while there were 78,000 state school teachers and 22,000 state medical staff.[68] The Russian administrative, military and professional elite was thus small compared to the size of the total population. The empire was developing, though such development depended heavily on state investment in and ownership of economic assets, as had been the case since Peter the Great. The growth in economic and social complexity was not accompanied by changes in government structure or behavior. For all practical purposes, therefore, Russia continued to be "governed as though it was the Tsar's private estate. . . ."[69] Even defeat at the hands of Japan (1904–6) in the Far East, bloody revolution in 1905, and humiliation in 1908 when Austria-Hungary annexed Bosnia-Herzegovina, failed to convince the czar that reform was needed. Such concessions as were made under the pressure of war and rebellion in 1905–6 were rolled back once the crisis passed.[70] The czar dismissed demands for diminution of autocracy as senseless daydreams. Heedless to good advice from his interior minister that Russia desperately needed peace, the czar, like other European leaders, blundered into the First World War in 1914. This decision would spell the end of the czarist system as the discipline of the army broke down under the relentless pressures of total war. In March 1917, the czar was forced to abdicate when his generals made it clear that they could no longer guarantee the loyalty of the army. About seven months later, radical social-ists led by Vladimir Lenin seized the opportunity to overthrow the pro-visional government and proclaim a communist revolution in Russia that they hoped would trigger similar upheavals elsewhere ushering in a global workers' utopia.

THE SOVIET UTOPIA, 1917–91

The communist revolutionaries who seized power after the fall of czarism were determined to build a utopia and use Russia as the launching pad for a global revolution that would usher in an era of equality and brotherhood for the human race. The state, the market, ownership, the class system, and religion would wither away before the march of progress that led to the com-munist utopia and the End of History. In actuality, Lenin and his fellow revo-lutionaries would succeed in replacing an autocratic police state legitimized by divine sanction with a totalitarian police state legitimized by a univer-sal ideology of redemption. Private property, never strong under the czars, would cease to exist. State enterprises, critical to the economy in czarist Rus-sia, would dramatically expand in scope and organization. Land, already organized on a communal or quasi-communal basis would be collectivized into larger farms where peasants would become employees. Bureaucracies and party cadres would multiply beyond the wildest expectations of those who launched a revolution that aimed to create an ordered society without a state. And above all else, police state terror tactics would kill tens of mil-lions and traumatize an entire nation to a degree that even the most vicious and arbitrary of Russia's old regime autocrats would have recoiled in horror. The Soviet Union was perhaps the most arbitrary state in human history, alongside Pol Pot's Cambodia or Maoist China, and like the despotic rulers of Russia's imperial past, the communists saw the population as "merely the building material for the establishment of a grand empire."[71]

Lenin, who is often exonerated by those sympathetic to the revolution for excesses committed under the Bolshevik regime, "seized the private property of the country" and ordered the destruction of files pertaining to ownership.[72] While a civil war (1918–20) raged between the communists and their opponents that claimed the lives of 10 million people, Lenin held two trump cards that ultimately saw the Reds through to victory. One was that the communists had seized the state gold reserves worth over one bil-lion gold rubles. Lenin decided how this wealth was to be spent and "much of it was dispensed on the authority of a simple note or even a word" from him.[73] The other was that with the collapse of czarism military officers came to see the Bolsheviks as the only faction with the cohesion and leader-ship to end the war and restore order to Russia. All told, some 75,000 czar-ist military officers, including 800 generals, joined the Red Army and thus help provide it with the leadership and expertise it needed to prevail.[74]

Guns and gold helped the Bolsheviks gain power and throw their ene-mies on the defensive. The Cheka, successor of the *Okhrana* and precursor of the KGB, was a major force in keeping the Bolsheviks in power. Political opponents were wiped out, some times in reprisal attacks such as those that followed an attempt on Lenin's life in August 1918. At the same time, entire groups of people were marked for destruction, either driven into exile or subjected to ferocious oppression. The Cossacks, who numbered about 3 million in 1897, were one such group and Lenin ordered the extermination of one-third of their population. Lenin's successor, Joseph Stalin (r. 1924–1953) would exterminate about 30 percent of Kazakhs and 15 percent of Ukrainians, as well as 5 million prosperous farmers and their families dur-ing collectivization in the 1930s.

Regarding collectivization, "In January 1930, Molotov planned the destruction of the kulaks, who were divided into three categories".[75] The first was to be "immediately eliminated," the second to be herded into concentration camps, the third, to be deported.[76] In 1930–31, about "1.68 million people were deported east and north" and "Within months Sta-lin's and Molotov's plan had led to 2,200 rebellions involving more than 800,000 people. Kaganovich and Mikoyan led expeditions into the coun-try- side with brigades of OGPU [*Obyedinyonnoye Gosudarstvennoye Politicheskoye Upravleniye* or Joint State Political Directorate] troopers and armoured trains like warlords. The magnates' handwritten letters to Stalin ring with the fraternal thrill of their war for human betterment against unarmed peasants. . . ."[77] By 1937, about 5.7 million households, or nearly 15 million people, "had been deported, many of them dead."[78] Real and imagined enemies of the regime had much to fear from informers employed by state security, whose ranks swelled to 11 million by 1952.[79] Party members were especially targeted for signs of disloyalty and it was generally assumed that telephones, public places, offices, and housing units were kept under surveillance.

The Party was the heart and brain of the system. Most of the important appointments in all walks of life were reserved for Party members and thus the state apparatus was a substantially politicized bureaucracy. There was no question of impartiality or neutrality given that those who resisted the official line were automatically rebels or subversives, destined to be crushed by the march of historical determinism embodied by the Party-State. The existence of the Party was, nonetheless, somewhat of an embarrassment and a negation of the great optimism at the time of the revolution that a new kind of harmonious society was being called into existence. The Party was the ruling class of a classless society, the privileged elite of an egalitarian utopia. Right from the inception of the communist regime in Russia special privileges were extended to the Party elite. While the Party and its privileges provided rich fodder for the Russian sense of humor they were also drivers of corruption, inefficiency, cynicism and institutionalized poverty. Country houses and estates left behind by the czarist nobility were converted into residences for the Party elite and senior functionaries. The Kremlin itself played host to the top leadership. Special medical and educational facilities were available for the elite as was access to a wider range of food, drink, entertainment and private transport.

The composition of the Party was a matter of some interest given that it claimed to represent the working classes. In July 1973, out of 15 million Party members, 14.7 percent were listed as collective farmers, 40.7 percent as workers, and 44.6 percent as "employees."[80] The "employees" category included white-collar workers such as civil servants, academicians, managers, engineers and the like. There was, however, a catch in that "a Party member is listed as a 'worker' throughout his Party career if that was his status when he joined."[81] Consequently, many top functionaries were listed as "workers" even though they had "long since left working-class jobs."[82] Within the Party politics was all about getting your people in the right jobs, developing a more powerful network of patronage so that you could do more favors, such as speeding things up, for clients. The most powerful persons in the Soviet Union were thus the General Secretary of the Communist Party of the Soviet Union, followed by his cronies in the Politburo and the regional party bosses. The operation of this system was quite similar to other arbitrary states. The ruler had his favorites, each favorite had his clique, and each clique competed for important positions within the Party-State nexus. In Stalin's time, only the General Secretary decided important matters and those who got on his worse side ended up dead or in concentration camps. One of his favorites was the spy chief Beria—a sadist, rapist and murderous sociopath who took immense pleasure in his work and was ultimately liquidated by Stalin's successors.[83] Of these successors, Brezhnev (r. 1964–82) proved far more easygoing and let Party discipline relax leaving regional bosses, many of whom were non-Russian, to carve out their own estates.[84]

The Party was not just an apparatus through which power was exercised and patronage distributed. It was also a Church with its prophets, apostles, martyrs, believers, teleology, and eschatology. Clearly inspired by the binary world-view of St. Augustine, the Party advocated Marxism-Leninism as the official creed and herald of the Communist Millennium. Ultimate triumph over liberalism, nationalism, capitalism, and traditionalism, was assured by elevating Marxist pseudo-science to the status of revealed wisdom. Party policy was to saturate the Soviet Union with propaganda that proclaimed the virtues and inevitable triumph of Marxism-Leninism and the vices that would lead to the ultimate demise of class, market, and state. The Communist Party justified its excesses and the need for its "'dictatorship' through purity of faith. Their scriptures were the teachings of Marxism-Leninism, regarded as 'scientific' truth. Since ideology was so important every leader had to be, or seem to be—an expert on Marxism-Leninism" so that they "spent their weary nights studying to improve their esoteric credentials, dreary articles on dialectical materialism."[85] Lenin was the focal point of this policy and his images and sayings were everywhere. Invocation and channeling of Lenin was essential if you wanted to make a speech or a presentation. Even technical specialists were obliged to explain how, for instance, computers worked better in a classless society or how Lenin's foresight had guided the Soviet Union's scientific development. Participation in rituals was compulsory and Party members were responsible for the political education of non-members in dreary and increasingly despised sermonizing.[86] The Marxist-utopia project sought to replace Orthodox Christianity with belief in "the no less absolutist" and monopolizing ideological fervor that glorified humanity "though there was little 'humanity' evident when some of these ideas became a ghastly reality for hundreds of millions of people."[87] Doublethink and double-speak were not and are not figments of George Orwell's imagination. They were and are helpful survival tools in any arbitrary state and essential in a totalitarian ideological police state such as the Soviet Union.

Lenin-mania, the Party-State complex, arbitrary rule from above, and the sheer terror of those caught in the system, were the main components of the Soviet Union's version of Russia's culture of power. Through such practices, the Soviet leadership pursued goals that would have been dear to the czars—territorial expansion and military preponderance over actual and potential rivals in Eurasia. The Soviet Union ran a permanent war economy and mobilized its manpower and natural resources to maintain a military numerous enough and strong enough to breakout of what it considered to be capitalist encirclement.[88] In a system as tightly controlled as the Soviet, it was possible to spend 12–25 percent of GNP on defense and defense-related enterprises and maintain an army that dwarfed others. This military-first approach did save the Soviet Union from defeat at the hands of Nazi Germany in the Second World War. This was in spite of Stalin's brutal purge of the Soviet military elite in 1937–8, which led to the execution or incarceration of nearly 37,000 officers, including more than 400 of the rank of Brigadier or above.[89] The initial confusion and paralysis that afflicted the Red Army was due in large measure to the purge, which had diminished the competence of the military officer corps, and the appointment of political commissars to oversee the fighting units and report signs of disloyalty. Soviet losses included some 20 million dead, the destruction of tens of thousands of villages and nearly two thousand cities and towns, and the devastation or displacement of Soviet industries. After victory, the occupation of Eastern Europe became permanent as did the imposition of the Soviet system on societies that were more advanced than the Soviet Union and unwilling to adopt its norms. Purges and liquidations soon followed, as did military interventions to put down rebellions against the Soviet Union's local stooges. These stooges were themselves trapped. For example, Eugen Loebl, Czech Deputy Minister for Foreign Trade in the Communist Party government formed after the Second World War was arrested and purged. Required to confess his crimes against communism,

Loebl found that "When I confessed . . . I always had to change the confession—because what was one day a crime, was the next day not a crime. But it was the Soviet political line."[90]

The Soviet Union did have several substantial achievements to its credit. Bureaucratic red tape notwithstanding, practically the entire population had some kind of housing. And while the quality of housing was poor by Western standards it was a big step up compared to what Russians were historically used to. Basic literacy was universal as was access to rudimentary health care facilities, though Soviet medicine lagged behind the West. Soviet citizens, from the 1960s onwards, also came to enjoy access to radio sets, televisions and refrigerators. After Stalin, the leadership relied much less on terror, went so far as to denounce the excesses of Stalinism (1956) and stopped employing genocide and starvation as instruments of state policy. Soviet achievements in sports as well as high technology, most notably in the Space Race, won global recognition. By 1985, the Soviet Union had 1.2 million researchers, over 2 million highly-trained technical personnel, spent 2 percent of its GNP on research, and rewarded its toilers of the mind with higher salaries, social prestige and settlement in elite communities.[91] The Soviet Union was quite effective when it came to organizing big projects and seeing them through to final outcomes for costs could be overcome, transferred or hidden. Where the Soviet Union failed quite badly was at managing day-to-day affairs, a front where shortages and corruptions were rife.

Michael Gorbachev, General Secretary from 1985 to 1991, sheds light on how the top leadership functioned. In summer 1982, Gorbachev proposed that the Politburo should establish an economic policy commission to propose reforms. Brezhnev's aides immediately thought that Gorbachev was trying to expand his power base through the creation of a new commission and so there was no follow up. Gorbachev kept pushing and met with more skepticism for no one believed that he was actually desirous of bringing about economic reforms. Brezhnev eventually decided to placate Gorbachev by letting him set up a section or department to examine this issue. Brezhnev's brain, moreover, was Chernenko, who had "always been at Brezhnev's side, anticipating all his wishes, his confidante, that is to say, his shadow. A powerful weapon in his hands was the omnipotent Party apparatus."[92] The Party apparatus did not want "to let go of power" for the functionaries who "determined targets and allotted resources" were seen as "tsar and god, potentate and benefactor."[93] Those in power "needed the shortages to be maintained" for without them their "monopoly, along with its fellow travelers- bribes, graft, mutual favors and so forth—would simply collapse."[94] Gorbachev realized that the Soviet Union could not continue to live as it was used to doing and felt that without reform of the political system and party bureaucracy it was not possible to bring about meaningful economic reforms. This analysis had merit, but without the General Secretary's autocratic sway any reforms that diluted central executive power would produce open factionalism and tear the Party apart. Since the Party *was* the state, such splintering posed an existential threat to the Soviet Union. Reforms, as they entailed weakening autocracy, derailed the entire system and led to Soviet collapse in 1991. The loss of territory in Central Asia and Eastern Europe was compounded by socioeconomic disintegration in Russia. The utopian project had ended in meltdown.

THE AFTERMATH OF UTOPIA AND THE RESTORATION OF AUTOCRACY

By 1998, Russia's GDP was about half of what it had been in 1991. Pensioners were economically wiped out. One fourth of the population said they lived in a "desperate situation."[95] Between 1995 and 2000 the number of books published fell by 65 percent, the circulation of newspapers fell by 80 percent and published magazines lost 90 percent of their readership.[96] Inequality rose prodigiously and hit home in intimate ways. In Soviet times nearly all children went for summer camp and an annual vacation was within the reach of most families. By the mid-1990s both had become "unusual" luxuries beyond the reach of all but the super-rich.[97] Economic, social and cultural collapse was accompanied by chaos and criminalization on an unprecedented scale. By the mid-1990s some 5,500 large criminal organization and 200,000 criminal groups were running amok in Russia.[98] Practically all retailers in cities paid protection money, as did four-fifths of banks and private companies.[99] One-fifth of petroleum output, one third of metals production, and seven-tenths of raw material shipped to Kaliningrad via Lithuania, were smuggled.[100]

The strip-mining of Russia's productive assets via vouchers that were extorted from ordinary Russians by gangsters working for politically connected oligarchs had no parallel in history. Thus, United Energy Systems, which produced as much power as a US\$ 50 billion power company was privatized for US\$ 200 million.[101] Other assets, worth billions, such as mines, metal works, and mechanical works were privatized for a few millions apiece. Those that benefited from this plunder, the oligarchs, rewarded the ruler of democratic Russia, Boris Yeltsin, by pouring US\$ 100 million into his 1996 re-election campaign, against the official spending limit of US\$ 3 million per candidate.[102] Phony banks set up by former officials and corrupt businessmen looted their depositors at will. A handful of well-connected individuals benefited, effectively becoming nobility albeit without any obligation of service. While a few made billions, real wages fell by 60 percent between 1991 and 1998, six out of ten workers were not paid on time and the real minimum wage was 20 percent of its 1991 level.[103] A 1995 survey found that 80 percent of respondents said that they lived in poverty.[104] In the countryside, agricultural output fell by one-third between 1992 and 1998, and while the government distributed title deeds to individual farmers most of the agricultural land remained under the control of "former *kolkhoz* in which individual farmers formally own shares."[105] The exact "meaning of these shares is ambiguous, and they are difficult to convert into property and cannot be used as collateral" while the "shareholders have little power to affect farm policy and change managers" for the farms depend on state support.[106] Equally galling for a society that prided itself on its scientific and cultural accomplishments, was that by the late-1990s, 32 percent of researchers and 49 percent of teachers lived below the poverty line, while spending on research fell by more than two-thirds and a million highly-educated Russians migrated abroad.[107] In such chaotic conditions it was hardly surprising that Russia's civil servants made the extraction of "as much personal revenue as possible" their top priority and helped politically connected people transfer wealth abroad.[108] If cynicism was a serious problem in the Soviet bureaucracy, it became overwhelming in the 1990s, with some US$ 33 billion a year being paid in bribes as civil servants "felt free of any moral obligations both to the public and to themselves due to ideological vacuum, overwhelming corruption from top to bottom" and unrelenting abuse of power.[109] Much of the bureaucratic leadership, especially at the regional level, was still a leftover from the Soviet period and had adapted to the anarchy that followed the 1991 collapse.[110]

Russia's descent into chaos was checked not by the gradual operation of procedural democracy and the emergence of a sustainable market economy but by ex-Soviet intelligence and security remnants (the *siloviki*) that had managed to reorganize themselves after the collapse. Leading the *siloviki* in their state-building mission was the Federal Security Bureau (FSB), the successor to the KGB. Serving and retired KGB/FSB officials, appalled by the ruin inflicted on their country by democracy and economic shock therapy, emerged as the only group with the organization and sense of loyalty to the state needed to restore order. Acting like a corporation or brotherhood on the basis of unquestioning mutual support, the *siloviki* emerged as a super-mafia. The lower ranking members of the 600,000 strong state security apparatus are blindly loyal to their bosses and are referred to as "serving people" in a style reminiscent of czarist Russia.[111] Led by Vladimir Putin, Russia's ruler since 2000, the *siloviki* became the new ruling class capable and willing to take on the oligarchs, rebuild Russia's military, restore national pride and ensure a measure of social stability. The new elite answers to Putin and operates above any law or contractual limitations and is thus immune to routine accountability. Through the use of coercion, Putin convinced oligarchs to support and subsidize government ventures, ranging from paying arrears of wages to workers and disbanding private security forces, to paying for building infrastructure for international sporting events hosted by Russia.[112] *Siloviki* control over the defense production sector was ratified in 2006 and was being contemplated for other key sectors while the state share in the total economy stood at 50 percent by 2009.[113] Hiring in the civil service picked up as the central government expanded its programs in the regions with the number of civil servants rising from 527,000 in 2001 to 878,000 in 2011.[114] Putin's restoration of autocracy mediated by a service-based elite answerable to the ruler, expansion of the state-operated economy, prioritization of the military and defense research, funneling the fruits of higher energy prices into welfare and boosting economic activity, are consistent with the practices of earlier Russian regimes.[115]

The rise of the service elite was accompanied by re-centralization.[116] In 2000, Putin launched a program of legal harmonization demanding that regions bring their laws in conformity with central government legislation and the national constitution. Presidential envoys to the regions were appointed to report directly to Putin on this and other issues. Though the volume of sub-legislation posed difficulties and caused complaints to emerge from Putin's supporters that the process was taking too long, 4138 legal acts were successfully amended in the North-West Federal District alone.[117] In 2005, Putin felt confident enough to restore the Council of State of czarist times, now called the Public Chamber, to advise the government. The Public Chamber has 126 members, one third chosen by Putin from eminent citizens and the rest elected by this appointed one third.[118] In Russia, an autocratic service state is being resurrected with considerable success after a period of social and economic catastrophe that has set the country back decades. The pain and humiliation of the 1990s, much of its blamed on Western advice and meddling, Gorbachev's naiveté, and Yeltsin's corruption and incompetence, set the stage for authoritarian rule albeit with a populist touch that employs democratic procedures as window dressing. If sustained, the gains made under Putin's leadership could well translate into a durable new "gathering" of Russia and thus vindicate its own traditions of governance.

CONCLUSION: THE RESILIENCE OF RUSSIAN AUTOCRACY AND THE SERVICE STATE

Russia's culture of power and historical experience of governance are similar to continental bureaucratic empires in West Asia, South Asia and East Asia. In the czarist Russian autocracy the country was the personal estate of the ruler. To manage this estate the autocrat relied on a nobility of service. This nobility of service was responsible for maintaining order and collecting taxes on the estates granted to it. Social position was determined by royal favor and entry into the higher nobility was restricted to the czar's favorites. In the absence of primogeniture, the service nobility never developed into a feudal aristocracy in the Western European sense, though it was superficially Europeanized by Peter the Great and his successors. Over time, the growth in the size of the nobility from about 50,000 in the mid-1700s (total population 20 million) to 1.20 million by the 1890s (total population about 130 million) meant that the loyalist social base grew faster than the population. It also meant that practically everybody who, in theory, had the capacity to resist czarist autocracy was dependent upon it. The Russian nobility did not even rise to the defense of serfdom once the czar decided to grant emancipation for there was no concept of privilege autonomous of the imperial will. The "pompous courtiers" that swarmed around the czar, observed the Marquis de Custine who visited Nicholas I's Russia, "were no more than slaves" that "could be made or broken in a day."[119] Their insecurity sustained and aggravated the "savage intensity" of competition characterized by "cruelty and officiousness towards underlings combined with the most extravagant obsequiousness towards people higher in position . . ."[120] for the czar's favor. The behavior of successive rulers, such as Catherine II Alexander I and Nicholas I, their formal evocation of Enlightenment pieties or the need for discipline, left little doubt that the czarist state "exemplified arbitrary rule . . . by ignoring all rules and consistently defying expectation, and by regularly changing the rules it constantly broke."[121]

Of the czar's servants, military officers played a vital role in the politics and administration of the country. This, again, corresponds to the praetorian cultures of power that prevailed in Persia, India, and the Middle East for the military was Russia's most organized entity. Successive rulers lavished attention and resources on it and gave its needs priority over other sectors. Russia's attempts at modernization, in czarist as well as Soviet times, were driven by defense needs to the neglect of the civilian economy. The Russian military repeatedly played the role of powerbroker and intervened as a matter of right in politics, often determining the succession of czars. The loyalty of the military to the czar depended on the czar's personality and his treatment of the forces deployed at or close to the center. Peter the Great broke the power of the *streltsy* and was idolized by the army, but many of his successors had a hard time asserting themselves against the imperial guards regiments that he created. It was not that the military opposed arbitrary rule, indeed it was its ultimate sanction and guarantor of autocracy. However, the ruler had to be very careful lest he disappointed the military or led it to feel that it was not his or her top priority.

Succession in Russia itself followed a pattern similar to that of the arbitrary monarchies of Asia. From Kievan Rus onwards, orderly succession was very difficult to manage. Brothers, uncles, sons, and nephews all felt entitled to a share of estates and to claim the throne. Naked power in the form of violence and conspiracy, rather than hereditary succession on the pattern of the absolute or feudal monarchies of Western Europe, determined who came out on top. Czarist Russia was no different in that the rulers couldn't even trust their own children and immediate relatives and could have profited greatly from Kautilya's advice, contained in the *Arthashastra*, about the need to keep family under surveillance and control, eliminating children found lacking in loyalty. In an arbitrary monarchy the wealth and power to be gained by occupying the throne combined with the absence of any right or status independent of the ruler's will destroys trust and creates a winner-take-tall mentality in politics. In contrast, even in an absolute monarchy like Louis XIV's France, the privileges of the nobility and clergy including considerable immunity from royal taxation, had to be respected by the ruler. In Russia, there was no legitimate right to autocratic power as that power itself created all rights. And even if a ruler was not overthrown and killed by his close relatives in cahoots with the military, assassination by malcontents was the other route out of imperial office.

In the absence of legitimate means of opposing the ruler, all opposition became rebellion. Rural discontent took the form of hundreds of localized uprisings against the excesses of the service nobility or the central government. Occasionally, these rebellions coalesced though conflicts within the rebel camp and superior imperial military power almost invariably carried the day. The Russian educated elite aspired to state service but some took up the cause of resisting czarist oppression, organizing themselves into revolutionary movements and assassinating officials as and when possible. While some lobbed bombs, the more typical response was to run away. Russians serfs fled their masters, Old Believers fled persecution, bourgeois liberals fled abroad, others ended up in internal exile, and the more religiously inclined took refuge in monasteries.

Religiously, Russia was a Christian county, the czar ruled by divine sanction, and the rich ceremonial culture of the Orthodox confession provided a spiritual center to Russian life. The Church organization itself, however, was increasingly an extension of the imperial state apparatus. Church administration for the last two hundred years of czarist rule was in the hands of lay officials appointed by the czar. The Church's wealth and offices were at the czar's disposal. There was little question of remonstrance after Peter the Great though later rulers did not seek to humiliate and intimidate the Church to the same extent. The Church was the propaganda instrument of the czarist regime and paid to legitimize the ruler and his actions projecting the czar as a divinely-guided and infallible overlord with Imperial Russia as the true successor of Byzantium representing a Third Rome.

Were it not for the First World War and the breakdown of czarist military power that it brought about, the Bolshevik revolution would never have been successful. Absent that tragedy, Russia might have evolved into a more progressively inclined autocracy had an enlightened ruler succeeded Nicholas II though it does not seem at all likely that it would have become a constitutional monarchy or developed a liberal-bourgeois society. The communists were themselves products of Russia's ideocratic and arbitrary culture of power and converted the czarist empire into the estate of Party elites. The General Secretary wielded arbitrary and autocratic power over the Party apparatus. Democratic centralism meant that the rest of the Party followed the lead set by its central cabinet, the Politburo. The civilian bureaucracy, the military, the internal security apparatus, and the professions, were politicized as Party membership or approval were vital to progression up the ladder. There was no question of private property or civil society or lawful resistance to the regime being tolerated. Compared to the czarist regime, the communists were utterly inhumane in their treatment of political or intellectual opposition and killed tens of millions and imprisoned millions more of their people. Such crimes were justified, indeed encouraged, by the ideological extremism of the Party under Lenin and Stalin. More so than czarist Russia, the Soviet Union was a hard ideological state saturated with pro-regime propaganda masquerading as social science. When the communist variant of ideocratic arbitrary rule collapsed in the late-1980s and early-1990s Russia lost much of her Central Asian and Eastern European empire and went into a domestic freefall.

Democracy meant internal chaos and international humiliation and set the stage for the reincarnation of the Russian service state, this time dominated by the *siloviki* and led by Putin, a former secret service officer.[122] Restrictions on media, the subordination of the oligarchs to the security elite, disciplining of the political system through securing a pliant majority in the parliament, and expansion of the central bureaucracy and state enterprises, and strong, ruthless, leadership, restored sanity to the proceedings. Between 2001 and 2008, Russia's GNP grew by about two-thirds, returning to the level it enjoyed in 1990 by 2007. This was not just regime publicity for the International Monetary Fund (IMF) and the World Bank (WB) confirmed that by 2010–11 Russia was once again one of the top ten economies in terms of the nominal size of its GNP, and by 2012–13 was, in terms of Purchasing Power Parity, the largest economy in Europe.[123] Though much of Russia's growth was driven by energy prices, Putin ensured that the growth was better distributed leading to increases in real wages and a 50 percent drop in the poverty level. While the *siloviki* regime is no longer as popular today as it was during its first decade in power the absence of credible alternatives and terrible experiences of the 1990s make it unlikely that it will be replaced anytime soon though, if Putin becomes a liability for the state security brotherhood he may well be replaced. Russia's steady resurgence is following a pattern similar to rallies in its past with the service state reordering and regimenting society to maximize national power and reclaim lost prestige for in Russia the state has long been an "overwhelming" force "arbitrarily imposed, commanding total obedience" except for "when deceit and trickery" enable "evasion", "feared but not respected" even under the most exceptional rulers.[124]

7   The Emergence and Crisis of the Japanese State of Harmony

INTRODUCTION: IMPASSE AND INNOVATION

Japan's historical experience of governance provides many unique insights into the modernization process of the past 500 years. Japan, owing to its isolation, relatively fractured geography, and the consequent difficulty of imposing an effective centralized state on the Chinese pattern over a large area, developed a kind of landlordism that resembled aristocratic feudalism in the European sense.[1] In outline at least the emergence of a centralizing state in the 1600s and 1700s under the Tokugawa shoguns after a period of particularly extreme warlord-dominated anarchy resembles the contemporaneous emergence of national monarchies, some constitutional others absolutist, in Europe. The remarkable success of the Tokugawa shoguns in demilitarizing Japanese society, creating a stable basis for agrarian and urban economic expansion upon which Japan's industrial revolution would build, and isolationism towards the outside world, laid the foundations for the modern Japanese Empire that emerged in the late 1800s. The modernization of the state and economy in the late 1800s and early 1900s, its rapid accumulation of military power and concomitant power projection in East Asia, meant that Japan was one of a handful of non-European states to enter the twentieth century with its sovereignty intact and the only one to be recognized as a Great Power by predatory Western states. Japan's growing militarism and economic clout, however, led Japanese elites to completely reverse their long-standing policy of isolationism and drew Japan into the fifteen-year war of 1931–45, which reached its climax in the US-Japan struggle for mastery over the Pacific (1941–45). Remarkably, defeat in World War II did not displace the Japanese elite. Rather, while militarism was shunned, Japan re-emerged as a constitutional monarchy with a dominant party political system that relied heavily on the civil service elite to formulate and implement policies. This new consensus had crystallized by 1955 with the emergence of the Liberal Democratic Party (LDP) as a wide-ranging conservative alliance enjoying the support of the civil service, the royal court and the United States of America. This consensus proved enduring and continued almost uninterrupted (with a brief hiatus in 1993) until 2010 when the main opposition Democratic Party of Japan formed a government after years of LDP failure to tackle Japan's burgeoning domestic debt and stagnant economy.

One can understand Japan's history as a series of transitions pulled off through the exertions of components of its elite at different points of time when the country seemed to have arrived at an impasse. The first such transition involved creating a semi-feudal, semi-bureaucratic monarchy as the solution to the problem of internal disorder and the threat of external penetration. The second transition entailed abandoning the policy of isolationism at a time when Japan's survival as an independent state was imperiled by the advent of 19th century Western empires, including that of the United States of America. The third transition, initiated under American occupation, involved establishing a Japanese variant of constitutional monarchy that was nonetheless committed to Japan's economic reemergence. At present, one might argue, Japan needs a fourth transition and since the early 1990s Japan's ruling elite has grappled unsuccessfully with breaking the country out of economic stagnation and rising maintenance costs that combined with a low birthrate and the consequent rapid graying of the population threaten to overwhelm the post-War Japanese welfare state. This chapter focuses on the transitional phases of Japanese history and argues that time and again the Japanese elite has succeeded in doing what was necessary to pull their country out of the impasse it found itself in.

JAPANESE GOVERNANCE UNDER THE TOKUGAWA SHOGUNS, 1600–1850

Japan was unified as a national state by a succession of military strongmen through a series of wars and political alliances that unfolded in the late 1500s and early 1600s. Oda Nobunaga started the process of state building, Toyotomi Hideyoshi completed the territorial unification of the country[2] and Tokugawa Ieyasu established his family's dynastic rule, consolidated the achievements of his predecessors, and formalized an elite consensus that would last 250 years. This government was therefore known as the Tokugawa Shogunate and in the process of its ascent its rulers had implemented a number of policies aimed at rescuing Japan from over a century of civil war and internal dissolution that had menacingly coincided with the first wave of overseas European penetration in East Asia.

The situation in Japan in the 1500s was dire. The country was divided into hundreds of domains under the control of lords (daimiyo) and their warrior-vassals (samurai). Between the arbitrariness and ambitions of the lords and the formidable martial ardor and endless personal vendettas of their samurai vassals, Japan was steadily being torn apart. In a dreadful real-life political drama this war of all against all could potentially continue for centuries. It was in this context of feudal anarchy and chivalry gone haywire that there emerged in the vicinity of present day Nagoya the lord of the Owari region—a brilliant, ruthless and determined warlord named Oda Nobunaga. Nobunaga was unquestionably a great general but what set him apart was his ability to consolidate the territories under his control and subdue the forces of feudal anarchy. The rising conqueror embarked "on a ruthless campaign of terror" that crushed fanatical autonomous Buddhist sects and cut his rival lords down to size.[3] Lesser lords were deprived of their estates and pensioned off while a survey of agricultural lands and the disarmament of villages heralded the advent of "a bureaucratic program of tax collection, so that his vassals did not collect revenue directly from villages."[4] In 1582, at the time of Nobunaga's death, some two-thirds of Japan had been unified under his regime with the authority of the state particularly effective in the Kanto plains region on the main island of Honshu.

Toyotomi Hideyoshi, a simple soldier who had risen from the ranks to become one of Nobunaga's lieutenants, succeeded his master and continued his work. Hideyoshi, however, moderated his predecessor's policy of terror and offered lords who submitted voluntarily to the new regime's authority the secure enjoyment of their lands, protection from arbitrary seizure, and a recognized feudal status that could be inherited by their male offspring. In exchange, the lords had to swear an oath of fealty to the new regime and send hostages to the capital as a guarantee that they would not renege on their commitment. A council of advisers was constituted to help run the affairs of state and at the time of Hideyoshi's death in 1598, Japan had become one country under a common government. At that point the entire unification and consolidation process almost came undone as civil war between the regime's generals erupted. This war of succession produced another military strongman, Tokugawa Ieyasu, who was formally recognized as Shogun in 1603 by the Japanese Emperor. Formally retiring in 1605, Ieyasu continued to rule till his death in 1617 from behind the scenes during his son's reign.

Ieyasu made a number of settlements that built upon the achievements of his predecessors. The lords were limited to one castle per domain and had to swear a personal oath of fealty to the shogun. Marriages in the nobility had to be approved by the shogun and inspectors were sent to the domains to ensure the loyalty of the landed elite. The lords were required to live in the capital and participate in a culture of conspicuous consumption at court that involved, among other things, lavish parties and the exchange of valuable gifts. Like the Sun King of France, half a world away, the shoguns appreciated the value of financially hemorrhaging their aristocrats and keeping them detached from their estates. Edo became to Japan what Versailles was to the Kingdom of France—an instrument of soft control over the socialization of a once turbulent and stubborn landed aristocracy. Between 20 and 25 percent of Japan's arable land was owned directly by the Tokugawa family or their immediate vassals while the rest was parceled out among 180 lords (the total rose to 266 lords in the 1850s). The samurai were granted stipends, official positions and settled in villages where they found their favorite pastime of private vendettas prohibited by the new regime. Following these reforms "Assignments to high office, and prospects for promotion" depended increasingly on "literacy, especially for samurai sons born into the middle and upper ranks."[5] In effect, the "samurai were transformed from warriors into bureaucrats" trading in their swords for brushes though those "on the bottom of the salary scale lived in very modest, often impoverished, circumstances."[6]

Japanese feudalism, therefore, contained "a strong bureaucratic infusion" with over 2 million samurai families depending directly on the government's pay roll for sustenance.[7] The shoguns proved remarkably enlightened in their taxation policy that helped pay for the court, the state machinery and the millions of samurai on the official pay rolls. Although taxes were settled on a village as a whole, the share of taxes to be collected was assessed in terms of fixed output and not as a proportion of output, as was the case in contemporary Timurid India.[8] Villages might have been collectively responsible for payment, and household groups were accountable for ensuring proper behavior on the part of all their members, but they could keep any surplus for themselves and so had an incentive to produce more. The rice merchant served as an important intermediary in this process and helped convert produce into cash as per the demands of the state. Relieved from the depredations of the lords and their samurai vassals, Japan experienced considerable economic growth.

By 1720, Japan's population, at some 26 million, was greater than that of the Russian Empire or France, and about 30–40 percent of Timurid India's. Even more impressive was the growth of cities, with the capital city of Edo growing to 1 million inhabitants, and Osaka and Kyoto approaching the 350,000–400,000 mark, in the 1720s.[9] One of the most tangible achievements of the shoguns was that they were able to balance the needs of Japan's natural environment with population growth and effectively presided over the reforestation of much of the country—an early example of environmentalism via administrative fiat.[10] This was achieved by cooperation between the shogun and the lords who collectively appointed hundreds of forest magistrates responsible for maintaining detailed records of forests and enforcing bans on slash and burn agriculture, logging, and grazing, while setting up a system of licenses and permits to use the forest sustainably.[11] The key to this was "the shogun's enforcement of peace within Japan" which "meant that people knew they couldn't meet their timber needs by seizing a Japanese neighbor's timber" combined with enlightened leadership at the top and an effective administration in the middle.[12]

At the heart of the Tokugawa administration was the bureau of finance, which was the "real nexus of decision-making" and served "as the interface between most of the actual administrative units."[13] In the domains forty regular salaried intendants oversaw the financial administration of the country.[14] Alongside the central financial administration and the intendants were inspectors responsible for "monitoring the behavior of other officials in the bureaucracy and impeaching them for offences."[15] These inspectors had the right to report their opinions not only to the Senior Council but also "to the shogun himself."[16] Thus, ten inspectors with an investigative staff of 150 officers had the power to "investigate the various government documents flowing from all quarters", helped with policymaking and eventually became more reform-minded than other groups in the state apparatus.[17] Overall, ". . . the decision-making procedures of the Tokugawa shogunate were highly bureaucratized."[18]

Bureaucratization coexisted with an official ideology that maintained that both the emperor and the shogun were divine rulers, although the latter practiced self-deification.[19] Certain aspects of Neo-Confucianism as expounded by the Chinese scholar Zhu Xi (1130–1200) and his philosophy of universal order were co-opted by the elite. These included the emphasis on order, hierarchy and obedience to superior authority. The Chinese ideal, and practice, of recruiting servants of the state through a competitive examination system was not, however, adopted by the shoguns and their regime remained a notionally aristocratic enterprise that presided over a practically caste-based society. Success or failure was taken as a sign of moral strength or weakness and the elite had an "obligation to leaven hierarchy with enough benevolence to allow peasants at least to survive."[20] Buddhist temples were regulated by the state and commoners had to register with a Buddhist temple which certified that the subject was religiously orthodox.[21] This was part of a successful program to expel Christianity from Japan and Buddhist temples submitted annual reports to the government on their localities.[22] In 1637–38, when the Christian stronghold of Shimabara (near Nagasaki) rebelled, the shogun's response was brutal suppression that left perhaps 37,000 dead.[23] Enemies of the state, once identified, deserved no mercy.

Acts of suppression and censorship, regulation and registration, were part of an overall policy of isolating Japan from undesirable influences and thereby preserving its uniqueness and purity. The ideocratic complex of the Tokugawa regime combined state religion, Confucian philosophy, ruler-worship, and a heavy dose of isolationism and xenophobia founded in a cultural narcissism and official paranoia that has few, if any, major parallels. This did not mean that the Tokugawa regime lacked information about the outside world—it actually knew much more about the Western imperial advent and Western science than the West knew about Japan. In essence, the Tokugawa policy was to maintain an asymmetry of information in its own favor when dealing with outsiders and it did so successfully for the better part of 300 years. Nevertheless, the second wave of Western imperial expansion in East Asia, which brought Indo-China under direct European rule and led to the humiliation and forced opening of China in the 1840s, meant that the Japanese elite had to reform or perish under the heels of European conquerors. The Tokugawa regime opted to open up

Japan in the 1850s but was soon overtaken by events such as the samurai rebellion, trends such as growing rural discontent, and the emergence of the belief that only the restoration of direct imperial rule could save Japan from destruction. The result was not a break with the past but a rapid acceleration of trends already in existence that led to the emergence by the late-1800s of an absolutist monarchy mediated through a powerful modernized military and bureaucracy and sanctified by a state religion and official ideology that established the emperor as the official center of Japan's political and ideological universe.

THE IMPERIAL WAY AND THE STEEL TETRARCHY

The decline and fall of the Tokugawa regime and the imperial restoration that emerged from the crisis-ridden period between 1853 and 1877 had important implications for Japan's culture of power and governance. These implications can be categorized as political, ideological, military, administrative and economic in nature, though they were by no means mutually exclusive and may actually have been mutually reinforcing.

The political implications are perhaps the most familiar and to outside observers the most obvious. The Tokugawa dynastic regime came to an end and the emperor formally assumed power over the state. A series of settlements, starting in March 1869, resulted in the lords giving up control of their domains in exchange for status and generous economic compensation. By August 1871 prefectures administered by appointed governors replaced the Tokugawa-era domains. The 1877 rebellion of dissatisfied samurai and lords was crushed by the Meiji state with some 20,000 rebels and 6,000 government troops losing their lives.[24] Caste discrimination was derecognized under law, samurai pensions were slashed, and a process initiated for the express purpose of framing a Japanese constitution that would culminate in the Meiji Constitution of 1889.

In the process of constitution-making the Japanese elite examined the laws and practices of different Western countries. One of the key ideas that were internalized in the process was that while a constitutional system could be autocratic (Germany), oligarchic (Britain) or democratic (the United States of America), the test of its success lay in its ability to create predictability in the running of the affairs of the state and thus reduce the level of arbitrariness in decision-making.[25] Equally important was the notion that constitutional changes ought to follow a gradual path of development and never lose sight of the local culture and traditions.[26] Loyalty to the state amongst the citizens was recognized as a prerequisite for the functioning of a constitutional system and was even more important in a parliamentary-representative dispensation than in an autocratic dispensation.[27] An autonomous, highly skilled and motivated bureaucracy was an essential need for a modern nation state, without which it would be impossible to simultaneously maintain order while modernizing the society rapidly.[28] And finally, the Japanese Emperor needed to have substantive authority so that if the need arose he could act to stabilize the political situation.[29]

The Meiji Constitution of 1889 reflected the above considerations. The normal objective of constitutionalism is to place limits on the power of the executive/head of state and render the government answerable before other institutions. The Meiji Constitution, however, empowered the emperor to exercise theoretically unlimited power. Articles I-X of the Meiji Constitution establish inter alia that the emperor does not merely reign but enjoys actual power over the government. These powers include the power to convene the Diet, sanction laws, rule by decree and decide "the organization of the different branches of the administration and the salaries of all civil and military officers" as well as appointing and dismissing "the same."[30] Articles XI-XVII further establish that the emperor commands the army and navy, declares war, negotiates peace, and approves treaties. In this regard, the emperor also "determines the organization and peace standing of the Army and Navy."[31] With all these powers concentrated in the hands of the supreme executive, it is hardly surprising that the Meiji Constitution is widely regarded as an exercise in legitimizing autocracy and as a document that is authoritarian in form and substance.

In practice, the presence of the *genro* or elder statesmen meant that "Frictions were smoothed over, faces saved, feathers unruffled, protégés pushed, and interests reconciled" behind "the veil of the imperial will."[32] The Meiji elite was intensely concerned with "building a consensus amongst its members" and using the emperor to unify the elite.[33] In effect, Japan adopted a "political tradition of autocratic rule combined with an ethos of restraint in its exercise."[34] Meiji "was indeed an autocrat" who "continued to support the military in disputes with the cabinet" even as "the *genro* continued to admonish him to restrain his exercise of despotic powers . . ."[35] Responsibility was diffused due to a culture of consensus and secrecy and it appeared that the emperor and his servants reflected each other's will. The apex political event and council that solemnized this diffusion of responsibility was the Imperial Conference:

> The imperial conference was *the* device for legally transforming the 'will of the emperor' into the 'will of the state.' And because everyone who participated in its deliberations could claim to have acted by, with, and under the unique authority of the emperor, while he could claim to have acted in accordance with the advice of his ministers of state, the imperial conference diffused lines of responsibility. In that sense it was the perfect crown to the Japanese practice of irresponsibility, for it sustained four separate fictions: (a) that the cabinet had real power; (b) that the cabinet was the emperor's most important advisory organ; and (c) that the cabinet and the military high command had reached a compromise agreement on the matter at hand, providing the emperor

with a policy that he (d) was merely sanctioning as a passive monarch. Reality was quite different: a powerless cabinet, an emasculated constitution, and a dynamic emperor participating in the palling of aggression and guiding the process . . . [36]

To put it less charitably, autocracy, irresponsibility, and institutional/clique rivalries meant that the vaunted "imperial will" was for all practical purposes a "screen around a snake pit."[37]

An ideological screen extended across the land and protected the state and the ruling elite from criticism, public opinion and external accountability. At the heart of this ideology was the notion that the emperor was a god, the Japanese people were his loyal subjects or *shinmin* and the state of Japan a vast family united by blood and the paternalism of the ruling house. The duty of the people was to serve the emperor and help him carry out grand plans for the greater glory of the national organism/polity (*kokutai*). Success was possible only through "social harmony" to ensure "the preservation of order" that would in turn be achieved through "a shared consciousness of racial homogeneity" combined with "military discipline and reverence for the emperor."[38] The Japanese state subscribed to a "theocratic ideal of the unity of religious rites and political administration (*saisei itchi*)" and consequently the emperor was the head of the official Shinto Buddhist sect.[39] The formal establishment of a Department of Shinto in 1868, a Shrine Office in 1900, and Peace Preservation Law of 1925, combined with educational policies that drilled emperor worship into the minds of young Japanese, served as the practical manifestations of indoctrination. A special higher police existed beyond the pale of accountability to weed out thought criminals who sought to modify the *kokutai*. Leftists and liberals were particularly targeted for political heresy and in March 1928, in an especially extensive crackdown, 1568 communists and labor activists were arrested.[40] The Japanese imperial servants and subjects were animated by the concept of "service to the *tenno* (lord of heaven)" while "the reforming oligarchs who were responsible for the end of the shogunate continued to emphasize the virtues of obedience, loyalty and acquiescence in service of one's superiors."[41] The 1890 Imperial Rescript on Education, which continued to be learnt by heart by students till 1948, served as the basic document for promoting nationalism, piety, Confucian ideals of ethics and obedience to the emperor.[42] The Japanese state proved successful in spreading literacy, numeracy and moral education as primary school enrolment for males and females rose from under 30 percent in 1871 to over 90 percent by 1907.[43]

While one can speculate about the degree to which official propaganda was successful in permeating and molding society at large, the impact of ideology was most keenly felt in the Japanese military, which steadily gained in power and influence following the Meiji Restoration. The introduction of compulsory military service in 1873, though it led to riots and the arrest of 100,000 protestors, was successfully imposed by the 1880s and equated "National education with military education. The samurai virtues were now applied nationally."[44] The 1882 Imperial Rescript to Soldiers and Sailors preached absolute obedience to the emperor and institutionalized emperor worship in the military.[45] The 1889 Meiji Constitution established the emperor as the commander of the military forces and ensured that the army and navy answered only to the head of state and were not subject to any parliamentary control. This meant that military involvement in politics was an integral component of the imperial system and that the corporate interests of the military as well as the sincere devotion of many officers and soldiers to their God Emperor dominated policy making. Perhaps the ultimate example of stoicism and devotion to the emperor was General Nogi, commander of the Japanese armies in the Russo-Japanese war of 1904–6, and later tutor to crown prince Hirohito. Nogi requested Meiji's permission to commit ritual patriotic suicide as he had lost his sons in the war against the Russians and was told that he would have to live so long as the emperor lived. Nogi accepted and true to his word, upon Meiji's death in 1912, committed suicide. This *bushido* spirit would wreak havoc upon Japan's military adversaries while greatly inflating Japanese casualties as its soldiers went on fighting long after other militaries would have surrendered.[46] This attitude, however, also furnished part of the reason for the contempt with which the Japanese military treated prisoners of war and for the view amongst the military officers that only they, by virtue of their readiness to die for the empire, truly knew how their fellow Japanese should live.

So great was the gravitational pull exercised by the military that by the 1930s politics in Japan had been warped by the domination of two factions, both rooted in the military. The more fanatical of the two was the Imperial Way faction, which sought to establish a military dictatorship under the emperor, overthrow the 1889 Meiji Constitution and liquidate the enemies of the state while pursuing overseas expansion through holy war. The less fanatical group was the Control faction, which sought to establish a military dictatorship under the emperor without overthrowing the 1889 Meiji Constitution while using police state methods to crush domestic dissent and vigorously expanding overseas. None of the 42 cabinets between 1880 and 1945 succeeded in subordinating the military to a civilian political process and the army/navy ministers—chosen from active duty generals and admirals—enjoyed the emperor's confidence and acted autonomously of their cabinet colleagues and the prime minister. Due to the military's rising influence and desire to turn Japan into a Naziesque national defense state, the 1930s witnessed the subversion of "independent political parties, business associations, producer cooperatives, labor unions, and tenant unions", which were "replaced by a series of state controlled mass bodies intended to mobilize the nation for its 'holy war' with China . . ."[47] In 1940, all political parties were abolished and merged into the Imperial Rule Assistance Association.

While Japan's military might was the most noticeable aspect of the country's modernization, the development of a powerful civilian bureaucracy recruited on merit was one of the most constructive of the Meiji era's accomplishments. To be sure "bureaucratic change" during the Meiji Restoration represented the acceleration of centuries of bureaucratic evolution already in evidence during the Tokugawa regime.[48] The introduction of a cabinet/ministerial system in 1885 was followed by the establishment of the Imperial University at Tokyo (1886) and the promulgation of the Regulations for Civil Service Examinations and Probationary Civil Officers/the Civil Service Code of 1887. Japan's reformers realized that the "existence of a modern bureaucracy and a recruitment system to staff it" was absolutely "indispensable" for Japan's modernization.[49] The birth of the Imperial University System was in some ways an affirmation of the Chinese ideal of meritocracy even as it spelled the end of administrative nobility and inherited social status as prerequisites for power and office. Henceforth, the servants of the emperor were to be chosen on merit, not birth, and the Japanese state was to be administered on more rational lines. The bureaucracy would act as the fulcrum of a "developmental dictatorship" that sought to institute "good government" in accordance with the benevolent wishes of the emperor and in the best interest of his loyal Japanese subjects.[50] The Meiji reformers "inherited a Tokugawa legacy of bureaucratic rule by civilianized samurai" and converted Japan into a full-fledged "bureaucratic state."[51]

One of the reasons for the reform of administration and politics in Japan was the need to modernize the country and do so quickly. State-led or guided industrialization was the order of the day and it may not be an exaggeration to say that the Japanese Meiji elite, not the Soviet Union, was the real progenitor of modern economic development administration. It was the Japanese state's intervention through investments in infrastructure, education, subsidies, incentives, legal reform and patronage of key industries that can be credited with Japan's economic lift-off. The emerging business elite was "socially and politically", though not legally, "inferior to the elite that ruled Japan."[52] At the same time, there was a strong trend towards concentrating wealth in the hands of the old landed elite that had accepted the loss of its lands as part of the Meiji reforms. In 1880, for instance, some 44 percent of stock in Japanese banks was held by *daimiyo* families transformed as they were by generous settlements into a capitalist class through state action.[53] The Japanese conglomerates, or *zaibatsu*, depended heavily upon the state for their wealth. Indeed, the "period of military hegemony" saw Japan's industrial output rise from 6 billion yen in 1931 to 30 billion yen in 1940, with the share of large scale manufacturing doubling from 38 percent to 73 percent during the same period.[54] Even as millions of Japanese subjects lost everything during the Second World War, "The four great *zaibatsu* firms, Mitsui, Mitsubishi, Sumitomo, and Yasoda, came out of the Second World War with total assets of more than 3 billion yen, compared with only 875 million in 1930."[55]

The preceding survey of Japanese history from the fall of the Tokugawa regime to the Second World War indicates that Japan's culture of power shifted its central focus from the shogun to the emperor and became increasingly authoritarian. For all practical purposes Japan was ruled by a small elite of court officials, military officers, civil servants and big businessmen—a steel tetrarchy—who shared a commitment to modernization from above. This reforming elite incorporated such aspects of modernity as they felt would enhance Japan's military and economic power quickly enough to enable it to survive in a world dominated by predatory and culturally confident Western powers. The Meiji reformists, by making the emperor the focal point of the entire system, made modernization appear to be mandated by the divine imperial will and projected it as a restoration of values lost under the decadent Tokugawa regime. In a sense, Japan experienced archaic modernization that entailed the fusion of a political religion with the interests and politics of the state, the democratization of the samurai spirit, and the regimentation of society for the attainment of national goals. The initial success of the reforms, underlined by victory over China and Korea in 1894–5 and Russia in 1904–6, unleashed an autocatalytic process whereby Japanese authoritarianism, militarism, corporatism, and bureaucratization, and theocracy gained momentum that fed off their own successes. The growing need for repression at home and expansion abroad undermined the viability of the system and let to serious indiscipline within the armed forces, which contributed to Japan being dragged into widening wars on the Asian continent that ultimately drew in the far more powerful United States of America. Ironically, Japan's capitulation at the end of the Second World War and its occupation by the United States military led to precisely the outcome that Japanese elites had sought to avoid—the subjugation and integration of Japan into the Western imperial system. Once again, Japan faced an impasse.

THE REBIRTH OF JAPAN: IMPERIAL DEMOCRACY AND THE IRON TRIANGLE

One of the most remarkable features of modern Japanese history is the way in which an alliance of conservative politicians, civil servants and large corporations managed to retain control of the state apparatus and political process even after a shattering defeat in the Second World War. This "Iron Triangle" has continued to rule Japan up to the present day and presided over what is regarded with both fear and admiration as one of the greatest economic miracles in history. The preservation of the imperial court and even the emperor who led Japan to defeat in the Second World War, albeit stripped of all substantive powers, meant the ruling dynasty reverted to the symbolic and ceremonial role of the Tokugawa period while governments became increasingly party-based.

The central component in this process of continuity and change has been Japan's civil service, which in some important ways benefited from the country's forced demilitarization. The Americans, while moving assiduously to remove the vestiges of militarism, left Japan's bureaucracy more or less intact after the war. Freed from the political and economic constraints of the militarist period "the new mandarinate" embarked upon Japan's transformation into a public construction state that, in turn, "would ensure that production served the interests of the whole nation, assume many of the functions hitherto performed by the *zaibatsu*, provide credit to worthy enterprises, encourage export competitiveness" that targeted foreign trade for planning and guidance by the state, while "modern scientific management" in the civil service replaced the "feudalistic" bureaucrats of the old regime.[56] The key element in Japan's post-War economic resurgence was an "elite bureaucracy" with enough autonomy to determine goals and implement policies and calibrate its market interventions under the aegis of the Ministry of International Trade and Industry (MITI).[57]

In every ministry an elite track of annually recruited civil service officers play the role of bureaucratic leadership. Recruitment depends for the most part on securing admission to the Tokyo University, getting top marks in recruitment exams/interviews conducted by individual ministries, and then undergoing rigorous training. The demanding selection process is designed to guarantee that these top civil servants are extremely competent and enjoy almost unparalleled social prestige. Within each ministry, those recruited on the elite track are given important assignments related to policy, general administration, research, and fiscal affairs. The year of recruitment determines the starting position within each elite track but within a few years those that demonstrate extraordinary potential are identified and given more important assignments with the aim of grooming them from an early stage to become administrative heads of their ministries. These "High-level Japanese bureaucrats, having complete job security and group esprit, are able to achieve self-confident and dynamic leadership" that leaves little room for ministerial interference in the running of the ministries.[58] Below the elite track is the regular civil service. This component of the civil service handles, within each ministry, the routine administrative work. Since civil servants are not transferred between ministries, the Japanese system ensures a high level of specialization and a superior quality of experienced bureaucratic leadership. It is the elite track civil servants that are responsible for meeting journalists, interacting with academia, consulting localities, preparing ministerial summaries, briefs and notes, and ensuring continuity in policies the most strikingly successful example of which was Japan's post-war economic miracle.

This planned economic transformation could only be achieved through political stability founded on administrative experience and practice. It is thus that the liberal-conservative consensus of 1955 established strong links between the ruling Liberal Democratic Party and the civil service.

The "party-bureaucracy complex" is essentially a direct link between civil servants in individual ministries and the ruling party's policymaking committees that circumvent ministers in the cabinet and therefore formal parliamentary control.[59] Thus, while adopting the form of a parliamentary democracy, the Japanese civil service and members of the ruling party in policymaking positions carried on with the business of state without real interference or supervision by members of parliament. Parliamentarians, for their part, sought to funnel development funds to their respective constituencies and factions via the local governments. Just as civil servants serve in varied capacities before leadership positions, politicians are also expected to serve on various boards and committees before rising to prominence as faction leaders. The apparent and substantive harmony of this process has led to the widespread notion that "leadership in Japan is group-oriented and decision-making consensual rather than personal."[60] This does not mean that there are no arguments or differences of opinion. The Japanese approach to disagreements is that they "can best be resolved not by adversary procedures and brilliant argument but by further gathering of information."[61] Although this approach has left twenty-first century Japan with a huge domestic debt, it also fuelled economic growth and raised standards of living far more equitably than in many Western democracies.

At a leadership level, the LDP drew its apex cadres from either career politicians with strong local roots and power bases, like Tanaka Kakuei, who remained the power behind the throne for twenty years after being forced to resign as prime minister due to corruption charges. The other main source of political leadership comes from "career bureaucrats-turned-politicians."[62] Between 1957 and 1972, the take-off period of Japan's post-war economic boom, the country was led by a succession of elite mandarins—Kishi, Ikeda and Sato—all ex-civil servants. Kishi had the added distinction of being on the list of most wanted Class-A war crimes suspects and had spent years in prison awaiting trial. The corporate culture of the new Japan reflected that of its civil service and political elite and was characterized by "permanently employed professional management staff . . ." that "was influenced by humanism, permanent employment, seniority and industry-specific" aptitudes.[63]

In the effective administration of law and order modern Japan probably surpasses all other large societies. The presence of a well-trained and well-funded police force deployed across thousands of local police stations and led by the National Police Agency is one side of the picture. The other side is that the high level of respect that state functionaries are held in combined with an acute sense of honor and social obligation enable the Japanese police and prosecutorial agencies to detect and punish crime with far greater regularity than is the case in other countries, even those with high levels of economic development. The relative homogeneity of Japan's population as well as its concentration in the highly-developed Kanto region enhanced the reach of the state. Moreover, the Japanese look down on litigation and when confronted with evidence of guilt can be easily shamed into confessing as a way of limiting damage to family honor. Other societies with different value systems that are more diverse and geographically spread out are far harder to police. Japan's wisdom in dealing with law and order has been to adapt formal structures to the requirements of its society while modernizing procedures, equipment, training and infrastructure. While these achievements are laudable, as comparisons between Japanese and European or North American crime statistics indicate, one cannot really see how the Japanese honor system, developed over centuries of social and historical conditioning, can be transplanted to other parts of the world.

The bureaucratic model of state-led economic development and leadership proved enormously successful in raising standards of living and catapulting Japan to the rank of the world's second largest economy by the early 1980s.[64] The major cost of this approach, as indicated earlier, was that the bulk of the national debt was incurred due to centrally-mandated expenditure by local governments.[65] Another example of the rising maintenance costs was the agricultural sector. By 1999/2000, 42,000 Ministry of Agriculture employees plus 320,000 workers in agricultural cooperatives nearly outnumbered the 426,000 households employed fulltime in agriculture.[66] By the early twenty-first century the public construction state had left Japan "full of unused tunnels, roads that go nowhere, lifeless rivers, bridges that nobody crosses . . ."[67] along with massive debt, a graying population that threatens to overwhelm the social welfare system erected after the Second World War, and stubbornly persistent economic stagnation and deflation.[68] In some ways it appears that after a period of extraordinary achievement the Japanese civil service state has arrived at an impasse and needs to reinvent itself. If the past is any guide to the future, there is every reason to hope that the Japanese elite will once again rise to the occasion and in so doing preserve the *kokutai*.[69]

8 The Freaks of History
The State of Laws and Britain's Culture of Power and Governance

INTRODUCTION: THE BASIS OF DIVERGENCE

Thus far the cultures of power and historical experiences of governance surveyed indicate that most of the major civilizations and powers in Eurasia took varied paths to becoming continental bureaucratic empires. In some cases this process unfolded thousands of years ago while in others, such as Japan, Western Europe or Russia, the development of bureaucratic states is a relatively recent phenomenon. These states, as we have seen, were and are very diverse in their details but reflect an underlying unity in that they came to rely on centralized or concentrated hierarchies of servants to govern their settled areas. There is, however, a very important exception that has exerted great influence on governance structures and practices on a global scale during the modern period. That exception is Britain and the emergence on British soil of a freakishly different solution to the problems of order, justice and financial administration amidst demographic pressure. That solution, in the form of the state of laws and a culture of power that consciously and subconsciously sought to minimize arbitrary power, diffuse authority, and encourage autonomous institutions, is in many respects the antithesis of the continental bureaucratic empire with its mania for arbitrariness, tendency towards either centralization or breakdown, and reliance on servile instruments. The effort here is to identify how a state of laws came into existence in Britain, what enabled it to survive, and what were/are the implications of this divergent evolution for history.

To begin with it is useful to present the contours of the stage upon which the state of laws would ultimately emerge. The Romans referred to the territory as Albion:

> . . . an island not widely sundered from the continent, and so tilted that its mountains lie all to the west and north, while the south and east is a gently undulating landscape of wooded valleys, open downs, and slow rivers. It is very accessible to the invader, whether he comes in peace or war, as pirate or merchant, conqueror or missionary.[1]

The area of the island is approximately 130,000 km² with more than 1800 km of coastline. The highest point is about 1000 meters above sea level while the lowest is some three meters below sea level.

There are three distinct geographic zones in Britain. The Pennines Chain is the main mountain range and stretches from Scotland to halfway down the length of England and is rich in coal. The South West Peninsula is a combination of a low plateau merging into highlands made of granite. The Lowlands comprise all those areas that the Pennines and Peninsula do not cover. They include the plains of Lancashire, Yorkshire, and the Midlands. The area around the Thames river valley is low, flat, and makes good farmland. The major rivers on the island include the Thames, Tee, Humber and Tyne, which flow into the North Sea, and the Mersey, Dee, Sevan, and Avon, which flow into the Irish Sea. Historically, the bulk of the population has resided in the Lowlands turning them into the center of political power and economic wealth.

The process of land clearance in the predominantly sylvan environment of Britain began in earnest with the arrival of iron-wielding Celtic groups from the European continent between 800 and 450 BC.[2] As conditions became more settled, towns gradually emerged as did trade between Celtic tribes on both sides of the channel.[3] The tribes did not make the transition to statehood and remained locked in armed conflict. It is possible that delegates from weaker tribes invited Julius Caesar, then Proconsul of Gaul, to invade and help contain the growing power of the Catuvellauni and Trinovantes.[4] Caesar's expedition of 55 BC to conquer Britain, the population of which was no more than half a million, at the head of fifty thousand Roman soldiers, proved abortive.[5] It was not until AD 43 that "the officials of highly competent departments" in Rome convinced Emperor Claudius, "a clownish scholar", to append Albion to the Roman Empire.[6]

The second Roman invasion, undertaken by fifty thousand troops representing about one-eighth of the empire's armed strength, was successful.[7] Many local chiefs collaborated with the imperialists and felt that the Roman presence "would strengthen rather than weaken their local authority".[8] Nevertheless, the pacification of the island took more than a generation and reached completion under Agricola, appointed governor in AD 78.[9] In AD 122, work had commenced on the construction of a wall, seventy-three miles long, seven to ten feet thick, and fifteen to twenty feet high, that ran from Solway Firth to the Tyne, and bears the name of Emperor Hadrian, who ordered its construction after a tour of inspection.[10]

The orientalization[11] of the Roman culture of power was quite advanced by the time Britain was annexed and brought under imperial administration. Roman republican institutions lost their power as the empire expanded. Sardinia and Sicily became the first Roman provinces in 227 BC.[12] By 112 BC, the republic had entered its terminal phase characterized by political instability, social unrest, and the emergence of dictators, like Sulla and Julius Caesar.[13] Continuous warfare and territorial aggrandizement caused power to drain away from the Senate to the administrators and generals in the provinces. Outside Italy, under the republic, despotism prevailed so that "Each province was like an immense estate left by its owner to an unprincipled agent, who abused his position to enrich himself and his followers."[14] Corruption was so pervasive that "it was said . . . a province had to yield three fortunes to its governor, one to pay his debts, one to bribe his judges," and one to compensate him for his "arduous and disinterested" efforts.[15] Each provincial governor was surrounded by "a hungry cohort of friends and adherents" and assaulted by a "greedy multitude" of speculators and tax farmers from Rome for favors.[16] Indeed, during the crisis-plagued final century of the republic,

> Nothing contributed so much to determine the course of the great constitutional changes which were impending over Rome as the vast powers of the provincial governors. Surrounded by devoted adherents, removed from the restraints of the capital, and living amongst subject peoples, the ruler of a Roman province wielded an authority which was virtually despotic.[17]

Perhaps the greatest achievements of the absolutist monarchical government that emerged in place of the republic in 27 BC was ". . . that the provincial administration was regularly organized, and vigilantly watched by the eye of the reigning sovereign."[18] One of the most important developments that led to the rise of absolutism was that in 107 BC, the Roman citizen-army recruited from the ranks of property-holding free men formally gave way to a salaried class of "poor volunteers".[19]

From the growing chaos there emerged, in 27 BC, a new order led by Octavian, a nephew of Julius Caesar, who established "behind a façade of republican piety"[20] the reality of an omnipotent continental bureaucratic empire. The provincial administration and military functions were entrusted to salaried officials reporting to the emperor. The Praetorian Guard was created and for the first time a military force, at the emperor's command, was stationed in Rome during peacetime. In 12 BC, Octavian, following Julius Caesar's footsteps, became "head of the official cult".[21] Octavian decided who was to be "elected" to the Senate and the emperor's legitimate jurisdiction was expanded to enable him to interfere in provinces that had no legions stationed in them.[22] In all parts of the Roman Empire other than the Italian peninsula, "all land . . . was ultimately the property of the emperor".[23] The cultivators were "imperial tenants" and "paid rents to Roman officials".[24]

Britain, which became the forty-fifth province of the Roman Empire, was ruled directly by the emperor's appointed governor and had legions stationed on its soil until AD 410, when the sack of Rome by Alaric the Goth forced the Romans to withdraw their forces from the island.[25] Britain was dotted with planned towns populated by fifteen to twenty thousand subjects,[26] and the local elite, once educated, aspired to join the state service, and lived comfortably in town houses with "engineered water supplies" unmatched in quality till the nineteenth century.[27] Estimates for the population of the island under Roman rule go as high as one and a half million, and it "seems certain" that the military, civil bureaucracy, "townsfolk", and the well-off, and their dependents, were three or four hundred thousand in number.[28] That Roman Britain had a highly cash-dependent economy compared to its successors is indicated by the fact that though coin hoards have been discovered "all over the country" very few of them date later than AD 400.[29]

The traditional account is that the calm of Roman bureaucratic despotism in Britain was broken in AD 367 by the combined assault of the Picts from Scotland, the Gaelic Dal Riata from Ireland, and the Anglo-Saxons from across the North Sea in Germany.[30] This version, though dramatic and consistent with the fall of the Roman Empire elsewhere, has been challenged quite effectively on the basis of archaeological and linguistic evidence.[31] The alternative view is that migrations from the continent took place gradually and on a much smaller scale leading to a gradual fusion of Celtic and Germanic cultures to produce a distinctly British hybrid. This debate need not detain us here for either way Roman Britain was dead by the seventh century and the Anglo-Saxons established themselves in a dominant position in the south and east of the island. The earliest surviving document of English law, dated to AD 600, deals with private property rights[32] and toward the end of the ninth century the Saxon lords, in response to the dire threat posed by the Vikings, overcame their differences and submitted to the authority of a single king.[33] Alfred the Great (r. 871–899) was the leader responsible for bringing about a semblance of political coherence over the strong-willed, armed, landowning aristocracy, of Saxon England. King Alfred founded the English navy, and issued regulations that grew into a body of laws, which, over centuries, evolved into the Common Law.[34] For his pivotal role in state-formation, and his exploits against the Vikings, Alfred earned the title of "Great"—a title that has not been given to any ruler of England since. The Anglo-Saxon rulers, in the Germanic tradition, governed the country with the help of the *witena gemot* or "council of the wise".[35] Major decisions were submitted to an assembly of freemen, or folkmoot, which met twice a year, and taxation and legislation required the consent of the "great" and the freemen.[36] It seems that the Germanic customs, of electing their magistrates and involving as much of the community as possible in decision-making were transplanted to Britain.[37]

When William, the Duke of Normandy, invaded England in 1066 and defeated the ruling class of four or five thousand Anglo-Saxon nobles,[38] pacified the country with "terror" and "bribery"[39], and institutionalized military feudalism, the process of divergent evolution slowed down. The *Domesday Book* of 1086, a detailed census record of every shire under Norman control, is one indicator of centralization. Another indicator was the Norman practice of considering the nobility not as landowners but as "tenants-in-chief" of the king, granted lands to maintain a quota of troops which, if not met, could entail confiscation by the crown and reassignment to a more competent person.[40] The normal practice, however, was that estates were held for life and inherited by the eldest son though, in the absence of a suitable heir, the widow could be forced by the king to remarry, and, if the children were too young, the lands would pass under the king's wardship. The Norman kings, their attention divided between the continent and the island, relied principally on customs duties, forests, and crown lands for finances.

The nobles were responsible for law and order on their estates and to decide cases the disputants would swear oaths, submit to an ordeal, or fight a duel that ended when one of the participants begged for mercy. The logic of the duel was that as God was on the side of justice, the person with the legitimate complaint would always win. Consequently, those individuals and groups that could afford it, maintained armed champions to handle litigation. Henry II (r. 1154–1189), the first of the Plantagenet line of Anglo-Norman kings, saw in this undeniably dismal state of affairs the opportunity to increase royal power. He did not have at his disposal enough armed strength to break the power of the great of the realm[41] through force. Nor was King Henry rich enough to reconcile his nobles by grants of wealth and offices. In 1175, for example, the royal income was twenty thousand pounds[42] or one-fourth of the income of the Roman Catholic Church in England, which, incidentally, also provided the king with one-seventh of the total military service owed by English landowners.[43]

King Henry, to draw freemen away from the manor courts, instituted the practice of trial by jury. As only the king could summon juries, they were available only to those who sought justice in royal courts. This innovation provided litigants with an option other than duel, ordeal, or oath. Furthermore, the royal courts administered "a law common to all England and all men"[44]. The jurymen were locals and selected because they were likely to know the plaintiff and defendant and be in a better position to ascertain the truth.[45] The principal advantages of the system of royal courts administering a common law with the assistance of locals were enhanced legal predictability and protection:

> . . . so long as a case has to be scrutinized by twelve honest men, defendant and plaintiff alike have a safeguard from arbitrary perversion of the law. It is this which distinguishes the laws administered in English courts from Continental legal systems based on Roman Law.[46]

King Henry's effort to make Churchmen accountable to royal courts misfired. In 1162, Thomas Beckett, the king's chancellor since 1155, became Archbishop of Canterbury. Contrary to the king's expectations, Beckett "went out of his way" to oppose the royal will and objected to the marriage of Henry's younger brother to a wealthy heiress because the couple were too closely related.[47] Beckett's opposition to the policy of making the clergy accountable before royal courts forced him to flee to France in 1164.[48] Beckett was murdered in 1170 by some of the king's overzealous partisans, and the outrage was sufficiently strong to compel Henry to humiliate himself by doing penance at his grave in 1174.[49]

Though the church may well have been "the greatest landlord and capitalist" in the realm, served as a semi-autonomous institution that posed as "constant challenge" to the king, and was not to be trifled with, the executive was not entirely at its mercy.[50] One advantage that the king had was that the church had to wait for his permission before it could elect new bishops and abbots.[51] In the interval, however, the crown collected the church's revenue and, thus, could prolong vacancies to boost its finances.[52] King John (r. 1199–1216), for example, kept the ecclesiastical office occupied by Hugh of Lincoln, who died in 1200, vacant until July 1202, and netted a profit of two thousand six hundred and forty-nine pounds.[53]

Another source of royal strength were the forests, which were royal monopolies administered by the king's officials. In addition to ferocious penalties for hunting, logging, and onerous rules and regulations for the subjects living near the forests, there were plenty of fines that could be imposed. The records of the forest courts show that the kings were "much more interested in taking their subjects' money than their lives and body parts."[54] The forest administration was headed by a Chief Forester, and run by justices of the forest and their deputies. When the king needed extra money, forest commissions would be sent and in 1175, Henry II managed to raise twelve thousand pounds through this medium.[55] Evidently, Henry didn't doubt "that his Chief Forester, Alan de Neville, would go to hell" given the sordid nature of the forest administration.[56]

King Richard the Lion Heart (r. 1189–1199), and his successor King John, were so beset with foreign entanglements that they started declaring districts disafforested[57] in exchange for a fee to raise money for war.[58] King John disafforested all of Cornwall for two thousand two hundred marks, Devon for five thousand marks, and Surrey for five hundred marks.[59] This process gained momentum "because people in those counties raised funds and petitioned for something they regarded as being of benefit."[60] However, even in areas that were disafforested, the locals were obliged to attend forest courts and the gross inequity of the system "united rich and poor alike in opposition to the crown."[61]

The example of the forests does help show that there existed a political process in the country and that a legitimate framework for opposition to the king had survived the Norman conquests. The Normans, notwithstanding their high regard for king's person and council, did not replace the Saxon system of local government. As the estates were hereditary and held for life, the nobility came to regard the land and people as their own. This, King John discovered to his dismay when his nobles refused to render military service in a "foreign" land like France since their feudal obligations applied only to England.[62]

The Norman nobility and English clergy were not the only classes that mattered from a political standpoint. Between 1066 and 1230, one hundred and twenty-five new towns were founded, and the burgesses, who bought plots of lands in the new towns, enjoyed the right of private property, were exempt from forced labor, and had the right to build their own hand-mills.[63] Most of these settlements were established by "wealthy landowners, bishops, abbots, and, above all, secular nobles", not the state.[64] The investment made by clerical and lay entrepreneurs represented a long-term commitment to the locality. The incentive was that once the town market became large enough it would generate enough dues to enrich both the burgesses and the founder, and, of course, pay for maintenance.[65]

The late twelfth and early thirteenth centuries marked the beginning of a "managerial revolution" in the countryside prompted by inflation caused by increased demographic pressure. As prices rose, more lords took over the management of their manors and began selling the surplus directly on the market for a profit because rents from land no longer sufficed to keep them solvent.[66] The earliest record or detailed financial account for a manor is from 1208, and the rising demand for trained specialists in financial affairs resulted in the opening of a school of business administration at Oxford in the thirteenth century.[67]

The first decade of the thirteenth century is important for the emergence on the English landscape of two creatures destined to play a vital role in the formation of England's culture of power. In 1209, a clerk studying the liberal arts at Oxford killed a woman and fled. The mayor had his housemates arrested and hanged in retaliation though they knew not where their companion had run away. Outraged, the masters and students, three thousand by one estimate, left the town in protest and formed a "university" (literally means corporation), which, like a borough, had legal rights and responsibilities.[68] The Common Law, in the meantime, had led to the creation of a permanent King's Bench at Westminster Hall where litigants came to plead their cases, and by 1200, there had emerged in London a group of attorneys prepared "to represent any client for a fee."[69]

It is in this context, that King John, eager to reclaim Normandy, which was lost to the French in 1204, began pushing his feudal prerogatives to unacceptable limits to raise money for a campaign of re-conquest. His seizures of church property, persecution of the clergy, rigorous collection of taxes, abuse of the forest laws, may have resulted in a temporary break with Rome, but they also drove his barons and senior clergymen into rebellion. The result of this episode, on June 15, 1215, was Magna Charta.

THE RISE OF THE STATE OF LAWS: 1215–1688

Magna Charta was the outcome of negotiation between the king and his nobles after the latter had rebelled to preserve the rights and liberties that were part of feudal custom. The nobles felt that the king had violated this custom by his arbitrary wielding of royal authority as evidenced by his taxation policy, military adventures, meddling with the inheritance of nobles, raising a mercenary army, and relying on foreign favorites from France. King John, when confronted by the prospect of rebellion, offered to make England a fief of the pope. The offer was accepted, and in return, all enemies of the king were to be excommunicated. Still, within England, the rebels enjoyed more support than the king, especially in London, the capital, then as now. Thus, the rebels drew up a charter and demanded that King John sign it. Sensing the popular mood and desirous of buying time, the king chose to accept the rebel demands and sign their charter.

The royal signature set a precedent that came to define the constitutional and political struggle from 1215 to 1688. In agreeing to a formal contract that limited royal power in theory and in practice, King John had set a legitimate threshold for rebellion and accepted the legal right of the aristocracy to dispute and question the monarch's conduct of policy. If the king violated the contract, the nobles had the legal, as well as the moral, right to resist with all the resources at their command. Magna Charta established a principle with which the kings,

> . . . as the highest justices of the land, could not conceivably quarrel: that the law was not simply the will or whim of the king but was an independent power in its own right . . . All this, in turn, presupposed something hitherto unimaginable: that there was some sort of English 'State' of which the king was a part (albeit the supreme part) but not the whole.[70]

King John's death in 1216, and the succession of a minor, Henry III (r. 1216–1272), meant that power passed into the hands of a regency council, which, in 1217, issued a Forest Charter that curtailed the king's arbitrary power over the forests. To distinguish the charter extorted from King John in 1215 from the Forest Charter the former was renamed Magna Charta. Magna Charta was reissued thirty-eight times, became the rallying point for legitimate opposition to the crown, and without it the principle that there is a law, here on earth, which the king cannot break, could not have taken hold as surely as it did in England.[71]

The sixty-three articles that comprise Magna Charta make for interesting reading. Articles Two through Six, tackle the power of the king to interfere with inheritance while Seven and Eight protect wealthy widows from forcible remarriage and provide them security of property. Articles Nine, Ten, and Eleven, set limits on the ability of the state to seize land due to default on debts, and provide some protection to private debtors that had taken loans from Jews.[72] Article Thirteen, assures all urban settlements in general, but specially the city of London, which with its empathy for the rebel cause did much to ensure its success, in particular, of rights, exemptions, and customs. Articles Twelve and Fourteen, assert that the king may not levy financial demands without summoning the higher nobility and clergy and securing their approval. Thirteen of the articles[73] place limits on the power of the king to appoint local officials such as sheriffs, ensure local supervision over law and order, require the production of "credible witnesses" to support charges, deprive constables and sheriffs of their powers to confiscate the property of subjects, and makes it illegal for any freeman to be imprisoned, exiled, or disgraced "except by lawful judgment of his peers or by the law of the land." Article Thirty-Five, standardizes weights and measures, and Article Forty-One guarantees merchants, foreign and local, safety of their person, the right to travel unhindered, and the freedom to buy and sell as they choose. Even in the event of war, merchants from a hostile country are to be detained "without damage to their person or goods." Articles Fifty and Fifty-One, expel powerful foreign nobles and "all alien" military forces from England.

The drift towards "arbitrary despotism" was checked, but the outcome was not "the withering anarchy of feudal separatism".[74] Even after Magna Charta, the king was powerful, indeed, "far stronger than any great lord, and stronger than most combinations of great lords".[75] This alone furnished an incentive for members of the nobility to break ranks in order to gain more power by courting the king's favor. An intelligent sovereign, by balancing and encouraging rivalry through the calculated distribution of his limited powers of patronage could steadily expand his power. That the eighteenth article of Magna Charta actually asks the king to send justices around the country four times a year, accompanied by four knights chosen from each county, to hear cases and dispense justice, is testament to the durability and wisdom of Henry II's reforms. The English king could, as his French counterpart did, use the royal justice system to uphold the rights of the weak against the local notables and in the process destroy the "aristocratic privilege" upon which local autonomy and political power rested.[76] Preventing the rise of personal rule by the king meant that the opposition needed a demographic base greater than that provided by the nobility and higher clergy[77] and an institutional framework that could concentrate and channel the power of the localities to act as a counterweight to the king. In the 1230s, the word "Parliament", derived from the term "to parley", entered the political discourse.[78]

After coming of age, Henry III extended patronage in the form of castles, offices, bishoprics, and land, to his foreign favorites.[79] The "baronial parliament" began "to assert" that it had "the right to approve, veto, or even dismiss" the king's appointments to offices.[80] In 1258, the King's Council of twenty-four was replaced by a council of fifteen, with the royal delegation reduced to a mere three while the remainder were to be elected by the baronage and higher clergy.[81] From each county knights were to be chosen, at the rate of four per shire, who would travel around the district, collect complaints, and deliver them to the Justiciar (Chief Legal Officer).[82] Sheriffs were to be chosen only from the county, appointed for one year, and "foreign undesirables" were marked for expulsion.[83] These changes were rejected by the king who raised an army of mercenaries and secured papal backing.[84] In July 1264, the leader of the opposition, Simon de Montfort, sounded the call to arms and raised a people's army.[85] The country gentry and lesser landlords, formed an association called "The Community of the Bachelors of England" and threw their support behind de Montfort, who now "rebuked the great lords" for the arbitrary exercise of power on their estates and extended to them the reforms already made in the royal administration.[86]

In 1264, the king's party, strengthened by barons who did not wish to see reforms on their estates, was defeated, King Henry and the heir apparent, the future Edward I (r. 1272–1307), were captured and a treaty was signed.[87] When Parliament met in January 1265 at London, de Montfort used the country gentry and townsmen "to override" the magnates and royalists.[88] Though de Montfort died in battle following a resumption of civil war, and Edward I ascended the throne a few years later and proved to be a strong king, the principle of parliamentary opposition had come to stay and the ranks of the politically active citizenry had been swelled by the inclusion of the country gentry and burgesses.

The reigns of Edward I, Edward II (r. 1307–27), and Edward III (r. 1327–77), regularized the practice of calling parliaments to raise taxes to meet extraordinary expenditures, and permanent departments of state were established for the Exchequer, Chancery, Privy Seal, and Wardrobe. In 1294, Parliament was called to raise taxes for war against France, which it did, quite willingly at first. Customs duties were imposed on leather and wool, cargo was impounded until the duties were paid, and the clergy were ordered to give the king half of their revenues.[89] When the king left for Flanders the opposition demanded the confirmation of both Magna Charta and the Forest Charter, and stipulated that henceforth, parliamentary consent was required for taxation, goods must not be impounded in the future, and the earls that had refused to serve abroad were not to be punished.[90]

Under Edward II the barons, powerful magnates, and royal household officials set up a committee called the "the Lords Ordainers."[91] Parliament, which was summoned about once a year during Edward II's reign, was able to gain power by throwing its weight behind the barons or the king. It thus came to hold the balance of political power even though, as an institution, it became progressively more different in composition and worldview from the baronage or crown party.[92] In 1327, the representatives of the shires and boroughs petitioned separately as a body and so gave birth to the House of Commons.[93] Under Edward III, the collective petitions by the Commons became the basis for legislation and Parliament gained recognition as an essential part of the fiscal and legal machinery of the state.[94]

The reign of Richard II (r. 1377–99) saw parliamentary power and the constitutional framework challenged by the executive. In 1380, a poll tax levied for defense against France precipitated a revolt of peasant proprietors, which turned into the Peasant's Rebellion of 1381, and culminated in a march on London to petition the sovereign.[95] King Richard bought time by making concessions but continued to rule through his favorites and ignored the need to keep a coalition of interests behind him.[96] In 1387, Parliament demanded that the king dismiss his councilors, which Richard declined to do having been fortified by "lawyers' advice" that Parliament had no legal right to interfere with the management of the court.[97] The king's efforts to arrest the Earl of Arundel, one of the main opposition figures, only made things worse and once it became clear that the royal troops could not subdue the "armed barons", the only option left was to surrender.[98] The "Merciless Parliament" that followed this successful resistance had Chief Justice Tresilian and four others responsible for the Nottingham Declaration, which supported royal supremacy, "hanged, drawn, and quartered."[99]

On May 3, 1389, a year after Parliament had so violently asserted its supremacy, Richard took his seat at the Council and "asked blandly to be told how old he was".[100] Upon being informed that he was twenty-three years old, Richard declared that "he had certainly come of age" and would now "manage the realm himself" as, indeed, was his legal right.[101] The erstwhile rebels, in response, handed over the Great Seal, and made way for the inclusion of royal "nominees" and favorites.[102] It was one thing to rebel to protect the law, and quite another to prevent the king from exercising his legitimate power. From 1389 to 1397, Richard II ruled as a constitutional monarch with the consent of the Lords and the Commons. After 1394, however, Richard began raising in Ireland "an army dependent upon himself"[103] and, in 1397, he struck back at the opposition leaders, who were killed or arrested.[104] A "praetorian guard" was established and the king set about replacing county officials that had local roots with "dependable hacks."[105]

In February 1399, John of Gaunt, the king's uncle, died. The king confiscated his properties, redistributed them among his favorites, and banished his uncle's son, Bolingbroke, from the realm. Parliament had already been strong-armed into suspending most constitutional rights and delegated its powers to a wrecking-crew of eighteen persons beholden to the king.[106] Having confiscated the greatest inheritance in the land, Richard II had violated his coronation oath and the contract between the king and nobles. The king, therefore, "needed to be stopped."[107] The lords and bishops "wanted a pragmatic, rather than an erratic, mystically self-absorbed king, a king who would understand that it had been man, rather than God, who had put the crown on his head."[108]

The rebellion was a success and before 1399 was out, Bolingbroke led the House of Lancaster to victory and was crowned Henry IV (r. 1399–1413). That the new king was technically a usurper played into the hands of Parliament for it alone could provide him with the legitimacy he needed.[109] Parliamentary control of finance increased and it began receiving accounts from the high officials of the state.[110] Henry V (r. 1413–1422) reorganized the fleet, recognized that laws needed the approval of the Commons,[111] and became the first king to send royal messages and letters in the English language.[112] Henry VI (r. 1423–1461) suffered reversals in France and thus defeats abroad combined with an economic crisis at home. The royal debt, for example, rose from one hundred and sixty-eight thousand pounds in 1433, to three hundred and seventy-two thousand pounds by 1449.[113] Soldiers returning from the war found employment in private armies raised by the aristocracy and from 1455 to 1485, England endured a civil war known as the Wars of the Roses, which ended when Henry VII (r. 1485–1509) of the House of Tudor, finally restored the king's peace. The civil war was,

> . . . for the landed aristocracy a social rather than a natural catastrophe, a bloodletting that severely weakened them and enabled the Tudor dynasty which emerged from the struggle to resume with greater success the process of consolidating royal power.[114]

The consolidation of royal power was matched, however, by the consolidation of land holdings carried out by lords through a "variety of legal and semi-legal means" and their conversion to enclosures that could raise sheep to sell wool on the market.[115] The "commercialization of agriculture" marked the beginning of the end for both the peasantry and the "feudal seigneur" who lived off rents, and the latter's gradual replacement by "an overlord who was closer to an acute man of business."[116] The Court of the Star Chamber and the Court of Requests, were two legal instruments used by the king to protect the status of the peasantry and, in the process, expand his power. The Star Chamber was a regular feature of Westminster, had two presiding justices, and tried cases that merited special consideration due to the "excessive might" of one of the litigants, as well as cases concerned with the maintenance of private armies and the corruption of juries.[117] Parliament gave Henry VII's royal council the powers to examine persons "without oath" and "condemn" subjects "on written evidence alone", treasurers were personally appointed by the king and submitted their accounts to him.[118] Unlike the French king, however, the English king could not raise taxes without parliamentary sanction, and possessed neither a standing army nor "a great artillery park."[119]

Henry VIII's reign (r. 1509–1547) saw the continuation of the process of centralization evident under his predecessor. Cardinal Wolsey, appointed Lord Chancellor in the winter of 1515, kept that position for twelve years during which Parliament was summoned only once.[120] The Star Chamber became more active, Common Law rules of evidence were dispensed with, and Justices of the Peace backed by royal sanction, became the king's instruments in the countryside.[121] The Foreign Service was re-vamped, an efficient intelligence network was set up on the Continent, and the navy was equipped with new cannon-bearing ships.[122] Wolsey enriched himself in a manner befitting the satraps and viziers of continental bureaucratic empires. His personal retinue numbered one thousand, he enjoyed an annual income of half a million pounds in "early twentieth century money", owned palaces that surpassed the king's own, enriched his relations, and showed a particularly extreme partiality for his illegitimate son, who held eleven Church appointments.[123] Wolsey's life ended in disgrace when the sovereign he served turned against him and many of his palaces were confiscated by the crown.

Henry VIII's clash with, and ultimate victory over, the Catholic Church, has earned him notoriety thanks, in no small part, to Hollywood movies that project him as a libidinous and capricious monster whose desire for Anne Boleyn led him to want the annulment of his marriage to Catherine of Aragon. The pope refused to grant this request and so the king broke with the Catholic Church, replaced it with the Church of England, and compelled the clergy, on February 7, 1531, to acknowledge him as "their protector" and "supreme head."[124] Church lands were seized, small monasteries were liquidated, and papal taxes were abolished. Those who refused to swear an oath of allegiance and submit to the new order of royal supremacy over ecclesiastical affairs were guilty of treason and to even verbally insult the king or queen became a crime.[125] "Visitors" were sent around the country to confiscate relics and religious ornaments because they represented "superstition".[126] Pilgrimages and saints days were banned, and relics were smashed in public.[127]

All of this was accomplished even though the "only centrally controlled armed force in England" were the Beefeaters at the Tower of London.[128] Henry VIII's advisors

> . . . knew very well that sooner or later, the pope would wheel his big gun, excommunication, into the battle, and if the king were to win he had better be prepared to fight back with something more or less novel in the language of politics, namely, patriotism . . . so it had to be the parliament, the voice of the nation, that enacted the laws instituting the royal supremacy.[129]

The Parliament certainly did enact in accordance with the king's wishes. It was in 1530 that the support of Parliament was made a prerequisite for statutes to become laws and Henry VIII relied on the Lords and the Commons to draft and vote the legislation that broke the back of the Catholic Church in England. The confiscations of monastic property were undertaken with parliamentary approval and two-thirds of the confiscated land was sold and became private property.[130] In this way, landowners and townsmen, quite literally, bought a share in the Tudor enterprise.

The reign of Elizabeth I (r. 1558–1603) can well be regarded as the golden age of monarchy in England. During this period, Crown revenue as a share of national revenue stood at nearly thirty percent,[131] religious conflict between Catholics and Protestants was contained, and England began making its presence felt as far away as the Ottoman Levant, Spanish America, and

India. Queen Elizabeth opened England's first stock exchange, and encouraged English privateers to raid Spanish treasure ships and ports. The Queen herself invested twenty thousand pounds in Francis Drake's expedition of September 1585.[132] When Drake returned from his expeditions to the Americas one of his ships carried loot equal in monetary value to two years' royal revenue.[133] Elizabeth, like her father Henry VIII, did not attempt to dispense with Parliament. Instead, she used it with great success to raise money for war with Spain. Between 1588 and 1601, Parliament approved two million pounds for the war effort.[134] Even though "Elizabethan England became Walsingham's national security state" with spies and agents "kept busy",[135] it appeared that the island had made it through the Reformation without losing its institutional balance. The queen was strong, inspired devotion, and gave Parliament its due, private enterprise was ascendant, the law continued to evolve, and excesses that were committed, such as the execution of four hundred and fifty rebels in 1569–70,[136] are exceedingly small in comparison to the decimation of populations that took place on the Continent at that time. In France, for example, ten thousand Protestants were murdered in 1572 in an event known as St. Bartholomew's Day Massacre.[137]

Joel Samaha's study of law and order in Elizabethan England is particularly instructive when it comes to understanding how an early modern state without a centrally controlled bureaucracy maintained its writ. The key to overcoming "the clear and present danger of massive lawlessness"[138] seems to have been the monarchy's cooption of both the aristocracy and the emerging middle class through grant of royally sanctioned positions as justices of the peace subject to judicial oversight.[139] Constables and juries, however, were locally elected while the administrative staffs of judges and justices of the peace were hired privately and were not on the government payroll.[140] Although the justices of the peace and constables had considerable legal powers these were subjected to checks in the form of juries and judges. Moreover, the constables were directly answerable to the courts and, as elected officials serving fixed terms in the locality where they lived, were also accountable to their neighbors.[141] Critically important to the success of this participatory model of law and order administration was the ability of local governments to lawfully resist demands imposed on them by the central government. Recurrent famines in pre-industrial Britain, due to the poverty of the soil and unpredictable weather, often led the central government to requisition food. However, the central government had no means of collecting the food directly. Justices, constables, and clerks, were local men, most of them were locally appointed or elected, and all of them were locally accountable. Thus, the "Privy Council's orders that Essex send corn to the capital during every food supply crisis and the county's polite but firm replies excusing itself from doing so" reflect the autonomy of local governments.[142]

Queen Elizabeth died heirless and so the crown of England passed to the House of Stuart, which then ruled Scotland. The first two Stuart kings, James I (r. 1603–1625) and Charles I (r. 1625–1649) suffered from illusions of omnipotence and regarded the principles of monarchial absolutism as moral and political imperatives. Curing the Stuarts of their illusions would take decades and trigger a series of political crises that would finally lead to the emergence of a state of laws.

James I believed that kings were above the law, possessed the divine right to tax their subjects and legislate as they chose, and should be able to govern through their appointed servants without being answerable to any temporal power. The English political reality was that Parliament controlled taxation and approved and drafted legislation, the nobility and gentry owned most of the land and wielded political power in the countryside, and the taxes of the upper classes were collected on the basis of self-assessment without bureaucratic interference.[143] Furthermore, the taxes collected by the crown were either from the king's private estates or from custom duties on major trade items such as wine and wool.[144] The right to collect custom duties was given to the king by Parliament, normally for life,[145] and "Attempts to circumvent parliamentary authority in taxation by extorting forced loans, made both by Henry VIII and Queen Mary[146] met with such fierce resistance that they had to be abandoned."[147]

When James I ascended the throne of England, the royal debt stood at four hundred thousand pounds.[148] In 1608, the debt stood at one million pounds and his expenditure during peacetime was equal to what Queen Elizabeth had spent "in a year of full war."[149] Some two hundred thousand pounds were spent in gifts for Scottish courtiers and favorites.[150] To meet rising expenses, James I sold six hundred and fifty five thousand pounds worth of crown land.[151] This practice provided liquidity in the short term but diminished the Crown's ability to generate revenue from its own estates.

In 1610, the judges, led by Chief Justice Coke, "launched a concerted campaign" against the king's avowed desire "to decide which channel of the law he would employ."[152] One of the first targets of the judges was the High Commission, a religious institution under royal control responsible for enforcing doctrinal conformity. The judges',

> . . . detailed complaints, that High Commission had no right to imprison or deprive except for heresy and schism, or that a royal commission could not create a new court, sink into insignificance beside their guiding principle; namely, that only Parliament could alter the law, and only common-law judges could interpret Acts of Parliament.[153]

King James declined to heed advice "against behaving like a foreign tyrant" and confided to the Spanish ambassador "his surprise that his predecessors had allowed the Commons to come into existence."[154] In 1610, Parliament, eager to remind the monarch of its existence, declared that sovereign authority rested with the "King-in-Parliament", not the "King-in-Council".[155] The king, confronted by an increasingly hostile Parliament, which was as upset by his pro-Spanish leanings as it was by his autocratic pretensions, resorted to the "prostitution of honors".[156] Two thousand three hundred knights were created, the peerage was increased from fifty-nine to one hundred, and, after 1614, he allowed his favorites to act as middlemen for the sale of noble titles.[157] To evade parliamentary control, King James began meddling with the cloth exporters with the result that by 1615 the value of their exports had fallen to "half of what they had been in 1610."[158] Not surprisingly, by 1615, traders refused to extend the crown any further credit.[159]

By the time Parliament met in 1621, relations with the king had become acrimonious. The Commons urged King James to marry the crown prince to a Protestant and enter the war raging on the Continent against the Habsburgs.[160] When the king read the riot act to the Commons for "meddling" in matters that did not concern them and declared that their existence and rights were due to his grace, the reply was that the Commons derived the power to speak freely on all matters, religion and foreign policy included, on the basis of its "privileges" as an institution and the "birthright" of the assembled representatives of the governed.[161] Infuriated, the king dissolved Parliament and "Coke, Phelips, Pym, were now added to those in custody, then the premier earl, Oxford, for words against royal policy, then Sage and Sele for instigating refusal of a benevolence."[162]

The volume of trade, in spite of the king's antics, continued to expand as did the returns from customs receipts. Historically, arable land has been the source of wealth and political power. In England, however, a transformation had been unleashed following the defeat of the Spanish Armada in 1588. From 1590 to 1623 receipts from customs rose from fifty thousand pounds to three hundred and twenty-three thousand pounds—a six-fold increase in little over a generation.[163] The king's income, at this rate of increase, could rise substantially enough to make him independent of Parliament within one or two generations.

Parliament was well aware of the implications of the rapid increase in the returns from customs duties. When Charles I ascended the throne and summoned Parliament, the income from his estates was just thirty thousand pounds.[164] On the continent assemblies such as the French Estates General and the Spanish Cortes were falling into disuse due to the increased financial autonomy of the crown. Thus, the Commons of 1625 broke with the tradition of granting the king the right to collect customs duties for life and, instead, limited the grant to only one year.[165] Parliament, when called the next year, proved hard to manage, and the defiant mood was reinforced by the poorly planned and clumsily executed military interventions on the continent. The third Parliament summoned by Charles complained bitterly of "un-parliamentary taxation, martial law, billeting of troops, and unregulated powers of imprisonment."[166] When La Rochelle, a Protestant enclave on the French Atlantic coast, fell, in 1629, the Commons were roused to frenzy against the king, and, on February 24, they held the Speaker down in his chair when he called for adjournment and locked the doors to the assembly hall. Royal guards were sent to restore order and in

March, Parliament was dissolved while the leaders of the opposition were sent to the Tower of London.

Charles I, like his French or Spanish counterparts, now ruled England through his Royal Council, appointed servants, and notables that saw gain in collaborating with the king. However, King Charles had "no standing army"[167] and a professional bureaucracy that numbered about twelve hundred, a tiny fraction of the forty thousand or so civil servants that the French king had at his command during the same period.[168] To make ends meet, King Charles sold six hundred and forty seven thousand pounds worth of royal land between 1625 and 1635, and by 1630, his income from the royal estates had plunged to ten thousand pounds.[169] Though peace was made with France in 1629, and Spain, in 1630, King Charles remained in desperate financial straits. He demanded "loans" from affluent subjects, with the result that "Hundreds refused to pay" and seventy-six were thrown in jail.[170] Through extortion and the collection of customs duties without parliamentary approval, Charles managed to increase the royal revenue to six hundred thousand pounds and incurred "a regular deficit".[171] The king, to gain legitimacy, "sustained the Church in its property" and in exchange the Church preached "the duty of obedience" and divine right.[172]

The crisis that plunged England into civil war and a spell of theocratic despotism was sparked by the imposition of "ship money", or taxes levied to raise money for the navy, on counties that were inland. In 1636, Charles got "his judges to rule that he could impose such a charge when the kingdom was in danger"—the catch was that the king was the sole judge of what constituted "danger."[173] Soon thereafter, John Hampden, a wealthy former Member of Parliament from Buckinghamshire, refused to pay the tax and argued that "even the best of taxes" are legitimate only if levied "with the consent of Parliament."[174] The protests that followed Hampden's arrest, trial, and imprisonment, were so widespread that whereas nine-tenths of the ship money assessed for 1637 was collected, only two-tenths of the assessment was paid in 1639.[175] Meanwhile, Scotland, the Stuart home base, spun out of control as Scottish notables, "shrewdly advised" by their lawyers, petitioned King Charles to withdraw the new Prayer Book from circulation.[176] In 1638, the General Assembly of Scotland "refused to dissolve" upon royal command.[177]

To gain some control over the situation, the Earl of Strafford, who was the king's First Minister, advised Charles to summon Parliament in the belief that the Commons could be managed. Parliament, when it met on April 13, 1640, was so hostile that the king hastened to dissolve it and hold fresh elections.[178] The election results were an even greater disaster for the king. The Scots had invaded England, two hundred and ninety-four out of four hundred and ninety-three members of the Short Parliament were returned, and many of the newcomers were unmanageably hostile as well.[179]

The City of London paid off the Scots, Strafford was executed, the king agreed to summon Parliament at least once in three years. The Star

Chamber was abolished,[180] and on June 1, 1642, the Nineteen Provisions stripped the king of "his whole effective sovereignty".[181] In response, the king issued orders for the raising of a royal army and on August 22, 1642, "Charles set up his standard at Nottingham".[182] Parliament raised a New Model Army, which was led by Oliver Cromwell, a Puritan member of the Commons. By the spring of 1646, armed resistance by the royalists was beaten down.

The king may no longer have posed a threat to Parliament but the New Model Army certainly did. The soldiers were restive, owed arrears by the government, and refused to disband until they received sufficient compensation. In autumn 1647, each regiment elected representatives who were to form a military assembly that would debate contentious issues, and a secretary was appointed to record the proceedings.[183] The danger of mutiny, however, was quelled not by points of order in a parliamentary-style debate, but by Cromwell's personal intervention and ability to command the confidence of some "twenty thousand resolute, ruthless, disciplined, military fanatics."[184]

Cromwell was dictator by 1653, England and Wales were divided into eleven districts headed by major generals responsible for policing, public order, and ensuring tax collection, Parliament was purged, and "Everywhere was prying and spying".[185] Scotland and Ireland were invaded, Cromwell styled himself as the "Lord Protector" and combined in his person supreme administrative, military, legislative, and religious powers, and had the support of a fanatic armed minority of Puritans. Cromwell's Holy Protectorate, fortunately for England, did not survive his death in 1658. Cromwell's legacy, which inadvertently contributed to parliamentary supremacy in the end, was that "What his sword had wounded never rose to its full life again, neither monarchy nor lords, Scottish Kirk nor Irish Catholics."[186] Furthermore, Charles I's execution, in 1649, "was a grisly reminder" for "subsequent English kings."[187]

In 1660, the "Rump" of the Long Parliament that had made it through Cromwell's Protectorate was dissolved by "its own consent", and a new Parliament was convened, which opted to offer the son of Charles I the throne.[188] The prince accepted this offer and ascended the throne of England as Charles II (r. 1660–1685). This momentous event,

> . . . was not only the restoration of the monarchy; it was the restoration of Parliament . . . the House of Commons had broken the Crown in the field; it had at length mastered the terrible army it had created for that purpose. It had purged itself of its own excesses, and now stood forth beyond all challenge, or even need of argument, as the dominant institution of the realm . . . the victory of the Commons and the Common Law was permanent.[189]

The army was disbanded, the new king relinquished his rights of escheat and wardship, an annual income of one million two hundred thousand pounds was settled on the king out of which he was to pay the salaries of the civil service and meet his own expenses, a public accounts committee was constituted, the Triennial Act of 1664 was approved, and the liberties of Englishmen were confirmed. Habeas Corpus became a full-fledged Act, and from 1668 onwards, the five principal office holders came to be called Cabinet Ministers. This anti-Puritan Parliament sat for eighteen years and though it "rendered all honor to the King", its members "had no intention of being governed by him".[190]

The State of Laws had finally come into being and after the Glorious Revolution of 1688, which was more of a palace coup staged by William of Orange and Mary Stuart with parliamentary support against James II (r. 1685–1688), whose Catholicism and pro-French leanings angered many powerful interests, its position became unassailable. In February 1689, Parliament passed the Declaration of Rights which stipulated, among other things, that the king could not suspend laws, raise taxes, or raise an army, without parliamentary consent, Protestant subjects had the right to bear arms, and Members of Parliament were assured of their right to speak freely.

THE STATE OF LAWS: 1688–1756

King William (r. 1689–1702) followed the custom of the Netherlands in summoning Parliament annually[191] and during this period, the share of the Crown in national revenue fell to one-fiftieth.[192] The National Debt and the Bank of England were created in 1693–94 and Parliament gained power over the dismissal and appointment of judges. Henceforth, no judge could be removed from office unless guilty of an offence or both Lords and Commons demanded his dismissal. In place of "the somber warfare of creeds and sects" came "the squalid but far less irrational strife of parties", represented by the Whigs and Tories.[193] Inter-party conflict meant that an organized opposition emerged within the assemblies directed at the group that had a majority and so exercised an internal check on the ability of the Commons to wield absolute power.

In 1720, came the South Sea Bubble, the world's first financial scandal of truly international proportions. The plan that went disastrously wrong was "dreamed up" by the South Sea Company and "required the privatization of a large portion of the National Debt".[194] People were encouraged to trade their long-term government bonds for stock in the South Sea Company which sold the idea "that the appreciation of South Sea Stock" would bring in more money than could ever be hoped for through long-term bonds.[195] The company was given a monopoly to trade in the West Indies and the South Sea even though it had no ships of it own.[196] Bribes were liberally distributed among the Lords, Commons, and even the Royal Court, to secure privatization. The hype generated by the exercise, the objections of the Bank of England notwithstanding, was so successful that between January and

June 1720, the value of South Sea Stock rose from one hundred and twenty-eight to nine hundred and fifty and peaked on June 24 at one thousand and fifty.[197] When "some prominent stockholders", including Isaac Newton and Thomas Guy, decided to cash in, a chain reaction set in.[198] From September 1 to October 1, the stock crashed from seven hundred and twenty-five to two hundred and ninety, and before the year was out, "The country was left drowning in worthless paper".[199] Into the chaos stepped Robert Walpole, a Whig party leader, and First Lord of the Treasury. The Bank of England and the Treasury took over the National Debt, the Sinking Fund was activated, and Walpole used his knowledge of how badly individual parliamentarians and court officials and favorites had been compromised to rally his party behind him, pacify his rivals, and overawe the king.[200]

Walpole was head of government from 1721 to 1742. During his twenty-one years in power a silent revolution occurred in the executive arm of the government, due partly to the fact that the Hanoverian kings who sat on the throne of England after Queen Anne (r. 1702–1714), didn't know very much about England, were preoccupied with their lands on the Continent, and let their ministers hold meetings unsupervised.[201] The term "Prime Minister" had been used by kings in earlier reigns, and most English monarchs had their ministerial favorites. What distinguished Walpole was his reliance on Parliament to reorganize the "great offices of state" and the fact that his fall from power was due not to the withdrawal of royal support but his inability to control the Commons.[202] After Walpole's fall from power, there were twenty changes of government, and fourteen different prime ministers, from 1742–1782.[203] Most of the individuals who held the position of head of government were, like Walpole, First Lords of the Treasury.[204] England had developed a dual executive that comprised king and prime minister and mirrored the division of the legislative assembly into Lords and Commons. The components balanced one another and Walpole, for one, deliberately avoided "great issues that might divide the country", had a healthy respect for the "mass of hostile opinion" that existed "in the manor-houses and parsonages of England" and was determined "not to provoke it".[205] Taxation was kept to the minimum required and the land tax, "anxiously watched by the Tory squires, was reduced by economy to one shilling."[206]

The English were conscious that their strength as a nation was based upon a "positive attitude towards trade" and, indeed, "this was a preeminence recognized by social hierarchy, as the great houses and estates of the merchant princes around London demonstrated . . . many of the greatest families owed their fortunes to trade and did not disdain to return to it or to marry merchants' daughters."[207] The sense of achievement provided by a nearly unbeatable entrepreneurial capacity was amplified "by the belief that the country's enemies were consumed by malicious envy."[208] One particularly important result of the depersonalization of credit achieved by the Bank of England was that by the mid-eighteenth century there were sixty thousand public creditors[209] out of a population of nine or ten million.[210] The contrast with France in the 1700s was significant:

> No one thought that any important business could be well-managed without the involvement of the state. The farmers themselves, people ordinarily very impatient of instruction, were brought to believe that if agriculture was not progressing, it was chiefly the government's fault, because it gave them neither enough advice nor enough help. One of them wrote to an intendant, in an irritated tone in which one can already hear the Revolution: "Why doesn't the government name inspectors who would go into the provinces once a year to see the state of crops, who would teach the farmers how to improve them, who would tell them what to do with their animals, how to fatten them, raise them, sell them and where one ought to market them? These inspectors ought to be well-paid. The farmer who showed the best crops would receive public honors." Inspectors and medals! This is an idea that would never occur to a Suffolk farmer.[211]

Another indicator of British priorities was the navy, which expanded in size from one hundred to one hundred and twenty-four ships of the line from 1689 to 1739, while its French rival fell in strength from one hundred and twenty to fifty during the same period.[212] Even the army expanded rapidly and rose from seventy-five thousand men in 1710 (compared to the Netherlands which had an army one hundred and thirty thousand strong and a population of less than two million) to two hundred thousand in 1756 (compared to three hundred and thirty thousand for France, which had a population of twenty one and a half million).[213] The astonishing ability of *perfide Albion* to raise finances and secure materials faster and more efficiently than absolute monarchies with vastly superior powers of taxation and legions of civil servants was due, according to Jacques Necker, the French Controller-General of Finance, to the fact that "taxation was viewed as a legitimate part of parliamentary government".[214] British self-government was, indeed, founded on the principle of self-taxation. The two made each other possible and provided the British State with a rational basis for legitimacy that enabled it in a crisis to command the loyalty and resources of the country in a manner scarcely comprehensible to the Sun Kings, First Servants, Czars, and Emperors of continental bureaucratic empires.

A corollary to self-government, self-taxation, and private enterprise, was "a frugal but functional court" that impressed observers by its simplicity.[215] The capital city of London, with its franchise of twelve to fifteen thousand, elections every seven years, two hundred printing presses, "thousands of public places", and a population of more than seven hundred thousand by the end of the eighteenth century, was a monument to "private money" and the power of commerce.[216] London stood in sharp contrast to Versailles, Vienna, or St. Petersburg, all of which were monuments to royal grandeur and stately magnificence. In the English countryside of the eighteenth century, "The political and economic supremacy of the larger landlords was partly the result of trends that long antedate the Civil War, chiefly the authority of local notables and the absence of a strong bureaucratic apparatus . . . even under the Tudors and Stuarts".[217]

The development of a strong parliamentary government in Britain by the late seventeenth and early eighteenth centuries parallels the rise of centralized bureaucratic states in France, Prussia, Russia, and, to a lesser degree, Austria. Britain, like these continental bureaucratic empires underwent a road construction boom following the establishment of an effective central government. The similarity, however, ends there. On the continent, roads were built by the state with public funds, maintained by taxes, and supervised by government officials. Louis XIV of France had a strong Royal Road Administration with a budget of nearly nine hundred thousand *livres* in 1700, which had risen to four million *livres* by 1770, and nine million *livres* by 1786.[218] The roads were built with forced labor imposed on communities by the state apparatus and the communications network that emerged from this effort "favored communications between Paris and the provinces".[219] Spain and Austria followed the French example and the state ownership and control of roads in continental bureaucratic empires from ancient times is a well-documented phenomenon. To develop their road network, however, the British set up turnpike trusts, which were "private companies authorized by Act of Parliament" to build, improve, and maintain roads and collect tolls in exchange for these services.[220] The eighteenth century was boom-time for these trail-paving entrepreneurs and by 1800, "no fewer than" sixteen hundred "turnpike trusts had been formed."[221] By 1754, it took only four days to travel from London to Manchester and between the 1740s and 1780s travel time from Birmingham to London fell from two days to nine hours.[222] Meanwhile, across the English Channel, in Bourbon France, "not even a charity workshop located in the depths of a far distant province could be established but that the controller-general wanted to directly supervise its expenses, write its regulations, and choose its location."[223] Furthermore, the ". . . paperwork was already enormous, and official procedure was so slow that . . . it always took at least a year for a parish to obtain authorization to rebuild its bell tower or repair its rectory; usually two or three years passed before the request was granted."[224]

The culture of power of the Anglo-Saxons was, by the mid-eighteenth century, anomalous in the European context, and freakishly different from the continental bureaucratic empires of East Asia, the Indian subcontinent, the Middle East, and North Africa. The divergence in evolution is explained to a great degree by geography and location. The land was not rich enough to allow the landed aristocracy to maintain or improve their lifestyles through rents alone once population pressure began driving prices up towards the end of the twelfth century. The relative poverty and scarcity of the land led the landlords towards raising sheep to sell wool on the market, which required little labor, and by the fourteenth century the wool traders were a powerful lobby. Location dictated that the south and the east of the home island could only be guarded by a strong navy, and armies were raised needed and packed off to France, Ireland, Germany, the Netherlands, or some far distant theatre of war. For long periods, England remained at peace with itself with no centrally controlled, organized, or equipped, standing army. The fact that primordial Germanic political traditions survived and developed far better in England than on the northern and eastern plains of Germany is another indicator of the decisive impact of geography and location on the development of cultures of power. The English contemporaries of Emperor Fredrick Hohenzollern, the Iron Chancellor Otto von Bismarck, and Nazi dictator Adolf Hitler, were Robert Walpole, Disraeli and Gladstone, and Winston Churchill, respectively. History furnishes few examples of greater divergence between peoples sharing the same religious, ethnic, linguistic, and cultural roots.

In continental bureaucratic empires, the servants of the state are the ruling class and consume the greatest portion of the country's wealth. The Anglo-Saxon historical experience of governance was marked by the conspicuous absence of a bureaucratic class and though state patronage was important, and many legislators were content to place a monetary value on their support and patronage, it was one of many potential sources of great economic wealth. Careers in trade, financial speculation, stocks, manufacturing, insurance, education, medicine, law, or raiding Spanish galleons, were in many respects more economically rewarding than state service. If anything, the state acted as the agent of private enterprise.

Private property, in both land and capital, further diminished the ability of the central authority to concentrate economic wealth. The Norman kings may have disliked the theoretical position of private property, but, in practice, could not reverse the trend in favor of it. The hereditary nature of fiefs granted to lords to maintain troops allowed time for a strong sense of association to develop between rulers and the ruled at the local level. Power, both legal and physical, was dispersed through the realm, and the nobility came to court not as craven supplicants in search of offices, confirmation of their lands, or remuneration for providing the king with a poetical ego-massage, but as politicians with the capacity to exert power independently of the crown, to which they were bound by a feudal contract that gave each party a legitimate sphere of action. Magna Charta and Parliament are both outgrowths of the will and the ability of the baronage and their allies in the clergy to preserve their lawful autonomy.

Parliament is central to the British culture of power for it is through this artifice that the baronage enlisted the support of the gentry and merchants to contain the central government without, however, destroying it or rendering it ineffective. Parliament has repeatedly come to the support of merchants being abused by the king and made it clear to more than one sovereign that placing arbitrary impositions on the property of merchants, extorting forced loans, or collecting custom duties without parliamentary approval, were violations of the contract between the king and his subjects. The security of private property helps explain why the landlord in England was willing to make long-term investments in founding boroughs or studying better business management methods. The conditions that prevailed in England meant that it was rational to save and invest in private enterprise and, after 1694, public credit, instead of consuming, wasting, and concealing wealth derived from the abuse of state power. By one estimate, the proportion of Englishmen that "lived by agriculture" was "probably not over fifty percent" by the mid-seventeenth century.[225]

The greatest achievement of Parliament was that it accelerated and completed the standardization of law begun by Henry II without necessitating the centralization of administrative power. The fact that England developed a relatively uniform judicial process, and the legitimate means to make changes to it, reduced the ability of the king to maneuver his way to arbitrary power by taking advantage of ambiguous and conflicting codes. Furthermore, where there is only one law, and a vocal class of lawyers and judges, it is easier to identify violations by the state, and in time consensus on interpretation can emerge. If Parliament drew up laws for the entire realm, the Common Law judiciary upheld Parliament's prerogative and received in return the right to interpret legislation. The wise sovereign worked through Parliament and accepted the fact of his or her subjection to an autonomous temporal reality, sustained by powerful landed and mercantile interests, and articulated by elected representatives in the form of laws. To deny or undermine this principle meant that the sovereign had broken the contract and rendered the inevitable Parliament-led rebellion that followed a legally and morally justifiable, if not imperative, exercise against tyranny.

The state of laws that emerged in 1689 was no longer in danger of dissolution by the executive and the emergence of political parties added an internal check on the ability of Parliament to attain consensus without compromise. The state of laws was one and indivisible. Self-government and self-taxation formed a virtuous cycle. Laws were made and changed by elected representatives. Wars were waged when necessary and with a level of efficiency that left the proud militarists of the Continent gaping with awe. Public participation in national political and economic life was greater than anywhere else in the world except, perhaps, England's colonies in North America. The aristocracy did not serve as a strong barrier to social mobility and contributed to the creation of an institutionally stable and gradually evolving political hierarchy that existed autonomously of the executive. In stunning contrast, the greatest handicap that continental bureaucratic empires have labored under through the ages is that the omnipotence of the executive reduces institutions to the level of mere instruments torn between servility, when the ruler is strong, and self-destruction, when he becomes weak.

That is not to say that the state of laws in Britain had attained perfection by 1756. The Reform Acts of 1832 and 1867, the American and French

Revolutions, the industrial revolution, and a host of other important constitutional, economic, political, and international events that would affect
the culture of power of the Anglo-Saxons still lay generations in the future.
The achievement, by 1756, was of a sense of purpose, direction, and process, combined with instituional means of progress by consensus, and the
freedom to pursue goals through reason, logic, observation, and laws.

Voltaire, in the *Philosophical Dictionary*, in 1756, asked, "Why can't
the world be more like England?"[226] Decades earlier, he had experienced
the delights of the Bastille for "publishing a satirical poem" and saw England, the place of refuge for tens of thousands of French Protestants after
Louis XIV revoked the Edict of Nantes in 1685, as "a model of freedom
and liberty".[227] He wondered, "Why can't the laws that guarantee British
liberties" be adopted elsewhere and enquiringly observed that coconuts,
which "bear fruit in India, do not ripen in Rome."[228] India and the Papal
States were very different in geography, soil, and climate, but in time, with
the application of reason, and careful cultivation, the coconut tree could
be made to bear fruit anywhere. The same was true of the state of laws
that Voltaire saw in Britain and was captivated by. It too, could become "a
universal model".[229] Voltaire, admittedly, "was more in love with the idea
of freedom and commercial enterprise than with its cruder manifestations.
What goes for the theatre (or American movies) applies to the press as
well."[230] However, he dismissed such incongruities and excesses as he saw
as "the bad fruits of a very good tree called liberty."[231]

THE EMERGENCE OF A CENTRAL BUREAUCRACY
AND PUBLIC SERVICE ETHOS, 1763–1945

After 1757, the British state underwent a steady transformation of its
administration and its politics. Administratively, Britain became more
bureaucratic as a permanent and eventually highly influential civil service
elite was constituted and sustained. Politically, Britain became more democratic and its system of representation was gradually expanded to accommodate the middleclass and the working class. Britain's culture of power
therefore evolved to create an equilibrium between a political elite that was
sufficiently pragmatic to make timely adjustments to the phenomenon of
modernization and a central administrative elite that remains to this day
the envy of other nations on account of its professionalism and integrity.
The successful symbiosis of the classical Anglo-Saxon state of laws with a
powerful central bureaucracy modeled on that of continental bureaucratic
empires is one of the most intriguing patterns of institutional development
in modern history and holds the key to understanding the stability and
progress of Britain during the 1800s and 1900s.

To begin with it is necessary to dispel the notion that Britain had a
weak state. In fact, Britain had, by the mid-1700s, developed a strong

state supported by the most powerful and upwardly-mobile elements of a strong society. A solid demonstration of this is provided by the British ability to raise large armies and a world-beating navy and fight protracted global and regional military conflicts against a far larger and wealthier France. In Continental Europe, more numerous bureaucracies yielded diminishing returns on account of corruption and social resistance to arbitrary demands. In Britain, proportionately far greater demands were imposed by a much smaller state apparatus that was able to perform better than its continental rivals as it enjoyed legitimacy derived from parliamentary sanction. The rise of the British "fiscal military state" in the 1700s was itself the result of a system that was more representative and legitimate and could on account of this demand and collect more from society even with quantitatively inferior means of extraction.[232] The centralization of tax collection was made possible by "the uncontested authority of Parliament"—an authority that had itself matured over many centuries and thus gained legitimacy.[233] In Britain, therefore, the tax collector, though hardly a popular figure, was the appointed agent of a lawful, representative and constitutional power, whereas elsewhere in the world, such officials were the personal servants of arbitrary and/or absolutist rulers. This combination of centralization and legitimacy in turn made possible the integration of local political interests and elites into a national order channelized through institutions. Thus, for example, in Scotland, MPs and local leaders lobbied the central government for subsidies, grants, posts in the state machinery, and access to jobs in the colonies and overseas corporations for their constituents, in exchange for facilitating and authenticating the fiscal centralization from which the government derived its wealth and its capacity for patronage.[234] Britain's need for manpower to fight wars of containment on the Continent and wars of expansion overseas also provided local leaders with the opportunity to gain from cooperating with the government's efforts at military recruitment. In Scotland, the local landed political elite were the principal organizers of such recruitment making them indispensible to the state as well as dependent on the state.[235] The party affiliations of the local leaders were important but by no means strong enough to preempt local cooperation due to a shared "apolitical commitment to a common statist polity."[236]

The ability of the British state to integrate its peripheries into a centralized national system of financial administration and military power was legitimated by Parliament and instrumented through a permanent civil service. Under parliamentary oversight and sanction, there was an expansion of the fiscal bureaucracy with the strength of "the excise establishment alone increasing from 1313 officers in 1690 to 4910 in 1783."[237] Recruitment to the bureaucracy depended on connections and political patronage.[238] The existence of a spoils system gave parliamentarians an important source of leverage over their constituents and, at least in theory, ensured that the civil servants remained subservient to the political class. In practice, this system was being overwhelmed by "the great and increasing accumulation of public business"[239] on account of greater population density, economic development and overseas expansion. It also had very high costs in terms of efficiency and honesty and was depriving the political leadership of a sound administrative platform capable of giving them informed advice and implementing policies effectively. In Britain, powerful families used their clout to secure civil service appointments for their "un-ambitious", "indolent" and "incapable" relations who were unable to make it on their own in one of the professions or as entrepreneurs and politicians.[240] The typical British civil servant cut a sorry figure, did not enjoy social prestige, was remunerated lightly, and secured appointment as a favor to the powerful by the powerful. This low median quality was the natural result of the unenlightened "discretion with which the heads of departments, and others who are entrusted with the distribution of patronage, exercise that privilege."[241] After recruitment, the clerical nature of the first assignments (typically as a glorified copyist) destroyed what little drive or initiative the new officer might possess, while salaries tied purely to seniority combined with departmental myopia helped create a situation in which departments were forced to recruit officers for key staff positions from outside the civil service.[242] It was therefore in the enlightened self-interest of the politicians to reorganize Britain's civilian bureaucracy on the more robust and competitive pattern of the military services or the Indian Civil Service.[243] The growing complexity of British society and the burden of governing a global empire meant that Britain could no longer afford to be administered by politically connected dilettantes and dullards. Instead, Britain needed an energetic, honest, and serious civil service secure against political interference, that would be remunerated well enough and enjoy sufficient social prestige to draw the best university graduates into its ranks. Doing so would require creating a central agency for conducting recruitment exams in a wide variety of subjects and substantially reducing the clerical aspects of work required from newly recruited officers. These recruits would then be transferred from one department to another in order to help them develop a synoptic understanding of how the state apparatus functioned. The emergence then in the mid-1800s of a civil service elite recruited on merit, promoted on the basis of a combination of seniority and performance, and rotated between departments so as to prevent fragmentation and produce a bureaucratic leadership able and willing to advise on matters on policy represented the rise of a "public service ethos".

This ethos was never formalized through acts of Parliament, a practice that is consistent with "the nature of the British political system and its unwritten constitution."[244] What ultimately sustains this ethos is a realization reinforced by practice shared by politicians and civil servants that they must work together to govern effectively while respecting the inherent difference between the requirements of politics and those of administration. The politicians hold responsibility for policy while the civil servants advise and apprise the government of the facts and concepts it needs to digest for this purpose. Policies framed, the politicians in government defend and explain, those in opposition criticize, and the civil service implements in the light of the law and the interests of the state. The politicians aggregate public opinion and sectional interests while the civil servants run the day-to-day affairs and deal with practical problems as they arise with minimal political interference. From this emerges a resilient equilibrium between bureaucratic autonomy and political leadership "based on a general code or ethos, which, although not explicitly codified, is nonetheless real and powerful."[245]

In practice the public service ethos depends on the ability of the civil service to be respected as politically neutral and therefore more objective about the affairs of state than the politicians. That objectivity, in turn, provides the civil service the opportunity to shape coherent departmental opinions. Ministers necessarily rely on their departments for information and guidance and find that civil servants have few qualms about entering into civilized disagreement with the political leadership. British ministers, since the mid-1800s, have been "to a degree rarely matched in other democracies, dependent on the assistance of a career bureaucracy whose members they have virtually no opportunity to select."[246] The social prestige, public esteem and esprit de corps of the civil service is such that even the most popular leader cannot wantonly interfere in the administration. Thus, when Prime Minister John Major entertained a proposal that would have had civil servants engaged as media advisers to the government, the move was effectively blocked on ethical grounds by the Cabinet Secretary. Later, when Prime Minister Tony Blair, sounded out the civil service on the possibility of having his party chief of staff appointed as Principal Private Secretary, the civil service successfully resisted the proposal. Even Prime Minister Margaret Thatcher, no fan of the civil service at the beginning of her tenure, was constrained to admit, at the end of the day, that it was "the sheer professionalism of the British Civil Service, which allows governments to come and go with a minimum of dislocation and a maximum of efficiency" and that this certainly is "something other countries with different systems have every cause to envy."[247]

The British central bureaucracy that emerged in the 1700s and underwent basic reorientation in the mid-1800s, was relatively small, numbering some 16,000 personnel at the time of the Northcote-Trevelyan reforms.[248] Over the decades that followed, the size and distribution of the civilian bureaucracy experienced quantitative expansion and qualitative refinement though a generalist core of central administrative officers remained powerful until the late-1960s. As the bureaucracy expanded questions arose as to the actual ability of Parliament and Cabinet to control the machinery that was technically subordinate to them. With a civil service numbering 732,000 in 1979 and a state sector that employed 30 percent of the workforce[249] the case may well have been made that Britain had become a civil service with a country rather than a country with a civil service. The problem in part had arisen from the post-Second World War socialistic reforms entailing the creation of a comprehensive welfare state, something that inevitably caused the ranks of state employees to swell. However, it would not be fair to attribute the marginalization of Parliament and even Cabinet in comparison to the bureaucratic machinery to socialistic reforms alone. In 1961, when Pakistan's Ambassador to Italy, S. K. Dehlavi, was tasked with preparing a report on administrative law, he found that Parliament had long conceded its law-making powers to the executive. In 1920, against 82 Acts of Parliament, 820 Statutory Rules and Orders were passed by the executive under the Rules Publication Act.[250] Taking cognizance of a situation in which Parliamentary and Cabinet control was being diluted, administrative tribunals were set up in the mid-1950s to check the expanding bureaucracy. The change was sufficiently great to merit the observation that the "law of England has become officialised and a system of administrative law in the guise of a great mass of administrative tribunals has come to exist."[251] Expansion of the bureaucracy, the prestige and esprit de corps of its elite services, and the popular criticism of the growth of officialdom, did not, however, mean that Britain ceased to be a state of laws. Rather, Britain's political elite was able to manage the challenge of administrative growth so that while the country's culture of power became more bureaucratic, it did not loose its touch with pre-industrial moorings.

PRAGMATISM AND GRADUALISM:
THE SYSTEM POLITICAL IN THE 1800s

While a cycle of bloody revolution, repression and reaction reigned supreme in Continental Europe, Britain's political elite adapted to the social and economic changes wrought by industrialization even though these changes had no precedent in history and thus their consequences were unforeseen. At the heart of the pragmatism and gradualism that characterizes Britain's political system in the 1800s and early 1900s was willingness on part of the elite to share power and concede popular demands before they assumed desperate and violent proportions. History has shown time and again that concessions made before social volcanism takes over have a stabilizing effect while concessions made after the tipping point has been crossed serve mainly to aggravate demands even further. Wisdom, therefore, lies in adapting before there is a violent test of strength between a regime and its subjects, though this is a lesson that was seemingly lost on most of the traditional rulers of Europe, as well as on the demagogues and adventurers who challenged them. There are a number of valid explanations for the wisdom with which the British state navigated the post-industrial landscape. Certainly, Britain had more than its fair share of farsighted political leaders willing to sacrifice themselves and their political popularity in order to do what was necessary to preserve the state. However, Britain's prime ministers do not have very much power, have to deal with cabinet colleagues who are parliamentarians in their own right, and are advised by an autonomous central bureaucracy whose esprit de corps makes imposition from the top a difficult proposition even at the best of times. Britain's great men, in other words, have never wielded great power on account of their country's institutional development.

The answer perhaps lies in the moderate temperament of the British political class. The leaders of a limited constitutional government that had acquired legitimacy through a longevity built on success were far more attuned to the needs of their society than the autocrats and theocrats that ruled elsewhere. The existence of chartered bodies, autonomous institutions, political parties, world-class private enterprise, and civil society, meant that Britain's peoples had a capacity for sustained mobilization. The British political elite, which itself emerged from a competitive process that was carried on by these entities, was willing to expand the scope of representation and introduce reforms as a way to broaden and deepen the social base that supported the state. Power sharing, to use a fashionable phrase, actually increased the power of the state by making its demands legitimate for a greater proportion of society.

An interesting indicator of this is the perseverance and adaptability of Britain's Conservative party and a recent study that uses the Conservative party as a benchmark that has demonstrated that British politics in the 1800s and 1900s operated in 28-year cycles. Thus, in the 1840s, 1870s, 1890s, 1920s-30s, early 1950s and more vigorously in the 1980s and 1990s, British conservatives reasserted their political dominance.[252] However, while the term "conservative" might conjure up images of refined aristocrats in powdered wigs conspiring against the public, Britain's conservatives would almost count as radicals by Continental European standards. From the repeal of the Corn Laws in 1846, to the electoral reforms of 1867, and more recently, Churchill's indelible heroism and Thatcher's assault on the complacent state socialism of the post-war era, Britain's conservatives have kept up with the times and made striking political comebacks. British conservatives, unlike those in many other countries, including those in the United States, do not seem to subscribe to utopian delusions about the past or the future. Their approach is far more inductive and therefore less ideologically driven. What this means in terms of practical politics is that the political leadership can take a surprisingly long view for a democratic country. The electoral cycle is, of course, very important, but it is not the dominant consideration in government calculations, especially when the incumbent has some control over when elections can be called. Thatcher's contempt for the "false squires" or "political calculators who see the task of conservatives as one of retreating gracefully before the left's inevitable advance",[253] while understandable, misses a very basic point. That is that the conservative "retreat" allowed Labor to exhaust its capital and overextend the state, laying the foundations for an enduring conservative revival between 1979 and 1997. Not only did conservative fortunes improve dramatically during this period but the British political mainstream also moved from left-of-center to right-of-center so that Labor had to rebrand itself as a market-friendly party.

The British political system's ability to simultaneously moderate opinion and facilitate change at critical moments apparently rests on three main factors. The first is that as power in Britain has long been limited by convention and the interplay of autonomous institutions, the stakes in political contests are kept within reasonable limits. In contrast, countries with long experience of arbitrary and autocratic rule gravitate towards a political mentality in which the desirability of staying in power is so great that it overrides considerations of constitutional propriety and state interest. The second is that over many centuries British society evolved participatory means of local government, civil society, and economic organization which, while regulated by the state were substantially autonomous of it. In contrast, in most other countries local privilege and socioeconomic autonomy were undermined when the rulers were strong and produced a rapid descent into chaos when the external force keeping the state going diminished. Britain's sustained argumentative tradition of politics and institutionalized experience of negotiation between social forces and the state that were deeply interdependent helped establish rules that in their collectivity *are* the state of laws. The third element is the deep social base of Britain's political parties, their internal democracy, sensitivity to local interests, and ability to relate these interests to a broader state rationality. The relative seriousness with which British political parties take local politics and the selection of councilors is instructive for in Britain efforts are made to search out competent people to fill local posts.[254] In other parts of the world, money power, vested interests and local patronage/kinship/sect/caste considerations determine how local politics play out, making it much harder for local cooperation to take root.

Some examples from the 1800s show the system in action with Parliament responding to public agitation and pressure. The repeal of the Combination Acts in 1824 allowed for the lawful formation of unions, with membership growing from a million in 1815 to 4 million by 1872.[255] In response to thousands of petitions and out of a desire to preempt a "French-style bourgeois-poor coalition", the Reform Act of 1832 was passed by Parliament, effectively "doubling the size of the electorate by lowering franchise requirements."[256] Increasingly sensitive to the danger posed to the state by a politically alienated working class, electoral reforms in the 1870s and 1880s lowered franchise requirements, expanded the electorate, and introduced secret ballots. Factory legislation, health reforms and, in 1870, the introduction of compulsory schooling up to age 13, were also intended as ways of expanding the social support base of the state. The effectiveness of these enactments, as well as the actual motivation behind them, was and remains contested. Marx, in particular, pokes numerous holes in the working of the Factory Act of 1850, which limited the workday to 10 hours.[257]

Under the Factory Act inspectors reporting to the home secretary were appointed and required by Parliament to publish reports every six-months. Factory owners, however, did all they could to frustrate the implementation of the law for the penalties were not greater than the benefits to be gained through violations. Health legislation aside, in 1863 the death rate per 100,000 for London's tailors and printers in the age group 45–55 years, at 2093 and 2367, respectively, was twice the rate for agricultural workers in England and Wales (1145 per 100,000).[258] Parliament, moreover, was hungry for property and privatized 3.5 million acres of common land between 1801 and 1831.[259] Of course, many other depredations and inequities can be cited as proof that Parliament was a den of insidious low-lives looking out only for themselves, and there is some truth in this. Such a perspective ignores the vital role that Britain's political system played in balancing fundamental conflicts and in allowing for the gradual development of institutions and conventions to drive a reform process forward that ultimately made the state more law-based and liberal in its behavior. The greatest test of this system with its old representative institutions and relatively new central bureaucracy, came in the 1900s when Britain's economic position, security and political temperament and traditions came under sustained assault, triggering and accelerating material decline at home and abroad.

THE ORDERLY MANAGEMENT OF DECLINE, 1900–PRESENT

A statement attributed to William Armstrong, Cabinet Secretary from 1968 to 1974 defines the role of Britain's government and civil service as managing "the decline of Britain in an orderly fashion."[260] This statement, was, and still is, taken as a sign of defeatism and conservatism and reflects a profound pessimism with respect to the fortunes of the British state in the global context. One can imagine that no political leader, even if their private views coincided with Armstrong's, could publicly concede the merit of his opinions. And yet, Armstrong's statement can also be taken as evidence of great wisdom and realism in British corridors of power for the erosion of Britain's global supremacy and pivotal role in the regional balance of power was ongoing since the late-1800s regardless of what the politicians or the public believed or thought.

Britain's decline had several interlocking components. One was the spread of industrialization to Continental Europe, the United States, and Japan, during the mid and late 1800s. The rapid industrialization of Germany and the United States, in particular, meant that by the 1890s Britain was no longer the workshop of the world and relative economic decline, evidenced by its falling share of world manufacturing output, had set in. Another component was the sheer size and complexity of the British Empire, the only truly global empire to have ever existed especially in terms of the vast areas under direct rule in the dominions of settlement and in the dominions of conquest. While impressive on the map, the size of the imperial core was small compared to the territories in orbit, and by 1900, with Germany developing a powerful navy and Japan rampaging through parts of East Asia, there was a question mark over Britain's ability to defend its possessions if it had to fight on more than one front. The third component was the European balance of power. Since 1815, no one state in Europe had been strong enough to dominate the entire Continent. This allowed Britain to focus on overseas expansion and avoid military entanglements on the Continent. But with the rise of Imperial Germany and with the post-Bismarck German leadership determined to pursue a global policy aimed at establishment a new pecking order, the balance of power in Europe was in danger of breaking down. The First World War underscored how strong Germany had in fact become for the combined might of the British, French and Russian empires proved insufficient to contain the Germans, leaving the achievement of victory dependent on the entry of the United States into the conflict. In the aftermath of this conflagration consequences emerged, ranging from a weak post-war economy to the rise of Bolshevism, fascism and Nazism, to confound attempts at stabilization. With the global political climate shifting, economics working in favor of other powers, and military challenges emerging from multiple points, Britain's imperial decline abroad, and industrial decline at home, were inevitable.

The decline and fall of the British Empire did not, of course, go smoothly, but compared to the disastrous legacy and declines associated with other empires, it could have been much worse. Rather than resisting the inevitable in a futile attempt to regain glory as the French tried to do, the British made a virtue out of necessity, transferring power to the elected representatives of India, Pakistan and Sri Lanka in 1947 and 1948. The Labor government elected in July 1945 moved very effectively to take the wind out of the Bolshevik challenge to Britain's domestic institutions by introducing comprehensive welfare reforms. In 1946, the National Insurance Act, Industrial Injuries Act, and National Health Act, followed in 1948 by the National Assistance Board, created the legislative matrix for the post-war welfare state. The government was able to sell welfare reforms as a means of helping people engage in "leveling up" and raising the average standard of living.[261] While the maintenance costs of the nanny state would grow faster than productivity and come in for criticism by the late 1970s, these reforms helped Britain rebuild and stabilize and acted as a firewall against more extreme views. Between 1951 and 1960, for instance, wages increased much faster than inflation and nearly doubled.[262] Britain's central bureaucracy played a critical role in the post-war planning process and by 1943 "the senior ranks of the civil service were consciously trying to apply the lessons they had learnt from the war economy in order to make what they regarded as proper provision for peace."[263] The politicians and the 2500-strong Administrative Class worked together to use state intervention in the economy to raise living standards and provide greater equality of opportunity though as this entailed the government taking on more functions even as each function became more technically demanding and complex, complaints arose that the bureaucracy needed to be reformed as it had become too powerful while losing its intellectual command over the issues it was now expected to address.

These criticisms were not entirely novel in the sense that alarm over the reliance on sub-legislation by executive agencies had led to the formation of a committee on ministerial powers as early as 1932.[264] Lord Haldane's committee had also expressed the opinion, with reference to wartime administrative exigencies that the expansion of the cabinet made effective control over the machinery of government rather more difficult than it was before.[265] It was not until 1968, when the civil service commission chaired by Lord Fulton, submitted its report that something was done about the problem, which, at any rate, had grown exponentially since 1945. The Fulton report observed that Britain's civil service was "still fundamentally the product of the nineteenth-century philosophy of the Northcote-Trevelyan Report."[266] That philosophy is that effective control and leadership of the state apparatus can best be secured by having a class of all-round administrators rotated between different departments in key command positions. The all-round administrators would thus acquire a synoptic understanding of the state and be in a position to provide direction to the executive and support staff below them *and* advise the politicians above them. This approach had given Britain's civil service a career orientation, immunized it from nepotism and "political jobbery", and earned for the service a social prestige and acknowledgement of its merit from the people at large.[267] These were no mean achievements for the esprit de corps, vitality, and autonomy of the civil service had become an essential part of governance in Britain.

The challenge was to adapt the administrative structure of Britain to the changing needs of society. Ironically, the very success of the generalist administration in creating a welfare state had led to accelerated social change and increased the complexity of administration that made the existing civil service pattern difficult to sustain. Over the years, engineers, doctors, scientists, technical specialists, and experts in nearly every conceivable field had been brought into the administrative structure to take care of highly technical functions. The Administrative Class was supposed to provide leadership to the specialists but the problem was that the former was no longer capable of mastering the knowledge needed to command the respect of the latter. While the Administrative Class lacked the knowledge now needed to govern effectively, the specialists had little or no experience of management and leadership. Thus, Britain's civilian bureaucracy was polarizing into a tiny administrative elite that knew about leadership and management and had the confidence to deal with the politicians but now lacked essential knowledge, and a much larger group of specialists who had the knowledge in their respective fields but lacked the leadership and management qualities of the Administrative Class. Fulton's advice was that

Britain needed to fuse the good qualities of the Administrative Class with the knowledge and expertise of the specialists and that this end could be achieved if the French pattern of "training and professionalism" for the specialist cadres were adopted.[268] This would help merge the familiarity "with the machinery of administration" that was the strong suit of the Administrative Class with the technical expertise of the specialists that was now vital to coping with the complexity and change characteristic of British society.[269] Some reforms, such as the creation of a special Civil Services Department to manage the civil service and examine issues of pay and service conditions more systematically were indeed implemented. For the most part, however, the civil servants pursued those reforms that enhanced their strength and autonomy and backpedalled on those recommendations that they felt would work to undermine their position.[270]

The conservatism of Britain's civil service elite arises in part from its autonomy being the result of practice and convention that evolved over the 1800s to make civil servants neutral advisers and executors of ministerial will. Seen another way, Britain's civil service was created to extend the ability of the cabinet to implement its decisions and to do so in a faithful, well-advised and lawful manner:

> Britain has no equivalent of the French conception of the civil service as the robust embodiment of the State, which by centralization liberates the peasants from the bondage of local *notables* and at the same time encourages its servants to enunciate general principles of equity and organization. The professionalization of thought and action took different forms on each side of the Channel. The assumptions of British civil servants were obviously related to the organization which became necessary in order to transform the service of individual ministers into a central government capable of carrying out its increased responsibilities.[271]

The British civil service, then, is an extension of the will of the cabinet and during the 1800s gained actual autonomy while remaining formally under ministerial control. Britain's political class was wise enough, and cautious enough, to realize that violating the neutrality of the civil service would jeopardize the very fabric of government. This allowed for a balanced working relationship to emerge between the political leadership and the civil service, especially the central bureaucratic elite. Britain's civil servants "are servants of the Crown which, today, means the duly-elected Government. They serve Ministers, not MPs nor Peers" and "they have no constitutional identity separate from that of the Government they serve."[272] For over 150 years, the British civil service has "been regulated by Orders in Council under the Royal Prerogative—that is the Government's not Parliament's rules."[273] This has, over time, produced "spontaneity and informality" and a cooperative moral relationship between politicians and civil servants with mutual trust and respect for each other's competence.[274] The existence of this relationship has allowed Britain's governments considerable leverage over the bureaucracy without, however, compromising civil service autonomy. Thus, during Thatcher's premiership, the government wanted to reduce the size of the civil service and had a popular mandate to do so. There was, however, no purge of the bureaucracy and no sudden shock to the system. Instead, the government and the civil service worked together on a plan that banned recruitment to many positions and departments followed by phasing out of positions once the incumbents left the service or retired. The result was that the numerical strength of the civil service was reduced by 100,000 and the share of the public sector in total employment fell from 30 percent in 1979 to 21 percent in 1990. Another example is the gradual transition of Britain from a centralized administration to an almost federal system of regional administrations, followed, more recently, by devolution of political power from the center.[275] The first such steps were occasioned by the establishment of the North Ireland Civil Service (NICS) in 1921 out of the former Irish Civil Service, and since then Scotland and Wales have also benefited from administrative devolution, though, in the regions, the bureaucracy has more power than it does in England. In Northern Ireland, owing to the disturbed law and order situation, "the department itself performs the function of a political head of department. The term 'minister' is a courtesy title—the incumbent has no formal constitutional powers."[276] Of course, the civil service itself does not have a formal constitutional standing as understood in other parts of the world. Rather, it exists as a creature of the government with an enviable and perhaps unmatched autonomy based on a tradition of political neutrality and professionalism that Britain's political class, motivated by its enlightened self-interest, has allowed to strike deep roots. Britain's institutional development is so precious and unique that it belongs in a separate category and is helpful as a study in contrast with the continent bureaucratic empires of Continental Europe and the rest of the world, excepting, of course, the dominions of settlement.

THE STRANGEST STATE: REFLECTIONS ON BRITAIN'S CULTURE OF POWER AND GOVERNANCE

The poverty of Britain's circumstances led it towards acquiring a wealth of institutions. This wealth of institutions provided Britain with a combination of political stability and socioeconomic dynamism that fuelled its rise out of the poverty of its circumstances and the marginality of its location towards an industrial breakthrough and global empire. That same extensive institutional development also ensured that Britain was able to weather the storms of the Age of Total War and the Cold War with its domestic stability intact and the legitimacy of its state resurgent. The last achievement in particular led Charles de Gaulle, in his address to the British Parliament to opine:

> [Your] outstanding role in the midst of the storm is owed not only to your profound national qualities but also to the value of your institutions. At the worst of moments, who among you challenged the legitimacy and authority of the State? . . . With self-assurance, almost without being aware of it, you operate in freedom a secure, stable political system. So strong are your traditions and loyalties in the political field that your government is quite naturally endowed with cohesion and permanence; that your Parliament has, throughout each term of office, an assured majority; that this government and this majority are permanently in harmony; in short, that your executive and legislative powers are balanced and work together by definition as it were. . . . Thus, lacking meticulously worked out constitutional texts, but by virtue of an unchallengeable general consent, you find the means, on each occasion, to ensure the efficient functioning of democracy without incurring the excessive criticism of the ambitious, or the punctilious blame of purists. Well! I can tell you that this England, which keeps itself in order while practising respect for the liberties of all, inspires trust in France.[277]

Britain as a state is perhaps the strangest of all time. It is the oldest major state in terms of the continuity of its constitutional processes, and yet one of the youngest in terms of its central bureaucracy and civil service structures. It has also proven itself to be one of the most resilient as well as one of the least arbitrary in world history. That Marx the revolutionary ideologue and Metternich the arch-reactionary would both end up as political refugees in Britain, secure from the violent hatreds raging on the Continent, is a most eloquent testimony to the security of person and opinion afforded by the British state of laws. What could possibly explain the uniqueness of this state of laws?

Our survey started by examining the geographical canvas on which British history unfolded. This canvas was fractured enough to sustain multiple power centers in pre-modern times, close enough to have easy access to markets and resources on the Continent, and yet just isolated enough to escape repeated invasions and conquests—the historical equivalent of a Goldilocks scenario. Owing to this relative security, the need for a permanent military was greatly diminished and with that Britain's rulers had to rely on taxation by the consent of their aristocrats and townsmen to pay for government and meet exigencies. An internal balance of power emerged in which no one individual or group was able to establish a monopoly over the state.

The institutional balance, arising from geography and environment, helped craft a special historical experience of governance in which efforts by monarchs to rule arbitrarily and autocratically were successfully resisted by the aristocracy and townsmen. Each episode of successful resistance led to these groups being given a greater share of representation in state affairs until, by the late 1600s, monarchists realized the futility of trying to imitate the absolutists on the Continent. Representation gave important elements of British society a sustained interest in simultaneously resisting attempts to establish arbitrary rule *and* a vested interest in maintaining the constitutional arrangements of the state of laws. Thus the state came to be felt as something distinct from the monarch or the government of the day and was strong enough to maintain order but had little interest in riding roughshod over the autonomy of political, social and economic institutions. On account of these institutions and their participation in government as parties, pressure groups and movements, the British state of laws steadily increased its effectiveness by expanding its social support base and moderating its culture of power. In Britain, the strength of the state came to rest upon the voluntary accord and legitimacy it enjoys in society, something evidenced by the 70 percent average turnout rates in general elections since 1945, and the participatory if somewhat sectional nature of local governments.

Until the mid-1800s, the administrative machinery was small and haphazardly staffed when compared to the bureaucratic states of Continental Europe. By the time Britain got around to reorganizing its bureaucracy on more efficient lines, its culture of power had matured and the inherent legitimacy of the state of laws meant that a ministerial civil service could emerge without threatening domestic stability. Unaccustomed to the arbitrary exercise of power, Britain's politicians saw that it was in their own interest to be advised and assisted by civil servants recruited on merit, trained to high standards, and encouraged to be politically neutral.[278] Britain's administrative elite soon gained a level of permanence, prestige and autonomy, built on the twin pillars of impartiality and competence, that made it indispensible to any government, however skeptical it may have been at first of the bureaucracy. Without such a bureaucracy, it is difficult to see how Britain could have avoided domestic collapse given the stress it was exposed to during the 1900s.[279]

Ultimately, Britain's place in history owes much to its state of laws and moderate culture of power, which, together, constitute its greatest political legacy. The export of Britain's institutional arrangements to the dominions of settlement through direct colonization, including the present-day United States of America alongside Australia, New Zealand and Canada, helped transform liberalism from a British peculiarity to a global force. The efforts made, with some success in India but often failure elsewhere, to introduce reforms inspired by the state of laws in the continental bureaucratic empires that became dominions of conquest, have had profound effects on state development on a global scale. So great is this change that at a theoretical level even the most autocratic regimes claim to be guided by the spirit of representation and the rule of law embodied in the state of laws that developed centuries ago on a small island separated by a channel from the Eurasian mainland.

Conclusion

In order to govern people in the present it helps enormously if those charged with this vital task, be they elected representatives, civil servants, ecclesiasts, or military officers, be aware of how governance has taken place in the past. History, as a record of power, of our successes and our failures, constitutes, to paraphrase the classical phrase, the mirror of, and school for, princes. Those who strike at the mirror, as the Timurid Emperor Shahjahan realized more than 350 years ago, only destroy themselves. The preceding chapters have sought to achieve three major objectives by way of presenting a survey of the exercise of power in Eurasia. The first is to test a framework developed to explain the culture of power and governance of South Asia against the historical experiences of other power-centers. The second is to place before the reader an interpretation of how and why the state evolved in different parts of the world. The third is to explain the contemporary implications of cultures of power and assess the weight of history on governance.

South Asia's traumatic and chaotic history punctuated by great imperial state formations is a superior point of reference for the purpose of studying other Eurasian polities. In contrast, the Western, and in particular, the American, experience, is sufficiently different that frameworks rooted in it are bound to breakdown when applied to most parts of Eurasia. It is time for a correction to be carried out and for South Asian scholars to break out of the established moulds on offer and free themselves from irrational tutelage. The arbitrary nature of governance in South Asia, the fact that rulers treat the state as a personal estate, the ascendance of ideological and religious sanction as the means of justifying the capricious exercise of power, are, among other factors, readily in evidence in other parts of Eurasia. Kautilya's *Arthashastra* is particularly instructive as a manual for running a complex bureaucratic empire, while the *Ain-i-Akbari* from some 1700 years later performs the same role in relation to the Timurid Empire. South Asia's alternation between periods of imperial order followed by far longer periods of chaos is a sobering reminder of how corrosive its indigenous norms are for political order in the region. The natural condition of South Asia is chaos and only extraordinary, and for the most part external, imperial elites have been able to surmount centripetal tendencies.

South Asia's relevance to students of world history and institutional development also stems from the experience of British imperial rule. Unlike earlier South Asian empires, the British Raj tried to introduce political and administrative reforms derived from Britain's own rather different and marginal culture of power. In trying to hybridize the continental bureaucratic state with the state of laws, the British laid the foundations for a constitutional parliamentary democracy in India. The stability of this order is creditable though the underlying behavioral pattern of India's post-colonial elite has steadily reverted to its pre-colonial grooves. Indian democracy demonstrates the difficulty, if not the near impossibility, of substantially altering the culture of power. The fact that India's two main parties consider Narendra Modi, architect of the Gujarat genocide, and Rahul Gandhi, a dynastic scion of questionable seriousness, as prime ministerial material, says much about the failure of democratic India to produce wise leadership. If anything, the quality of leadership has steadily declined since Nehru's death in 1964. India represents a brave new kind of hybrid polity—an arbitrary democracy that combines constitutional stability and regular multi-party elections with the classical behavioral pattern of South Asian ruling elites. If democracy were to spread in the Arab world or Central Asia one can imagine that it would, at its very best, resemble India, or, more likely, Pakistan.

The similarities between the South Asian historical experience of governance and that in Persia and West Asia are striking. Arbitrary regimes with absolute rulers operating hierarchical instruments and legitimized by ideological or divine sanction have been, and still are, the norm. Like South Asia, these regions were exposed to invasion and fragmentation and plunged into chaos for long periods. The intervals between imperial restorations often lasted centuries, thus aggravating insecurity and making effective despotism the only viable option as a mechanism for maintaining order. Location, in the case of Persia and the Ottomans was a major challenge, far more so than was the case with South Asia. Persia's empires were exposed on two major land fronts to migrations and invasions from Central Asia and Mesopotamia. During periods when South Asia was ruled by a great empire Persia's southern and eastern frontiers had to be carefully watched as well. The Ottomans were exposed in the east to rival Turkish emirates, to the west lay the European powers, to the south lay *mamluk* Egypt and Syria and to the east Persia. In addition to these land fronts, the Mediterranean was up for grabs and the Ottomans faced a coalition of navies ranged against them. South Asian empires had it comparatively easy, as there was only one major invasion and migration route, which lay to the northwest. This route was mountainous and could be blocked by keeping a watch on major passes even though small-scale infiltration was then, as now, impossible to stop. The discomfiture produced by their unfavorable location drove the Persians and Ottomans to build enduring empires rooted in organizational superiority, religious and ideological fervor, and hardiness. In contrast, South Asian potentates, often locked in mutual rivalry, failed to patrol and control the major invasion routes with catastrophic consequences. The wealth, ease, and mutual distraction of political life in the plains of South Asia, produced enervation and softness as soon as the imperial will holding things together relaxed. While sharing a common tradition of arbitrary rule with South Asia, the Persians and Ottomans developed powerful reserves of frenetic zeal and Platonic elitism that their wealthier, more populous, but flabby counterparts on the other side of the Hindu Kush did not. Persia's empires have been triumphs of will that sought, and still seek, to convert defensive vulnerability into offensive momentum and moral insecurity into fanatical determination. The Ottoman Sultanate combined greater flexibility and pragmatism with the calculated use of force and cultural assimilation to produce the coherence denied to it by location and circumstances.

China, a continental bureaucratic empire encapsulating a civilization, offers several important lessons by way of contrast with South Asia. One contrast is continuity for since 221 BC China has spent much of its history unified or largely unified under effective regimes. Another is the development of a merit-based civil service recruited through competitive exams that was entrusted with running the state and advising the rulers. China's ideocratic complex combined performance legitimacy with Confucian piety and was far more humanistic and rational than that of almost any other Eurasian polity. From an epistemological perspective, China and Japan had far less trouble adjusting to the demands of the modern scientific rationality that arose in the West after the Renaissance and Reformation—indeed, less trouble than the West itself. It was, for the Chinese, a very unhappy coincidence that European power peaked just as the Celestial Empire went into decline and that China's rulers, unmindful of the nature of the threat and overconfident on account of their past achievements underestimated the challenge and delayed a response (unlike the more vulnerable Japanese). The consequences of such hubris were, as Herodotus would have expected, invasions, defeats, humiliations, rebellions, massacres, provinces spinning out of the center's control, and exhaustion. It took more than a hundred years of pulverization (1840–1978) before China's renewal began under the wise authoritarianism of Deng Xiaoping. This renewal has followed the classical pattern of guidance from above, meritocracy, statism, and long-term planning, in which the state and society are viewed as extensions of each other and part of the same moral and political order. Contemporary China has enormous problems, ranging from ecological degradation to rising income inequality and workers' protests against sweatshop conditions as expectations rise. However, unlike South Asia, China has a state with the will and capacity to govern, discipline, and lead, and is at ease with humanism and rationalism (unlike Iran), albeit not with political liberalism, and is considerably insulated from the threat of majority-mandated regression (as has happened in Pakistan, and is threatening to take place in Turkey).

Continental Europe, unlike China, has basically remained politically and administratively fragmented on account of geography, relative poverty, and demographic diversity. The Roman Empire managed to overcome these constraints for a while at the cost of sacrificing its state of laws and developed into a despotic state in the Persian style. Nevertheless, the state started falling apart in the early 200s, effectively split up by the early-300s, and had collapsed in the West by AD 476. Since then, Napoleonic and Nazi interludes aside, Europe has remained divided. Political disunity after the Roman collapse was reinforced by cultural differences between the north and south of Europe, which crystallized into religious differences after the Protestant Reformation. Combined with the unique legacy of a thousand years of aristocratic feudalism and Christian theo-centric continuity, a situation emerged in which the state, as would have been comprehensible to a Chinese, Indian, Persian, or Turkish, sovereign, did not reemerge until the 1500s. When royal authority revived it did so slowly and in alliance with merchants that brought additional sources of revenue as much of the land was already under the domain of the Church and the aristocracy. Even at this slow rate, royal absolutism became fashionable in Europe by the mid-1600s though this kind of governance was not nearly as arbitrary or autocratic as what prevailed elsewhere in Eurasia. The steady growth of Europe's wealth on account of expansion of trade, manufacturing and services, enabled governments to consolidate internal control over limited areas, undermine the aristocracy, and start fielding regular armies and employing central bureaucracies. Even though European absolutism was half-baked and contested it helped restore the state to a point where it became stronger than society. The development of that society into the masses and the advent of industrialism furnished additional wealth with which even more powerful states could be constructed. If Europe's experience is any guide to what will happen elsewhere with industrialization, it seems that the process will greatly strengthen the state and make society far more dependent on it, with or without democracy. It could also lead to the emergence of radical fascistic regimes equipped with the power and technology of industrial civilization as happened in Europe during the 1920s and 1930s, and continued in Eastern Europe until the end of the Cold War. The Continental European transition from Roman Empire to feudal decentralization and modern industrialized bureaucratic states led to terrible wars and upheavals which ended only in 1945 with the Soviet and American partition of Europe. Attempts at bridging internal divisions through economic integration, which gained a huge boost after the collapse of the Soviet Union, have recently come to grief on account of the diversity of work ethics and attitudes towards power within Europe.

The Russian Empire, like Persia and the Ottoman Sultanate, originated in a disadvantageous location open on most sides to attack. Russia is vast but lacks natural boundaries that can form a reliable defensive perimeter. The population is, alternately, concentrated in a few fertile regions or then spread thin across a huge territorial expanse. Climatically, Russia is outside the temperate zone and exposed to harsh rainy and winter conditions for much of the year. In order to survive in these conditions the Russian state simply could not afford parleys and discussions as methods of governance. It thus evolved into the quintessential garrison and security state and sought peace of mind in the subjugation of groups on its elastic periphery, who, if left unmolested, would probably attack, enslave, and conquer the Russians. Russia thus became an autocratic military state legitimized by divine sanction and ruled by the czar through his servants. In modern times, this traditional autocracy was overthrown and replaced by the Bolsheviks who transformed Russia into the ideological police state and militarized empire called the Soviet Union. After the Soviet collapse in 1991, arbitrary democracy with criminality and corruption that would make a South Asian politician blush tried to take root. This transition was aborted by the state security elite, which restored the substance of autocracy while retaining the form of democratic elections.

Japan is an exceptional state in that it gradually acquired a bureaucratic organization and became the first non-Western country to industrialize. Once its industrial take-off had happened, Japan acquired an overseas colonial empire and evolved into an ideological, militarized, police state ruled by an emperor regarded as divinity incarnate. As was the case with Continental Europe, the emergence of a powerful bureaucratic state was a consequence of industrialization though in Japan this process was pursued consciously and moved much more quickly on account of the Tokugawa legacy. Defeat in the Second World War knocked the military out of the government process and allowed an alliance of civil servants, corporations and conservative politicians, the "Iron Triangle", to take charge. With minor disruptions, this triumvirate has ruled Japan since the mid-1950s, and provided stability with prosperity and periodic elections. Of all the states in our survey Japan is probably the least arbitrary, the most consensus-oriented and merit-based and, for a large, densely populated society, uniquely harmonious. At the same time, the state is highly bureaucratic, elitist, and authoritarian, while the political process has perpetuated a de facto one-party rule for almost sixty years.

Britain is the great exception in our survey and the modern home of the marginal Eurasian tradition of the state of laws. Unlike Continental Europe, Britain did not have to maintain large standing armies on home soil and sought security, instead, through naval power taking full advantage of its geographic position. Like the states on the continent, Britain possessed the structures of aristocratic feudalism. Take away the need for a standing army and the basis for royal authority is greatly diminished. Instead of royal authority mediated by civil servants and military officers, Britain was able to craft and sustain a state comprising multiple autonomous institutions. In this political order the monarch was the head of state but the lords, temporal and ecclesiastical, and wealthy commoners, formed large councils or houses to aggregate their views and protect their interests. Executive power was thus distributed between the king, the aristocracy, the Church, and the commoners. No one pillar was able to overpower the others and thus all needed cooperation to make the state function. Island status meant that stability and protection from invasion (since 1066) was practicable while the risk of secession was remote. The poverty of the soil also meant that lords could not live solely off rents, a fact that greatly enhanced the importance of market towns, traders, and manufacturers. Attempts by the king to increase his powers, raise additional revenues, revoke charters, manhandle the judiciary, or dilute the nobility, were met with effective opposition in the name of upholding the law to which even the sovereign was supposed to adhere. After 1688, the formation of rival parties within the assemblies helped consolidate the political process and enabled changes of government from one party to another in the modern sense. These developments would have remained interesting but essentially irrelevant to the wider world were it not for the establishment of the British Empire, which, in dominions of settlement, saw the transplantation of the state of laws through large-scale migration. This transfer meant that the British variant of the state of laws spread to North America, Australia, and New Zealand for the settlers took with them their political heritage and moderate culture of power. The indigenous inhabitants they encountered were decimated by disease, lacked organized states, and were overpowered by guns. Dominions of conquest like India, were a rather different matter and here a sustained effort was made to introduce some of the norms of the state of laws into the continental bureaucratic empire. This attempt, as examined earlier, has in South Asia both succeeded and failed while the material success of Britain and her dominions of settlement produced a considerable amount of imitation all around the world.

Integrating the historical experience of governance of the eight centers in the survey helps advance an interpretative framework. Geography and environment shape the initial conditions in which societies develop and thus constitute primordial causes of what happens later. The technique or method employed to meet the initial challenge posed by nature creates early structures and patterns that need to be sustained and expanded if the society is to survive. As the society grows it needs to master more complex organization and requires some kind of central direction. Since there are other predators swirling around at the edges it also needs defense and the means to pay for that protection. This is the likely origin of a state and once the advantages of central direction become evident in terms of superiority in war and greater wealth for those entrusted with authority the resulting historical experience generates self-reinforcing continuities in the exercise of power. Over time, these become habits, and come to represent a culture of power that determines the range of responses to, and expectations of, the state. Human agency is important in all this but a lot of our freedom depends on the cooperation or compulsion of others and is circumscribed by the context in which we find ourselves. While it certainly is not possible to predict the precise behavior of individuals, or even small groups of individuals, at any point in time, as we move from the micro to the macro the degree to which any random individual can affect outcomes rapidly becomes inconsequential. And if we talk of specific individuals in positions of authority, then it is the structure through which they exercise it that merits study.

This study does not conform to the opinions that the past is not really relevant or that it is merely a collection of arbitrary and subjective narratives. To accept that premise does grievous harm to the claim of social sciences that they constitute a valid body of knowledge, and deprecates the value of subjects like history that are, if nothing else, rational accounts of human irrationality. Humanity's capacity to understand itself depends a great deal on the past not merely in the political sense but also in terms of the role of objective factors and our responses. Imagine, for instance, a thirty-year-old person who only remembers what has happened to him or her over the past one year. It is, of course, true, that the recent past is far more relevant to our daily functioning that the remote past. However, without knowledge of that more distant past we would lose so much of what makes us who we are, all those layers accumulated over our personal *longue durée* would either vanish from our limited memory or else be deemed irrelevant. This would clearly be unacceptable for as any psychiatrist or psychologist will tell you, our formative experiences in childhood, adolescence, and young adulthood, are profoundly and directly relevant to our present and our future. We can suppress, ignore, or otherwise marginalize the importance of our past, but such willful denial of reality would only harm us by making self-comprehension much more difficult. Our early experiences cast a long shadow regardless of whether we acknowledge them or not. In a like manner the early and apparently distant experiences of a state, society, or empire, have a tremendous impact on their subsequent development. History adds depth and breadth to our perspective and knowledge, geography helps us understand the contours of the stage on which events and trends unfold, logic and reason enable us to make connections, and our human nature, which is the same as that of our ancestors, enables us to empathize with and relate to what has gone before. And while not everything has a future it does have a past so that a student of world politics who only knows about developments since 1945, or a social scientist acquainted with the latest jargon but not with the classics, stand handicapped by insufficient historical knowledge.

That knowledge has, perhaps due to boredom and tenure squabbles in the advanced countries, come under assault and been declared to be nothing more than a potentially infinite set of narratives. At one level this approach can make for peaceful coexistence in that everyone is entitled to his or her own narrative and as there are no objective criteria for determining the superiority of one over the other we can all live smugly ever after. The problem with this approach is that it renders subjects such as history essentially meaningless. One can, operating from this premise, treat the Nazi "Final Solution" and Operation Barbarossa, or the brutal wars of Containment during the Cold War, or the Atlantic slave trade, as figments of a subjective imagination that subscribe to a particular narrative. Intriguingly, the lengths to which the Nazis went to destroy evidence, including files, pertaining to their genocide of the Jews, Russian POWs, Poles, Gypsies, and others, indicates that they were trying to cover up the reality betrayed by documentation. The storm of controversy generated by modern leaks of classified information by whistleblowers like Snowden and Wikileaks is due to the fact that people in power reveal their actual thoughts and actions only when secure that they will not be exposed. While fashionable social scientists are free to eviscerate the epistemological basis of their disciplines, this study has focused on the state and how historical experience can help draw meaningful conclusions.

One conclusion that can be drawn is that Eurasian cultures of power have for much of history shown a broad convergence or tendency towards arbitrariness, and that the dominant power configuration has been the continental bureaucratic state. The continental bureaucratic model is extremely resilient because it concentrates power in the executive who operates through appointed servants, exercises universal proprietorship, and is legitimized by divine sanction or ideology. Its simplicity in terms of the principle that animates it, namely, obedience to an omnipotent executive, also makes it highly adaptable enabling it to take root in practically any sedentary society with access to a moderate amount of arable land. A basic unity in principle granted, this adaptability has led to variation in details. Thus while Persia and China were and are both continental bureaucratic empires with arbitrary governance, the former has much stronger religious structures while the latter relies on a merit-based bureaucracy. This variability holds true for the state of laws as well for the Ancient Greek, Ancient Roman, Renaissance Italy, and Anglo-Saxon versions are different from each other in their details. Another conclusion is that arbitrary cultures of power are remarkably resilient and basically immune to change through legislation that is not backed by wisdom and political will over a long period. It is easier to become more arbitrary rather than the reverse for human nature seeks the greatest freedom when placed in power. The state of laws with its moderate culture of power is a fragile plant that takes a long time to nurture and can be uprooted or reduced to ritual fairly easily.

This brings us to the implications of this study for the contemporary era. The first is that the world is likely to revert to multiple historical trajectories with the gradual decline of Western power in this century. Pre-fabricated solutions to problems in different parts of the world, which are dished out by leading international institutions and Western governments, need to be abandoned in favor of a more historical and rational approach. The belief that industrialization outside the West will produce a more uniform world, one that conforms to the West's values, is sadly mistaken. Even if every country in the world were to introduce multiparty democracy their indigenous cultures of power, not parliamentary statutes, would determine the actual behavior of the state. The second is that the spread of democracy is fragile—Voltaire's proverbial coconuts are far from having acclimatized to their new homes and environments. Democracy in India should serve as a powerful corrective to the notion of liberal universalism for it demonstrates that arbitrary governance and wholesale plunder can coexist quite well with elections and a multi-party system. Third, geography and ecology enabled the rise of states and civilizations but humanity's very success at temporarily circumventing Malthusian constraints has placed growing and unsustainable pressure on the environment. If ecocide is not stopped then catastrophe on a global scale is inevitable. In catastrophic conditions only the most disciplined, authoritarian, and motivated, states will be likely to survive. Eurasia is no stranger to terrible calamity and the collapse of states and empires accompanied by the slaughter of tens of millions. Regional and trans-regional collapses have occurred in the past and there is no reason to think that we have been inoculated against a recurrence of disintegration in the future. It is precisely these harsh conditions that have helped consolidate and perpetuate the continental bureaucratic state as the normal variant adopted by Eurasian empires. The state of laws, with its cumbersome procedures, limited authority, and checks and balances, is unlikely to survive environmental collapse under present conditions and expectations. Only humility, reason, and a clinical understanding of history, can potentially rescue us from the consequences of arrogance, blind selfishness, and mistaken belief in our immunity from nemesis.

Notes

NOTES TO THE INTRODUCTION

1. For Ibn Khaldun, the terms "dynasty" and "state" were interchangeable for "A state exists only insofar as it is held together by the dynasty; when the dynasty disappears the state collapses." Ibn Khaldun, *The Muqaddimah (An Introduction to History)*, trans. Franz Rosenthal, ed. N. J. Dawood (London: Routledge and Kegan Paul, 1978), xi.

2. A class of priests known as the Magi existed in Achaemenid Persia. Their functions were the enforcement of religious orthodoxy and providing the rulers with legitimacy. They enjoyed a relatively privileged position in Persian society. Michael Axworthy, *Empire of the Mind: A History of Iran* (London: Hurst and Company, 2007), 10. Sassanid Persia, which lasted from the third to the seventh centuries AD and ruled the same core territories as its Achaemenid predecessor, maintained a theocratic establishment of some twenty-five thousand salaried priests and ecclesiastical officials. David L. Lewis, *God's Crucible: Islam and the Making of Europe, 570 to 1215* (New York: W. W. Norton, 2008), 20.

3. The back and forth movement in Turkey has not been greater than that experienced by France between 1790 and 1958. Indeed, France, the greatest and most enlightened continental bureaucratic state in Europe, experienced four republics, two Napoleonic Empires, one Consulate, one Directory, two Bourbon monarchies, and one Orléanist monarchy, before stabilizing under the Fifth Republic after Charles de Gaulle's overthrow in 1968–69. Establishing a state of laws, even in Western Europe, was very hard and often unrewarding work. Those in Europe who criticize Turkey for using the coercive power of the state apparatus to move towards a state of laws forget their own, often tragic, historical failures. What is important is that Turkey has pursued a coherent vision for much of its history since 1924. This consistency, which is one of the greatest legacies of Kemalism, has enabled Turkey to overcome vicissitudes inherent in meaningful and fundamental reforms. The powerful central state in Turkey, like its counterpart in France, acted, and continues to act, as both the anchor of order and the engine of change.

4. "In each European nation, the transition from aristocracy to democracy involved a different kind of amalgam of the original elements of European society—feudal aristocracy, the self-governing cities or communes, royal power, and the Church . . . Those different amalgams have, in turn, left their mark on the political cultures of each nation, giving each what 200 years ago would have been called its own genius. Thus, Dutch democracy has been oligarchical and confessional, German democracy decentralized and

parliamentist, French democracy bureaucratic and at times populist, Italian democracy communal and even anarchical." Larry Siedentop, *Democracy in Europe* (London: Allen Lane, the Penguin Press, 2000), 230–31.

5. With the rise of the intelligence apparatus and the obsession with internal security, which was reinvigorated after the terrorist attacks on the Pentagon and World Trade Center in September 2001, the United States appears to be in the process of becoming a bureaucratic state like those in Eurasia. George Washington "feared that the United States might develop a state apparatus, comparable to those of the autocratic states of Europe, that could displace the constitutional order. This would inevitably involve a growth in federal taxes to pay for the armies and bureaucracies of the state, a shift in political power from the constituent states of the union to the federal government, and a shift within the federal government from the preeminence of the Congress to that of the president, resulting in what we have come to call the 'imperial presidency'." Chalmers Johnson, *The Sorrows of Empire: Militarism, Secrecy, and the End of the Republic* (New York: Metropolitan Books, Henry Holt and Company, 2004), 44. In effect, like the Roman Republic, the United States needs imperial institutions at home to command an imperial system abroad. By 2001, officials at the Pentagon estimated that some US $ 1.1 trillion could not be accounted for, while after the Vietnam War the United States shifted from a citizen army of conscripts to a standing army of volunteers. Ibid., 58–60. Recent revelations, such as those orchestrated by Wikileaks or by Edward Snowden, have confirmed the irrelevance of civil liberties and the end of privacy in the United States as well as the concentration of power in the hands of more than a dozen intelligence agencies employing hundreds of thousands of officials with high level security clearance.

6. For a fine effort at linking geography to history see Robert D. Kaplan, *The Revenge of Geography: What the Map Tells us about Coming Conflicts and the Battle against Fate* (New York: Random House, 2012).

7. Jared Diamond, *Guns, Germs and Steel: A Short History of Everybody for the last 13,000 Years* (London: Vintage, 2005), 87.

8. Tom Standage, *An Edible History of Humanity* (New York: Walbert Company, 2009), 17.

9. Ibid., 23.

10. Jared Diamond, *The Rise and Fall of the Third Chimpanzee: How our Animal Heritage Affects the Way we Live* (London: Vintage Books, 2002), 222.

11. Jack Goody argues that Europe and Asia, rather than being seen as distinct units, ought to be seen as part of a whole with ideas and inventions circulating from one end to the other producing an alternating pattern of rise and decline. Societies that fall behind play catch-up and overtake those who are further ahead sharing, in the process, science, philosophy, religion, technology and material exchanges, in a sort of meta-historical circulation. Jack Goody, *The Eurasian Miracle* (Cambridge: Polity Press, 2010).

12. Darwin contends: "the difficulty of framing autonomous states on an ethnic basis, against the gravitational pull of cultural or economic attraction (as well as disparities of military force), has been so great that empire (where different ethnic communities fall under a common ruler) has been the default mode of political organization through most of history." John Darwin, *After Tamerlane: The Global History of Empire since 1405* (London: Penguin Books, 2007), 23. Thus, the earliest states that expanded within continental landmasses were imperial states making empire as old as civilization.

13. For more on the relationship between technological asymmetries and imperialism see Daniel R. Headrick, *Power over Peoples: Technology, Environments, and Western Imperialism, 1400 to Present* (Princeton: Princeton University

Press, 2010). Headrick's argument is that "The innovation of the West came from two sources. One is a culture that encouraged the domination of nature through experimentation, scientific research, and the rewards of capitalism. The other is the competitive nature of the Western world, in which states powerful enough to challenge one another—Spain, France, Britain, Germany, Russia and the United States—at one time or another vied for dominance over Europe." Ibid., 4.

14. Herodotus reveals that Menes, the first pharaoh (c.3200 BC), "raised the dyke which protects Memphis from the inundation of the Nile" and that these waterworks, thousands of years later in his own time (c. 450 BC) when Egypt was a satrapy of Achaemenid Persia, were ". . . guarded with the greatest care by the Persians." Herodotus, *Histories*, trans. George Rawlinson (Hertfordshire: Wordsworth Editions Limited, 1996), 155–56.

15. For a fine history of innovation and ideas that have changed the world (not necessarily for the better) see Peter Watson, *Ideas: A History from Fire to Freud* (London: Weidenfeld and Nicolson, 2005). One of the truly grand ideas to emerge in history was that of a merit-based civil service recruited through competitive exams—a Chinese idea steadily refined by successive dynasties. Ibid., 305–7.

16. "It is a common optical illusion of a highly individualistic world that people see themselves as self-made and independent. The order that states provide [in the developed world since 1945] is so taken for granted that we barely notice how much we are protected from gunmen and bandits, plagues and currency collapses . . ." Geoff Mulgan, *Good and Bad Power: The Ideals and Betrayals of Government* (London: Allen Lane, Penguin Books, 2006), 15.

17. "To speak on behalf of the state has not been a comfortable assignment in recent times. Lenin called for the state to be 'smashed'; if the state continued to be necessary after the revolution and under the Dictatorship of the Proletariat, it would soon 'wither away'. Stalin created the state as an all-dominant totalitarian monster. In American politics, the right warns against statism as the enemy of freedom; the left favors government but fears the state's designs on civil liberties. Feminists declare it to be 'male' and so by definition illegitimate. Anarchists and libertarians oppose the state altogether." Charles Hill, *Grand Strategies: Literature, Statecraft and World Order* (New Haven: Yale University Press, 2010), 15.

18. The United States is often presented as an example of such a state, emerging out of a contract amongst the governed. While that contract employed "the language of liberty and equality" in order to "unite just enough whites to fight a Revolution against England" it scrupulously avoided "ending either slavery or inequality." Howard Zinn, *A People's History of the United States, 1492-Present* (New York: Harper Perennial, 2005), 58. Indeed, a case can be made that in light of a ban imposed on private purchases of Native American land (1763) and the Somerset Case (1771–72) that established in Britain that slavery had no basis in the Common Law, American elites in the thirteen colonies had every right to be wary of the mother country, lest it abolish slavery and accommodate the Native Americans in the imperial structure.

19. The state is not a modern construct or creation and "there are fundamental commonalities between the states of millennia before and those around us today. Granted, the nature of the state is hard to grasp, but unless it is understood in a classical way, we cannot shore up the contemporary state or understand that there is no replacement for it." Hill, *Grand Strategies*, 15.

20. In Ancient Egypt "it is clear that the existence of officials to run the granary [system] was extremely important in the Old Kingdom . . . This must surely

be associated with the importance to Egypt of the management of the grain supply necessary for a stable society." Nigel Strudwick, *The Administration of Egypt in the Old Kingdom: The Highest Titles and their Holders* (London: KPI Limited, 1985), 254.

21. For a fashionable account of regimentation at the state level see Michel Foucault, *Discipline and Punish: The Birth of the Prison*, trans. Alan Sheridan (New York: Vintage, 1995), esp. 3–31, and 195–228. For the antidote, see Francis Wheen, *How Mumbo-Jumbo Conquered the World: A Short History of Modern Delusions* (London: The Fourth Estate, 2004).

22. At the same time, there is no great redeemer in the form of market principles in the modern age for "Without some form of government intervention, where there are negative externalities, like pollution, markets produce too much, and where they are positive externalities, as is the case of basic research, they produce too little." Joseph E. Stiglitz, *The Roaring Nineties: Seeds of Destruction* (London: Allen Lane, the Penguin Press, 2003), 104. The creation and perpetuation of asymmetries of information are inherent in economies and mean that markets tend to behave corruptly unless regulated. Ibid., 128. Indeed, the South Asian experience indicates that markets are *more* corrupt than the state, or, rather, cannot be expected to be less corrupt than the state they operate in.

23. The Stanford Prison Experiment demonstrated how ordinarily "good" people change in their behavior when placed in positions of power, devoid of accountability, over others. Philip Zimbardo demonstrates the importance of structure to morality and demolishes the "Fundamental Attribution Error that locates the inner qualities of people as the main source of their actions." Philip Zimbardo, *The Lucifer Effect: How Good People Turn Evil* (London: Rider, 2007), 445. Practically everybody is corruptible, the differences lie in degree and circumstances.

24. These worldviews are often resistant to reform and generally do not undergo meaningful transformation without external pressure, which is why reforms or revolutions, are stimulated by danger rather than tranquility. In the modern period, the European assault on other parts of Eurasia stimulated soul searching and adaptation though, like Europe itself, the path to resistance often necessitated the strengthening of the state and the imposition of ideologies that sought to legitimize real or pseudo modernization. Darwin, *After Tamerlane*, 270.

25. Animals too respond to conditioning—in Japan I was amazed at how fish in the moat surrounding the Imperial Palace were unafraid of people and actually approached them. I can't imagine fish in Pakistan anywhere responding in the same way. In a like manner, in India, monkeys boldly occupy government offices and make a nuisance of themselves in cities confident that their sacred status will protect them. The same, of course, cannot be said for India's 170 million untouchables.

26. "For an analogy, consider our physical environment. It certainly changes: mountains, rivers, glaciers and coastlines gradually shift. But so slow is this process that none of us perceive it with the naked eye . . . The lives of countries and civilizations, and their psychological or spiritual attitudes of peoples, are not so seemingly immutable; yet generations succeeds generation without really radical change." Fernand Braudel, *A History of Civilizations*, trans. Richard Mayne (New York: Penguin, 1995), xxxvi.

27. China's ancient Zhou Dynasty (BC 1046–256) lasted longer than the Ottoman Sultanate, but for most of its history it exercised nominal power and was in no position to govern.

NOTES TO CHAPTER 1

1. This chapter is a summary of Ilhan Niaz, *An Inquiry into the Culture of Power of the Subcontinent* (Islamabad: Alhamra, 2006) and updates and revises the first chapter of Ilhan Niaz, *The Culture of Power and Governance of Pakistan, 1947–2008* (Karachi: Oxford University Press, 2010).

2. Reference India and Pakistan, Kaplan argues that the two warring states have a mutually shared perception that the other poses an existential threat and that Pakistan, in particular, represents "the threat of another Mughal onslaught without the Mughal's redeeming cosmopolitanism." Kaplan, *The Revenge of Geography*, 241.

3. Ibn Khaldun, *The Muqaddimah*, 263.

4. Ibid.

5. Ibid.

6. Harappa was one of the most important cities and located at the centre of the Indus Valley civilization.

7. Karen Armstrong goes so far as to describe states such as Magadha and Kosala as "modern kingdoms" with "streamlined bureaucracies and armies" loyal to the monarch. They were thus "far more efficiently run" than the tribal oligarchies and aristocracies. Karen Armstrong, *Buddha* (London: Phoenix, 2002), 20.

8. Different versions and editions of Ancient India's compendium on statecraft include: Kautilya, *The Arthashastra*, trans. L. N. Rangarajan (New Delhi: Penguin Books, 1992); Kautilya, *Arthashastra* trans. R. Shamasastry's (Bangalore: Government Press, 1915); and B. P. Sinha, *Readings in Kautilya's Arthasastra* (New Delhi: Agam Publishers, 1976). Kautilya was the prime minister to Chandragupta Maurya, the founder of the Maurya Empire, about 320 BC.

9. The *Arthashastra* is often "mistakenly believed" to be "a text on Hindu political thought." This is incorrect given that Kautilya is not concerned with presenting a philosophy of government. In fact, the treatise is "a text-book on administration in a monarchical state." Romila Thapar, *Cultural Pasts: Essays in Early Indian History* (New Delhi: Oxford University Press, 2005), 411.

10. Kautilya, *The Arthashastra*, trans. Rangarajan, 154.

11. Ibid.

12. Ibid.

13. Ibid., 157–58.

14. Thapar, *Cultural Pasts*, 430.

15. Kautilya, *The Arthashastra*, trans. L. N. Rangrajan, 246.

16. Ibid., 205.

17. Ibid.

18. Ibid., 498.

19. Ibid.

20. In his edicts Ashoka entrusts "officers" and "rural officers" as well as "rural chiefs" to assemble the people and explain to them the principles of Buddhism and the new thinking. Thapar, *Cultural Pasts*, 427.

21. Ibid., 436.

22. Ibid., 434.

23. Bharat Karnad, *Nuclear Weapons and Indian Security: The Realist Foundations of Strategy* (New Delhi: Macmillan, 2002), 325. In this groundbreaking and informative work, Karnad demolishes most popular notions of Hindu-Indian pacifism, and Gandhian and Nehruvian idealism.

24. Thapar, *Cultural Pasts*, 227.
25. The intermediate forms of resistance included renunciation, flight, "philosophical acrobatics", migration, violating existing caste regulations and joining another sub-sect. Ibid., 213–32. The nature of the dissent itself indicates that the relative power of the state was significant. One might also consider that the ability of a rural and caste-ridden society to resist a determined armed minority keen to impose demands on it in the form of taxes and compulsory service would not be very great.
26. A rare window into this period is provided the Chinese Buddhist monk Fa-Hien, who set out to find Buddhist texts. His account naturally focuses on Buddhist religious establishments, which he was pleased to see were still functioning. One feature of India that struck him was its flatness: "From where (the travelers) crossed the Indus to South India, and on to the Southern Sea, a distance of forty or fifty thousand le, all is level plain." Fa-Hien, *A Record of Buddhistic Kingdoms*, trans. James Legge (Islamabad: Lok Virsa, n.d.), 47. Ideal country for invaders with cavalry once they got down from the mountain passes lying undefended since the fall of the Guptas.
27. The term "Sultanate" is a bit misleading. The Delhi Sultanate was a succession of dynastic states that rose and fell between 1206 and 1526. The dynasties were the Shamsids (Slave Dynasty), Ghiyathids, Khaljis, Tughluqids, Sayyids and the Lodhis. Most of these dynasties had only one great ruler under whom the Delhi Sultanate exercised effective control of the Indo-Gangetic plain and penetrated the Deccan. The total period of effective central authority for the Delhi Sultanate is about a century and a half. However, the maximum total period of continuous, effective, rule from a single center is about sixty years (1325–88).
28. Hugh Kennedy, *The Court of the Caliphs: When Baghdad Ruled the Muslim World* (London: Phoenix, 2005), 214.
29. Mu'tasim then moved the capital from Baghdad to Samarra: "The new regime was established in Samarra, and the new army and the bureaucracy were moved there. Mu'tasim was now master in his own capital, surrounded by the troops who owed everything to him. Baghdad with its turbulent inhabitants and vigorous commercial life, was well out of the way. He could not have realized how this isolation in the middle of his troops would make Samarra a prison and ultimately a death trap for his successors." Ibid.
30. Peter Jackson, *The Delhi Sultanate: A Political and Military History* (Cambridge: Cambridge University Press, 1999), 241.
31. This system, of Ancient Persian origin, was extensively employed by the Arab imperial states. The second Abbasid ruler, Mansur, "relied heavily on an organization called the *barid*. This is usually translated as 'post', but though it did carry official correspondence its remit ran much wider. The agents of the *barid* operated in every city and district a sort of alternative government structure, reporting directly to the caliphs on the behaviour of the governor, the *qadi* or judge and such mundane but important matters as the movement of prices of essential commodities." Kennedy, *The Court of the Caliphs*, 15. When Harun al Rashid, the Abbasid ruler immortalized in the *Arabian Nights*, died in 809 at Tus, some 1900 kilometres from the capital, Baghdad, the news was transmitted through the *barid* and arrived at the imperial palace in eleven or twelve days. Ibid., 85.
32. Ibn Battuta, *Travels in Asia and Africa 1325–54* (London: Routledge and Keagan Paul, 1929; reprint Lahore: Services Book Club, 1985), 181.
33. Ibid.

34. K. A. Nizami, ed., *Politics and Society During the Early Medieval Period: Collected Works of Professor Mohammed Habib,* vol. 2 (New Delhi: Peoples Publishing House, 1981), 369–70.

35. K. M. Ashraf, *Life and Conditions of the People of Hindustan* (New Delhi: Munshiram Manoharlal, 1959), 77.

36. The combination of passive acceptance and flight from contact with the state finds expression in the Sufi traditions and orders of South Asia. While some Sufi orders became instruments in the hands of arbitrary rulers during the Delhi Sultanate, the Chisti order opted for asceticism and aloofness from a political power that was irredeemably corrupt and self-serving. Under energetic sultans, like Muhammad bin Tughluq (1325–1351), the Delhi Sultanate pursued those who refused to pander to the imperial court and the "Chisti shaykhs tried to evade the official directives but at the same time tried to avoid conflict with the political authorities or the state." Tanvir Anjum, *Chisti Sufis in the Sultanate of Delhi, 1190–1400: From Restrained Indifference to Calculated Defiance* (Karachi: Oxford University Press, 2011), 281.

37. Ashraf, *Life and Conditions of the People of Hindustan* 2.

38. Ibid., 36.

39. Babur was a descendent of Amir Timur, who led the second wave of Mongol invasions. These invasions, in the late fourteenth and early fifteenth centuries, devastated the Muslim world. In 1398–99, The Timurid armies conquered and sacked Delhi, a blow from which the sultanate, then undergoing dynastic failure, never truly recovered. After Timur's death in 1405, his empire disintegrated into hundreds of petty despotisms. The first Timurid Empire drew it strength from two major groups of imperial servants. The war machine was administered by the nomadic Turco-Mongol warrior elite whose tribal rivalries were manipulated in order to ensure loyalty to Amir Timur. The settled districts, cities, towns and trade routes were managed by a Persian or Persianized bureaucracy. By balancing and encouraging rivalries within the imperial apparatus and employing an extensive network of spies and couriers on the classical Persian pattern, Amir Timur made his will prevail over all others. He *was* the system and "power was exercised personally, rather than through institutions." Justin Marozzi, *Tamerlane: Sword of Islam, Conqueror of the World* (London: Harper Collins, 2004), 204–5.

40. Akbar can be credited with leading the Timurids to paramount power status in the subcontinent. Ishtiaq Husain Qureshi, *Akbar: The Architect of the Mughul Empire* (Karachi: Ma'aref Limited, 1978). More recent research into the 'documentary evidence' has 'only tended to confirm and underline the standard propositions about the elements of centralization and systematization' in the Timurid Empire. M. Athar Ali, *Mughul India: Studies in Polity, Ideas, Society and Culture* (New Delhi: Oxford University Press, 2007), 87–88.

41. During the reign of Humayun (1530–56) the Timurids experimented with sharing different provinces amongst the royal princes instead of plunging into a fratricidal civil war. The consequences for the Timurid dominion were almost fatal as dissension between the brothers crippled the state and led to humiliation and exile at the hands of the Afghan Sher Shah Suri (1540–45). Ultimately, Humayun had to defeat his brothers and re-conquer northern India, which was, at the time of his death in 1556, still far from complete.

42. Abu'l Fazl Allami, *A'in-I Akbari*, trans. H. Blochmann (Calcutta: Calcutta Madrassah, 1873; reprint, Lahore: Sang-e-Meel Publications, 2003), 65.

43. Ibid.

44. Irfan Habib, *Essays in Indian History: Towards a Marxist Perspective* (New Delhi: Tulika, 1995), 97.

45. Standard silver currency units.
46. Inayat Khan, *Shahjahan-nama*, trans. A. R. Fuller, eds., W. Begley and Z. A. Desai (Delhi: Oxford University Press, 1990), 282.
47. Ibid., 232.
48. François Bernier, *Travels in the Mogul Empire: AD 1656–1668*, trans. Irving Brock, revised and improved edition, Archibald Constable (London: Archibald Constable and Company, 1891; reprint, Karachi: Indus Publications, n.d.). 204.
49. Ibid.
50. Tapan Raychaudhuri and Irfan Habib, eds., *The Cambridge Economic History of India*, vol 1, *c1200 to c1750* (Cambridge: Cambridge University Press, 1982), 173.
51. M. Athar Ali, *The Mughal Nobility Under Aurungzeb* (New Delhi: Asia Publishing House, 1970), 155–56.
52. Abu'l Fazl, *A'in-I Akbari*, trans. H. Blochmann, 225.
53. Raychaudhuri, *The Cambridge Economic History of India*, vol 1, *c1200 to c1750*, 179. The total revenues are estimated at 130 million rupees under Akbar, 220 million rupees under Shahjahan, and 380 million rupees during the later half of Aurungzeb's reign.
54. Ibid., 181.
55. Abraham Eraly, *The Last Spring: The Lives and Times of the Great Mughals* (New Delhi: Viking, 1997), 815.
56. Athar Ali, *Mughul India*, 68.
57. This point is driven home by Yoginder Sikand. He argues that the local converts to Islam were regard as *ajlaf* by the Muslim elite, or *ashraf*, in pre-British India. Until the decline of Turco-Persian imperial power in the eighteenth century the *ashraf* didn't even consider it possible for the "Natives" to become *real* Muslims. Yoginder Sikand, *The Origins and Development of the Tablighi-Jama'at, 1920–2000: A Cross-country Comparative Study* (New Delhi: Orient Longman, 2002).
58. Ibn Hasan, *The Central Structure of the Mughal Empire and its Practical Working up to the Year 1657* (Karachi: Oxford University Press, 1967), 85.
59. Nizam-ud-din Ahmed, *Tabakat-i-Akbari*, trans. Sir H. M. Elliot (n.p. 1871 reprint; Lahore: Sind Sagar Academy, 1975), Book I, 86.
60. Ibid., Book II, 89.
61. Ibid., 96.
62. Ibid.
63. "Keeping records is an excellent thing for a government; it is even necessary for every rank of society. Though a trace of this office may have existed in ancient times, its higher objects were but recognized in the present reign." Abu'l Fazl, *A'in-I Akbari*, trans. H. Blochmann, 245.
64. Bernier, *Travels in the Mogul Empire: AD 1656–1668*, 231.
65. "My *wazirs* informed me that the whole amount of the revenue of India is six *arbs*; now each *arb* is a 100 *kror*, and each *kror* is 100 *lacs*, and each *lac* is a 100,000 *miskals* of silver. Some of the nobles said: 'By the favour of Almighty God we may conquer India, but if we establish ourselves permanently therein, our race will degenerate and our children will become like the natives of those regions, and in a few generations their strength and valour will diminish." Timur, *Tuzak-i-Timuri*, trans. H. M. Elliot, ed. John Dowson (Lahore: Sang-e-Meel, 2004), 13. The Timurid Empire in India sought to stave off racial decay through encouraging the migration of fresh recruits from Central Asia and Persia.
66. "No dignity is higher in the eyes of God than royalty; and those who are wise, drink from its auspicious fountain . . . royalty is a remedy for the spirit

of rebellion, and the reason why subjects obey. Even the meaning of the word Padishah shows this; for *pad* signifies stability and possession, and *shah* means origin, lord." Abu'l Fazl, *A'in-I Akbari*, trans. H. Blochmann, 58.

67. Athar Ali, *The Mughal Nobility Under Aurungzeb*, 99.

68. Ibid.

69. Ibid.

70. "In *Asia*, the great are never approached empty-handed. When I had the honour to kiss the garment of the great Mogol *Aurung-zebe* (Ornament of the Throne), I presented him with eight *roupies,* as a mark of respect; and I offered a knife-case, a fork and a pen-knife mounted in amber to the illustrious *Fazal-Khan* . . . a Minister charged with the weightiest concerns . . . on whose decision depended the amount of my salary as a physician." Bernier, *Travels in the Mogul Empire: AD 1656–1668*, 200.

71. A more detailed account of Britain's culture of power is provided in eighth chapter.

72. Simon Schama, *A History of Britain: At the Edge of the World? 3000 BC-AD 1603* (London: BBC Worldwide Ltd., 2000), 162.

73. Charles de Secondat, *The Spirit of Laws* (New York: Prometheus Books, 2002), 152.

74. Ibid., 160.

75. "Tocqueville, believing the strength of American democracy to lie in its local institutions, travelled almost exclusively in the provinces, greatly neglected the organs of the central authority, visited Washington only briefly, towards the end of his journey, and with only perfunctory interest. Custine, coming to a country where power was centralized as nowhere else in the Christian world, quite properly and naturally confined his attention largely to the capital city, the court, and the central apparatus of government.'" George F. Kennan, *The Marquis de Custine and his 'Russia in 1839'* (London: Hutchinson, 1972), 19.

76. Alexis de Tocqueville, *Democracy in America*, trans. George Lawrence, ed., J. P. Mayer (New York: HarperCollins, 2000), 39, 43.

77. Maya Jasanoff, *Liberty's Exiles: American Loyalists in the Revolutionary World* (New York: Alfred A. Knopf, 2011), provides a remarkable account of the loyalist Diaspora and its role in helping to recast the British Empire after the successful revolt of the Thirteen Colonies.

78. In 1895, Winston Churchill, on his first visit to the United States was struck by the superior quality of communications in New York as compared to a rather unimpressive currency: "The communication of New York is due to private enterprise while the state is responsible for currency: and hence I came to the conclusion that the first class men of America are in the counting houses and the less brilliant ones in the government." Martin Gilbert, *Churchill: A Life* (London: Minerva, 1990), 57. In continental bureaucratic empires, which account for the overwhelming preponderance of human historical experience, the equation between the "palace" and the "counting house" was precisely the opposite.

79. G. W. Forrest, ed., *Selections from the State Papers of the Governor-General of India*, vol I, *Hastings* (London: Constable & Co. Ltd., 1910), 161.

80. Conor Cruise O'Brien, *The Great Melody* (London: Minerva, 1993), 351.

81. Ibid., 354.

82. Ibid., 376.

83. Jeremy Bernstein, *Dawning of the Raj: The Life and Trial of Warren Hastings* (London: Aurora Press Ltd., 2000), 166.

84. Montesquieu, *The Spirit of Laws*, 115.

85. Eric Stokes, *The English Utilitarians and India* (New Delhi: Oxford University Press, 1982), 4.

86. A. Aspinall, *Cornwallis in Bengal* (New Delhi: Uppal Publishing House, 1987), 24.
87. Ibid., 16–17.
88. Ibid., 30.
89. *Selection of Papers from the Records at the East India House Relating to the Revenue, Police and Civil and Criminal Justice under the Company's Governments in India*, vol I (London: E. Cox and Son, 1820), 59.
90. Ibid., 15
91. Ibid.
92. Ibid., 16.
93. Ibid., 26.
94. The Cornwallis Code of 1793.
95. Stokes, *The English Utilitarians and India*, 152.
96. *Selection of Papers from the Records at the East India House Relating to the Revenue, Police and Civil and Criminal Justice under the Company's Governments in India*, vol I, 65.
97. Ibid.
98. Ibid.
99. Lawrence James, *Raj: The Making and Unmaking of British India* (London: Abacus, 2003), 153.
100. G. B. Malleson, *Administration of British India under Lord Wellesley* (New Delhi: Daya Publishing, 1988; original edition, 1889), 102.
101. Niall Ferguson, *Empire: How Britain Made the Modern World* (London: Allen Lane the Penguin Press, 2003), 56.
102. Thomas Munro, a collector, and later governor of the Madras Presidency.
103. H. H. Dodwell, ed., *The Cambridge History of India*, vol. 5, *British India 1497–1858* (Cambridge: Cambridge University Press, 1921; reprint, New Delhi: S. Chand & Company (Pvt.) Ltd., 1987), 470.
104. *Selection of Papers from the Records at the East India House Relating to the Revenue, Police and Civil and Criminal Justice under the Company's Governments in India*, vol. I, 211.
105. Ibid.
106. C. H. Philips, ed., *The Correspondence of Lord William Cavendish Bentinck: Governor-General of India 1828–1835*, vol. I, *1828–1831* (Oxford: Oxford University Press, 1977), xxv.
107. Ibid., xxv.
108. Ibid., 111.
109. *Selection of Papers from the Records at the East India House Relating to the Revenue, Police and Civil and Criminal Justice under the Company's Governments in India*, vol II (London: E. Cox and Son, 1820), 187.
110. Ibid.
111. In the Punjab the collapse of Timurid authority facilitated the rise of the Sikhs, a military brotherhood professing a blend of Islam and Hinduism. During the eighteenth century the Sikh *khalsa*, or army of the pure, gained prominence and successfully challenged the Afghans and Timurids for control of the Punjab. During the early nineteenth century, under the leadership of Ranjit Singh, the Sikhs established a kingdom with its capital at Lahore that was strong enough to defeat the Afghans and check British expansion. The *Khalsa Sarkar* was a single-mindedly military government devoid of many of the cultural refinements of its Timurid predecessor. Even the most sympathetic reading of events leaves little doubt in this regard. See for instance Khuswant Singh, *Ranjit Singh: Maharaja of the Punjab* (New Delhi: Penguin Books India, 2001; original edition, 1962).

112. *Report of the Commissioners Appointed to Inquire into the Organisation of the Indian Army, Together with the Minutes of Evidence and Appendix* (London: Her Majesty's Stationery Office, 1859), xi.

113. Ibid., xi.

114. *The Indian Army Commission Report of Major General Hancock* (London: Her Majesty's Stationery Office, 1859), 14–16.

115. Ibid., 27–28.

116. Ibid., 30.

117. The Company's Charter required it to 'protect' Indians 'in the free exercise of their religions' and was interpreted by its officials as a mandate for 'non-interference' in religious affairs. Avril Powell, *Muslims and Missionaries in Pre-Mutiny India* (Surrey: The Curzon Press, 1993), 80.

118. Indeed, the East India Company and its officials feared "the consequences of allowing would-be missionaries" access to the parts of India under British rule. The missionaries often harped on 'the sinfulness and vanity of all other religious paths' and were thus guaranteed to offend Hindus, Muslims and other religious communities in India. Ibid., 76.

119. Ibid., 283.

120. Ferguson, *Empire*, 155.

121. Powell, *Muslims and Missionaries*, 284.

122. David Cannadine, *Ornamentalism: How the British Saw Their Empire* (New York: Oxford University Press, 2001), 89–90.

123. Over the past forty years there has been a consistent attempt to read a great many things into the British Indian state's attempts at acquiring knowledge about its subjects. The broad thrust of the argument made is that in conducting censuses or compiling gazetteers at the local or regional levels the British somehow defined Indians into new categories that ossified into political identities. Thus, the 1871–72 census of India is taken as the starting point for the development of a distinctly "Muslim" or "Hindu"identity because people in India were asked to indicate their religious affiliation. Given the religious complexity and fractiousness of Indian society it was only logical that the British would want to know the number of people of different faiths in territories under their control. The idea that the British could impose identities on ancient and deeply ingrained religious and cultural traditions borders on the absurd especially if one is familiar with these traditions. A recent example of this line of inquiry is Alex Padamsee's *Representation of Indian Muslims in British Colonial Sources* (New York: Palgrave MacMillan, 2005).

124. *East India (Advisory and Legislative Councils)* Vol. II, Part II, *Replies of the Local Governments, Enclosures XXI to XXX to Letter from the Government of India, No. 21, dated the First of October 1908* (London: His Majesty's Stationery Office, 1908), 78.

125. Ibid., 81.

126. Ibid.

127. Ibid., 47.

128. Evan Maconchie, *Life in the Indian Civil Service* (London: Chapman and Hall, 1926), 251.

129. Following the end of the European imperial age the post-colonial states that emerged "found it natural to base their political legitimacy on the rejection of empire as an alien, evil and oppressive force." Marozzi, *After Tamerlane*, 23. The rejection of empire rarely had much substance given that nearly all the post-colonial states were empires in their own right with a miniscule elite ruling a diverse multitude of ethnicities and religions.

130. In Africa, the colonial state was far lighter on the ground than in India. In effect Africa was left "to the mercy of commercial or settler interests" whose rapacity and ignorance were an embarrassing contrast to the probity and efficiency of the Indian administration. Ibid., 315–16.

131. "In contrast to the erupting turmoil across the subcontinent, the scene between imperial lord and victorious revolutionary, that night was one of astonishing civility. For half a century Nehru has devoted his life to the single goal of throwing off the yoke of the British Empire. Now it was done, and his first act as Prime Minister was to pay a call to the power he had just displaced—and offer it a job." Alex von Tunzelmann, *Indian Summer: The Secret History of the End of an Empire* (London: Simon & Schuster, 2007), 5.

132. Prime amongst these was dealing with post-war reconstruction in the UK and managing the situation on the European continent.

133. Peter Clarke, *The Cripps Version: The Life of Sir Stafford Cripps* (London: Allen Lane the Penguin Press, 2002), 397. Cripps was a wealthy man by background—one of countless Marxists, including Friedrich Engels, whose ideological superstructure had very little to do with class or economic base. Cripps was a member of the coalition government formed under Churchill's leadership during the Second World War. In that capacity he served as a minister in the cabinet and handled portfolios that included Aircraft Production and the Board of Trade. A member of the Labor Party, which was ideologically closer to the Indian National Congress, he was sent to India in 1942 to negotiate with Gandhi. After Churchill's defeat in the July 1945 elections, Cripps was entrusted with the task of leading a Cabinet Mission (1946) to negotiate a solution to the deadlock between the Muslims and the Hindus while maintaining the unity of India. As a member of the Cabinet Mission, Cripps reported to Pethick-Lawrence.

134. Clarke, *The Cripps Version*, 393.

135. Ibid., 399.

136. Ibid., 470.

137. B. B. Misra, *The Indian Political Parties: An Historical Analysis of Political Behavior up to 1947* (Delhi: Oxford University Press, 1978), 611–12.

138. It is generally accepted that about ten million were displaced and hundreds of thousands were killed. A war broke out between India and Pakistan over Kashmir in 1948. Gandhi was assassinated by a Hindu fundamentalist on January 30, 1948, Pakistan's founder and first Governor-General, Mohammed Ali Jinnah passed away on September 11, 1948, Sardar Patel, the only serious alternative to Nehru in Congress, died in 1950, and Pakistan's first prime minister, Liaqat Ali Khan, was assassinated in 1951.

139. A. G. Noorani, *Citizens' Rights, Judges and State Accountability* (New Delhi: Oxford University Press, 2002), 1.

140. Armed services chiefs serve standard three-year terms with no extensions. The seniority principle is strictly adhered to and political interference in promotions is minimal. There were rumors of a possible coup attempt in the mid-1970s but nothing came of them.

141. The Emergency of 1975–77.

142. India's first prime minister, he served from 1947 until his death in 1964.

143. Mark Tully and Zareer Masani, *From Raj to Rajiv: 40 Years of Indian Independence* (London: BBC Books, 1988), 24.

144. Ibid.

145. Ibid., 49.

146. In connection with securing a sales-tax deferral for the Reliance Group's fiber processing plant at Planyanga. Agreeing to this request would have entailed the loss of one billion rupees to the state exchequer and it had been reported

that the actual capacity of the plant was much larger than the declared capacity. Cajoling and bribes were followed by threatening phone calls and death threats. Madhav Godbole, *Unfinished Innings: Recollections and Reflections of a Civil Servant* (New Delhi: Orient Longman, 1996), 170.

147. Orchestrated by Rajesh Pilot, the Union Minister of State for Home Affairs.
148. Godbole, *Unfinished Innings*, 4.
149. Dan Banik, "The Transfer Raj: Indian Civil Servants on the Move", *The European Journal of Development Research*, Vol. 13, No. 1, June 2001, 109.
150. Ibid., 110.
151. Ibid., 113–14.
152. Ibid., 122.
153. Ibid., 120.
154. Ibid.
155. Paul R. Brass, *The New Cambridge History of India: The Politics of India since Independence* (Cambridge: Cambridge University Press, 1992), 53.
156. Rajesh Tandon and Ranita Mohanty, eds., *Does Civil Society Matter? Governance in Contemporary India* (New Delhi: Sage, 2003), 83.
157. Tully, *Raj to Rajiv*, 51.
158. Alternatively, the share of indirect taxes rose from about sixty to eighty-four percent during the same period. David Shelbourne, *An Eye to India: The Unmasking of a Tyranny* (Suffolk: Penguin Books, 1977), 428.
159. For a fascinating insight into the role of the state and its distribution agencies in ensuring that two hundred million Indian's go hungry every day, and perhaps as many more suffer from the consequences of malnutrition, see Bill Pritchard, Anu Rammohan, and Madhushree Sekher, "Food Security as a Lagging Component of India's Human Development: A Function of Interacting Entitlement Failures", *South Asia: Journal of South Asian Studies*, Vol. 36, No. 2, 2013, 213–28.
160. "India's Tax-GDP ratio one of the lowest", March 26, 2013, *The Business Standard*. http://www.business-standard.com/article/economy-policy/india-s-tax-gdp-ratio-one-of-the-lowest-113032500376_1.html (Accessed July 30, 2013).
161. Ashok Mody and Michael Walton, "The Inflation Elixir", January 16, 2013, *The Business Standard*. http://www.business-standard.com/article/opinion/ashoka-mody-michael-walton-the-inflation-elixir-113011700092_1.html (Accessed July 30, 2013).
162. Ibid.
163. 1947–1972.
164. Dilip Hiro, *Inside India Today* (London: Routledge & Kegan Paul, 1976), 32.
165. Tandon and Mohanty, eds., *Does Civil Society Matter?*, 93.
166. Hiro, *Inside India Today*, 35.
167. Tully, *Raj to Rajiv*, 33.
168. Ibid., 65.
169. Indira Gandhi, Jawaharlal Nehru's daughter, served as prime minister from 1966 to 1977 and 1980 to 1984.
170. Tandon and Mohanty, eds., *Does Civil Society Matter?*, 93–94.
171. For detailed analysis of what this has meant for the emerging metropolitan hub of Gurgaon, near Delhi, see Tathgata Chatterji, "The Micro-Politics of Urban Transformation in the Context of Globalisation: A Case Study of Gurgaon, India", *South Asia: Journal of South Asian Studies*, Vol. 36, No. 2, 2013, 273–87. ". . . it is a most unusual city: it has no discernible centre or visible urban structure; instead, it is a motley collection of privately developed gated enclaves, separated from each other by old village *abadis*

(settlements), which have been turned into slums, stretching endlessly along the Delhi-Jaipur highway." Ibid., 274.

172. Bal Mundkar, "Incredible India: The Inconvenient Truth", *Asian Affairs*, 42: 1, 91.

173. Ibid., 87.

174. Ibid.

175. Ramchandra Gupta, *India After Gandhi: The History of the World's Largest Democracy* (London: MacMillan, 2007), 683.

176. Francine R. Frankel, *India's Political Economy, 1947–2004: The Gradual Revolution* (New Delhi: Oxford University Press, 2005), 592.

177. Mundkar, "Incredible India: The Inconvenient Truth", 91.

178. Swapna Banerjee-Guha, "Accumulation and Dispossession: Contradictions of Growth and Development in Contemporary India", *South Asia: Journal of South Asian Studies*, Vol. 36, No. 2, 2013, 170. Fascinatingly, the infrastructure built for the 2010 Commonwealth Games in New Delhi required 1.2 million workers out of which only 22,000 were "legally registered as eligible to receive wages as per the Minimum Wage Act; the rest, numbering more than 1.1 million were labeled 'illegal' by the government that was using their services." Ibid., 172.

179. Ranging from taxi-drivers to prostitutes

180. Arun Gandhi, ed., *The Morarji Papers: Fall of the Janata Government* (New Delhi: Vision Books, 1983), 132. There was also an established prostitution racket involving senior officials and politicians that involved offering girls in state-owned educational institutions an improvement of their grades in exchange for sexual favors.

181. Primila Lewis, *Reason Wounded: A Personal Account of India's Emergency* (Lahore: Vanguard Books Ltd., 1979), 113.

182. Ibid., 119.

183. Ibid., 142.

184. Brass, *The New Cambridge History of India: The Politics of India since Independence*, 56–57.

185. Senior Advocate, Indian Supreme Court, Tagore Professor of Law at Calcutta University, Indian ambassador to the United States 1977–79, Honorary Member of the Academy of Political Science, New York.

186. N. A. Palkhivala, *We, the People* (Bombay: Strand Book Stall, 1988), 34.

187. Ibid., 3.

188. Stephen P. Cohen, *India: Emerging Power* (Washington D.C.: Brookings Institute Press, 2001), 116.

189. Tandon and Mohanty, eds., *Does Civil Society Matter?*, 108.

190. Noorani, *Citizens' Rights, Judges and State Accountability*, 3.

191. Ibid., 120.

192. Ibid., 123.

193. Mundkar, "Incredible India: The Inconvenient Truth", 90.

194. For a fine account of how the state and local political fixers help cheat local people out of their lands in order to service the needs of India's rich, see Patrik Oskarsson, "Dispossession by Confusion from Mineral-Rich Lands in Central India", *South Asia: Journal of South Asian Studies*, Vol. 36, No. 2, 2013, 199–212.

195. Brass, *The New Cambridge History of India: The Politics of India since Independence*, 55.

196. This puts the ratio of police officers to population at roughly two per thousand.

197. Hiro, *Inside India*, 205.

198. Ibid.

199. Javed Hassan, *India: A Study in Profile* (Rawalpindi: Services Book Club, 1990), 176.

200. For an insider's account of Indian-held Kashmir see Basharat Peer, *Curfewed Night* (London: Random House, 2008). Written as a personal narrative rooted in a collective tragedy *Curfewed Night* brings home what the post-1990 Indian paramilitary and military deployment has meant for tens of thousands of families. Of course, the wider world has no interest and as the West seeks to assist India in its efforts to project a "soft" image, hard realities, and those who expose them, are unwelcome.

201. For a searing account of how India's democracy upholds order, see Arundhati Roy, *Listening to Grass-hoppers: Field Notes on Democracy* (Rawalpindi: Services Book Club, 2011). The draconian Prevention of Terrorism Act (POTA) has effectively replaced investigation with torture as far as suspected enemies of the state are concerned. After the state sponsored massacre of Muslims in Gujarat in 2002, 287 persons were charged with offenses under POTA—astonishingly, 286 were Muslims and one was a Sikh! Ibid., 28. Related to this is the sustained employment of the Armed Forces Special Powers Act, which is a stricter and more arbitrary version of colonial-era legislation, in large swathes of the country, including the North East and Kashmir. The military can imprison and torture people on suspicion and has been doing so with impunity for decades. "The fact that despite all this, India sustains its reputation as a legitimate democracy—in the international community and amongst its own middleclass—is a triumph." Ibid., 29.

202. The Golden Temple is the holiest shrine of the Sikh religion. Amritsar is a major urban center in the Indian Punjab, about an hour's drive from Lahore, the capital of Pakistani Punjab.

203. An estimated three thousand civilians and insurgents were killed in the operation in addition to about seven hundred Indian soldiers. Kuldip Nayar and Khushwant Singh, *Tragedy of Punjab: Operation Bluestar and After* (New Delhi: Vision Books Pvt., Ltd., 1984), 108–9.

204. Ibid. About one in twelve Indian soldiers is a Sikh.

205. Ibid., 181. Estimates of the number killed range from the hundreds to more than ten thousand.

206. Marc Galantier, *Law and Society in Modern India*, ed., Rajeev Bhavan, (Delhi: Oxford University Press, 1988), xxii.

207. Ibid.

208. Ibid., xxvi.

209. Palkhivala, *We, the People*, 296.

210. Ibid., 298.

211. Tandon and Mohanty, eds., *Does Civil Society Matter?*, 85.

212. Ayesha Jalal, *Democracy and Authoritarianism in South Asia: A Comparative and Historical Perspective* (Lahore: Sang-e-Meel Publication by arrangement with the Cambridge University Press, 1995), 47.

213. Ibid., 47–48.

214. Speaking at a police conference on June 10, 1981, the British Home Secretary, William Whitelaw, elucidated important aspects of the Anglo-Saxon culture of power and state of laws: "I think . . . that it is highly desirable that the enforcement of the criminal law should not be subject to political control or influences. As Home Secretary, I cannot give direction to chief constables on operational matters. . . . I do not believe that the majority of people in this country would welcome or would tolerate the situation in which local or national politicians could direct the police operations or influence decisions on who should be prosecuted." Noorani, *Citizens' Rights, Judges and State Accountability*, 135. Noorani observes "The law in India is no different

from that in Britain. What is different is the actual set-up which is brazenly violative of the law." Ibid., 136. The "set up" refers to the broad category of responses to the state and the exercise of authority that comprise cultures of power. Laws can be changed overnight. Cultures of power change, if at all, at a glacial rate.

215. Ibid., 18–19.
216. Ibid., 71.
217. Ibid., 56, 68.
218. Ibid., 126–27.
219. Palkhivala, *We, the People*, 354.
220. One survey found that 91% of the population thought of politicians as corrupt. Gupta, *India After Gandhi*, 686.
221. Lewis, *Reason Wounded*, 113.
222. The 1970 campaign slogan was "Eliminate Poverty."
223. Jalal, *Democracy and Authoritarianism in South Asia*, 76.
224. Tandon and Mohanty, eds., *Does Civil Society Matter?*, 145.
225. Ibid., 150.
226. Ibid., 147.
227. Ibid., 149. Emphasis in original.
228. Ibid., 151–52.
229. Mundkar, "Incredible India: The Inconvenient Truth", 86.
230. Ibid., 84.
231. An illiterate mother of nine. When she first became Chief Minister, she swore in a cabinet with seventy-five ministers.
232. Patna, the ancient capital of the Mauryas.
233. Incidentally, Uttar Pradesh and Bihar are amongst India's poorest and most lawless states
234. Another interesting example are the bicycle rickshaw drivers of New Delhi. In 2006, their number was estimated at 500,000. Under the law, there is a ceiling of 99,000 permits. Instead of raising "the permit ceiling or abolish the quota altogether, the state ensures that more than 400,000 people continued to operate illegally. In order to do so the rickshaw drivers have to pay regular bribes to the police each month." Edward Luce, *In Spite of the Gods: The Strange Rise of Modern India* (London: Little, Brown Group Ltd., 2006), 80.
235. Khalid Mahmud, *Indian Political Scene, 1989: Main Contenders for Power* (Islamabad: Institute of Regional Studies, 1989), 32.
236. Ibid., 33.
237. Ibid., 34.
238. Ibid., 36.
239. Godbole, *Unfinished Innings*, 105.
240. Ibid., 91.
241. Sanjay Gandhi, Indira's Gandhi's son and political heir apparent, died in an air crash in 1980. If Sanjay Gandhi had lived then he would succeeded his mother after her assassination in 1984.
242. Tandon and Mohanty, eds., *Does Civil Society Matter?*, 114.
243. Ibid.
244. Ibid., 109.
245. Founded in 1925.
246. A. G. Noorani, *The RSS and the BJP: A Division of Labour* (New Delhi: LeftWord Books, 2000), 9.
247. Ibid., 12.
248. Ibid., 26.
249. M. J. Akbar, *India: The Siege Within, Challenges to a Nation's Unity* (Suffolk: Penguin Books Ltd., 1985), 305.

250. The basic concept is to recast Hinduism "as a masculine, aggressive and violent faith . . . India's slavery had to be explained" and "this was done in terms of loss of masculinity of the Hindus." Jyotirmaya Sharma, *Hindutva: Exploring the Idea of Hindu Nationalism* (New Delhi: Penguin Books, 2006), 9.

251. Balbir K. Punj, "Hindu Rashtra," *South Asian Journal* (October-December 2003), 12.

252. Praful Bidwai, "A Critique of Hindutva," *South Asian Journal* (October-December 2003), 20.

253. Sharma, *Hindutva*, 46.

254. Bidwai, 30. Never mind that the Hindus themselves had little interest in their own history and the task of bringing Ancient India above the historical horizon fell upon the British.

255. Ibid., 21.

256. Ibid., 30.

257. Ibid.

258. Ibid., 26.

259. Ghanshyam Shah, Mario Rutten, and Hein Streefkerk, eds., *Development and Deprivation in Gujarat* (New Delhi: Sage Publications, 2002), 37.

260. Mahatma Gandhi and Quaid-i-Azam Mohammed Ali Jinnah, going by their national titles.

261. Shah, Rutten, and Streefkerk, eds., *Development and Deprivation in Gujarat*, 40.

262. Ibid., 37.

263. Ibid., 50–51.

264. Ibid., 59, 62.

265. Ibid. Advani has served as the BJP-led government's Union Home Minister and was the deputy prime minister.

266. Khushwant Singh, *The End of India* (New Delhi: Penguin Books, 2003), 3–4.

267. Tandon and Mohanty, eds., *Does Civil Society Matter?*, 109.

268. Bidwai, "A Critique of Hindutva," *South Asian Journal*, 31.

269. Shelbourne, *An Eye to India*, 94.

270. Ibid., 101.

271. Susan Bayly, *The New Cambridge History of India: Caste, Society and Politics from the Eighteenth Century to the Modern Age* (Cambridge: Cambridge University Press, 2000), 3.

272. An excellent example is Amartya Sen's *The Argumentative Indian: Writings on Indian History, Culture and Identity* (London: Allen Lane the Penguin Press, 2005). Sen argues that India has indigenous liberal traditions and cites Kautilya and Akbar as prime examples of these traditions in action. To anyone familiar with the substance of Kautilya's work or Akbar's reign, this assertion seems more like wishful thinking. Yes, there are some facets of pre-modern South Asia can be identified as pluralistic, but, for the most part, that tradition in arbitrary and autocratic.

273. V. S. Naipaul, *An Area of Darkness* (London: Pelican Books, 1968), 73, 81.

274. Ibid., 81.

275. Mundkar, "Incredible India: The Inconvenient Truth", 85.

276. Raghav Bhal, *Superpower? The Amazing Race between China's Hare and India's Tortoise* (London: Portfolio/Penguin, 2010) is a recent exercise towards this end. The basic argument is that China is growing too fast and too much for it be sustained while India has a far more balanced model of growth that is likely to reach the finish line while China goes under, like a hare pumped up on steroids.

277. For a comparative perspective, see Siedentop, *Democracy in Europe*. Particularly relevant is Chapter I "Democratic Liberty on a Continental Scale?", 1–24.

278. Macaulay's speech in the House of Commons on 10 July 1833. Later, as the Law Member of Bentinck's council, Macaulay advised the government not "to leave the natives to the influence of their own hereditary prejudices," stop spending money on publishing works in Arabic and Sanskrit for which there was hardly any market demand, and reorient public education towards instruction in English and the vernaculars. C. H. Philips, ed., *The Correspondence of Lord William Cavendish Bentinck: Governor-General of India 1828–1835*, vol. II, 1832–1835 (Oxford: Oxford University Press, 1977), 1409–12.

279. For the author's take on Pakistan see Niaz, *The Culture of Power and Governance of Pakistan, 1947–2008*.

280. The BJP does not have to secure a clear majority of the popular vote to command a two-thirds majority in the central legislature. Congress, for example, has never secured more than 48.1 percent of the popular vote, although it enjoyed two-thirds majorities in 1952, 1957, 1962, 1971, and 1984.

NOTES TO CHAPTER 2

1. "China has existed for several millennia, certainly for two, arguably even three thousand years" and according to Chinese propaganda, for as much as five millennia. While debating the exact antiquity of Chinese civilization is not our purpose, China "is far and away the oldest continuously existing polity in the world, certainly dating back to 221 BC, in some respects, rather longer." Martin Jacques, *When China Rules the World: The End of the Western World and the Birth of a New Global Order*. (London: Penguin, 2012), 244.

2. During China's decline during the early 20th century, the Japanese attempted to understand Chinese administrative law, which resulted in *"The Administrative Law of the Qing Empire . . . An* encyclopedia-style work . . . created collaboratively by Meiji Japanese jurists and Sinologists." The objective was to understand Chinese law in the context of developments in Europe that had affected legal reforms in Japan and to educate the Chinese about these advances. As it turned out, Chinese imperial administrative law fell into several distinct categories including "general codes", "ministerial precedents", "precedents for provinces", and "miscellaneous". The Chinese empire was a "democratic despotism" in the sense that while the ruler was above the law, his subjects, including his officers, were equally subject to it. Cheng Yi, "Enacting the 'Incomprehensible China': Modern European Jurisprudence and the Japanese Reconstruction of Qing Political Law", *Law & Social Inquiry*, Vol. 33, Issue 4, Fall 2009, 956, 974, 977. One particularly interesting aspect of the Chinese legal system was that any claim of entitlement by one subject against another or against the state, especially for money or property, required the registration of the assets in question in the government record—if unregistered property came to the notice of the state it could be legally confiscated. Ibid., 986.

3. For more on how the Chinese state has viewed the rest of the world, see Odd Arne Westad, *Restless Empire: China and the World since 1750* (London: The Bodley Head, 2012), esp, 1–53.

4. So much so that "When European intellectuals first started thinking seriously about China, in the seventeenth century, most felt humbled . . . If China's

eighteenth century emperors had known that European philosophers such as Voltaire were writing poems praising them, they would probably have thought that that was exactly what French philosophers ought to be doing." Ian Morris, *Why the West Rules—for Now:The Patterns of History and what they Reveal about the Future* (London: Profile Books, 2010), 13.

5. In 5 BC, the total size of the imperial bureaucracy was about 130,000. In about 30 BC there were some 57,000 officials employed to manage two hundred ancestral shrines as part of the legitimation exercise of the Han imperial state. John Keay, *China: A History* (London: HarperCollins, 2009), 146–47.

6. The Chinese "belief in ancestral spirits encouraged a similar respect for and veneration of the state as an immortal institution which represented the continuity of Chinese civilization." Jacques, *When China Rules the World*, 156.

7. Si Ma Qian, *Records of the Grand Historian: Qin Dynasty*, trans. Burton Watson (New York: Columbia Press, 1993), provides all the materials relevant to the rise and fall of Qin in one convenient volume. Si Ma Qian states: "Qin began as a small state in a far-off region" and was originally considered a semi-barbarian state. In spite, or perhaps because of, its cultural handicaps, it developed a ferocious military and administrative capability and "in the end united the whole world under its rule." Ibid., 86.

8. The seven warring states were: Han, Wei, Chu, Qi, Zhao, Yan and Qin. Qin was the western-most and exposed to barbarian attacks. Wei, Qi and Han occupied more central positions, while Chu fell to the south and Yan and Zhao to the north and northwest. Until 400 BC, the states of Wei and Qi were in a more dominant position as compared to Qin.

9. Lord Shang's advice, as "records on bamboo strips recovered" from the period "show that the laws were enforced in all their savagery." Morris, *Why The West Rules-For Now*, 265.

10. It was the height of folly for a ruler "to confer office, to give rank and to grant salaries, without regard to merit. . . ." Shang Yang, *The Book of Lord Shang*, trans. J. J. L. Duyvendak (London: Wordsworth Classics, 1998), 194.

11. Jonathan Clements, *The First Emperor of China* (Gloucestershire: Sutton Publishing, 2004), 24.

12. Ibid., 57.

13. Morris, *Why the West Rules-For Now*, 266.

14. Clements, *The First Emperor of China,* 58.

15. Ibid., 100.

16. Julia Lovell, *The Great Wall: China Against the World, 1000 BC- AD 2000* (New York: Grove Press, 2006), 51.

17. Ibid., 59.

18. Ibid.

19. The other major dynasties were: Han (206 BC—AD 220), Sui (AD 581–618), Tang (618–907), united (Northern) Song Empire (960–1127) and Southern Song (1127–1263), Yuan (1263–1368), Ming (1368–1644), and Qing (1644–1911).

20. One such example of effective counting helps explain the outbreaks of disease: "Epidemics of infectious diseases first appeared around 2000 B.C.E. in centers of unusually dense human populations where there existed domesticated animals. However, the magnitude of the burden of epidemics on people's everyday life is not well known, especially before 1800. There are, to my knowledge, no reports of how frequent the outbreaks were and whether their density evolved across time. In other words, there is no description of how the pressures of epidemics on societies grew over the last 4000 years. This knowledge deficit stems mainly from a lack of accurate long-term

monitoring of epidemic outbreaks in most regions of the world. However, there is a major exception: a catalogue of dates and places of outbreaks of epidemic diseases is available for China between 243 B.C.E. and 1911 C.E., i.e. over about 2000 years. The records encompass the entire duration of the Chinese Empire, from the 'First Emperor' of the Qin (Qin Shi Huang-di—from 221 to 206 B.C.E.), to the last Emperor of the Manchu or Qing Dynasty (1644–1911)." A. Morabia, "Epidemic and Population Patterns in the Chinese Empire (243 B.C.E. to 1911 C.E.): Quantitative Analysis of a Unique but Neglected Epidemic Catalogue", *Historical Review* (Cambridge: Cambridge University Press, 2009), 1362–63.

21. Ibid., 1365–66.
22. The Han were the first to effectively extend China's writ into the far west, settling through force and inducement some 700,000 farmers west of the Yellow River, and deploying tens of thousands of soldiers to protect them while fortifying outlying positions. In punitive campaigns against assorted Inner Asian nomads and pastoralists the Han were prepared to suffer 90 percent casualties in pursuit of wearing down their enemies through attrition and settlement. Keay, *China: A History*, 138.
23. Chinese society was, and is, divided in clans/lineages, reflected in the modern surnames. About one hundred such surnames cover 85 % of the Han Chinese population, against 70,000 surnames covering 90 % of Americans. Jacques, *When China Rules the World*, 310. The term "Han Chinese" is a modern construction, coined by the scholar Zhang Taiyan (1868–1936) and not a real ethnicity. In fact, China comprises different racial sub-groups that over time assimilated into the cultural and political matrix of the imperial civilization-state. Under assault from outsiders in the 1800s and 1900s, the Han Chinese ethnicity emerged as a response designed to provide modern nationalist underpinnings to the pre-modern cultural and civilization identities. Jacques, *When China Rules the World*, 307–310.
24. W. M. Spellman, *Monarchies: AD 1000—2000* (London: Reaktion Books, 2001), 20.
25. Frank Ching, *Ancestors: The Story of China through the lives of an Extraordinary Family* (London: Rider, 2008).
26. Barrington Moore, *The Social Origins of Dictatorship and Democracy: Lord and Peasant in the Making of the Modern World* (Boston: Beacon Press, 1967), 172.
27. Jens Kaalhauge Nielsen, "The flower that didn't bloom: why did the industrial revolution happen in Europe and not in China?", *Journal of Chinese Economic and Business Studies*, 8: 1, (2010), 23–44 is one recent example of this hypothesis. Nielsen argues: "that the key reasons why China's development was blocked is to be found in the structural 'freeze' between China's cultural pattern and its political system. This freeze implied three things. (a) The cultural system and the political system were locked together, so that the political system was 'overloaded' with cultural symbolism and with socio-cultural functions. (b) It also implied that the political system was not (sufficiently) differentiated from the societal community, so that one important outcome of this lack of differentiation was the weak nature of Chinese civil society. As a result, the stratification of society tended to fossilize around a state-centered bureaucracy. Hegel has illustrated this problem by saying that China was a state without a society. (c) The freeze also blocked important differentiation processes within the cultural system itself, including those processes Max Weber has called 'rationalization processes', and was manifested in the way that Chinese philosophy according to Frederick Mote is characterized by an interlinking 'organismic' worldview." Ibid., 24.

28. The Neo-Confucian ethic dictated that "fulfillment comes from action in this world" and subjects like geography and economics were added to the compulsory subjects for competitive examinations. Money supply in China rose from 300 million coins in 983 to 1.83 billion coins in 1000 and agriculture, thanks to an excellent canal system, was able to reap three harvests a year, against the two common in South Asia, and one common in Europe. Block printing had unleashed millions of cheap books on the market and by 1024 a banking system complete with currency notes was in place. Iron output rose from 20,000 tons in 800 to 125,000 tons in 1078—greater than Europe's total output till 1700. "One well-documented foundry, at Qicunzhen, employed three thousand workers to shovel 35,000 tons of ore and 42,000 tons of coal into furnaces each year." Morris, *Why the West Rules-For Now*, 374–80. One can go on giving examples in this respect as Morris does, such as that of the silk-reeling machine comparable in design to an eighteenth century French flax spinning machine, that indicate the early phase of an industrial revolution in China.

29. Moore, *The Social Origins of Dictatorship and Democracy*, 175.

30. Lovell, *The Great Wall*, 194.

31. Ibid., 195.

32. John King Fairbank and Merle Goldman, *China: A New History* (Cambridge, Massachusetts: Harvard University Press, 2006), 121.

33. Lovell, *The Great Wall*, 229, 126, 83.

34. James Mulvenon, "The PLA in the New Economy" in David M. Finkelstein and Kirsten Gunness, eds., *Civil-Military Relations in Today's China: Swimming in a New Era* (New Delhi: Pentagon Press, 2009), 216.

35. Or the path of *Ren*, that is rational humaneness based on humility, respect for seniority, and devotion to one's family and one's country.

36. Tingyang Zhao, "Rethinking Empire from a Chinese Concept 'All Under Heaven' (Tian xia)", *Social Identities*, Vol. 12, No. 1, 34 (2006).

37. Ibid., 35.

38. Ibid., 31.

39. Ibid.

40. Spellman, *Monarchies*, 28.

41. Ching, *Ancestors*, 136.

42. Ibid., 35.

43. "In China, those who add murder to robbery are cut in pieces: but not so the others; to this difference it is owing that though they rob in that country they never murder. In Russia, where the punishment of robbery and murder is the same, they always murder. The dead, they say, tell no tales." Charles de Secondat, *The Spirit of Laws*, Vol I, 90. In the second volume, Montesquieu expresses admiration for the Confucian philosophy in its skepticism towards the immortality of the soul and focus on issues in this life. Ibid., Vol. II, 38.

44. Voltaire illustrates the relative vulgarity of Western culture in his *Philosophical Dictionary*: "In 1723, a Chinese visited Holland. This Chinese was a man of letters and a merchant; which two professions ought not to be incompatible, but which have become so among us, thanks to the extreme regard which is paid to money, and the little consideration which mankind has ever shown, and will ever show, for merit." Ben Ray Redman, ed., *The Portable Voltaire* (New York: Penguin, 1978), 128.

45. Wenxian Zhang, "Dang An: A Brief History of the Chinese Imperial Archives and its Administration", *Journal of Archival Organization*, Vol. 21, ½, 2004, 18.

46. Ibid.

47. Ibid., 23.

48. Ibid., 24.
49. Ibid., 26.
50. Ibid.
51. Ibid., 27.
52. Ibid.
53. Ching, *Ancestors*, 20–21.
54. Ibid., 214.
55. Clements, *The First Emperor of China*, 69.
56. Ibid.
57. Jared Diamond, *Collapse: How Societies Choose to Fail or Survive* (London: Penguin, 2006), 374.
58. Lovell, *The Great Wall*, 147.
59. Clements, *The First Emperor of China*, 97.
60. Ibid., 100.
61. Fairbank, *China: A New History*, 129–30.
62. Ibid., 130.
63. Ibid.
64. Ibid., 132.
65. Ching, *Ancestors*, 43.
66. Ibid.
67. It was still, however, a large apparatus by the high point of the Qing dynasty with some 40,000 officers, 1.2 million clerks and 500,000 runners. Karl Wittfogel, *Oriental Despotism: A Comparative Study of Total Power* (New Haven: Yale University Press, 1963), 307.
68. Fairbank, *China: A New History*, 130.
69. John Man, *Kublai Khan: The Mongol King who Remade China* (London: Transworld Publishers, 2006), 111, 148–49.
70. Spellman, *Monarchies*, 45.
71. Man, *Kublai Khan*, 130.
72. Ibid., 131.
73. Ibid.
74. Clements, *The First Emperor*, xi.
75. Ibid., 154.
76. In order to the build the Grand Canal the Sui government mobilized at least 1 million workers. Wittfogel, *Oriental Despotism*, 34.
77. Adam Smith makes the case that China set the standard for large-scale projects such as canals and roads as these greatly facilitated the expansion of agriculture and from it the land revenue also increased. Adam Smith, *The Wealth of Nations*, ed., Edwin Cannan (New York: Bantam Classics, 2003), 925–26.
78. An interesting statistic from the Han dynasty is that of the civil servants about whose career information is available, 21 percent were imprisoned, 35 percent died violent deaths outside the battlefield, 12 percent were murdered or tortured and 9 percent committed suicide. Beneath the Confucian veneer was the harshness of Qin legalism. Wittfogel, *Oriental Despotism*, 338.
79. In 1599, in order to punish Yang Yinglong, an errant pacification minister who had set up a brutal regime of terror and gotten away with it for twenty years, the Ming dispatched an expedition of 250,000 troops, which succeeded in reasserting central authority over Bozhou and brought it back "within the standard system of directly administered prefectures." Keay, *China: A History*, 404.
80. The fallout of these trends on the population of the core areas is open to question, for, in 1598, "the Italian Father Matteo Ricci had opted for the Grand Canal" route to travel to Beijing from Nanjing. Ricci had spent sixteen years

in Guangdong, was familiar with the country, and knew the language. "He was nevertheless amazed by the volume of shipping on the canal. It was said that 10,000 vessels were engaged in transporting the tax produce of Shandong and the Yangzi provinces to Beijing, and Ricci saw no reason to doubt it. He was equally impressed by the 'great number of well known cities' he passed. As for the banks of the canals, they were lined by 'so many towns, villages and scattered houses that one might say the entire route is inhabited'. Throughout a distance of around 1700 kilometers (1060 miles), the commercial activity never ceased." Ibid., 412.

81. Ching, *Ancestors*, 180.
82. Ibid.
83. Ibid., 181.
84. Ibid.
85. Lovell, *The Great Wall*, 233–34.
86. Ibid., 253.
87. "You, O King, live beyond the confines of many seas; nevertheless, impelled by your humble desire to partake of the benefits of our civilization, you have dispatched a mission respectfully bearing your memorial. . . .As to your entreaty to send one of your nationals to be accredited to my Celestial Court and to be in control of your country's trade with China, this usage is contrary to all usage of my Dynasty and cannot possibly be entertained. . . .If you assert that your reverence for our Celestial Dynasty fills you with a desire to acquire our civilization, our ceremonies and codes of laws differ so completely from your own that, even if your envoy were able to acquire the rudiments of our civilization, you could not possibly transplant our manners and customs to your alien soil." Cited from Arnold J. Toynbee, *A Study of History*, abridged, D. C. Somervell (New York: Dell Publishing, 1978), Vol. 1, 55
88. Philip Short, *Mao: A Life* (London: Hodder & Stoughton, 1999); Li Zhisui, *The Private Life of Chairman Mao*, trans. Tai Hung-Chao (New York: Random House, 1994), and Jung Chang and Jon Halliday, *Mao: The Unknown Story* (New York: Alfred A. Knopf, 2005) are three particularly outstanding examples available in the English language. Short and Chang present external perspectives while Li Zhisui, Mao's personal physician, provides remarkable details about Mao's inner circle and his personal life.
89. These include, Mao Tse-Tung, *Selected Readings from the Works of Mao Tse-Tung* (Peking: Foreign Language Press, 1967), and Mao Tse-Tung, *Selected Works of Mao Tse-Tung*, Vols. I-V (Peking: Foreign Language Press, 1975).
90. The Cultural Revolution technically continued until 1978 when it was repudiated by the post-Mao leadership.
91. Christian Taylor, *Wild West China: The Untold Story of a Frontier Land* (London: John Murray, 2004), 132–33.
92. The Maoist slaughter of the Uighur elite and later colonization of the region by Han settlers was presaged by the policy of the Qing against the Zunghars or Western Mongols. The 1689 treaty between China and Russia, the first that involved recognition of sovereign equality from the Chinese side, was designed to secure Russian neutrality as the Chinese government unleashed genocide and colonization against the Zunghars. This "turned out to be a remarkably successful grand bargain" from the Qing and Russian perspectives "though the Zunghars, slaughtered to almost the last man, woman, and child by the 1750s, would have disagreed." Westad, *Restless Empire*, 33.
93. Short, *Mao: A Life*, 630–31.
94. The details of the millions of individual tragedies that unfolded as a consequence of Mao's psychopathic and ruinous policies constitute a record of

suffering paralleled only by the excesses of Nazism and Stalinism. One such episode is as follows: "Hua Lanhon, a modernist who had worked with Le Corbusier in the 1930s, went to a China he had never seen to become deputy head of the city planning bureau in Beijing in 1949. Hua oversaw much of the destruction of Ming-dynasty city in the 1950s. He was later purged as a promoter of Westernization, and spent twenty years buiding outhouses for rural communities when he was not brought out to be publicly humiliated as a representative of 'deviant architecture.' Hua was finally able to go back to France in 1977." Westad, *Restless Empire*, 243–44.

95. You Ji, "Unraveling Myths about Commissars", in Finkelstein, ed., *Civil-Military Relations in Today's China*, 153.

96. James Mulvenon, "The PLA in the New Economy", in Ibid., 217.

97. Ibid., 219.

98. Cheng Li, "The New Military Elite", in Ibid., 55.

99. Ibid., 49.

100. Yu Bin, "The Fourth Generation Leaders and the New Military Elite", in Ibid., 77.

101. One estimate is that in 2001 some 240,000 Chinese scholars were more or less permanently employed in studying Marxism or variants thereof. Gordon G. Chang, *The Coming Collapse of China* (London: Century, 2001), 225.

102. Mao's rejection of even Soviet advisors by the mid-1960s and the Great Leap Forward were manifestations of the refusal to accept that it would take a long time for China to modernize. Mao wanted to move quickly and believed that those who argued for a steady but more gradual approach were revisionists rather than true revolutionaries. Indeed, Mao seemed to have adopted the policy of permanent revolution in one country, combining the worst of Trotskyism with Stalinism. The crusade against revisionism led to widespread incrimination and imprisonment for criticizing earlier excesses or even making innocent remarks about how good imported shoe polish was. Westad, *Restless Empire*, 321.

103. At the end of the Mao era, "The average per capita income of Chinese peasants, who made up 80 per cent of the population, was then only US$ 40 per year. The amount of grain produced per person had fallen below what it had been in 1957." Ezra F. Vogel, *Deng Xiaoping and the Transformation of China* (Cambridge, Massachussetts: The Belknap Press of Harvard University Press, 2011), 1.

104. Deng Xiaoping formally rose to power at The Third Plenary Session of the XI Party Central Committee in December 1978. This event "is usually regarded as a milestone of China's reform and opening up. The plenary session decided to put an end to the 'Cultural Revolution,' to shift the principal work of the Party from class struggle onto economic development and to elect Deng Xiaoping as the top leader of the Party and the state. The basic reason why the Session made so many important decisions within 5 days, according to some specialists on the history of the CCP, is that before the Session a 36-day working conference was held, at which participants had reached great consensus on important issues after heated argument and intense conflict. The Session did approve the decisions of the working conference and Mr. Deng Xiaoping's keynote speech at the working conference was acknowledged officially as 'the main speech of the Third Plenary Session'." Yu Keping, "Toward an Incremental Democracy and Governance: Chinese Theories and Assessment Criteria", *New Political Science*, 24: 2, (2002), 183.

105. Which is not to say that the statistics are unimportant: "The yearly average growth rate of China's GDP in 20 years from 1978 till 1998 surpassed 9.8%. In 1998 China's GDP reached 7.955,3 billion Yuan while it was merely 358.8

billion Yuan in 1978. The rapid economic growth resulted in an enormous rise in the standard of living of the Chinese people. The average per capita income of peasants increased from 133.6 Yuan in 1978 to 2,160 Yuan in 1998, 4.3 times as much as the 1978 figure. The average per capita income of urban residents in the cities amounted to 5,425 Yuan in 1998, 3.5 times as much as the 1978 figure . . . Although the investment proportion of SOEs in terms of total fixed assets remains to be over 70%, 60% or more of the increase of the GNP in recent years came from the non-state enterprises, because over 70% of the SOEs operate at a loss. Second, China reformed the management and operational system. In the countryside, the People's Commune system was abolished and replaced by a variety of contract or subcontract systems; in urban areas cities, the egalitarian production and distribution systems were replaced by the new job responsibility with different payments." Ibid., 185

106. A ruthlessness evidenced by the crackdown on student demonstrators on June 4, 1989, at Tiananmen Square in Beijing. Deng felt the demonstrators, by refusing to vacate the square even during Gorbachev's visit had proven that they lacked patriotism. Deng personally took charge of the containment operation and the crackdown that left, according to different estimates, hundreds or thousands of demonstrators dead. Vogel, *Deng Xiaoping, 599*, 630–31.

107. Cheng Li, "The New Military Elite", in Finkelstein, ed., *Civil-Military Relations in Today's China*, 55.

108. Jacques, *When China Rules the World*, 283.

109. Yu Bin, "The Fourth Generation Leaders and the New Military Elite", in *Civil-Military Relations in Today's China*, 79.

110. Vogel, *Deng Xiaoping*, 540–41.

111. Yu Bin, "The Fourth Generation Leaders and the New Military Elite", in Finkelstein, ed., *Civil-Military Relations in Today's China*, 79.

112. Jacques, *When China Rules the World*, 283.

113. Yongfei Zhao and Guy Peters, "The State of the State: Comparing Governance in China and the United States", *Public Administration Review*, Dec. 2009, Special Issue, S124.

114. Ibid.

115. Yu Keping, "Toward an Incremental Democracy and Governance: Chinese Theories and Assessment Criteria", 193.

116. Yongfei Zhao, "The State of the State: Comparing Governance in China and the United States", S125.

117. Ibid.

118. Ran Tao and Ping Qin, "How has Rural Tax Reform Affected Farmers and Local Governments in China", *China and World Economy*, Vol. 15, No. 3, 2007, 21.

119. Oppression by state functionaries was and perhaps still is one of the major causes of rural-urban migration and congestion in the cities: "Another strong incentive to leave the countryside is the misery inflicted by greedy, tyrannical local officials. Abuses against farmers grew to be one of the country's most explosive issues when a Chinese magazine published a report in December 2003 by Chen Guidi and Wu Chuntao . . ." Ted C. Fishman, *China Inc.: The Relentless Rise of the Next Great Superpower* (London: Simon & Schuster, 2006), 56.

120. Bill K. P. Chou, "Does 'Good Governance' Matter? Civil Service Reform in China", *Journal of Public Administration*, 31:1, (2007), 54–55.

121. This stability is, however, threatened by growing inequality. China's Gini Coefficient rose from 0.30 in 1978 to 0.47–0.50 in 2009, while internally,

the GDP ratio between the richest and poorest provinces is 10 to 1, more than Brazil's 8 to 1. Jacques, *When China Rules the World,* 195.

122. One of these achievements is the revival of the state's share of the total GDP raked in by revenues. In 1978, some 34 percent of GDP was taken by the state as revenues, which fell to 10.8 percent by 1995 on account of runaway economic growth. This was followed by more effective tax collection, with the result that by 1999 revenues were 14 percent of GDP and by 2006, 22 percent. Ibid., 197.

123. Some aspects of this comeback are particularly disliked by the West: "China's failure to police intellectual property, in effect, creates a massive global subsidy worth hundreds of billions to dollars to its businesses and people. Seen another way, China's vast counterfeiting schemes act on the rest of the world the way colonial armies once did, invading deep into the economies of their victims, expropriating their most valued assets, and in so doing, undermining their victims' ability to counter." Fishman, *China Inc.,* 252.

124. Referring to China, Goody observes that productivity was often stimulated by the demands and incentives provided by the state: "The textile industry in China was a secondary seasonal activity for more than 2000 years, stimulated not only by local needs but also by the fact that, for the greater part of its history, the government demanded taxes in kind in the form of textiles, which it could then export." Goody, *The Eurasian Miracle,* 19.

125. "The Chinese state remains a highly competent institution, probably superior to any other state-tradition in the world and likely to exercise a powerful influence on the rest of the world in the future." Jacques, *When China Rules the World,* 574.

126. To do so will require great wisdom and prudence, two qualities that China's strategists, civil servants, and rulers, have prized though not always managed to practice, and the avoidance of military conflicts until such time that China's demographic and economic pull renders such exercises irrelevant to the ultimate result. Kissinger summarizes the differences between the Chinese and Western approaches thus: "Where Western strategists reflect on the means to assemble superior power at the decisive point, Sun Tzu addresses the means of building a dominant political and psychological position, such that the outcome of a conflict becomes a foregone conclusion. Western strategists test their maxims by victories in battles; Sun Tzu tests by victories where battles have become unnecessary." Henry Kissinger, *On China* (London: Penguin books, 2012), 26.

NOTES TO CHAPTER 3

1. The major periods in Persian history being the Achaemenian (559 BC—330 BC), the Seleucid (312 BC—160 BC in Persia and till 63 BC in Syria), the Parthian (240s BC—AD 224), the Sassanid (224—644), the Arab Empire and Turkish Sultanates (644–1258), the Mongol/Timurid conquests (1220s-1400s), the Safavids (1501-1722), the Qajars (1796-1926), the Pahlavis (1926—1979) and the Islamic Republic (1979—Present). The earlier dates may vary but fall within the same range.

2. A recent example of which is Anothy Pagden, *Worlds at War: The 2500-year Struggle between East and West* (Oxford: Oxford University Press, 2009).

3. René Labat, "Elam and West Persia", in I. E. S Edwards, C. J. Gadd, N. G. L. Hammond, et. al., eds, *The Cambridge Ancient History: The Middle East and the Aegean Region c1380–1000 BC* (Cambridge: Cambridge University Press, 1980), Vol. 2, Part 2-A, 484.

4. Ibid., 491.
5. Percy Sykes, *A History of Persia*, vol. I (London: Routledge and Kegan Paul, 1969), 157.
6. Tom Holland, *Persian Fire: The First World Empire and the Battle for the West* (London: Little, Brown, 2005), 24.
7. Herodotus, *Histories*, 261.
8. Ibid., 262.
9. Cyrus's policies invite comparison with Akbar the Great of the Timurid (Mughal) Empire in India. Akbar's move away from Islamic orthodoxy and relaxation of restrictions and punitive taxation on Hindus was resented by the conservative ulema. Later rulers gravitated towards orthodox Islam culminating in the Islamic-oriented policies of Aurungzeb Alamgir.
10. Herodotus, *Histories*, 649.
11. Sykes, *A History of Persia*, vol. I, 164.
12. R. C. Zaehner, *The Dawn and Twilight of Zoroastrianism* (New York: Phoenix, 2003), 301.
13. Ibid., 21.
14. Ibid., 158.
15. For a contemporary corroboration of Herodotus's *Histories* and exploration, see Justin Marozzi, *The Way of Herodotus: Travels with the Man who Invented History* (London: DA CAPO Press, 2008), esp., 1–27.
16. A unit of measurement, one Babylonian talent was about 30 kilograms.
17. Herodotus, *Histories*, 266.
18. Ibid.
19. Ibid.
20. Ibid., 267.
21. Ibid.
22. Ibid.
23. Ibid.
24. Ibid.
25. Ibid.
26. Ibid.
27. Ibid., 268.
28. Ibid.
29. K. Nefedkin, "The Tactical Development of Achaemenid Cavalry", *Gladius*, XXVI (2006), 7.
30. Ibid., 12.
31. Ibid.
32. Herodotus, *Histories*, 537.
33. Axworthy, *Empire of the Mind*, 46.
34. Sykes, *A History of Persia*, vol. I, 407.
35. Ibid., 415.
36. David Levering Lewis, *God's Crucible: Islam and the Making of Europe, 570 to 1215* (New York: W. W. Norton, 2008), 20.
37. Zaehner, *The Dawn and Twilight of Zoroastrianism*, 284.
38. J. H. Iliffe, "Persia and the Ancient World", in A. J. Arberry, ed., *The Legacy of Persia* (London: Oxford University Press, 1968), 30–31.
39. Richard N. Firye, *The Golden Age of Persia: The Arabs in the East* (London: Weidenfeld and Nicholson, 1977), 7.
40. Lewis, *God's Crucible*, 20.
41. Ibn Khaldun describes the ruinous effects of excessive arbitrariness, especially with regard to the confiscation of property noting "When attacks on (property) are extensive and general, affecting all means of making a livelihood, business inactivity, too becomes general." Ibn Khaldun then refers to

the reign of the Sassanid Shah Bahram II (r. 276–293) who is reputed to have been extremely unjust and greedy at the start of his reign and confiscated farms and bestowed them on his favorites without regard to merit. Bahram eventually realized the folly of his arbitrary confiscations and seized the property from his favorites and gave it back to the previous owners. Ibn Khaldun, *The Muqqadimah*, 238–39.

42. Ibid. 40–41.
43. Centered on oases and wells.
44. J. J. Saunders, *A History of Medieval Islam* (London: Routledge, 1965; reprint, 1996), 5.
45. "The First Caliphs did not appoint distinctive Muslim judges" and "the Arabs took over the legal and administrative institutions and practices of the conquered territories, both Roman-Byzantine and Sasanian-Persian, whose cultures were highly developed." Hans Kung, *Islam: Past, Present and Future*, trans. John Bowden (Oxford: Oneworld, 2007), 182.
46. The Arabs "took over not only legal institutions and legal practices but also particular juristic terms and maxims, methods of argument and basic ideas" include the one about expert opinion dear to the Roman legal tradition. Ibid.
47. The fourth Caliph, Ali (r. 656–661), revered by Sunnis and Shia alike, took a stand against the rise of Umayyad interests that had occurred during the Caliphate of Usman (r.644–656). Ali reversed his predecessor's "centralized control of the incomes of the provinces and ensured a more equitable distribution of the income from taxation and the plunder of war." Ibid., 183.
48. Nizami, ed., *Politics and Society During the Early Medieval Period*, 4.
49. Ibid., 7.
50. Ibid., 11.
51. Ibid., 10.
52. Ibid., 9.
53. Ibid.
54. Ibid., 14–15, 19.
55. Ibid., 22.
56. Ibid.
57. Ibn Khaldun quotes extensively from the note written by Abd-al Hamid the *sahib al-insha*, or chief secretary, to the last Ummayad rulers. Abd-al Hamid was killed during the Abbassid takeover, so his advice apparently didn't have the desired effect. It does however, shed light on the bureaucratic nature of the Ummayad state. Abd-al Hamid wrote: "He gave to you, secretaries, the great opportunity to be men of education and gentlemen, to have knowledge and good judgment. You bring whatever is good in the caliphate and straighten out its affairs. Through your advice, God improves the government for the benefit of human beings and makes their countries civilized. The ruler cannot dispense with you. You alone make him a competent ruler. Your position with regard to rulers is that you are the ears through which they hear, the eyes through which they see, the tongues through which they speak, and the hands through which they touch." Ibn Khaldun, *The Muqaddimah*, 203.
58. Hugh Kennedy, *The Court of the Caliphs*, 65.
59. Ibid., 71.
60. Carl Brockelmann, *History of the Islamic Peoples* (New Delhi: Munshiram Manoharlal Publishers, 1995), 163.
61. Ibid., 163–64.
62. Ibid., 164.
63. Saunders, *A History of Medieval Islam*, 68–69.

64. Brockelmann, *History of the Islamic Peoples*, 165.
65. With the decline of Abbasid power, the Turkish-led military effectively went on a rampage that lasted until 935, when Ibn Raiq assumed the mantle of political power as the *Amir-al-Umara*. The Abbasids were allowed to exist by the Turkish *amirs* in order to acquire divine sanction. Thus, the Abbasids were kicked upstairs to the highest position within the ideocratic complex of the Turkish warrior-elite's state.
66. Saunders, *A History of Medieval Islam*, 120–21.
67. Hugh Kennedy, *The Court of the Caliphs*, 287.
68. Ibid., 290.
69. Saunders, *A History of Medieval Islam*, 149.
70. Brockelmann, *History of the Islamic Peoples*, 168.
71. Ibid.
72. Sachau, *Alberuni's India*, vii.
73. Ibid., viii.
74. Ibid.
75. Nizami, ed., *Politics and Society During the Early Medieval Period*, 69.
76. Ibid.
77. Sachau, *Alberuni's India*, 3.
78. Ibid.
79. With reference to the difficulties between Firdausi and Sultan Mahmud, the story goes that the former was so disappointed with the meager sum given to him (20,000 dirhams) that he gave away the entire amount, fled to Herat, stayed in hiding there for six months, and then went to Tabiristan where Shahriyar of the House of Baiwind granted him refuge. There, Firdausi wrote a satire on Sultan Mahmud that Shahriyar had the sense to purchase for 10,000 dirhams and prevent it from being circulated. Edward G. Browne, *A Literary History of Persia* Vol. II, *From Firdausi to Sa'di* (Lahore: Sang-e-Meel, 2003; first published, 1906), 135–36.
80. Kumar, ed., *Local Governments and Administration During Muslim Rule in India*, 66.
81. Ibid.
82. Ibid., 67.
83. Ibid.
84. Ibid.
85. Ibid., 68.
86. Nizami, ed., *Politics and Society During the Early Medieval Period*, 83.
87. Ibid., 90.
88. Omid Safi, *Religion and Politics in Saljuq Iran: Negotiating Ideology and Religious Inquiry* (Karachi: Oxford University Press, 2007), 56–57.
89. For more on the conflict between the Sunni orthodox Seljuks and their Ismaili rivals see Peter Wiley, *Eagle's Nest: Ismaili Castles in Syria and Iran* (London: I. B. Tauris, 2005), esp. 21–23. Ultimately, it was the Mongols who crushed the Ismailis, though the Seljuks also devoted considerable time and resources to this same end.
90. Safi, *Religion and Politics in Saljuq Iran*, 67.
91. Kumar, ed., *Local Governments and Administration During Muslim Rule in India*, 69.
92. Nizami, ed., *Politics and Society During the Early Medieval Period*, 84.
93. Ibid., 85.
94. Ibid.
95. Ibid.
96. Ibid.
97. Ibid., 86.

98. Sachau, *Alberuni's India*, xviii.
99. Ibid., 20.
100. Ibid., 21.
101. Ibid., 22.
102. Ibid., 27.
103. Ibid., 133–35
104. Ibid., 184–85.
105. Ibid., 210.
106. Ibid.
107. Brockelmann, *History of the Islamic Peoples*, 147.
108. Ibid.
109. One consequence of this was arbitrary spending and conspicuous consumption amongst the elite. During the reign of the Abbasid Caliph Ma'mum on the occasion of his wedding, lavish gifts worth millions of dinars were distributed and some 30,000 boats were prepared to carry guests and their retinues along the Tigris. Ibn Khaldun, *The Muqaddimah*, 139.
110. Hugh Kennedy, *The Court of the Caliphs*, 26.
111. Ibid., 21.
112. Axworthy, *Empire of the Mind*, 104.
113. For more on the encounter see Walter J. Fischel, *Ibn Khaldun in Egypt: His Public Functions and his Historical Research, A Study in Islamic Historiography* (Berkeley: University of California Press, 1967), 42–65. Ibn Khaldun explained to Amir Timur the philosophy of history as it revolved around the waxing and waning of *asabiyah* or group solidarity that was itself rooted in a combination of kinship/blood relations and ideology/religion.
114. Roger Savory, *Iran Under the Safavids* (Cambridge: Cambridge University Press, 1980), 22.
115. Ibid., 29.
116. Edward G. Browne, *A Literary History of Persia*, Vol. IV, *Modern Times, 1500–1924* (Lahore: Sang-e-Meel, 2003; first published, 1924), 22.
117. David Blow, *Shah Abbas: The Ruthless King who Became an Iranian Legend* (London: I. B. Tauris, 2009), 4.
118. Ismail I believed himself to be "God's mystery", the son of the Caliph Ali, "Pir of the Twelve Imams", and the living embodiement of Jesus, for good measure. Andrew J. Newman, *Safavid Iran: Rebirth of a Persian Empire* (London: I. B. Tauris, 2009), 13–14.
119. Browne, *A Literary History of Persia*, Vol. IV, *Modern Times, 1500–1924*, 55.
120. Ibid., 61.
121. Savory, *Iran under the Safavids*, 34.
122. These rivalries were initially between the Turkish Qizilbash tribes and the Tajik-dominated bureaucracy, though later, the raising of a slave corps added a third element. The Shia ulema might be considered a fourth group though their role as an integral part of the power structure is questionable. Newman, *Safavid Iran*, 15.
123. Maria Szuppe, "Kinship ties between the Safavids and the Qizilbash Amirs in Late Sixteenth-Century Iran: a Case Study of the Political Career of Members of the Sheral al-Din Oghli Tekelu Family", in Charles Melville ed., *Safavid Persia: The History and Politics of an Islamic Society* (London: I. B. Tauris, 1996), 81–85, 91, 94.
124. "In 1629, of the top thirteen members of the cabinet by office, five were Tajiks, five were *ghulams*, and three had tribal connections." Newman, *Safavid Iran*, 71.
125. Blow, *Shah Abbas*, 25.

126. Ibid., 33.
127. In order to stimulate the economy and raise revenues from what was a narrow agricultural and demographic base, the Safavid state invested in cermaics products, the silk trade, and carpet weaving, in addition to levying transit duties wherever possible. Newman, *Safavid Iran*, 67.
128. Blow, *Shah Abbas*, 42.
129. Ibid., 43.
130. Qazvin was the former Safavid capital and of great strategic importance as it dominated the ancient road that connected Khorasan to the rest of the Iranian plateau. Qazvin had been used by the Sassanids as a military strongpoint while the Seljuks had also employed it as the center of their military efforts against the Ismailis. Ehsan Echraqi, "Le Dar al-Saltana de Qazvin, deuxieme Capitale des Safavides", in Melville ed., *Safavid Persia*, 105–8.
131. Blow, *Shah Abbas*, 44.
132. Ibid., 45.
133. Halil Inalcik, *The Ottoman Empire: The Classical Age, 1300–1600* (London: Phoenix, 2000), 59. The toll such confinement took on the Ottoman princes was considerable though it did keep them alive it also drove many of them insane.
134. Willem Floor and Patrick Clawson, "Safavid Iran's Search for Silver and Gold", *International Journal of Middle Eastern Studies*, 32 (2000), 347–48. The population of Safavid Persia is estimated at between 5 and 8 million.
135. Ibid., 348.
136. Ibid.
137. Michael Axworthy, *The Sword of Persia: Nader Shah, from Tribal Warrior to Conquering Tyrant* (London: I. B. Tauris, 2009), 27.
138. Ibid., 43.
139. It is very fashionable to focus on British depredations in Bengal and the transfer of wealth that they occasioned, but far more of South Asia was plundered and devastated by the Persian, Afghan, ex-Timurid elite, Sikhs and Marhattas, during the 1700s.
140. Ibid., 270.
141. Ibid., 271. One gold *toman* was equal to about four Indian gold *mohars*, or about 44–45 grams.
142. Hasan-i-Fasai, *Farsnama-ye Naseri (History of Persia under Qajar Rule)* trans. Heribert Busse (New York: Columbia University Press, 1972), 39.
143. Ibid., 65.
144. Ibid., 67.
145. Ibid., 70.
146. Ibid., 71.
147. Vanessa Martin, *The Qajar Pact: Bargaining, Protest and the State in Nineteenth Century Persia* (London: I. B. Tauris, 2005).
148. Homa Katouzian, *State and Society in Iran: The Eclipse of the Qajars and the Emergence of the Pahlavis* (London: I. B. Tauris, 2000).
149. Martin, *The Qajar Pact*, 16.
150. Ibid., 17.
151. Gene R. Garthwaite, *Khans and Shah: A History of the Bakhtyari Tribe in Iran* (London: I. B. Tauris, 2009), 38.
152. Ibid., 43.
153. Ibid., 45.
154. Ibid., 49.
155. Ibid., 73.
156. Ibid., 96.
157. Katouzian, *State and Society in Iran*, 9.

158. Ibid.
159. Ibid.
160. John Walbridge, "The Babi Uprising in Zanjan: Causes and Issues", *Iranian Studies*, Vol. 29, No. 3–4, Fall/Winter 1996, 339.
161. Katouzian, *State and Society in Iran*, 68.
162. Katouzian, *State and Society in Iran*, 315.
163. Ibdi.
164. Homa Katouzian, *The Political Economy of Modern Iran: Despotism and Pseudo-Modernism, 1926–1979* (London: MacMillan, 1981), 123.
165. Ibid.
166. Ibid., 115.
167. Ibid., 116.
168. Donald N. Wilber, *Riza Shah Pahlavi: The Resurrection and Reconstruction of Iran, 1878–1944* (Hicksville, New York: Exposition Press, 1975), 133.
169. Ibid., 131. Wilber is referring to the leftist movement within Iran as well as anyone associated with it.
170. Ibid., 145.
171. Ibid., 133, 153.
172. Ibid., 181.
173. Ibid., 231.
174. Katouzian, *State and Society in Iran*, 317.
175. Wilber, *Riza Shah Pahlavi*, 228.
176. Katouzian, *State and Society*, 319.
177. Robert Fisk, *The Great War for Civilization: The Conquest of the Middle East* (London: Harper Perennial, 2006), 120.
178. Ibid., 121.
179. Katouzian, *The Political Economy of Modern Iran*, 208, 219.
180. Fisk, *The Great War for Civilization*, 121.
181. Marvin Zonis, *The Political Elite of Iran* (Princeton: Princeton University Press, 1971), 55.
182. Ibid., 30.
183. Ibid., 260.
184. Ibid., 230.
185. Baqer Moin, *Khomeni: Life of the Ayatollah* (London: I. B. Tauris, 2009), 97.
186. A comparison with Saudi Arabia is instructive. The Saudi regime is a very conservative monarchy backed by the Wahabi ulema. The Saudi regime is also subservient to Western interests in the Middle East and has close links with the United States. In spite of this, however, the Saudi regime is strictly religious in its internal administration and gives the ulema an important role to play, patronizing them with positions in the state and resources. Pahlavi Iran, in contrast tried *to simultaneously serve Western interests while humiliating the ulema and insulting the religious sensibilities of the masses.*
187. Ghoncheh Tazmini, *Khatami's Iran: The Islamic Republic and the Turbulent Path to Reform* (New York City: I. B. Tauris & Co., 2010), 27.
188. Saiyyid Ruhollah Musavi Khomeni, *Islam and Revolution: Writings and Declarations of Imam Khomenei*, trans. & annotated by Hamid Algar (Berkley: Mizan Press, 1981), 55.
189. Ibid., 59.
190. Ibid., 116.
191. Ibid., 147.
192. Moin, *Life of Khomeini*, 158.
193. Ibid., 207.
194. Fisk, *The Great War for Civilization*, 135.
195. Tazmini, *Khatami's Iran*, 105.

NOTES TO CHAPTER 4

1. For a semi-cyclical account of Europe's historical development of mentality see Giambattista Vico, *The New Science*, trans. Thomas Goddard Bergin and Max Harold Fisch (Ithaca, New York: Cornell University Press, 1948). Vico argued that we could know history scientifically owing to the fact that it was created by our own thoughts and actions. History, at least in Europe, had, according to Vico, developed in sets of three stages with ages of God, Heroes, and Man, following each other, subject to a recourse during the age of Man brought about by catastrophe that caused a new age of God to begin. Thus, Europe's first age of God corresponded to the mythological period of the Greeks and Romans, its first age of Heroes corresponded to the rise of the city-states and their wars, and the first age of Man was the *Pax Romana*. The disintegration of the Roman Empire and the rise of Christianity in its wake represented a second age of God, while the emergence of feudalism represented a second age of Heroes. Vico's own age, that of the Scientific Revolution and Enlightenment, was the beginning of a second age of Man.
2. David Landes, *The Wealth and Poverty of Nations* (London: Abacus, 1998), 156.
3. Morris, *Why the West Rules for Now*, 13.
4. Landes, *The Wealth and Poverty of Nations*, 21–22, 26.
5. Cicero, *The Republic and The Laws*, trans. Niall Rudd (Oxford: Oxford University Press, 2008), xii.
6. Ibid., 19.
7. Ibid.
8. Jean-Jacques Rousseau, *The Social Contract or Principles of Political Right*, trans. Maurice Cranston (London: Penguin Classics, 1968), 53.
9. Ibid.
10. Edward Gibbon, *The Decline and Fall of the Roman Empire*, abridged, Frank C. Bourne (New York: Dell Publishing, 1963), 34.
11. Ibid.
12. Ibid.
13. Ramsay MacMullen, *Corruption and the Decline of Rome* (New Haven: Yale University Press, 1988), 59.
14. Ibid.
15. Cicero, *The Republic and The Laws*, 24.
16. J. Donald Hughes, "Social Structure and Environmental Impact in the Roman Empire", *Capitalism, Nature, Socialism,* Vol. 15, No. 3, 2004, 31.
17. Caesar, *The Gallic War*, trans. Carolyn Hammond (New York: Oxford University Press, 2008), xii. The popular interest would refer to that of the plebian masses.
18. Ibid., xvii.
19. Morris, *Why the West Rules for Now*, 229.
20. Soldiers were, however, paid when on campaign for otherwise they might desert to look after their families.
21. Caesar, *The Gallic War*, 23.
22. Ibid., 59.
23. Morris, *Why the West Rules for Now*, 229.
24. Which is not to say that it did not happen. Julius Caesar's troops were tired after the Gallic War and did not relish the prospect of prolonged campaigning against other Roman armies. When Caesar heard of this discontent he "summoned the grumblers into his presence, and reduced them to obedience by a single word: 'I grant what you desire', he said, 'Citizens, you may go.' At

the sound of that peaceful title, which seemed to them a bitter humiliation, the soldiers repented of their rebellious mood and begged to be received back into their commander's favor." H. L. Havell, *Ancient Rome: The Republic* (New Lanark: Geddes and Grosset, 2003), 487.

25. Ibid., 492.
26. These relatively unassuming titles were chosen in order to avoid politically charged terms like "king" or "dictator" that were likely to arouse resentment.
27. Two famous victims of the proscription of 43 BC were Marcus Tullius Cicero and his brother Quintus Tullius Cicero. Having earlier aligned themselves with Pompey, they were forgiven by Caesar, only to betray him in 44 BC. Octavian and Antony felt that Caesar's generosity had been misplaced. Marcus and Quintus Cicero were among more than 2000 victims of this proscription. Cicero, *The Republic and The Laws*, xxiv.
28. Gibbon, *The Decline and Fall of the Roman Empire*, 163.
29. Tacitus, *The Annals: The Reigns of Tiberius, Claudius, and Nero*, trans. J. C. Yardley (Oxford: Oxford University Press, 2008), 3.
30. Ibid.
31. Basic Roman currency unit, made of bronze during the principate. 100 sesterces were equal to 1 aureus or gold coin. The denarius was a silver coin, 25 of which were equal to 1 aureus.
32. Tacitus, *The Annals*, 8.
33. Ibid., 11.
34. Ibid.
35. Ibid., 14. Nearly thirty colonies were set up within Italy by Augustus, and many others were planted in Africa, Spain, Asia, Syria, etc.
36. Ibid., 15.
37. Gibbon, *The Decline and Fall of the Roman Empire*, 74.
38. Tacitus, *The Annals*, 13.
39. Ibid., 49.
40. Ibid., 109.
41. Ibid., 111.
42. Paul Du Plessis, "The Protection of the Contractor in Public Works Contracts in the Roman Republic and Early Empire", *The Journal of Legal History*, Vol. 25, No. 3, 2004, 287, 294. Thus, close relatives of a magistrate could not apply for contracts to be decided by him, and public announcements and notices made known who had been contracted for which project.
43. Tacitus, *The Annals*, 152.
44. Ibid., 175.
45. Ibid., 190–200.
46. Ibid., 194.
47. Ibid.
48. Nero's adviser, the philosopher Seneca, amassed a fortune of 300 million sesterces "within a four-year period of friendship" with the emperor. In Rome "the wills of childless men were being caught in his net, while Italy and the provinces were being drained by his unscrupulous usury." Ibid., 293.
49. Gibbon, *The Decline and Fall of the Roman Empire*, 73.
50. The censors were two magistrates appointed for eighteen-month terms responsible for maintaining the register of citizens that was used for taxation and representation purposes. These officials acquired "a sort of inquisitorial jurisdiction over the lives and manners of Roman citizens, corresponding in this respect to the Council of Areopagus at Athens." Havell, *Ancient Rome*, 86.
51. Gibbon, *The Decline and Fall of the Roman Empire*, 49.

52. M. Alexander Speidel, "Roman Army Pay Scales", *The Journal of Roman Studies*, Vol. 82, 1992, 87–106.
53. Morris, *Why the West Rules for Now*, 315.
54. Gibbon, *The Decline and Fall of the Roman Empire*, 43.
55. Ibid., 46.
56. Ibid., 68.
57. Hughes, "Social Structure and Environmental Impact in the Roman Empire", 33.
58. Ibid.
59. Gibbon, *The Decline and Fall of the Roman Empire*, 83.
60. Ibid., 99.
61. Ibid., 101.
62. Ibid., 107.
63. Hughes, "Social Structure and Environmental Impact in the Roman Empire", 33.
64. Ibid.
65. Cicero, *The Laws and The Republic*, 162.
66. Du Plessis, "The Protection of the Contractor in Public Works in the Roman Republic and the Early Empire", 303.
67. Gibbon, *The Decline and Fall of the Roman Empire*, 107.
68. MacMullen, *Corruption and the Decline of Rome*, 132.
69. Gibbon, *The Decline and Fall of the Roman Empire*, 122.
70. That is, with reference to South Asian history, the period of chaos that erupted in the Sikh Kingdom after the death of Maharaja Ranjit Singh in 1839. Rival military commanders vied for supremacy leading to internal conflict, instability in succession, and inflation in the number of troops.
71. MacMullen, *Corruption and the Decline of Rome*, 144.
72. Ibid.
73. Ibid., 146.
74. Gibbon, *The Decline and Fall of the Roman Empire*, 191–92.
75. Morris, *Why the West Rules for Now*, 315.
76. MacMullen, *Corruption and the Decline of Rome*, 33–34.
77. A drachma was about the same value as a denarius, so eight drachma would equal roughly seven denarii.
78. About 36 liters.
79. Hughes, "Social Structure and Environmental Impact in the Roman Empire", 33–34.
80. Ibid., 34.
81. Michael Grant, *The Fall of the Roman Empire* (London: Phoenix, 2005), 57–58.
82. Ibid., 56.
83. For a convenient and sympathetic abridgment of St. Augustine's work see F. R. Montgomery Hitchcock, *St. Augustine's Treatise on the City of God* (New York: The Macmillan Company, 1922).
84. Landes, *The Wealth and Poverty of Nations*, 21–22.
85. Morris, *Why the West Rules for Now*, 419.
86. Ibid., 380.
87. Alexis de Tocqueville, *The Old Regime and the Revolution*, trans. Alan S. Kahan, Edited and with an Introduction by François Furet and Françoise Mélonio (Chicago: University of Chicago Press, 1998), 103.
88. Montesquieu devotes a lot of effort to explaining aristocracies and their organization around the principle of honor and mutual obligation. For more see Charles de Secondat, *The Spirit of Laws*, Vol. II, 171–268.

89. Landes, *The Wealth and Poverty of Nations*, 34.
90. Pipes, *Property and Freedom*, 106.
91. David A. Warner, "Ideals and Action in the Reign of Otto III", *Journal of Medieval History*, Vol. 25, No. 3, 1999, 10.
92. Ibid.
93. Ibid., 11–12.
94. Ibid., 16.
95. Ibid.
96. Ibid., 16–17.
97. George T. Beech, "The Lord/Dependent (vassal) Relationship: A Case Study from Aquitaine, c. 1030", *Journal of Medieval History*, Vol. 24, No. 1, 1998, 1–30.
98. Ibid., 20.
99. Ibid., 19.
100. Ibid.
101. Mark Hagger, "How the West was Won: The Norman Dukes and the Cotentin, c. 987–1087", *Journal of Medieval History*, Vol. 38, No. 1, 2012, 24.
102. Ibid., 29.
103. Ibid., 46.
104. Robert Portass, "The Contours and Contexts of Public Power in the tenth-century Liebana", *Journal of Medieval History*, Vol. 38, No. 4, 2012, 394.
105. Ibid.
106. Ibid.
107. Ibid., 395.
108. Ibid., 401.
109. Ibid.
110. Gianluca Raccagni, "The Teaching of Rhetoric and the Magna Carta of the Lombard Cities: The Peace of Constance, the Empire and the Papacy in the works of Guido Faba and his leading Contemporary Colleagues", *Journal of Medieval History*, Vol. 39, No. 1, (2013), 61.
111. Ibid.
112. Ibid., 68.
113. Ibid., 70.
114. Ibid., 76.
115. "If we judge medieval philosophy by its content alone, then there was no philosophy in the Middle Ages, only the faith of the church." John Inglis, "Philosophical autonomy and the historiography of medieval philosophy", *British Journal for the History of Philosophy*, Vol. 5, No. 1, 1997, 23.
116. Fukuyama, *The Origins of Political Order*, 238.
117. Ibid.
118. Ibid., 269.
119. Damien Kempf, "Paul the Deacon's *liber de episcopis Mettensibus* and the role of Metz in the Carolingian Realm", *Journal of Medieval History*, Vol. 30, No. 3, 2004, 295
120. Ibid., 282
121. Constant J. Mews, "Gregory the Great, the Rule of Benedict and Roman Liturgy: The Evolution of a Legend", *Journal of Medieval History*, Vol. 37, No. 2, 2011, 125–44.
122. C. M. A. West, "Unauthorized Miracles in the mid-ninth century: Dijon and the Carolingian Church Reforms", *Journal of Medieval History*, Vol. 36, No. 4, 2010, 297–98.
123. Matthias Becher, *Charlemagne* (London: Yale University Press, 2003), 118.
124. Ibid., 66–67.

125. Cullen J. Chandler, "Heresy and Empire: The Role of the Adoptionist Controversy in Charlemagne's Conquest of the Spanish March", *The International History Review*, Vol. 24, No. 3, 2002, 510.
126. Ibid.
127. Ibid.
128. Ibid., 517.
129. Norman Tanner and Sethina Watson, "Least of the Laity: The Minimum Requirements for a Medieval Christian", *Journal of Medieval History*, Vol. 32, No. 4, 2006, 397.
130. Ibid.
131. Ibid., 404.
132. Ibid.
133. West, "Unauthorized Miracles in the mid-ninth century", 297.
134. Ibid., 304.
135. Becher, *Charlemagne*, 91–92. Actually, the dispute with the Second Council of Nicaea was due to a poor translation of its decision into Latin, which made it appear that religious icons ought to be venerated as substitutes for the real thing.
136. Philip Zimbardo, *The Lucifer Effect: How Good People Turn Evil* (London: Rider, 2007), 9
137. David Ogg, *Europe in the Seventeenth Century* (London: Adam and Charles, 1967), 367–68.
138. Zimbardo, *The Lucifer Effect*, 9.
139. Fernand Braudel, *The Perspective of the World: Civilization and Capitalism 15th-18th Century*, Vol. 3, trans. Sian Reynolds, (London: Phoenix Press, 2002), 119.
140. Ibid., 120.
141. Ibid.
142. Fernand Braudel, *The Wheels of Commerce: Civilization and Capitalism 15th-18th Century*, Vol. 2, trans. Sian Reynolds, (London: Phoenix Press, 2002), 408.
143. Geneva is an important example of this. The struggle between the Dukes of Savoy and the Bishop of Geneva resulted in the wealthy commoners gaining a charter from the Church in 1387. Attempts by the Dukes of Savoy to assert their control ended in failure and turned Geneva into an independent city-state. During the Reformation, Geneva broke off from the Catholic Church as well.
144. Siedentop, *Democracy in Europe*, 13.
145. Ibid.
146. "For the process of state formation was, especially on the continent, essentially a despotic one. It involved the creation of instruments for government from above—government by lawyers, bureaucrats and 'experts' . . . France epitomized this process." Ibid., 119.
147. Braudel, *The Wheels of Commerce*, 516.
148. Carsten, ed., *The New Cambridge Modern History*, vol 5, *The Ascendancy of France 1648–88*, 225.
149. W. F. Reddaway, *A History of Europe from 1610 to 1715* (London: Methuen and Co. Limited, 1967), 268.
150. Harold J. Grimm, *The Reformation Era: 1500–1650* (London: The MacMillan Company, 1969), 24.
151. Reddaway, *A History of Europe from 1610 to 1715*, 95.
152. Ogg, *Europe in the Seventeenth Century*, 62.
153. Ibid., 63.
154. Ibid.

155. Ibid., 64–66.
156. Ibid., 65. The *livre* was the French pound, originally established by Charlemagne as the equivalent of one pound of silver. It was divided into twenty *sous*, each, in turn, subdivided into twelve *derniers*.
157. Ibid.
158. In an average French town of 3,000 people the officials included the *bailli*, the *prévot*, the *lietenant*, the *procurer-fiscal*, six notaries, twelve procurers, four *greffiers* and a "host of clerks". Ibid., 23.
159. Ibid., 193.
160. Carsten, ed., *The New Cambridge Modern History*, vol 5, *The Ascendancy of France 1648–88*, 222.
161. Parlements were judicial bodies staffed by aristocrats. The offices were hereditary, for life, and could not be lawfully interfered with by the king.
162. Richelieu exiled even Marie de Medicis, the Queen Mother, for conspiring against him.
163. Ogg, *Europe in the Seventeenth Century*, 197.
164. Ibid., 195.
165. Ibid., 197.
166. Carsten, ed., *The New Cambridge Modern History*, vol 5, *The Ascendancy of France 1648–88*, 236. That is, the intendant of police, justice, and finance, or collector-magistrate.
167. Ibid.
168. There were also territories recently conquered by France in which the king collected taxes directly. These were the *pays d'imposition*.
169. Ogg, *Europe in the Seventeenth Century*, 199.
170. Ibid., 200.
171. For more on this see, James H. Kitchens, III, "Judicial Commissaires and the Parlement of Paris: The Case of the Chambre de l'Arsenal", *French Historical Studies*, Vol. 12, No. 3, 1982, 323–50.
172. Pipes, *Property and Freedom*, 139. His English counterpart, with four million subjects, had a royal bureaucracy that numbered about one thousand two hundred.
173. Michael S. Kimmel, *Absolutism and its Discontents: State and Society in Seventeenth Century France and England* (Piscataway, NJ: Transaction Publishers, 1988), 96.
174. Ibid.
175. Ibid.
176. Ibid., 97–98.
177. Ibid., 101.
178. Ibid.
179. Ibid.
180. Ibid.
181. Ogg, *Europe in the Seventeenth Century*, 215.
182. Conscious of his own mortality and the need to shore up his legacy, "Louis XIV devoted a considerable amount of time to preparing his memoirs, based on the early years of his personal reign" with the object of educating his successors in how to govern. The "*Mémoires* is first and foremost a set of instructions which, in the case of the king's premature death, would arrive to the Dauphin as a message from the other side of the grave." Hall Bjornstad, "The Marginalization of the *Mémoires* of Louis XIV", *The European Legacy*, Vol. 17, No. 6, 2012, 780, 786.
183. Ogg, *Europe in the Seventeenth Century*, 219.
184. Carsten, ed., *The New Cambridge Modern History*, vol 5, *The Ascendancy of France 1648–88*, 238.

185. T. C. W. Blanning, *The Culture of Power and the Power of Culture: Old Regime Europe 1660–1789* (Oxford: Oxford University Press, 2002), 33. A *livre* was a French currency unit comparable to an English pound.
186. Tocqueville, *The Old Regime and the Revolution*, 120.
187. Carsten, ed., *The New Cambridge Modern History*, vol 5, *The Ascendancy of France 1648–88*, 232.
188. Ibid.
189. Ibid., 233.
190. The desertion rate in the French army was about two percent in the 1780s. In contrast, about 18% of the British army deployed in Ireland deserted every year. Geoffery Best, *War and Society in Revolutionary Europe, 1770–1870* (Suffolk: Fontana Paperbacks, 1982), 33.
191. Ogg, *Europe in the Seventeenth Century*, 235.
192. Ibid.
193. The French system for maritime service could mobilize 12,000 sailors at once, 40,000 in one month, and 70,000 in two months, from coastal communities. This system, managed by the royal bureaucracy, was "efficient, humane and equitable" by the standards of the day and "not notably unpopular." The British system for recruiting sailors was "impressment" of criminals, debtors, and abductees. This naturally led to a high desertion rate in the British navy. Between 1774 and 1780, 42,000 out of 176,000 British navy recruits deserted. Best, *War and Society in Revolutionary Europe, 1770–1870*, 40–41.
194. Ogg, *Europe in the Seventeenth Century*, 235–36.
195. Tocqueville, *The Old Regime and the Revolution*, 188.
196. Best, *War and Society in Revolutionary Europe, 1770–1870*, 16.
197. Ian Davidson, *Voltaire in Exile: The Last Years, 1753–78* (London: Atlantic Books, 2004), 149. There were two levels of torture, ordinary and extraordinary, that could be applied with or without a doctor present. Ibid.
198. Keeper of the Seals
199. J. G. Lindsay, *New Cambridge Modern History*, vol VII, *The Old Regime 1713–63* (Cambridge: University Press, 1970), 218.
200. Antoine Lavoisier, the father of modern Chemistry, for instance, was a tax farmer. He used the money to finance his scientific experiments.
201. Tocqueville, *The Old Regime and the Revolution*, 168.
202. Ibid.
203. Ibid., 159.
204. Ibid., 166.
205. Ogg, *Europe in the Seventeenth Century*, 23.
206. Reddaway, *A History of Europe from 1610 to 1715*, 452.
207. Ogg, *Europe in the Seventeenth Century*, 287.
208. Ibid., 288.
209. Ibid., 291–93.
210. Best, *War and Society in Revolutionary Europe, 1770–1870*, 26.
211. Carsten, ed., *The New Cambridge Modern History*, vol 5, *The Ascendancy of France 1648–88*, 239–40. Many of the governors were kept at the capital so that the king could keep a close eye on them.
212. Tocqueville, *The Old Regime and the Revolution*, 231.
213. The roads were built to facilitate official communications and so linked the center with the provinces rather than the provinces to each other. The compulsory labor formerly owed to feudal lords by the peasants was now also demanded by the central government.
214. Tocqueville, *The Old Regime and the Revolution*, 231.
215. Ogg, *Europe in the Seventeenth Century*, 308.

216. Ibid., 307.
217. Ibid.
218. Carsten, ed., *The New Cambridge Modern History*, vol 5, *The Ascendancy of France 1648–88*, 227.
219. Moore, *Social Origins of Dictatorship and Democracy*, 57.
220. Tocqueville, *The Old Regime and the Revolution*, 184–85.
221. Pierre Birnbaum, *The Idea of France* trans. M. B. DeBevoise (New York: Hill and Wang, 2001), 11.
222. Ogg, *Europe in the Seventeenth Century*, 305.
223. Lindsay, *New Cambridge Modern History*, vol VII, *The Old Regime 1713–63*, 220.
224. Ogg, *Europe in the Seventeenth Century*, 283.
225. Ibid., 283–84.
226. During the Old Regime "the only effective feature of enlightened despotism in France was its often remarkable administrative staff" that created a layer of uniformity and direction when properly led over a society divided by "aristocratic bodies, parlements, clerical assemblies, and provincial estates." After Louis XIV, the administrative organs were not improved while the quality of leadership withered. The result was that in 1789, Louis XVI "ruled through virtually the same ministries and councils that Louis XIV had used." Georges Lefebvre, *The French Revolution*, Vol. 1, *From its Origins to 1793*, trans. Elizabeth Moss Evanson (New York: Columbia University Press, 1962), 89.
227. Lindsay, *New Cambridge Modern History*, vol VII, *The Old Regime 1713–63*, 226. Louis XIV also had mistresses and enjoyed lavish entertainment. The difference was that Louis XIV did not allow his favorites and family members to interfere in government affairs and spent most of his day working at his desk or inspecting his realm.
228. Ibid., 226–27.
229. Claude Manceron, *Twilight of the Old Order*, trans. Patricia Wolf (New York: Alfred A. Knopf, 1977), 229.
230. Ibid.
231. Ibid., 57.
232. Ibid., 117.
233. Ibid.
234. Munro Price, *The Fall of the French Monarchy: Louis XVI, Marie Antoinette, and the baron de Breuteuil* (London: Pan Macmillan, 2002), 33.
235. Manceron, *Twilight of the Old Order*, 231.
236. In March 1788, the total expenditure of the Old Regime was 629 million *livres*, total income was 503 million *livres*, annual deficit was 126 million *livres*, and debt servicing accounted for 318 million *livres* per year. The only way to avoid fiscal collapse was to equalize taxation and cut wasteful expenditure. Lefebvre, *The French Revolution*, Vol. 1, *From its Origins to 1793*, 97.
237. The eventual violence of that overthrow would turn opinion against the Revolution in France as it became more democratic. "Of this, I am certain, that in a democracy, the majority of citizens is capable of exercising the most cruel oppressions upon the minority, whenever strong divisions prevail in that kind of polity, as they often must; and that oppression of the minority will extend to far greater numbers, and will be carried on with much greater fury, than can almost ever be apprehended from the dominion of a single sceptre." Edmund Burke, *Reflections on the Revolutions in France*, ed. J. C. D. Clark (Stanford: Stanford University Press, 2001), 292.
238. The Revolution itself occurred on account of the limited nature of royal power as the price of absolutism in France was the continued perpetuation of

social and economic privileges for an aristocratic elite that had lost its utility in terms of the actual exercise of power. Albert Soboul, *Understanding the French Revolution* (London: The Merlin Press, 1988), 4.

239. "Hence, in order that the social pact shall not be an empty formula, it is tacitly implied in that commitment—which alone can give force to all others—that whosoever refuses to obey the general will shall be constrained to do so by the whole body, which means nothing other than that he shall be forced to be free." Rousseau, *The Social Contract*, 64.

240. Vincent Cronin, *Napoleon* (London: HarperCollins, 1994), 195.

241. Ibid.

242. Ibid., 196.

243. Ibid., 201.

244. Ibid., 200–1.

245. Ibid., 200.

246. Ibid., 200–1.

247. To further this end, Napoleon strengthened the *Ecole Polytechnique*, originally established in 1794 at Paris with the objective of providing "a general scientific education for future mining engineers, geographers, civil architects, and eventually teachers of mathematics and science." Napoleon became cognizant of the quality of the school as his Egyptian expedition (1798–99) included forty of its students. The pressure of war meant that many of the graduates were sent to the military even though they "had always preferred the civilian services" amongst which "the Bridges and Roads service was the most popular." Margaret Bradley, "Scientific Education versus military training: The Influence of Napoleon Bonaparte on the *Ecole Polytechnique*", *Annals of Sciences*, Vol. 32, No. 5, 1975, 415, 417, 424.

248. Cronin, *Napoleon*, 194.

249. "La Chaise remarked, with a touch of adulation, 'God made Bonaparte, and then rested.' To which the émigré Comte de Narbonne retorted: ' God should have rested a little sooner.'" Ibid.

250. Napoleon's "self-given task" was to reorganize the French people through "the reconstruction of corporate bodies and hierarchies that mediated the relationship between state and citizen. In Napoleon's own words, the state must be founded upon 'blocks of granite', not ... grains of sand." This entailed establishing a Legion of Honor in 1802, an Imperial Nobility in 1808, encouraging Freemasonry, and setting up "professional bodies for lawyers and engineers" that were legitimated "on the basis of their utility to the state and not, as under the old regime, in terms of autonomous historical rights." Michael Rowe, "Debate: Napoleon and the post-Revolutionary Management of Sovereignty", *Modern & Contemporary France*, Vol. 8, No. 4, 2000, 511.

251. Between 1800 and 1815, some 750,000 French soldiers died in Napoleon's campaigns. Best, *War and Society in Revolutionary Europe, 1770–1870*, 114.

252. J. F. Bernard, *Talleyrand: A Biography* (London: Collins, 1973), 301.

253. Ibid.

254. For a critical insight into Napoleonic mistakes and Russian resilience, see J. David Markham, "Napoleon in Russia: Questionable Judgment and Critical Errors", *The RUSI Journal*, Vol. 148, No. 6, 2003, 62–69. The central error was the delay at Moscow followed by withdrawal.

255. For a detailed account of Napoleon's downfall see Robert Asprey, *The Rise and Fall of Napoleon Bonaparte* Vol. II, *The Fall* (London: Abacus, 2002).

256. Bernard, *Talleyrand* 313.

257. Isser Woloch, "Introduction: The Ambiguities of Revolution in the Nineteenth Century," in Isser Woloch, ed., *Revolution and the Meanings of Freedom in the Nineteenth Century* (Stanford: Stanford University Press, 1996), 10.
258. Bernard, *Talleyrand: A Biography*, 428.
259. Ibid.
260. The Charter established a constitutional monarchy with considerable power vested in the royal office. It also recognized civil liberties and basic rights. Eligibility for membership of the Chamber of Deputies or Chamber of Peers depended on payment of taxes and a minimum age of 40 years. To be eligible to vote one had to pay three hundred francs per year in taxes and be at least thirty years of age. The text of the Charter can be found at: http://www.napoleon-series.org/research/government/legislation/c_charter.html (Accessed: April 6, 2013).
261. André Jardin, *Tocqueville: A Biography*, trans. Lydia Davis and Robert Hemenway (London: Peter Halban, 1988), 21.
262. Ibid., 28.
263. Ibid., 29.
264. Ibid., 55.
265. Ibid., 88–89.
266. Ibid., 89.
267. Ibid., 351.
268. Ibid., 343.
269. The Second Empire (1851–1870) used police repression to consolidate power and carried out 26,000 political arrests in the 1850s. Bayly, *The Birth of the Modern World*, 146.
270. R. S. Alexander, "The Hero and Houdini: Napoleon and Nineteenth Century Bonapartism", *Modern & Contemporary France*, Vol. 8, No. 4, 2000, 463.
271. Richard Vinen, *A History in Fragments: Europe in the Twentieth Century* (London: Abacus, 2002), 62.
272. Jean LaCouture, *De Gaulle: The Ruler, 1945–1970,* trans. Alan Sheridan (London: Harvill, HarperCollins Publishers, 1991), 16.
273. Ibid., 206.
274. Ibid., 211.
275. In 1990, some 70 percent of French citizens had a positive perception of the military, its competence, and its devotion to the state. This perception rose to being shared by 81 percent of citizens in 2000. The army, of course, is the ultimate guarantor of the political order of the Fifth Republic. Pascal Vennesson, "Civil-Military Relations in France: Is there a Gap?", *Journal of Strategic Studies*, Vol. 26, No. 2, 2003, 34–35.
276. Ibid., 526.
277. Ibid., 536.
278. Ibid., 541.
279. Birnbaum, *The Idea of France*, 10.
280. S. K. Dehlavi, "Report on the Administrative Law and Courts in England, France, Germany, Switzerland, Italy, Holland, Belgium, Sweden and Spain", (Rome-Islamabad: Ministry of Foreign Affairs, Government of Pakistan, 1961), 29.
281. Ibid., 30.
282. Ibid.
283. Ibid., 34. Thus, in 1961, when de Gaulle removed one member of the Council of State, it had been a century since the executive had exercised its legal prerogative.
284. Ibid., 36.

285. Ibid.
286. Birnbaum, *The Idea of France*, 191.
287. Ibid., 165.
288. Ibid., 175.
289. The Archbishops of Mainz, Cologne, and Trier, the Margraves of Saxony and Brandenburg, the Elector Palatine of the Rhine, and the King of Bohemia where the seven electors.
290. Bavaria, Swabia, Franconia, the Upper Rhine, Westphalia, Lower Saxony, the Lower Rhine, Upper Saxony, Burgundy, Austria, plus Bohemia and Hungary.
291. The exhaustion of Spain as a result of this process combined with growing religious fanaticism to effectively cut it off from the Scientific Revolution and the Enlightenment. Taxes levied by the Spanish crown were punitive and ruined commerce as the primary interest of the monarch was to acquire gold and silver bullion with which to pay for warfare. This wealth also enabled the ruler to dispense with the feudal assemblies that had previously raised taxes and advised the government. Since wealth was being extracted from the colonies in the form of gold and silver, the ruler became irresponsible. The Church and its Holy Office (the Inquisition) supported the monarchy and by 1538 there were nineteen local branches in addition to the central office operating in Spain. The accused were denied legal rights and put to torture to extract confessions.
292. Perhaps as much as one-third of Germany's population died during the Thirty Years War.
293. Fukuyama, *The Origins of Political Order*, 329.
294. Lindsay, *New Cambridge Modern History*, vol VII, *The Old Regime 1713–63*, 156.
295. Ibid.
296. Ibid.
297. Ibid., 159.
298. Istvan Deak, "Lawful Revolutions and the Many Meanings of Freedom in the Habsburg Monarchy", in Isser Woloch ed., *Revolution and the Meanings of Freedom in the Nineteenth Century*, 288.
299. Ibid.
300. Blanning, *The Culture of Power and the Power of Culture in Old Regime Europe*, 54.
301. Ibid.
302. Paul Kennedy, *The Rise and Fall of the Great Powers: Economic Change and Military Conflict 1500–2000* (London: Fontana Press, 1989), 280. Thus the Habsburg Empire was as much a bureaucratic society as it was a bureaucratic state.
303. Alan Palmer, *Metternich: Councillor of Europe* (London: Phoenix, 1997), 122.
304. Ibid., 225. Known as the Metternich System constituted by the Carlsbad Decrees of 1819.
305. Ibid., 182.
306. Ibid.
307. Ibid., 233.
308. Lindsay, *New Cambridge Modern History*, vol VII, *The Old Regime 1713–63*, 293.
309. Ibid.
310. Ibid., 296.
311. Ibid.
312. Ibid., 298.

313. Ibid.
314. Edgar Feuchtwanger, *Bismarck* (New York: Routledge, 2003), 14.
315. Ogg, *Europe in the Seventeenth Century*, 441–44.
316. Max Weber's understanding of the ideal type of administration would depend heavily on Europe's experience in which bureaucracy was associated with modernization and industrialization. However, this did not mean that in actual terms the state became more rationalistic or legalistic in its attitude. For more see Cristiana Senigaglia, "Max Weber and the Parliamentary Bureaucracy of his time", *Parliaments, Estates and Representation*, Vol. 31, No. 1, 2011, 54. Thus the ten characteristics of the ideal type of modern bureaucracy (obedience to official functions, a fixed hierarchy, a fixed set of competencies, contractual nature of employment, job-specific knowledge verified through examinations, regular pay and pensions, administrative work as the only occupation of an official, career advancement on merit, inability to convert the office into a personal holding, and oversight/discipline) were not necessarily met anywhere, nor perhaps can be met. Ibid., 56.
317. Lindsay, *New Cambridge Modern History*, vol VII, *The Old Regime 1713–63*, 317.
318. Ibid., 312.
319. Feuchtwanger, *Bismarck*, 19.
320. Ibid., 57.
321. Ibid., 70.
322. Patricia Kollander, "Constitutionalism or Staatssreich? Bismarck, Crown Prince Frederick William, Crown Princess Victoria and the Succession Crisis of 1880–85", *European Review of History*, Vol. 8, No. 2, 2001, 187.
323. Ibid., 187–88.
324. Many "Europeans admired the English ruling class. Freedom of speech, of the press, and of association, which the British enjoyed, were political ideals to which the cultured classes of the continent aspired." Spencer M. Di Scala and Salvo Mastellone, *European Political Thought, 1815–1989* (Boulder, Colorado: Westview Press, 1998), 18. Aspiration, of course, did not mean that Continental European elites were necessarily keen on practicing the values they admired.
325. Kollander, "Constitutionalism or Staatssreich? Bismarck, Crown Prince Frederick William, Crown Princess Victoria and the Succession Crisis of 1880–85", 192.
326. Michael Strumer, *The German Empire* (London: Weidenfeld and Nicolson, 2000), 29.
327. Feuchtwanger, *Bismarck*, 188.
328. Ibid., 191, 207.
329. Ibid., 243.
330. Moore, *Social Origins of Dictatorship and Democracy*, 35.
331. Strumer, *The German Empire*, 23.
332. Ibid., 37.
333. Eric von Manstein's memoirs, aptly titled *Lost Victories*, capture the contradictions faced by the German leadership and military. Stronger than any of its neighbors, Germany's location meant that it faced the dilemma of a central power and wisdom dictated a policy of restraint and peaceful development. Domestic material success, nationalism, and the evident weakness of neighbors created the illusion of opportunity for expansion. The result was tactical brilliance and strategic disaster. Eric von Manstein, *Lost Victories: The War Memoirs of Hitler's most Brilliant General*, trans. Anthony G. Powell, (Minneapolis: Zenith Press, 2004).
334. Strumer, *The German Empire*, 69.

335. Lindsay, *New Cambridge Modern History*, vol VII, *The Old Regime 1713–63*, 312.

336. For a solid history of the German century that begins with the movement for national unification in the mid-1800s and ends with catastrophe in 1945, see Gordon A. Craig, *Germany, 1866–1945* (Oxford: Oxford University Press, 1978).

337. The internal security aspect of this regime, reference the Gestapo and Gestapo tactics, has earned notoriety and captured the public imagination. However, relatively little work has been done on German intelligence history. For more see Wolfgang Krieger, "German Intelligence History: A Field in Search of Scholars", *Intelligence and National Security*, Vol. 19, No. 2, 2004, 185–98.

338. Wilhelm Reich, *The Mass Psychology of Fascism* (Lahore: Gautum Publishers, 1995).

339. Michael Burleigh, *The Third Reich: A New History* (London: Macmillan, 2000), 348.

340. Ibid., 392.

341. Most Western "Theories of modernization are not scientific hypotheses but theodices—narratives of providence and redemption—presented in the jargon of social science. John Gray, *Black Mass: Apocalyptic Religion and the Death of Utopia* (New York: Farrar, Straus and Giroux, 2007), 75.

342. Michael Burleigh, *Earthly Powers: Religion and Politics in Europe from the Enlightenment to the Great War* (London: HarperCollins Publishers, 2005), 8.

343. In Germany, "The bulk of secondary students were almost certainly on the right, though—as in my own school—not necessarily on the National Socialist right. Among the university students support for Hitler was notoriously strong." Eric Hobsbawm, *Interesting Times: A Twentieth Century Life* (London: Allen Lane, the Penguin Press, 2002), 70.

344. The Soviet state sought to restore the equality of conditions in an advanced industrialized setting but created a state so powerful that it perpetuated new inequalities. The idealization of primitive equality which operated "at an equal distance from the stupidity of brutes and the fatal enlightenment of civilized life" has deep roots though it wasn't until modern times that European states possessed the organizational capacity to tax and redistribute on the scale needed to restore this conditions. Jean-Jacques Rousseau, *A Discourse on Inequality*, trans Maurice Cranston (London: Penguin Classics, 1984), 115.

345. German strategic planners would have done well to heed Clausewitz's advice that uncertainty in the aftermath of the unleashing of armed force made outcomes difficult to predict. Being over-confident was thus the surest path to defeat as was ignoring the real strengths of the adversary. Carl von Clausewitze, *On War*, ed. and trans. Michael Howard and Peter Paret (Princeton: Princeton University Press, 1989, 86.

346. In East Germany, the Stasi (Ministry for State Security), successor to the Gestapo kept exhaustive files on the population. The Stasi "left about 180 kilometers of files" after the collapse of East Germany in 1990. Krieger, "German Intelligence History", 187.

347. Tony Judt, *Postwar: A History of Europe since 1945* (London: William Heineman, 2005), 318.

348. On account of the Party's domination of the economy and the tying of privileges to the administrative positions that made life bearable for state functionaries.

349. Judt, *Postwar: A History of Europe since 1945*, 361.

350. Ibid., 362.

351. Ibid., 367.

352. Ibid., 368.
353. Ibid.
354. Vinen, *A History in Fragments,*, 357.
355. Ibid., 446.
356. Judt, *Postwar: A History of Europe since 1945, 558.*
357. That is to say, the average for *all* twenty-seven member-states of the European Union. Actual rates of taxation are much higher in some countries while punitive levels of taxation (more than half of one's income) kick in at relatively low levels. For more, see James Rogers and Cécile Philippe, *The Tax Burden of Typical Workers in the EU 27* (Paris-Brussels: Institute Économique Molinari, 2011).
358. Democracy and prosperity in Europe emerged from intensive state penetration of all sectors and development of limited local resources. This was necessary as in Europe without massive state intervention a moderate and liberally inclined middleclass could not emerge. This was very different from "American circumstances" that were "conducive to liberty", which included "plentiful opportunities for moderate wealth, which gives men a concrete interest in liberty; the open frontier, which provides a safety valve against conflict; and the lack of foreign enemies, which reduces the need for a strong state" and a standing army deployed at home. David Meskill, "Self-Interest Properly Felt: Democracy's Unintended Consequences and Tocqueville's Solution", *Critical Review: A Journal of Politics and Society*, Vol. 19, No. 1, 2007, 119.
359. Rogers and Cécile Philippe, *The Tax Burden of Typical Workers in the EU 27,* 7. Rates of 45–50 percent are relatively light in the European Union.
360. Judt, *Postwar: A History of Europe since 1945, 325.*
361. James J. Sheehan, *Where have all the Soldiers Gone? The Transformation of Modern Europe* (New York: Houghton Mifflin Company, 2008), 162.
362. For more on the building up of supporting networks, see Carl J. Friedrich, *Europe: An Emergent Nation?* (New York: Harper and Row, 1969).
363. Vinen, *A History in Fragments,* 331–32.
364. Ibid., 330, 392.
365. Dimitri A. Sotiropoulis, "Southern European Public Bureaucracies in Comparative Perspective", *West European Politics*, Vol. 27, No. 3, 2004, 411.
366. Ibid.
367. For more on the effect of institutional design on corruption and maladministration see Ellen V. Rubin and Andrew Whitford, "Effects of the Institutional Design of the Civil Service: Evidence from Corruption", *International Public Management Journal*, Vol. 11, No. 4, 2008, 404–25. There is evidently a direct correlation between security of tenure and corruption so that as insecurity of tenure and politicization increase, bureaucratic corruption grows and competence declines.
368. Sotiropoulis, "Southern European Public Bureaucracies in Comparative Perspective," 410.
369. "A glance at the occupational statistics of any country of mixed religious composition brings to light with remarkable frequency . . . the fact that business leaders and owners of capital, as well as the highest grades of skilled labor, and even more the higher technically and commercially trained personnel of modern enterprises, are overwhelmingly Protestant." Max Weber, *The Protestant Ethic and the Spirit of Capitalism*, trans., Talcott Parsons (London: Butler and Tanner Ltd., 1950), 35. The divergence between the profit-seeking capitalist north and rent-seeking indolent south was due, according to Weber, to the abolition of transactional morality by the Protestant Reformation. This meant, that hard work and honesty, if rewarded by material success in this life, represented a sign from God that

the recipient of the reward was one of the elect, pre-destined to be saved on Judgement Day.

370. Sotiropoulis, "Southern European Public Bureaucracies in Comparative Perspective," 409.
371. Ibid.
372. Ibid., 409–10.
373. Ibid., 410.
374. Ibid.
375. Ibid., 413–14.
376. Including Spain, Portugal, Greece and Ireland.
377. The evolution of the Swedish state is in this respect instructive. With a relatively small nobility and a free peasantry, the Swedish monarchy became absolute in the mid-1600s and highly militarized with an army of 100,000 out of a population of perhaps 1.5 million in the early 1700s. The Swedish bureaucracy was organized into colleges or ministries at the central level that coordinated with local governments. While inefficient by later standards, it was at the time highly regarded and even imitated by the Russians.
378. For more on the Euro-zone crisis see: http://www.guardian.co.uk/business/debt-crisis (Accessed: April 5, 2013).
379. http://www.telegraph.co.uk/news/worldnews/europe/france/9839529/Most-French-people-agree-their-country-is-totally-bankrupt.html (Accessed: April 7, 2013). The French are trying to cut spending while further increasing taxes over the next five years. The spending cuts are likely to slow down the economy, which depends heavily on state expenditure. The tax increases will add to already high rates of taxation.
380. Siedentop, *Democracy in Europe*, 230.

NOTES TO CHAPTER 5

1. Or *yildrim*, which means lightening that shoots across the sky.
2. Damascus itself is one of the oldest cities in the world, dating to at least the mid-1400s BC.
3. One of the most striking features of Timur's decision-making is its coldness even when it entailed extinguishing tens of thousands of lives. In 1398–99, his armies approached Delhi and skirmishes ensued between the forces of the Sultanate of Delhi and the Timurids. The captives in Timur's camp, some 100,000 in number, made the mistake of cheering for the Delhi side. Amir Jahan Shah, Suleiman Shah, and other senior commanders noted before Timur that if they were to attack the city, the 100,000 "infidel prisoners might attempt to rebel and thus compromise the safety of their camp. They advised Timur to put them all to death. Timur agreed and issued the order to massacre all the prisoners: "When I heard these words I found them in accordance with the rules of war, and I directly gave my command for the *tawachi*s to proclaim throughout the camp that every man who had infidel prisoners was to put them to death, and whosoever neglected to do so should himself be executed, and his property given to the informer . . . Maulana Nasir-ud-Din Umar, a counselor and man of learning, who in all his life had never killed a sparrow, now slew with his sword in execution of my order, fifteen idolatrous Hindus, who were his captives." The slaughter continued all night and by the following day all 100,000 captives were dead. Timur, *Tuzuk-i-Timuri*, trans. H. M. Elliot and John Dawson, 53–54.
4. Walter S. Fischel, *Ibn Khaldun in Egypt*, 46.
5. Ibid., 48.

6. Ibid., 51.
7. Ibid., 53.
8. Ibid., 57.
9. Pure gray mules were specially provided to religious judges in Egypt.
10. Fischel, *Ibn Khaldun in Egypt*, 60.
11. Ibid., 104–5.
12. In 1528, some 87 percent of the arable land in the empire belonged to the sultan or was in the possession of his servants in exchange for the maintenance of provincial cavalry. Fukuyama, *The Origins of Political Order*, 218.
13. See M. Naeem Qureshi, *Pan-Islam in British India* (Karachi: Oxford University Press, 2009). In the aftermath of the First World War, the Indian Muslims launched a mass movement to help the Turkish nationalists and convince the British not to dismantle the Ottoman Sultanate. As it turned out, once the nationalists were victorious, they threw the Ottomans out anyway.
14. The Abbasid state was the temporal "manifestation of the might of Islam". The Abbasid Caliph exercised "monetary and other forms of royal patronage" over religious life so that the caliph's "interests coalesced with those of the scholars". This ensured compliance with the caliph's wishes and religious legitimacy for his arbitrary power. During wars of successions choosing which contender to back could be tricky, though normally the clerical supporters of the losing prince switched allegiance to the victor. For instance, "Many a preacher active in propaganda *against* al-Ma'mun during the civil war simply changed sides . . . after al-Ma'mun turned out to be victorious." Muhammad Qasim Zaman, *Religion and Politics under the Early Abbasids* (Leiden: Brill, 1997), 189–93.
15. The letter of Harun al-Rashid to the Byzantine Emperor Constantine VI (r. 780–797) enjoining him to convert to Islam pointed out the many benefits of such a conversion—among other things, the Abbasid Caliphate was the most successful state in the world and Islam was its religion, while, as a Muslim ruler of non-Muslim subjects, Constantine could increase his revenues through the poll tax on non-Muslims. Ibid., 188.
16. Peter B. Golden, "Khazar Turkic Ghulams in Caliphal Service", in C. E. Bosworth, ed., *The Formation of the Classical Islamic World*, Vol. 9, *The Turks in the Early Islamic World* (Hants: Ashgate Publishing, 2007), 137.
17. Ibid., 138.
18. Ibid., 151, 156.
19. Ibid., 158.
20. C. E. Bosworth, "The Turks in the Islamic Lands up to the mid-11th century", in Ibid., 201.
21. Ibid., 202.
22. The period of political disarray and fragmentation did not lead to cultural regression or the decline of education. Many of the outstanding scholars of the Muslim world lived during the period of Abbasid decline and were patronized by Turkish potentates who sought to imitate the caliph's patronage of scholars. Ibn Fadlan, Ibn Sina, al-Khwarizmi, al-Mawardi, al-Razi, Juzjani, Firdausi, and al-Beruni, were some of the luminaries of this period. In the 900s, some seventy well-known translators were employed at the House of Wisdom in Baghdad and paid five hundred gold dinars per month for their work. The Fatimids in Egypt sought to match the Abbasids and maintained a royal library with some two million volumes, 18,000 of which were on the Greeks alone. Cordoba, the seat of the Umayyad Emirate, had, at the same time, some seventy libraries. For more see, Amira K. Bennison, *The Great Caliphs: The Golden Age of the Abbasid Empire* (London: I. B. Tauris, 2011), and Stewart Gordon, *When Asia was the World* (Philadelphia: DACAPO Press, 2008).

23. From Indian pan-Islamists in the early 1900s to the Salafi revival in the contemporary era, the idea of a united Muslim world under strong central leadership continues to enjoy appeal. Such a state, owing to geography, demography, and entrenched sectarian differences, can, thinking in conventional terms, only come about if a core Muslim state takes up the challenge of creating a new Islamic Caliphate. Al-Qaeda and its offshoots are in several respects post-modern attempts at reviving a united Islamic world by provoking Western retaliation against Muslim countries through acts of terrorism against the West or its vital interests. This retaliation, animated by a combination of fear, greed and hubris, helps spread instability and chaos in the Muslim world that cohesive and highly motivated non-state actors, representing a contemporary variant of *asabiya* can exploit to their own advantage. For a solid account of this, and related phenomena, see, Abdel Beri Atwan, *The Secret History of al Qaeda* (Los Angeles: University of California Press, 2006).
24. For two very different but substantial histories of the Seljuk polities see John Freely, *Storm on Horseback: The Seljuk Warriors of Turkey* (London: I. B. Tauris, 2008) and Safi, *Religion and Politics in Saljuq Iran*.
25. P. H. Newby, *Saladin in his Time* (London: Phoenix Press, 2001), 60–61, 79.
26. Ibid., 97.
27. "War and unbearable Mongol taxation caused peasants to flee the land in desperation and the once fertile land which had fed Baghdad became a wasteland." Bennison, *The Great Caliphs*, 204. Iraq's population, as late as 1960, was about 6.7 million, probably about the same as it had been in 1000. The increase in population since then (presently 33 million) was made possible by oil wealth and massive investments in infrastructure by the Ba'thist regime. For more on the Ba'thist party and its brutal politics see Charles Trip, *A History of Iraq* (Cambridge: Cambridge University Press, 2001). For an excellent overview of the history of the regions presently comprising Iraq, see William R. Polk, *Understanding Iraq: A Whistle-stop Tour from Ancient Babylon to Occupied Baghdad* (London: I. B. Tauris, 2005).
28. Inalcik, *The Ottoman Empire,* 13.
29. Ibid.
30. Ibid., 65.
31. Ibid., 73.
32. David Goffman, *The Ottoman Empire and Early Modern Europe: New Approaches to European History* (Cambridge: Cambridge University Press, 2002), 49.
33. Under the Abbasids, the Turkish slave-soldiers were manumitted and converted to Islam but "they continued to be known as *mamluks*," unlike other freedmen. In theory, "cultural disassociation and personal dependence" supposedly "obliterated the soldier's public personality" and led to the "extinction of the soldier's autonomy." This made the *mamluks* "a superb instrument" of their "master's will when it was coupled with personal obedience", but the loss of this obedience due to weakness on part of the master was all the more disastrous for there were no intermediary loyalties in a "servile army", quite unlike the "feudal" militaries of medieval Europe. In effect, "*mamluk* armies are essentially body guards writ large" and so "they have all the virtues of elite troops at their best, but all the vices of private servants and foreign mercenaries at their worst." Patricia Crone, *Slaves on Horses: The Evolution of the Islamic Polity* (Cambridge: Cambridge University Press, 1980), 78–79, 84.
34. The Ottomans, like the Abbasids, faced an apparently impossible contradiction that was reconciled only by the arbitrary power of the ruler: "The *sharia* caught the Abbasids in an insoluble dilemma. To the extent that it was

the core of Islam, an Islamic empire must of necessity represent the norms embodied in it; yet were the Abbasids to abide by its norms, an Islamic empire could not be created." Ibid., 63.

35. Caroline Finkel, *Osman's Dream: The Story of the Ottoman Empire, 1300–1923* (London: John Murray, 2006), 73.
36. Inalcik, *The Ottoman Empire*, 103.
37. Finkel, *Osman's Dream*, 45.
38. Roger Crowley, *1453: The Holy War for Constantinople and the Clash of Islam and the West* (New York: Hyperion, 2005), 6.
39. Beyazid II had, quite possibly, facilitated his father's demise, at the age of forty-nine, by having him poisoned. The alternative, open rebellion against a formidable military commander like Mehmed "The Conqueror", would have amounted to suicide.
40. The contrast between development outcomes in East Asia, where countries like South Korea, Vietnam, Japan, and China, devastated by military conflicts and often lacking in natural resources vital to industrialization have modernized, and other parts of the world, better endowed with natural resources, is due in part to the tradition of high quality authoritarian rule. Thus, in 1954, Nigeria and South Korea had about the same per capita income. Between 1960 and 2010, Nigeria earned some US $300 billion of oil revenue, even though, between 1975 and 1995, its per capita income actually fell. South Korea, on the other hand, emerged as the world's twelfth largest economy by 1997. Fukuyama, *The Origins of Political Order*, 470.
41. Inalcik, *The Ottoman Empire*, 154.
42. Traditionally, a city that had to be taken by storm was sacked for three days, but in this case, Mehmed called it off after one day. His soldiers fell in line rapidly once the order was given to halt the pillaging.
43. Crowley, *1453*, 233.
44. The contest between the Ottoman janissaries and the Egyptian *mamluk*s is often one whose outcome in favor of the former is attributed to firearms. The Egyptian *mamluk*s were slower to adopt firearms and cannons as primary weapons than the Ottomans, though it is not clear whether the weapons themselves were vital to the result of the 1516 and 1517 military campaigns. The Ottoman's steadfastness and discipline seemed to be more important, especially considering that they were attacking and the *mamluk*s were defending. Robert Irwin, "Gunpowder and Firearms in the Mamluk Sultanate", in Michael Winter and Amalia Levanoni, eds., *The Mamluks in Egyptian and Syrian Politics and Society* (Leiden: Brill, 2004), 136–37.
45. Kaplan goes so far as to argue that in the future the world might become a more interconnected version of the *millet* system in which diverse communities live among each other without necessarily sharing the same civil and religious institutions and beliefs. Kaplan, *The Revenge of Geography*, 345.
46. Between 1516 and 1918 Syria comprised several provinces under different governors and the effectiveness of the state depended a great deal on the officials dispatched by Istanbul. In the 1830s, the Egyptian army, led by Ibrahim Pasha, occupied Syria and tried to establish a strong government there. In the 1850s and 1860s, the Ottomans reasserted their authority and introduced local government reforms. After the First World War, the Syrian provinces were amalgamated into a Syrian Mandate (1920–1946) under French control. The Syrian Ba'ath Party, founded in 1940, emerged as the most cohesive force after the French withdrawal, which saw instability until Hafiz al-Assad's coup in 1970. Assad was supported by the *jamaa* (company) drawn primarily from the Alawite Shia minority. Assad built Syria into a military state with a tightly controlled economy. For more see, Moshe Maoz

and Avner Yaniv, *Syria Under Assad: Domestic Constraints and Regional Risks* (Kent: Croom Helm Ltd., 1987). Prior to the Syrian Civil War (2011-Present), Syria maintained armed forces with an active strength of 300,000, and an armored corps equipped with some 5000 main battle tanks. Anthony H. Cordesman, *The Israeli and Syrian Conventional Military Balance: An Overview* (Washington D.C.: Center for Strategic and International Studies, 2008), 12, 14.

47. Albert Hourani, *A History of the Arab Peoples* (London: Faber and Faber, 2002), 226.
48. Afat Lutfi al-Sayyid Marsot, *Egypt in the Reign of Muhammad Ali* (Cambridge: Cambridge University Press, 1984), 5.
49. Hourani, *A History of the Arab Peoples*, 217.
50. Ibid.
51. Joseph Dorey, "Founding a new Mamlaka: Some Remarks Concerning Safed and the Organization of the Region in the Mamluk Period", in Winter and Levanoni, eds., *The Mamluks in Egyptian and Syrian Politics and Society*, 169–85.
52. The Ottoman's piracy fleet in the 1500s had 120 galleys plus a complement of sailing vessels and ranged across the Western Mediterranean. Slaving expeditions helped pay for the maintenance of the fleet and reduced pressure on Istanbul's resources. Thus, in 1534, thousands were enslaved from coastal Italy. In 1535, 1800 were carried off into slavery from Minorca. In 1544, 7000 were enslaved from Naples. In 1551 some 5000 were enslaved from Gozo. In 1554, another 6000 were taken from Calabria. In 1566, 4000 were enslaved from Granada. Roger Crowley, *Empires of the Sea: The Siege of Malta, the Battle of Lepanto, and the Contest for the Center of the World* (New York: Random House, 2009), 71.
53. Kenan Inan, "The Making of Kanun Law in the Ottoman Empire, 1300–1600", in Günther Lottes, Eero Medijainen, Jón Viðar Sigurðsson, eds., *Making, using and resisting the law in European history* (Pisa: Pisa University Press, 2008), 67.
54. Cited in Ibid.
55. Carl F. Petry, "The Estate of al-Khuward Fatima al-Khossbekkiyya: Royal Spouse, Autonomous Investor", in Winter and Levanoni, eds., *The Mamluks in Egyptian and Syrian Politics and Society*", 279–80.
56. Hourani, *A History of the Arab Peoples*, 220.
57. Finkel, *Osman's Dream*, 55.
58. Ibid.
59. Ibid., 148.
60. Ibid., 165.
61. Ibid., 178.
62. Ibid.
63. Ibid., 131.
64. Ibid.
65. Inalcik, *The Ottoman Empire*, 59.
66. Finkel, *Osman's Dream*, 211.
67. Noel Barber, *Lords of the Golden Horn: The Splendors of Islam and the Fall of the Mighty Ottoman Empire* (London: MacMillan, 1973), 101.
68. Koprulu Mehmed, grand vizier, 1656–1661. Fazil Ahmad, son of Koprulu Mehmed, grand vizier, 1661–1676. Merzifonlu Kara Mustafa, son-in-law of Fazil Ahmad, grand vizier, 1676–1683. Siyarus, son-in-law of Fazil Ahmad, grand vizier, 1687. Fazil Mustafa, younger son of Koprulu Mehmed, grand vizier, 1689–1691. Amcazade Huseyn Pasha, nephew of Korprulu Mehmed on his brother's side, grand vizier, 1697–1702.

69. Andrew Wheatcroft, *The Ottomans* (New York: Viking, 1993), 76.
70. Qureshi, *Pan-Islam in British India*, 4. The requirement of Quraysh descent was waived by the ulema to help validate the Ottoman assumption of the caliphate.
71. For more on the Gallipoli campaign that made Mustafa Kemal's reputation as the *ghazi* pasha, see Robert Rhodes James, *Gallipoli* (London: Pan Books, 1965). Written fifty years after the Allied failure, *Gallipoli* provides a comprehensive account of the campaign and explains how the Turks, operating from a position of strategic inferiority on almost every account (technology, wealth, control of the seas, firepower) were able to exploit the weaknesses of an unimaginative Allied military leadership and win a historic triumph. Of course, this triumph did not change the ultimate outcome, but it demonstrated the toughness and determination of the Turkish military and established Mustafa Kemal as the hero capable of defeating Turkey's enemies.
72. Mustafa Abbasi, "The Aristocracy of the Upper Galilee: Safed Notables and the Tanzimat Reforms", in Itchuk Weismann and Fruma Zachs, eds., *Ottoman Reforms and Muslim Regeneration* (London: I. B. Tauris, 2005), 175.
73. Ibid., 169.
74. Ibid.
75. Ibid.
76. Nimrod Luz, "The Re-making of Beersharba: Winds of Modernization in the late Ottoman Sultanate", in Ibid., 187–89.
77. Hourani, *A History of the Arab Peoples*, 252.
78. Ibid., 229.
79. Ibid.
80. Ibid., 235.
81. Jane Hathaway, *Beshir Agha: Chief Eunuch of the Ottoman Imperial Harem* (Oxford: Oneworld Publishers, 2009), 43.
82. Ibid., 69.
83. Finkel, *Osman's Dream*, 391. The levies were abolished in 1775.
84. Hathaway, *Beshir Agha*, 69.
85. Ibid., 81.
86. Ibid.
87. Ibid., 76.
88. The field organization of the *mamluk* sultanate in Egypt merits attention. The *mamluk* sultanate was divided into governorates headed by centrally appointed governors that were subject to transfer and removal at the sultan's whim. The governors presided over an official hierarchy that included a variety of administrative designations. Some of the more important posts were: castle commanders, chief chamberlain, district/town garrison commanders, town/city police chiefs, district police chiefs, tax collector for royal estates, commander of the post, commander of the tribes, castle treasurers, protocol/hospitality officer, officer in charge of military lands, officer in charge of religious endowments, financial overseer (pay master), inspectors (for bridges, agriculture, irrigation, markets), chief of the secretaries, minor correspondents, major correspondents, officer in charge of ratifying official documents, superintendant of revenue assignments, financial controller, supervisor of the state treasury, chief judges (one for each of the major schools of Sunni jurisprudence), deputy judges, religious/legal counsel, prayer leaders, and preachers. *Mamluk* Egypt was thus already a bureaucratic state and the Ottoman advent meant that the existing apparatus could be taken over by the new dynasty.
89. Marsot, *Egypt in the Reign of Muhammad Ali*, 7.
90. In terms of wealth, the janissary and *mamluk* emirs of Egypt were the wealthiest section of society, their power securing for them enormous riches.

Between 1679 and 1700, fourteen beys had a combined wealth of 25.3 million *paras* (silver currency units), which makes for an average of 1.81 million *paras*. Sixty-one aghas had a combined wealth of 20.24 million *paras*, which makes for per capita assets of 331,880 *paras*. Thirty-eight *katkhudas* had a total wealth of 15.80 million *paras*, or an average of 415,737 *paras*. A total of 113 elite commanders and officers had a combined wealth of 61.375 million *paras*, which works out to about 543,143 per head. In contrast, "For the same period, the 468 estates of artisans and merchants . . . amount to an average of 138,272 *paras*—four times lower" than the average for the elite military officers. André Raymond, "The Wealth of Egyptian Emirs at the end of the Seventeenth Century", in Winter and Levanoni, eds., *The Mamluks in Egyptian and Syrian Politics and Society*, 361.

91. Marsot, *Egypt in the Reign of Muhammad Ali*, 8.
92. Ibid.
93. Ibid., 11.
94. Ibid.
95. Ibid., 15.
96. Ibid., 65.
97. Ibid., 181.
98. Ibid., 191.
99. Ibid., 192.
100. Ibid., 160.
101. Ibid., 217.
102. Wheatcroft, *The Ottomans*, 132–35.
103. The problem of economic development in the Eastern Mediterranean, with special reference to catching up to the West, may have something to do with the weakness of financial institutions, particularly banks. Here, however, the problem is that in the nineteenth and early twentieth centuries, "the Middle East did not lack banks" and was fairly open to foreign as well as local financial houses opening branches. The post-1945 leaderships in many Arab countries, however, identified foreign as well as local bankers as agents of international capitalism and neo-colonialism and sought nationalization of the banking system, effectively closing off their financial systems to foreign investment. The real problem lay with trade and the terms of trade imposed during the colonial period. Adrian E. Tschoegl, "Financial Integration, Disintegration, and Emerging Re-integration in the Eastern Mediterranean, c. 1850 to the Present", *Financial Markets, Institutions and Instruments*, Vol. 13, No. 5, 2004.
104. Dina Rizk Khoury, *State and Provincial Society in the Ottoman Empire: Mosul 1540–1834* (Cambridge: Cambridge University Press, 1997), 114–15.
105. Ibid., 6.
106. Inalcik, *The Ottoman Empire*, 103. This decline was itself the product of the intensely political economy of the Ottoman Sultanate. The center's demand for gold and silver outstripped supply and led to the debasement of the currency.
107. Khoury, *State and Provincial Society in the Ottoman Empire*, 5.
108. Wheatcroft, *The Ottomans*, 63.
109. Rai Shakil Akhter, ed., *Turkey in New World Perspective: A Cultural-Historical Analysis* (Lahore: Sang-e-Meel, nd), 7–15.
110. 73.60 million/1600 million.
111. US $ 790 billion/5700 billion.
112. Charles Swallow, *The Sick Man of Europe: Ottoman Empire to Turkish Republic 1789–1923* (London: Ernest Benn, 1973) 13.

113. Ibid.
114. Wheatcroft, *The Ottomans*, 89.
115. Swallow, *The Sick Man of Europe*, 13.
116. Shakil Akhter, ed., *Turkey in New World Perspective*, 15.
117. Swallow, *The Sick Man of Europe*, 14.
118. Ibid., 14.
119. Cronin, *Napoleon*, 150–51.
120. Ibid., 151.
121. Ibid., 152.
122. Ibid., 152.
123. For a critique of European historiography in relation to the Ottoman Empire see, Goffman, *The Ottoman Empire and Early Modern Europe*.
124. Swallow, *The Sick Man of Europe*, 14.
125. Wheatcroft, *The Ottomans*, 122.
126. Ibid., 122–23.
127. Ibid., 123.
128. Ibid., 124–25.
129. Ibid., 125.
130. Ibid., 126.
131. Ibid., 129.
132. Ibid., 136.
133. Shakil Akhter, ed., *Turkey in New World Perspective*, 19.
134. Swallow, *The Sick Man of Europe*, 84.
135. Ibid., 86.
136. Mohammed Rashid Feroze, *Islam in Modern Turkey* (Islamabad: Islamic Research Institute, 1968) 51–53.
137. Ibid., 52.
138. Shakil Akhter, ed., *Turkey in New World Perspective*, 24.
139. Feroze, *Islam in Modern Turkey*, 55–56.
140. Ibid., 52.
141. Patrick Kinross, *Atatürk: The Rebirth of a Nation* (London: Weidenfeld and Nicolson, 1966), 304–5.
142. Ibid., 340.
143. Shakil Akhter, ed., *Turkey in New World Perspective*, 34.
144. Swallow, *The Sick Man of Europe*, 84.
145. Ibid., 84–85.
146. Wheatcroft, *The Ottomans*, 197.
147. Swallow, *The Sick Man of Europe*, 87.
148. Shakil Akhter, ed., *Turkey in New World Perspective*, 20.
149. Barber, *Lords of the Golden Horn*, 181.
150. Swallow, *The Sick Man of Europe*, 88.
151. Ibid., 89.
152. Ibid.
153. Barber, *Lords of the Golden Horn*, 196–97.
154. Ibid., 196.
155. Shakil Akhter, ed., *Turkey in New World Perspective*, 21.
156. Kinross, *Atatürk*, 527.
157. Ibid.
158. Ibid., 216, 219.
159. Ibid., 272.
160. Ibid., 343.
161. Ibid., 344, 528.
162. Ibid., 528.
163. Shakil Akhter, ed., *Turkey in New World Perspective*, 31.

164. Ibid., 32.
165. Kinross, *Atatürk*, 384
166. In September 1833, at Münchengratz, Czar Nicholas I of Russia asked Chancellor Metternich of the Habsburg Empire, ". . . what do you think of the Turk? Is he not a sick man?" Metternich, who did not want to pursue the Eastern Question at that time, replied, "Is Your Majesty addressing the doctor or the heir." Neither the Russian Czar nor the Habsburg Chancellor could have imagined that the decrepit Ottoman Sultanate would outlast their dynastic empires. Palmer, *Metternich,* 261.
167. Kinross, *Atatürk*, 528.
168. Ibid., 397.
169. Ilter Turan, "Continuity and Change in Turkish Bureaucracy: The Kemalist Period and After", in Jacob M. Landau, ed., *Atatürk and the Modernization of Turkey* (Boulder, Colorado: Westview Press, 1984), 103.
170. Ibid., 105.
171. Ibid., 108.
172. Ibid., 107.
173. Metin Heper, "Atatürk and the Civil Bureaucracy", in Ibid., 91.
174. Ibid., 92.
175. Metin Heper, *Ismet Inonü: The Making of a Turkish Statesman* (Leiden: Brill, 1998), 168.
176. Ibid., 173.
177. Ibid., 99.
178. Erik J. Zurcher, *Turkey: A Modern History* (London: I. B. Tauris, 1998), 216.
179. Z. Y. Hershlag, *Turkey: The Challenge of Growth* (Leiden: E. J. Brill, 1968), 44.
180. Ibid., 57.
181. Ibid., 71.
182. Kinross, 529.
183. Ibid., 465.
184. Ibid., 468.
185. Ibid., 529.
186. Ibid., 473.
187. Shakil Akhter, ed., *Turkey in New World Perspective*, 36.
188. Ibid., 37.
189. Ibid.
190. Zurcher, *Turkey: A Modern History*, 227–28.
191. Ibid., 222.
192. Shakil Akhter, ed., *Turkey in New World Perspective*, 39.
193. Zurcher, *Turkey: A Modern History*, 233.
194. Ibid., 239.
195. Shakil Akhter, ed., *Turkey in New World Perspective*, 38.
196. Ibid., 40.
197. Heper, *Ismet Inonü*, 23.
198. Ibid.
199. Shakil Akhter, ed., *Turkey in New World Perspective,* 41.
200. Ibid., 42.
201. Ibid.
202. Ibid., 42–46.
203. Frank Tachau, "The Political Culture of Kemalist Turkey", in Landau, ed., *Atatürk and the Modernization of Turkey*, 72.
204. Shakil Akhter, ed., *Turkey in New World Perspective*, 46.
205. Andrew Mango, *The Turks Today*, (New York: The Overlook Press, 2004), 81.

206. Ibid.
207. Ibid.
208. Ibid.
209. Ibid., 83.
210. For more on the training and service structure of Turkey's civil bureaucracy see Muhittin Acar and Huseyn Ozgur, "Training of Civil Servants in Turkey: Progress, Problems, and Prospects", in *International Journal of Public Administration*, Vol. 27, No. 3, 2004, 197–218. Successive government have integrated improvement of training and provision of opportunities to build expertise in their central economic plans. The State Employees Act of 1965 provides "the main legal and administrative framework for managing public personnel" in Turkey, with training units attached to all state organizations covered by the Act. The State Personnel Authority (SPA), which was established in 1960, oversees the training programs. State employment is secured through open competitive exams, followed by training, and then promotions are to be determined by performance. Here, however, Turkey suffers from a disconnect "between training and pay and promotion" on account of political interference in the administration as well as bureaucratic politics. Ibid., 202–4.
211. Ibid., 188.
212. As in South Asia, "Political interference is the bane of the administration. It makes for discontinuity in policies, programs and personnel, and swells the public sector with the clients of ruling politicians." Ibid., 187. Again, local democracy means pilferage of state resources with 23.5% of electricity being stolen, and nearly one-third of investments used as bribes. Ibid., 143.
213. Shakil Akhter, ed., *Turkey in New World Perspective*, 49.
214. Mango, *The Turks Today*, 93.
215. Shakil Akhter, ed., *Turkey in New World Perspective*, 48.
216. Mango, *The Turks Today*, 144.
217. Ibid., 142–43.
218. Ani Sarkissian and S. Ilgu Ozler, "Democratization and the Politicization of Religious Civil Society in Turkey", *Democratization* (2012).
219. Mango, *The Turks Today*, 134.
220. For a fascinating and deeply informative account of the Turkish Council of State see Esin Orucu, "*Conseil D'État*: The French Layer of Turkish Administrative Law", *International and Comparative Law Quarterly*, Vol. 49, July 2000. The Turkish Council of State is called the *Danistay* and presides over a hierarchy of regional administrative courts and taxation courts. The Turkish *Danistay* is also responsible for ensuring that the government does not pass legislation in contravention of the principles of Kemalism. Thus, in 1998, the *Danistay* annulled amendments that would have allowed children in the fifth year of schooling to attend religious instruction classes. The *Danistay* struck down the amendment as it violated the Law on Eight Years of Continuous Education which ensures "that young minds that have not yet fully grasped positive sciences and contemporary education should not be given a theocratic education before reaching full consciousness and also to fulfill the requirements of the Law on the Unity of Education." Cited in Ibid., 688.
221. Mango, *The Turks Today*, 95.
222. Mango, *The Turks Today*, 111.
223. http://www.worldbank.org/en/country/turkey (Accessed: July 14, 2013).
224. Piotr Zalewski, "The Turkish Media's Darkest Hour." *Foreign Affairs*. 14 June 2013. Web. 14 July 2013. http://www.foreignaffairs.com/articles/139505/piotr-zalewski/the-turkish-medias-darkest-hour (Accessed: July 14, 2013).
225. Ibid.

226. Swallow, *The Sick man of Europe*, 123.
227. Shakil Akhter, ed., *Turkey in New World Perspective*, 150.
228. Ibid., 118.
229. Here it might be pertinent to mention that democracy is not one of the six principles of Kemalism (secularism, revolutionism, populism, statism, republicanism, nationalism). Thus, the preservation of the state, its secular character, the republican ethos, as well as the revolution, all override democracy if the elected government attempts to subvert these principles.
230. For an interesting study of the relationship between military spending and the economy in Turkey see Jülide Yildirim and Selami Sezgin, "Military Expenditure and Employment in Turkey", *Defence and Peace Economics*, Vol. 14, No. 2, 2003, 129–39. Rapid economic growth has reduced the importance of the military in terms of its role in generating employment and income though, with universal military service still in place, Turkey remains very much an *Ordu Millet* (a nation that is an army).
231. Kinross, *Atatürk*, 227, 434.
232. According to the United Nations Development Program (UNDP) Turkey was well on the way to achieving a high level of human development. According to the 2001 *Human Development Report* Turkey's HDI Rank was 82, Life expectancy at birth was about 70 years, adult literacy rate was more than 85 percent, GDP per capita (PPP $), 6,974. For more see *The United Nations Human Development Report 2001*, http://hdr.undp.org/en/reports/global/hdr2001/ (Accessed: November 30, 2013).

NOTES TO CHAPTER 6

1. Probably starting with the Ambassador of the Holy Roman Empire to the Russian court in 1517 and continuing down the Kremlinologists of the Cold War era, Western scholars, diplomats, journalists and statesmen have struggled to understand the Russian state and group mind. Ronald Hingley, *The Russian Mind* (London: The Bodley Head, 1977), 21. The ambassador observed of the czar that he "holds unlimited control over the lives and property of all his subjects." Ibid., 163. George F. Kennan's "Long Telegram" of February 1946 is probably one of the most influential assessments of Russian intentions and capabilities and argued that Russian intransigence was rooted in the country's domestic institutions, which, unless they were discredited and overthrown, would continue to seek confrontation with the West. The full text is available on line: http://www.gwu.edu/~nsarchiv/coldwar/documents/episode-1/kennan.htm (Accessed, September 29, 2012).
2. Eric Hobsbawm sees the 1900s as essentially a struggle between those loyal to the Bolshevik "World Revolution" in Russia and those loyal to the old order. Eric Hobsbawm, *The Age of Extremes*, esp. 51–84.
3. For a fast paced and readable account of the global communist movement led by the Soviet Union see Rober Harvey, *Comrades: The Rise and Fall of World Communism* (London: John Murray, 2003), esp 181–220, which covers the softening of Soviet Communism before the complexities of trying (and failing) to manage an industrial economy.
4. The 1767 *Nakaaz* (Instruction to the legislative commission) of Catherine II pronounces Russia to be a European country—the fact that such a statements needed to be asserted publicly indicated that in reality Russia was *not* a European country. It was, and remains, a transcontinental semi-European and semi-Asian empire ruling over diverse nationalities through a combination of force and patronage. The *Nakaaz* can be accessed online at

http://novaonline.nvcc.edu/eli/evans/HIS241/Documents/Nakaz.pdf. (Accessed, September 29, 2012).

5. As Jared Diamond brilliantly demonstrates, diffusion of technology and techniques proceeds much slower along a North/South Axis than an East/West Axis. This is due to climatic changes that moving north or south occasion—much less of a problem when moving from east to west. For more see, Jared Diamond, *The Rise and Fall of the Third Chimpanzee.*

6. For a taste of Byzantium and its arbitrary culture of power see Procopius, *The Secret History*, trans. G. A. Williamson and Peter Sarris (London: Penguin Books, 2007), esp. Part III "Anatomy of a Regime", 78–124. Written as an invective against Justinian and Theodora, *The Secret History* reveals an autocracy managed by spies and ruled through fear in which no one upon whom the rulers fixed their gaze was safe.

7. One argument, which is perhaps excessive with regard to Kievan Rus, is that "From its inception in the 9th century as a sovereign state of the Kievan Rus to the dissolution of the Soviet Union in 1991, centralized governance, strong statesmanship, and authoritarian leadership were very distinctive characteristics of the Russian politics and business environment." Anatoly Zhuplev and Vladimir I. Shein, "Russia's Evolving Corporate Governance in the Cultural Context", *Journal of Transnational Management*, 10:3 (2005), 25.

8. Nicholas A. Riasanovsky, *A History of Russia* (New York: Oxford University Press, 1977), 32.

9. Hereditary succession from one brother to another is practiced in some monarchies even today—Saudi Arabia and Kuwait are two prominent examples of this. Jordan too would have followed this practice but shortly before his death, King Hussain altered the succession in favor of his son, now King Abdullah.

10. Philip Longworth, *Russia's Empires: Their Rise and fall from Prehistory to Putin* (London: John Murray, 2005), 45.

11. For more see Ibn Khaldun, *An Introduction to History: The Muqaddimah*, The premise from which Ibn Khaldun writes is that "History makes us acquainted with the conditions of past nations as they are reflected in their national character." Ibid., 11. Driving the cycle of dynastic change is the ebb and flow of group solidarity as determined by blood ties and religious or ideological motivation. The greater the sense of solidarity (*asabiya*) the greater the potential strength of an imperial elite.

12. The Mongol Empire founded by Genghis Khan broke up into a number of smaller, but still very formidable dynastic states. The most famous of these was the Yuan Dynasty in China whose greatest ruler, Kublai Khan, was visited by Marco Polo. Persia became part of the Emirate of the Il-Khans, while Russia was subjugated by the Golden Horde.

13. Hugh Seton-Watson, *The Russian Empire, 1801–1917* (Oxford: Oxford University Press, 1988), 529.

14. The serfs were all state property, some managed directly by the czar on crown or state lands and others managed on the czar's behalf by military and civil officials. Pipes, *Property and Freedom*, 185.

15. The Ottomans retook Azov in 1641.

16. Robert K. Massie, *Peter the Great: His Life and World* (London: Cardinal, 1989), 12.

17. Alexander Chubarov, *The Fragile Empire: A History of Imperial Russia* (New York: Continuum International Publishing Group, 1999), 12.

18. Alex de Jonge, *Fire and Water: A Life of Peter the Great* (London: Collins, 1979), 26.

19. Merle Fainsod, "Bureaucracy and Modernization: The Russian and Soviet Case", in Joseph LaPolambara ed., *Bureaucracy and Political Development* (Princeton: Princeton University Press, 1963), 240.

20. The Old Believers opposed reforms introduced by the Patriarch Nikon in the mid-1600s. These changes were primarily ritualistic, involving the manner in which the sign of the cross was made, directions of processions, spelling, etc. At the time such changes created serious opposition and led to those who wanted to stick to the old rituals splitting from the main body of the Church. Persecutions, repression and punitive taxation drove many Old Believers into exile away from the main concentrations of the Russian population.
21. Massie, *Peter the Great*, 235.
22. Ibid., 390.
23. Ibid.
24. Reaching the top eight ranks conferred hereditary nobility, while attaining the lower six personal nobility. Service to the state was compulsory and the nobility's power "came from their office, and from the emperor's confidence, not their noble birth." Seton-Watson, *The Russian Empire*, 15.
25. These attributes were not, however, shared by his second wife, Czarina Catherine I, who quite enjoyed all the refinements that an imperial court could bring.
26. Massie, *Peter the Great*, 769.
27. Seton-Watson, *The Russian Empire*, 23.
28. Ibid.
29. C. A. Bayly, *The Birth of the Modern World, 1780–1914: Global Connections and Comparisons* (Oxford: Blackwell Publishing, 2004), 33. The Prussian bureaucracy was, however, much more territorially concentrated though Prussia's population, at 6 million, was one-fifth or one-sixth of Russia's population. Austria's central government, during the same period, employed about 10,000 civil servants.
30. Henri Troyat, *Catherine the Great,* trans. John Pinkham (New York: E. P. Dutton, 1980), 129.
31. Ibid., 154.
32. Ibid., 161.
33. Ibid., 173.
34. Ibid., 345–46.
35. Ibid., 345.
36. Ibid.
37. Simon Sebag Montefiore, *Prince of Princes: The Life of Potemkin* (London: Phoenix Press, 2001), 20.
38. Ibid., 51.
39. Ibid., 205.
40. Ibid., 382.
41. Seton-Watson, *The Russian Empire*, 23. The figures refer to male serfs, including their families, the totals rise significantly.
42. Ibid., 25.
43. Ibid.
44. The *Nakaaz* stated that autocracy was necessary for in Russia "The Extent of the Dominion requires an absolute Power to be vested in that Person who rules over it. It is expedient so to be that the quick Dispatch of Affairs, sent from distant Parts, might make ample Amends for the Delay occasioned by the great Distance of the Places." http://novaonline.nvcc.edu/eli/evans/HIS241/Documents/Nakaz.pdf . (Accessed, September 29, 2012).
45. Troyat, *Catherine the Great*, 346.
46. Joan Haslip, *Catherine the Great* (London: Weidenfeld and Nicholson, 1977),
47. Chubarov, *The Fragile Empire*, 41–42.
48. Ibid., 43.
49. Seton-Watson, *The Russian Empire*, 80.

50. Ibid., 106.
51. Ibid., 105.
52. Ibid., 156.
53. Ibid., 161.
54. Ibid.
55. Ibid.
56. Edward Crankshaw, *The Shadow of the Winter Palace: The Drift to Revolution, 1825–1917* (London: MacMillan, 1976), 18.
57. Seton-Watson, *The Russian Empire*, 214.
58. Hingley, *The Russian Mind*, 99.
59. Ibid., 131.
60. J. M. K. Vyvyan, "Russia in Europe and Asia", *The New Cambridge Modern History*, Vol. X, *The Zenith of European Power* (Cambridge: Cambridge University Press, 1968), 358.
61. Ibid., 362. The Russian state was kept much busier on this front between 1855 and 1861 when it crushed 474 peasant rebellions. Ibid.
62. Crankshaw, *Shadow of the Winter Palace*, 40.
63. Ibid.
64. Ibid., 57.
65. Ibid., 259.
66. Nicholas II and his entire family, including princess Anastasia, met their doom at the hands of the Bolsheviks in July 1918. The entire family was executed by the communist regime to eliminate any possibility of a dynastic restoration or provide the White Russian forces with a unifying symbol.
67. Seton-Watson, *The Russian Empire*, 534.
68. Ibid.
69. Crankshaw, *Shadow of the Winter Palace*, 299.
70. For a superb account of the reassertion of czarist autocracy and the dismantling of the concessions granted under pressure of the 1905 rebellion, see Abraham Ascher, *The Revolution of 1905: Authority Restored* (Stanford: Stanford University Press, 1992). It becomes clear the czar did not see the rebellion as anything more than the rebellions that had occurred in the past, and he thus obstructed his own advisers, such as Stolypin, from implementing reforms and from taking the Duma seriously. When czarism collapsed in March 1917, there was thus no autonomous institution capable of filling the void thus created—an ideal opportunity for a highly motivated armed minority to seize power. Ibid., 216–63.
71. Chubarov, *The Fragile Empire*, 202.
72. Dmitri Volkogonov, *The Rise and Fall of the Soviet Empire* (London: HarperCollins, 1999), 5.
73. Ibid., 52.
74. Longworth, *Russia's Empires*, 240.
75. Simon Sebag Montefiore, *Stalin: The Court of the Red Tsar* (London: Phoenix, 2003), 47
76. Ibid.
77. Ibid.
78. Ibid., 87. The enormity of Soviet crimes make the construction of the 227 kilometers long Baltic-White Sea canal was accomplished in the early 1930s by the forced labor of 170,000 workers, of whom 25,000 died every year, appear to be one of the more humane projects undertaken.
79. Volkogonov, *The Rise and Fall of the Soviet Empire*, 64.
80. Hedrick Smith, *The Russians* (London: Sphere Books, 1976), 356.
81. Ibid.
82. Ibid.

83. Beria had joined the Cheka in 1920 and became Stalin's favorite "Prosecutor" and became head of the NKVD (Narodnyy Komissariat Vnutrennikh Del, or People's Commissariat for Internal Affairs) in 1938. Once in power Beria settled old scores, personally tortured and executed his enemies and forced countless women to service him sexually or be sent to the camps or be executed. For more see, Montefiore, *Stalin*, 287–304.

84. Brezhnev had "the psychology of a middle-ranking Party functionary", was "vain", "wary", "conventional", devoted to achieving military-strategic parity with the West regardless of the wider costs and "was not only a reluctant writer" but "also found reading a chore." Volkogonov, *The Rise and Fall of the Soviet Empire*, 264, 268.

85. Montefiore, *Stalin*, 89.

86. Outside the Soviet Union "For many young intellectuals, Communism was less a matter of conviction than an affair of faith." Moscow was the spiritual center and the military might and global influence of the Soviet Union after the Second World War provided the faith with an example of secular achievement. Soviet-inspired "Communism operated on the principle that writers need not *think*" but only accept and propagate the profound insights of Marxism-Leninism. Judt, *Postwar*, 200–1.

87. Burleigh, *Earthly Powers*, 12. Other utopian projects, from nationalism to Nazism, produced comparably "ghastly" results.

88. Written in September 1946, Ambassador Novikov's telegram to his masters in Moscow laid out the Soviet perception of US foreign policy as being driven by "monopolistic capital" with its objective being the encirclement of the Soviet Union. The full text of the telegram is available online at: http://academic.brooklyn.cuny.edu/history/johnson/novikov.htm. (Accessed September 29, 2012).

89. Antony Beevor, *Stalingrad* (London: Penguin, 1999), 23.

90. Michael Charlton, ed. & comp., *The Eagle and the Small Birds: Crisis in the Soviet Empire from Yalta to Solidarity* (London: BBC, 1984), 77.

91. Michael R. Intriligator, Serguey Braguinsky and Vitaly Shvydko, "Human Capital", in Lawrence R. Klein and Marshall Power, eds., *The New Russia: Transition Gone Awry* (Stanford: Stanford University Press, 2001), 404.

92. Mikhail Gorbachev, *Memoirs* (London: Bantam Books, 1997), 199.

93. Ibid., 297.

94. Ibid.

95. Georgi Arbatov, "Origins and Consequences of 'Shock Therapy'", in *The New Russia*, 173–74.

96. Ibid., 174.

97. Ibid. 173.

98. Svetlana P. Glinka, Andrei Grigariev, and Vakhtang Yakobidze, "Crime and Corruption", in Ibid., 237.

99. Ibid.

100. Ibid., 237–38.

101. Ibid., 239.

102. Ibid., 241.

103. Vladimir Mikhalev, "Poverty and Social Assistance", in Ibid., 251, 257.

104. Ibid., 253.

105. Geliy Shmeliov and others, "Agriculture" in Ibid., 342.

106. Ibid.

107. Intriligator, Serguey Braguinsky and Vitaly Shvydko, "Human Capital", in Ibid., 405.

108. Pavel A. Makeyenko, Vatche Gabrelian and March Holzer, "The New Russian Bureaucracy: What is new about it?", *International Journal of Public Administration*, Vol. 22, No. 1 1999, 25.

109. Ibid., 28.
110. A 1995 study by the Russian Academy of Sciences found that 82 percent of regional officials "were drawn from the old Soviet *nomenklatura*, the higher proportion of all elite categories." T. H. Rigby, "Russia's Provincial Bosses: A Collective Career Profile", *Journal of Communist Studies and Transition Politics*, Vol. 17, No. 4, 2001, 3.
111. Stephen Blank, "Russia's Geo-economic future: The Security Implications of Russia's Political and Economic Structure", *Journal of Slavic Military Studies*, Vol. 24, No. 3, 2011, 353.
112. Ibid., 355.
113. Ibid., 357.
114. Ibid., 358.
115. In 2003, the Kremlin launched an "assault on the Yukos oil company and its 'oligarch' chief executive and owner, Mikhail Khodorkovskii, who was charged with fraud and tax evasion . . . businessmen have viewed the affair as giving tax bureaucrats the go-ahead to interpret tax laws as they like." Marc P. Berenson, "Rationalizing or Empowering Bureaucrats? Tax Administration Reform in Poland and Russia", *Journal of Communist Studies and Transition Politics*, Vol. 24, No. 1, 2008, 147. In 2006, taxation departments were granted the power to fine entrepreneurs up to 5000 rubles and firms up to 50,000 rubles without a court decision, thereby increasing the power of the civilian bureaucracy over the private sector and making it easy for punitive payments to be imposed. Ibid., 148.
116. Siedentop observes that "Perceived injustices can easily become motors of centralization. For it is usually the most remote and general agency of government that is appealed to on the grounds that it is best placed to overcome local or regional prejudice, defining higher standards of conduct or provisions, and enforcing them in a uniform way across the political system." Siedentop, *Democracy in Europe*, 21.
117. Elena A. Chebankova, "The Limitations of Central Authority in the Regions and the Implications for the Evolution of Russia's Federal System", *Europe-Asia Studies*, 57:7, 2005, 934.
118. Hans Oversloot and Ruben Verheul, "Managing Democracy: Political Parties and the State in Russia", *Journal of Communist Studies and Transition Politics*, Vol. 22, No. 3, 2006, 387.
119. Kennan, *The Marquis de Custine and his 'Russia in 1839'* , 78.
120. Ibid., 79.
121. Laura Engelstein, "Revolution and the Theater of Public Life in Imperial Russia," in Isser Woloch, ed., *Revolution and the Meanings of Freedom in the Nineteenth Century*, 315.
122. Russia, argue Steven Rosefielde and Romana Hlouskova, is not a democracy though it does hold elections. The United Russia Party dominates parliament with a two-thirds majority, the media is under state influence or control, non-government organizations are under pressure to submit to state control or pack their bags, especially if they receive foreign funding, and since December 1999, when Putin took over as prime minister, thirteen journalists have been murdered in contract-style killings with no convictions being secured by the prosecution. For more, see Steven Rosefielde and Romana Hlouskova, "Why Russia is Not a Democracy", *Comparative Strategy*, Vol. 26, No. 3, 2007, 215–29.
123. http://data.worldbank.org/country/russian-federation (Accessed: August 16, 2013). Russia's current nominal GDP is about US$ 2 trillion, per capita income about US$ 12,700.
124. Hingley, *The Russian Mind*, 161.

NOTES TO CHAPTER 7

1. In Japan, as in China, a "peasant" society dominated by a Confucian, or Neo-Confucian ethos emerged alongside a strong state, strengthening the logic of its development. Thus, Japanese aristocratic feudalism did not develop along lines parallel to European feudalism, and once a strong state backed by a service class and supported by a peasantry started to take shape in the late-1500s and early 1600s, the power of the lords declined rapidly: "Historically, two features set peasant societies in East Asia apart from agricultural societies in other regions. One was the absence of the system that grew up in, for example, medieval and early-modern Europe, of large-scale management of extensive domains held by feudal lords. Broadly speaking, direct management of land by a political ruling elite who controlled vast tracts did not develop in East Asia, even though this pattern did become established not only in many parts of medieval and early-modern Europe but in West Asia and Latin America as well. Ruling elites in East Asia certainly had their share of large landowners, including many shidafu in China and *yangban* 両班 (scholar-official status group, resembling shidafu) in Korea, but generally large estate holders rented land to tenant farmers rather than directly managing it themselves. What distinguished East Asia in this respect from other regions, then, was the sustained and entrenched tendency to leave land management to tenant farmers.

   The second feature of East Asia's peasant societies was scale: agricultural labourers, cultivators working on land they did not manage independently, were comparatively small in number. Compare that with, for example, the neighbouring area from Southeast Asia across to the Indian subcontinent. There, farm labourers have continued to make up an extremely high proportion of the agricultural population, which still poses major problems in these regions today. In East Asia farmers generally managed the land themselves; if they owned none, they rented land and worked it directly." Hiroshi Miyajima, "The Emergence of Peasant Societies in East Asia", *International Journal of Asian Studies*, Vol. 2, No. 1. (2005), 4.

2. Control over the northern island of Hokkaido was patchy until the mid-1800s.

3. Andrew Gordon, *A Modern History of Japan from Tokugawa Times to the Present* (New York: Oxford University Press, 2003), 10.

4. Ibid.

5. Ibid, 15.

6. Ibid.

7. Moore, *The Social Origins of Dictatorship and Democracy*, 231–32.

8. Ibid., 259.

9. Gordon, *A Modern History of Japan from Tokugawa Times to the Present*, 21.

10. Diamond, *Collapse: How Societies Choose to Fail or Survive*, 301.

11. Ibid.

12. Ibid., 305.

13. Mitani Hiroshi, *Escape from Impasse: The Decision to Open Japan*, trans. David Noble (Tokyo: International House of Japan, 2006), xxix.

14. Moore, *The Social Origins of Dictatorship and Democracy*, 231.

15. Mitani, *Escape from Impasse*, xxix.

16. Ibid.

17. Ibid., xxix–xxx.

18. Ibid., xxxiii.

19. Gordon, *A Modern History of Japan from Tokugawa Times to the Present*, 34–35.

20. Ibid., 29.
21. Ibid., 15.
22. Ibid., 17.
23. Ibid.
24. Ibid., 87.
25. Takii Kazuhiro, *The Meiji Constitution: The Japanese Experience of the West and the Shaping of the Modern State*, trans., David Noble (Tokyo: International House of Japan, 2007), 39.
26. Ibid., 34–35.
27. Ibid., 83.
28. Ibid., 76.
29. Ibid., 83.
30. Ibid., 150.
31. Ibid., 152.
32. Ian Buruma, *Inventing Japan: From Empire to Economic Miracle* (London: Weidenfeld & Nicholson, 2003), 54.
33. Najmul Saqib Khan, *Japanese Experience and Nation-Building in South-west Asia* (Tokyo: The Japan Times, 1993), 28.
34. Herbert Bix, *Hirohito and the Making of Modern Japan* (New York, New York City: HarperCollins Perennial, 2001), 28.
35. Ibid., 29.
36. Ibid., 329.
37. Buruma, *Inventing Japan*, 54.
38. Ibid., 65.
39. Bix, *Hirohito and the Making of Modern Japan*, 57–58.
40. Ibid., 206.
41. Spellman, *Monarchies, 1000–2000*, 64.
42. It reads: "I, the Emperor, think that my ancestors and religion founded my nation a very long time ago, with its development a profound and steady morality was established. The fact that my subjects show their loyalty to me and show filial love to their parents in unison with the hearts of several millions of my subjects, which accumulates virtue generation after generation is indeed a pride of my nation, and is a profound and basic idea of education.

    You, my subjects form full personalities by showing filial love to your parents, by making good terms with your brothers and sisters, by being intimate with your friends, by making couples who love each other, by trusting your friends, by reflecting upon yourselves, by conveying a spirit of philanthropy to other people and by studying to acquire knowledge and wisdom.

    Thus, please obey always the constitution and other laws of my nation in your profession in order to spread the common good in my nation. If an emergency may happen, please do your best for my nation in order to support the eternal fate and future of my nation. In this way, you are my good and faithful subjects, and you come to appreciate good social customs inherited from your ancestors. The way of doing this is a good lesson inherited from my ancestors and religion which you subjects should observe well together with your offspring.

    These ideas hold true for both the present and the past, and may be propagated in this nation as well as in the other countries. I would like to understand all of this with you, my subjects, and hope sincerely that all the mentioned virtues will be carried out in harmony by all of you subjects." October 30, 1890 (23rd year of Meiji Era) (Translated by Shizuya Sato) http://www.ne.jp/asahi/moriyuki/abukuma/ref/jp_ref/imperial_rescript_en.html (Accessed, July 27, 2010)

43. Najmul Saqib Khan, *Japanese Experience and Nation-Building in South-west Asia*, 30–31.

44. Buruma, *Inventing Japan*, 41.

45. It reads: "We are your supreme Commander-in-Chief. Our relations with your will be most intimate when We rely upon you as Our limbs and you look up to Us as your head. Whether We are able to guard the Empire, and so prove Ourself worthy of Heaven's blessings and repay the benevolence of Our Ancestors, depends upon the faithful discharge of your duties as soldiers and sailors." And concludes that "Moreover these five articles are the "Grand Way" of Heaven and earth and the universal law of humanity. . . ." The articles themselves deal with loyalty to the emperor, loyalty to superior officers, maintenance of courage and discipline, eschewing luxuries and serving the best interests of the state. Soldiers are also formally prohibited from participating in politics though the extensive militarism of the Meiji regime and its successors made that particular prohibition a dead letter to begin with. For more see http://www.facstaff.bucknell.edu/jamesorr/ImpResSold-Sailors1882web.htm (Accessed on July 27, 2010).

46. One of the most moving accounts, made famous due to its incorporation in the 2006 Clint Eastwood Film *Letters from Iwo Jima* is a book by the same name, which follows the Japanese defense of the island in February-March 1945. The entire Japanese garrison, over 20,000 men, was wiped out in the course of a ferocious and brilliantly executed inland defense. "By March 14, the Japanese had nine hundred men left in their last stronghold in the northern end of the island. These were not the only Japanese troops left on the island. Men were still alive in bunkers in areas that the Americans had passed across, and many of them fought guerrilla style even though their units were scattered and there was no one left to lead them. Although the Americans urged them to surrender, no one complied." Kumiko Kakahashi, *Letters from Iwo Jima: The Japanese Eyewitness Stories that Inspired Clint Eastwood's Film* (London: Weidenfeld & Nicholson, 2006), 184.

47. Gordon, *A Modern History of Japan from Tokugawa Times to the Present*, 182.

48. Joseph LaPalombara, ed., *Bureaucracy and Political Development* (Princeton: Princeton University Press, 1963), 18–19.

49. Kazuhiro, *The Meiji Constitution*, 92.

50. Ibid, 118.

51. Gordon, *A Modern History of Japan from Tokugawa Times to the Present*, 64.

52. Moore, *The Social Origins of Dictatorship and Democracy*, 288.

53. Ibid.

54. Ibid, 301–2.

55. Ibid, 302.

56. John Dower, *Embracing Defeat: Japan in the Wake of World War II* (New York: W. W. Norton & Company, The New Press, 1999), 539.

57. Najamul Saqib Khan, *Japanese Experience and Nation-building in South-west Asia*, 78.

58. Ezra F. Vogel, *Japan as Number One: Lessons for America* (Cambridge, Massachusetts: Harvard University Press, 1979), 59.

59. Eisuke Sakakibara, *Structural Reform in Japan: Breaking the Iron Triangle* (Washington D.C Brookings Institution Press, 2003), 55.

60. Najamul Saqib Khan, *Japanese Experience and Nation-building in South-west Asia*, 78.

61. Vogel, *Japan as Number One*, 51.

62. Gordon, *A Modern History of Japan from Tokugawa Times to the Present*, 301.
63. Eisuke, *Structural Reform in Japan*, 64.
64. The state-led development that helped Japan industrialize during the Meiji Era, and guided Japan to a rapid economic recovery after defeat in the Second World War, exploited access to the US market and built upon Japanese traditions of workmanship and entrepreneurship developed over centuries. The Japanese civil service elite maximized the advantages that Japan's prior economic experience had accumulated. This is precisely the reason why Japan's pre-war industrialization and post-war miracle are not readily replicable in other societies, even if those societies share a common Confucian or East Asian heritage. For more, see, Aurelia George Mulgan, "Japan's Interventionist State: Bringing Agriculture Back In", *Japanese Journal of Political Science*, Vol. 6, No. 1, (2005), 29–61.
65. Eisuke, *Structural Reform in Japan*, 124.
66. Ibid, 138.
67. Buruma, *Inventing Japan*, 142–43.
68. "This is where agriculture can be brought back in—not as a singular model of intervention, but as an exemplar of Japan's interventionist state. The similarities between structures of intervention across industry and agriculture are suggestive of the existence of such a common interventionist model. The key point is that the institutional, legal, financial and other characteristics of the Japanese system of state intervention in the economy are not specific to particular industries, but are cross- sectoral. This proposition is supported by other research that reveals the generic mechanisms of state intervention in the Japanese economy." Mulgan, "Japan's Interventionist State: Bringing Agriculture Back In", 55.
69. Matsutani Akihiko argues that the traditional paradigm of economics, which almost assumes population growth and is fixated on GNP increases as the key objective of economic policy will have to be abandoned in favor of a new approach that organizes the economy to adjust, even benefit from, natural population decrease. Akihiko asserts that Japan's decreasing population is an "opportunity to redress Japan's biggest economic flaw: the failure of economic growth to produce commensurate improvements in the quality of life" due to overcrowding and overconcentration of the total population in a small percentage of the national territory. Mastutani Akihiko, *Shrinking Population Economics: Lessons from Japan*, trans. Brian Miller (Tokyo: International House of Japan, 2006), xi. Japan may well become the first country to experience a rise in per capita income and quality of life alongside decline in its total population over the long-term.

NOTES TO CHAPTER 8

1. Winston S. Churchill, *A History of the English-Speaking Peoples*, vol. 1, *The Birth of Britain* (London: Cassell, 1956; reprint, London: Cassell, 2002), viii.
2. Keith Feiling, *A History of England From the Coming of the English to 1918* (Trowbridge & Esher: Book Club Associates., 1975), 6.
3. Schama, *A History of Britain: At the Edge of the World?*, 24–25.
4. Ibid., 26.
5. Churchill, *A History of the English-Speaking Peoples*, vol. 1, *The Birth of Britain*, 4.
6. Ibid., 15.

7. Schama, *A History of Britain: At the Edge of the World?*, 31.
8. Ibid., 28.
9. Churchill, *A History of the English-Speaking Peoples*, vol. 1, *The Birth of Britain*, 23.
10. Schama, *A History of Britain: At the Edge of the World?*, 33.
11. The Roman Emperor came to resemble the Pharaohs of Egypt, and God-Kings of Persia and India.
12. Roberts, *History of the World*,185.
13. Ibid., 191.
14. Halvell, *Ancient Rome,* 332.
15. Ibid.
16. Ibid., 333.
17. Ibid.
18. Ibid.
19. Roberts, *History of the World*, 190.
20. Ibid., 195.
21. Ibid.
22. Ibid.
23. Pipes, *Property and Freedom*, 123.
24. Ibid.
25. Schama, *A History of Britain: At the Edge of the World?*, 43.
26. Ibid., 38.
27. Ibid., 40.
28. Churchill, *A History of the English-Speaking Peoples*, vol. 1, *The Birth of Britain*, 30.
29. Ibid., 38.
30. Schama, *A History of Britain: At the Edge of the World?*, 41.
31. Roger Osborne, *Civilization: A New History of the Western World* (London: Jonathan Cape, 2006), 40–41.
32. Pipes, *Property and Freedom*, 125.
33. Schama, *A History of Britain: At the Edge of the World?*, 57.
34. Churchill, *A History of the English-Speaking Peoples*, vol. 1, *The Birth of Britain*, 94–95.
35. Pipes, *Property and Freedom*, 123.
36. Ibid., 125.
37. Osborne, *Civilization*, 39.
38. Schama, *A History of Britain: At the Edge of the World?*, 67.
39. Ibid., 107.
40. Pipes, *Property and Freedom*, 126.
41. The nobility.
42. Danzinger, *1215*, 126.
43. Ibid., 146.
44. Churchill, *A History of the English-Speaking Peoples*, vol. 1, *The Birth of Britain*, 170–72.
45. Ibid., 173.
46. Ibid.
47. Danzinger, *1215*, 139.
48. Ibid., 139–40.
49. Ibid., 142.
50. Churchill, *A History of the English-Speaking Peoples*, vol. 1, *The Birth of Britain*, 162.
51. Danzinger, *1215*, 143.
52. Ibid.
53. Ibid.

54. Ibid., 125.
55. Ibid., 126.
56. Ibid.
57. Declared that a district was no longer considered as a forest for administrative purposes.
58. Danzinger, *1215*, 127.
59. Ibid.
60. Ibid.
61. Ibid., 127–28.
62. Churchill, *A History of the English-Speaking Peoples*, vol. 1, *The Birth of Britain*, 195.
63. Danzinger, *1215*, 52–53.
64. Ibid., 54.
65. Ibid.
66. Ibid., 42–43.
67. Ibid., 45–46.
68. Ibid., 83–84.
69. Ibid., 193.
70. Schama, *A History of Britain: At the Edge of the World?*, 162.
71. Churchill, *A History of the English-Speaking Peoples*, vol. 1, *The Birth of Britain*, 200.
72. The Jews were expelled from England in 1290.
73. Articles 23, 24, 28, 29, 30, 31, 38, 39, 40, 44, 45, 48, and 54.
74. Churchill, *A History of the English-Speaking Peoples*, vol. 1, *The Birth of Britain*, 198.
75. Ibid., xv.
76. Siedentop, *Democracy in Europe*, 18.
77. Churchill, *A History of the English-Speaking Peoples*, vol. 1, *The Birth of Britain*, xv.
78. Schama, *A History of Britain: At the Edge of the World?*, 169.
79. Ibid., 173.
80. Ibid.
81. Ibid. 176.
82. Ibid., 177.
83. Ibid
84. Ibid., 178.
85. Ibid., 180–81.
86. Churchill, *A History of the English-Speaking Peoples*, vol. 1, *The Birth of Britain*, 217.
87. Ibid., 218–19.
88. Ibid., 220–22.
89. Ibid., 231.
90. Ibid., 233.
91. Ibid., 246.
92. Ibid., 249.
93. Ibid., 282.
94. Ibid., 283.
95. Schama, *A History of Britain: At the Edge of the World?*, 246–9.
96. Ibid., 249.
97. Ibid., 256.
98. Ibid., 257.
99. Churchill, *A History of the English-Speaking Peoples*, vol. 1, *The Birth of Britain*, 299.
100. Ibid., 300.

101. Ibid.
102. Ibid.
103. Ibid., 301.
104. Schama, *A History of Britain: At the Edge of the World?*, 260.
105. Ibid.
106. Churchill, *A History of the English-Speaking Peoples*, vol. 1, *The Birth of Britain*, 303.
107. Schama, *A History of Britain: At the Edge of the World?*, 262.
108. Ibid.
109. Churchill, *A History of the English-Speaking Peoples*, vol. 1, *The Birth of Britain*, 308.
110. Ibid., 310.
111. Ibid., 316.
112. Ibid., 322.
113. Feiling, *A History of England From the Coming of the English to 1918*, 300.
114. Moore, *Social Origins of Dictatorship and Democracy*, 5.
115. Ibid., 9.
116. Ibid., 10.
117. Winston S Churchill, *A History of the English-Speaking Peoples*, vol. 2, *The New World* (London: Cassell, 1956; reprint, London: Cassell, 2002), 19.
118. Ibid.
119. Ibid., 23.
120. Ibid., 33.
121. Ibid.
122. Ibid., 34.
123. Ibid., 32.
124. Ibid., 45.
125. Schama, *A History of Britain: At the Edge of the World?*, 308.
126. Ibid., 310.
127. Ibid., 315.
128. Churchill, *A History of the English-Speaking Peoples*, vol. 2, *The New World*, 36.
129. Schama, *A History of Britain: At the Edge of the World?*, 308.
130. Pipes, *Property and Freedom*, 134.
131. Ibid., 147. The exact share was 28.83 percent.
132. Giles Milton, *Big Chief Elizabeth: How England's Adventurers Gambled and Won the New World* (London: Hodder and Stoughton, 2001), 158.
133. Pipes, *Property and Freedom*, 134.
134. Ibid., 135.
135. Schama, *A History of Britain: At the Edge of the World?*, 378.
136. Ibid., 365–68.
137. Birnbaum, *The Idea of France*, 12.
138. Joel Samaha, *Law and Order in Historical Perspective: The Case of Elizabethan Essex* (New York: Academic Press, 1974), 11.
139. Ibid., 41–42.
140. Ibid., 90–92.
141. Ibid., 85.
142. Ibid., 4.
143. Pipes, *Property and Freedom*, 133.
144. Ibid., 133.
145. Ibid.
146. Ruled from 1553 to 1558
147. Pipes, *Property and Freedom*, 135–36.
148. Feiling, *A History of England From the Coming of the English to 1918*, 445.

149. Ibid.
150. Ibid.
151. Pipes, *Property and Freedom*, 136–37.
152. Feiling, *A History of England From the Coming of the English to 1918*, 445.
153. Ibid.
154. Ibid., 446.
155. Pipes, *Property and Freedom*, 135.
156. Feiling, *A History of England From the Coming of the English to 1918*, 449. i.e. the sale of titles and ranks.
157. Ibid.
158. Ibid.
159. Pipes, *Property and Freedom*, 136–37.
160. Feiling, *A History of England From the Coming of the English to 1918*, 451. The war in question was the Thirty Years War (1618–1648) that pulverized central Europe and killed thirty percent of the German population.
161. Ibid.
162. Ibid.
163. Pipes, *Property and Freedom*, 140.
164. Ibid., 138.
165. Feiling, *A History of England From the Coming of the English to 1918*, 452.
166. Ibid., 454.
167. Churchill, *A History of the English-Speaking Peoples*, vol. 2, *The New World*, 155.
168. Pipes, *Property and Freedom*, 139.
169. Ibid., 138.
170. Ibid., 141.
171. Feiling, *A History of England From the Coming of the English to 1918*, 456.
172. Churchill, *A History of the English-Speaking Peoples*, vol. 2, *The New World*, 159.
173. Feiling, *A History of England From the Coming of the English to 1918*, 457.
174. Churchill, *A History of the English-Speaking Peoples*, vol. 2, *The New World*, 158.
175. Ibid.
176. Ibid., 163.
177. Ibid.
178. The Short Parliament.
179. Churchill, *A History of the English-Speaking Peoples*, vol. 2, *The New World*, 170.
180. Moore, *Social Origins of Dictatorship and Democracy*, 17.
181. Churchill, *A History of the English-Speaking Peoples*, vol. 2, *The New World*, 185.
182. Feiling, *A History of England From the Coming of the English to 1918*, 474.
183. Churchill, *A History of the English-Speaking Peoples*, vol. 2, *The New World*, 215.
184. Ibid., 219.
185. Ibid., 248.
186. Feiling, *A History of England From the Coming of the English to 1918*, 508.
187. Moore, *Social Origins of Dictatorship and Democracy*, 17.
188. Churchill, *A History of the English-Speaking Peoples*, vol. 2, *The New World*, 259.

189. Ibid., 261.
190. Ibid., 267.
191. Pipes, *Property and Freedom*, 150.
192. Ibid., 147. The exact share was 1.98%.
193. Churchill, *A History of the English-Speaking Peoples*, vol. 2, *The New World*, 259. The term "Whig" meant "clever, bigoted, greeted Scots Presbyterian", while Tory meant "Irish Papist Bandit".
194. Simon Schama, *A History of Britain: The British Wars 1603–1776* (London: BBC Worldwide Ltd., 2001), 352.
195. Ibid., 353.
196. Ibid.
197. Ibid.
198. Ibid.
199. Ibid.
200. Ibid., 355.
201. Harold Wilson, *The Governance of Britain* (London: Book Club Associates, 1976), 12.
202. Ibid., 13.
203. Ibid., 14.
204. Ibid.
205. Winston S Churchill, *A History of the English-Speaking Peoples*, vol. 3, *The Age of Revolution* (London: Cassell, 1956; reprint, London: Cassell, 2002), 96.
206. Ibid., 97.
207. Blanning, *The Culture of Power and the Power of Culture*, 303.
208. Ibid., 304.
209. Ibid., 307.
210. Kennedy, *The Rise and Fall of the Great Powers*, 128.
211. Tocqueville, *The Old Regime and the Revolution*, 143.
212. Kennedy, *The Rise and Fall of the Great Powers*, 129.
213. Ibid., 128.
214. Blanning, *The Culture of Power and the Power of Culture*, 307.
215. Ibid., 318.
216. Ibid., 328.
217. Moore, *Social Origins of Dictatorship and Democracy*, 22.
218. Blanning, *The Culture of Power and the Power of Culture*, 127.
219. Ibid.
220. Ibid., 128.
221. Ibid.
222. Ibid.
223. Tocqueville, *The Old Regime and the Revolution*, 138.
224. Ibid.
225. Feiling, *A History of England From the Coming of the English to 1918*, 509.
226. Ian Buruma, *Voltaire's Coconuts or Anglomania in Europe* (London: Phoenix, 2000), 20.
227. Ibid.
228. Ibid.
229. Ibid., 23.
230. Ibid., 31.
231. Ibid.
232. Andrew Mackillop, "The Political Culture of the Scottish Highlands from Culloden to Waterloo", *The Historical Journal*, Vol. 46, No. 3, 2003, 521.
233. Ibid.

234. Ibid., 522.
235. Ibid., 526.
236. Ibid., 528.
237. Ibid., 521.
238. *Report on the Organisation of the Permanent Civil Service* (London: Her Majesty's Stationery Office, 1854), 5.
239. Ibid., 3.
240. Ibid., 4.
241. Ibid., 6.
242. Ibid., 7–8.
243. Ibid., 8.
244. David Richards and Martin J. Smith, "The Public Service Ethos and the role of the British Civil Service", *West European Politics*, Vol. 23, No. 3, 2000, 47.
245. Ibid., 49.
246. Anthony Barker and Graham K. Wilson, "Whitehall's Disobedient Servants: Senior Officials' Potential Resistance to Ministers in British Government Departments", *British Journal of Political Science*, Vol. 27, No. 2, 1997, 224.
247. Richards and Smith, "The Public Service Ethos and the role of the British Civil Service", 62.
248. Exclusive of the military services.
249. Margaret Thatcher, *The Downing Street Years* (New York City: HarperCollins, 1993), 45–46.
250. Dehlavi, "Report on the Administrative Law & Courts in England, France, Germany, Switzerland, Italy, Holland, Belgium, Sweden & Spain", 6–7.
251. Ibid., 7.
252. Samuel Merrill III, Bernard Groffman, and Thomas L. Brunell, "Do British Party Politics Exhibit Cycles?", *British Journal of Political Science*, Vol. 41, No. 1, 2011, 50.
253. Thatcher, *The Downing Street Years*, 104.
254. Jack Brand, "Party Organization and the Recruitment of Councilors", *British Journal of Political Science*, Vol. 3, No. 4, 1973, 476.
255. Aditi Bagchi, "Political Citizenship in Britain and Germany", *German Politics* Vol. 9, No. 3, 2000, 169.
256. Ibid.
257. Marx, *Capital*, 152.
258. Ibid., 281.
259. Ibid., 369.
260. Richards and Smith, "The Public Service Ethos", 59.
261. David Childs, *Britain since 1945: A Political History* (London: Routledge, Taylor & Francis, 2001), 18.
262. Ibid., 79.
263. J. M. Lee, "The British Civil Service and the War Economy: Bureaucratic Conceptions of the 'Lessons of History' in 1918 and 1945", read at the Society's Conference, September 15, 1979, *Transactions of the Royal Society*, 188.
264. Ibid., 194.
265. *Report of the Machinery of Government Committee* (London: His Majesty's Stationery Office, 1918), 5.
266. *Report of the Committee, 1966–68*, Vol. 1, *The Civil Service* (London: Her Majesty's Stationery Office, 1968), 9.
267. Ibid.
268. Ibid., 22.
269. Ibid.

270. Childs, *Britain since 1945*, 120–21.
271. Lee, "The British Civil Service and the War Economy", 197.
272. George Jones, "Against a Civil Service Act", *Public Money and Management*, Vol. 22, No. 4, 2002, 5.
273. Ibid.
274. Ibid., 6.
275. Janice McMillan and Andrew Massey, "Beyond Westminster: The New Machinery of Subnational Government: A Regional Future for the UK Civil Service", *Public Money and Management*, Vol. 21, No. 2 2001, 26.
276. Paul Carmichael, "Beyond Westminster: The New Machinery of Subnational Government: The North Ireland Civil Service", *Public Money and Management*, Vol. 21, No. 2, 2001, 34.
277. Address to British Parliament, April 7, 1960, cited in Wolfram Kaiser, "The political reform debate in Britain since 1945: The European dimension", *Contemporary British History*, Vol. 12, No. 1, 1998, 53.
278. Britain self-imposed restraint with regard to fiscal deficits and overspending have had important consequences for the fiscal outlook, which, if current trends hold, will result in a surplus budget by 2017–18, from a fiscal deficit of 6.0 percent of GDP in 2013. This has been achieved through anti-populist measures that have aggravated inequality and led to demands for increased public spending and could well cost the current Conservative-led coalition government the next elections. And yet, the ability of British leaders to commit political suicide in order to secure the long-term interests of the state is a factor that has contributed to the survival of constitutional and representative order in the United Kingdom. For more on fiscal stabilization see, *Office for Budget Responsibility, Economic and Fiscal Outlook* (London: Her Majesty's Stationery Office, March 2013). In 2011–12, in the United Kingdom, the wealthiest fifth of households have an average annual income of about £ 78,000, while the bottom fifth have an average annual income of £ 5400. The top 40 percent of households pay more in taxes than they receive in benefits, while the remainder receives more in benefits than they pay in taxes. http://www.bbc.co.uk/news/business-23253092 (Accessed: August 16, 2013).
279. For instance, in Britain, the share of government expenditure as percentage of GDP, rose from 34.2 percent to 41.5 percent between 1950 and 1973 and "The overwhelming bulk of this increase in spending went on insurance, pensions, health, education and housing." Judt, *Postwar*, 361.

Selected Bibliography

Ahmed, Nizam-ud-din. *Tabakat-i-Akbari*, trans. H. M. Elliot. Lahore: Sind Sagar Academy, 1975.

Ahsan, Aitzaz. *The Indus Saga and the Making of Pakistan*. Lahore: Nehr Ghar Publications, 2001.

Allami, Abu'l Fazl. *A'in-I Akbari*, trans. H. Blochmann. Calcutta: Calcutta Madrassah, 1873; reprint, Lahore: Sang-e-Meel Publications, 2003.

Allami, Abu'l Fazl. *The Akbarnama*, trans. H. Beveridge, vol 1. Lahore: Islamia-al-Saudia Printers, 1984.

Allen Charles. *Buddha and the Sahibs: The Men who Discovered India's Lost Religion*. London: John Murray, 2002.

Ali, Athar M. *The Mughal Nobility Under Aurungzeb*. New Delhi: Asia Publishing House, 1970.

Ali, Parveen Shaukat. *Pillars of British Imperialism: A Case Study of Sir Alfred Lyall 1873–1903*. Lahore: Aziz Publishers, 1976.

Anjum, Tanvir. *Chisti Sufis in the Sultanate of Delhi, 1190–1400: From Restrained Indifference to Calculated Defiance*. Karachi: Oxford University Press, 2011.

Arberry, A. J. ed. *The Legacy of Persia*. London: Oxford University Press, 1968.

Ascher Abraham. *The Revolution of 1905: Authority Restored*. Stanford: Stanford University Press, 1992.

Ashraf, K. M. *Life and Conditions of the People of Hindustan*. New Delhi: Mushiram Manoharlal, 1970.

Askari, Syed Hasan. *Medieval India: A Miscellany*. New Delhi: Asia Publishing House, 1969.

Aspinall, A. *Cornwallis in Bengal*. New Delhi: Uppal Publishing House, 1987.

Asprey, Robert. *The Rise and Fall of Napoleon Bonaparte* Vol. II, *The Fall*. London: Abacus, 2002.

Atwan, Abdel Beri. *The Secret History of al Qaeda*. Los Angeles: University of California Press, 2006.

Axworthy, Michael. *Empire of the Mind: A History of Iran*. London: Hurst & Company, 2007.

———. *The Sword of Persia: Nader Shah, from Tribal Warrior to Conquering Tyrant*. London: I. B. Tauris, 2009.

Aziz Ahmed, *An Intellectual History of Islam in India*. Edinburgh: Edinburgh University Press, 1969.

Aziz, K. K. *The British in India: A Study in Imperialism*. Islamabad: NCHCR, 1975.

Barber, Noel. *Lords of the Golden Horn: The Splendors of Islam and the Fall of the Mighty Ottoman Empire* (London: MacMillan, 1973.

Battuta, Ibn. *Travels in Asia and Africa 1325–54*. London: Routledge and Keagan Paul, 1929; reprint Lahore: Services Book Club, 1985.

Bayly, C. A. *The Birth of the Modern World: 1780–1914*. Oxford: Blackwell Publishing, 2004.

Bayly, Susan. *The New Cambridge History of India: Caste, Society and Politics from the Eighteenth Century to the Modern Age*. Cambridge: Cambridge University Press, 2000.

Becher, Matthias. *Charlemagne*. London: Yale University Press, 2003.

Beevor, Antony. *Stalingrad*. London: Penguin, 1999.

Bennison, Amira K. *The Great Caliphs: The Golden Age of the Abbasid Empire*. London: I. B. Tauris, 2011.

Bernard, J. F. *Talleyrand: A Biography*. London: Collins, 1973.

Bernier, François. *Travels in the Mogul Empire: AD 1656–1668*, trans. Irving Brock, revised and improved edition, Archibald Constable (London: Archibald Constable and Company, 1891; reprint, Karachi: Indus Publications, n.d.).

Bernstein, Jeremy. *Dawning of the Raj: The Life and Trial of Warren Hastings*. London: Auram Press Ltd., 2000.

Best, Geoffery. *War and Society in Revolutionary Europe, 1770–1870*. Suffolk: Fontana Paperbacks, 1982.

Raghav Bhal. *Superpower? The Amazing Race between China's Hare and India's Tortoise*. London: Portfolio/Penguin, 2010.

Birnbaum, Pierre. *The Idea of France* trans. M. B. DeBevoise. New York: Hill and Wang, 2001.

Bix, Herbert. *Hirohito and the Making of Modern Japan* (New York, New York City: HarperCollins Perennial, 2001.

Blanning, T. C. W. *The Culture of Power and the Power of Culture: Old Regime Europe 1660–1789*. Oxford: Oxford University Press, 2002.

Blow, David. *Shah Abbas: The Ruthless King who Became an Iranian Legend*. London: I. B. Tauris, 2009.

Bosworth, C. E. ed. *The Formation of the Classical Islamic World*, Vol. 9. *The Turks in the Early Islamic World*. Hants: Ashgate Publishing, 2007.

Brass, Paul R. *The New Cambridge History of India: The Politics of India since Independence*. Cambridge: Cambridge University Press, 1992.

Braudel, Fernand. *A History of Civilizations*. Trans. Richard Mayne. New York: Penguin Group, 1995.

———. *Civilization and Capitalism 15th-18th Century*. Trans. Sian Reynolds. Vol I. *The Structures of Everyday Life*. London: Phoenix Press, 2002.

———. Vol. II. *The Wheels of Commerce*. London: Phoenix Press, 2002.

———. Vol. III. *The Perspective of the World*. London: Phoenix Press, 2002.

Brockelmann, Carl. *History of the Islamic Peoples*. New Delhi: Munshiram Manoharlal Publishers, 1995.

Browne, Edward G. *A Literary History of Persia*, Vol. IV, *Modern Times, 1500–1924*. Lahore: Sang-e-Meel, 2003; first published, 1924.

Buckland, C. E. *Dictionary of Indian Biography*. Lahore: Sang-e-Meel Publications, 1985.

Burke, Edmund. *Reflections on the Revolutions in France*, ed. J. C. D. Clark. Stanford: Stanford University Press, 2001.

Burleigh, Michael. *Earthly Powers: Religion and Politics in Europe from the Enlightenment to the Great War*. London: HarperCollins Publishers, 2005.

———. *The Third Reich: A New History*. London: Macmillan, 2000.

Buruma, Ian. *Inventing Japan: From Empire to Economic Miracle*. London: Weidenfeld & Nicholson, 2003.

———. *Voltaire's Coconuts or Anglomania in Europe*. London, Phoenix, 2000.

Caesar. *The Gallic War*. Trans. Carolyn Hammond. New York: Oxford University Press, 2008.

Cannadine, David. *Ornamentalism: How the British Saw Their Empire*. New York: Oxford University Press, 2001.

Carsten, F. L. ed. *The New Cambridge Modern History.* Vol V. *The Ascendancy of France 1648–88.* Cambridge: University Press, 1969.

Chang, Gordon G. *The Coming Collapse of China.* London: Century, 2001.

Chang, Jung and Jon Halliday. *Mao: The Unknown Story.* New York: Alfred A. Knopf, 2005.

Charlton, Michael ed. & comp. *The Eagle and the Small Birds: Crisis in the Soviet Empire from Yalta to Solidarity.* London: BBC, 1984.

Childs, David. *Britain since 1945: A Political History.* London: Routledge, Taylor & Francis, 2001.

Ching, Frank *Ancestors: The Story of China through the lives of an Extraordinary Family.* London: Rider, 2008.

Chubarov Alexander. *The Fragile Empire: A History of Imperial Russia.* New York: Continuum International Publishing Group, 1999.

Churchill, Winston S. *A History of the English-Speaking Peoples.* vol. 1, *The Birth of Britain.* London: Cassell, 2002.

———. Vol. 2, *The New World.*

———. Vol. 3, *The Age of Revolution.*

———. Vol. 4, *The Great Democracies.*

Cicero. *The Republic and The Laws.* Trans. Niall Rudd. Oxford: Oxford University Press, 2008.

Clarke, Peter. *The Cripps Version: The Life of Sir Stafford Cripps.* London: Allen Lane the Penguin Press, 2002.

Clausewitz, Carl von. *On War.* Ed. & Trans. Michael Howard and Peter Paret. Princeton: Princeton University Press, 1989.

Clements, Jonathan. *The First Emperor of China.* Gloucestershire: Sutton Publishing, 2004.

Clive, John. *Macaulay: The Shaping of a Historian.* Cambridge: The Belknap Press of Harvard University Press, 1987.

Cohen, Stephen P. *India: Emerging Power.* Washington D.C.: Brookings Institute Press, 2001.

Cotterfell, Arthur. *China: A History.* London: Pimlico, 1995.

Craig, Gordon A. *Germany, 1866–1945.* Oxford: Oxford University Press, 1978.

Crankshaw, Edward. *The Shadow of the Winter Palace: The Drift to Revolution, 1825–1917.* London: MacMillan, 1976.

Cromwell, Daniel W. *The SEWA Movement and Rural Development.* New Delhi: Sage, 2003.

Crone, Patricia. *Slaves on Horses: The Evolution of the Islamic Polity.* Cambridge: Cambridge University Press, 1980.

Cronin, Vincent. *Napoleon.* London: HarperCollins, 1994.

Crowley, Roger. *1453: The Holy War for Constantinople and the Clash of Islam and the West.* New York: Hyperion, 2005.

———. *Empires of the Sea: The Siege of Malta, the Battle of Lepanto, and the Contest for the Center of the World.* New York: Random House, 2009.

Danzinger, Danny and John Gillingham. *1215: The Year of Magna Carta.* London: Hodder and Stoughton, 2003.

Darwin, John. *After Tamerlane: The Global History of Empire since 1405.* London: Penguin Books, 2007.

Davidson, Ian. *Voltaire in Exile: The Last Years, 1753—78.* London: Atlantic Books, 2004.

Dewey, Clive. *Anglo-Indian Attitudes: The Mind of the Indian Civil Service.* London: Hambeldon Press, 1993.

Dodwell, H. H., ed. *The Cambridge History of India, vol 5, British India 1497–1858* Cambridge: Cambridge University Press, 1921; reprint, New Delhi: S. Chand & Company (Pvt.) Ltd., 1987

————. ed. *The Cambridge History of India*, vol 6, *The Indian Empire 1858–1919 with Additional Chapters 1919–1969*. Cambridge: Cambridge University Press, 1932; reprint, New Delhi: S. Chand & Company (Pvt) Ltd., 1987.

Diamond, Jared. *Collapse: How Societies choose to Fail or Survive*. London: Penguin, 2006.

————. *Guns, Germs and Steel: A Short History of Everybody for the last 13,000 years*. London: Vintage, 2005.

————. *The Rise and Fall of the Third Chimpanzee: How our Animal Heritage Affects the way we Live*. London: Vintage, 2002.

Dower, John. *Embracing Defeat: Japan in the Wake of World War II*. New York: W. W. Norton & Company, The New Press, 1999.

Edwards I. E. S, C. J. Gadd, N. G. L. Hammond, et. al., eds. *The Cambridge Ancient History: The Middle East and the Aegean Region c1380–1000 BC*. Cambridge: Cambridge University Press, 1980, Vol. 2, Part 2-A.

Eisuke Sakakibara. *Structural Reform in Japan: Breaking the Iron Triangle*. Washington D.C Brookings Institution Press, 2003.

Embree, Ainslie T., ed. *Sources of Indian Tradition*, vol 1, Second Edition, *From the Beginning to 1800*. New Delhi: Penguin Books, 1992.

Eraly, Abraham. *The Last Spring: The Lives and Times of the Great Mughals*. New Delhi: Viking, 1997.

————. *The Mughal World: India's Tainted Paradise*. London: Weidenfeld & Nicolson, 2007.

Fa-Hien. *A Record of Buddhistic Kingdoms*. Trans. James Legge. Islamabad: Lok Virsa, n.d.

Fairbank, John King and Merle Goldman. *China: A New History*. Cambridge, Massachusetts: Harvard University Press, 2006.

Farrell, Nicholas. *Mussolini: A New Life*. London: Phoenix: 2003.

Feiling, Keith. *A History of England From the Coming of the English to 1918*. Trowbridge & Esher: Book Club Associates. 1975.

Feroze, Mohammed Rashid. *Islam in Modern Turkey*. Islamabad: Islamic Research Institute, 1968.

Fest, Joachim C. *Hitler*. Trans. Richard and Clara Winston. London: Penguin, 1974.

Feuchtwanger, Edgar. *Bismarck*. New York: Routledge, 2003.

Ferguson, Niall. *Civilization: The West and the Rest*. London: Allen Lane, the Penguin Press, 2011.

————. *Empire: How Britain Made the Modern World*. London: The Penguin Press, 2003.

Finkel, Caroline. *Osman's Dream: The Story of the Ottoman Empire, 1300–1923*. London: John Murray, 2006.

Finkelstein, David M. and Kirsten Gunness, eds. *Civil-Military Relations in Today's China: Swimming in a New Era*. New Delhi: Pentagon Press, 2009.

Firye, Richard N. *The Golden Age of Persia: The Arabs in the East*. London: Weidenfeld and Nicholson, 1977.

Fischel, Walter J. *Ibn Khaldun in Egypt: His Public Functions and his Historical Research, A Study in Islamic Historiography*. Berkeley: University of California Press, 1967.

Fishman, Ted C. *China Inc.: The Relentless Rise of the Next Great Superpower*. London: Simon & Schuster, 2006.

Fisk, Robert. *The Great War for Civilization: The Conquest of the Middle East*. London: Harper Perennial, 2006.

Forrest, G. W., ed. *Selections from the State Papers of the Governor-General of India*. Vol. 1. *Hastings*. London: Constable & Co. Ltd., 1910.

Foucault, Michel. *Discipline and Punish: The Birth of the Prison*. Trans. Alan Sheridan New York: Vintage, 1995.

Freely, John. *Storm on Horseback: The Seljuk Warriors of Turkey.* London: I. B. Tauris, 2008.

Froembgen, Hanns. *Kemal Ataturk: A Biography.* Trans. Kenneth Kirkness. Karachi: Indus Publications, 1980.

Fukuyama, Francis. *After the Neocons: America at the Crossroads.* London: Profile Books, 2006.

———. *The Origins of Political Order: From Prehuman Times to the French Revolution.* London: Profile Books, 2012.

———. *Trust: The Social Virtues and the Creation of Prosperity.* New York: The Free Press, 1995.

Galantier Marc, *Law and Society in Modern India*, ed., Rajeev Bhavan. Delhi: Oxford University Press, 1988.

Gandhi, Arun, ed. *The Morarji Papers: Fall of the Janata Government.* New Delhi: Vision Books, 1983.

Garret, H. L. O. and G. L. Chopra, eds. *Events at the Court of Ranjit Singh 1810–1817: Translated from the Papers in the Alienation Office, Poona.* Lahore: Sang-e-Meel, 2002.

Garthwaite, Gene R. *Khans and Shah: A History of the Bakhtyari Tribe in Iran.* London: I. B. Tauris, 2009.

Gibbon, Edward. *The Decline and Fall of the Roman Empire*, Abridged and with an Introduction by Frank C. Bourne. New York: Dell Publishing Co., 1963.

Gilbert, Martin. *Churchill: A Life.* London: Minerva, 1990.

Gilmour, David. *Curzon.* London: John Murray, 1994.

———. *The Ruling Caste: Imperial Lives in the Victorian Raj.* London: John Murray, 2005.

Godbole, Madhav *Unfinished Innings: Recollections and Reflections of a Civil Servant.* New Delhi: Orient Longman, 1996.

Goff, Jacques Le. *Medieval Civilization: 400–1500*, trans. Julia Barrow. Oxford: Basil Blackwell, 1984.

Goffman, Daniel. *The Ottoman Empire and Early Modern Europe: New Approaches to European History.* Cambridge: University Press, 2002.

Goody, Jack. *The Eurasian Miracle.* Cambridge: Polity Press, 2010.

Gorbachev, Mikhail. *Memoirs.* London: Bantam Books, 1997.

Gordon, Andrew. *A Modern History of Japan from Tokugawa Times to the Present.* New York: Oxford University Press, 2003.

Gordon, Stewart. *When Asia was the World.* Philadelphia: DACAPO Press, 2008.

Grant, Michael. *The Fall of the Roman Empire.* London: Phoenix, 2005.

Gray, John. *Black Mass: Apocalyptic Religion and the Death of Utopia.* New York: Farrar, Straus and Giroux, 2007.

Griffiths, Percival. *To Guard my People: The History of the Indian Police.* London: Ernest Benn Limited, 1971.

Grimm, Harold J. *The Reformation Era: 1500–1650.* London: The MacMillan Company, 1969.

Gupta, Anandswarup. *The Police in British India: 1861–1947.* New Delhi: Concept Publishing Company, 1979.

Habib, Irfan. *Essays in Indian History: Towards a Marxist Perspective.* New Delhi: Tulika, 1995.

———, ed. *Medieval India: Researches in the History of India 1200–1750.* Delhi: Oxford India Paperbacks, 1999.

Hali, Hussain. *Hayat-i-Javed*, trans. David J. Mathews. Panipat: n.p. 1902; reprint, Delhi: Rupa & Co., 1994.

Halvell, H. L. *Ancient Rome: The Republic.* New Lanark: Geddes & Grosset, 2003.

Harle, J. C. *The Art and Architecture of the Indian Subcontinent.* London: Penguin Books, 1986.

Haroon, Sana. *Frontier of Faith: Islam in the Indo-Afghan Borderland*. London: Hurst and Company, 2007.

Harvey, Robert. *Comrades: The Rise and Fall of World Communism*. London: John Murray, 2003.

Hasan-i-Fasai. *Farsnama-ye Naseri. History of Persia under Qajar Rule)* trans. Heribert Busse. New York: Columbia University Press, 1972.

Hasan, Mubashir. *The Mirage of Power: An Inquiry into the Bhutto Years, 1971–1977*. Karachi: Oxford University Press, 2000.

Haslip, Joan. *Catherine the Great*. London: Weidenfeld and Nicholson, 1977.

Hathaway, Jane. *Beshir Agha: Chief Eunuch of the Ottoman Imperial Harem*. Oxford: Oneworld Publishers, 2009.

Headrick, Daniel R. *Power over Peoples: Technology, Environments, and Western Imperialism, 1400 to Present*. Princeton: Princeton University Press, 2010.

Hennessy, H. F. *Administrative History of British India*. New Delhi: Neeraj Publishing House, 1983.

Heper, Metin. *Ismet Inonü: The Making of a Turkish Statesman*. Leiden: Brill, 1998.

Herodotus. *Histories*. Trans. George Rawlinson. Hertfordshire: Wordsworth Editions Limited, 1996.

Hershlag, Z. Y. *Turkey: The Challenge of Growth*. Leiden: E. J. Brill, 1968

Hill, Charles. *Grand Strategies: Literature, Statecraft and World Order*. New Haven: Yale University Press, 2010.

Hingley, Ronald. *The Russian Mind*. London: The Bodley Head, 1977.

Hiro, Dilip. *Inside India Today*. London: Routledge & Kegan Paul, 1976.

Hirschmann, Edwin. *White Mutiny: The Ilbert Bill Crisis in India and the Genesis of the Indian National Congress*. New Delhi: Heritage Publishers, 1980.

Hitchcock, F. R. Montgomery. *St. Augustine's Treatise on the City of God*. New York: The Macmillan Company, 1922.

Hobsbawn, Eric. *The Age of Extremes: A History of the World, 1914–1991*. New York: Vintage Books, 1996.

———. *Interesting Times: A Twentieth Century Life*. London: Allen Lane the Penguin Press, 2002.

———. *On History*. London: Abacus, 1997.

Holland, Tom. *Persian Fire: The First World Empire and the Battle for the West*. London: Little, Brown, 2005.

Hourani, Albert. *A History of the Arab Peoples*. London: Faber and Faber, 2002.

Humphreys, R. Stephen. *Mu 'awiya Ibn Abi Sufyan: From Arabia to Empire*. Oxford: Oneworld, 2009.

Hussain, Mushahid and Akmal Hussain. *Pakistan: Problems of Governance*. Lahore: Vanguard, 1993.

Ibn Hasan. *The Central Structure of the Mughal Empire and its Practical Working up to the Year 1657*. Karachi: Oxford University Press, 1967.

Inalcik, Halil. *The Ottoman Empire: The Classical Age 1300–1600*. London: Phoenix, 2000.

India Office List for 1935. London: Harrisons and Sons Ltd., 1935.

Jackson, Peter. *The Delhi Sultanate: A Political and Military History*. Cambridge: Cambridge University Press, 1999.

Jacques, Martin. *When China Rules the World: The End of the Western World and the Birth of a New Global Order*. London: Penguin, 2012.

Jalal, Ayesha. *Democracy and Authoritarianism in South Asia: A Comparative and Historical Perspective*. Lahore: Sang-e-Meel Publications, 1995.

Jamaluddin, Syed. *The State Under Timur: A Study in Empire Building*. New Delhi: Har Anand Publishers, 1995.

James, Lawrence. *Raj: The Making and Unmaking of British India*. London: Abacus, 2003.

————. *The Rise and Fall of the British Empire*. London: Abacus, 2001.

James, Robert Rhodes. *Gallipoli*. London: Pan Books, 1965.

Jardin, André. *Tocqueville: A Biography*. Trans. Lydia Davis and Robert Hemenway. London: Peter Halban, 1988.

Jeep, John M, ed. *Medieval Germany: An Encyclopedia*. New York: Garland Publishing Inc, 2001.

Jeffery, Keith. *MI6: The History of the Secret Intelligence Service, 1909–1949*. London: Bloomsbury Publishing, 2010.

Johnson, Chalmers. *The Sorrows of Empire: Militarism, Secrecy, and the End of the Republic*. New York: Metropolitan Books, Henry Holt and Company, 2004.

Joint Committee on Indian Constitutional Reform Session 1933–34, vol I, part I. London: His Majesty's Stationery Office, 1934.

Jonge, Alex de. *Fire and Water: A Life of Peter the Great*. London: Collins, 1979.

Judt, Tony. *Postwar: A History of Europe since 1945*. London: William Heineman, 2005.

Kaplan, Robert D. *The Revenge of Geography: What the Map tells us about Coming Conflicts and the Battle against Fate*. New York: Random House, 2012.

Katouzian, Homa. *The Political Economy of Modern Iran: Despotism and Pseudo-Modernism, 1926–1979*. London: MacMillan, 1981.

————. *State and Society in Iran: The Eclipse of the Qajars and the Emergence of the Pahlavis*. London: I. B. Tauris Publishers, 2000.

Kaura, Uma. *Muslims and Indian Nationalism: The Emergence of the Demand for India's Partition 1928–1940*. New Delhi: Manohar Book Service, 1977.

Kautilya. *The Arthashastra*, trans, L. N. Rangaraja. New Delhi: Penguin Books, 1992.

Kautilya, *The Arthashastra*, trans, R. Shamasastry. Bangalore: Government Press, 1915.

Keay, John. *China: A History*. London: HarperCollins, 2009.

————. *India: A History*. London: HarperCollins, 2000.

————. *India Discovered*. London: William Collins & Sons, 1988.

Kejariwal, O. P. *The Asiatic Society of Bengal and the Discovery of India's Past: 1784–1838*. Delhi: Oxford University Press, 1988.

Kemp, Barry J. *Ancient Egypt: Anatomy of a Civilization*. London: Routledge, 2002.

Kennan, George F. *The Marquis de Custine and his 'Russia in 1839'*. London: Hutchinson, 1972.

Kennedy, Charles. *Bureaucracy in Pakistan*. Karachi: Oxford University Press, 1987.

Kennedy, Hugh. *The Court of the Caliphs: When Baghdad Ruled the Muslim World*. London: Phoenix, 2005.

Kennedy, Paul. *The Rise and Fall of the Great Powers: Economic Change and Military Conflict 1500–2000*. London: Fontana Press, 1989.

Ibn Khaldun. *An Introduction to History (The Muqaddimah)*. Trans. Franz Rosenthal. Ed. N. J. Dawood. London: Routledge and Kegan Paul, 1978.

Khan, Asghar M. *We've Learnt Nothing from History: Pakistan Politics and Military Power*. Karachi: Oxford University Press, 2005.

Khan, Hamid. *The Constitutional and Political History of Pakistan*. Karachi: Oxford University Press, 2002.

Khan, Inayat. *Shahjahan-nama*, trans. A. R. Fuller, eds., W. Begley and Z. A. Desai. Delhi: Oxford University Press, 1990.

Khan, Khafi. *History of Alamgir*, trans., S. Moin-ul-Haq. Karachi: Pakistan Historical Society, 1975.

Khan, Najmul Saqib. *Japanese Experience and Nation-Building in Southwest Asia*. Tokyo: The Japan Times, 1993.

Khan, Saqi Mustad. *Maasir-i-Alamgiri*, trans. Jadunath Sarkar. Calcutta: Royal Asiatic Society of Bengal, 1947 reprint; New Delhi: Munshiram Manoharlal, 1985.

Khan, Syed Ahmed. *The Causes of the Indian Revolt*, trans., Colonel Graham and Auckland Clovin, with an introduction by Francis Robinson. Karachi: Oxford University Press, 2000.

Khomeni, Saiyyid Ruhollah Musavi. *Islam and Revolution: Writings and Declarations of Imam Khomenei.* trans. & annotated by Hamid Algar. Berkley: Mizan Press, 1981.

Khoury, Dina Rizk. *State and Provincial Society in the Ottoman Empire: Mosul 1540–1834.* Cambridge: Cambridge University Press, 1997.

Kimmel, Michael S. *Absolutism and its Discontents: State and Society in Seventeenth Century France and England.* Piscataway, NJ: Transaction Publishers, 1988.

Kinross Patrick. *Atatürk: The Rebirth of a Nation.* London: Weidenfeld and Nicolson, 1966.

Kissinger, Henry. *Diplomacy.* New York: Simon & Schuster, 1994.

———. *On China.* Penguin: London, 2012.

Klein, Lawrence R. and Marshall Power, eds. *The New Russia: Transition Gone Awry.* Stanford: Stanford University Press, 2001.

Kochanek, Stanley A. *Interest Groups and Development: Business and Politics in Pakistan.* Karachi: Oxford Univesity Press, 1983.

Kosambi, D. D. *The Culture and Civilization of Ancient India in Historical Outline.* New Delhi: Vikas Publishing House, 1985.

Korbel, Josef. *Danger in Kashmir.* Princeton: Princeton University Press, 1954; reprint, Karachi: Oxford University Press, 2003.

Kulke, Hermann and Dietmar Rothermund. *A History of India.* New Delhi: Manohar Publications, 1991.

Kumar, Dharma. *The Cambridge Economic History of India*, Vol II, *c. 1757—c. 1970.* Cambridge: The Press Syndicate of the Cambridge University, 1982; reprint, Delhi: Orient Longman, 1984.

Kumar, Raj, ed. *Local Government and Administration during Muslim Rule in India.* New Delhi: Anmol Publications Pvt. Ltd., 2000.

Kumiko Kakahashi. *Letters from Iwo Jima: The Japanese Eyewitness Stories that Inspired Clint Eastwood's Film.* London: Weidenfeld & Nicholson, 2006.

Kung, Hans. *Islam: Past, Present and Future.* Trans. John Bowden. Oxford: Oneworld, 2007.

Kuper, Adam and Jessica Kuper, eds. *The Social Science Encyclopedia.* Lahore: Services Book Club, 1989.

LaCouture, Jean. *De Gaulle: The Ruler, 1945–1970.* Trans. Alan Sheridan. London: Harvill, HarperCollins Publishers, 1991.

Lambrick, H. T. *Sir Charles Napier and Sind.* Oxford: Clarendon Press, 1952.

Landau Jacob M, ed. *Atatürk and the Modernization of Turkey.* Boulder, Colorado: Westview Press, 1984.

Landes, David. *The Wealth and Poverty of Nations.* London: Abacus, 1998.

Lane-Poole, Stanely. *Mediaeval India Under Muhammaden Rule.* Lahore: Sang-e-Meel, 1991.

LaPolambara, Joseph ed. *Bureaucracy and Political Development.* Princeton: Princeton University Press, 1963.

Lefebvre, Georges. *The French Revolution*, Vol. 1, *From its Origins to 1793.* Trans. Elizabeth Moss Evanson. New York: Columbia University Press, 1962.

Lewis, David Levering. *God's Crucible: Islam and the Making of Europe, 570 to 1215.* New York: W. W. Norton, 2008.

Lewis, Primila. *Reason Wounded: A Personal Account of India's Emergency.* Lahore: Vanguard Books Ltd., 1979.

Li, Zhisui. *The Private Life of Chairman Mao*. trans. Tai Hung-Chao. New York: Random House, 1994.

Lindsay, J. G., ed. *New Cambridge Modern History*, vol VII, *The Old Regime 1713–63*. Cambridge: University Press, 1970.

Locke, John. *An Essay Concerning Human Understanding*. Ed. Roger Woolhouse. London: Penguin, 2004.

Longworth, Philip. *Russia's Empires: Their Rise and fall from Prehistory to Putin*. London: John Murray, 2005.

Lord, John. *The Maharajas*. New York: Random House, 1971.

Lovell, Julia. *The Great Wall: China Against the World, 1000 BC–AD 2000*. New York: Grove Press, 2006.

Luce, Edward. *In Spite of the Gods: The Strange Rise of Modern India*. London: Little, Brown, 2007.

Machiavelli, Niccolo. *The Discourses*. Trans. Leslie J. Walker. Ed. Bernard Crick. Rev. Brian Richardson. London: Penguin Books, 2003.

MacMullen, Ramsay. *Corruption and the Decline of Rome*. New Haven: Yale University Press, 1988.

Maconchie, Evan. *Life in the Indian Civil Service*. London: Chapman and Hall, 1926.

Mahmud, Khalid. *Indian Political Scene, 1989: Main Contenders for Power*. Islamabad: Institute of Regional Studies, 1989.

Major, Andrew J. *Return to Empire: Punjab under the Sikhs and British in the mid-Nineteenth Century*. Karachi: Oxford University Press, 1996.

Majumdar R. C., H. C. Raychaudri, and Kalikinkar Datta, *An Advanced History of India*, 3rd ed. Macmillan Student Editions. London: Macmillan, 1967.

Malleson, G. B. *Administration of British India under Lord Wellesley*. New Delhi: Daya Publishing, 1988.

Man, John. *Kublai Khan: The Mongol King who Remade China*. London: Transworld Publishers, 2006.

Manceron, Claude. *Twilight of the Old Order*. Trans. Patricia Wolf. New York: Alfred A. Knopf, 1977.

Mango, Andrew. *The Turks Today*. New York: The Overlook Press, 2004.

Manstein, Eric von. *Lost Victories: The War Memoirs of Hitler's most Brilliant General*. Trans. Anthony G. Powell. Minneapolis: Zenith Press, 2004.

Mao Tse-Tung. *Selected Readings from the Works of Mao Tse-Tung*. Peking: Foreign Language Press, 1967.

———. *Selected Works of Mao Tse-Tung*, Vols. I-V. Peking: Foreign Language Press, 1975.

Maoz Moshe and Avner Yaniv, eds. *Syria Under Assad: Domestic Constraints and Regional Risks*. Kent: Croom Helm Ltd., 1987.

Marozzi, Justin. *Tamerlane: Sword of Islam, Conqueror of the World*. London: HarperCollins, 2004.

———. *The Way of Herodotus: Travels with the Man Who Invented History*. London: DA CAPO Press, 2008.

Marsot, Afat Lutfi al-Sayyid *Egypt in the Reign of Muhammad Ali*. Cambridge: Cambridge University Press, 1984.

Martin, Vanessa. *The Qajar Pact: Bargaining, Protest and the State in Nineteenth Century Persia*. London: I. B. Tauris, 2005.

Marx. Karl. *Capital: A New Abridgement*. Ed. David McLellan. London: Oxford University Press, 2008.

Massie, Robert K. *Peter the Great: His Life and World*. London: Cardinal, 1989.

Mastutani Akihiko. *Shrinking Population Economics: Lessons from Japan*. Trans. Brian Miller. Tokyo: International House of Japan, 2006.

McGrath, Allen. *The Destruction of Pakistan's Democracy*. Karachi: Oxford University Press, 1996.

Melville, Charles ed. *Safavid Persia: The History and Politics of an Islamic Society*. London: I. B. Tauris, 1996.

Merne, Cecil. *The Development of Self-Government in India 1858–1914*. Chicago: The University of Chicago Press, 1922.

Metcalf, Thomas R. *The New Cambridge History of India: Ideologies of the Raj*. Cambridge: Cambridge University Press, 1994.

Milton, Giles. *Big Chief Elizabeth: How England's Adventurers Gambled and Won the New World*. London: Hodder and Stoughton, 2001.

———. *Nathaniel's Nutmeg: How One Man's Courage Changed the Course of History*. London: Hodder and Stoughton, 1999.

Mishra, Pankaj. *Temptations of the West: How to be Modern in India, Pakistan, Tibet and Beyond*. New York: Farrar, Straus and Giroux, 2006.

Mitani Hiroshi. *Escape from Impasse: The Decision to Open Japan*. Trans. David Noble. Tokyo: International House of Japan, 2006.

Montefiore, Simon Sebag. *Prince of Princes: The Life of Potemkin*. London: Phoenix Press, 2001.

———. *Stalin: The Court of the Red Tsar*. London: Phoenix, 2003.

Moin, Baqer. *Khomeni: Life of the Ayatollah*. London: I. B. Tauris, 2009.

Moon, Penderel. *The British Conquest and Dominion of India*. London: Duckworth, 1989.

Moore, Barrington Jr. *Social Origins of Dictatorship and Democracy: Lord and Peasant in the Making of the Modern World*. Boston: Beacon Press, 1967.

Mujeeb, M. *The Indian Muslims*. London: George Allen & Unwin Ltd., 1967.

Mukherjee, Sipra. *Indian Administration of Lord William Bentinck*. New Delhi: K. P. Begchi & Company, 1994.

Mulgan, Geoff. *Good and Bad Power: The Trials and Betrayals of Government*. London: Allen Lane, Penguin Books, 2006.

Naipaul, V. S. *An Area of Darkness*. London: Pelican Books, 1968.

Nayar, Kuldip and Khushwant Singh. *Tragedy of Punjab: Operation Bluestar and After*. New Delhi: Vision Books Pvt., Ltd., 1984.

Newby, P. H. *Saladin in his Time*. London: Phoenix Press, 2001.

Newman, J. Andrew. *Safavid Iran: Rebirth of a Persian Empire*. London: I. B. Tauris, 2006.

Niaz, Ilhan. *An Inquiry into the Culture of Power of the Subcontinent*. Islamabad: Alhamra Publishing, 2006.

———. *The Culture of Power and Governance of Pakistan, 1947–2008*. Karachi: Oxford University Press, 2010.

Nichols, Robert. *A History of Pashtun Migration, 1775–2006*. Karachi: Oxford University Press, 2008.

Nizami, K. A. ed. *Politics and Society During the Early Medieval Period: Collected Works of Professor Mohammed Habib, vol 2. New Delhi: Peoples Publishing House, 1981*.

Noorani, A. G. *Citizens' Rights, Judges and State Accountability*. New Delhi: Oxford University Press, 2002.

———. *The RSS and the BJP: A Division of Labour*. New Delhi: LeftWord Books, 2000.

O'Brien, Conor Cruise. *The Great Melody*. London: Minerva, 1993.

Ogg, David. *Europe in the Seventeenth Century*. London: Adam and Charles, 1967.

Orwell, George. *Orwell: The Observer Years*. London: Atlantic Books, 2003.

Osborne, Roger. *Civilization: A New History of the Western World*. London: Jonathan Cape, 2006.

Padamsee, Alex. *Representations of Indian Muslims in British Colonial Discourses*. New York: Palgrave MacMillan, 2005.

Pagden, Anothy. *Worlds at War: The 2500-year Struggle between East and West.* Oxford: Oxford University Press, 2009.

Palkhivala, N. A. *We, the People.* Bombay: Strand Book Stall, 1988.

Palmer, Alan. *Metternich: Councillor of Europe.* London: Phoenix, 1997.

Peer, Basharat. *Curfewed Nigh.* London: Random House, 2008.

Penner, Peter and Richard Dale McLean, eds. *The Rebel Bureaucrat: Frederick John Shore (1799–1837) as Critic of William Bentinck's India.* Delhi: Chanakya Publications, 1983.

Philips, C. H. ed. *The Correspondence of Lord William Cavendish Bentinck: Governor General of India 1828–1835.* Oxford: Oxford University Press, 1977.

Pipes, Richard. *Property and Freedom.* New York: Alfred A. Knopf, 1999.

Plutarch. *The Rise and Fall of Athens: Nine Greek Lives.* Trans. Ian Scott-Kilvert. London: Penguin Books, 1965.

Polk, William R. *Understanding Iraq: A Whistle-stop Tour from Ancient Babylon to Occupied Baghdad.* London: I. B. Tauris, 2005.

Possehl, Gregory ed. *Harappan Civilization: A Contemporary Perspective.* New Delhi: Oxford and IBH Publishing Co., 1982.

Price, Munro. *The Fall of the French Monarchy: Louis XVI, Marie Antoinette, and the baron de Breuteuil.* London: Pan Macmillan, 2002.

Procopius. *The Secret History.* Trans. G. A. Williamson and Peter Sarris. London: Penguin Books, 2007.

Punj, Balbir K. "Hindu Rashtra", *South Asian Journal.* October-December 2003.

Pye, Lucian W. and Mary W. Pye. *Asian Power and Politics: The Cultural Dimensions of Authority* Cambridge, Massachusetts: The Belknap Press of Harvard University Press, 1985.

Qureshi, I. H. *Akbar: The Architect of the Mughul Empire.* Karachi: Ma'aref Limited, 1978.

———. *Ulema In Politics: A Study Relating to the Political Activities of the Ulema in the South Asian Subcontinent from 1556—1947.* Karachi, Inter-services Press Ltd., 1972.

Rahman, Tariq. *Language, Ideology and Power: Language-Learning Among the Muslims of Pakistan and North India.* Karachi: Oxford University Press, 2002.

Rapoport, Yousaf and Shahab Ahmed, eds. *Ibn Taymiyya and His Times.* Karachi: Oxford University Press, 2010.

Rapson, E J., ed. *The Cambridge History of India.* vol 1. *Ancient India.* Cambridge: Cambridge University Press, 1921; reprint, New Delhi: S. Chand & Company (Pvt.) Ltd., 1987.

Raychaudhry, Tapan and Irfan Habib, eds. *The Cambridge Economic History of India,* vol 1, *c1200 to c1750.* Cambridge: Cambridge University Press, 1982.

Read, Anthony and David Fisher. *The Proudest Day: India's Long Road to Independence.* London: Jonathan Cape, 1997.

Reddaway, W. F. *A History of Europe from 1610 to 1715.* London: Methuen and Co. Limited, 1967.

Redman, Ben Ray, ed. *The Portable Voltaire.* New York: Viking Penguin Inc., 1977.

Reich, Wilhelm. *The Mass Psychology of Fascism.* Lahore: Gautum Publishers, 1995.

Report of the Committee, 1966–68. Vol. 1, *The Civil Service.* London: Her Majesty's Stationery Office, 1968.

Report of the Machinery of Government Committee. London: His Majesty's Stationery Office, 1918.

Report on the Organisation of the Permanent Civil Service. London: Her Majesty's Stationery Office, 1854

Riasanovsky, Nicholas V. *A History of Russia.* New York: Oxford University Press, 1977.

Roberts, Andrew. *Hitler and Churchill: Secrets of Leadership.* London: Phoenix, 2003.

Roberts, J. M. *History of the World.* New York: Oxford University Press, 1993.

Roberts, Nick. *The Corporation that Changed the World: How the East India Company Shaped the Modern Multinational.* Hyderabad: Orient Longman Private Limited, 2006.

Robinson, Chase F. *'Abd al-Malik.* Oxford: Oneworld, 2006.

Rogerson, Barnaby. *The Heirs of the Prophet Muhammad and the Roots of the Sunni-Shia Schism.* London: Little, Brown, 2006.

Rousseau, Jean-Jacques. *A Discourse on Inequality.* Trans. Maurice Cranston. London: Penguin Classics, 1984.

———. *The Social Contract or Principles of Political Right.* Trans. Maurice Cranston. London: Penguin Classics, 1968.

Roy, Arundhati. *Listening to Grass-hoppers: Field Notes on Democracy.* Rawalpindi: Services Book Club, 2011.

Russel, Bertrand. *Power: A New Social Analysis.* London: Unwin Books, 1960.

Sachau, Edward C. *Alberuni's India: An account of the Religion, Philosophy, Literature, Geography, Chronology, Astrology, Customs, Laws, and Astrology of India About AD 1030*, vol 1. Lahore: Ferozesons, 1962.

Safi, Omid. *Religion and Politics in Saljuq Iran: Negotiating Ideology and Religious Inquiry.* Karachi: Oxford University Press, 2007.

Samaha, Joel. *Law and Order in Historical Perspective: The Case of Elizabethan Essex.* New York: Academic Press, 1974.

Saran, P. *The Provincial Government of the Mughals: 1526–1658.* Allahabad: Kitabistan, 1941; reprint Lahore: Faran Academy, 1976.

Saunders, J. J. *A History of Medieval Islam.* London: Routledge, 1965; reprint, 1996.

Savory, Roger. *Iran Under the Safavids.* Cambridge: Cambridge University Press, 1980.

Scala, Spencer M. Di and Salvo Mastellone. *European Political Thought, 1815–1989.* Boulder, Colorado: Westview Press, 1998.

Schama, Simon. *A History of Britain: At the Edge of the World? 3000 BC- AD 1603.* London: BBC Worldwide Ltd., 2000.

———. *A History of Britain: The British Wars 1603–1776.* London: BBC Worldwide Ltd., 2001.

Secondat, Charles de. *The Spirit of Laws.* New York: Prometheus Books, 2002.

Sen, Amartya. *Identity and Violence: The Illusion of Destiny.* New York: W. W. Norton and Company, 2006.

Seton-Watson, Hugh. *The Russian Empire, 1801–1917.* Oxford: Oxford University Press, 1988.

Shah, Ghanshyam, ed. *Dalit Identity and Politics: Cultural Subordination and the Dalit Challenge*, vol 2. Sage Publications: New Delhi, 2001.

Shah, Ghanshyam, Mario Rutten, and Hein Streefkerk, eds. *Development and Deprivation in Gujarat.* New Delhi: Sage Publications, 2002.

Sharma, Jyotirmaya. *Hindutva: Exploring the Idea of Hindu Nationalism.* New Delhi: Penguin Books, 2006.

Sharma, Mukul, ed. *Improving People's Lives: Lessons in Empowerment from Asia.* New Delhi: Sage, 2003.

Sheehan, James J. *Where have all the Soldiers Gone? The Transformation of Modern Europe.* New York: Houghton Mifflin Company, 2008.

Shelbourne, David. *An Eye to India: The Unmasking of a Tyranny.* Suffolk: Penguin Books, 1977.

Short, Philip. *Mao: A Life.* London: Hodder and Stoughton, 1999.

Siddiqi, A. H. *Caliphate and Sultanate in Medieval Persia.* New Delhi: Adam Publishers, 2010.

Siddiqui, Tasneem Ahmad. *Towards Good Governance.* Karachi: Oxford University Press, 2001.

Siedentop, Larry. *Democracy in Europe.* London: Allen Lane Penguin Press, 2000.

Sikand, Yoginder. *The Origins and Development of the Tablighi-Jama'at, 1920–2000: A Cross-country Comparative Study.* New Delhi: Orient Longman, 2002.

Singh, Khushwant. *The End of India.* New Delhi: Penguin Books, 2003.

———. *Ranjit Singh: Maharaja of the Punjab.* New Delhi: Penguin Books, 2001.

Skinner, Quentin. *Visions of Politics.* Vol. I, *Regarding Method.* Cambridge: Cambridge University Press, 2002.

———. *Visions of Politics.* Vol. II, *Renaissance Virtues.* Cambridge: Cambridge University Press, 2002.

———. *Visions of Politics.* Vol. III, *Hobbes and Civil Science.* Cambridge: Cambridge University Press, 2002.

Smith, Adam. *The Wealth of Nations.* Ed., Edwin Cannan. New York: Bantam Classics, 2003.

Smith, Bosworth R. *Life of Lord Lawrence.* Vols. I and II. London: Smith, Elder & Co., 1883.

Smith, Hedrick. *The Russians.* London: Sphere Books, 1976.

Soboul, Albert. *Understanding the French Revolution.* London: The Merlin Press, 1988.

Spellman, W. M. *Monarchies: AD 1000—2000.* London: Reaktion Books, 2001.

Srivastava, Kamal S. *Some Aspects of Indian History.* Varanasi: Sangeeta Prakashan, 1998.

Standage, Tom. *An Edible History of Humanity.* New York: Walbert Company, 2009.

Stiglitz, Joseph E. *The Roaring Nineties: Seeds of Destruction.* London: Allen Lane the Penguin Press, 2003.

Strudwick, Nigel. *The Administration of Egypt in the Old Kingdom: The Highest Titles and their Holders.* London: KPI Limited, 1985.

Stokes, Eric. *The English Utilitarians and India.* Delhi: Oxford University Press, 1982.

Strumer, Michael. *The German Empire.* London: Weidenfeld and Nicolson, 2000.

Swallow, Charles. *The Sick Man of Europe: Ottoman Empire to Turkish Republic 1789–1923* (London: Ernest Benn, 1973.

Sykes, Percy. *A History of Persia,* Vol. I. London: Routledge and Kegan Paul, 1969.

Tacitus. *The Annals: The Reigns of Tiberius, Claudius, and Nero,* trans. J. C. Yardley. Oxford: Oxford University Press, 2008.

Takii Kazuhiro. *The Meiji Constitution: The Japanese Experience of the West and the Shaping of the Modern State.* trans. David Noble. Tokyo: International House of Japan, 2007.

Tandon, Rajesh and Ranita Mohanty, eds. *Does Civil Society Matter? Governance in Contemporary India.* New Delhi: Sage, 2003.

Taylor, Christian. *Wild West China: The Untold Story of a Frontier Land.* London: John Murray, 2004.

Tazmini, Ghoncheh. *Khatami's Iran: The Islamic Republic and the Turbulent Path to Reform.* New York City: I. B. Tauris & Co., 2010.

Thapar, Romila. *Cultural Pasts: Essays in Early Indian History.* New Delhi: Oxford University Press, 2005.

———. *The Penguin History of Early India: From the Origins to AD 1300*. London: Penguin Books, 2002.

Thatcher, Margaret. *The Downing Street Years*. New York City: HarperCollins, 1993.

Timur, *Tuzuk-i-Timuri: The Autobiography of Timur*. Trans. H. M. Elliot and John Dawson. Lahore: Sang-e-Meel, 2004.

Tocqueville, Alexis de. *Democracy in America*, trans. George Lawrence, ed., J. P. Mayer. New York: HarperCollins, 2000.

———. *The Old Regime and the Revolution*, trans. Alan S. Kahan, Edited and with an Introduction by François Furet and Françoise Mélonio. Chicago: University of Chicago Press, 1998.

Toynbee, Arnold J. *A Study of History*. Abridged, D. C. Somervell. New York: Dell Publishing, 1978.

———. *A Study of History*. Vol. VI. London: Oxford University Press, 1956.

Travelyan, Raleigh. *The Golden Oriole*. New York: Viking, 1987.

Trench, Charles Chevenix *The Indian Army and the King's Enemies 1900–47*. London: Thames and Hudson, 1988.

Tripp, Charles. *A History of Iraq*. Cambridge: Cambridge University Press, 2001.

Troyat, Henri. *Catherine the Great*. Trans. John Pinkham. New York: E. P. Dutton, 1980.

Tunzelmann, Alex von. *Indian Summer: The Secret History of the End of an Empire*. London: Simon & Schuster, 2007.

Tusi, Nizam-ul-Mulk. *The Book of Government or Rules for Kings: The Siyasatnama or Siyar al-Muluk of Nizam al-Mulk*. Trans. Hubert Drake. London: Routledge and Kegan Paul, 1960.

Tully, Mark and Zareer Masani. *From Raj to Rajiv: 40 Years of Indian Independence*. London: BBC Books, 1988.

Tuzuk-i-Jahangiri, trans. Alexander Rogers, ed., Henry Beveridge, vol 1, Years 1–13 (n.p. 1909–1914 reprint; Delhi: Munshiram Manoharlal Publishers, 1978).

Vico, Giambattista. *The New Science*. Trans. Thomas Goddard Bergin and Max Harold Fisch. Ithaca, New York: Cornell University Press, 1948.

Vinen, Richard. *A History in Fragments: Europe in the Twentieth Century*. London: Abacus, 2002.

Vogel, Ezra F. *Deng Xiaoping and the Transformation of China*. Cambridge, Massachussetts: The Belknap Press of Harvard University Press, 2011.

———. *Japan as Number One: Lessons for America*. Cambridge, Massachusetts: Harvard University Press, 1979.

Volkogonov, Dmitri. *The Rise and Fall of the Soviet Empire*. London: HarperCollins, 1999.

Peter Watson. *Ideas: A History from Fire to Freud*. London: Weidenfeld and Nicolson, 2005.

Weber, Max. *The Protestant Ethic and the Spirit of Capitalism*. Trans., Talcott Parsons. London: Butler and Tanner Ltd., 1950.

Weismann, Itzhuk and Fruma Zachs, eds. *Ottoman Reforms and Muslim Regeneration*. London: I. B. Tauris, 2005.

Westad, Odd Arne. *Restless Empire: China and the World since 1750*. London: The Bodley Head, 2012.

Wheatcroft, Andrew. *The Ottomans*. London: Viking, 1993.

Wheeler, Mortimer. *The Indus Civilization*. London: Book Club Associates, 1976.

Wheen, Francis. *How Mumbo-Jumbo Conquered the World: A Short History of Modern Delusions*. London: The Fourth Estate, 2004.

Wilber, Donald N. *Riza Shah Pahlavi: The Resurrection and Reconstruction of Iran, 1878–1944*. Hicksville, New York: Exposition Press, 1975.

Wilson, Harold. *The Governance of Britain*. London: Book Club Associates, 1976.

Winter, Michael and Amalia Levanoni, eds. *The Mamluks in Egyptian and Syrian Politics and Society.* Leiden: Brill, 2004.

Wittfogel, Karl A. *Oriental Despotism: A Comparative Study of Total Power.* New Haven: Carl Purington Rollins Printing Office of the Yale University Press, 1963.

Woloch Isser, ed. *Revolution and the Meanings of Freedom in the Nineteenth Century.* Stanford: Stanford University Press, 1996.

Woodruff, Philip. *The Men Who Ruled India,* vol 2, *The Guardians.* Norwich: Jarrold and Sons Ltd., 1965.

Yasin, Muhammad. *A Social History of Islamic India: 1605–1748.* Lucknow: n.p., 1958 reprint; Lahore: Book traders, n.d.

Yong, Tan Tai. *The Garrison State: The Military, Government and Society in Colonial Punjab, 1849–1947.* Lahore: Vanguard, 2005.

Zachariah, Benjamin. *Nehru.* London: Routledge, 2004.

Zaehner, R. C. *The Dawn and Twilight of Zoroastrianism.* New York: Phoenix, 2003.

Zaman, Muhammad Qasim. *Religion and Politics under the Early Abbasids.* Leiden: Brill, 1997.

Zimbardo, Philip. *The Lucifer Effect: How Good People Turn Evil.* London: Rider, 2007.

Zinn, Howard, *A People's History of the United States: 1492-Present.* New York: Harper Perennial, 2005.

Zonis, Marvin. *The Political Elite of Iran.* Princeton: Princeton University Press, 1971.

Zurcher, Erik J. *Turkey: A Modern History.* London: I. B. Tauris, 1998.

ARTICLES IN JOURNALS

Acar, Muhittin and Huseyn Ozgur. "Training of Civil Servants in Turkey: Progress, Problems, and Prospects." *International Journal of Public Administration.* Vol. 27. No. 3. 2004.

Alexander, R. S. "The Hero and Houdini: Napoleon and Nineteenth Century Bonapartism." *Modern & Contemporary France.* Vol. 8. No. 4. 2000.

Bagchi, Aditi. "Political Citizenship in Britain and Germany." *German Politics.* Vol. 9. No. 3. 2000.

Banerjee-Guha, Swapna. "Accumulation and Dispossession: Contradictions of Growth and Development in Contemporary India." *South Asia: Journal of South Asian Studies.* Vol. 36. No. 2. 2013.

Banik, Dan. "The Transfer Raj: Indian Civil Servants on the Move." *The European Journal of Development Research.* Vol. 13. No. 1. 2001.

Barker, Anthony and Graham K. Wilson. "Whitehall's Disobedient Servants: Senior Officials' Potential Resistance to Ministers in British Government Departments." *British Journal of Political Science.* Vol. 27. No. 2. 1997.

Beech, George T. "The Lord/Dependent (vassal) Relationship: A Case Study from Aquitaine, c. 1030." *Journal of Medieval History.* Vol. 24. No. 1. 1998.

Berenson, Marc P. "Rationalizing or Empowering Bureaucrats? Tax Administration Reform in Poland and Russia." *Journal of Communist Studies and Transition Politics.* Vol. 24. No. 1. 2008.

Binbas, Ilker Evrim. "The Anatomy of a Regicide Attempt: Shahrukh, the ʿurufīs, and the Timurid Intellectuals in 830/1426–27." *Journal of the Royal Asiatic Society.* Series 3. August. 2013.

Bjornstad, Hall. "The Marginalization of the *Mémoires* of Louis XIV." *The European Legacy.* Vol. 17. No. 6. 2012.

Blank, Stephen. "Russia's Geo-economic future: The Security Implications of Russia's Political and Economic Structure." *Journal of Slavic Military Studies.* Vol. 24. No. 3. 2011.

Bradley, Margaret. "Scientific Education versus military training: The Influence of Napoleon Bonaparte on the *Ecole Polytechnique.*" *Annals of Sciences.* Vol. 32. No. 5. 1975.

Brand, Jack. "Party Organization and the Recruitment of Councilors." *British Journal of Political Science.* Vol. 3. No. 4. 1973.

Carmichael, Paul. "Beyond Westminster: The New Machinery of Subnational Government: The North Ireland Civil Service." *Public Money and Management.* Vol. 21. No. 2. 2001.

Chandler, Cullen J. "Heresy and Empire: The Role of the Adoptionist Controversy in Charlemagne's Conquest of the Spanish March." *The International History Review.* Vol. 24. No. 3. 2002.

Chatterji, Tathagata. "The Micro-Politics of Urban Transformation in the Context of Globalisation: A Case Study of Gurgaon, India." *South Asia: Journal of South Asian Studies.* Vol. 36. No. 2. 2013.

Cheng Yi. "Enacting the 'Incomprehensible China': Modern European Jurisprudence and the Japanese Reconstruction of Qing Political Law." *Law & Social Inquiry.* Vol. 33. No. 4. 2009.

Chou, Bill K. P. "Does 'Good Governance' Matter? Civil Service Reform in China." *Journal of Public Administration.* Vol. 31. No 1. 2007.

Floor, Willem and Patrick Clawson. "Safavid Iran's Search for Silver and Gold." *International Journal of Middle Eastern Studies.* Vol. 32. No. 3. 2000.

Hagger, Mark. "How the West was Won: The Norman Dukes and the Cotentin, c. 987–1087." *Journal of Medieval History.* Vol. 38. No. 1, 2012.

Hiroshi Miyajima. "The Emergence of Peasant Societies in East Asia." *International Journal of Asian Studies.* Vol. 2. No. 1. 2005.

Hughes, J. Donald. "Social Structure and Environmental Impact in the Roman Empire." *Capitalism, Nature, Socialism.* Vol. 15. No. 3, 2004.

Inglis, John. "Philosophical autonomy and the historiography of medieval philosophy." *British Journal for the History of Philosophy.* Vol. 5,.No. 1. 1997.

Jones, George. "Against a Civil Service Act." *Public Money and Management.* Vol. 22. No. 4. 2002.

Kaiser, Wolfram. "The political reform debate in Britain since 1945: The European dimension." *Contemporary British History,* Vol. 12. No. 1. 1998.

Kempf Damien. "Paul the Deacon's *liber de episcopis Mettensibus* and the role of Metz in the Carolingian Realm." *Journal of Medieval History,* Vol. 30. No. 3. 2004.

Kollander, Patricia. "Constitutionalism or Staatssreich? Bismarck, Crown Prince Frederick William, Crown Princess Victoria and the Succession Crisis of 1880–85." *European Review of History.* Vol. 8. No. 2. 2001.

Krieger, Wolfgang. "German Intelligence History: A Field in Search of Scholars." *Intelligence and National Security.* Vol. 19. No. 2. 2004.

Mackillop, Andrew. "The Political Culture of the Scottish Highlands from Culloden to Waterloo." *The Historical Journal.* Vol. 46. No. 3. 2003.

Makeyenko, Pavel A. Vatche Gabrelian and March Holzer. "The New Russian Bureaucracy: What is new about it?" *International Journal of Public Administration.* Vol. 22. No. 1. 1999.

Markham, J. David. "Napoleon in Russia: Questionable Judgment and Critical Errors." *The RUSI Journal,* Vol. 148. No. 6. 2003.

McMillan, Janice and Andrew Massey. "Beyond Westminster: The New Machinery of Subnational Government: A Regional Future for the UK Civil Service." *Public Money and Management.* Vol. 21. No. 2 2001.

Merrill III, Samuel, Bernard Groffman, and Thomas L. Brunell. "Do British Party Politics Exhibit Cycles?" *British Journal of Political Science*. Vol. 41. No. 1. 2011.

Meskill David. "Self-Interest Properly Felt: Democracy's Unintended Consequences and Tocqueville's Solution." *Critical Review: A Journal of Politics and Society*. Vol. 19. No. 1. 2007.

Mews, Constant J. "Gregory the Great, the Rule of Benedict and Roman Liturgy: The Evolution of a Legend." *Journal of Medieval History*. Vol. 37. No. 2. 2011.

Mundkar, Bal. "Incredible India: The Inconvenient Truth." *Asian Affairs*. Vol. 42. No. 1. 2011.

Mulgan, Aurelia George. "Japan's Interventionist State: Bringing Agriculture Back In", *Japanese Journal of Political Science*. Vol. 6. No. 1. 2005.

Nefedkin, K. "The Tactical Development of Achaemenid Cavalry." *Gladius*. Vol. XXVI. 2006.

Nielsen, Jens Kaalhauge. "The flower that didn't bloom: why did the industrial revolution happen in Europe and not in China?" *Journal of Chinese Economic and Business Studies*. Vol. 8. No. 1. 2010.

Orucu, Esin. "*Conseil D'État*: The French Layer of Turkish Administrative Law." *International and Comparative Law Quarterly*. Vol. 49. 2000.

Oskarsson, Patrik. "Dispossession by Confusion from Mineral-Rich Lands in Central India." *South Asia: Journal of South Asian Studies*. Vol. 36. No. 2. 2013.

Oversloot, Hans and Ruben Verheul. "Managing Democracy: Political Parties and the State in Russia." *Journal of Communist Studies and Transition Politics*. Vol. 22. No. 3. 2006.

Plessis, Paul Du. "The Protection of the Contractor in Public Works Contracts in the Roman Republic and Early Empire." *The Journal of Legal History*. Vol. 25. No. 3. 2004.

Portass, Robert. "The Contours and Contexts of Public Power in the tenth-century Liebana." *Journal of Medieval History*. Vol. 38. No. 4, 2012.

Pritchard, Bill, Anu Rammohan and Madhushree Sekher. "Food Security as a Lagging Component of India's Human Development: A Function of Interacting Entitlement Failures." *South Asia: Journal of South Asian Studies*. Vol. 36. No. 2. 2013.

Raccagni, Gianluca. "The Teaching of Rhetoric and the Magna Carta of the Lombard Cities: The Peace of Constance, the Empire and the Papacy in the works of Guido Faba and his leading Contemporary Colleagues", *Journal of Medieval History*. Vol. 39. No. 1. 2013.

Ran Tao and Ping Qin. "How has Rural Tax Reform Affected Farmers and Local Governments in China." *China and World Economy*. Vol. 15. No. 3. 2007.

Richards David and Martin J. Smith. "The Public Service Ethos and the role of the British Civil Service." *West European Politics*. Vol. 23. No. 3. 2000.

Rigby, T. H. "Russia's Provincial Bosses: A Collective Career Profile." *Journal of Communist Studies and Transition Politics*. Vol. 17. No. 4. 2001.

Rosefielde. Steven and Romana Hlouskova. "Why Russia is Not a Democracy." *Comparative Strategy*, Vol. 26. No. 3. 2007.

Rowe, Michael. "Debate: Napoleon and the post-Revolutionary Management of Sovereignty." *Modern & Contemporary France*. Vol. 8. No. 4, 2000.

Sarkissian, Ani and S. Ilgu Ozler. "Democratization and the Politicization of Religious Civil Society in Turkey." *Democratization* (2012).

Senigaglia, Cristiana. "Max Weber and the Parliamentary Bureaucracy of his time." *Parliaments, Estates and Representation*. Vol. 31. No. 1. 2011.

Sotiropoulis, Dimitri A, "Southern European Public Bureaucracies in Comparative Perspective." *West European Politics*. Vol. 27. No. 3. 2004.

Speidel, M. Alexander. "Roman Army Pay Scales." *The Journal of Roman Studies.* Vol. 82. 1992.

Tanner, Norman and Sethina Watson. "Least of the Laity: The Minimum Requirements for a Medieval Christian." *Journal of Medieval History.* Vol. 32. No. 4. 2006.

Tingyang Zhao. "Rethinking Empire from a Chinese Concept 'All Under Heaven' (Tian xia)." *Social Identities.* Vol. 12. No. 1. 2006.

Tschoegl, Adrian E. "Financial Integration, Dis-integration, and Emerging Re-integration in the Eastern Mediterranean, c. 1850 to the Present" *Financial Markets, Institutions and Instruments.* Vol. 13. No. 5. 2004.

Vennesson, Pascal. "Civil-Military Relations in France: Is there a Gap?" *Journal of Strategic Studies.* Vol. 26. No. 2. 2003.

Walbridge, John. "The Babi Uprising in Zanjan: Causes and Issues." *Iranian Studies.* Vol. 29. No. 3–4. 1996.

Warner, David A. "Ideals and Action in the Reign of Otto III.",*Journal of Medieval History.* Vol. 25. No. 3. 1999.

Wenxian Zhang. "Dang An: A Brief History of the Chinese Imperial Archives and its Administration." *Journal of Archival Organization.* Vol. 21. No. ½. 2004.

West, C. M. A. "Unauthorized Miracles in the mid-ninth century: Dijon and the Carolingian Church Reforms." *Journal of Medieval History.* Vol. 36. No. 4. 2010.

Whitford, Andrew. "Effects of the Institutional Design of the Civil Service: Evidence from Corruption." *International Public Management Journal.* Vol. 11. No. 4. 2008.

Yildirim, Jülide and Selami Sezgin. "Military Expenditure and Employment in Turkey." *Defence and Peace Economics.* Vol. 14. No. 2. 2003.

Yongfei Zhao and Guy Peters. "The State of the State: Comparing Governance in China and the United States." *Public Administration Review.* Dec. 2009, Special Issue.

Yu Keping. "Toward an Incremental Democracy and Governance: Chinese Theories and Assessment Criteria." *New Political Science.* Vol. 24. No. 2. 2002.

Zhuplev, Anatoly and Vladimir I. Shein. "Russia's Evolving Corporate Governance in the Cultural Context." *Journal of Transnational Management.* Vol. 10. No. 3. 2005.

Index

An environmentally friendly book printed and bound in England by www.printondemand-worldwide.com

This book is made entirely of sustainable materials; FSC paper for the cover and PEFC paper for the text pages.

#0020 - 290514 - C0 - 229/152/25 [27] - CB